Israel – the Apartheid State of the Middle East.
Jan – April 2019

Compiled by Godot Hussein

First Published   April 2019

Published & Distributed by Lulu

www.lulu.com

© Godot Hussein 2019

The right of Godot Hussein to be identified as the author of this work has been asserted in accordance with the UK Copyright, Design & Patents Act 1988

All rights reserved. No part of this publication may be reproduced, stored in a retrieval system, or transmitted, in any form or by any means, electronic, mechanical, photocopying, recording or otherwise, without the prior permission of the publishers.

ISBN   978-0-244-77748-7

Introduction.

Another year of Zionist madness, apartheid, house demolitions, killings, brutality against civilians and the usual list of land thefts.

Israel the totally failed nation. The nation which puffs its chest out in 2019 and pretends to be great and powerful. In practice it's built on land thefts and apartheid …. It's as simple as that.

In reality, most of the world hates and despises both the place, the country, its rulers and many of its citizens. It's only "real" friend in the world is America – at least for the time being – but even this is beginning to change this year somewhat.

This is a state that never learns, never learns that one day they are going to lose their dream country – and they'll deserve to lose it. Really Dumb!

As with all the earlier books compiled by Godot Hussein, this volume will be made available at cost price only. Godot makes not a cent from its sale. **Promise.**

All of these books are merely a record of freely available articles on the internet, in newspapers and magazines over a period of time, that monitor the situation in Israel/Palestine. I want a record kept of the atrocities which are being committed in the name of the Zionist State of Israel. Web sites often close or become unavailable over periods of time and people forget the facts of what actually happened on the ground at a particular period. Hence these volumes.

The compiler, although fiercely pro-Palestinian, tries his very best to ensure that anti-semitism plays NO part whatsoever in these publications …. it is however totally and utterly anti-Zionist.

Anyone who doesn't know the difference between these concepts needs to broaden their education somewhat.

Don't be fooled by Zionists who will endlessly tell you that all Zionists are Jews and all Jews are Zionists …. as I've been told for decades. This is just NOT true in any shape or form and a brief search on Google will show you the truth. One day I just may write another book on this very subject …. But not right now. There's too much else to record.

…… Godot Hussein, April 2019.

The Berlin Wall and the Israeli wall …. Just the same nastiness and evilness – which hopefully will both end with the same result …. Gone - and good riddance.

This is what Apartheid looks like in reality – yet Israelis will tell you they are not an Apartheid State .... endlessly ... they do lie endlessly! Total racists - however much they bleat otherwise.

■ **Imagine that you are standing at a bus stop alongside one other person, waiting for the bus to arrive. You are both heading in the same direction, but when the bus pulls up, you are not permitted to board. It pulls away without you. Why? Because you were born with the wrong ID.**

■ **This scenario is a reality in the West Bank, where Israeli-operated buses travel and pick up passengers on Palestinian land, yet do not serve Palestinians who hold West Bank IDs. These buses are part of a segregated infrastructure and transport system that helps Israeli settlers move efficiently through the heart of occupied territories, while Palestinians in the same area are denied their right to freedom of movement.**

The five defining moments of the Israeli occupation in 2018
By Zena Tahhan From Middle East Eye. 30th Dec 2018

Middle East Eye takes a look at the five biggest political developments of 2018 in Israel's occupation of the Palestinian territories

Israeli settlement in the West Bank considered illegal according to UN resolutions (AFP)

In the volatile reality of Israel's ongoing occupation and campaign of ethnic cleansing against Palestinians, the news cycle never stops. The nightly military raids, arrests of young men, killing of civilians and home demolitions have continued – as they have for the past 70 years.

But 2018 also saw substantial political changes that will keep this year etched in the memory of many Palestinians.

Many believe that while Israel has merely continued to enact policies consistent with its Zionist ideology, this year saw such practices become even more flagrant.

"What stood out the most in 2018 is that Israeli policies have become completely overt," Nisreen Elayyan, a Palestinian lawyer based in Jerusalem, told Middle East Eye. "It no longer tries to disguise its policies and goals, particularly with violating basic human rights."

Here are the five biggest political events in the occupied Palestinian territory to have taken place this year.

Great March of Return in the Gaza Strip

Palestinians have been demonstrating for nine months near the fence separating Gaza from Israel (MEE/Mohammed al-Hajjar)

In the ongoing Palestinian struggle for freedom, the Great March of Return protests in the besieged Gaza Strip have been one of the biggest developments of the year.

On 30 March, thousands of Palestinians in Gaza gathered on the boundary with Israel in a mass demonstration movement known as the Great March of Return.

The demonstrations were organised to coincide with Land Day, which marks the events of 30 March 1976 when Israeli police killed six Palestinian citizens of Israel who were protesting against land theft.

The Great March of Return, which continues until today, has called for the right of return of Palestinian refugees to their homes, from which they were expelled during the Nakba - or catastrophe - amid the establishment of the state of Israel in 1948. The protests also called for an end to the 11-year siege of Gaza and Palestinians' right to dignity and freedom.

Some two-thirds of Gaza's two million inhabitants are refugees from towns and cities in present-day Israel such as Jaffa and Asqalan - since renamed Yafo and Ashkelon. The small Palestinian territory is highly impoverished, with more than 80 percent of its population relying on humanitarian aid.

Since the beginning of the protests, Israeli forces have killed at least 230 Palestinians in the besieged coastal enclave - at least 190 of whom were killed during the March of Return demonstrations - and wounded more than 25,000 people.

"In 2018, we saw Israel continue its unlawful killing of demonstrators in Gaza. Officers repeatedly fired on protesters who posed no imminent threat to life, pursuant to expansive open-fire orders from senior officials that contravene international human rights law standards," Omar Shakir, the Israel and Palestine director for Human Rights Watch, told MEE.

Israel passes Nation-State law

Demonstrators attend a rally to protest against the nation-state bill in Tel Aviv on 14 July 2018 (AFP)
On 19 July, the Israeli parliament, known as the Knesset, passed the nation-state bill into its Basic Law - Israel's equivalent to a constitution - affirming that the right to national self-determination in the state of Israel was "unique to the Jewish people", a move decried by rights groups and Palestinians alike as an apartheid policy.

The nation-state law also states that Israel "views the development of Jewish settlement as a national value, and shall act to encourage and promote its establishment and strengthening" - despite settlements being deemed illegal under international law.

For Jamal Zahalqa, a Palestinian-Israeli member of the Knesset, the law's passing was the most important development of 2018 for Palestinians, especially Palestinian citizens of Israel, who make up some 20 percent of the country's population.

"What Israel did is transfer the concept of the nation-state law from the state to the cities," Zahalqa told MEE. "The law indicates that settlements are not a choice for the state, but it is the state's obligation. Today, the law forces the state to encourage and financially support settlements."

Zahalqa pointed to the Israeli town of Afula, whose municipality has openly pushed to "preserve the Jewish character" of the city following the passage of the nation-state law, "meaning that they would prevent Palestinians from living there and from entering the public parks there".

"This law gives legality to the occupation, to the Judaisation of Jerusalem. It opens the door for much more. We must monitor the implementation of this dangerous law in 2019."

Shakir agreed with the Knesset member: "In 2018, we saw the further entrenchment of the two-tiered discriminatory system that treats Palestinians unequally - not only in the West Bank but also inside Israel proper.

"The nation-state law enshrined as a constitutional mandate Jewish supremacy over non-Jews, which has effectively guided Israeli policy for years."

Trump moves US embassy to Jerusalem

Israeli Prime Minister Benjamin Netanyahu at the US embassy opening on 14 May (Reuters)

On 6 December 2017, US President Donald Trump broke with decades of American policy towards the Palestinian-Israeli conflict and recognised Jerusalem as the capital of Israel - announcing that his country would move its embassy from Tel Aviv to the holy city. On 14 May, which marked the 70th anniversary of the Nakba - and Israel's Independence Day - the US moved its embassy to Jerusalem, infuriating the diplomatic community and sparking protests in Gaza that were put down violently by Israeli troops, leaving 68 dead.

Due to Jerusalem's importance to followers of the three Abrahamic religions, the city's status has long been the main sticking point in the Israeli-Palestinian conflict.

Israel occupied the eastern half of the city, which houses the Old City and religious landmarks such as the al-Aqsa Mosque compound, the Church of the Holy Sepulchre and the Western Wall, in 1967. It then proceeded to annex Jerusalem in contravention of international law, and in 1980 proclaimed it as its "eternal, undivided capital".

Until Trump's move, Israel's control and sovereignty over the city had not been recognised by any country in the international community, and all embassies were based in Tel Aviv.

In the wake of the US decision Guatemala and Paraguay also moved their embassies to Jerusalem - although Paraguay later rescinded the move. A number of politicians in other countries have also since called for their states to follow suit.

The Palestinian leadership, which has long called for the establishment of a Palestinian state with East Jerusalem as its capital as part of a two-state solution, saw Trump's declaration and embassy move as a fatal blow to the already stalled peace process.

Elayyan said the transfer of the embassy "implicitly translated into an encouragement for Israel to continue and intensify its racist policies against Palestinians in the city.

"The state has employed more violence, became bolder and was encouraged to transfer more Israelis into Palestinian neighbourhoods in Jerusalem," she explained.

In the long term the embassy move, Elayyan said, will have "many adverse political dimensions on the Palestinian people - both inside and outside Palestine".

She added that the move would make it much more difficult in the future to establish a Palestinian state, especially if other countries followed suit.

Israel attempts to demolish Khan al-Ahmar village

Israeli policemen detain a Palestinian girl in Khan al-Ahmar, West Bank on 4 July 2018 (Reuters)
In 2018, the Palestinian Bedouin village of Khan al-Ahmar, east of Jerusalem in the occupied West Bank, came under threat of demolition by Israeli authorities - and saw solidarity pour in from local and international activists and diplomats.

The village, home to some 200 residents and an eco-friendly school that serves children from surrounding communities, stands in the way of Israel's plans to create a contiguous bloc of illegal settlements in the central West Bank just east of Jerusalem.

Due to Khan al-Ahmar's strategic location in the last corridor between the occupied West Bank and Jerusalem, Israel's demolition would mean the division of the West Bank in half - and the final nail in the coffin of the two-state solution.

When Israeli bulldozers have approached the village, activists and residents stood their ground and blocked soldiers from razing the community to the ground; many were beaten and arrested.

Israel's security cabinet eventually put the demolition on hold, but Prime Minister Benjamin Netanyahu vowed his government would still go ahead with the plans, without saying when the move would take place.

Several European governments and human rights organisations said the demolition of the village would constitute a war crime though the forcible displacement of an occupied civilian population.

"The problem of Khan al-Ahmar is bigger than the village itself. It is about the establishment of a Palestinian state. The so-called peace efforts depend on this village. If this village is demolished, then the Palestinian dream crumbles," Eid Khamis, the community spokesperson and leader, wrote for MEE earlier this year.

It remains unclear whether the demolition will take place in 2019, but activists have kept a close eye on the situation, monitoring any developments.

Rights groups have warned that if Israel succeeds in destroying Khan al-Ahmar, at least 8,000 other Palestinians in similar communities may face the same fate.

Airbnb announces it will remove listings from Israeli settlements

In November, the global online rental marketplace Airbnb announced it would begin a process to remove listings from illegal Israeli settlements in the occupied West Bank.

"We concluded that we should remove listings in Israeli settlements in the West Bank that are at the core of the dispute between Israelis and Palestinians," Airbnb said in a statement.

"US law permits companies like Airbnb to engage in business in these territories. At the same time, many in the global community have stated that companies should not do business here because they believe companies should not profit on lands where people have been displaced," the statement read.

"We know that people will disagree with this decision and appreciate their perspective. This is a controversial issue."

A road sign points towards an Airbnb apartment, located in the Esh Kodesh outpost, near the Jewish settlement of Shilo and the Palestinian village of Qusra in the occupied West Bank on 20 November 2018 (AFP)

Airbnb has since been pressured by Israel to rescind its decision.

Human rights groups have long shamed Airbnb and other companies for doing business in the occupied Palestinian territories, exposing how it contributes to a two-tiered system of discrimination.

"Airbnb took the only course of action that it could to comply with its responsibilities under the UN guiding principles on business and human rights - not to directly facilitate and profit from rights abuse," said Shakir of Human Rights Watch.

"I think it's an important message - not only to other businesses that continue to do business in and with settlements, but also to the Israeli government - that the international community will not be a party to the abuses associated with its ongoing ugly occupation of the West

Criticise Israel and you immediately trigger its army of outraged partisans

An army of social media trolls are at the ready to denounce legitimate criticism of Israel's occupation and settlement enterprise

By Kamel Hawwash in Middle East Eye 12th December 2018

A handout photo of Israeli troops (AFP)

Israel was created through violence and terror, which it continues to heap on Palestinians to this day, as it works to fulfil the dream of Zionism - a Jewish state from the river to the sea.

How, then, does it continue to portray itself as the victim, while painting the actual victims - Palestinians - as the aggressors?

It has become a tired and broken record, one that Israel and its ardent supporters play, regardless of the rationality of their arguments. Any criticism of Israel, or any peaceful act to put pressure on the state, draws the same outrage, expressed through carefully thought out, yet irrational, talking points.

Total impunity

Anyone, or any organisation, who dares to criticise the self-proclaimed "only democracy in the Middle East" is accused of being motivated by anti-semitism. Any critical act or protest aimed at pressing Israel to uphold international law, no matter how peaceful, is denounced.

Israel's treatment with kid gloves is not new; what is new, however, is its launching of the bullying trigger button within seconds of an attack.

While access to the nuclear button is normally reserved for the head of state, any pro-Israel civilian can launch the bullying trigger button, and they are encouraged to do so by Israel. An army of social media trolls linked to Israeli missions abroad have their fingers hovering over this button, ready to defend as soon as they perceive an attack. It's a button they have pressed repeatedly in recent days.

Take the case of Airbnb. The holiday property listings company enraged the bullying army by withdrawing listings for properties built in illegal Israeli settlements from its website. Pro-Israel critics claimed that Airbnb was singling out Jewish Israeli properties, and therefore, this was anti-semitic.

Breaking international law

The reality is that the settlement enterprise itself is racist, because homes are only built for Jewish Israelis. Imagine the outcry if Britain built homes only for white Christians, banning other inhabitants of Britain from acquiring them. Settlements are also illegal under international law.

Airbnb said it took action because settlements were at the "core of the dispute between Israelis and Palestinians".

A statement from the company noted: "US law permits companies like Airbnb to engage in business in these territories. At the same time, many in the global community have stated that companies should not do business here because they believe companies should not profit on lands where people have been displaced."

A reasonable person would see clear logic in that stance. However, the bullying trigger button was pressed, and an illegal settler is now bringing a lawsuit against Airbnb. Consider that for a moment: an illegal settler is suing a company for a moral and legal act.

It was then the turn of British Quakers to enrage the pro-Israel lobby. Their crime? Divesting from companies that profit from

Israel's illegal occupation. Paul Parker, recording clerk for Quakers in Britain, said in a statement: "With the occupation now in its 51st year, and with no end in near sight, we believe we have a moral duty to state publicly that we will not invest in any company profiting from the occupation."

More pressure needed

This time, it was the Board of Deputies of British Jews that pressed the bullying trigger button. In a statement, the board's president, Marie van der Zyl, condemned the decision: "The appalling decision of the Friends House hierarchy to divest from just one country in the world – the only Jewish state – despite everything else going on around the globe, shows the dangers of the obsessive and tunnel-visioned approach that a narrow clique of church officials have taken in recent years."

Any reasonable person who knows the Quakers would realise that they would have reflected seriously before making such a decision, and that it was based on their deep knowledge of the situation over decades. Divesting from companies that profit from an illegal occupation is moral and legal.

Israeli soldiers photographed beating Palestinian in West Bank (Reuters)

Israel does not recognise that the West Bank and East Jerusalem are occupied. Prime Minister Benjamin Netanyahu has deemed it absurd to talk of an occupation, and the long-advertised US "deal of the century" will likely reflect this by avoiding a call to end the occupation.

This will certainly not lead to peace. What is needed is more pressure on Israel to comply with international law and to finally end the occupation of Palestinian land. Airbnb was correct to identify the settlements as a core issue, and it is time that others follow suit.

Whither free speech?

The bullying trigger button will now be pressed regularly, judging by the number of moves to ban trade with illegal Israeli settlements.

Chile's congress overwhelmingly passed a resolution demanding that the government "forbid the entry of products manufactured and coming from Israeli colonies in the occupied Palestinian territory". This follows hot on the heels of Ireland's senate passing a bill banning the import of products from illegal Israeli settlements.

The vicious attack on CNN contributor Marc Lamont Hill, fired for standing with Palestinians, shows that Israel is being singled out not for criticism, but rather for protection from accountability.

Free speech, it seems, is a value that most claim to uphold - except those who blindly support Israel. Speak if you want to, they say, but the price will be high. The bullying trigger button can be pressed by anyone in defence of Israeli apartheid.

*- **Kamel Hawwash** is a British-Palestinian engineering professor based at the University of Birmingham and a longstanding campaigner for justice, especially for the Palestinian people. He is a regular columnist and appears regularly in the media as a commentator on Middle East issues. He runs a blog at www.kamelhawwash.com and tweets at @kamelhawwash. He writes here in a personal capacity.*

The views expressed in this article belong to the author and do not necessarily reflect the editorial policy of Middle East Eye.

Israeli occupation: More of the same in 2019

The Israeli government will assure us that there is no partner for peace and that to even dare breath the word "apartheid" is nothing but an antisemitic lie

by <u>Ben White</u>, first published in Middle East Eye 25th Dec 2018

On 13 December, shortly after two Israeli soldiers had been shot dead outside an illegal Israeli settlement in the occupied West Bank, Yaakov Katz, editor-in-chief of The Jerusalem Post tweeted the following: "They celebrate death and we celebrate life. That is the core of this conflict".

Katz's tweet encapsulated the dehumanisation of Palestinians, and utter denial about the reality of occupation and colonialism, that is unfortunately all too common amongst Jewish Israelis.

The occupied and occupation

"Incitement", "brainwashing", "religious fervour", "extremism", "social media", "family problems" – variations on familiar refrains are trotted out, time and time again. Anything to avoid facing an equation familiar to every colonial power throughout history: The occupied always reject occupation.

It's doubtful whether Katz, or any of the other apartheid apologists, ever imagine what it must be like to be a Palestinian in the West Bank, to have so much of your life controlled by a soldier's whim and a general's decision. Your house? Demolished. Your child? Shot dead. Your colleague? Jailed.

Israeli politicians and "security" officials tell us that Palestinian youth are fed a diet of hatred and incitement – at schools, in mosques, and online. But Palestinian children do not need to be taught to hate when settlers attack them on their way to school, or when Israeli soldiers shoot their classmates, or when military judges jail their parents. Living under occupation is its own education – and it lasts a lifetime.

It is hard to understate the extent to which Israel's colonial occupation degrades and brutalises Palestinians. Their homes and properties can be taken. Their bodies can be tortured. Their lives can be extinguished. And all of the above with total impunity.

In its daily activities, the "Israel Defence Forces" is, first and foremost, above all else, a colonial army.

A military regime

According to former officers, "the number of soldiers the army needs to keep in the West Bank amounts to more than half, and occasionally two thirds, of its regular forces engaged in operational duties." And 80 percent of those forces "are involved in direct protection of the settlements".

Of the 14 Israelis killed by Palestinians this year, seven were uniformed soldiers, and seven were settlers – all were killed in the occupied Palestinian territory. According to Israeli authorities' own figures, out of 330 "terrorist attacks" in October (a category that includes throwing Molotov cocktails at occupation forces), not a single one was "executed within the Green Line".

Yet rather than draw the obvious conclusions from the above data – namely, that a military regime dedicated to protecting a settler population and apartheid system will necessarily engender a dynamic of revolt and repression – Israel only knows how to double down on occupation.

Over the second week of December, for example, many Israelis have complained that the army's "deterrence has been lost", with demands from politicians and settlers for fresh collective punishment policies.

These include further limits on freedom of movement for Palestinians, home demolitions, sanctions on the Palestinian Authority, and, in addition, a boost to the colonisation of Palestinian land through settlement expansion and outpost authorisation.

The only concern for Israeli authorities weighing up such options – especially the military and bodies like the Shin Bet – is an anxiety not to upset the "equilibrium" to which so many resources are dedicated: Enough repression to subdue resistance, but not enough to provoke a wider uprising.

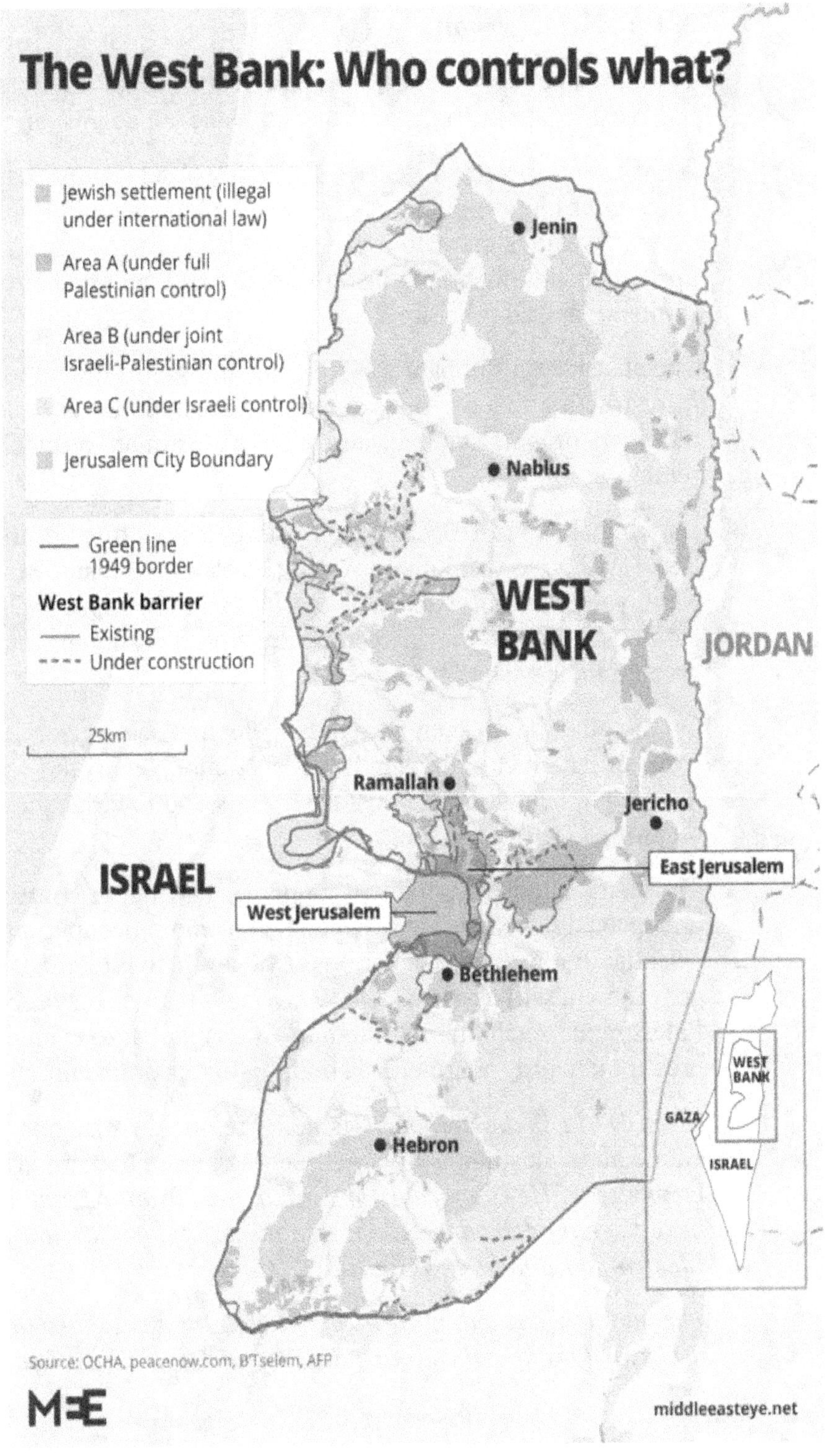

The West Bank: Who controls what?
Jewish settlement (illegal under international law)
Area A (under full Palestinian control)
Area B (under joint Israeli-Palestinian control)
Area C (under Israeli control)
Jerusalem City Boundary
Green line 1949 border
West Bank barrier
Existing
Under construction
25km
Jenin
Nablus
WEST BANK
JORDAN
Ramallah
Jericho
ISRAEL
East Jerusalem
West Jerusalem
Bethlehem
Hebron
WEST BANK
GAZA
ISRAEL
Source: OCHA, peacenow.com, B'Tselem, AFP
MEE
middleeasteye.net

2019: A wider revolt

Though Israeli analysts have fretted over a 'spike' in violence in the West Bank, the odds are currently stacked against an intifada.

As Mouin Rabbani wrote back in 2015, "observations that the Palestinians have not had it so bad since 1948 should reference not only the various indicators that would lead one to suggest another uprising is imminent, but also those factors that together conspire against renewed rebellion".

The absence, in Rabbani's words, of "an organisational infrastructure that can once again channel popular fury and mobilize, organize, and sustain a new Palestinian intifada", remains.

Looking ahead to 2019, the next year promises more of the same. Israel will go to the polls in April, and Prime Minister Benjamin Netanyahu will not want to be outflanked to his right by Jewish Home; the settlers urging a crackdown on Palestinians may be granted their wish.

On the other hand, keen to avoid an election season dominated by a wave of Israeli casualties in the West Bank, Netanyahu will also be inclined to heed the warnings from army and intelligence officials regarding fuelling a wider revolt.

The status quo is thus likely to prevail – barring, of course, an unexpected development – which means more occupation and periodic, but limited, escalations. And all the while, the Israeli government will assure us that there is no partner for peace, the Palestinians teach their children to hate, and that to even dare breath the word "apartheid" is nothing but an antisemitic lie.

*- **Ben White** is the author of* Israeli Apartheid: A Beginner's Guide *and* Palestinians in Israel: Segregation, Discrimination and Democracy. *He is a writer for Middle East Monitor and his articles have been published by Al Jazeera, al-Araby, Huffington Post, the Electronic Intifada, the Guardian's Comment is Free and more.*

The views expressed in this article belong to the author and do not necessarily reflect the editorial policy of Middle East Eye.

Israeli politicians cower before Jewish terror

By **Shlomi Eldar** January 8, 2019 in Al Monitor.

Protesters hold sticks as they stand on a roof during the evacuation of Jewish settler families from the outpost of Netiv Ha'avot in the occupied West Bank, June 12, 2018.

About 15 years ago, Idith Zertal and my fellow Al-Monitor columnist Akiva Eldar wrote "Lords of the Land." In their in-depth book they investigated the settlement enterprise and showed how the settlers receive preferential treatment over the rest of the nation, delineating the perks and privileges they enjoy. Today the situation is even worse. The prime minister and political leaders are simply afraid of the settlers.

There were two dramatic events this past week: another evacuation of the Amona outpost in the West Bank (evacuated by court order in February 2017) and the arrest of Jewish teenagers on suspicion of terrorism. These events and their fallout show that the State of Israel has become the land of the settlers, and its elected leaders their servants.

In the 1999 elections, in which Benjamin Netanyahu lost to Ehud Barak, Netanyahu created the slogan "They are afraid," a contemptuous reference to Israeli media outlets and his critics. Now he himself is so afraid to lose the far-right settler votes that to appease them over Amona, he was willing to humiliate his military secretary, Brig. Gen. Avi Blot.

The Amona outpost, north of Ramallah, has become notorious in Israel even though it was populated by a mere 40 families. In the years between its establishment and its 2017 evacuation and even after, right-wing Knesset members behaved like the Amona settlers' servants. They paid visits to the outpost to encourage the residents and went out of their way to compensate them for their "distress and anguish" in the forced evacuation.

The original Amona was built on private Palestinian land and after endless petitions, extensions and appeals, it was evacuated about two years ago. Following the evacuation, the government authorized a generous compensation package to the settlers to the tune of a dozen of millions of shekels and decided to found a permanent, alternate locality named Amichai.

Amichai was founded, but last month, a group of settlers returned to Amona in reaction to the shooting terror attacks near the Ofra settlement. When the Frontier Guard and police forcibly evacuated Amona once again Jan. 3, Netanyahu grew concerned for right-wing criticism and worried that the settlers might take revenge in the upcoming April 2019 elections. And so, Netanyahu blamed Blot (himself a resident of a settlement), accusing him of failing to relay the prime minister's instruction to suspend the eviction in time. As a result, IDF Chief of Staff Gadi Eizenkot officially reprimanded Blot.

This is not the end of the groveling before the Lords of the Land. In the course of the evacuation, 23 policemen were injured, including a police officer who was stabbed in the hand with a sharp instrument. Some were sent to the hospital for treatment. Seven settlers were detained but immediately freed. None of them were brought before a judge for attacking and wounding policemen. As far as is known at this time, none of them have been indicted.

Recall the young Palestinian girl Ahed Tamimi, who was arrested, investigated, tried and sentenced to eight months in prison for slapping and kicking an Israeli soldier. Her lawyer's requests for early release were refused on the grounds that Tamimi maintains an "extremist ideology."

On Jan. 6, it was released for publication that five teens from the Pri Ha'Aretz yeshiva in Rechelim are under suspicion of causing the death of Aisha Rabi, a Palestinian resident of Biddya and mother of a large family in October 2018. Rabi was killed near Rechelim as a result of stone-throwing at the family car being driven by her husband. Only 24 hours after the incident, four prominent right-wing activists from the Yizhar settlement drove — violating the Sabbath — to Rechelim to prepare the yeshiva students to be cross-examined by members of the Shin Bet's Jewish Department. It took the Shin Bet almost three months to arrest the perpetrators.

When the settler youths were first arrested, they were denied the opportunity to meet with a lawyer, just like Palestinian security detainees. In reaction, a whole campaign was orchestrated on their behalf. Justice Minister Ayelet Shaked, for example, spoke on the phone to the mother of one of the arrested teens who asked that her son be allowed to meet with a lawyer. Shaked told her that she talked to State Prosecutor Shai Nitzan twice, saying, "I relayed to him your cry and made the point clear to him." She added that she would do everything she could to help them. On Jan. 7 it was reported that Shaked also met in person with the parents.

True, the teens' culpability has not yet been proven, but the protests over the conditions of their arrest on suspicion of terrorism, complete with harsh verbal attacks on the Shin Bet, are unprecedented. "Every day stones are thrown at vehicles in Judea and Samaria and if you are wondering why you don't hear about it, it's because it is tweeted Likud Knesset member Nava Boker. "But when Jewish youths are suspected of throwing stones, suddenly they experience KGB investigation methods. It would be better if the Shin Bet spent its time trying to prevent murderous Palestinian terror and not torturing Jewish boys."

Last week, they were brought before the Magistrate Court in Rishon Lezion and the Central District Court in Lod to discuss the case. Rght-wing activists protested nearby and clashed with police.

A demonstration in support of the detainees was held in Jerusalem with the participation of rabbis and senior members of the religious Zionist stream. Rabbi Ephraim Meir, a professor from Bar Ilan University, said at the demonstration, "Our wonderful hilltop youths, continue following your paths. You are the pioneers of the generation. We are not terrorists."

Simultaneously, important Zionist figure Rabbi Haim Druckman published a video in which he argues to Netanyahu that the youths "are not terrorists" and that they should be investigated like anyone else in Israel, not interrogated by the Shin Bet.

Did Netanyahu back up the Shin Bet for its work in arresting Jewish perpetrators of terror? Has anyone among pro-settler HaBayit HaYehudi, the New Right party or the Likud supported the Shin Bet? So far, no, not even after the intelligence agency shared documentation of some of the youths destroying the Israeli flag. This is the way things go when the prime minister and his ministers are servants instead of masters.

Shlomi Eldar is a columnist for Al-Monitor's Israel Pulse. For the past two decades, he has covered the Palestinian Authority and especially the Gaza Strip for Israel's Channels 1 and 10, reporting on the emergence of Hamas. In 2007, he was awarded the Sokolov Prize, Israel's most important media award, for this work.
Eldar has published two books: "Eyeless in Gaza" (2005), which anticipated the Hamas victory in the subsequent Palestinian elections, and "Getting to Know Hamas" (2012), which won the Yitzhak Sadeh Prize for Military Literature. He was awarded the Ophir Prize (Israeli Oscar) twice for his documentary films: "Precious Life" (2010) and "Foreign Land" (2018). "Precious Life" was also shortlisted for an Oscar and was broadcast on HBO. He has a master's degree in Middle East studies from the Hebrew University.

Encountering Peace: The Gaza dilemmas
By Gershon Baskin, January 10, 2019 in Jerusalem Post

When Hamas implemented a coup d'état in Gaza in 2007 and kicked out the Fatah forces of the Palestinian Authority, Israel responded by designating Gaza as an "enemy territory" and implemented a policy it called "differentiation" (bidul in Hebrew). The basic idea of the policy was to enable the Palestinians to understand that if they supported moderation, the PA, there would be prosperity, openness, economic development and political opportunities. But if they supported Hamas, there would be economic closure, no development, territorial restrictions on movement and access, and no political opportunities. This is collective punishment against the Palestinian people for electing a Hamas government. The policy failed. Hamas has remained in power and has strengthened their hold on Gaza since the inception of the policy. The failure was not only because collective punishment rarely works, but also because the situation in the West Bank has not developed into the peace and prosperous reality that was supposed to be the "difference" that the Palestinian people would see between the reality on the ground in both Palestinian territories.

The realization of the failure has led Israel to engage together with the assistance of Egypt in trying to manage the relations with Gaza and the Hamas regime there. Egypt, which has genuine leverage of Hamas, serves as the primary access point for Gazans to the rest of the world. Egypt has managed to get Hamas to dissociate itself entirely from its roots of the Muslim Brotherhood. Egypt also succeeded in getting Hamas to modify its covenant in which it eliminated some of its antisemitic content and i accepted a Palestinian state in the West Bank, Gaza and east Jerusalem, without committing to peace with Israel. Egypt has successfully and repeatedly pressured Hamas into ceasefire understandings with Israel. With the assistance of Qatar, Israel has bought six months of quiet with Gaza for the price of $15 million a month of Qatari money as well as additional Qatari fuel that comes from Israel and provides Gaza with electricity.

Israel is clearly interested in weakening Hamas. Despite Hamas being in deep political and financial crisis, it is not being weakened. The PA has come to the realization that there are very little chances of reconciliation between it and Hamas and have returned to a policy of sanctions against the Hamas regime. President Abbas is seeking support of Egypt and other Arab leaders to agree to pressure Hamas. Hamas has refused to accept Abbas's demands to turn over the control of its military wing to a single-headed Palestinian government led by Abbas. In principle, Israel's interests and policies of wishing to weaken Hamas should give credence and support to Abbas's demands and needs. But this is not the case – mainly because if Gaza continues to deteriorate – it will end up with rockets being shot into Israel's civilian communities and could easily develop into another war. So while Israel does not wish to empower Hamas, it finds itself working towards understandings with Hamas that will postpone the next round of violence.

This is truly a dilemma for Israel. In the absence of any genuine peace process – which is the only thing that I believe could have a chance of weakening Hamas – Israel correctly wants to avoid another war in Gaza. The main reason is that there is no real strategic advantage of another war. There is no intention or even a real consideration of re-occupying Gaza. Israel does not want to get bogged down and does not want the responsibility to provide health, education and welfare services for two million Palestinians in Gaza, nor have thousands of Israelis soldiers policing the densely populated neighborhoods of Gaza. Nor can Israel deliver a defeated Gaza to the PA – no Palestinian leader will ride on the back of Israeli tanks to attempt to control Gaza.

Prime Minister Benjamin Netanyahu has not yet seen a political advantage in the election season to engage in another war, although if he gets indicted on corruption charges it may be an option. But this is a very dangerous one, even if it is clear that Israel would win the war, no one can predict the results on the ground, particularly because Hamas's main weapon, the Qassam rocket is a statistical weapon – it can fall anywhere – even on a school bus, a kindergarten or a shopping mall. Most of the time it gets shot down or falls in open spaces.

An agreement to a negotiated ceasefire would be supported by the Left. The agreement would anger Netanyahu's base and the Right, who would view it as next to capitulation. This is also why it is very unlikely, during the next six months at least, that there will be a negotiated agreement with Hamas to return the bodies of IDF soldiers Hadar Goldin and Oron Shaul and the live Israeli civilians Abera Mengisto and Hisham A-Sayed. To achieve that Netanyahu would have to agree to release a limited number of Palestinian prisoners including some Hamas members, who were originally released in the Schalit prisoner exchange deal and rearrested in June 2014. Bringing the soldiers bodies home and the civilians who are alive would be a victory for Netanyahu, but the payment would strengthen Hamas once again and that would not be a victory.

The choices are not easy. The one consideration that will not be weighed is the welfare of the two million Palestinians in Gaza. That is truly a pity. Perhaps when we and our leaders begin to think about those people as human beings and as neighbors and not as the enemy, the situation on the ground will have a chance of improving and with it, the strategic options that decision-makers will face.

The writer is a political and social entrepreneur who has dedicated his life to the State of Israel and to peace between Israel and her neighbors. His latest book In Pursuit of Peace in Israel and Palestine was published by Vanderbilt University Press.

Pro-settler rabbis ignore Jewish values, democracy
by Akiva Eldar January 10, 2019 in Israel Pulse, Al Monitor

Palestinians carry the body of Aisha Rabi, who died after the car she was traveling in was hit by stones thrown by a group of Israeli settlers, during her funeral in Biddya, West Bank, Oct. 13, 2018. (JAAFAR ASHTIYEH/AFP/Getty Images)

Agents of the Shin Bet security service have developed a particularly thick skin over the years. The Shin Bet generally ignores human rights activists who accuse it of torturing Palestinian detainees or issues a laconic denial, at most. Shin Bet usually does the same whenever a radical right-wing Jewish group accuses it of using outlawed methods to interrogate Jewish suspects.

On Jan. 6, however, the Shin Bet deviated from its practice, as it reacted to the right-wing outcry against the detention of five Jewish minors suspected of causing the death of Aisha Rabi, a Palestinian mother of eight from the West Bank village of Biddya. Rabi and her husband were attacked by a group of settlers who threw stones at their car. In a statement about the detention, the Shin Bet lashed out at the "deliberate and continuing effort by interested elements to denigrate the organization and its employees and delegitimize its activities." Taking an unusually harsh tone, the organization said it conducts all its counterterrorism activity in accordance with the law and values of the state and it expects "condemnation" of those who malign it.

This should send shock waves through the country as this is not some one-off incident. It is a distress call by a key security agency tasked with protecting the State of Israel from a subversive organization that does not recognize the country's laws and rules. According to official data, Israeli West Bank settlers and right-wing activists carried out 482 documented attacks against Palestinians in 2018 (up to mid-December), more than three times the 2017 figure. These include throwing stones, damaging homes and cars, cutting down trees and spraying graffiti. Israeli human rights activists operating in the West Bank claim this information is not complete because many incidents of harassment by thugs from Israeli outposts go unreported given Palestinian mistrust of the Israeli Police.

These very same assailants and their supporters are now crying foul at the arrest of several Israeli teens suspected of complicity in the rock throwing that killed Rabi. They are the ones to whom the Shin Bet was referring in demanding that its critics be condemned. Obviously, the organization expected that its direct boss, Prime Minister Benjamin Netanyahu, would rush to its defense. However, it took Netanyahu two days to issue a half-hearted defense of the organization — and then only because he had no choice in light of its success in hunting down and killing a wanted Palestinian terrorist.

"It [the Shin Bet] does its work with professionalism and dedication. There is no place for attacks on it," Netanyahu said Jan. 8.

It is easy to guess how Netanyahu would have slandered the Arab minority if minors from the Israeli Arab village of Kfar Kassem, for example, were suspected of killing a Jewish woman. Suffice it to recall what Netanyahu said after a January 2016 terror attack by an Arab Israeli in Tel Aviv. "I will not accept two nations within Israel: a lawful nation for all its citizens and a [second] nation within a nation for some of its citizens, in pockets of lawlessness," he said, speaking at the scene of the attack.

On Jan. 3, upon his return from Brazil, a jet-lagged Netanyahu was quick to demand that Israel Defense Forces Chief of Staff Lt. Gen. Gadi Eizenkot reprimand the prime minister's military secretary, Brig. Gen. Avi Blot, for the delay in conveying Netanyahu's instructions to the army to stop the evacuation of the outlawed settler outpost of Amona. Netanyahu does not seem to have visited the 23 members of the security forces injured in clashes with the settlers opposing their evacuation, and he did not comment on the violence in this "pocket of lawlessness" whose residents are allowed free rein.

Justice Minister Ayelet Shaked cannot afford to lag behind the prime minister in the campaign for the hearts and minds of the Jewish lawbreakers. She took time off from the election campaign of her fledgling New Right party for a phone call with the mother of one of the teen suspects; she then met with the parents. The minister said on the phone that she had spoken twice with the state prosecutor about the youths. "I relayed to him your cry and made the point clear to him," Shaked told the mother.

A Jewish law opinion issued by a group of rabbis after the death of Rabi reveals the side taken by the prime minister, the defense minister, the justice minister and their supporters in the rearguard battle to save Israel's democratic values and its Jewish image as envisioned in the Declaration of Independence. Traveling on the Sabbath by car violates Jewish laws and is not permitted under almost any circumstances, unless someone's life is in danger. Still, well-known rabbis justified a decision by right-wing activists to desecrate the Sabbath by driving to Rehelim yeshiva in the West Bank on the day following the attack on Rabi. The activists assessed that the Shin Bet would arrest students from that yeshiva over Rabi's death, and went there to coach the youths on dealing with Shin Bet interrogators.

To cover for the youths suspected of violating the "Thou shall not kill" commandment (Exodus 20:13), Rabbi Dov Lior, one of the leaders of religious Zionism, Rabbi Yehoshua Schmidt of the settlement of Shavei Shomron and the head of the Bircas Hatorah yeshiva gave a post-factum blessing to violation of another commandment — "Remember the Sabbath day, to keep it holy" (Exodus 20:8). Over the centuries, Jews gave up their lives in order to abide by the Sabbath commandment, mindful of the biblical injunction that "Everyone who profanes it must surely be put to death. Whoever does work on that day must be cut off from his people" (Exodus 31:14).

These "rabbis" — like the ones who decreed that Prime Minister Yitzhak Rabin was fair game for assassination because he was willing to cede parts of the biblical Land of Israel to the Palestinians — should be qualified as "villains in the service of the Torah." In other words, these are people who misleadingly and incorrectly use Jewish law to justify their villain deeds. But some rabbis reacted to that. Consequently, Rabbis for Human Rights announced that it was considering taking the rabbis to a religious arbitration court.

In fact, Rabbis for Human Rights made the correct distinction between moral and human rights on the one hand, and preventing injustice on the other. On the detention of the settler youths, the group rejected the use of any illegitimate methods of interrogation and the blocking of the right to meet with an attorney, the same way it criticizes the countless violations of rights that Palestinian suspects suffer.

The country's political and judicial leadership, on the other hand, is burying its head in the ballot box. Ignoring this situation enables the Israeli leadership to ignore the vile statements excoriating the state and its laws, made in broad daylight in the outposts of the radical right zealots. These zealots are growing in number, growing in power, growing in extremism. They are, to paraphrase the Jewish sages, "Villains in the service of the authorities." It will not be long before this monster rises up against its creators.

Akiva Eldar *is a columnist for Al-Monitor's Israel Pulse. He was formerly a senior columnist and editorial writer for Haaretz and also served as the Hebrew daily's US bureau chief and diplomatic correspondent. His most recent book (with Idith Zertal), Lords of the Land, on the Jewish settlements, was on the best-seller list in Israel and has been translated into English, French, German and Arabic.*

Israeli minister calls for annexation of the West Bank

Yoav Galant dismisses the possibility of a future Palestinian state, saying 'settlements are the new Zionism of the 21st century'

Monday 14 January 2019 in Middle East Eye

Yoav Gallant holding a press conference near the border with the Gaza Strip, 26 March 2010 (AFP)

Palestinian state in the West Bank and called for the occupied territory to be annexed.

"Settlements are the new Zionism of the 21st century," Migration and Integration Minister Yoav Galant said.

During an election campaign stop in an illegal Israeli settlement in the West Bank, Galant said: "I am clearly saying no to a Palestinian state. It is not possible to have more than one state west of the Jordan River."

"We will work to apply sovereignty in all of Judea and Samaria and to strengthen the settlements," he added, using the terms Israel uses for the West Bank.

"Only settlement is the key to holding onto sovereignty and Zionism. Judea and Samaria are the eastern defence belt of the State of Israel."

Israel captured the West Bank, along with East Jerusalem and the Gaza Strip, in 1967 and has occupied it ever since. In contravention of international law, Israel has settled hundreds of thousands of Israelis on Palestinian land.

There are almost 834,000 Israeli settlers living in settlements in the West Bank and East Jerusalem.

The number of settlers has almost tripled since the Oslo Accords of 1993, when settlers' number estimated 252,000. Illegal settlements have leapt from 144 to 515 in that time.

Israel's nation-state law that passed last July stated that building and strengthening the settlements is a "national interest."

Galant was appointed to his position last week after leaving Kulanu party and joining Prime Minister Benjamin Netanyahu's Likud party.

He is formerly the commander of the Israeli army's Southern Command and led Israel's war in the Gaza Strip in March 2010 that killed 1,400 Palestinians.

Israel's thugs beat me, but they only strengthened my dream of Palestinian freedom

Most Western commentators still refuse to recognise Palestinians in Israel as subjugated by the same colonialist regime that oppresses people in the West Bank and Gaza

Friday 11 January 2019, Middle East Eye

A Palestinian protester carrying a national flag uses a slingshot to hurl stones during demonstrations in southern Gaza on 14 December (AFP)

In 1983, three Israeli civilian-dressed men entered the Jerusalem-based English al-Fajr newspaper office where I was working, and asked: "Are you Awad?" I replied, "Yes, I am."

They said they had an order from the Israeli internal security minister banning me from entering the West Bank and Gaza Strip for six months, for security reasons. They refused my suggestion to sign the order in our office, as I had done previously, and insisted that I accompany them to a local police station.

I was pushed towards a Jeep, and the three men began attacking me brutally, uttering nasty and sexist words against my mother, wife and whole family. I almost fainted, but that was not the end.

In the detention compound, they renewed their brutal physical and verbal assault until I fell to the ground, almost unconscious. It was shocking that this second round of abuse occurred after a lawyer who had been asked to accompany me to the station had left.

Fighting for liberty

This brutal episode lasted only two hours, but the impact on me - mentally, politically and intellectually - was huge and continues to this day. The sense of humiliation was immense. But later on, it only consolidated my determination and resilience to adhere to my path: the path of a colonised people fighting for freedom, liberty and a decent life.

This wasn't the first time I was arrested, for a few hours or days, for my views and political activities - but it was the first time I encountered such barbaric behaviour from the Israeli occupation against a university graduate and former English teacher fired for his political views. The interrogators' claim that I was a traitor to Israel for working at a Palestinian newspaper, though licensed and legal, stunned me.

It made me realise their true view of Palestinian citizens of Israel. The Israeli regime wants us to be disconnected from the rest of our Palestinian people beyond the pre-1967 borders of Israel; they simply want us to be collaborators, or at least passive and docile, while we are systematically discriminated against, robbed of our land, and denied the rights to equality and to preserve our collective memory.

Since that experience, along with my brothers, wife and sons, I have experienced further arrests and physical assaults at the hands of Israel's repressive regime. My last detention, which lasted 11 days, began on 18 September 2016. Yet, I have never been convicted in court. This has been true for many Israeli Palestinian activists, young and old, and their leaders.

International lip service

Although more people in Western countries have begun to learn about the plight of the 1.5 million Palestinians living in Israel proper, most are unwilling to acknowledge that we are part of the historical conflict, and our plight must be addressed accordingly. They still act as though Israel is a normal democracy that behaves equally towards all its citizens, regardless of ethnicity or religion, and relate only to the struggle of the illegal occupation of the West Bank and Gaza.

Regrettably, the so-called international community has merely paid lip service to opposing occupation, while endorsing the ever-hastening colonisation of the Palestinian territories. Thus, the temporariness of the Israeli occupation has turned into permanent settler-

Israeli soldiers confront Palestinians protesting against Israeli land seizures for Jewish settlements in the village of al-Mughir, in the occupied West Bank, on 4 January (AFP)

Israel's true nature, and more importantly the absence of peace with the Palestinian people and the Arab world, can be understood only by looking deeply into the ideological, political and legal structure of the state of Israel, and to how this structure functions towards its non-Jewish citizens.

After the 1948 Nakba, only around 150,000 of nearly a million Palestinians survived the ethnic cleansing to remain in Israel; hundreds of thousands were made refugees. Though the number of those who remained was small, and their leaders and relatives had been forced out, the new Jewish state looked at them with suspicion. It was not acceptable to expel them too, after Israel signed on to the UN Partition Plan, so instead the leaders of the new state endorsed a tight system of control and surveillance, involving military rule, massive land confiscation, denationalisation and political repression.

Grassroots struggles

The state of Israel has taken more than 90 percent of our land, destroying traditional socioeconomic structures and turning Palestinians into cheap labourers for Jewish enterprises. At the same time, internal colonisation has been ongoing, encircling Arab towns with Jewish settlements as Arab homes are destroyed. Meanwhile, the teaching curricula imposed on Arab schools bears no mention of the history of the Palestinian people.

However, in recent decades, Palestinians in Israel have waged grassroots struggles, built political parties and become more assertive of their national identity.

Frustrated at the failure of its repressive strategy, the Israeli regime has enacted new racist laws, such as the apartheid-enshrining nation-state law, and administrative measures to curb this ever-growing political awareness. The nation-state law openly perpetuates the inferiority of Palestinian citizens of Israel, threatening their very existence.

Israel was originally born as an apartheid and colonial state, a model without which the occupation and colonisation of the rest of Palestine in 1967 wouldn't have taken place.

No peace or justice is achievable without firstly acknowledging that Israel is a Jewish and colonial entity, and secondly endorsing the deconstruction of the apartheid Zionist regime and the construction of a truly democratic state where Arabs and Israeli Jews can live in equality.

- Awad Abdelfattah is a political writer and the former general secretary of the Balad party. He is the coordinator of the Haifa-based One Democratic State Campaign, established in late 2017.

The views expressed in this article belong to the author and do not necessarily reflect the editorial policy of Middle East Eye.

Israeli settlers attacks against Palestinians in West Bank tripled in 2018: Report

Haaretz says 482 incidents, including damaging homes, cars and farmers' trees, reported by mid-December, compared to 140 for 2017

Sunday 6th Jan 2019 from MEE & agencies

The phrase "Jews rise up" was spray-painted in Hebrew on a car in the Palestinian village of Yasuf in December (Screengrab)

Violence by Jewish settlers and right-wing activists against Palestinians in the occupied West Bank tripled last year, with 482 such incidents reported by mid-December, compared to 140 for 2017.

In addition to beating up and throwing stones at Palestinians, more frequently the offences consisted of painting nationalist and anti-Arab or anti-Muslim slogans, damaging homes and cars and cutting down trees belonging to Palestinian farmers, Israel's Haaretz newspaper reported.

Such incidents decreased sharply in 2016 and 2017 from previous years, with the decline attributed to the response of the authorities after the firebombing of a home in the West Bank village of Duma.

Saad and Riham Dawabsheh and their 18-month-old baby, Ali, were killed in that attack, while the couple's four-year-old son,

Ahmed, was the sole survivor.

After the attack the Shin Bet security service arrested several extremist right-wing activists living in the northern West Bank who were suspected of involvement in violence and incitement to violence against Arabs.

A series of actions taken during that time - including detention without charges, restraining orders keeping suspects out of the West Bank and in a few cases the granting of permission to interrogate suspects using harsh methods - enabled the authorities to crack a number of cases, according to Haaretz, which acted as a deterrent and brought down the rate of violence against Palestinians.

However, over the past year, after the activists were released, as well as due to the rise of new, younger groups, violent acts increased once again.

Revenge attacks

Haaretz said the rise in the number of violent incidents also seems connected to a desire for revenge by Israelis after Palestinian attacks.

Such incidents increased after two attacks early last year and again after the murder of two Israelis in an attack in the Barkan industrial zone in October.

A few days after the murder at Barkan, Aisha al-Rabi, a Palestinian mother-of-seven, was killed near Nablus by stones thrown by Israeli settlers at the car in which she was travelling.

On Sunday, it was reported that five Jewish seminary students had been arrested in connection with Rabi's death.

In another case, a failed attempt was made to set fire to a mosque.

'Price tag' attacks

After a string of violent incidents that occurred in the West Bank last month, Israeli settlers have increased their use of so-called price tag attacks and blocked roads across the territory.

Local media and activists have reported several incidents on roads in the Ramallah and Nablus areas, where settlers have ambushed

Palestinian drivers, hurling rocks at their vehicles and causing damage and injuring drivers and passengers.

Hebrew posters have also appeared in the Nablus-area town of Huwwara, which is surrounded by several illegal Israeli settlements, calling for the death of Palestinian President Mahmoud Abbas, who is labelled as a "supporter of terrorists".

Last month, Palestinians in the village of Yasuf woke to find their car tyres slashed and homes covered in racist, Hebrew-language graffiti, in what residents told Middle East Eye they believe was an attack by Israeli settlers.

Nashaat Abed al-Fattah, Yasuf's 37-year-old mayor, told MEE that a group of Israeli settlers raided the village before dawn.

"They slashed the tyres of 24 vehicles and sprayed graffiti on many homes, including mine, as well as the village mosque," he said.

"Price tag", "Revenge" and "Death to Arabs" were among some of the messages spray-painted on homes throughout the village, Abed al-Fattah said.

'Hilltop youth'

On Friday, the UN condemned the throwing of stones at the Palestinian prime minister on Christmas Day, allegedly by Israeli settlers in the occupied West Bank, calling it "absolutely unacceptable".

Prime Minister Rami Hamdallah's convoy was hit with a number of stones on 25 December as he was returning home from attending Christmas Eve mass in Bethlehem, a Palestinian government spokesman said.

Two of Hamadallah's bodyguards were wounded, the spokesman said in a statement on Thursday.

Regarding the tripling in the number of attacks last year, Haaretz reported that defence officials said that the most extreme group of right-wing activists, the "hilltop youth," most of whom live in West Bank outposts, are estimated to number about 300.

Out of these, a few dozen are suspected of involvement in violence.

The majority of the suspects are quite young, 15 or 16.

Most of last year's violent acts were allegedly committed in the area of outposts in the Shiloh Valley area between Ramallah and Nablus, near the illegal settlements of Yitzhar near Nablus and around the evacuated outpost of Amona near Ramallah.

Israeli activist who slapped Ahed Tamimi's prosecutor wants a political trial

Yifat Doron says she slapped the IDF prosecutor to defend her friend. 'We are not punished the same way the Palestinians are for the same actions.'

By Oren Ziv, ,January 14, 2019 from +972

Israeli activist Yifat Doron. '(Oren Ziv/Activestills.org)

A few minutes before an Israeli military court sentenced teenager Ahed Tamimi to eight months in prison, an Israeli activist, Yifat Doron, approached the military prosecutor, shouted "who are you to judge her?" and slapped the lieutenant colonel across the head.

Doron was released on her own recognizance just two days after being arrested for slapping the prosecutor in March of last year. Tamimi had been denied bail for four months while awaiting trial, also for slapping an Israeli soldier a few months earlier.

Ahed is Palestinian. Yifat is Israeli. Ahed was put into Israel's military court system. Yifat —despite slapping a military officer in the occupied West Bank, just like Ahed — was charged in a civilian court inside Israel.

When Israel occupied the West Bank in 1967, it applied military law to the territory. Technically, military law and the military court system have jurisdiction over Palestinians and Israelis alike in the occupied territory. In practice, a Palestinian and an Israeli who commit the exact same crime in the exact same territory are subject to different laws, different legal procedures, are tried in different courts, and are given different rights and protections.

Unlike Ahed's slap, which was the subject of headlines around the world, and seemingly embarrassed *the* Israeli military establishment and national pride, there was no video documentation of Doron's act.

Her trial, for assaulting a public servant under aggravated circumstances, began at the Jerusalem Magistrate's Court last Tuesday. The prosecution is asking for prison time.

Outside the courtroom in Jerusalem last week, Doron said that she wasn't trying to make a political statement when she slapped the Israeli officer last year: "The way I see it, this was in reaction to seeing my friend in distress." Nevertheless, she added, what followed was an example of apartheid.

"We are not punished the same way the Palestinians are punished for the same actions," she explained.

Doron is representing herself in the trial.

"Because the arrest happened in a political context, I have no interest in entering into all kinds of legal arguments," she said of her decision to decline counsel. "I'm going to represent myself politically — I understand politics."

The legal system is one of the primary tools Israel uses to oppress Palestinians, Doron added, and she hopes to make the trial about that. She particularly hopes to highlight the disparate ways Palestinians and Israelis are treated in the dual, separate legal systems.

Yifat Doron and Nariman Tamimi embrace on the day Tamimi was released from prison, July 28, 2018. (Oren Ziv/Activestills.org)

Doron will not oppose the prosecution's request to imprison her, she said. "There are people who accept imprisonment peacefully, like many of my Palestinian friends, who experience the reality of imprisonment, either personally or through their loved ones, on a daily basis." Prison is simply a part of their lives, she explains.

Over the past few years, Doron visited the Palestinian village of Nabi Saleh almost every week. She participated in the village's regular demonstrations against the occupation, and attended the funerals of Palestinian residents killed by Israeli forces for protesting illegal settlement expansions. Dozens of people from Nabi Saleh, including minors, have been arrested and sent to prison for their involvement in the village's weekly demonstrations over the past decade.

"In the end, the point is basically to stand by my friends," Doron concludes.

The next hearing in her trial will be in September — eight months from now. Unlike Ahed, who was held in prison while awaiting trial, Doron will remain free until then.

A version of this article was first published in Hebrew on Local Call.

Pro-settler rabbis ignore Jewish values, democracy
A group of rabbis supports settler youths suspected in causing the death of a Palestinian woman, instead of condemning their act and defending human rights and democracy

By Akiva Eldar, Al Monitor, January 10, 2019

Palestinians carry the body of Aisha Rabi, who died after the car she was traveling in was hit by stones thrown by a group of Israeli settlers, during her funeral in Biddya, West Bank, Oct. 13, 2018. JAAFAR ASHTIYEH/AFP/Getty Images

Agents of the Shin Bet security service have developed a particularly thick skin over the years. The Shin Bet generally ignores human rights activists who accuse it of torturing Palestinian detainees or issues a laconic denial, at most. Shin Bet usually does the same whenever a radical right-wing Jewish group accuses it of using outlawed methods to interrogate Jewish suspects.

On Jan. 6, however, the Shin Bet deviated from its practice, as it reacted to the right-wing outcry against the detention of five Jewish minors suspected of causing the death of Aisha Rabi, a Palestinian mother of eight from the West Bank village of Biddya. Rabi and her husband were attacked by a group of settlers who threw stones at their car. In a statement about the detention, the Shin Bet lashed out at the "deliberate and continuing effort by interested elements to denigrate the organization and its employees and delegitimize its activities." Taking an unusually harsh tone, the organization said it conducts all its counterterrorism activity in accordance with the law and values of the state and it expects "condemnation" of those who malign it.

This should send shock waves through the country as this is not some one-off incident. It is a distress call by a key security agency tasked with protecting the State of Israel from a subversive organization that does not recognize the country's laws and rules. According to official data, Israeli West Bank settlers and right-wing activists carried out 482 documented attacks against Palestinians in 2018 (up to mid-December), more than three times the 2017 figure. These include throwing stones, damaging homes and cars, cutting down trees and spraying graffiti. Israeli human rights activists operating in the West Bank claim this information is not complete because many incidents of harassment by thugs from Israeli outposts go unreported given Palestinian mistrust of the Israeli Police.

These very same assailants and their supporters are now crying foul at the arrest of several Israeli teens suspected of complicity in the rock throwing that killed Rabi. They are the ones to whom the Shin Bet was referring in demanding that its critics be condemned. Obviously, the organization expected that its direct boss, Prime Minister Benjamin Netanyahu, would rush to its defense. However, it took Netanyahu two days to issue a half-hearted defense of the organization — and then only because he had no choice in light of its success in hunting down and killing a wanted Palestinian terrorist.

"It [the Shin Bet] does its work with professionalism and dedication. There is no place for attacks on it," Netanyahu said Jan. 8, 2019

It is easy to guess how Netanyahu would have slandered the Arab minority if minors from the Israeli Arab village of Kfar Kassem, for example, were suspected of killing a Jewish woman. Suffice it to recall what Netanyahu said after a January 2016 terror attack by an Arab Israeli in Tel Aviv. "I will not accept two nations within Israel: a lawful nation for all its citizens and a [second] nation within a nation for some of its citizens, in pockets of lawlessness," he said, speaking at the scene of the attack.

On Jan. 3, upon his return from Brazil, a jet-lagged Netanyahu was quick to demand that Israel Defense Forces Chief of Staff Lt. Gen. Gadi Eizenkot reprimand the prime minister's military secretary, Brig. Gen. Avi Blot, for the delay in conveying Netanyahu's instructions to the army to stop the evacuation of the outlawed settler outpost of Amona. Netanyahu does not seem to have visited the 23 members of the security forces injured in clashes with the settlers opposing their evacuation, and he did not comment on the violence in this "pocket of lawlessness" whose residents are allowed free rein.

Justice Minister Ayelet Shaked cannot afford to lag behind the prime minister in the campaign for the hearts and minds of the Jewish lawbreakers. She took time off from the election campaign of her fledgling New Right party for a phone call with the mother of one of the teen suspects; she then met with the parents. The minister said on the phone that she had spoken twice with the state prosecutor about the youths. "I relayed to him your cry and made the point clear to him," Shaked told the mother.

A Jewish law opinion issued by a group of rabbis after the death of Rabi reveals the side taken by the prime minister, the defense minister, the justice minister and their supporters in the rearguard battle to save Israel's democratic values and its Jewish image as envisioned in the Declaration of Independence. Traveling on the Sabbath by car violates Jewish laws and is not permitted under almost any circumstances, unless someone's life is in danger. Still, well-known rabbis justified a decision by right-wing activists to desecrate the Sabbath by driving to Rehelim yeshiva in the West

Bank on the day following the attack on Rabi. The activists assessed that the Shin Bet would arrest students from that yeshiva over Rabi's death, and went there to coach the youths on dealing with Shin Bet interrogators.

To cover for the youths suspected of violating the "Thou shall not kill" commandment (Exodus 20:13), Rabbi Dov Lior, one of the leaders of religious Zionism, Rabbi Yehoshua Schmidt of the settlement of Shavei Shomron and the head of the Bircas Hatorah yeshiva gave a post-factum blessing to violation of another commandment — "Remember the Sabbath day, to keep it holy" (Exodus 20:8). Over the centuries, Jews gave up their lives in order to abide by the Sabbath commandment, mindful of the biblical injunction that "Everyone who profanes it must surely be put to death. Whoever does work on that day must be cut off from his people" (Exodus 31:14).

These "rabbis" — like the ones who decreed that Prime Minister Yitzhak Rabin was fair game for assassination because he was willing to cede parts of the biblical Land of Israel to the Palestinians — should be qualified as "villains in the service of the Torah." In other words, these are people who misleadingly and incorrectly use Jewish law to justify their villain deeds. But some rabbis reacted to that. Consequently, Rabbis for Human Rights announced that it was considering taking the rabbis to a religious arbitration court.

In fact, Rabbis for Human Rights made the correct distinction between moral and human rights on the one hand, and preventing injustice on the other. On the detention of the settler youths, the group rejected the use of any illegitimate methods of interrogation and the blocking of the right to meet with an attorney, the same way it criticizes the countless violations of rights that Palestinian suspects suffer.

The country's political and judicial leadership, on the other hand, is burying its head in the ballot box. Ignoring this situation enables the Israeli leadership to ignore the vile statements excoriating the state and its laws, made in broad daylight in the outposts of the radical right zealots. These zealots are growing in number, growing in power, growing in extremism. They are, to paraphrase the

Jewish sages, "Villains in the service of the authorities." It will not be long before this monster rises up against its creators.

Akiva Eldar is a columnist for Al-Monitor's Israel Pulse. He was formerly a senior columnist and editorial writer for Haaretz and also served as the Hebrew daily's US bureau chief and diplomatic correspondent. His most recent book (with Idith Zertal), Lords of the Land, on the Jewish settlements, was on the best-seller list in Israel and has been translated into English, French, German and Arabic.

While Palestinians build, Israelis love to demolish!

Israeli troops, this week, have demolished:

- dozens of Palestinian-owned shops in the Shufat refugee camp, in occupied East Jerusalem
- a Palestinian-owned family home, workshop, and a structure, in the Negev
- a Palestinian home in the Duma village, Nablus
- a Palestinian-owned carwash in Hebron

All under the pretext that the structures were built on Palestinian land without the difficult-to-obtain Israeli permit.

The Palestine Project

Preserving a racist character in Israel

Haaretz Editorial • Nov 27, 2018

" Israel has a long history of insularity, exclusion and discrimination not only toward the Arab minority but also toward Mizrahi Jews and other groups.

Against the backdrop of the enshrining of Jewish supremacy and Arab inferiority, and the racist incitement that has become typical of Benjamin Netanyahu's government, we should get used to the terrible idea that these will only spread. "

The Palestine Project

Israel to seize 34 acres of land in Ramallah for settlement

January 10, 2019 from Middle East Monitor

Israel's Ministry of Finance has authorised a plan to illegally annex part of the Palestinian village of Deir Dobwan, east of the West Bank's administrative city of Ramallah.

The authorisation was revealed by the Land Research Centre in Jerusalem today, which reported that 139 dunams of land – equivalent to 34 acres or 139,000 square metres – is to be seized by a local illegal settlement.

The revelation comes amid an increased authorisation and building of Jewish settlements in the West Bank since US President Donald Trump took office in 2017.

"The feeling of the government is everything is allowed, that the time to do things is now because the [Trump] administration is the most pro-settlement you can ever have," said Hagit Ofran, of the Israeli anti-settlement monitoring group Peace Now in its Settlement Watch programme.

As a result of years of settlement projects and constant violation of international law, over 450,000 illegal settlers now live in the West Bank, as well as 200,000 in occupied East Jerusalem.

It is feared that the Israeli government is using its vast network of settlements by linking them together for the purpose of increasing ease settler access to illegal settlements in the West Bank and occupied Jerusalem.

Israel's 'Apartheid Road' opens in West Bank, separating Palestinian and Jewish settlers
January 10, 2019 in Middle East Monitor

Israel has opened a road connecting areas of illegal Jewish settlements in the West Bank with Jerusalem, making settler access from the occupied Palestinian territory to the holy city easier. Route 4370, which had been closed and out of use for years since it was built over a decade ago due to staffing disputes between the police and army, was opened to traffic yesterday and is the first part of the eastern ring of Jerusalem. It will significantly ease congestion around northern Jerusalem by providing an extra or alternate route to the city from the illegal settlements.

Israel's Minister of Transport and Intelligence Yisrael Katz said that his department had invested more than 30 million shekels ($43 million) on Highway 4370. "The paving of the road constitutes an important step in connecting the residents of the [illegal West Bank settlements in the so-called] Binyamin region to Jerusalem and in strengthening the metropolitan area of Greater Jerusalem, following the opening of the Adam and other initiatives promoted by the Ministry of Transportation in recent years."

The re-opened route is, essentially, a way to further connect the settlers in the West Bank with the Israeli mainland and its newly proclaimed "capital" Jerusalem, in pursuit of Israel's overall aim of increasing its sovereignty over Palestinian territories. Interior Minister Gilad Erdan said: "This is one of many other steps to strengthen the services of the Ministry of Public Security on its bodies to the residents of Judea and Samaria [the West Bank] and to strengthen sovereignty in the area…We will continue to work to expand Israeli sovereignty throughout the entire area, while maintaining strict and consistent security needs."

The new route will also redirect Palestinian traffic through a new security checkpoint en route to Jerusalem and away from an existing road in the unbuilt area of E1 in the West Bank, effectively separating Palestinians and Jewish settlers from using the same routes.

Since US President Donald Trump recognised Jerusalem as the new capital of Israel in 2017, Israel has been increased projects and initiatives which prepare for its annexation of large parts of the occupied West Bank, critics have warned.

Encountering Peace: My wishes for Aviv Kochavi

By Gershon Baskin, Jerusalem Post, January 17th 2019

On Tuesday, Lt.-Gen. Aviv Kochavi took over as the IDF's new chief of staff. My first wish for him, and for us, is that he will not have to have "his war." It is clear that his first responsibility is to make sure that the army is prepared for war and if there is a war, that the army will win with as few casualties as possible (on all sides). Prime Minister Benjamin Netanyahu and the new chief of staff, in their speeches at the ceremony for the changing of the guards, said the IDF would be stronger than ever and more deadly than ever. What a wish.

Perhaps the main goal of any army has to be its success in the battlefield. As Netanyahu said, the first goal of the IDF under Kochavi is to win the next war. That is the best tactical approach to the battlefield. But a more strategic approach, which should be the main focus of the political echelon and backed by the actions of the army should be to prevent the next war. Preventing the next war is a function of what every military person calls "building deterrence," which essentially means making sure the enemy understands the depth of death and destruction that they will receive if they dare to take aggressive actions against us.
The other main aspect of preventing the next war is to provide what has been called in Israel a "political horizon," meaning having a reason to hope that through moderation and diplomacy the other side can achieve more for their cause and their people than using aggression, force and violence.

The primary contact point between Palestinian civilians and officials is the Israeli army. The IDF has been known to engage in activities that at times have provided political and economic horizons. There have been senior officers who understand that as the sovereign in the occupied territories, there is a lot of power in the hands of the army not only for using "sticks," but also for using "carrots."

Toward the end of the Second Intifada, after experiencing years of horrific terrorist attacks inside of Israel, and after the Palestinians felt the pains of destruction as a result of Operation Defensive Shield in which the Palestinian Authority was crushed and the whole area was reoccupied by the IDF, the military launched new procedures to lesson friction at the checkpoints. A new function of "humanitarian officers" was created at the main checkpoints into Israel.

Reservist Arabic-speaking officers, usually in their 40s and 50s, were stationed to assist when the contact between the young soldiers and Palestinian civilians erupted into heightened tension and animosity. I have personally heard hundreds of stories of the sense of humiliation felt by Palestinians at Israeli checkpoints. I experienced this myself many times over many years and as recent as this week when I arranged to pick up a Palestinian work colleague outside of the Beit El checkpoint, which was closed, after being opened the day before.

The behavior of the soldiers at the checkpoints where Palestinians cross, which I see often, is usually disgraceful. Of course there are exceptions, but the rule is behavior of disrespect, aggression, looks of hatred, gross and improper use of a few words in Arabic and as an Israeli citizen who served in the army and educated officers – it is disgraceful and an embarrassment.
When I kindly suggested to a solider at the checkpoint that he could speak more calmly and less aggressively to my Palestinian colleague and others nearby, that he didn't have to shout at people, he responded by pointing his gun at me and yelling at me in the same tone and words that he used to the Palestinians.

Suggesting that he should speak to people with respect, I also noted that I could be his father. His response was: you could never be my father, my father would not have your opinions! He did not know me or my opinions, but that fact that I have Palestinian colleagues was enough for him to understand that he had the license to treat me with total disrespect. If I were his officer, he would be sent to prison for his behavior – unfitting of a soldier of the Israeli army.

DURING MY reserve duties before the Second Intifada, I was often brought to lecture to officers and soldiers who staffed joint patrols (which existed before the Second Intifada as part of the Oslo agreements). In those days there were specific orders and

training for officers who commanded soldiers who had contact with the Palestinian civilian population. They were trained to be sensitive and to treat people with respect. That does not seem to exist anymore – at least I don't see it or hear about it.
Changing the behavior of the soldiers is only a small part of what the army could do to create a climate that could encourage paths toward renewing a political negotiating process. While the primary decisions are in the hands of the prime minister and his government, it is the IDF that is the legal sovereign in the occupied territories and the soldiers that have the direct contact with the Palestinian civilian public. There were attempts in the past to find ways to ease the movement of people and goods around the occupied territory. Those steps are essential for economic stabilization and growth, without which there will be more frequent rounds of violence.

The solutions for our conflict with the Palestinians are not really in making a more comfortable occupation. The real solutions must be political and aimed at ending Israel's control over the Palestinian lands and people. Political steps must be complemented with economic and social steps that remove tension and open opportunities for more human contact that is less filled with animosity, fear and hatred. This is a long process and the IDF has a key role to play in that process.

I wish and recommend to the new chief of staff that the spirit of the IDF needs not only to be about being victorious in battle, but also being respectful of human life and to treat people, including Palestinian people, with respect and dignity.

The writer is a political and social entrepreneur who has dedicated his life to the State of Israel and to peace between Israel and her neighbors. His latest book, In Pursuit of Peace in Israel and Palestine, was published by Vanderbilt University Press.

In a clear and blatant violation of international law, Israeli authorities have demolished 16 Palestinian structures in Jerusalem's Shuafat neighborhood. (21 November 2018)

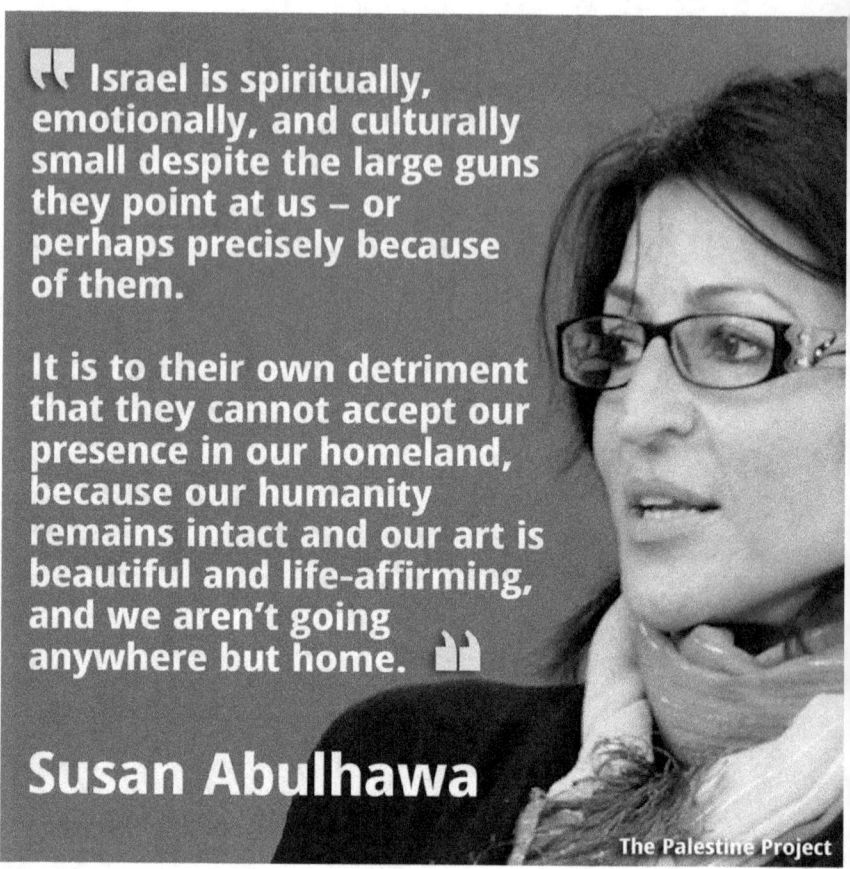

Samir Mourad - What the state of Israel is doing is harming the Jews in the world

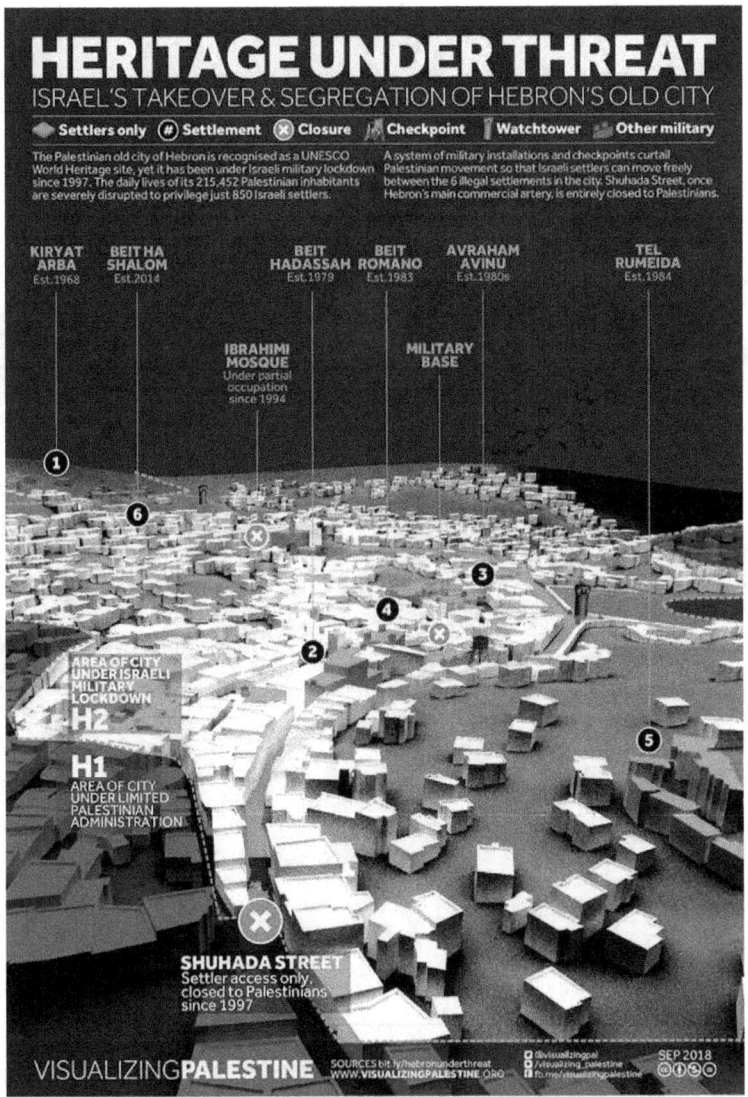

Israel has placed 6 illegal #settlements, 95 physical structures, and 2200 Israeli soldiers to privilege 850 illegal settlers. #visualizingpalestine's latest visual highlights Israel's takeover of Palestinian #AlKhalil #Hebron

Download the visual at: http://bit.ly/Heritage-under-threat

The development of the map was based on the interactive platform "Mapping Hebron's apartheid" https://www.hebronapartheid.org/

In Jerusalem's Silwan, Palestinians fear looming ethnic cleansing

Despite living in their homes for decades, Israel is set to evict hundreds of Palestinian residents from a historic neighbourhood of the city

Zuheir Rajabi shows photograph of homes currently settled by Israelis in the midst of Batn al-Hawa in Silwan (MEE/Zena Tahhan)

By Zena Tehhan in Middle East Eye

In the narrow, two-way winding roads of Batn al-Hawa, some 84 Palestinian families, nestled in homes on a steep slope south of the Old City of Jerusalem, live in fear of being displaced by Israeli settlers.

Last Wednesday, Israel's High Court of Justice paved the way for the settler group Ateret Cohanim to continue legal proceedings to evict at least 700 Palestinians living in the Batn al-Hawa area of East Jerusalem's Silwan neighbourhood.

Israeli rights group B'Tselem said the high court was "sanctioning the broadest move to dispossess Palestinians since 1967", when Israel occupied the city, the West Bank and Gaza Strip.

The court ruled the case should be solved in the Jerusalem magistrate court rather than the high court, in response to a petition by Batn al-Hawa's residents against their eviction orders, which have been systematically issued since 2014.

The Palestinian families have been there since the 1950s and have papers to prove it, including contracts. But Silwan's proximity to the Old City and its importance to Israeli settler groups attempting to consolidate Jewish control over Palestinian neighbourhoods around it make the families a target of ethnic cleansing.

'The fight isn't over'

Zuheir Rajabi, a Palestinian homeowner, sits in his modest living room flicking through security camera feeds, some 10 metres away from an Israeli settler building and police station.

He is the spokesperson for the Batn al-Hawa Committee, a group created to form a united front against Ateret Cohanim in Israeli courts.

Zuheir Rajabi in his Silwan home (MEE/Zena Tahhan)
"We have no choice but to resist through the so-called legal system here. We have no alternative. If we surrender, we'll be thrown on the streets," he tells Middle East Eye.

"The fight isn't over yet. We will continue petitioning and maybe even turn to international courts. Some 80 percent of the residents here are refugees of 1948 from all over Palestine, and now they want to displace us again?"

Silwan is a relatively poor and overpopulated neighbourhood, but the lack of sanitation and ghettoisation of Batn al-Hawa and nearby areas is particularly striking. The roads have no sidewalks and are barely wide enough to fit one car.

"We pay taxes like every other Israeli, but the municipality does not collect the trash. We have sewage on the streets and rats. This is how they pressure us to leave," says Rajabi.

Batn al-Hawa and Silwan as a whole have long been a target of Ateret Cohanim, which pressures Palestinians into leaving their homes by offering large sums of money for land, and waging lengthy and costly legal battles against the residents who refuse to be bought out.

Some 80 percent of the residents here are refugees of 1948 from all over Palestine, and now they want to displace us again?

- Zuheir Rajabi, Silwan resident

The group was largely funded by the late American Jewish millionaire Irving Moskowitz. It has stated aims of working with Israeli authorities to reinforce control over the "historic basin" of the Old City, in order to thwart any chance of these areas becoming part of a Palestinian capital in East Jerusalem.

The Israeli justice system is vastly weighted in the settlers' favour. In 2002, the Israeli justice ministry silently transferred ownership of the Batn al-Hawa families' lands to Ateret Cohanim without informing the Palestinian residents.

A year prior to the land transfer, three members of the settler group were appointed as trustees to the Benvenisti Trust, a Jewish fund that Ateret Cohanim claims owned the property in the 19th century and settled Yemeni Jews there.

With the current legal system in Israel allowing Jews to claim property that was owned prior to the 1948 war that created the Israeli state – while denying the same to Palestinians – Ateret Cohanim and the trust effectively control the fate of at least 84 families who have lived in Silwan for decades, some for 60 years.

The families, who have borne the brunt of the legal battle, submitted a petition in June signed by 104 Palestinians from the neighborhood, arguing that under the Ottoman law which applied at the time, only the homes and buildings – which no longer exist - were owned by the trust, but not the land itself.

In that month, the Israeli government admitted that the justice ministry had failed to investigate the trust and the Ottoman-era law before issuing title deeds to the Benvenisti Trust in 2002.

Settlers move in

Today, some 20 Israeli families have moved in between Palestinian homes in six different apartments and buildings, after purchasing land from Palestinian homeowners for huge sums of money. According to Rajabi, those who sold their properties were paid between three million to 30 million shekels ($800,000 to $8 million).

According to Haaretz, Ateret Cohanim employees have offered residents the services of sex workers in return for selling their property, and often threaten to publicise negotiations, endangering the owner's life if he refuses to sell.

Ateret Cohanim hopes to Judaise the neighbourhood by settling more Israelis in the homes of Palestinians targeted in the latest court case for 84 families.

The presence of settlers, who are legally allowed to carry weapons, has led to devastating effects on the Palestinian community.

Following their arrival, the government built a police station near one of the settler homes. The settlers, along with the army and police, routinely invade the privacy of Palestinians in their home, and attack and arrest residents, including children.

A Palestinian child walks in the streets of Batn al-Hawa (MEE/Zena Tahhan)

Najah Awad, a 65-year-old widow who lives with her children and nephews, was handed an eviction notice. She lives in a building attached to an apartment occupied by Israeli settlers.

The bottom floor of her house, under the settler home, reeks of sewage, and the paint on the walls is peeling away.

"Their bathrooms leak and the urine is coming down into our walls," she says. "We've complained to the police, but they did nothing."

"The soldiers come into our homes and arrest our boys. The settlers can do whatever they please, but for us, we live in a police station. We're not allowed to fix our homes or live peacefully," Awad continues, glancing at the distressed white walls.

Awad has lived in her home for 50 years and says she has nowhere else to go.

"We're not saying we want new homes – we want our own homes. We just want Israel to leave us alone."

Najah Awad stands in the bottom floor of the building she and her family live in (MEE/Zena Tahhan)

Similarly, 38-year-old Jadallah al-Rajabi, brother of Zuheir, faces eviction despite having the home's proof of purchase from 1966.

"My father was working two jobs and he bought this house with his blood, sweat and tears," he tells MEE in a community centre built for the Palestinian children of Batn al-Hawa, where he works.

"I didn't kill a Jew, or kick anyone out of their home. We bought our home legally and have lived in it all our lives. They will have to kill us before we give up our homes," he continues.

We bought our home legally and have lived in it all our lives. They will have to kill us before we give up our homes

- Jadallah al-Rajabi, Silwan resident

"I know everyone here, I know this neighbourhood. This is my life, I am happy here. You say you want peace? Where is it? You're coming into our neighbourhoods and forcing people out, throwing them on the streets."

The father of four says children in the neighbourhood have become depressed and violent, often failing to achieve good grades at school.

"If they're playing football, they have to stop until the Israelis pass with the security guards. How am I supposed to explain this situation to my children?" he asks.

"I was beaten and arrested in front of my kids for speaking out about the situation here. What am I supposed to tell my child? Do I tell them that we want peace with them? They can see the injustice with their own eyes."

Changing East Jerusalem

The settler colonialism faced by the residents of Batn al-Hawa is rampant across Silwan and East Jerusalem. Some 200,000 Israeli settlers live in occupied East Jerusalem, many in the midst of Palestinian neighbourhoods.

According to Israeli NGOs Peace Now and Ir Amim, between 2009 and 2016, 68 Palestinian families were evicted from Sheikh Jarrah, Silwan and the Muslim Quarter of the Old City.

And Israel is coming up with new methods to Judaise Palestinian areas.

Last week, the Knesset, Israel's parliament, approved an amendment that enables residential construction in national parks.

The bill was promoted by settler group ELAD that manages the City of David Park, which includes the Wadi Helweh area of Silwan that lies under the al-Aqsa Mosque's gaze.

As the Israeli government has designated Wadi Helweh part of the national park, the land, which is privately owned by Palestinians, has been off-limits for building.

However the new law will allow ELAD to construct settler homes in the area, where Palestinians risk demolition if they resort to building without permits near impossible to obtain from Israeli authorities.

"They claim a historic and cultural heritage to Silwan - that this was the City of David. It is tied to the history, religion and politics of the situation here," Khalil Tufakji, a map and settlements expert in East Jerusalem, tells MEE.

The al-Aqsa Mosque seen from Silwan (MEE/Zena Tahhan)

"Israel and settler groups began building settlement homes in the midst of Palestinian areas to solidify Israel's hold on Jerusalem and cut off Palestinians from the city."

Back in Batn al-Hawa, many families suffer from sleepless nights as they await their unknown fate.

"Sometimes I lie awake and imagine what would happen to my family and children if we are evicted," says Jadallah al-Rajabi.

"They gave away our land without even informing us. Is this not discrimination?"

This article is available in French on Middle East Eye French edition.

Before talks with Palestinians, Israel must fulfill agreements

Akiva Eldar in עברית *January 15, 2019*

Years of occupation and settlement expansion render the possibility of reaching an agreement with the Palestinians very slim, but Israel can reach out to them by implementing past agreements.

An Israel flag is seen hanging on a house as an Israeli settler looks at Palestinians in Hebron, in the occupied West Bank, March 27, 2018. REUTERS/Mussa Qawasma

Some say the upcoming elections are mainly a lifeline to save Prime Minister Benjamin Netanyahu from criminal conviction. Others believe that on April 9, Israel's citizens will choose between perpetuating the rule of a right-wing, clerical government and supplanting it with a centrist, liberal one. President Donald Trump's much-touted "ultimate deal" between Israelis and Palestinians, which was supposed to prioritize resolution of the Israeli-Arab conflict, will instead merit a footnote in the annals of the 2019 election campaign, at most. Jewish politicians who roll around the word "peace" on their tongue, or mutter the letters o-cc-u-p-a-t-i-o-n, are considered weird, at best, and dyed-in-the-wool leftists, at worst.

Internal Palestinian struggles are also contributing their share to the growing doubt by Israelis and Palestinians of the two-state blueprint. Calls for a unilateral annexation of the West Bank by the Israeli side and for a one-state solution between the Mediterranean and the Jordan River on the Palestinian side are filling the diplomatic vacuum. The result is identical: death, violence, suffering, theft and despair. But contrary to prevailing public and political discourse, such a fate is not predestined. There is a way out of it.

Indeed, the prospects of the next government, whatever its makeup, vaulting over all the obstacles and reaching the finish line of negotiations with the Palestinians are about as likely as leftist Meretz Party leader Tamar Zandberg replacing Netanyahu in the Prime Minister's Office — in other words, slim to nil. A decade of rule by the settlers and their political representatives, led by Netanyahu, has deepened Palestinian mistrust of the diplomatic option. That is understandable. The most significant change in half a century of Israeli occupation, affected by the 1993 Oslo Accord and thousands of hours of negotiations in the ensuing quarter of a century, is the addition of over 300,000 Israeli settlers in the West Bank.

And so, the only way to convince the Palestinians and the rest of the world that the two-state solution is a viable option is to change the facts on the ground. Seeing a handful of thugs evacuated from their outlawed hilltop outposts on stolen Palestinian land in the West Bank is far better than listening to numerous news reports of a "breakthrough" in Israeli-Palestinian negotiations.

All the political parties to the left of the Likud theoretically support a diplomatic solution to the Israeli-Palestinian conflict. The platform of the centrist Yesh Atid party warns that the stalemated negotiations and investments in distant, isolated settlements constitute a real threat to Israel's survival as a Jewish and democratic state. The center-left Zionist Camp (before it was dismantled this month) called for renewed negotiations with the Palestinians on a permanent arrangement based on the principle of separation and two national states for two people. Even the platform of the center-right Kulanu Party, which is a member of the Netanyahu government, supports a territorial compromise (although there is currently no mention of this on the party's website).

But what will these parties do if and when they win the trust of the Israeli electorate in order to restore the trust of the Palestinian public in Israel's willingness to pay the price for peace, not only as lip service? Former chief of staff, Lt. Gen. Benny Gantz, currently considered a political threat to Netanyahu's victory, must address this crucial issue.

As an initial step in proposing change and offering hope, these parties would have to implement an international agreement bearing the signature of none other than Netanyahu. Under the terms of the Oct. 23, 1998, Wye River Memorandum, Netanyahu committed to handing over to the Palestinians 13% of the part of the West Bank under total Israeli control (some 60% of the West Bank, known as Area C). One percent of the territory would be handed over to full control by the Palestinian Authority (PA) (what is known as Area A of the West Bank), and 12% to an area of the West Bank under joint Israeli-Palestinian control (Area B). Israel also committed to transferring 14.2% of Area B to Area A.

However, under pressure from the settlers, Netanyahu got cold feet and stopped the process after handing over only 2% of Area C to Area B, and 7.1% of Area B to Area A. Prime Minister Ehud Barak, who replaced Netanyahu after the 1999 elections, committed in September of that year to an accelerated timetable for implementation of the Wye River deal (the Sharm El Sheikh Memorandum), but he was also unable to withstand the pressure of his right-wing, pro-settler government coalition partners.

Handing over Area C to the Palestinians should begin with the isolated Israeli settlements in the West Bank and the Jordan Valley. A comprehensive survey at the end of 2013 showed that 28.8% of the estimated 100,000 residents of the isolated settlements east of the security fence would like to move away from them in return for monetary compensation. Surveys conducted in 2008 and 2012, also conducted by the Macro Center for Political Economics together with the Blue White Future group, indicated similar results. The 2013 survey shows that the Jewish settlers in the Jordan Valley and the Dead Sea area display the most willingness to evacuate their homes as soon as possible; 43.1% would like to vacate their homes in return for compensation prior to any diplomatic agreement and regardless of such a deal.

Former Israeli Shin Bet agency chief Ami Ayalon, one of the founders of Blue White Future, spoke about that with Al-Monitor this week. He referred to data showing that many Israeli-Jews support territorial concessions (to the Palestinians). For instance, said Ayalon, internal surveys he has that were conducted in late 2015 during the ''individual intifada'' period showed the willingness of some 60% of Israeli Jews to divide Jerusalem and hand over the Palestinian neighborhoods (in east Jerusalem) to Palestinian control. Another internal survey, conducted in the summer of 2018, showed that 50% of people questioned prefer the two-state solution compared with only 4% who support a one-state solution. The rest — more than 40% — are undecided.

Unlike the unilateral 2005 Israeli withdrawal from the Gaza Strip and northern Samaria area of the West Bank, evacuation of West Bank isolated settlements must be coordinated with the PA. Parallel to the implementation of the Wye River and Sharm memoranda, the new Israeli government will have to launch serious negotiations with the Palestinians on resolving all the core issues of the conflict, including future borders, the fate of the settlements and of Jerusalem, Palestinian refugees and security measures. Any attempt to separate these two paths is a sure-fire recipe for the perpetuation of the bloody Israeli-Palestinian conflict and the apartheid regime in the occupied territories. There is no greater moral corruption and no greater threat to democracy. The parties of the left and center must unite against this threat on April 9 and on the morning after.

Akiva Eldar is a columnist for Al-Monitor's Israel Pulse. He was formerly a senior columnist and editorial writer for Haaretz and also served as the Hebrew daily's US bureau chief and diplomatic correspondent. His most recent book (with Idith Zertal), Lords of the Land, on the Jewish settlements, was on the best-seller list in Israel and has been translated into English, French, German and Arabic.

Palestinians protest against Israeli demolition policy
From Middle East Monitor, January 24, 2019

Image of Palestinians protesting against demolition of homes by Israel [Nedal Eshtayah/Apaimages]

Residents of Al-Issawiya in occupied Jerusalem organised a rally on Wednesday in protest against the Israeli demolition of the Palestinian homes in the district, *Safa* news agency has reported. "The rally was organised outside one of the houses which has a demolition order," explained Mohammad Abul Hommos, a member of the local Follow-up Committee. He noted that the Israeli municipality in Jerusalem handed over six demolition orders on Tuesday under the pretext of their owners building them without permits.

One of the buildings belongs to Mahmoud Eliyan, who built three apartments nine months ago. Fourteen people will be made homeless when the building is demolished.

The 20,000 Palestinians who live in Al-Issawiya are sometimes obliged to build new homes or extend existing buildings to accommodate growing families, but the Israel occupation authorities rarely, if ever, grant permits for them to do so. Illegal Jewish settlements in Jerusalem and the other occupied Palestinian territories are not only given the go ahead but also get government support.

Israel's policy of demolishing Palestinian-owned homes is seen by critics as one way to force the indigenous population to leave the towns, cities and districts of their birth, as part of the occupation state's Judaisation plan.

Israel charges Jewish teenager over 'racist' killing of Palestinian mother
From The New Arab, 24th Jan 2019

Aisha Rabi, 48, died after a stone thrown by a Jewish settler broke through the windshield of the car she was travelling in with her husband and nine-year-old daughter.

Israeli prosecutors on Thursday charged a Jewish 16-year-old settler with manslaughter after he allegedly threw a stone at a car in the occupied West Bank and killed a Palestinian woman.

Prosecutors announced the indictment for the October incident in a statement, alleging the unnamed suspect threw the stone in an anti-Palestinian attack "as part of an act of terror".

He was also charged with stone-throwing and intentional sabotage of a vehicle, both "under terrorist circumstances".

The attack was "based out of an ideological motive of racism and hostility toward Arabs everywhere", the indictment said.

Aisha Rabi, 48, died after the stone broke through the windshield of the car she was travelling in with her husband and nine-year-old daughter in the occupied West Bank on October 12.

The mother of nine was struck on the head and died later at a hospital in the city of Nablus. The stone weighed about two kilograms, according to prosecutors.

Her husband managed to continue driving and make it to a Palestinian clinic, prosecutors said.

Israeli authorities arrested the suspect on December 30. Four other suspects arrested as part of the investigation have been released to house arrest.

Israeli investigations into "Jewish terrorism" - as such cases are often referred to by Israeli media - are highly sensitive.

Israeli authorities have been accused by rights activists of dragging their feet in such cases in comparison to investigations into Palestinian attacks.

Settler violence against Palestinians in the occupied West Bank is routine, with the UN reporting over 220 incidents of assault or damage to property in 2018.

Over 90 percent of complaints filed by Palestinians regarding settler violence are closed by Israeli authorities without an indictment.

Stone-throwing incidents implicating Israeli settlers have risen of late, according to Palestinian security sources.

Nearly 450,000 Jewish settlers live in the Israeli-occupied West Bank, which is also home to more than 2.5 million Palestinians.

Hundreds protest new Palestinian evictions in Sheikh Jarrah

Israeli and international activists march in solidarity with the East Jerusalem neighborhood as families brace for a new wave of evictions.

By +972 Magazine Staff, 18th January 2019

Hundreds of activists marched from West Jerusalem to the East Jerusalem neighbourhood of Sheikh Jarrah to stop the eviction of Palestinian families there, on January 18, 2018. (Activestills.org)

Hundreds of Israeli and international activists marched from central West Jerusalem to Sheikh Jarrah, a Palestinian neighbourhood in East Jerusalem, on Friday, in solidarity with the families there who Israeli authorities want to evict.

In late November, Israel's Supreme Court rejected the Sabag and Hamad families' appeals against their evictions. Residents of Sheikh Jarrah fear that decision could lead to a new wave of evictions affecting as many as 11 families and 500 people.

"We were shocked," Muhammad Sabag, 74, said in an interview in December. "We waited for a decision for a long time, but we were not ready for such a blow."

Residents of the neighborhood and activists with Free Jerusalem, a group organizing against Israel's military occupation, initiated Friday's action in order to bring attention to the families' cases and to try and stop their evictions. Other organizations, including Peace Now and Combatants for Peace, also participated in the protest, said Sahar Vardi, an organizer with Free Jerusalem.

Israeli, international, and Palestinian activists march in the East Jerusalem neighborhood of Sheikh Jarrah against an expected new wave of demolitions, January 19, 2019. (Activestills.org)

As protestors were gathering at their meeting point, a man grabbed one of the activists' glasses off his face and crushed them in his hands, said activist Daniel Roth, who participated in Friday's demonstration. People who were opposed to the action also yelled hateful, racist statements as the protesters marched into Sheikh Jarrah, added Roth.

When demonstrators reached the neighborhood, Palestinian residents and organizers joined the action. Toward the end of the protest, while activists were standing outside one of the homes of the families facing eviction, Israeli police attacked a man holding a Palestinian flag, said Roth. Activists then stood between the man and police forces, and began chanting "end the occupation" until police backed off.

"At the core of this whole thing is the idea that all people have a right to a home, and what's going on here is that the powers that be are taking homes from some people because of their national identity, period," said Roth in a phone interview after activists dispersed. "What we're looking at is racist policy and action around people's very homes, and that should wake people up to stand up with these folks."

Hundreds of activists marched from West Jerusalem to the East Jerusalem neighborhood of Sheikh Jarrah to stop the eviction of Palestinian families there, on January 18, 2018. (Photo courtesy of A. Daniel Roth)

In the 19th century, a small Jewish community lived Sheikh Jarrah. By 1948, most of its Jewish residents abandoned the area as East Jerusalem came under Jordanian rule. In 1956, 28 Palestinian refugee families from West Jerusalem were settled there through an agreement reached between Jordan and UNRWA.

When Israel occupied East Jerusalem in 1967, the Palestinian families who had been living in the neighborhood since the 1950s were allowed to stay. But in recent years, several of these families were evicted as a result of Israeli court decisions to recognize pre-1948 ownership claims made by two Jewish bodies, the Sephardic Community Committee and the Knesset Israel Committee.

In 2003, a U.S.-based company named Nahalat Shimon purchased the land from the two Jewish community councils. It is unclear who owns Nahalat Shimon. What is clear is that it is trying to put Israeli settlers in homes currently occupied by Palestinians.

In response to these evictions, Palestinian and Israeli activists started a protest movement in 2009 that eventually mobilized thousands to demonstrate in the neighborhood every week against both evictions. The struggle led to pressure in the media and the international community and the evictions came to a halt. Since then, Israeli authorities have evicted only one family in Sheikh Jarrah.

Although implemented according to Israeli legal and justice systems, the evictions set a political double standard that justifies Jewish claims to property held before 1948, but does not allow Palestinians to make similar claims to properties they were forced to leave in West Jerusalem.

A new framework for viewing Israel's regime in the West Bank

The existing frameworks we have for addressing Israel's rule over the Palestinians are flawed and becoming less relevant. Comparing it to other regimes that share one of its prominent characteristics, institutionalized discrimination, can create space for new ideas.

By Yariv Mohar, 31st January 2019 from +972 Blog

Israeli troops check the ID of a Palestinian woman and her child at a checkpoint in the occupied West Bank, May 18, 2018. (Wisam Hashlamoun/Flash90)

In the 51 years since Israel seized control of the West Bank and Gaza, Palestinians, Israelis, and the international community have come up with various frameworks for understanding and trying to resolve the situation. While the international community still prefers to think about Israel's military control as a form of temporary occupation, more and more people have begun framing Israel, and particularly its rule over the West Bank, as a form of apartheid.

And yet, neither framework captures precisely the kind of regime that Israel has built over the past five decades. Rather than belligerent military occupation or apartheid, I propose viewing Israel's rule in the West Bank as a "regime of discrimination." A comparative study I conducted for Rabbis for Human Rights, which sought to rank discriminatory regimes globally, concluded that Israel's rule over the West Bank is the third-most discriminatory regime in the world today.

The study ([Hebrew](#)) analyzes cases of institutional discrimination and aims at opening up a relatively new and potentially more effective understanding of the issue at hand. By comparing the situations in various regimes around the world, the study analyzes and compares the treatment of minorities in terms of: legal status, political opportunities, and suffrage (i.e. the right to vote and be elected or, in non-democratic regimes, the option of gaining senior positions in the political establishment), the right to freedom of movement and the freedom to live anywhere in the country, and the allocation of resources.

According to the criteria laid out in the study, Israel's rule in the West Bank came in behind Lebanon's treatment of Palestinian refugees and Myanmar's treatment of its Rohingya minority. Along the same criteria, Israel's regime in the West Bank was ranked as more discriminatory than Morocco's treatment of the Sahrawis in Western Sahara, Russia's treatment of the Chechnyans and Crimean Tatars, Pakistan's treatment of Pashtuns, China's treatment of Tibetans, Turkey's treatment of the Kurds, and India's treatment of the Kashmiris.

It is important to note that the study did not deal with levels of oppression (which, in cases like Myanmar, is far more severe than in the West Bank) or violence. It sought to create a framework that looked exclusively at regimes that institutionalize discrimination.

A flawed discourse

Beyond ranking, these findings provide us with a new framework to think about Israel's regime in the West Bank, especially as existing paradigms become less relevant. The classic framework used among international institutions vis-à-vis the occupied territories is based on the legal and conceptual framework of a military occupation amid security concerns and territorial disputes. This type of framework is used when describing various similar cases around the world, including West Sahara or Kashmir. What usually results from this framing is a single solution to the Israeli-Palestinian conflict: Israeli withdrawal from the West Bank following a political agreement.

Such framing legitimates the endless and fruitless cycles of "peace negotiations," which give the occupation a "temporary" veneer. And yet the occupation endures, lasting a lifetime for many Palestinians. In a sense, the occupation framework creates the conditions for its own persistence.

In the past few years, we have seen the "apartheid" analogy, which seemingly prescribes sanctions on Israel, similar to South Africa's apartheid regime, gain momentum internationally. Yet the apartheid discourse remains on the political margins, partly because Israel's regime is in so many ways different than the South African case.

In contrast, framing Israeli rule as a regime of discrimination means it is not bound to one specific historical example and its particularities. Instead, it allows us to view the regime in the West Bank as a general state of affairs, making it harder to dismiss and easier to utilize in comparative studies.

Thus, I propose understanding Israel's rule over the West Bank as a "regime of discrimination." As this study suggests, doing so will help us expose just how unexceptional yet severe Israel's rule over the West Bank truly is. And perhaps, viewing it through a different framework could lead to innovative ways of resolving it.

Yariv Mohar is the head of the media and research department in Rabbis for Human Rights and a PhD student in sociology at Ben Gurion University.

The Gaza protest casualties are not just statistics; where is the colonial context, UN?

By Ramona Wadi January 22, 2019 from Middle East Monitor

Israeli forces fire at Palestinians who are protesting at the Gaza border on 14 December 2018 [Mohammed Asad/Middle East Monitor

The UN Office for the Coordination of Humanitarian Affairs in the occupied Palestinian territories (OCHA) released statistics on Monday showing that 254 Palestinians have been killed in Gaza since the start of the Great March of Return protests in March last year. A total of 23,603 Palestinian women, children and men have also injured by Israel's snipers on the nominal border of the enclave in the same period.

By way of contrast, the stats show that two Israelis have been killed and 52 wounded, illustrating the asymmetric nature of the conflict between Israel and the Palestinians. This fact is usually concealed by imposing equivalence on all loss of life, as well as the tendency to generalise the tally of killed and injured Palestinians while going into specifics when it comes to Israeli casualties. However, the prevailing difference in numbers should prompt the entire international community to review its deliberate acceptance of Israel using sophisticated military weapons against unarmed

Palestinian civilians while creating a hypocritical furore about the rudimentary "incendiary kites".

OCHA's introduction to its graphics and statistics is completely dissociated from Israel's colonial presence and intent. There are only two references to Israel with regard to the "perimeter fence with Gaza" and "excessive use of force by Israeli troops", the latter, according to OCHA, having "raised concerns". But the Gaza protest casualties are more than just statistics; where is the colonial context, UN?

Not for the first time, the legitimate Palestinian right of return is absent from the presentation. Instead, OCHA has focused on the protests and their aftermath in terms of humanitarian assistance without a colonial political context. The brief report states, "Despite significant assistance provided, addressing the resulting multi-sectoral needs of the mass influx of casualties remains challenging due to lack of funds, years of blockade, the internal divide and a chronic energy crisis."
What UN organisations identify as reasons behind the difficulties in offering humanitarian assistance are manifestations of colonial violence that have been trivialised by the international community as ongoing issues that do not deserve urgent political intervention. Almost a year since the protests started, the UN has made it a point to separate them from their right of return about which the Palestinians are demonstrating.

For the sake of convenience, as far as the UN is concerned the Palestinian right of return must remain confined to the relevant resolutions imbued with conditional agreements incumbent upon the Palestinians themselves. As long as the right of return is viewed, even by Palestinians, as a right conferred by the international community, the UN will continue to define both protests and Palestinian rights for an international audience, thus suffocating Palestinian voices and their role as a collective force striving for their liberation. If the UN truly wants an end to the killings, it must take several steps back to allow the Palestinian right of return to take shape on Palestinians' terms.

The statistical impact will also be lost within such a framework, due to its contribution towards simplifying collective aims and struggle into numbers. All that can be expected out of such reports are regular updates as snipers continue their murderous target practice. It is shameful that the UN is still voicing concern and expecting Palestinians to resort to its institutions when the international community's role is clearly to continue shaping the tragedy approved collectively prior to 1948.

UN: 254 Palestinians killed, 23,000 injured in Gaza protests
January 22, 2019 in Middle East Monitor

Palestinian take cover as Israeli forces fire at protesters at the Gaza border on 14 December 2018 [Mohammed Asad/Middle East Monitor]

More than 250 Palestinians have been killed by Israeli army fire and over 23,000 injured since the start of the "Great March of Return" protests in the besieged Gaza Strip on 30 March until the end of last year, UN OCHA revealed in a report yesterday. "Since 30 March 2018, the Gaza Strip has witnessed a significant increase in Palestinian casualties in the context of mass demonstrations and other activities along Israel's perimeter fence with Gaza, taking place as part of the Great March of Return."

The Israeli constant attack on Gaza – Cartoon [Sabaaneh/MiddleEastMonitor]

OCHA confirmed that "254 Palestinians were killed in Gaza between 30 March and 31 December, among them 180 killed during the March of Return protests at the Gaza border with Israel and the rest in other circumstances but also by Israeli gunfire. Among those killed 44 were children and four were women."

The report pointed out that "23,603 Palestinians were injured during the same period, almost all of them during the March of Return protests and included 5,183 boys, 464 girls, and 1,437 women."

"The largest number of fatalities and injuries occurred in May (80 deaths and 5,981 injuries) during mass protests against the relocation of the United States embassy in Israel from Tel Aviv to Jerusalem."

OCHA stressed: "The large number of casualties among unarmed Palestinian demonstrators, including a high percentage of demonstrators hit by live ammunition, has raised concerns about excessive use of force by Israeli troops. Exposure of children to violence and lack of protection for medical teams are also of concern."

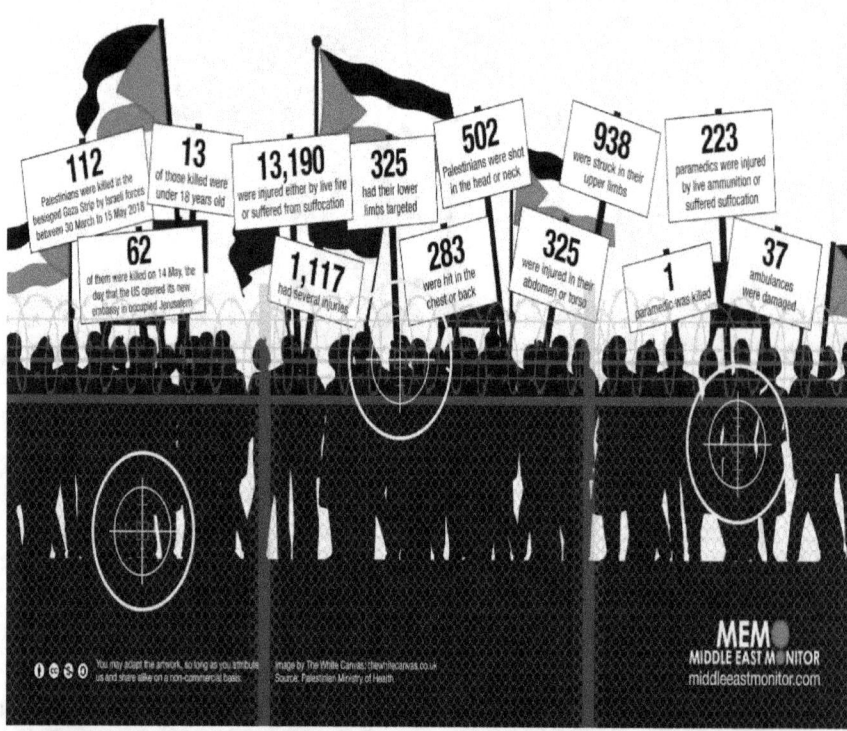

Encountering Peace: How low can we go?

By Gershon Baskin in The Jerusalem Post, January 24th 2019

So far, as a concerned citizen, this is the most uninteresting and shallow election season that I have experienced in my 40 years in Israel.

In fact, it is completely boring, despite the intrigues that the media focuses on with the breakup of political parties, the establishment of new ones, the announcements of veteran politicians leaving the race and the addition of news ones to the field. The inundation of surveys, which are completely irrelevant, and the constant pestering of surveyors, almost always anonymous, in our email and through Whatsapp, have contributed to the decline of the essence of what elections are supposed to be about.

Elections are supposed to be a celebration of democracy and the ability of citizens to weigh in on the issues, to take positions, to debate in public, to advocate policies and to determine our shared future. Elections are supposed to be about hope. They are supposed to be about believing that our voice matters and that people who wish to represent us want to know what we think. It is about debating and determining public policy priorities. Elections should be about the issues that determine who we are and the differences between political parties and politicians should be clear and focused.

In Israel, in these times, the elections must also focus on the integrity and honesty of the politicians and their respect for the law and for the rule of law. We have never before faced elections with a prime minister under such intense criminal investigation and who, by all signs, seems very likely to be indicted on charges of corruption. It does not seem very relevant if the indictment is before or after the elections, or if there is a hearing before or after the elections. Netanyahu has had ample time to make his case to the public and what we have heard so far is very far from convincing.

This has distracted us all from the real issues that need to be discussed and weighed and decided on. The personality cult that has developed around Netanyahu and his choir of submissive and parrotlike cohorts has brought us to a new low point in our already challenged democracy. The Likud party of law and order and respect for democracy does not exist anymore. For the sake of Israel, why don't we hear voices from within the prime minister's own camp telling him that he needs to step down and focus on defending himself instead of dragging the country down into the circus that these elections are becoming? Netanyahu is not the only person in this country who has the ability to be prime minister. He has already led the country for many years. It is time for change and it is time for us to return to ourselves and to allow us to get back to focusing on the real issues.

Our elections now seem to be focused more than ever on the face of the leader of each party instead of the issues. And Israel has serious issues to face – first and foremost being, as always, issues of peace and issues of security. The Israeli army has never been stronger and more technologically advanced. We saw another amazing achievement this week with the successful testing of the Arrow-3 anti-missile system. Israel has built its military deterrence – but where is it building a peace strategy?

Israel, even after 70 years, has no permanent border on its east. Seventy years of being a state with a provisional border seems impossible to imagine. Israel must make decisions about its control over the Palestinian people and the Palestinian lands. We must have a chance to re-evaluate our national priorities.

What are our priorities? Where should our financial resources be invested? Do we continue to build settlements in the occupied territories and invest in infrastructure to serve the needs of half a million Israeli settlers, or do we focus our priorities on Israel's economic and social peripheries? Do we continue to invest in infrastructure of private vehicles or do we seek to help people to rid themselves of cars in favor of fast and efficient public transportation? Can we wrestle better with questions of religion and state?

Let's put the issue of public transportation on Shabbat on the debate agenda. Let's focus on the tremendous inequalities that continue to exist in our society, such as discrimination against women in their paychecks, or the obvious discrimination against Israel's Palestinian citizens in every field of life in this country. Let's discuss in public how Israelis of Ethiopian descent can and must be equal citizens and if we should bring their remaining relatives in Ethiopia to Israel. Let's argue and decide about granting asylum to the 30,000-40,000 asylum-seekers or let us return to the UN plan that Netanyahu accepted and then rejected overnight.

How about dealing seriously with our collapsing public health system? Shouldn't we be concerned about political parties that exist in our democracy but lack democracy within their own ranks? Shouldn't the fact that there are political parties that ban women from their ranks of leaders be an issue that we confront head on? Or what about our very problematic public education system? With the genius and innovation that exists in Israel, the country should be leading the world in education and health. Instead we hold the lowest ranks in the OECD. Doesn't that bother us? Shouldn't these be the issues that we are dealing with in these elections?

Instead, our elections, early on, are focused on the "look" of the leader, his smile, his slogan in a competition over who will say less. We, the citizens, have to demand more. Political parties that don't say what they stand for should not be supported. They are insulting our intelligence and taking us for granted.

Elections are an opportunity for us to make course corrections or course changes. There are deep divisions in our society, disparate points of views and value systems. Elections are divisive, no doubt, but if we are going to argue and we are going to point out our differences, shouldn't this process actually be about real issues? We, the citizens, have to raise the level of what the politicians are dishing out to us. We, the citizens, must demand better.

The author is a political and social entrepreneur who has dedicated his life to the State of Israel and to peace between Israel and her neighbors. His latest book In Pursuit of Peace in Israel and Palestine was published by Vanderbilt University Press.

Can the Shin Bet stop hilltop youths' march to Armageddon?

By Ben Caspit *January 25, 2019 from Al Monitor*

Jewish settlers stand at a point overlooking the West Bank village of Duma, near Yishuv Hadaat, a Jewish settler outpost, Jan. 5, 2016

On Jan. 24, Israel filed a charge of manslaughter against a student from the Pri HaAretz yeshiva in the West Bank settlement of Rehelim. The indictment states that on Oct. 12, 2018, the 16-year-old threw a heavy rock at a car driven by a Palestinian family on Highway 60 between the Rehelim and Tapuah intersections. The rock killed Aisha Rabi, a mother of eight.

The investigation into the incident by the Shin Bet and the Nationalist Crimes Unit of the Israel Police lasted more than three months. At the investigation's launch, leaders of the settler movement deemed it a witch hunt and began one of their own with the backing of members of Prime Minister Benjamin Netanyahu's government. They leveled harsh criticism against the Shin Bet and police, with claims that they had employed brutal tactics against the suspects, who were all minors. No means were considered out of bounds, they said, even alleging that the suspects had been prevented from meeting with their attorneys.

In point of fact, the situation was the opposite. The real witch hunt was conducted against the Shin Bet, with Netanyahu, the highest authority over the intelligence agency charged with ensuring Israelis' security, failing to back it. Several days passed before he even mumbled his way through a few words of generic support. Ministers and Knesset members from Netanyahu's party also targeted the Shin Bet and police, in an effort to appease the settlers and win a few more votes in the upcoming Likud primary, in less than two weeks.

Some 98% of all terrorist activity in the West Bank is conducted by Palestinians against Israelis, and 95% of the Shin Bet's activity is aimed at thwarting attacks and resolving cases. At the same time, the Shin Bet also considers Jewish terrorism to be a serious problem.

"Attacks by Jews against Arabs create tensions on the ground, result in retaliatory attacks by Arabs and could set the whole region on fire," said a senior source in the Shin Bet speaking to Al-Monitor on the condition of anonymity. "It is our responsibility to do everything we can to prevent them."

Having solved Rabi's murder, the Shin Bet released an unusually direct statement on Jan. 24, with observers noting that it included a hint of criticism aimed at Israeli decision-makers. The statement said that the Shin Bet had conducted the investigation while "engaging the heads of the yeshiva and other sources in dialogue, but these activities faced a concerted and ongoing effort by many parties with an interest in thwarting the investigation." As part of this effort, the Shin Bet said, on a Saturday, one day after the murder, a group of extremist activists drove from the far right-wing settlement of Yitzhar to Rehelim "to brief the boys studying in the yeshiva how to prepare and deal with Shin Bet interrogations." In other words, Orthodox Jews received special permission to violate the Sabbath, by driving, in order to "save lives."

The statement also claimed that "interested parties" had tried to interfere in the investigation by slandering and denigrating the security forces conducting it even though the entire investigation was taking place under judicial scrutiny. The Shin Bet determined that Rabi's murder was "an act of terrorism in every sense of the term" and asserted that it treated similar acts conducted by Arab minors in the same way.

The Shin Bet's statement only reveals the tip of the iceberg of Jewish extremism in the West Bank. The goal of these extremists is to set the region on fire, dragging the Jewish and Arab populations to Armageddon. These so-called hilltop youth consist of several hundred young Jews who are driven by "messianic activism" and who consider the state and its institutions to be an enemy that must be overthrown. In short, they want to topple Israel's democratic government and replace it with a "kingdom of Halacha," that is, an entity ruled by Jewish law.

To achieve their goal, the young extremists are striving to create as many violent hotspots as possible to incite a War of Armageddon, which, they believe, will culminate in the Redemption. They do not serve in the Israel Defense Forces, do not recognize the Israeli government, and have no qualms about attacking Israeli security forces. They live a Spartan, semi-military lifestyle, based on how they believe early Jews lived in biblical times. The Shin Bet has been fighting this phenomenon for many years.

"One of the milestones that led to the growth of this movement," former Shin Bet Director Yoram Cohen told Al-Monitor, "was the [2005] disengagement from Gaza and northern Samaria. These young people, who have an anti-institutional worldview, decided that the settler leadership at the time did not take the fight against the disengagement seriously, so they came up with their own idea of the "price tag" brand, which they used to attack Arab civilians in revenge for Arab terrorism. As soon as they saw that this did not work, they switched to an approach based on inciting religious chaos by burning down churches and mosques, so that 'good comes from evil.' Once this tactic failed, they moved on to even more brutal attacks, culminating in throwing the Molotov cocktail that burned a Palestinian family to death in the village of Duma [in retaliation for the shooting death of Malachi Rosenfeld of the Kochav HaShahar settlement by Palestinians]. These young people living in tents and caves decided to avenge his death, so they went to the nearby village, threw a Molotov cocktail and burned a family to death."

Cohen further stated, "These attacks result in devastating harm being caused directly to their perpetrators, because the Palestinians respond immediately with retaliatory attacks of their own." The problem is that the hilltop youth have no problem with acts of vengeance, and they receive logistical assistance from a wider circle of thousands of supporters. Their ultimate goal is all-out war pitting everyone against each other.

Meanwhile, the Shin Bet has had a hard time infiltrating their ranks. It is almost impossible to plant agents among them. The extremists are determined and well trained, study the Shin Bet's methodology in depth and are prepared to sacrifice themselves "as martyrs." In the case of the Rabi murder, for instance, the Shin Bet used the most sophisticated means imaginable to identify the perpetrator, including staging a big scuffle with Palestinians, who were actually Shin Bet agents. This won the trust of the yeshiva students from Rehelim and led to the breakthrough in the investigation, identification of the minor whose DNA was found on the rock that killed Rabi.

Most worrying is the sense that members of the Israeli political establishment are utterly indifferent as they watch this phenomenon gather momentum and that they are too afraid to take serious measures against these lawbreakers. A senior security source speaking to Al-Monitor on the condition of anonymity more than a year ago warned that the Shin Bet's ability to discourage the hilltop youth is dissipating.

"They are losing all sense of boundaries and fear," the source said. "They receive orders banning them from entering the territories, only to go back the next morning. The police are failing to enforce these orders, leaving them to do as they please, and their brashness is growing from moment to moment."

While the security source did not say as much, everyone in Israel is aware of the fear shared by every leader on the right, both secular and religious — that they could lose the support of settlers, particularly in an election season. The only person who has dared to express an opinion on this phenomenon, and who did so vocally, is former Defense Minister Moshe Ya'alon. He has already been marginalized, paying a steep political price for his views.

One can only hope that Israel's leadership wakes up before these lawless settlers succeed in setting the West Bank on fire.

The following comment was written on the Al Monitor website in response to the above article.

Of course the Shin Bet CAN stop a bunch of teenage terrorists from the settlements. But DO THEY WANT TO? No. Of course not. Everything they do is just for show. A Palestinian teen can get 20 years time or a life sentence in administrative detention. A Jewish Terrorist Teen (JTT) will get around 3-4 days and a kiss on the head. Fair? No. Cruel and sadistic? Yes.

Pressured by settlers, Netanyahu ejects Hebron observers

READ IN: עברית
By **Shlomi Eldar** *January 30, 2019 in Israel Pulse, Al-Monitor*

Prime Minister Benjamin Netanyahu surprised everyone Jan. 29 by announcing that he had decided not to extend the mandate of the multinational observer force in Hebron. The force was established in the wake of Baruch Goldstein's massacre of Muslim worshippers in the Cave of the Patriarchs in February 1994, and after the United Nations Security Council demanded that an international force be stationed in Hebron to monitor events in the most volatile city in the West Bank. The force was first stationed there in May 1994, but it was forced to leave that August, after Israel and the Palestinian Authority under Yasser Arafat could not reach an agreement on what troops would constitute the force and what its precise mandate would be. It returned to the city after the signing of the Hebron Accords in 1997 by then-Prime Minister Benjamin Netanyahu and Palestinian leader Arafat.

The Temporary International Presence in Hebron (TIPH) now consists of several dozen unarmed observers from Norway, Italy, Sweden, Switzerland and Turkey. They are tasked with documenting events on the ground and writing situation reports, but these have had no real impact on the town. In fact, most reports written by TIPH get very little attention.

A staff member fixes the flag of the Temporary International Presence in Hebron at its headquarters in Hebron, the West Bank, Jan. 29, 2019. Reuters

On the other hand, quite a lot of information about what happens in Hebron is disseminated to the public. Video clips showing clashes between Palestinians and the settlers in Hebron are published frequently. Israeli human rights organizations such as B'Tselem and Breaking the Silence place activists in Hebron specifically so that they can report to the world about what is happening there. So, for instance, in 2016, they filmed a soldier, Elor Azaria, shooting a neutralized terrorist in the head. Ten years earlier, in 2006, dozens of settlers were filmed throwing rocks at Palestinian homes, in response to plans to evict Jewish families squatting in houses in the local wholesale market, as well as in the illegal outpost of Amona. Furthermore, Breaking the Silence organizes tours of the city for anyone who is interested. Recently, they also released "Occupying Hebron," a collection of testimonies from soldiers, describing the impossible situation in the city. The bottom line is that with such extensive documentation already circulating, written reports by the multinational force do not contribute much to the discussion.

Over the years, the international observers tried hard not to upset the Israelis too much, so that they could continue to cooperate with the Israel Defense Forces (IDF) and the civil administration. As a result, reports produced by the various human rights organizations were usually much more severe than anything TIPH produced. But Hebron is still Hebron; it is impossible to ignore what is happening there.

In December 2018, journalist Uri Blau published in Haaretz a report by TIPH, claiming that Israel was violating international law and harming the Palestinian population on a regular basis. According to the report, no attempts are made by Israel anywhere in the city to restore "a normal life," particularly not in the Old City. As an example, the report mentions the old Palestinian vegetable market, which has been turned into an Israeli military zone "that is frequently taken over by settlers and serves as a playground for their children."

From the settlers' point of view, this report was too much. True, it would be impossible for them to kick B'Tselem and Breaking the Silence out of Hebron. The most anyone can do is try to discredit them by calling them leftists and enemies of Israel. But when it comes to international observers from Europe, who are already suspected of anti-Israel sentiment, there is something that can be done.

As a result, the leaders of the settlers began pressuring Netanyahu (again) to act against TIPH. Similar pressure applied over the years, until recently, had little result, even though the settlers claimed that the international observers were being hostile to them. In 2017, for instance, Palestinian security cameras caught an observer puncturing the tires of a car belonging to a family of settlers in Hebron. At the time, the incident was considered to be so marginal and uncommon that nothing was done with the video footage. It only made the headlines in the last few months, as part of the settlers' efforts to throw the undesirable organization out of Hebron once and for all.

Still, Netanyahu refused to acquiesce to the settlers' requests, at least until this week. Then, without informing anyone in the security forces, the civil administration, the Foreign Ministry or even UN Middle East envoy East Nikolay Mladenov, Netanyahu announced that the observers' role in Hebron was over. He did this even though he himself, together with Arafat, first decided to station them there 20 years ago.

The Israeli right celebrated of course. The Yesha Council, the umbrella organization of the settlement movement, released a statement priding itself on the success of the public struggle it waged, together with other right-wing organizations: "We are pleased to see that all the effort we poured into this, together with the Land of Israel lobby in the Knesset, the "My Israel" movement and the Jewish community of Hebron, finally bore fruit."

The chairman of the Knesset Subcommittee for Judea and Samaria (in the West Bank), Knesset member Moti Yogev (HaBayit HaYehudi), is a resident of the settlement of Dolev, who once proposed that the Supreme Court be torn down with a D9 tractor. He said smugly that "the IDF and the Israeli Police will ensure security and public order in Hebron better than any other force in the world."

"This isn't just about the observers. It is part of a much broader and bigger effort," Avner Gvaryahu, the executive director of Breaking the Silence, told Al-Monitor. He said that several dramatic events have taken place in the city over the past four years, noting that anyone who still believes the occupation will end one day "should come to Hebron to see exactly what is preventing that from happening."

Gvaryahu claims that neither the settlers nor the government want the world to see what is actually taking place in the city. "There is a deep-rooted process underway to empty downtown Hebron of its Palestinian residents and turn it into a ghost town," he said. "From Hebron the evil will come forth."

Now that he is in election mode, Netanyahu wants to appease the settlers as much as he possibly can. During a visit Jan. 28 to the West Bank area in the Etzion settlement bloc, where an alternative settlement is scheduled to be built for the evacuees of the Netiv Ha'avot settlement neighborhood, Netanyahu apologized for the Hebron Accords of 1997, claiming that they were "a mishap." He said, "As far as I am concerned, there will not be anymore uprooting of communities or the cessation of [building in] communities, but rather the exact opposite. The Land of Israel is ours and it will remain ours. What has fallen will be rebuilt."

The settlers really understand the situation. They know that once the election is over, they will not be able to get everything that they can get now, with Netanyahu so susceptible to pressure. So far, they can take credit for one big victory.

Gantz, peace and the West Bank landscape

By Akiva Eldar January 31, 2019 on Al Monitor

This section of the Israeli-built separation barrier severs Eastern Jerusalem neighborhoods from the West Bank town of Abu Dis, July 16, 2004. Reuters

Benny Gantz, chair of the new Israel Resilience party, delivered his maiden speech on Jan. 29 and on the occasion avoided uttering "Palestinian state," a term the political right has turned into a catchphrase for left-wing sympathies verging on treason. Also notably, the new candidate, vying to replace Benjamin Netanyahu as Israel's prime minister, chose to use the term "separation fence" rather than "security fence," the official designation of the barrier. He pledged to "maintain security in the entire Land of Israel," but added, "We will not allow the millions of Palestinians living beyond the separation fence to endanger our security and our identity as a Jewish state."

The choice of words regarding the barrier is not semantic quibbling. Gantz, a former military chief of staff, obviously knows the official name of the structure, a combination of fencing and wall that Israel began building in 2002 on parts of the occupied West Bank and on its own territory around it. In fact, authorities have been so determined to ensure the use of the official terminology to brand the barrier's purpose that in 2009 the Foreign Ministry forced the national airline, El Al, to stop distributing maps to passengers until it replaced the term "separation wall" with "security fence."

The demarcation between Israel and the 2.5 million Palestinians on the West Bank is one of the major political challenges that would confront a center-left government if Gantz manages to oust Netanyahu in the April 9 elections. The barrier that such a government would inherit could constitute a solution for separating Israelis from Palestinians, but its route would be a major diplomatic headache.

At present, most of the fence — 85%, constituting the segments already completed and those planned – deviates from Israel's 1967 borders because its 442-mile route is twice the length of the Green Line delineating Israel's pre-1967 border. As a result, the barrier deprives Palestinians of 9.4% of West Bank land, including land Israel annexed 51 years ago to Jerusalem's municipal boundaries.

A government striving for regional peace, like the one Gantz has pledged to lead, would have to reach an accommodation with the Palestinians based on the 1967 borders, on annexation of the West Bank settlement blocs and on land swaps. That would mean dismantling significant parts of the barrier and rebuilding them along the new border.

In addition to confronting the intrusive route of the barrier, the new government would also find roads built in recent years across the West Bank as annexation measures disguised as responding to "security needs." One such example is a road northeast of Jerusalem between Hizme and al-Zaim that opened this month with separate sections for Israeli traffic and for Palestinian traffic.

As noted by Shaul Arieli, a researcher focusing on the Israeli-Palestinian conflict, the road was designed to lead to Mevaseret Adumim, a new neighborhood in the contested West Bank area known as E1, situated between the Maale Adumin settlement and

East Jerusalem. The planned neighborhood is part of a road map to create a contiguous Jewish presence between Jerusalem and the Maale Adumim, a vast area east of Jerusalem that would eventually be annexed to the city. The new construction plan is controversial, because it will physically separate the West Bank and its Palestinian population from East Jerusalem.

What would a government under Gantz do with the tens of thousands of Palestinians living in that area of the security fence, given that the coalition would likely include right-wing Knesset representatives, for instance former Llikud minister Moshe Ya'alon, former government secretary Zvi Hauser and former Netanyahu communication adviser Yoaz Hendel? A quick glance at the map clearly indicates that annexation of the area would thwart plans for a Palestinian state by instead creating Bantustan-style Palestinian enclaves. In other words, annexing that area would cut through any future Palestinian state, fracturing the territory into small, confined regions.

South of E1 near Bethlehem, members of the new government would find another annexation initiative, designated as area E2, launched under the guise of plans to widen Route 60. On Dec. 26, the state informed the Supreme Court that it had allocated 1,182 dunams of land (292 acres) for Givat Ha-Etam, a new settlement with 2,500 housing units.

The Palestinian Authority claims in "Besieging Bethlehem," a report issued this month, that Israel — having cutting off the Palestinian city of Bethlehem from Jerusalem with a string of settlements — is now planning to cut Bethlehem off from Hebron and from the villages west of the town. The plan threatens land belonging to the Palestinian towns and villages of Beit Jala, al-Khader and Massara. In addition, environmental groups warn that it would damage part of Battir, a Palestinian village recognized by UNESCO in 2014 as a World Heritage Site. Archaeological finds around the village have been dated to the Middle Bronze Age and the Iron Age, and remnants of a 7th-century town from the early Arab period have been found there. Battir has been an important site for vegetable cultivation since the 12th century.

How will Gantz respond to UNESCO's warning that construction of the separation barrier in Battir as currently planned could cause irreparable damage to stone terraces dating back thousands of years and rob Palestinian farmers of the fields and orchards nurtured by a traditional subterranean watering system? Will the new government boycott UNESCO and thumb its nose at its decisions like the current government has done? Will Gantz sit on the fence while Israeli contractors build a cement wall on ancient stone terraces?

Like every politician eyeing the political center, Gantz could not avoid pledging to keep Jerusalem "unified for eternity." The separation fence, however — the one he cited as the buffer between Israel and millions of Palestinians — runs deep into the heart of "unified Jerusalem." Misleading voters with slogans about a united Jerusalem will not address the problem of sewage flowing through the streets of the Shuafat refugee camp, which Israel annexed to Jerusalem, and will not ease the neglect in the annexed East Jerusalem neighborhood of Walaja.

A responsible and reasonably decent government will have to decide, sooner rather than later, how to deal with the 100,000-150,000 Palestinians from East Jerusalem who hold Israeli ID cards but are separated from the city by the barrier. The mystery of their exact number is characteristic of their isolation and neglect.

New parties, like Israel Resilience, can hold out the promise of "change." Such change, however, will require a fundamental reassessment of the geopolitical reality created by successive Israeli governments in the occupied territories by erecting walls, building roads for Israelis only and expropriating Palestinians' land. To prevent Israel from plunging into the abyss of occupation and moral decline on the verge of which it now teeters, the wheel must be turned. Gantz, in his speech, failed to indicate whether he has the strength or will to do so.

Palestinian teen shot dead after alleged stabbing attack

January 31, 2019 from Middle East Monitor

Israeli border police opened fire on Samah Zuheir Mubarak, a student from the West Bank city of Ramallah, at the al-Zaeem checkpoint [Maannews]

Israeli forces have shot dead a 16-year-old Palestinian girl after she allegedly attempted to stab a border policeman at a checkpoint between the occupied West Bank and Jerusalem, according to local media and police reports.

Israeli border police opened fire on Samah Zuheir Mubarak, a student from the West Bank city of Ramallah, at the al-Zaeem checkpoint, which separates an illegal Jewish settlement in the West Bank from a neighbourhood that lies in occupied East Jerusalem.

Mubarak's family, based in the Gaza Strip, told local media that Israeli forces killed their daughter in "cold blood".

In a video released by Israeli police, Mubarak is seen walking towards the checkpoint. In another clip, she is seen standing near a vehicle and a group of Israeli forces. After what appears to be a brief exchange, the police officer backs away, Mubarak is shot by Israeli forces at close range and falls to the ground.

Another clip shows Israeli forces searching through her belongings including books and school supplies as they emptied her bag.

Yoram Halevi, Israel's Jerusalem police chief, said the Palestinian girl pulled out a knife and tried to "stab" Israeli soldiers at the al-Zaeem checkpoint, and was shot.

"It's not clear what the background is, what is the reason [behind her arrival to the checkpoint]," he said, adding the incident is being "investigated".

The incident comes days after at least three other Palestinians were killed by Israeli forces and settlers.

On Saturday, 38-year-old Hamdi Naasan succumbed to his wounds in the West Bank village of al-Mugheir after Israelis from a nearby settlement fired shots.

Ayman Hamed, 18, was laid to rest in his village of Silwad after the Israeli army shot and killed him on Friday for allegedly throwing stones.

Israeli police also killed Riyad Shamasneh during a high-speed chase near the Old City's Damascus Gate in East Jerusalem on Saturday morning.

A number of local and international human rights groups have raised concerns that Israeli security forces have used excessive force when confronting Palestinians who carried out attacks or were suspected of doing so.

The Israeli police relaxed its open-fire regulations in December 2015, permitting officers to open fire with live ammunition on those throwing stones or firebombs as an initial option, without having to use non-lethal weapons first.

Besieging Bethlehem.
Latest Israeli Settlement Developments in Bethlehem.
A document by The State of Palestine, PLO Negotiations Affair Dept.
January 28th 2019

Bethlehem, located 10 kilometers to the south of Jerusalem, has been one of the most hard-hit Palestinian governorates by Israeli colonial-settlement policies. Being surrounded by 18 illegal colonial settlements, the iconic Bethlehem, birthplace of Jesus and home to an important number of religious, archeological and cultural sites, has been separated from its twin city of Jerusalem by the construction of three illegal settlements between both occupied cities (Gilo, Giv'at Hamatos and Har Homa), in addition to the illegal Annexation Wall. Today, the Israeli occupation advances plans in order to further fragment the hinterland of the city by separating it from its western villages as well as from Hebron to the south. This brief describes the latest Israeli colonial-settlement steps in the Bethlehem Area.

Threatening Battir, a World Heritage Site1:

Battir is a Palestinian village of about 5,000 inhabitants dating back to Canaanite times. It is home to Roman springs, hand-made terracing, ancient irrigation systems, baths, and captivating hiking trails. In addition, the village features other fascinating elements such as Roman graves, stone houses, watchtowers, olive trees, and vineyards. It was historically known as the "agricultural basin" of Jerusalem. In June 2014, Battir was inscribed as a World Heritage

Site on the List of World Heritage in Danger. The name of the site is "Palestine, Land of Olives and Vines: Cultural Landscape of Southern Jerusalem, Battir". The World Heritage Site also includes the lands of Beit Jala, in what is known as the "Makhrour Valley".

In 1996, three years after the Oslo Interim Agreement was signed, Israel built a bypass road for Israeli settlers to facilitate the traffic of settlers toward southern West Bank areas. Road 60 became an important element in settlement growth in the area, particularly the settlements in the Western Bethlehem Area.

These cases include the settlements of Beitar Illit and Efrat, that from the signing of the Accords, the populations have drastically increased from 5,500 and 3,500 respectively, to populations of over 50,000 and 10,000 today. Road 60, including its bridges and tunnels, is just one of many tools pulled out of Israel's toolbox in its attempts to annex the western Bethlehem areas of occupied Palestine.

In July 2017, members of the Israeli government coalition introduced a bill to the Israeli parliament for a further unilateral expansion of the Israeli Jerusalem Municipality towards other areas of the West Bank around Jerusalem, including the western Bethlehem Area (known by Israel as the "Gush Etzion Bloc"), where the World Heritage Site is located. This bill has been considered an initiative towards the annexation of the area.

On 22 October 2018, the Israeli Government approved plans to expand Bypass Road 60, threatening Palestinian lands of Beit Jala, Al-Khadder and Al-Ma'sara. This new development directly threatens the protected World Heritage Site of Battir. As part of the same plan, the Israeli occupying authorities plan to build an additional bridge in the nearby site of the Cremisan Valley, further devastating Palestinian olive groves in the area.

On 19 December 2018, a group of armed Israeli settlers entered the World Heritage Site from Beit Jala in an attempt to establish a new colonial-installation in the heart of the area, between Beit Jala and Battir, and parallel to the illegal colonial-settlement of Har Gilo about 500 meters. They opened a road approximately 300 meters long.

The settlers returned on Christmas Eve, 24 December, to attempt to build a colonial-installation through violent means. While their attempts failed, there are justifiable concerns that violent settlers will return to the area, especially in the context of the upcoming Israeli elections.

SHRINKING BETHLEHEM
(SPEPTEMBER 2015)

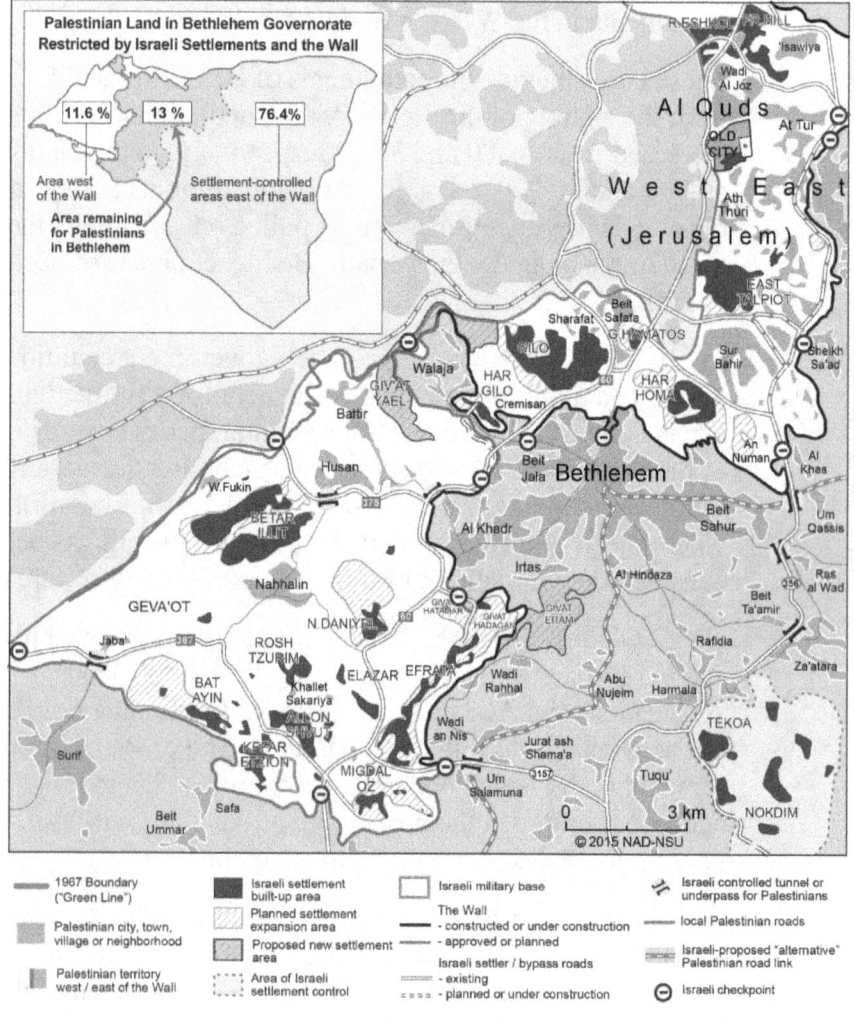

Separating Bethlehem from Hebron

Illegally established in 1980, on the eastern side of Road 60 and south of the city of Bethlehem, the illegal colonial-settlement of Efrat has prevented Palestinian natural growth in the southern

Bethlehem area. Its largest expansion came following the signing of the Oslo Agreement.

This illegal colonial settlement is part of what Israel refers to as the "Gush Etzion Bloc", linking colonial-settlements to the west, as well as to the east, of Bethlehem Governorate ("Etzion East").

On 16 December 2018, the Israeli Government publicly announced that they had allocated an area of about 1,182 dunums (an unofficial calculation highlights it is likely closer to 1,300 dunums) for the construction of a new illegal colonial settlement named "Givat Eitam", nearby Efrat. This is located in the area of A-Nahla, one of the last areas left for the development of Bethlehem, close to the historic village of Artas.

The aim of the new settlement would be to consolidate the role being played by the colonial-settlement of Efrat, creating territorial contiguity between the illegal Israeli colonial settlements from the east and west parts of Bethlehem, effectively closing the area for Palestinian presence. This plan has been referred by some as "E-2", in relation to the "E-1" settlement areas that would effectively divide and further fragment the occupied West Bank.

Israeli Settlements are Illegal

Colonial-settlements are a grave violation of international humanitarian law. There is consensus about the illegality of Israeli colonial settlement activities. From the Fourth Geneva Convention[5], to the Rome Statute[6], the Hague Regulations[7], the UN Charter and several UN resolutions, including UNSC Resolution 2334 (December 26, 2016), as well as the 2004 Advisory Opinion of the International Court of Justice.

Cultural Property is Protected under International Law

Cultural Property is not only valuable to the sovereign State in which territory it stands, rather it is valuable to all human kind. Consequently, the international community has sought its protection through multiple international instruments. These include Hague IV on the Laws and Customs of War on Land, The Hague Convention on Protection of Cultural property in the Event of Armed Conflict, Additional Protocol I to the Geneva Conventions, and the Rome Statute of the International Criminal Court which classifies "Intentionally directing attacks against buildings dedicated to religion, education, art, science or charitable purposes, historic monuments, hospitals and places where the sick and wounded are collected, provided they are no military objectives" as a war crime.

Responsibility to Act

While there is a broad consensus among the members of the international community about the illegality of Israel's colonial-settlement enterprise, Israel has been able to continue to act with full impunity. Products made in such settlements, including several companies located in the Bethlehem area, continue to be traded in international markets; foreign companies continue to work as part of this illegal enterprise, and a number of foreign organizations continue to fund illegal colonial activities in the occupied State of Palestine.

In the case of the protected World Heritage Site of "Palestine, land of Olives and Vines: Cultural Landscape of Southern Jerusalem, Battir", there is an additional responsibility to prevent the destruction of the site by the occupying power, including through the Convention Concerning the Protection of the World Cultural and Natural Heritage.

As far as Israel's continues to be treated as a state above the law, Tel Aviv will continue to expand its colonial enterprise in Palestine, thus eliminating the prospects of a just and lasting peace.

Ending Apartheid in Palestine: An Interview With BDS Australia's Hilmi Dabbagh

By Paul Gregoire | 02/02/2019 from the Sydney Criminal Lawyers web pages

Amnesty International has taken aim at online booking companies for "fuelling human rights violations against Palestinians" by listing hundreds of accommodation options, attractions and tours in Israeli settlements in Occupied Palestinian Territories.

Released this week, the <u>Destination: Occupation report</u> calls on Airbnb, TripAdvisor, Expedia and Booking.com to stop doing business in the Israeli settlements, which it stresses are deemed illegal under international humanitarian law.

Amnesty outlines that these digital companies are actually misleading their customers by failing to consistently indicate when accommodation is situated within the settlements, which is leading to a situation where tourists have no idea they're holidaying on stolen land.

Israel's strategic affairs and public security minister Gilad Erdan <u>tweeted</u> that in its report Amnesty is attempting to "distort facts, deny Jewish heritage and delegitimise Israel". The minister also accused the human rights group as being a front for the Boycott, Divestment and Sanction (BDS) movement.

Established in 2005, the BDS movement is a global campaign promoting the boycotting of Israel in various ways in order to bring a halt to the human rights violations Palestinian people in the region are subjected to.

An open air prison

Meanwhile, in the Gaza Strip today, two million Palestinians are living in what amounts to a giant open prison. After the withdrawal of its military presence in 2005, Israel instigated a number of sanctions two years later that have amounted to an ongoing blockade by land, air and sea.

In 2017, the United Nations reported that those living in Gaza are down to two hours electricity a day, youth unemployment was up around 60 percent, and the region's only water source will be "irreversibly depleted" by next year.

At the same time that the US controversially opened its embassy in Jerusalem on 14 May last year, Israeli forces just 70 kilometres away at the Gaza border killed 58 unarmed Palestinian demonstrators, who were demanding the right to return to their homelands and an easing of the blockade.

Boycotting the oppression

BDS Australia is a coalition of Palestinian associations from around the country. Along with the movement's other branches across the globe, it's "challenging international support for Israeli apartheid and settler-colonialism".

The Israeli parliament effectively enshrined Israel's decades-old system of apartheid in the nation's Basic Laws – its de facto constitution – when it passed the Nation-State Law on 19 July last year. The legislation states that only Jewish people have the right to self-determination in Israel.

BDS is inspired by the South African anti-apartheid movement. Its local chapter is currently calling on SBS Australia to stop its broadcast of the Eurovision Song Contest this year as it's set to be held in Tel Aviv.

Sydney Criminal Lawyers spoke to BDS Australia convener Hilmi Dabbagh about the plight of the Palestinian people, the impact that the movement has had in its time, as well as the opposition it faces in this country.

Firstly, Boycott, Divestment and Sanction Australia has recently been campaigning so that SBS refrains from broadcasting the 2019 Eurovision Song Contest as Israel is set to host it. And you've also been asking Australian contestants to stop taking part.

Hilmi, can you outline how this campaign is going? And how is BDS trying to achieve its aims?

For the Eurovision campaign, BDS Australia is part of a global campaign. The campaign was launched by the BDS National Committee in Palestine. We work in coordination with BDS teams in other countries.

Unfortunately, SBS insists that it will broadcast Eurovision, which is going to be held in Tel Aviv in May. We think this is a very unfortunate decision.

We keep asking SBS to live up to its charter and reflect the ethical values of the Australian people. We will also continue to ask all people to support international law and human rights to premise these values.

Similarly, we are asking supporters to contact the contestants, and the winner, when Australia decides who has won, and tell them not to participate.

We are employing a range of strategies and actions to educate the Australian public about this campaign and why SBS should not take part in it.

We are also planning a counter concert on the same evening as the May Eurovision final concert broadcast.

We coordinate all our actions with international teams around the world. So, sometimes something will come up from other countries which we will implement.

In July last year, the Israeli government passed the Nation-State Law, which, as BDS Australia has pointed out, effectively enshrined the apartheid system in Israeli law.

How would you describe the plight of Palestinian people living in Israel? And further, the situation of those Palestinians living in the Occupied Palestinian Territories?

In Israel itself, even before this Nation-State Law – which is literally an apartheid law, because it gives self-determination only to Jewish citizens – there were some 65 laws that discriminate against Palestinians. These laws are in relation to land ownership, residency and many other aspects.

The situation of Palestinian-Israeli citizens is evident to any visitor. If you visit Israel, you go through Israeli towns and villages, which are modern with western style facilities.

But, if you pass by villages that are predominantly populated by Palestinians, you easily notice the difference in the infrastructure and housing, as well as the disgraceful lack of services.

Half of the Palestinian population in general – which is estimated at about 14 million – live in diaspora and half of them live in Palestine. There are 2 million Palestinians in Israel and 3 million in the West Bank, with roughly 2 million in Gaza.

It's important to know about the Palestinians in the occupied territories. If we talk about the West Bank, there's the confiscation of Palestinian prime agricultural land to massive settlements and also, hundreds of checkpoints and roadblocks, which impact very aggressively on any freedom of movement.

Palestinians have to use an inferior road system, while there are modern freeways that link the illegal settlements to Israel. Palestinians are not allowed to use these freeways. This is a clear example of the apartheid system that operates throughout the area.

The illegal settlements use up to 20 times more water resources than the local Palestinian villages, some of which have to actually buy water, because their wells have been declared off limits and destroyed as they are located on the land that has been taken for settlement.

There are the arrests of Palestinians, including children, at night time. There are the assassinations and summary executions of Palestinians, who Israel believe have no right to resist the occupation. These are very commonplace practices.

Peaceful demonstrations aren't tolerated. And protesters, including children, are regularly teargassed and shot with rubber bullets.

There are currently more than 6,000 Palestinian security prisoners and detainees in Israel, including more than 200 children. Individuals are often detained in prison for an indefinite time, with no charge or trial, as Israel uses mandatory detention as a tool of oppression and as a way of silencing Palestinian leaders and politicians.

Palestinians in the West Bank and East Jerusalem are subject to military law and a military court system, while all settlers are subject to civilian law, even when they attack or kill Palestinians. The unemployment rate is 30 percent. It's a terrible situation.

I can't talk about the plight of Palestinian people without talking about people in Gaza. It is enough to say it has been under almost full blockade for some 12 years, since 2007.

In addition, attacks against Gaza have caused thousands of deaths and tens of thousands of injuries, with massive destruction to housing and infrastructure. And limited construction material is allowed in to rebuild.

There is a United Nations Relief and Works Agency 2012 report titled <u>Gaza in 2020</u> and it advises that Gaza will not be fit for habitation by next year. But, are the international community responding positively? They are not even condemning it, let alone, taking any action to alleviate the situation.

And I can't really talk about the plight of Palestinians without talking about the diaspora. Those who live in countries around Palestine are in camps that are not fit for humans.

And people who managed to get another citizenship – such as myself living a decent life in this lovely country – we suffer enormous emotional damage from being away from our homeland, family and friends.

How is it fair for anyone with Jewish European heritage – who has no links to the Middle East whatsoever – to have automatic rights to Israeli citizenship now, while I have all my ancestors on record as residents of Jaffa and I can't return to my parents' home.

Back in October last year, prime minister Scott Morrison flagged a proposal for Australia to move its embassy in Israel to Jerusalem, following the United States having done the same in May.

Then Morrison announced in mid-December that Australia was recognising West Jerusalem as the capital of Israel, however the embassy wouldn't be moving straightaway. What did you think about these developments?

It's a move that was advised by former Australian ambassador to Israel Dave Sharma, who was also the Liberal candidate in the Wentworth byelection.

Fortunately, they lost the byelection. And it is good that the Labor Party said they don't support this.

It was an election move, which was very shocking for people who even support the Liberal Party, because it's against the ethos on their website. It has nothing to do with genuine politics, it had to do with the matter of the election.

On 16th of this month, BDS Australia sent a letter to the Sydney Opera House chairperson in relation to the Israeli dance company L-E-V performing at the venue over a four night period ending this Sunday.

Your organisation has asked the Opera House not to host events featuring performers representing Israel in the future. Why is it important to stop a dance company like L-E-V playing in Australia?

Because we are trying to counter effect the Israeli government's conscious program to use artists and cultural events to promote Brand Israel. They have this strategy to brand the country as a democratic progressive society. L-E-V has received Israeli government funding in the past.

In general, with this Brand Israel, the Israeli government seeks to normalise Israel. And show that it is a country that has values similar to the west, when in fact, all that they're trying to do is justify the discrimination, occupation, land theft and army violence against Palestinians, as a legitimate action to maintain Israeli security.

And besides what we've already covered, what other campaigns and boycotts are BDS Australia running at present?

Currently, we are partnering with the global campaign against Hewlett Packard, HP: the company that produces computers and IT equipment.

Why? Because HP technology and support are essential for the occupation: the checkpoints, the ID cards, and the Israeli Navy's illegal siege of Gaza. It all relies on HP technology.

Later this year, we will launch our campaign for a ban on weapons and military equipment trade between Israel and Australia.

The UK Labour Party has agreed it will implement a ban if it wins the next election. And we know Australians would support the Labor Party here doing the same.

We will also press for superannuation funds to divest from companies that support the occupation and the ongoing oppression of Palestinians.

BDS is a global movement launched by 170 Palestinian organisations in 2005. What would you say the campaign's impact has been?

BDS has massively raised awareness. And, like in South Africa, Israel must cease its illegal and immoral actions and negotiate for peace or face the consequences by becoming ever more recognised as a pariah state.

Every week, somewhere in the world another council or church or sporting team says no to Israel.

In comparison, in South Africa, the boycott phenomenon started around 1949. They got their freedom and apartheid finished in 1994 – 45 years later.

There are commentators who think what the BDS movement has achieved against Israel has been much faster. It can be understood because of the social media and the modern communications we have at this time.

We are hoping we will get our freedom, similar to South Africa.

Pro-Israel lobby groups are said to hold a lot of sway in Australia. What sort of opposition does your campaign face here?

First and foremost, they have a standard line, which is that it is anti-Semitic. It is an intentionally conflated concept that Israelis and Jewish people are one. In my own view, this is anti-Semitic by itself.

There are so many Jewish people around the world – including those who participate in BDS – that don't see Israel as their state.

The Israeli lobby has been operating effectively throughout Australia for many decades since the creation of Israel in 1948. Politicians, journalists and union leaders have been effectively managed by key organisations that have maintained a fierce attack on anyone or any political party that criticises Israel.

The Australian media mostly ignores the plight of Palestinians, but social media is an effective means to counter this long-term bias and expose the everyday experience of Palestinians.

There's a recent example of this in a [New York Times article](#) by journalist Michelle Alexander. She says many public figures and cultural leaders still worry about clearly supporting Palestinian human rights, as they feel this may damage their careers.

We ask these politicians, celebrities and everyone who has a conscience to see life through Palestinian eyes and to stand on the right side of history, as with what occurred in South Africa.

And lastly, Hilmi, you've just mentioned that awareness of the Palestinian people's plight is growing globally, however developments like the US embassy move have occurred and the illegal expansion of Israeli settlements in the West Bank continue.

What do you foresee happening in the near future in regard to the Israel-Palestine conflict?

All I know is that Palestinians everywhere will continue to resist, organise and we will keep finding allies as the BDS movement grows.

It is happening in the USA: in universities, churches and some Congress members are putting BDS on the agenda for the first time ever. A similar thing is happening in Europe. And we hope we will grow in Australia.

If you look at the news and what's happening, it's not promising. But, we can see a real change at the grassroots level. Polls in Australia say that there has been a significant increase in the support of the Palestinian cause.

Justice and equal rights are the expectation of most people regarding this issue. And I know our movement will continue to grow, putting pressure on the Israeli state until it stops being a rogue country above international law.

Encountering Peace: Moving forward without negotiations – for now
Gershon Baskin, January 31, 2019, Jerusalem Post

This week, the Israel Institute of National Security Studies (INSS), headed by former Military Intelligence chief Maj.-Gen. (res.) Asher Yadlin, issued a new plan for confronting the Israeli-Palestinian conflict. The INSS plan is called "A Political-Security Framework for the Israeli-Palestinian Arena."

In its introduction they state: "Although Israel has never been stronger and more secure, it today faces a severe external national security threat in the form of a one-state reality, which would perforce be either non-Jewish or non-democratic. However, the Israeli political system of recent years has failed to address this threat seriously.

"While the Israeli Right continues to lead Israel toward a one-state reality that threatens to destroy the Zionist dream of a Jewish democracy, the Left still believes that reaching peace is possible. However, the Palestinian parameters for agreement are clearly unacceptable to the vast majority of people in Israel, fall short of assuring sufficient security and demographic conditions, and fail to guarantee the end of the conflict.

"Thus, both of the traditional two paradigms are unrealistic, and the dichotomy between them is artificial... The main advantages of the INSS plan... is in its very essence: defining a clear strategic goal for Israel as a Jewish, democratic, secure, and just state, and arresting the slide toward a one-state reality. The second advantage is in its modular, flexible, and phased implementation strategy. This strategy can breach the current impasse in the political process and enjoy critical flexibility of maneuver between various alternatives, while suiting the ever-changing strategic environment."

The INSS correctly assesses that with the current leadership in Israel and Palestine there is no possibility of bridging the gaps between them at this time on the fundamental core issues that must be agreed upon. There have not been any genuine Israeli-Palestinian political negotiations during the entire terms of the past two Netanyahu governments. There have also not been any Israeli political initiatives toward the Palestinians or initiatives aimed at setting a political border between Israel and Palestine.

During all this time Israeli settlements, not only in the settlement blocks, have been expanding. Israeli infrastructure for Israelis throughout the West Bank (roads, water and electricity networks) have also grown enormously. Proposals for annexation of most of the West Bank (area C, which equals 62% of the area) have taken root inside of Israel's Right wing and have trickled down to the mainstream.

THE NON-JEWISH majority "between the river and the sea," which is subject to Israeli control and domination, does not enjoy the benefits of Israel's democracy, and thus Israel, under the continued right-wing Jewish religious population is destroying Israel's own self-definition as the democratic nation-state of the Jewish people. The one-state reality is materializing before our eyes.

It is already questionable if there remains a viable two-states solution. It is difficult to find Palestinians who still believe in that solution, which most thinking Palestinians now call a political fiction. The facts on the ground since the signing of the Oslo agreements, of continued Israeli settlement building, expanded land expropriations, house demolitions, removal of Palestinians from area C, entrenching the Israeli occupation and control over the Palestinians, prove to the Palestinians that Israel never had a real intention of allowing them to have a state of their own.

Israelis who know the reality on the ground also have real difficulty imagining how a two-states solution could be feasible without the Palestinians agreeing to at least 10% of the West Bank being annexed to Israel, and east Jerusalem never being the capital of Palestine. Under the current reality, and in the absence of any clear Israeli peace initiative, there is no acceptable starting point for entering into negotiations.

These were the issues that the INSS team of military and security experts placed on the table when they confronted Israel's strategic options. The continuation of the status quo, which is not static but all the time moving toward annexation, essentially means that Israel either becomes non-democratic, apartheid-like, or it no longer can claim to be the nation-state of the Jewish people. If at the current time, with the current leaderships, there is no possibility of Israeli-Palestinian negotiations, does it mean that Israel cannot take actions to improve the situation on the ground, create better conditions to facilitate possible genuine negotiations in the future, and to prevent the horrendous effects of annexation?

The lessons from the strategic negative impacts of previous Israeli unilateralism, both in the withdrawal from Lebanon and from Gaza, have been learned. And so the question addressed is how to achieve a better result for Israel without handing territories over to the possibility of becoming areas for attacking Israel? The central element for mitigating the risks of Israeli withdrawal, according to the INSS, is to define a political border, which is not permanent; declare that the permanent border will be negotiated between the two states in the future; and to keep full Israeli military control of the Jordan Valley and freedom of military action within the entire area under Palestinian control for countering terrorism.

THE OTHER central element of the mitigation of risks is to continue to coordinate security with the Palestinian security forces, even to enhance that coordination and to take steps for enlarging Palestinian territorial assets with contiguity, without Israeli settlements inhibiting free movement, and without Israeli checkpoints in and around Palestinian cities. These steps, according to the INSS plan, would increase the chances for a functioning governable Palestinian state in the future.

The INSS also went beyond the regular separation paradigm of "Us here and them there," recognizing that cross-border Israeli Palestinian cooperation in all fields – economic and others – would be mutually beneficial and could help to create the environment which would enable future negotiations. The INSS plan overcomes the Israeli habit of calling for divorce and hopefully recognizes that: 1) there was never a marriage, and 2) eventual peace is not built by walls and fences but rather by bridges of understanding and cooperation. The plan calls to "demonstrate Israel's intention to promote political and territorial separation from the Palestinians and promote conditions for a two-state reality, thus improving Israel's strategic position even without bilateral political progress."

While the plan does not undertake enough emphasis for rebuilding Israeli-Palestinian partnerships – something that an institute like INSS could play a very positive role in doing – this is the best option for Israel under a government led by the Right wing, yet cautious enough not to completely cave in to the demands of the Israeli settler's movements. A more left-leaning government could do a lot more to create a more positive climate for genuine negotiations that would have to include dealing with Jerusalem, Gaza, refugees and a swap of territories with much broader cross-border cooperation in everything from water, energy and the environment to security. =

Renewing genuine negotiations, even with the current Fatah-led leadership, would not be impossible, but it would also demand Israeli initiative and demonstration of real intentions to create a viable two-states solution based on rebuilding partnerships of real cross-border cooperation. Giving a significant push to Palestinian economic development and seriously improving the lives of Palestinians on the ground by enabling more freedom is largely in Israel's hands. New positive initiatives by serious people, like those in the INSS, are most welcome.

The fight for Sheikh Jarrah continues as residents battle second wave of evictions

By _Yumna Patel_ on January 29, 2019 from Mondoweiss

It has been an agonizing few weeks for 70-year-old Mohammed Sabbagh and his family, who live in the occupied East Jerusalem neighborhood of Sheikh Jarrah.

On January 12, Israeli authorities handed an eviction order to the Sabbagh family, who number 47 people living in five adjacent homes.

Mohammed Sabbagh, his four brothers, their wives, children, and grandchildren were given until January 23 to leave their homes, to make way for Israeli settlers who would be moving in.

Israeli authorities agreed to an appeal filed by the family's lawyers to freeze the eviction until a final decision was reached within a month.

Mohammad Sabbagh in front of his family home in Sheikh Jarrah (Photo: Saleh Zghari)

"It bought us some more time, but we still know that eviction is inevitable," Sabbagh told Mondoweiss in the living room of his family home, where he has lived since 1956, when he was eight-years-old.

Sabbagh's family is originally from the town of Jaffa, now in present day Israeli territory. They were forcibly expelled, like hundreds of thousands of other Palestinians, during the Nakba in 1948.

When Jordan assumed control over the West Bank and East Jerusalem, the Jordanian government partnered with UNRWA to provide apartments for 28 refugee families, including the Sabbaghs, in Sheikh Jarrah. "We were forced out of our homes by the occupation when I was a boy, and now in my old age they are expelling me again," Sabbagh said. "It's another Nakba."

Fighting the law

The Sabbagh family, like many others in Sheikh Jarrah and neighborhoods across East Jerusalem, have been embroiled in legal battles with Israeli settler organizations for decades.

After the Nakba and establishment of Israel in 1948, the state enacted the Absentee Property Law, which transferred Palestinian refugees' property into the hands of the state.

Although their original homes in Haifa are still standing, the Sabbagh family cannot reclaim ownership of them.

The law, however, does not apply to small percentage of Jewish families that left their homes in 1948 for West Jerusalem and other Jewish-majority parts of Israel. Under Israeli law, those Jewish families could reclaim their properties, like the ones in Sheikh Jarrah.

Following the Israeli occupation of the city in 1967, parts of Sheikh Jarrah and other neighborhoods where Jews once lived prior to 1948 were handed over to Israel's Custodian of Absentee Property.

Israeli settler groups began making claims to the land and homes, using the Israeli legal system to try and kick Palestinian families out of their homes in East Jerusalem. Given that they were refugees not originally from East Jerusalem, the Sabbagh family homes were among the easier prey for the settler groups.

In 1972, settlers quietly registered the land where the Sabbagh family homes are located under their names, and in 2003, those settlers sold the property to settler company Nahalat Shimon.

"That is when everyone's troubles really began," Sabbagh told Mondoweiss, adding that in 2009, the family was served with their first notice of an eviction lawsuit being filed against them.

"The settlement organization was claiming that they have been the owners of this land since 1885," he said, "and they presented documents claiming they are the owners."

The Sabbagh family home (Photo: Saleh Zghari)

But Sabbagh believes the documents were forged, telling Mondoweiss that the alleged Jewish owners of the land pre-1948 were actually renting the land from a Palestinian landowner.

"With those forged documents, and the discriminatory legal system in Israel," the settlers have been trying to kick us out."

"I am not optimistic"

Using those same documents, settler organizations were able to evict three Palestinian families from Sheikh Jarrah in 2009, the same year the Sabbaghs were given their first eviction notice.

Despite the family's lawyers presenting proof to the courts that the settler documents were forged, Israel's lower courts refused to rule on the family's eviction, citing statute of limitations.

"They sent us to the High Court, and when we finally went in November 2018, the judges rejected our claims of ownership saying that we should have demanded ownership back in 2003 when the properties were sold to the settler company," Sabbagh said.

After the High Court decision, the family was given their most recent eviction notice. Their only hope now, Sabbagh says, is the freese that their lawyers were able to secure.

"There are 11 other families in Sheikh Jarrah fighting eviction," Sabbagh said. "If all of us file an appeal or motion with the Magistrate Court to open the ownership files of the families, we could buy more time and extend the freeze."

But even when Sabbagh speaks of the chances the family has of remaining in their homes, he expresses little hope. "I am not very optimistic," he said.

"One of the three judges who ruled on our case in the High Court is herself a settler," he said. "So what do you honestly expect to happen?"

The 'Judaization' of East Jerusalem

The story of the Sabbagh family and Sheikh Jarrah is a microcosm of the Israeli occupation and its decades-long efforts to "Judaize" East Jerusalem.

Rights groups and activists have long criticized the government for its housing and zoning policies that actively work to push Palestinians out of the city, which Israel has declared as its "undivided capital."

"The Israeli occupation authorities and leaders have designed the laws in in accordance with their interests, which is making Jerusalem a demographically Jewish city," local Palestinian activist Omar al-Shalabi, 48, told Mondoweiss.

"The racism of the Israeli government is blatantly obvious to anyone who looks at the double standards they have for Muslim and Christian Palestinians, versus Jews," al-Shalabi said.

Pointing to absentee property laws, zoning laws that restrict Palestinian construction in the city, home demolitions, lack of municipal services for Palestinian areas, and the over-policing of Palestinian communities, al-Shalabi argued that the Israeli government actively searched for "a thousand pretexts" under which they can drive out Palestinians from Jerusalem.

Israel's Jerusalem Municipality has zoned only 15% of the land in East Jerusalem for residential use, despite the fact that Palestinians make up 40% of the city's population.

According to UN documentation, at least a third of all Palestinian homes in East Jerusalem lack an Israeli-issued building permit, placing over 100,000 Palestinians at risk of displacement.

"As Palestinians in Jerusalem, we face roadblocks at every turn," al-Shalabi said. "But for the settlers, everything is allowed, and encouraged by the politicians and security forces who assist them in their takeover of the city."

Israeli settlers claim another Palestinian life: Father of four shot and killed in West Bank village

Yumna Patel on January 27, 2019 from Mondoweiss

Israeli settlers shot and killed a Palestinian father of four during a raid on the al-Mughayyir village in the central occupied West Bank district of Ramallah on Saturday night.

Palestinian officials and local media outlets reported that a group of Israeli settlers raided the village under the protection of armed

Israeli soldiers — a common occurrence in areas of the West Bank located close to settlements — causing clashes to erupt with Palestinian residents of the village, who tried to fend off the settlers.

During the confrontations, a settler reportedly shot and killed 38-year-old Hamdi Saadeh Naasan.

The Palestinian Ministry of Health said in a statement that Naasan, a father of four young children and a former prisoner, arrived to the hospital in critical condition and succumbed to his wounds shortly afterwards.

The ministry also said that Israeli settlers shot Naasan in his back with live ammunition.

Ma'an News Agency quoted local sources who said that Israeli settlers attempted to raid the village's northern entrance, descending from a mountaintop into the outskirts of the village, "under the heavy protection of Israeli forces."

In response, locals from al-Mughayyir and villagers from the nearby Khirbet Abu Falah rushed to the mountaintop in attempts to push back the settlers and prevent them from attacking the homes on the edge of the village.

"Israeli forces repeatedly fired live bullets, rubber-coated steel bullets, and stun grenades towards the Palestinians to disperse them," Ma'an News reported, adding that at least 30 other Palestinians were injured during the attack, including six who were shot with live ammunition.

Meanwhile, the Israeli military released statements saying that a "confrontation" between settlers and Palestinians resulted in the light injury of a settler.

"Initial details suggest that shortly thereafter, a conflict erupted between Israeli civilians and Palestinians in the area, in which live rounds were fired by the civilians. One Palestinian died and several others are injured," they said in a statement, adding that an investigation has begun.

Videos released on social media of the incident, however, corroborate Palestinian accounts of the events, showing Israeli settlers and soldiers to be the initial instigators of the confrontations.

Palestinian president, Mahmoud Abbas, condemned the killing, saying it "will lead to serious consequences, further tension and the creation of a dangerous and uncontrollable atmosphere."

UN Special Coordinator for the Middle East Peace Process, Nikolay Mladenov, condemned the killing of Naasan on Twitter, calling it "shocking and unacceptable."

"Israel must put an end to settler violence & bring those responsible to justice. My thoughts and prayers go out to the family of the Palestinian man killed and those injured," he said.

Senior PLO official Hanan Ashrawi condemned the "heinous murder" of Naasan, and held the Israeli government "fully responsible" for his death.

"The political climate in Israel negates Palestinian rights and expresses objectionable racism against the Palestinian people," she said.

"As such, the marked escalation of terror attacks by armed groups of Israeli settlers against Palestinian civilians is a natural outcome of the culture of hate and atmosphere of incitement and violence against Palestinians that this extremist Israeli government espouses and promotes."

Al-Mughayyer is surrounded by eight Israeli settlements and outposts from all sides, and is frequently subject to settler attacks on the people of the village and their property.

Attacks like the one on Saturday night are a common occurrence in the West Bank, which is home to some 600,000 nationalistic and right-wing Israeli settlers living in illegal settlements and outposts.

Rights groups, local media, and grassroots activists have thoroughly documented such attacks, which often fit the profile of Saturday's attack: Israeli settlers wielding guns, bats, and rocks descend on a village from a mountaintop, under the protection of the Israeli army, and attack Palestinians and their property.

2018 saw a steep rise in anti-Palestinian hate crimes carried out by Israeli settlers in the West Bank. As of mid-December, 482 such incidents had been reported, more than triple the reported 140 incidents in 2017.

Rights groups and activists have long accused the Israeli state and security officials of fostering a "culture of impunity" for Israelis committing violent acts against Palestinians, who are rarely prosecuted for their crimes.

Meanwhile, Palestinian minors have repeatedly been sentenced to decades in prison if they are found guilty of attacking or killing Israelis.

Yumna Patel is a multimedia journalist based in Bethlehem, Palestine. Follow her on Twitter at @yumna_patel

Israel kicks out international monitoring force in Hebron

Ahmad Melhem February 5, 2019 from Middle East Monitor

Palestinians take part in a protest against Israeli Prime Minister Benjamin Netanyahu's decision not to renew the mandate of the Temporary International Presence in Hebron, in the Israeli-occupied West Bank town of Hebron, Jan. 30, 2019. Reuters.

The Israeli government is expelling the Temporary International Presence in Hebron (TIPH) force, the civilian observation mission that has monitored the divided city in the southern West Bank for more than 20 years.

Israeli Prime Minister Benjamin Netanyahu decided Jan. 28 not to renew the TIPH mandate. "We will not allow the presence of the TIPH force that operates against us," Netanyahu said in a statement to the press. Israel's Public Security Ministry accused the TIPH of cooperating with extremists and interfering with soldiers and police.

The TIPH's mandate is normally renewed twice a year, in January and June, by the Palestinian Authority (PA) and Israel. The TIPH reports to its five founding countries — Turkey, Norway, Sweden, Switzerland and Italy — as well as the PA and Israel, on breaches of agreements on Hebron, as well as on violations of international humanitarian and human rights laws.

Saeb Erekat, secretary-general of the PLO Executive Committee, said at a press conference Jan. 31 that he had personally signed the renewal of the TIPH mandate Jan. 27. He confirmed, however, that the TIPH received the Israeli government's decision to terminate its mission.

The Israeli decision raised the PA's concern over possible repercussions on Palestinians in Hebron. The PA fears Israeli settlers will launch more attacks on Palestinian residents in the absence of a third-party observer. The PA also fears the decision will encourage Israelis' settlement activities, specifically in the old quarter and the southern area of Hebron.

Nabil Abu Rudeineh, spokesman for PA President Mahmoud Abbas, warned in a Jan. 28 press release of the impact Israel's decision could have on the situation in Hebron. "Israel's disregard of all signed agreements and its refusal to abide by its commitments create an atmosphere of tension and chaos, with unpredictable consequences," he said.

In a Jan. 29 press release, Erekat said Israel's decision is a preliminary step toward abolishing all bilateral agreements reached since the Oslo Accord on Palestinian autonomy in the 1990s. He described the nonrenewal of the TIPH's mandate as a move toward the illegal annexation of the West Bank and the imposition of Greater Israel on Palestine's historic land, demonstrating clear contempt for the UN and international laws.

Erekat said Netanyahu's decision represents "an open invitation to commit more massacres" that will give Israeli settlers the freedom to act against Palestinians without any supervision.

The TIPH was deployed in Hebron after the UN Security Council issued Resolution 904 in March 1994 in the wake of a massacre at the Hebron Mosque of Ibrahim. On Feb. 25, 1994, Israeli settler Baruch Goldstein gunned down 29 Palestinian worshipers and injured 125 others. The UNSC resolution called for "measures to be taken to guarantee the safety and protection of the Palestinian civilians throughout the occupied territory, including, [among other things], a temporary international or foreign presence."

Representatives of the PA and Israel held bilateral negotiations in 1994 and asked Italy and Norway to deploy international observers temporarily in Hebron. The first TIPH mission began that May and withdrew from the city that August.

The signing of the Oslo II Interim Agreement on Sept. 28, 1995, called for a partial redeployment of the Israeli security forces in Hebron, along with a temporary international presence. On Feb. 1, 1997, the TIPH started operating in Hebron.

After Netanyahu's announcement, Norwegian Foreign Minister Ine Marie Eriksen Soreide told Reuters, "The one-sided Israeli decision can mean that the implementation of an important part of the Oslo Accord is discontinued." She noted, "[The] situation in Hebron is unstable and characterized by conflict," adding that the TIPH's expulsion is "worrying."

Hebron Deputy Gov. Khalid Dudin told Al-Monitor, "The TIPH is the only international witness that monitors attacks by the Israeli army and settlers in the old city of Hebron and the southern area. This did not please the settlers and the army." He added, "The presence of the TIPH comforted Palestinian citizens, especially as the mission would document all acts on the ground."

According to Dudin, the TIPH suspension ends the remainder of the Oslo agreement and the Hebron Protocol of 1997, and kills any potential chance for international protection of Palestinians, because Israel will not allow it. "The governorate is in contact with the PLO, the Ministry of Foreign Affairs and the Palestinian Mission at the UN to ask the UN and the world to pressure Israel into reneging on its decision."

Netanyahu's decision comes in the midst of a fierce election campaign in Israel. All candidates, including Netanyahu, aspire to win the support of settlers.

"Netanyahu ... is leading a battle to win every vote amid his difficult situation, against the background of his investigation on corruption charges," said Antoine Shalhat, director of the Israeli Scene Unit at the Palestinian Forum for Israeli Studies (MADAR). "In the last elections, Netanyahu relied on a right-wing base of settlers to become prime minister and he is trying to preserve this base for the legislative elections slated for April 9."

Shalhat added, "The settlers in Hebron who incite against TIPH are the largest and the most radical part of this electoral base. This is why Netanyahu saw the expiry of TIPH as an opportunity to get rid of it and assert his loyalty to the settlers."

Tayseer Khaled, a member of the PLO Executive Committee, told Al-Monitor that Netanyahu's decision demonstrates Israel's total disregard of international law and UN resolutions.

He pointed out that the TIPH provides no physical protection to the Palestinian people on the ground, but rather monitors events and documents them in its reports. "The international community doesn't act or show any reaction to these reports. Yet Israel keeps rejecting the TIPH," Khaled added, noting that the suspension of the TIPH mandate should be a problem acknowledged by the international community.

As the PA relentlessly calls for international protection for the Palestinian people, Netanyahu's decision to expel the TIPH forces seems to turn those hopes into a far-fetched dream.

Jerusalem Archbishop: 'Everything Palestinian is targeted by Israel's occupation'
February 2, 2019 in Middle East Monitor

The Palestinian Archbishop of Jerusalem's Greek Orthodox Church, Atallah Hanna, said yesterday that "everything Palestinian in Jerusalem is targeted by the Israeli occupation".

During a meeting with a delegation from Médecins Sans Frontières (Doctors without Borders, MSF), Hanna explained the dangers threatening Palestinians' existence and identity in the Holy City, *Al-Wattan Voice* reported.
"Everything is in danger in Jerusalem," Hanna said, adding: "The Islamic and Christian holy sites and endowments are targeted in order to change our city, hide its identity and marginalize our Arabic and Palestinian existence."

Hanna added that "recently, the Israeli occupation cancelled a planned celebration on the 50th anniversary of establishing Al-Maqased Hospital," noting that the Israeli occupation had cancelled many other Palestinian events planned to take place in Jerusalem.

The Archbishop said that Palestinians "are living under severe torture and harsh persecution," pointing to Israel's closure of Palestinian institutions in the city. "It seems that they wanted us to give up Jerusalem and submit to their polices, measures and practices," he added.

Archbishop of Jerusalem's Greek Orthodox Church, Atallah Hanna [centre], seen during a protest in the West bank city of Hebron January 22, 2015 [Muhesen Amren / ApaImages]

Hanna continued: "Jerusalem is for us and will remain for us. We will never give up our rights in Jerusalem and we will defend it against Israeli oppression."

Addressing the MSF staff, he said: "We want you to know closely the suffering of the Palestinians and the oppression inflicted by the Israeli occupation on them in Jerusalem. We want our message to reach all the people around the world as we want more friends for the Palestinians."

14 Palestinians homeless as Israel forces 2 Jerusalem homes to be torn down

February 1, 2019 from Middle East Monitor

Majdi Abu Tayeh was forced to demolish his own home in order to avoid demolition costs of near $1,400 from the Israeli occupation on 30 January 2019 [Silwanin.net]

Fourteen Palestinians were left homeless yesterday after the Israeli Civil Administration ordered for their homes to be demolished in the occupied East Jerusalem neighbourhood of Silwan.

The Wadi Hilweh Information Centre in Silwan said that Israeli bulldozers stormed the neighbourhood and demolished the home of Issa Jaafra.

Eight members of his family, including five children, lived in the house, which measured 70-square-metres.

Silwan resident Majdi Abu Tayeh demolished his own home in order to avoid incurring large demolition fees from the Israeli Civil Administration.

The Israeli Civil Administration ordered the demolition of both homes under the pretext that they were built without the nearly-impossible to obtain Israeli permits.

The centre confirmed that despite the fact that Abu Tayeh lived in the home for the past four years along with five members of his family, four of whom are children, he was forced to carry out the demolition himself.

Israel rarely grants Palestinians permits to build in East Jerusalem.

Israel steps up attacks on Palestinian schools
By Maureen Clare Murphy, 5 February 2019 from Electronic Intifada

When Israeli occupation forces shot three secondary school students, critically injuring two of them, last week, it was hardly an isolated incident.

The students were injured after soldiers raided Tuqu village near the West Bank city of Bethlehem, surrounding a high school. The military fired tear gas and live ammunition after being confronted by youths.

The frequency of such violence in or near Palestinian schools in the West Bank has increased during the current academic year.

"Incidents of interference in schools by Israeli forces" include "threats of demolition, clashes on the way to school between students and security forces, teachers stopped at checkpoints, and the violent actions of Israeli forces and settlers on some occasions," according to a statement by United Nations officials.

The bulk of the 111 "interferences to education" in the West Bank documented by the UN in 2018 took place in the last four months of the year.

"More than half of the verified incidents involved live ammunition, tear gas and stun grenades fired into or near schools by Israeli forces, impacting the delivery of education or injuring students," according to the UN officials.

Israeli forces demolished or seized five Palestinian schools in the West Bank, including East Jerusalem, last year, and 50 more are under threat of demolition.

"Orief secondary school for boys near Nablus has also been forced closed twice due to settler violence, and children from this school have been hospitalized with multiple injuries, including from gunshots," the UN officials add.

Regular violence in Hebron
In the H2 area of Hebron, where Palestinians live in close proximity to hostile Israeli settlers, "tear gas is regularly used around schools, and new measures are being applied at checkpoints that expose students and teachers to violence – at one particularly affected H2 school, more than 20 such incidents were documented in 2018."

Video published by the human rights group B'Tselem shows heavily armed Israeli Border Police forces apprehending students in Hebron's city center as they were leaving school in December:

Two of the students detained by the Israeli officers were under the age of 12.

One of the boys, 13 years old, was taken to a police station, where he was "interrogated with no parent or other adult acting on his behalf present."

He was held overnight without being given food or drink until the morning. He was released that afternoon after his father posted bail at a military court, deposited by the soldiers far away from his home.

Soldiers drove the boy to the entrance to al-Arroub refugee camp and removed his handcuffs. One of the soldiers punched the child on the head, causing him to fall to the ground, before they drove off.

Demolitions on permit pretext
Human Rights Watch also emphasizes Israel's violations of Palestinian children's right to education in its shadow report to the UN Committee on Economic, Social and Cultural Rights review of Israel.

Israeli forces have demolished or confiscated Palestinian school buildings or property in the West Bank at least 16 times since the beginning of this decade, according to the rights group.

"Israeli authorities have justified the destruction or damage to schools on the basis that they lacked building permits from the Israeli military, but the military almost never grants Palestinians building permits in Area C, the 60 percent of the West Bank where it exercises exclusive control," Human Rights Watch states.

More than a third of Palestinian communities in Area C do not have primary schools and some 1,700 children are forced to walk five or more kilometers to school due to road closures and lack of infrastructure.

"The long distances and fear of harassment by settlers or the military lead some parents to take their children out of school," Human Rights Watch adds.

Gaza schools attacked
The Israeli military also disrupts Palestinian children's education in Gaza.

Schools in both Gaza and southern Israel were closed for at least one day during a three-day military escalation in the coastal enclave last November and some incurred severe damage.

More than half of Gaza's schools were damaged during Israel's 51-day assault on the territory in summer 2014.

"Israeli restrictions on the delivery of construction materials to Gaza and a lack of funding have impeded reconstruction of damaged or destroyed facilities," Human Rights Watch notes.

During that military offensive, Israel hit three schools administered by UNRWA, the UN agency for Palestine refugees, being used as shelters, killing 45, including 17 children.

"The Israeli military alleged that Palestinian fighters were operating near the school, or had fired mortars 'from the vicinity' of it, but it has offered no information or evidence to support that claim," Human Rights Watch adds.

One rocket fired from Gaza during that offensive hit a building used as a daycare in southern Israel, but caused no casualties.

Israelis to turn historic mosque into museum
Israel has demolished hundreds of Palestinian mosques, cemeteries and other religious sites since the state's creation in 1948.
February 5, 2019 in Middle East Monitor

The Israeli authorities in Tiberias have broken into the historic Al-Bahr Mosque in order to start turning it into a museum, *Al-Resalah* reported on Monday. The move violates a 2000 agreement between the authorities and the Palestinian community in Israel to maintain the status quo at the mosque, which has been closed ever since.
One fifth of all Israeli citizens are Palestinians, the so-called "Arab-Israelis", and face institutionalised discrimination at the hands of the state.
Israel has demolished hundreds of Palestinian mosques, cemeteries and other religious sites since the state's creation in 1948. Dozens have been turned into bars and night clubs in Jaffa, Lod, Al-Ramla, Ashkelon and other cities with no regard for their religious significance.

According to *Arab48.com*, the agreement reached in 2000 has been violated several times, with attacks on the building, including arson. Largely left unguarded, it has been used by drug addicts. "We have to go to Tiberias and stop the desecration of the holy site which aims to erase any Palestinian symbols in the city," insisted Mohammad Baraka, the Chairman of the High Committee for Arab Citizens. He said that the Arab citizens in Israel would never accept such a move and pledged to protect the mosque and other holy places.

"Those who forget the agreement to maintain the status quo should know that it was not easy to reach," said Kamal Al-Khatib, the head of the freedoms sub-committee in the Arab Follow up Committee. "It seems that the right-wing trend is within the mindset of [Israeli Prime Minister Benjamin] Netanyahu and the head of Tiberias municipality, which is known for its right-wing stances."

Al-Bahr ("The Sea") Mosque was built in 1743 by the Muslim ruler of Tiberias, Al-Zaher Omar. It is located on the shore of Lake Tiberias, also known as the Sea of Galilee. Since the Israeli occupation of Palestine in 1948, the mosque has been abandoned and no Muslims have been allowed to enter it. Having been turned into a bar, an agreement was reached in 2000 between the Tiberias municipality and the Palestinian citizens of Israel, including Arab parliamentarians. However, it was abandoned again and Palestinians are not allowed to enter even to clean it.

Netanyahu whitewashing far-right activists

By Shlomi Eldar, February 7, 2019 from Israel Pulse Al-Monitor

Since he first served as prime minister from 1996 to 1999, Benjamin Netanyahu has warned voters of a dangerous tide of "leftism." He utters the word with contempt and fear, as he would the name of a communicable disease. Netanyahu, along with his fellow Likud members and those to the right of them (HaBayit HaYehudi and New Right parties), all see a "leftist virus" spreading and threatening to infect all Israelis. The way they see it, anyone who is not one of them has probably come down with the "leftism" disease. "Whoever says he's not right and not left, is left," Netanyahu claimed following the Jan. 29 maiden speech by his rival Benny Gantz, who urged voters to put the good of the state before divisive partisanship. Netanyahu's close ally, Regional Cooperation Minister Tzachi Hanegbi, went further, declaring on Feb. 2, "Anyone who is not Likud is left."

However, Netanyahu is still unhappy. According to Israeli law, votes cast in favor of a party that does not reach the Knesset entry threshold are lost. And so, fearing a loss of votes for his right-wing bloc in the April 9 elections, the prime minister is busy extending its borders and is even willing to include those once considered the "forbidden right." These are disciples and admirers of radical activist Rabbi Meir Kahane, whose Kach party platform called for a forceful expulsion of Israel's Arab citizens. In 1984, Kahane was elected to the Knesset, but when he got up to speak, Likud lawmakers, including then-Prime Minister Yitzhak Shamir, would often walk out in protest.

Shamir, a right-wing stalwart, was unwilling to hear Kahane spew anti-Arab vitriol. Ahead of the 1988 elections, Kahane's party was banned because of its racist platform. In 1994, the government declared it a terror organization and outlawed Kach. Kahane himself was shot and killed in 1990 by a Muslim assassin.

Israeli Prime Minister Benjamin Netanyahu attends the weekly Cabinet meeting in Jerusalem, Feb. 3, 2019. Reuters

Netanyahu, however, no longer sees red lines. As far as he is concerned, anything and everything goes. After former army chief Rabbi Rafi Peretz was named on Feb. 5 to head HaBayit HaYehudi, the Likud urged the party to join forces with Otzma Leyisrael, which consists of Kahane's disciples and fans, to prevent the weakening of the right. Netanyahu thus bleached the mark of shame that Israeli society had imprinted on Kahane's racist movement, granting his successors a political clemency that they probably never imagined was possible.

Otzma Leyisrael, Hebrew for "power to Israel," is a union of two parties formed by former Knesset members Michael Ben-Ari and Aryeh Eldad ahead of the 2013 elections to the 19th Knesset. However, the party did not win sufficient votes to get into the Knesset. Its campaign slogan was "We will wipe out a thousand terrorists and not a single hair on the heads of our soldiers will fall." Ahead of the 2015 elections to the 20th Knesset, one of its members, Baruch Marzel, a student of Kahane and chair of the Kach party, was named to fourth place on the Knesset slate of a party established by the former head of the ultra-Orthodox Shas party, Eli Yishai. This party, too, did not garner sufficient votes to get into the Knesset.

Otzma Leyisrael is now headed by its founder, Michael Ben-Ari, who holds a Ph.D. in Israel studies and archaeology. While still in high school, he was active in the Kach movement. In the run-up to the 2009 Knesset elections, he laid out his philosophy in an interview with the Ynet website. "The saying, 'Kahane was right,' has already been used up. You can practically see how what Rabbi Kahane brought up 24 years ago has now become the central issue of this election campaign," he said. Ben-Ari espouses undermining the standing and rights of Israel's Arab minority. He calls for their transfer to other countries, as well as for Israeli soldiers to disobey orders to evacuate Jewish settlements.

Another senior party figure is attorney Itamar Ben-Gvir, who gained notoriety over his role in the wild incitement against Prime Minister Yitzhak Rabin in the mid-1990s. Television reporter Hezi Mahlev documented him at the age of 19 participating in a demonstration of radical activists, most of them residents of the West Bank city of Hebron, against Rabin. In a particularly memorable photo, he is seen brandishing an emblem he took off Rabin's armored Cadillac, saying, "Just as we reached this emblem, we can reach Rabin." A few months later, in November 1995, a right-wing assassin killed Rabin.

Ben-Gvir, who was a parliamentary aide to Ben-Ari during his short term, carried out many of the provocations he engineered over the past 20 years with Marzel, the last chair of Kach before it was banned. In 2015, Ben-Gvir said he had been served with 53 indictments for disruption of public order, destroying property, inciting racism, supporting a terror organization and more. He was convicted in eight of the indictments.

After spending years as a radical activist, Ben-Gvir studied law at the Kiryat Ono Academy and was admitted to the bar. He has since represented radical right-wingers in courts, among them one of the suspects in the July 2015 murder of the Palestinian Dawabsheh family by Israeli Jewish terrorists, and the Israeli youth suspected of killing a Palestinian woman, Aisha Rabi, from the West Bank village of Bidya in October 2018.

Yet another member of Otzma Leyisrael is Bentzi Gopstein, also a Kahane disciple and founder of Lehava, a movement dedicated to "preventing assimilation in the holy land," in other words, the coupling of Jews with Arabs. Gopstein has extended his party's activities over time to Jewish boycotts of Arab-owned businesses.

There is not enough time or space to describe the crimes and misdeeds of this party's members. Most did not do their mandatory military service, and the Shin Bet security agency monitors their activity, viewing them as dangerous individuals motivated by hatred of Arabs and xenophobia.

This week, the members of this radical group could not believe their luck when Netanyahu handed them a seal of approval. Ben-Gvir told a radio interviewer that his party is open to any kind of union. What does he have to lose after Otzma Leyisrael failed in all its past incarnations to overcome the electoral threshold and make it into the Knesset? After all, Netanyahu might even offer them a spot in his next government. Their criminal records, radical views and ongoing incitement against Arabs have all been forgiven.

Even Knesset member Bezalel Smotrich, the newly elected chair of the National Union party, a radical rightist in his own right, was put off by Netanyahu's unity call. He realizes that Ben-Ari, Marzel, Ben-Gvir and Gopstein are too dangerous even for his party. In response, Smotrich proposed snidely that the Likud adopt Otzma Leyisrael to prevent the loss of any votes, obviously a non-starter.

After turning those who do not support the Likud into dangerous leftists, and endorsing those on the margins of the right once considered beyond the pale, Netanyahu appears willing to do anything to ensure victory. There is room for racists, Arab haters and criminals with records as long as they can boost his power and buy him more time as prime minister.

Settlers to Palestinian laborers: 'Work with human rights groups and lose your job'

Flyers posted in villages near Gush Etzion warn Palestinian laborers they will be banned from nearby settlements should they cooperate with anti-occupation groups.

By [Edo Konrad](#) Published February 4, 2019 from +972

Palestinian construction workers build a new house in the West Bank settlement of Har Gilo, on the southern outskirts of Jerusalem, September 7, 2009. (Kobi Gideon/Flash90)

Settlers in the southern West Bank posted flyers warning Palestinian laborers not to cooperate with Israeli human rights activists or organizations if they want to keep their jobs.

Tazpit News Agency, a settler-aligned English-language news outlet, [reported](#) earlier this week that Israeli settlers in the Gush Etzion settlement bloc have been posting these intimidating flyers around Palestinian villages nearby. The flyers threaten to ban Palestinians who cooperate with human rights groups from working in settlements there.

According to the flyer, which was printed in Arabic, Palestinians who want to "provide a living" for their families must refuse cooperation with the organizations and people listed. The flyer includes photos and names of prominent Israeli and Palestinian activists, and singles out Ta'ayush and Rabbis for Human Rights, two organizations that accompany and protect Palestinians in the occupied West Bank from threats of settler violence.

The flyer reads:

"Do you wish to keep working in the settlements? Do you want to provide a living for your families from the Jews? Whoever cooperates with any one of these individuals and organizations (Ta'ayush and Rabbis for Human Rights) will never be allowed to enter the settlements for work. Be warned!"

"On the one hand this is a classic divide and conquer tactic," says Guy Butuvia, an Israeli activist with Ta'ayush, an Israeli-

Palestinian volunteer grassroots group founded during the Second Intifada. "They want to create a division between Palestinians and human rights workers who support the Palestinian struggle to remain on their land, so as not to disturb the land theft that is taking place."

"On the other hand," he continues, "over the years, the occupation has made it difficult for Palestinians to make a livelihood, whether it's by taking their land, resources, water, or strangling their economy. Now those who are forced to work in the settlements are being threatened. This is part of an attempt to limit the rights of Palestinians as well as their access to legal recourse."

Since the Second Intifada, Israeli authorities have significantly limited the entry of Palestinian laborers into Israel. In West Bank settlements, however, Palestinian workers are able to enter and work more freely. Around 36,000 Palestinians work in settlements in the West Bank, many in construction, where they earn up to three times the average Palestinian wage.

According to TPS, the flyers are a reaction to Palestinians who have been working at the behest of "extreme leftist" organizations and "illegally taking over lands around and within Israeli communities in the eastern part of Gush Etzion." TPS further reported that a Hebrew translation of the ad was distributed to settlers in the area, and that a list of Palestinian families working in settlements there will be distributed to allow each employer to "make his own decision" — presumably over whether or not to continue employing them.

Butuvia says similar flyers were distributed in the same area a year ago by members of far-right group Im Tirzu. Those flyers personally targeted Israeli human rights workers for their "anti-Israel activism" and their "activities against the IDF."

"These flyers are yet another reminder that we are a target of far-right groups, which get their marching orders from the Israeli government. The goal is clear: to expel Palestinians from their Area

C of the West Bank [under full Israeli military control – E.K.] and minimize their ability to defend themselves."

While settlers are busy threatening Palestinians over alleged land theft in Gush Etzion, the Israeli government has been busy allocating around 300 acres for the planning of a new neighbourhood that would expand the settlement of Efrat, widely considered the capital of the bloc. The new Givat Eitman neighborhood is expected to expand the built-up area in Gush Etzion up to Bethlehem's southern outskirts, effectively surrounding the city with settlements.

During a recent visit to Netiv Ha'avot, an outpost in Gush Etzion that was partially demolished after the High Court of Justice found that six of its structures were built on private Palestinian land, Prime Minister Benjamin Netanyahu said that if it was up to him, "There won't be any more uprooting or halting settlements — just the opposite: The Land of Israel is ours, and will remain ours."

Israel intensifying 'settlement ring' around Jerusalem's Old City, NGO says
February 14, 2019 from Middle East Monitor

Israel is "intensifying" its settlement activity in and around Jerusalem's Old City, according to NGO Ir Amim.
Publishing a new map yesterday, Ir Amim described an "accelerated, intensifying chain of new facts on the ground in the most historically contested and politically sensitive part of Jerusalem: the Old City and adjacent ring of Palestinian neighbourhoods".

Ir Amim pointed to "a mounting number of state-sponsored settlement campaigns inside Palestinian neighbourhoods", as well as "settler-initiated evictions of Palestinians, takeovers of their homes, and the expansion of settler compounds", as well as the use of "touristic settlement sites" as "key points along a ring of tightening Israeli control".

According to the group, the Israeli authorities have struggled over the decades to advance plans for settlements due to "the population density in the built-up areas of the Old City". Some 100,000 Palestinians live in the Old City and its immediate environs, compared to 6,000 Israelis.

In these circumstances, Ir Amim stated, tourism and supposed archaeology projects "assume a central role in Israeli settlement policy".

A view of construction works in Ramot, a Jewish settlement in East Jerusalem on October 04, 2018. (Mostafa Alkharouf - Anadolu

Handing over management of such projects to settler organisations allows Israel "to exploit tourism as a tool for reinforcing settlement initiatives in the Old City and its environs, erasing the significant Palestinian presence there, promulgating the idea of the entire area as an Israeli environment, and imposing a nationalistic Israeli character that blurs the multi-religious and multi-cultural nature of the space, primarily to the detriment of the Muslim sites and presence", Ir Amim said.

Ultimately, the NGO added, "this use of national parks and tourist sites serves the goal of transforming the Palestinian neighbourhoods in and around the Old City – including Silwan, A-Tur, Ras al-Amud and Sheikh Jarrah – from a densely populated Palestinian area into one sprawling tourist site that bolsters Israeli control of the area and access to it".

In Hebron, Israel removes the last restraint on its settlers' reign of terror

Jonathan Cook on February 13, 2019 Palestine Project

You might imagine that a report by a multinational observer force documenting a 20-year reign of terror by Israeli soldiers and Jewish settlers against Palestinians, in a city under occupation, would provoke condemnation from European and US politicians.

But you would be wrong. The leaking in December of the report on conditions in the city of Hebron, home to 200,000 Palestinians, barely caused a ripple.

About 40,000 separate cases of abuse had been quietly recorded since 1997 by dozens of monitors from Sweden, Norway, Switzerland, Italy and Turkey. Some incidents constituted war crimes.

Exposure of the confidential report has now provided the pretext for Israeli prime minister Benjamin Netanyahu to expel the international observers. He shuttered their mission in Hebron this month, in apparent violation of Israel's obligations under the 25-year-old Oslo peace accords.

Israel hopes once again to draw a veil over its violent colonisation of the heart of the West Bank's largest Palestinian city. The process of clearing tens of thousands of inhabitants from central Hebron is already well advanced.

Any chance of rousing the international community into even minimal protest was stamped out by the US last week. It blocked a draft resolution at the United Nations Security Council expressing "regret" at Israel's decision, and on Friday added that ending the mandate of the Temporary International Presence in Hebron (TIPH) was an "internal matter" for Israel.

The TIPH was established in 1997 after a diplomatic protocol split the city into two zones, controlled separately by Israel and a Palestinian Authority created by the Oslo accords.

The "temporary" in its name was a reference to the expected five-year duration of the Oslo process. The need for TIPH, most assumed, would vanish when Israel ended the occupation and a Palestinian state was built in its place.

While Oslo put the PA formally in charge of densely populated regions of the occupied territories, Israel was effectively given a free hand in Hebron to entrench its belligerent hold on Palestinian life.

Several hundred extremist Jewish settlers have gradually expanded their illegal enclave in the city centre, backed by more than 1,000 Israeli soldiers. Many Palestinian residents have been forced out while the rest are all but imprisoned in their homes.

TIPH faced an impossible task from the outset: to "maintain normal life" for Hebron's Palestinians in the face of Israel's structural violence.

Until the report was leaked, its documentation of Israel's takeover of Hebron and the settlers' violent attacks had remained private, shared only among the states participating in the task force.

However, the presence of observers did curb the settlers' worst excesses, helping Palestinian children get to school unharmed and allowing their parents to venture out to work and shop. That assistance is now at an end.

Hebron has been a magnet for extremist settlers because it includes a site revered in Judaism: the reputed burial plot of Abraham, father to the three main monotheistic religions.

But to the settlers' disgruntlement, Hebron became central to Muslim worship centuries ago, with the Ibrahimi mosque established at the site.

Israel's policy has been gradually to prise away the Palestinians' hold on the mosque, as well the urban space around it. Half of the building has been restricted to Jewish prayer, but in practice the entire site is under Israeli military control.

As the TIPH report notes, Palestinian Muslims must now pass through several checkpoints to reach the mosque and are subjected to invasive body searches. The muezzin's call to prayer is regularly silenced to avoid disturbing Jews.

Faced with these pressures, according to TIPH, the number of Palestinians praying there has dropped by half over the past 15 years.

In Hebron, as at Al Aqsa mosque in Jerusalem, a Muslim holy site is treated solely as an obstacle – one that must be removed so that Israel can assert exclusive sovereignty over all of the Palestinians' former homeland.

A forerunner of TIPH was set up in 1994, shortly after Baruch Goldstein, an Israeli army doctor, entered the Ibrahimi mosque and shot more than 150 Muslims at prayer, killing 29. Israeli soldiers aided Goldstein, inadvertently or otherwise, by barring the worshippers' escape while they were being sprayed with bullets.

The massacre should have provided the opportunity for Yitzhak Rabin, Israel's prime minister of the time, to banish Hebron's settlers and ensure the Oslo process remained on track. Instead he put the Palestinian population under prolonged curfew.

That curfew never really ended. It became the basis of an apartheid policy that has endlessly indulged Jewish settlers as they harass and abuse their Palestinian neighbours.

Israel's hope is that most will get the message and leave.

With Israeli Prime Minister Benjamin Netanyahu in power for a decade, more settlers are moving in, driving out Palestinians. Today Hebron's old market, once the commercial hub of the southern West Bank, is a ghost town, and Palestinians are too terrified to enter large sections of their own city.

TIPH's report concluded that, far from guaranteeing "normal life", Israel had made Hebron more divided and dangerous for Palestinians than ever before.

In 2016 another army medic, Elor Azaria, used his rifle to shoot in the head a prone and badly wounded Palestinian youth. Unlike Goldstein's massacre, the incident was caught on video.

Israelis barely cared until Azaria was arrested. Then large sections of the public, joined by politicians, rallied to his cause, hailing him a hero.

Despite doing very little publicly, TIPH's presence in Hebron had served as some kind of restraint on the settlers and soldiers. Now the fear is that there will be more Azarias.

Palestinians rightly suspect that the expulsion of the observer force is the latest move in efforts by Israel and the US to weaken mechanisms for protecting Palestinian human rights.

Mr Netanyahu has incited against local and international human rights organisations constantly, accusing them of being foreign agents and making it ever harder for them to operate effectively.

And last year US President Donald Trump cut all aid to UNRWA, the United Nations' refugee agency, which plays a vital role in caring for Palestinians and upholding their right to return to their former lands.

Not only are the institutions Palestinians rely on for support being dismembered but so now are the organisations that record the crimes Israel has been committing.

That, Israel hopes, will ensure that an international observer post which has long had no teeth will soon will soon lose its sight too as Israel begins a process of annexing the most prized areas of the West Bank – with Hebron top of the list.

A version of this article first appeared in the National, Abu Dhabi.

'There are no foreigners left': Israeli settlers rampage in Hebron following expulsion of human rights observers

By Yumna Patel on February 14, 2019 from Mondoweiss

Dozens of Israeli settlers launched an attack on Palestinians in the Old City of Hebron in the southern occupied West Bank on Tuesday night, yelling "death to Arabs!" in the street and hurling rocks at Palestinian homes.

According to locals, more than 100 settlers accompanied by over 70 armed Israeli forces began marching down Shuhada street at 9pm in the Old City, heading towards the Palestinian neighborhood of Tel Rumeida.

"They were chanting anti-Arab slogans, calling for the expulsion of all Palestinians from the area, saying this is the land of Israel, and saying we should all die," Badee Dweik, 46, Co-Founder of the Human Rights Defenders group in Hebron told *Mondoweiss*.

According to Dweik, who witnessed the events, settlers began harassing and throwing stones at any Palestinians who were walking outside. Shortly after, the settlers began hurling rocks at the windows of Palestinian homes.

"Here in the Old City we are used to such attacks, so the Palestinians all have bars on their windows so that the settlers can't break through," Dweik said.

He added that no one was badly injured, but several people sustained bruises on their faces and bodies from being physically assaulted by the settlers.

The attack lasted until just after midnight, Dweik said. "When the soldiers saw lots of Palestinians beginning to congregate in the area, they started to push the settlers back and control them."

"They only interfered, not to protect the Palestinians, but to protect the settlers."

Dweik said he believes that the attack was a direct result of the lack of presence of international volunteers and observers in the area.

"The settlers, who are already extremely violent, are becoming more and more aggressive since the Israeli government decided to expel the TIPH mission in Hebron," he said.

"Getting rid of TIPH was a greenlight for settlers to be more violent, not just against Palestinians, but also against any internationals that they see here."

According to Dweik, two volunteers with the International Solidarity Movement (ISM) were detained by Israeli forces for 10 hours after the notoriously violent settler Anat Cohen claimed the ISM volunteers tried to slap her.

"The soldiers only released them after forcing them to sign a paper that they're not allowed to be in the H2 area for 15 days," Dweik said, adding that the Ecumenical Accompaniment Programme in Palestine and Israel (EAPPI) pulled their observers out of Hebron's Old City after their staff were targeted by settlers.

"There are only two Christian Peacemaker Teams (CPT) staff left in the Old City now after Israel deported them," Dweik said. "All the internationals are a target more than before."

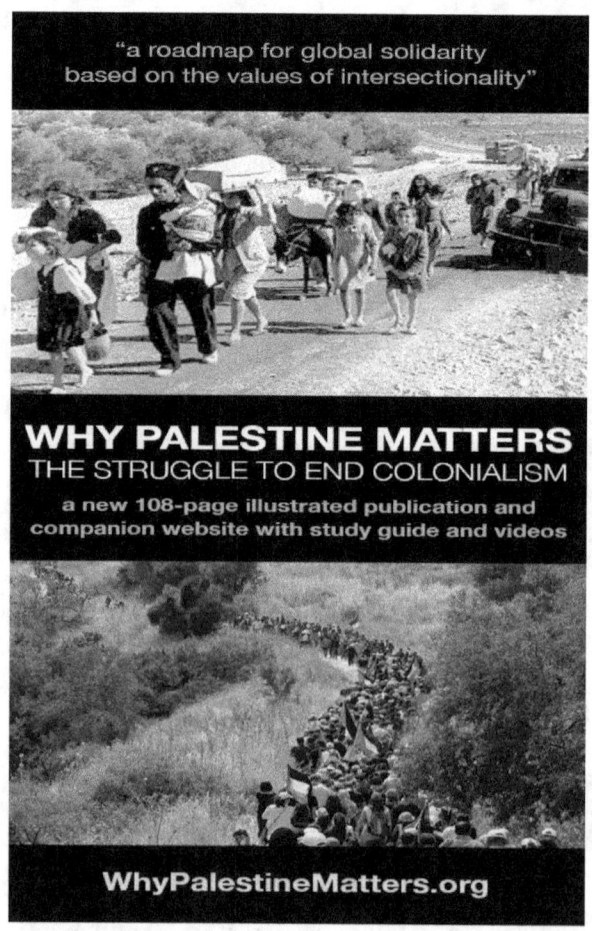

Thousands of Palestinian Bedouins have no access to vote in upcoming Israeli elections

By <u>Yumna Patel</u> on February 11, 2019 from Mondoweiss

As the Israeli campaign trail moves full speed ahead to the upcoming April 9th elections, rights groups are demanding authorities provide thousands of Palestinian Bedouin citizens of Israel with adequate access to polling stations.

Adalah – The Legal Center for Arab Minority Rights in Israel released a statement Monday saying the group is appealing to the Israeli Central Elections Committee Chairman and Interior Minister, demanding that polling stations be placed in 11 "unrecognized" Bedouin villages in the Negev desert.

The 11 villages, which are home to some 40,000 Palestinian Bedouins who have Israeli citizenship, currently have no polling stations or public transportation to reach existing stations.

"Some of their thousands of residents will have to travel up to 50 kilometers to vote in the upcoming national elections on 9 April 2019," Adalah said.

The group added that many of the villages' residents would have to travel on foot, given that the communities lack public transportation and many residents do not own private vehicles.

"The absence of polling stations in the Bedouin villages is one of the main reasons for the low voter turnout among this population," Adalah said, adding that "harming citizens' access to polling stations constitutes a grave and disproportionate violation of the constitutional right to vote enshrined in Israel's Basic Law: The Knesset (Article 4)."

According to Adalah, the group filed a similar appeal before the last national elections, but were rejected on the basis that the public transportation lines situated along main highways were "sufficient."

The group, however, has maintained that low voter turnout from the previous elections "indicate that this failed to remedy the situation."

Further commenting on the situation, Adalah Attorney Sawsan Zaher criticized the government's lack of accommodations for its Palestinian Bedouin citizens as "another indication of Israel's efforts to pressure Bedouin citizens to leave their homes and villages."

"The Central Elections Committee must allow all citizens to vote without having to embark on unreasonable journeys in order to do so," Zaher said.

More than half of the approximately 160,000 Negev Bedouins reside in villages "unrecognized" by the state of Israel, according to the Association for Civil Rights in Israel (ACRI).

Due to the fact that many Bedouins generally lack titles to the lands their ancestors historically grazed and lived on, it is difficult for them to prove their right to live and work on the lands, which were declared property of the state of Israel in 1948.

As a result, Bedouin communities in the Negev are constantly at risk of forcible displacement at the hands of Israeli authorities.

Last month, Israeli authorities announced a plan to forcibly transfer 36,000 Palestinian Bedouins living in unrecognized villages in the Negev region in order to expand military training areas and implement so-called "economic development" projects.

Rights groups have claimed that such actions in Bedouin communities are an Israeli policy aimed at removing the indigenous Palestinian population from the region to make room for the expansion of Jewish-Israeli communities.

Encountering Peace: Dumped deal
By Gershon Baskin, February 14, 2019 in The Jerusalem Post

Tweets coming out of Washington this past week notified the world that the Trump Israeli-Palestinian peace plan was "finished." Furthermore, the tweets informed us that Jared Kushner, special adviser and the president's son-in-law, together with Attorney Jason Greenblatt, would be traveling to the region to present the plan to Arab leaders to get them on-board with the plan.

Undoubtedly, the Trump "deal of the century" was conceived hand-in-hand with Prime Minister Benjamin Netanyahu. The Palestinian leadership was not consulted or taken into account by the Trump administration. It is hard to imagine a Trump Israeli-Palestinian peace plan that is not a non-starter for the Palestinians.

The Trump strategy, similar to Netanyahu's own Middle East views seems to be based on getting the weigh-in from the Arab states – the Saudis, Egypt, Jordan, UAE, Bahrain, Qatar, and Oman. The basic idea is that the Arab states would force the Palestinians to accept a proposal, which is a priori unacceptable to them.

The Trump mind-set translates everything into money and every deal has to be a money maker for those involved. Based on this strategy, Trump is essentially "selling" Palestine for economic benefits to the Arab states and to Israel. This follows the belief that the Palestinians will settle for less than they have demanded until now, because they will gain economically from the deal.

If the Palestinians reject the plan, as planned, everyone, including the Arabs would blame them, and then all of the Arab states could heap on the table all the deals that they have already tried making with Israel before.

If the Palestinians refuse, it doesn't really matter to Trump. Once again, Netanyahu will state that there is no Palestinian partner for peace, leaving the deal on the table. Trump and Netanyahu believe that the common cause in the region coalesces around reining in Iranian power and believes that any influence will overtake Arab loyalty to the Palestinian cause.

There is no doubt that the importance of the Palestinian issue has declined significantly in the post-Arab spring era. The decline of the Muslim brotherhood and their allies also brought about a deterioration in regional support for palestine. The continued division between Fatah and Hamas has also impacted the ability of the Palestinians to keep their issue high on the Arab agenda. Furthermore, the rejection of President Abbas by Trump and Netanyahu has cut down the stature and political worth of Abbas in the international community and in the Arab region.

The internal political stagnation in Palestinian is also a contributing factor to the decline of the Palestinian issue. But the long reign of Netanyahu and the understanding in the international community is that Netanyahu is not interested in a genuine peace process with the Palestinians. This has also led to a waning international will to apply any real pressure on Israel to compromise with the Palestinians.

The basic understanding is that the maximum that Netanyahu is willing to give is far less than the Palestinians will ever accept. The international community, including the Arab world, has largely backed the Palestinian demands for an independent sovereign state on 22% of the land between the Jordan river and the Mediterranean sea based on the June 1967 borders with east Jerusalem as the capital of Palestine and west Jerusalem the capital of Israel. But there is no Israeli partner for a deal based on those parameters.

It is conceivable that the Arab states could accept a Trump proposal for less than the Palestinians have demanded in terms of territory and sovereignty. Jerusalem, however; is another issue. It is totally inconceivable that the Arab states, including the Saudis under the rule of Crown Prince Mohammed Bin Salman could agree to a deal that grants Israel control over al-Aqsa Mosque and the Old City of Jerusalem. Even if Bin Salman agrees to that, al-Aqsa and Al-Quds is too symbolic, holy and sacred for Muslims to allow their leaders to agree to allow Israel to receive legitimization for their control.

While the Arab states may not have a lot of genuine sympathy for the Palestinian people, Jerusalem is a symbol and could unite Arabs all over the region against the deal of the century. As Jerusalem expert Attorney Danny Seidemann recently posted on Twitter, "However much Sunni states are willing to sell the Palestinians in a quixotic pursuit of the 'Grand Alliance' against Iran, Jerusalem will not let them."

According to some Washington insiders, the Trump plan will be unveiled on May 14 or 15, a historic date marking the founding of the State of Israel and the US Embassy move to Jerusalem last year. This is also the act that led to the formal cutting of ties between the Palestinians and the US. On Tuesday, Jason Greenblatt tweeted: "Sorry @FoxNews & @TreyYingst your sources gave you bad info. While the plan is close to complete, we aren't there yet & we'll continue to refine it until release. 175 pages is also inaccurate. It's a very detailed political/economic plan but not that long."

Regardless of its length, it may never be presented and is unlikely to be accepted by the Palestinians. The best chance of ever reaching a deal will return to the principal understanding that they must negotiate directly. It is very unlikely to happen while Netanyahu is leading the Israelis and as long as Abbas remains the leader of the Palestinians.

Perhaps the Israeli elections will bring new leadership and new opportunities. The Palestinians also need their own elections and fresh new leadership to bring about new opportunities.

The Trump deal of the century will probably still be born . But we Israelis and Palestinians will remain here, with no deal, and no future, unless we come to terms with each other's existence.

The author is a political and social entrepreneur who has dedicated his life to the State of Israel and to peace between Israel and her neighbours. His latest book In Pursuit of Peace in Israel and Palestine was published by Vanderbilt University Press.

Israeli Elections and the Big, Fat Palestinian Elephant in the Room

Hardened by terror and frustrated by failed peace efforts, Israelis don't want to hear about the evils of occupation or ways of ending it

By <u>Chemi Shalev</u> in Haaretz Feb 17th 2019

A Palestinian man carries the national flag during a demonstration near the fence along the border with Israel, east of Gaza City, February 8, 2019. AFP

As of 2019, there are 6.7 million Jews in Israel, the occupied territories and Gaza, and 6.7 million Arabs, according to the latest official estimates.

Of the Arabs – or Palestinians, if you will – nearly 1.9 million are Israeli citizens, another 1.9 million live under a ruthless Hamas regime fixated on fighting Israel and 2.9 million live in the hybrid West Bank, under military occupation or the semi-autonomous rule of the Palestinian Authority.

An objective observer might surmise that Israel is caught between a rock and hard place, with a sword hanging over its head to boot. It won't recapture Gaza but won't release it from its stranglehold either. It won't surrender the West Bank, for both religious and security reasons – and because Israelis are convinced that it would soon turn into another Gaza as well.

Israel won't annex the West Bank either, less because of concerns over the international backlash and more because such a move entails enfranchisement of the Palestinians, which would upset the demographic balance, upend Israel's democracy and jeopardize the country's continued existence as a Jewish state.

An Israeli soldier keeps position during clashes with Palestinian protesters following a demonstration against Jewish settlements in the West Bank village of Urif, February 15, 2019.AFP

History shows that prolonged periods of relative – very relative – peace and quiet, however, are always a prelude to flare-ups of violence and significant loss of Israeli lives. Our dispassionate outsider might surmise, therefore, that Israelis are clamouring for a solution and pressing their leaders to come up with new ideas, especially during an election campaign. He (or she) couldn't be more wrong.

The Palestinian problem, in fact, is hardly being mentioned, other than as a club with which the right browbeats leftist politicians and portrays them as defeatist and even treacherous. Politicians run away from discussing potential solutions – never mind actual peace – as if it was the plague. And it's not because they're all out of fresh ideas, though they are: They know the Israeli public is in collective denial and that voters won't reward those who dare snap them out of their reverie. Those who are might be tempted to cry out "The emperor has no clothes" will first be shushed and then sent home, consigned to political oblivion.

Exceptions to the rule can be found on the fringes alone, from the hard right that advocates annexation come what may, to the hard left, both Zionist and Arab-Israeli, which is gradually gravitating toward a one-state solution – with all its inherent risks. But in most of the Jewish political arena, from right to left, the Palestinian issue is like a dead man zone, which no man dare enter. If pressed to the wall, supporters of Benjamin Netanyahu will praise the current status quo as the best of all possible worlds. But given their opponents' fear of upsetting voters and being branded traitors, they don't get pressed very often.

Israelis are not blind to the fact that there is a big, fat Palestinian elephant in their living room. After decades of devoting election campaigns to discussing what to do with it, they now prefer to go about their lives and ignore it. At best, it will disappear on its own and at worst it will need to be subdued. But the odds are that it will remain inert and paralyzed, with occasional spasms meant to remind the world of its existence. As Scarlett O'Hara famously said in "Gone With the Wind," Israel will think about it tomorrow.

It's not that Israelis don't want peace either. Most polls show that a solid majority of Israelis, and a distinct plurality of Israelis Jews, support a two-state solution, while only a small minority backs outright annexation. With all due deference to President Donald Trump's impending and "ultimate" deal, peace is regarded today as a pie in the sky aspiration for the far future. In practice, most Israelis believe that achieving it is a mission impossible, and therefore unworthy of their attention or energy.

They have arrived at this conclusion based on what they perceive as Israel's countless and futile efforts to negotiate peace with the Palestinians, from Camp David I to Oslo, from Camp David II to Annapolis, from Jimmy Carter to John Kerry et al. Many on the right are convinced the Palestinians regard "peace" as a gateway to Israel's destruction, but even those that reject such views now regard the most minimal Palestinian demands as exceeding Israel's maximal concessions.

Israelis still carry the scars and trauma of the second intifada, which ravaged Israel at the start of the last decade, when suicide bombings terrified them, turned their cities to hell, their buses to death traps and their Palestinian neighbors to inhuman adversaries, unworthy of concessions and incapable of compromise.

Yasser Arafat, Yitzhak Rabin and Bill Clinton during the signing of the Oslo Accords, September 13, 1993.\ REUTERS FILE PHOTO/ REUTERS

And while the world might regard the occupation and Palestinian violence as chicken and egg, Israelis have managed to convince themselves it's the other way round: It's not the occupation that sows the seeds of terror and violence, but rather the Palestinian propensity for terror and violence that justifies and mandates continued occupation.

The savagery of the suicide bombings, coupled with the despondence over past failures to achieve peace, have effectively erased whatever remained of the Israeli left's compassion for Palestinians and sympathy for their plight. The injustice of the occupation played a prominent role in driving left-wing support for Palestinian independence and/or territorial compromise in the first few years after the territories were occupied during the 1967 war. But perceived Palestinian intransigence, coupled with the traumas of terror, have gradually hardened the most leftist of hearts. Until they learn to behave, Israelis tell themselves, the Palestinians have got it coming.

The flip side of this post-1967 perspective was the dire assessment of many leading figures on the left, from Yeshayahu Leibowitz to Amos Oz, from David Ben-Gurion to Yitzhak Rabin, of the inevitable corrosive influence of the occupation on Israeli society and democracy. The impact of lording over another people and sending Israel's soldiers to police them, they warned, could not remain quarantined in the streets of Nablus and Ramallah; it would permeate throughout pre-1967 Israel, distorting its democracy, brutalizing its politics and propelling it to embrace Jewish nationalism and ethnocentrism.

But by the time this pervasive leftist pessimism was fully borne out and vindicated – as Netanyahu's last term in office amply shows – moderate Israelis have themselves forgotten the direct link their predecessors made between cause and effect. Even the most moderate of Israeli politicians no longer contends that occupation is the original virus responsible for many of the ailments plaguing Israeli democracy today. They prefer to blame Netanyahu and, in doing so, to convince themselves that his removal would produce a catchall cure.

The scene of an attack during the second Intifada, Jerusalem, Israel, 2001. Eyal Warshavsky / BauBau

In this regard, there is some truth in describing the Israeli left as well as its political leaders as "defeatist" – not vis-à-vis the Palestinians, but toward their political rivals on the right.

The numbers are indeed daunting: For most of the past 40 years, Labor and its allies have either been in the opposition or shared power as a junior or equal partner in coalitions with Likud. Since the first Likud victory 42 years ago, the "left" has held power for only six years – and even those were due to the decidedly hawkish, militaristic and decidedly non-leftist appeal of Yitzhak Rabin and Ehud Barak, two former army chiefs of staff.

In the April 9 ballot, the role of former army commander challenging right-wing hegemony is being filled by Benny Gantz, who has shunned politicians such as Tzipi Livni for being too "leftist" but embraced the ultra-right former Defense Minister Moshe Ya'alon, who believes the very concept of peace is a dangerous illusion. Gantz is following in the footsteps of Labor leader Avi Gabbay, who initially lurched to the right after his election but has since re-centered himself after alienating large parts of his own base. The upshot, however, is that when the left tries to emulate the right, voters tend to prefer the original to the impersonation.

Israel's Prime Minister Benjamin Netanyahu, former Lt. Gen. Benny Gantz and former Defense Minister Moshe Yaalon in Jerusalem, Israel, August 27, 2014.\ NIR ELIAS/ REUTERS

Even the distinctly ideological left-wing Meretz, while formally remaining committed to a two-state solution, is wary of the potential fallout of advocating forcefully in its favor. Like Labor, it has selected a Knesset slate heavy on social advocacy and general support for democratic principles enunciated in the Declaration of Independence – as opposed to the controversial nation-state law – while steering clear of the injustice of occupation and the evils it has wrought on Israeli society and democracy.

Instead, Netanyahu's rivals have fallen into his trap of making the elections all about him rather than the issues themselves. The current election campaign has so far been marked by Netanyahu's efforts to harness his position in order to tout his achievements – a risky endeavour, as proven by his recent scandal-plagued and mishap-rich participation in the U.S.-brokered anti-Iranian summit in Warsaw. And it has been dominated by anticipation for, and speculation over, the attorney general's impending decision whether to indict the prime minister for bribery.

Once the decision is made public, apparently within the next two weeks, the preoccupation with Netanyahu's legal predicament is bound to reach fever pitch. The few and isolated efforts to place the Palestinian problem on center stage will be swept away by the expected tsunami of saturation media coverage of Netanyahu's affairs and the politicians' tendency to go where the news takes them.

The Palestinian elephant will continue to be ignored, consigned to a collective Israeli attitude reminiscent of the Ottoman fleet that was sent by Sultan Suleiman the Magnificent in the mid-16th century to reconnoiter the island of Malta and to ascertain the reason for its steadfast resistance to his superior forces. The famous response of the commander sent on the mission was to tell his sultan "Malta yok" – Malta does not exist.

It will take a leader made of sterner stuff than the current offerings in order to jolt Israelis out of their collective denial – unless the Palestinians do so earlier, at deadly cost. Until then, Israelis will continue to adhere to their "groupthink" – a phenomenon of mass psychology first detailed by the late Prof. Irving Janis of Yale and Berkeley, who wrote that it occurs "when concurrence-seeking becomes so dominant in a cohesive in-group that it tends to override realistic appraisal of alternative courses of action."

In societies overtaken by groupthink, a term derived from George Orwell's "1984," Janis wrote that "independent critical thinking will be replaced by groupthink, which is likely to result in irrational and dehumanizing actions directed against out-groups." More than the powerful lobby of Jewish settlers, the rabble-rousing nationalism espoused by the right and the general frustration with efforts to achieve peace, it is the willful ignorance of the Israeli public that is the chief enabler of the occupation and the ongoing disenfranchisement of the Palestinian "out-group."

Netanyahu and his allies have come to learn and exploit the Israeli groupthink to their heart's content, and for the perpetuation of their rule.

After Israeli anchor calls out brutality of 'occupation', political leaders land hard on her

By Jonathan Ofir on February 19, 2019 on Mondoweiss

This is a big story in Israel. On Saturday, Channel 13 anchorwoman Oshrat Kotler commented on a case of sadistic Israeli soldier beatings of a Palestinian father and son in occupied territory, saying:

They send children to the army, to the territories, and get them back human animals. That's the result of the occupation.

The response was immediate. Thousands of expressions of rage streamed in from audiences, and many leaders on the right were condemnatory. Prime Minister Benjamin Netanyahu tweeted:

Proud of IDF soldiers and love them very much. Oshrat Kotler's words should be roundly condemned.

Education Minister Naftali Bennett Bennett wrote:

Oshrat, you're confused. IDF soldiers give their lives so you can sleep peacefully. Human animals are the terrorists who murder children in their beds, a young girl on a walk or a whole family driving on the road. IDF soldiers are our strength. Our children. Apologize.

"After they finished, they started dancing"

The story goes back to January 8th, when Israeli combat soldiers arrested a Palestinian father and his 15-year-old son in the village of Abu Shukheidim in the West Bank. The two, unnamed in news reports, were suspected of aiding As'am Barghouti, a Palestinian accused of killing two soldiers from the same Israeli battalion in December, but the two were said not to be directly involved in the attack.

The two were handcuffed and blindfolded, and the soldiers punched and kicked them, and hit them with their weapons, causing severe wounds. One soldier filmed the event. The soldiers were in fact indicted, and last week, Ynet published some of the testimonies.

The son testified that he was beaten by four soldiers in the face, chest, stomach and legs.

They hit my knee with the gun barrel and my chest, knees, thighs and groin with the butt end... I couldn't open my left eye. My mouth was full of blood and my shirt was soiled as well. I also bled from my nose.

He added that some of the abuse was verbal as well.

One of the soldiers asked me to say 'In spirit, in blood, we will redeem Palestine' while I watched him beat up my father. The soldier told me 'Look at your dad. He deserves to be beaten. You think you're patriotic.'

He added that no one had intervened to stop the abuse, and that "after they finished, they started dancing."

The father testified that he was cursed at and hit with a belt. "When I asked them why they were beating me up, they hit me with the butt end of their weapons and one of the soldiers stepped on my face and broke my nose. I bled profusely and wasn't allowed to speak. I shouted at them but they told me to shut up. I was then hit in the face and lost consciousness."

"Settling scores"

The commander of the battalion clarified that he does not regret sending his soldiers on the mission. In his investigation, he said that he has no doubt that it was necessary in order to "settle scores" with the assailant who had killed two fighters from his battalion and that this was necessary in order to "create a feeling of success amongst the fighters."

He also said that their behavior was unacceptable and that he suspended them from duty. Although the arrest of the other soldiers has been extended until today, the IDF Spokesperson said that the commander of the battalion is no longer under arrest.

Death threats to Kotler and condemnation from top executives

Channel 13 has assigned bodyguards to Kotler due to death threats. She now risks trial for Defamation, and has also been called in for disciplinary hearings by the news station's executives.

Executive Yulia Shmuelov Berkovitch of the Second Authority (which monitors commercial television stations for adherence to ethics), condemned Kotler for "expressing her opinion" (Haaretz, Hebrew):

Oshrat Kotler is an anchor, not an interpreter. She definitely overstepped her authority.

Berkovitch did not refer directly at all to the "human animals" expression, but rather to "occupation":

It's not alright what she said. If she speaks about 'occupation', let her go to politics. Soon they are closing the lists for the parties [for elections], let her find her place there.

Haaretz interviewer Itai Stern wondered:

Is it not permitted to say the word "occupation" in broadcast anymore? Is that an illegitimate expression of opinion?

Berkovitch:

What do you mean? There's a wide public in Israel that doesn't agree with this definition, so of course there's a political statement here. See, this is really the point of it all. It's not that these soldiers behaved like "human animals", that is, with unfathomable sadistic barbarism. That's not the issue at all. The issue is that Kotler said "occupation".

Israel's freezing of Palestinian tax funds "collective punishment"
by Maureen Clare Murphy, Rights and Accountability, 18 February 2019 from Electronic Intifada

Palestinians protest the siege on Gaza at Erez checkpoint in the northern Gaza Strip, February 2018. Yasser Qudih APA images

Israel's freezing of millions of dollars in Palestinian tax revenue will cause the dire situation in Gaza to deteriorate even further, Al Mezan, a human rights group in the territory, warned on Monday.

Thousands of civil servants in the coastal enclave, its population of two million plunged into poverty after more than a decade of economic blockade, have already had to contend with salary cuts and late payments due to "discrimination" by the Palestinian Authority in the West Bank.

Now Israel is planning to withhold some $138 million in taxes it collects on behalf of the PA as a form of sanctions over stipends to political prisoners.

The freezing of tax fund transfers will be a "dangerous contribution to the deterioration of humanitarian and economic conditions," according to Al Mezan.

Israel in "sole control" over borders
Legislation passed last year allows Israel to deduct payments made to Palestinian prisoners and their families from Palestinian Authority tax revenue, which Israel controls.

Israel has intermittently frozen tax transfers to the Palestinian Authority since the Oslo accords were signed 25 years ago.

Israel's withholding of Palestinian tax revenue is a violation of Israel's obligations under the Oslo accords Paris Protocol, Al Mezan stated.

Under that protocol Israel collects taxes on behalf of the Palestinian Authority, giving the military occupier "sole control over the external borders and collection of import taxes and VAT," as described by the human rights group B'Tselem.

The customs union framework of the Paris Protocol was implemented because Israel "did not want to establish an economic border with the Palestinian Authority, an act that would give a clear flavor of sovereignty," B'Tselem adds.

The Palestinian Authority estimates that the West Bank and Gaza economy loses at least $350 million per year due to Israel's implementation of the Paris Protocol.

The Palestinian economy has lost $540 million in revenue since 2006 due to administrative fees imposed by Israel alone, according to the PA.

Last year the PA demanded $360 million in unpaid taxes from businesses operating in so-called Area C – the 60 percent of the West Bank under full Israeli military control.

The World Bank acknowledged in 2016 that the PA "suffers from substantial revenue losses under the current revenue sharing arrangements" amounting to $285 million, or 2.2 percent of the Palestinian GDP.

Israel moreover treats the occupied West Bank and Gaza Strip as captive markets for its own products including food and pharmaceuticals, thus generating immense revenue from near-monopoly access to Palestinian markets.

Collective punishment
Sanctioning Palestinian tax revenue "is tantamount to collective punishment prohibited under international law," Al Mezan stated.

Stipends to Palestinian prisoners "are considered a form of social security for families that lost their main breadwinner," the rights group added.

The tax revenue freeze is the latest financial blow to Palestinians living in the occupied West Bank and Gaza Strip and in refugee camps in Syria, Jordan and Lebanon.

Last year, the Trump administration in Washington slashed $300 million in aid to the already under-funded UNRWA, the United Nations agency for Palestine refugees, as well as $200 million in bilateral aid to the Palestinians.

New legislation signed into law by Trump last October effectively disqualifies the Palestinian Authority from receiving US funding "unless it agrees to pay court judgments of sometimes up to hundreds of millions of dollars on behalf of American victims of Palestinian attacks," as reported by the Associated Press.

Aid as leverage
President Donald Trump has admitted to using humanitarian aid as political leverage to advance his administration's Israeli-Palestinian "peace deal."

Israeli media have reported that Trump's long-delayed plan – now shelved until after Israel's general election in early April – will include the annexation of Israel's major settlement blocs in the West Bank.

The Israeli government, under the leadership of Benjamin Netanyahu, who is running for re-election, plans to significantly expand settlements in the West Bank, including outposts built without formal authorization.

All Israeli settlements in the West Bank, including East Jerusalem, violate international law, which prohibits an occupying power from transferring its civilian population to the territory it occupies.

In 2016 the UN Security Council reaffirmed that Israeli settlement-building in the occupied West Bank "has no legal validity and constitutes a flagrant violation under international law."

Settlers, soldiers seize Jerusalem home from Palestinian family

Tamara Nassar, 18 February 2019. From Electronic Intifada

Israeli forces expelled a Palestinian family from their home in the Muslim Quarter of occupied East Jerusalem's Old City on Sunday and handed it to Jewish settlers.

The Abu Asab family received eviction orders earlier this month demanding they vacate the building by 12 February.

Hatem Abu Asab was able to postpone his family's expulsion until 28 February through his lawyers, but Israeli police paid no heed.

On Sunday, with no prior warning, Israeli forces surrounded the house and blocked the road leading to it, eyewitnesses told Wattan TV.

They then stormed the house to forcibly evacuate it and prevented family members from collecting their belongings.

"They destroyed me. They destroyed my life. They took everything I own here. My entire life is here," Rania Abu Asab said in a video after she was kicked out of her house.

"They did not give us time to organize our things. They came in barbarically, attacked my husband, attacked my children and beat my aunt," she added. Hatem Abu Asab's son was also arrested. Local media circulated pictures of the arrest as well as Israeli settlers taking over the Abu Asab house:

Settlers raised the Israeli flag on the roof of the house after seizing it:

Nakba survivors
The Abu Asab family lived in the house for the past 67 years.

They were forcibly displaced from their home in the Baqa neighborhood in western Jerusalem after the notorious massacre by Zionist forces in the village of Deir Yassin on 9 April 1948 and moved near the Damascus Gate in Jerusalem's Old City.

The expulsion of tens of thousands of Palestinians from western Jerusalem and the takeover of their homes was part of the 1948 Nakba – the ethnic cleansing of Palestinians carried out by Zionist forces to establish the state of Israel in their place.

The family then moved to their home in eastern Jerusalem in 1952, which was then under Jordanian control, and shared it with the Tuffaha family, until the latter moved elsewhere.

Israel then conquered eastern Jerusalem in 1967, when it occupied the West Bank, Gaza Strip, Golan Heights and Egypt's Sinai Desert.

The home was originally owned by the Palestinian Nuseibeh family, which leased the property to Jewish residents before 1948, for 99 years, according to Wattan TV.

Despite the expiration of the lease, Israeli settlement groups launched a legal effort to seize the property in 2014.

In October last year, Israel's high court ruled in favor of the settlers.

The court's ruling is made possible by Israel's 1950 Absentee Property Law, which allows Israel to seize land and property owned by Palestinian refugees who fled or were expelled from their homes during and after the Nakba.

Under a 1970 amendment to its law, Israel allowed Jews to reclaim Jerusalem properties they left in 1948, but did not allow the same right to Palestinians – a blatantly racist measure.

The settlers who are being given the Abu Asab house are not related to the previous Jewish occupants.

The Jewish family who originally lived in the home handed the property to a trust.

"A few years ago, settlers managed to appoint themselves as directors of this trust, and in their name they sued the family who lived in the property," according to the Israeli group Peace Now. "With this crooked legal situation, the court granted the settlers the house and the Abu Asab family became refugees for the second time."

The Abu Asab family paid rent consistently to the guardian of the absentee property, and was surprised by the 2014 campaign for their eviction.

Under discriminatory Israeli law, the Abu Asab family cannot return to their original home in Baqa or even demand compensation.

Another Palestinian family, the Sabbaghs, also faces imminent eviction from its home in occupied East Jerusalem's Sheikh Jarrah neighborhood.

The family had received an order from occupation authorities that if they did not leave their house, which is also wanted by settlers, by 23 January, then they would also face forced removal. That could happen any day.

Entrenching occupation
There has been an increase in forced evictions of Palestinians in Jerusalem's Old City and surrounding areas by Israel and settlement organizations, according to Ir Amim, an Israeli group that documents settlement activity in the city.

An Israeli government settlement agency has allocated $55 million for projects in Jerusalem.

The so-called Company for the Reconstruction and Development of the Jewish Quarter will use the money to renovate several Jewish religious sites under the guise of improving tourism routes.

"The privatization of project management to nationalist settler organizations enables the Israeli government to exploit tourism as a tool for reinforcing settlement initiatives in the Old City and its environs, erasing the significant Palestinian presence there," Ir Amim stated.

Ir Amim published a map showing Israel's expansion of a settlement ring around Jerusalem's Old City to further entrench its control.

Israel is "promulgating the idea of the entire area as an Israeli environment, and imposing a nationalistic Israeli character that blurs the multi-religious and multicultural nature of the space, primarily to the detriment of the Muslim sites and presence."

Israeli occupation forces also placed new locks on the Bab al-Rahma entrance to the al-Aqsa mosque compound on Sunday to prevent the Islamic Waqf, or trust, from using the site.

Palestinians were planning a prayer near the site as form of resistance to the occupation's incursions in the city.

Firas al-Dibs, a spokesperson for the Islamic Waqf, said that Israeli police also closed the gates to the al-Aqsa mosque compound, attacked worshippers inside its courtyard and arrested Palestinians, as shown in pictures

Palestinians prayed in front of the gate on Monday in defiance of Israeli measures.

On Monday afternoon, Palestinian youths broke the chains placed by occupation forces and opened Bab al-Rahma to worshippers.

Israel must not be allowed to use Eurovision as a propaganda tool
Brian Eno, 18th Feb 2019, in The Guardian

A protester outside the BBC in London this month. Photograph: Penelope Barritt/Rex/Shutterstock

Those of us who make art and culture for a living thrive on free and open communication. So what should we do when we see culture becoming part of a political agenda? "Music unites," says UK Eurovision entrant Michael Rice. What happens when a powerful state uses art as propaganda, to distract from its immoral and illegal behaviour? Everybody involved in the Eurovision song contest this year should understand that this is what is happening.

European broadcasters, including the BBC, are pushing ahead with plans to hold the contest in Tel Aviv this May, as if broadcasting a hugely expensive entertainment spectacle from an actively repressive apartheid-like state is no problem at all. Eurovision, says the European Broadcasting Union, is a "nonpolitical" event. It's impossible to reconcile what the EBU is saying with reality. Israel is a state that sees culture as a political instrument: its prime minister, Benjamin Netanyahu, praised Netta Barzilai, Israel's 2018 Eurovision winner, as someone who has done "exceptional foreign relations work".

Then there's Israel's war against the Palestinians and their culture. In March and April last year, Israel's snipers targeted and killed journalists who were filming the peaceful protests in Gaza. In August its F16 jets destroyed the Said al-Mishal Centre in Gaza, a place of music, theatre and dance. Palestinian artists, actors and musicians are routinely denied permission to travel by the Israeli occupation authorities, or, as in the case of the poet Dareen Tatour, imprisoned for "inciting terrorism". Meanwhile the Israeli culture minister accuses dissident Israeli cultural organisations of subversion, and threatens to cut funding unless they modify their programmes to suit government tastes. In 2017, for instance, the Acre theatre festival withdrew a play about Palestinian prisoners of Israel rather than face the minister's financial revenge; since then galleries and film festivals have been similarly menaced.

These threats to cultural production are part of a wider pattern that undermines the claim that Eurovision 2019 will embody values of inclusion, diversity and friendship. The EBU's code of ethics promotes Eurovision as a safe space, where "human rights, freedom of expression, democracy, cultural diversity, tolerance and solidarity" can thrive. If that is really the intention, having Israel as the host is absurd: the briefest inquiry would show broadcasters that these principles had long been abandoned there.

Reporters Without Borders notes that Israeli journalists are subject to "military censorship" – gag orders. And as for "inclusion" – Israel's myriad restrictions on the movement of Palestinians will ensure that almost all of them are excluded from the Eurovision festivities.

Last year Israel's acclaimed theatre actor-director, Itay Tiran, was moved to urge international support for the growing Boycott, Divestment and Sanctions (BDS) movement, called for by Palestinian civil society; and tens of thousands of people across Europe, fans and musicians, have signalled that they will be campaigning to disengage their countries from the events in Tel Aviv. I understand Rice's joy at being selected as Britain's Eurovision representative. But when he believes "it's not my place to say" whether Israeli treatment of the Palestinians means Eurovision should be relocated, I think he's underestimating his power. He could help to ensure that Eurovision 2019 will be remembered as an occasion of principled protest, not another episode of cultural whitewashing.

• Brian Eno is a musician, composer, producer and visual artist. He is a supporter of Artists for Palestine UK

The Palestinian activists protecting Hebron from settler violence

After Israel boots the only internationally mandated human rights observer group in Hebron, Palestinian volunteers step up to monitor settler attacks amid a sense of heightened hostility. By Steven Davidson, 18th Feb 2019, in +972 magazine

Israeli Settler Ofer Ohana argues with Palestinian activists in the West Bank city of Hebron, February 10, 2019. (Wisam Hashlamoun/Flash90)

About a dozen Palestinian volunteers in blue vests identifying themselves as "human rights observers" made their way toward the Israeli army's Checkpoint 56 on Shuhada Street in the occupied West Bank city of Hebron early last week. They were escorting children on their way to the Qurtuba school 100 meters away, enduring harassment and kicking by settlers as they let the schoolchildren pass.

Up until late last month, this was a task for international observers, but on January 28, Israeli Prime Minister Benjamin Netanyahu announced that he will not renew the mandate for the Temporary International Presence in Hebron (TIPH), accusing the mission of "acting against Israel" in a tweet.

"When they kicked TIPH out, it was like they kicked us in the face," said Palestinian activist Izzat Karaki.

The Oslo II Accord of 1995 called for an international presence in Hebron following the 1994 Ibrahimi Mosque massacre, in which a Jewish settler killed 29 Palestinian worshipers in the city. TIPH mission was tasked with monitoring the human rights situation in the city, which Oslo divided into two areas: H1, home to most of the city's Palestinian residents, is governed by the Palestinian Authority; and H2, where hundreds of Israeli settlers live among tens of thousands of Palestinians, and which is under the control of the Israeli army.

TIPH was the only observer group in Hebron with an official international mandate renewed every few months by Israel and the PA. Its staff included observers from Norway, Sweden, Switzerland, Turkey and Italy. The organization, which was also the best-funded and well-staffed in the city, produced over 40,000 monitoring reports in 22 years, among other humanitarian duties. Right-wing pressure against TIPH increased in Israel after two incidents by observers in which one slashed a settler's tires and another slapped a child's face. Both were removed by TIPH.

With TIPH's exit, other volunteer international observation groups are now concerned about their safety in Hebron. According to Peter Prove, director of the Commission of the Churches on International Affairs at the World Council of Churches (WCC), "the same day as the announcement, there was a noticeable spike in harassment and threats from members of the settler community" against observers from the WCC Ecumenical Accompaniment Programme in Palestine and Israel (EAPPI). Within days, the WCC decided to pull out their international observers from the IDF-controlled H2 area of Hebron, severely curtailing their ability to carry out their intended monitoring.

Prove called EAPPI's return to H2 "imminent," saying they will reintroduce their observers "step-by-step" after they implement measures to increase their observers' safety.

About a dozen Palestinian volunteers escorted children to the Qurtuba school in Hebron after Israeli Prime Minister Netanyahu decided not to renew TIPH's mandate in Hebron on Jan. 28, 2019. (Catherine Curran-Groome)

In the interim, a group of Palestinian volunteers is trying to fill the monitoring gap left behind by the recent departures of the two international observer organizations. The new group, Kifah, or "struggle," is named after Kifah Owewi, a Hebron activist who passed away recently, and was the brainchild of Tel Rumeida community leader Issa Amro. Kifah is reviewing volunteer applications and training Palestinians on how to properly handle settler provocations.

But as Palestinians under military law — and without the official international mandate of TIPH — Kifah volunteers have little power to monitor human rights abuses. On their third day at Checkpoint 56, for example, soldiers demanded the Palestinian group leave, declaring the area a closed military zone for 24 hours. The order was seemingly enforced only that morning in order to remove the Palestinian observers, with the army allowing normal movement on Shuhada Street to resume a few hours later.

The next morning, soldiers waited outside the Youth Against Settlements house in Tel Rumeida, where Kifah volunteers had gathered before leaving to monitor the checkpoint. They prevented the Palestinian group from leaving the house by declaring the area a closed military zone. The soldiers again stopped the Palestinian volunteers when they tried to reach the school from another direction.

Because TIPH was part of an internationally mandated force, Israeli soldiers generally did not force them out of such closed military zones. "Now, we are weaker," said Issa Amro. "We can't replace TIPH, an international mission. We can't do what they could."

With the military declaring closed military zones around Qurtuba school each day, Amro said they plan to monitor other schools in the morning instead. On Thursday, they were joined by other Palestinian committees to monitor three separate locations in H2. They will continue to patrol the area at night and offer a hotline for locals whenever there are any settler attacks.

In other areas, TIPH helped fund community projects around Tel Rumeida, including a kindergarten, a garden, a playground, and a health clinic, according to Bassem Abu Aisha, president of the Popular Committee of Tel Rumeida. The organization also supported education classes for adults, organized communal feasts on Ramadan, and took children on field trips, he said. Now that TIPH is gone, "we have no money for projects in our community. These problems will worsen in the coming months," said Abu Aisha.

The few remaining non-official international observers in Hebron described a "frightening" atmosphere in the city following TIPH's departure. All volunteers interviewed asked that their names and the organizations they are with not be published.

Earlier this month, the IDF detained two activists from the International Solidarity Movement (ISM) and banned them from

H2 for two weeks. Others have been forced to leave checkpoint locations this week.

Amid the hostile environment, remaining observers are going "underground and incognito," said one international volunteer, adding that many are afraid to identify themselves. Observers from organizations like Christian Peacemaker Teams (CPT) no longer wear their vests identifying them or their organization, fearing reprisal or banishment.

With many incoming volunteer observers being denied entry at the Israeli border, resources were already being stretched thin for monitor groups before TIPH and EAPPI left. "Our focus has been shifted to covering as many checkpoints as we can," said John. "Previously, our teams were bigger, so people can do home visits, write reports, but with the denials at the border spreading every organization thin, those things aren't happening."

To compensate for the losses and heightened hostility, remaining observer organizations are in constant communication with each other, calling to exchange information and cover for each other at checkpoints.

When harassing Amro and other Kifah observers, the settlers' taunts at times seem celebratory. Minutes after he was forced to leave Checkpoint 56 near Qurtuba school, Amro told media "settlers attack the school from time to time."

"A lot of times! A lot of times!" interrupted Israeli settler Ofer Ohana, who had been taunting and taping Amro and the Kifah volunteers the previous 30 minutes in an effort to provoke them. Ohana is a well-known Israeli settler from nearby Kiryat Arba who was infamously videotaped kicking a knife toward the body of the incapacitated Palestinian man executed by Israeli soldier Elor Azaria in March 2016.
During a recent settler attack, in which several threw stones at Palestinian homes in Tel Rumeida, Amro said settlers told him and others, "TIPH is not here anymore. We can do whatever we want with you."

Some families are taking time off from work to bring their children to school, fearing settler violence now that there aren't international observers at checkpoints. Abdullah Gharib's children go to Qurtuba, and he said he is considering pulling them out of the school altogether. "We are scared for our children and women and properties," said Gharib. "We don't have any resources to defend ourselves."

For now, Gharib and other families are "standing together" and tightening communication with one another. But there isn't much they can do, said his wife, Haiam. "Any attack the settlers wanted to do, when TIPH was there, the settlers couldn't do it so freely," said Haiam. "We will suffer much more over time. The coming days will be bad for us," she added.

Hours later that night, a group of Israeli settlers threw stones at the windows of several Palestinian homes around the corner from the Gharib house and at passersby. Palestinians describe increasing settler incidents in the days since.

Haiam recalled how in September 2018, a settler ran over their 16 year-old son, Montaser, outside their neighbor's house in Tel Rumeida, moderately wounding him. Afterwards, TIPH directed them to lawyers and helped monitor their case in court. "Who will care for us now? We are just swinging in the air. We don't know where to go," said Haiam.

"We used to feel more secure when [TIPH] was here," she added. "Now, there's no security. It's gone."

Steven Davidson is a freelance journalist based in the Middle East. His work has appeared in the Forward, the Times of Israel, Haaretz, Salon, and +972 Magazine, among others. You can find him on Twitter @sdavidson169.

Netanyahu pretends occupation does not exist
by Akiva Eldar February 19, 2019 from Al Monitor

Israeli Prime Minister Benjamin Netanyahu speaks at the Conference of Presidents of Major American Jewish Organizations Leadership Mission to Israel, Jerusalem, Feb. 18, 2019.

The April 9 elections to the 21st Knesset will be the 15th time since the 1967 Arab-Israeli War that Israel's citizens and soldiers will exercise their democratic right while ruling over millions of disenfranchised Palestinians. There were times when the exhortation "down with the occupation" merited a place of honor in the political discourse, alongside the word "peace." Under the decadelong regime of Prime Minister Benjamin Netanyahu, such talk has made way for a discourse of annexation and incitement. It is as if not saying the word makes the occupation disappear.

On Feb. 16, Channel 13 news anchor Oshrat Kotler, referring to a report about Israeli soldiers who beat up two Palestinian detainees, commented that 18-year-old soldiers were deployed in the territories and "come back human animals. That's the result of the occupation." Her comment generated outraged reactions on the political right, not because she had used the word "occupation" — they were careful to sideline that — but because she had "dishonored Israeli soldiers." Her bottom line — "that's the result of the occupation" — was ignored. According to the right-wing worldview, if you do not react to the occupation, it does not exist.

How does a state that boasts of being a democracy deal with its continued control of another people? There are various ways. Netanyahu, for example, depicts an alternative reality. Thus, in a March 2018 speech at the annual convention of the pro-Israeli American Israel Public Affairs Committee lobby in Washington, he had the supreme gall to compare the values instilled in Americans by Abraham Lincoln and Martin Luther King — "freedom, justice, peace and hope" — with those cherished by Israel, while ignoring Israel as an occupying, discriminatory power that oppresses and depresses. It would be interesting to know what value he thinks is embodied in his warning to right-wing voters on election day in March 2015 that Israel's Arab citizens "are heading to the polling stations in droves."

The chair of the New Right party, Naftali Bennett, wondered in 2013 how anyone could call Israel an occupier in its own home. "After all, this is our home," he said. Two years later, Deputy Foreign Minister Tzipi Hotovely of the Likud Party demanded that Israeli diplomats "return to the basic truth about our right to this land" when representing the country abroad. In addition to discussing Israel's security and diplomacy needs, she added, "You should stress the biblical and historic link of the Jews to the Land of Israel."

The secular right has its own ways of justifying the occupation. There is the argument that the Palestinians repeatedly reject Israel's terms (all justified, they think). Then there is the one that the Palestinians are a bunch of terrorists who will turn the West Bank into another Gaza Strip and threaten residents of the nearby central Israeli town of Kfar Saba as they do residents of the Gaza border communities in the south. The real pros cite updated legal arguments against the "fake occupation" from a 2012 report by former Supreme Court Justice Edmond Levy whom Netanyahu appointed to examine the status of the settlements in Judea and Samaria (the biblical names of the West Bank).

Levy's three-member committee determined that "Judea and Samaria" are not under military occupation because the 1917 Balfour Declaration, the 1920 San Remo conference and the 1922 British Mandate issued by the League of Nations all designated the land as part of a future Jewish state. The panel also concluded that although the 1947 UN Partition Resolution designated land for the establishment of an Arab state alongside the Jewish one, the resolution for an Arab state was never implemented and thus its validity had expired. That same argument, according to the panel, holds for the Jordanian annexation of the area in 1950, which the international community never recognized. Nonetheless, the committee avoided defining the status of the West Bank, noting that successive Israeli governments had avoided its annexation.

The committee failed to mention that in 2003, the UN Security Council unanimously adopted the road map for peace in the Middle East (Resolution 1515), saying a permanent solution to the Israeli-Palestinian conflict would "end the occupation that began in 1967." According to the road map, a peace agreement would be based, inter alia, on the principle of land for peace and on the 2002 Arab Peace Initiative that offered Israel security and normalized relations with the Arab world in return for the establishment of a Palestinian state within the 1967 borders. (In later negotiations, the words "land swaps" were added.)

Netanyahu was a senior member of the defense Cabinet under Prime Minister Ariel Sharon, which approved the road map with certain reservations (which were rejected). "You can dislike the word 'occupation,'" Sharon told critics within the Likud in 2003, "but that is what is happening … keeping 3.5 million Palestinians under occupation is a terrible thing — both for Israel and the Palestinians. … This cannot continue endlessly." Sharon asked his colleagues whether they want Israel to remain forever in the Palestinian towns of Jenin, Nablus, Ramallah and Bethlehem. The Israeli right of 2019 would have answered, "Why not?" In fact, who's going to stop them? Israel's friend US President Donald Trump? Israel's allies from the central European Visegrad Group? The Jewish voters who are convinced there is no such thing as an occupation? The monthly Peace Index survey conducted on the 50th anniversary of the 1967 war found that 62% of Israelis believe Israel's control of the territories is not an occupation. On the political right and center, only a minority — 12% and 37%, respectively — believe it is an occupation.

Israeli media has come to the conclusion that stories about human rights abuse in the West Bank bore the Israeli readers and audience. Thus, reports about land theft by settlers or about assaults against

Palestinian shepherds have disappeared from the newspapers and TV headlines.

Only on the left, the smallest of the three political blocs, a sweeping majority (86%) believes the correct definition of the situation is "occupation." However, many on the left are troubled mostly by the occupation's damage to Israeli Jews. For example, Brig. Gen. (Res.) Ilan Paz, who was head of the Civil Administration in the West Bank, wrote this week on Facebook that occupation corrupts, as anchor Kotler said. Few on the left talk about the suffering inflicted by the occupation on millions of Palestinians who have never known a day of freedom. In fact, only very few ever visit the territories and listen to its residents, jailed as they are among Israeli settlements and outposts.

Raya Yaron, the spokeswoman of Machsom Watch, an organization that monitors Israeli troop conduct in the territories, told Al-Monitor that not a single Knesset member had ever joined a tour offered by the group in the region. Dean Issacharoff, the spokesman of the anti-occupation group Breaking the Silence, told Al-Monitor the organization enjoys support from the left-wing Meretz Party and the Arab Joint List. He made favorable mention of Knesset member Ksenia Svetlova, a member of the Hatnua Party led by Tzipi Livni, the one-time Likud member who crossed the lines to become one of the peace camp's most prominent advocates. Livni and Svetlova realized that the occupation is the greatest threat to Israel's democracy and its Jewish identity. Livni announced Feb. 18 that the party will not run in the upcoming April elections. And so, neither she nor Svetlova will be returning to the Knesset after the elections. Nor is there any guarantee that Meretz will be there, either.

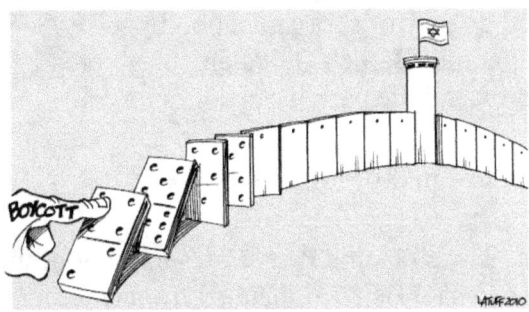

Netanyahu Just Invited Israel's Equivalent Of The KKK To Join The Government

By [Batya Ungar-Sargon](), February 20, 2019 from the "Forward" web site

The Israeli election cycle currently underway has been awash in anti-Arab racism for a while now. But things just got much, much worse.

On Wednesday, Haaretz reported that Israel's Prime Minister Benjamin Netanyahu pushed the Jewish Home Party to join another party, the "Jewish Power" party, which inherited its leaders and politics from the well-known racist Meir Kahane.

Kahana's Kach party was outlawed in 1994, the same year it was listed as a terrorist organization by the U.S. State Department, after a supporter, Baruch Goldstein, massacred 29 Arabs at prayer in Hebron and the party issued its support.

And now, in 2019, it's back.

If the Jewish Home Party votes in favor of the merger, it will mean that Michael Ben-Ari, banned from entering the U.S. for belonging to a terrorist organization, will be part of the ruling coalition of the

Jewish State. It will mean that Itamar Ben Gvir, convicted of inciting racism and supporting terrorism, will be welcomed in the halls of the Knesset as a lawmaker.

It will mean that Kahana's legacy — including his attempts to strip non-Jewish Israelis of their citizenship, ban marriage between Jews and non-Jews, and transfer Israel's Arab population out of Israel — will once again have advocates in the Israeli government.

For shame.

These are the David Dukes and the Richard Spencers of the Jewish State, people who believe that Jewish sovereignty depends on the oppression, ethnic cleansing and even murder of Israel's Arab population. And with this merger, Netanyahu's willingness to sell out any and all values in order to ensure his political survival has reached a new low.

But Netanyahu's move to include avowed racists in the ruling coalition, though horrifying, should not surprise us.

Netanyahu has spent the better part of the last two years leading Israel down an ugly road of increased ethnonationalism. From the Nation State bill, which ratifies Jewish supremacy over Israel's minorities, to the whitewashing of Holocaust revisionists in Poland and Hungary, to the embrace of racist premieres of other countries like the Philippines and Brazil, Netanyahu has put all his eggs in the racist, ethnonationalist basket.

The embrace of a party literally called Jewish Power is only the last in a long line of betrayals of Jews, Jewish history and Jewish values. What is the lesson of Jewish history if not that the rights of minorities must be vigorously, vigorously protected? What are Jewish values if not the Torah's exhortation that we pursue justice, justice at all costs? What are Jews if not the descendants of the most hounded people in history, ourselves the victims of ethnic cleansing time and again?

And now, the ruling coalition of the Jewish State will welcome members who wish to ethnically cleanse Palestinians, already dispossessed of civil rights by the millions, the victims of a brutal occupation in the West Bank and blockaded in Gaza.

For shame.

Meanwhile, regardless of Israel's descent into ethnonationalism, we in the Diaspora are expected to continue to provide unwavering support for a Jewish state that's embracing the very worldview — the supremacy of a country's majority over its minorities — that has ensured our destruction for millennia.

Contrary to Netanyahu's cynical view, Jewish rights need not come at the expense of the Palestinians. But when we balk at this request for unconditional support, when we demand accountability for Israel's descent into this ugliest form of nationalism, we are told that we don't have the right to speak up because we are assimilating and wont exist in three generations, or because we haven't served in the Israeli military, or because we don't speak Hebrew, or because we don't live in Sderot.

You don't need to live in Sderot to know a racist when you see one. You don't need to speak Hebrew to know that ethnic cleansing is wrong, and welcoming its advocates into the halls of the Jewish State's government is a *shanda*.

Netanyahu is not only betraying Jewish history with his embrace of ethnonationalism. He is betraying living, breathing Diaspora Jews. For the rise of populist nationalist leaders across the globe has brought with it an astounding and terrifying rise in anti-Semitic incidents, including vandalism, assault, murder, and mass murder — as it always does.

Across the world, anti-Semitism is on the rise in shocking ways, egged on by leaders like Hungary's Viktor Orban and the United States' own President Trump alike, both of whom hate minorities and espouse anti-Semitic conspiracy theories as Jewish bodies pile up. Both of whom have been embraced by Netanyahu.

Orban, a close ally of Netanyahu's, famously cast George Soros as his opponent throughout his campaign in nakedly anti-Semitic terms. And at a campaign stop, Orbán used well-worn anti-Semitic tropes to demean his enemies. "They are not national, but international; they do not believe in work, but speculate with money; they have no homeland, but feel that the whole world is theirs," he said.

This didn't stop Netanyahu from welcoming Orban to Yad Vashem and even sanctioning a new Holocaust-revision museum.

And Trump, who couldn't bring himself to condemn neo-Nazis and who initially blamed Jews for their own massacre in the Tree of Life synagogue, pushed the anti-Semitic conspiracy theory that George Soros was funding the Central American caravan making its way to the U.S., a conspiracy theory that animated the Tree of Life shooter. And to whitewash his responsibility in the event, Trump bragged about how much he's done for Israel, and how much Netanyahu likes him.

Netanyahu has certainly leaned into Trump's support, bragging about it on huge billboards overlooking Tel Aviv. But when he stands with anti-Semitism-enabling ethnonationalists like Trump and shares photo-ops with Orban, he gives a Jewish stamp of approval to the very forces that endanger Jewish lives.

For shame.

Jewish safety and sovereignty cannot come at the expense of Palestinian rights, freedoms, and dignity. The opposite; ethnonationalism will always come for Jews in the end. If the dignity of our Palestinian brothers and sisters isn't enough to move you, then let Jewish history do so.

Just as those who fight for Palestinian rights must cleanse their ranks of anti-Semitism, so too must Jews anxious about our past, present and future call out this appalling normalization of racism in the Jewish state.

This will not be done in my name.

For shame.

Batya Ungar-Sargon is the opinion editor of the Forward.

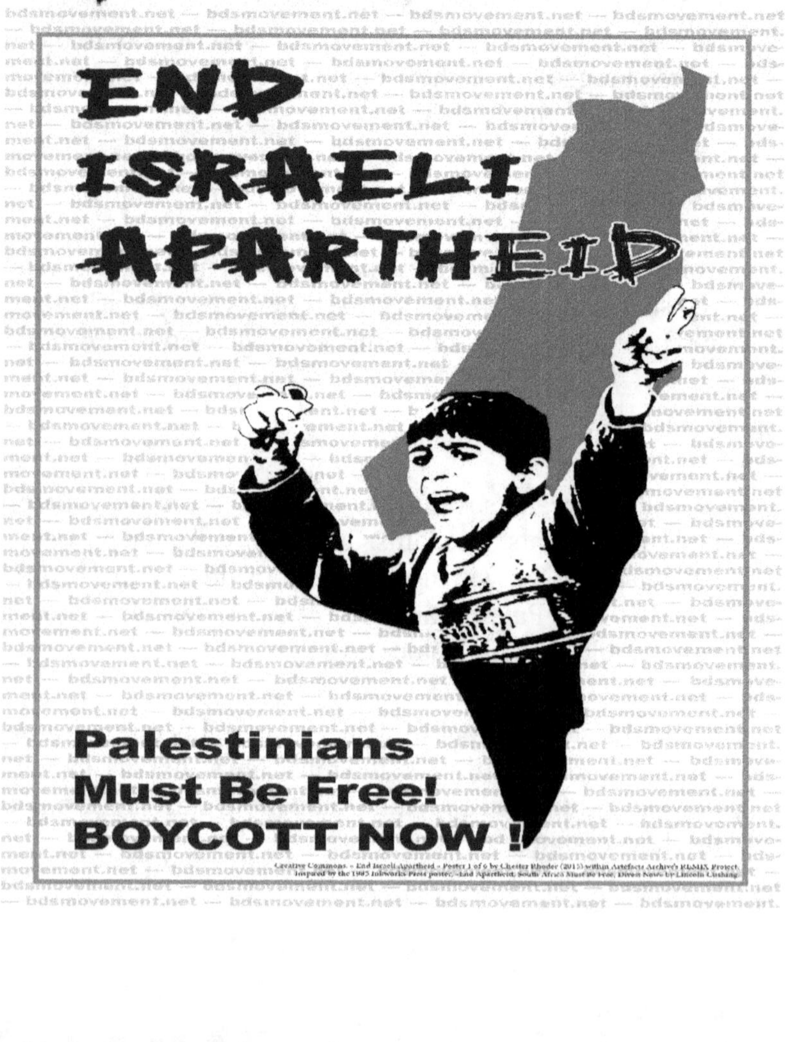

The Future is Palestinian: On Sumud and Benny Morris' Prophecies

By RamzyBaroud February 22, 2019, Middle East Monitor

Palestinians ride horses as they hold Palestinian flags during a demonstration to show solidarity with Jerusalem and Al-Aqsa Mosque in Gaza City, Gaza on 2 August 2017 [Ali Jadallah/Anadolu Agency]

In an interview with the Israeli newspaper, Haaretz, prominent Israeli historian Benny Morris predicted a grim future for his country.
"This place will deteriorate into a Middle Eastern state with an Arab majority," he said referring to Israel and Palestine. "The violence between various populations inside the state will continue to increase … The Arabs will demand the return of the refugees. The Jews will remain as a small minority in a large Arab sea of Palestinians – a persecuted minority or a slaughtered minority, as it was when they lived in Arab countries."

"In another 30 to 50 years, they will overcome us, one way or another," he added.

It doesn't matter whether Morris' prediction was meant to manipulate existing fears among his countrymen, to hype the sense of victimisation that continues to define the collective Israeli Jewish mindset or to communicate his honest feelings.

Either way, his statement explains why Israel acts against the Palestinian identity with such a great sense of urgency, intensifying attacks on Palestinian culture, speeding up annexation of Palestinian land, expanding Jewish settlements and Jewish-only roads, renaming streets and marginalising the Arabic language.

For Israel, erasing Palestine and writing the Palestinian people out of the history of their homeland have always been a strategic endeavour.

"Considered as a major accomplishment of modern Jewish nationalism, the 'Hebraicization of Israel' usually refers to the revival of the Hebrew language undertaken by and associated with Zionism as a restorative project of nation-building," Israeli academics Maoz Azaryahu and Arnon Golan wrote in their paper "(Re)naming the Landscape: the Formation of the Hebrew Map of Israel".

"A lesser known aspect of the 'Hebraicization of Israel', however, has been the 'Hebraicization of the map', a state-promoted national project whose objective was "to Judaize (sic) the map of Israel and to affix Hebrew names to all geographical features in the map of Israel".

This is as true in the case of Palestine, as it was in the case of all colonised nations. And like other settler-colonialist powers, Israel is well aware of the important rapport between places, names and collective identities of the indigenous, colonised people.

As Canadian historian Kaleigh Bradley pointed out in a recent essay: "For indigenous peoples, place names act as mnemonic devices, embodying histories, spiritual and environmental knowledge, and traditional teachings. Place names also serve as boundary markers between home and the world of outsiders."
The Israeli Zionist campaign to rename Palestinian places, destroy Palestinian heritage sites, claim Palestinian culture, undermine the Arabic language and erase cultural contributions of the Palestinian people has continued for over 70 years now.

More recently, the Israeli army has used its violent military assaults on Palestinians not only to take Palestinian lives but also to destroy cultural monuments and places of worship of historical significance. According to official Palestinian reports, Israel destroyed 73 mosques in the 51-day war on the besieged Gaza Strip in 2014.

Palestinian activists demonstrate against the Israeli occupation and Gaza blockade in front of a tower which was destroyed during the 2014 war between Israel and Hamas in Gaza city on 1 April 2017 [Mohammed Asad/Apaimages]

Some of these mosques, like al-Omari Mosque in Jabaliya, are ancient structures that date back more than a thousand years. Al-Omari Mosque was built nearly 1365 years ago and has served as a symbol of hope for Palestinians in Gaza, a reminder of past grandeur.

The Israeli authorities have also increased pressure on Islam's third-holiest site: Al-Aqsa Mosque. It has facilitated the forceful incursions of the Temple Mount Faithful, an extremist Jewish group, into the Haram al-Sharif compound, where the mosque is located. The group has declared that it is keen on destroying al-Aqsa Mosque to build a "Third Temple on Temple Mount" – something the Israeli government also wishes for.

There have been various attacks on Palestinian cultural heritage in Nablus, al-Khalil (Hebron), Ariyha (Jericho), Yaffa (Jaffa), Haifa and many other Palestinian towns and villages.

Despite all of this destruction, on intellectual and political levels, Israel remains insecure about its past and uncertain of its future.

But the foretold demise of Israel as a "Jewish state" – as prophesied by Morris – will come not as a result of the Arab majority "slaughtering" the "persecuted minority", but as a result of Israel's reckless actions. Before the Zionists, there were many other invaders. Many fled, but many others chose to stay and were naturally integrated into the fabric of the diverse Palestinian society.

Israel refuses to accept the fact that the Palestinians' relationship with their land cannot be dictated or terminated by violence, Knesset bills or army decrees. To the contrary, the more aggression is unleashed onto the Palestinians, the stronger the Palestinian sense of nationhood grows. The late Palestinian poet Mahmoud Darwish in his seminal poem, "ID Card" was able to capture this Palestinian spirit of resistance brilliantly:

I am a name with no honorific.
Patient in a land
Where everything lives in bursting rage
My roots were planted before time was born
Before history began
Before the cypress and the olive trees
Before grass sprouted

Palestinian "sumud" (steadfastness) has turned out to be far superior and more powerful than any of Israel's military and political stratagems. And it is this steadfastness that will guarantee that Morris' prediction comes true. The great Palestinian sea will swallow the occupier.

The integration of Israel

By _Lorenzo Meigs_, *February 22, 2019 from "The Bowdon Orient"*

Swastikas were painted onto nearly a hundred Jewish graves in France and the British Labour party splintered over the release of Jeremy Corbyn's nasty 2013 remarks on Jews, anti-Semitism in Europe boiled over yet again this week. Meanwhile, in America, we continued to wrestle with our own issues of anti-Semitism in light of Representative Ilhan Omar's (D-Minn.) tweet last week about the Washington consensus around support for Israel being "all about the Benjamins." These incidents are by no means equally bad—Omar's remark, for example, seems like a genuine mistake, free of hatred—yet these incidents do all underscore a fact the Western left seems to be rapidly forgetting: the need for a Jewish state remains strong.

Seventy years after the World War Two, many Jews still do not feel safe in their nations, and rightly so. The events of these last few weeks pale in comparison to the Tree of Life massacre in Pittsburgh last year and the 2014 siege of the Don Abravanel synagogue in Paris. Now more than ever, the Jews of the world need and deserve a strong state—a state where they are guaranteed sanctuary and a state that will advocate for their interests abroad. Unfortunately, Israel may soon no longer be that state.

Israel was always an unstable and controversial project. Its founding resulted in the horrifying expulsion of 700,000 Palestinians and, surrounded by nations that want it gone, its continued existence has forever been a fight. Yet, somehow, this parched piece of land has become a wonderful modern state. Indeed, to visit it is to fall in love with it. The energy of Tel Aviv, the beauty of Haifa, the thickness of community in the still-thriving Kibbutzim—these goods constitute the manifestation of a dream that has been millennia in the making. The chosen people have finally returned to their land and built themselves a home.

However, this home is rotten and fast decaying. As unarmed Palestinians fighting for freedom continue to be gunned down, the mask of Western values Israel has been hiding behind for decades is finally starting to slip, and the world is beginning to grasp the sorry fact that Israel is—and has been for years—an unapologetic apartheid state.

In 2010, Prime Minister Benjamin Netanyahu and his Likud party gave up on preventing further settlements in the West Bank, and since then the ostensibly Palestinian territory has swollen to hold some 400,000 Jewish settlers. These settlers are full Israeli citizens, represented in the Knesset (Israeli's Parliament), and they can drive in and out of the West Bank almost without noticing they are moving across state lines.

Palestinians, meanwhile, are subject to strict movement controls, denied equal access to water and governed by Israeli military law—not the civil law settlers are subject to. In Gaza, Jewish settlements were removed, but Israel has also maintained complete functional control, preventing the region from developing through the imposition of a decade-long economic blockade. A United

Nations report recently found that the area may be rendered "unlivable" as soon as next year.

In short, Israel has conquered Palestine and unilaterally implemented its own twisted vision of a one-state solution. If you squint, Israel is the sole democracy in a region of autocracy, but if you open your eyes, it's hard to see anything but a humanitarian disaster. J-Street, a Jewish-American lobbying organization, and the rest of the international community can continue breathlessly debating how to implement a two-state solution, but that possibility died years ago: 400,000 settlers cannot be moved, and the Palestinians are totally incapable of supporting themselves. Thus, to support a two-state solution now is to support the status quo, for there will never be any real movement towards those two states—Netanyahu has already said as much. This is a tragedy of epic proportions, but ignoring it will not solve it.

To be sure, the current state of affairs cannot be blamed solely on Israel-Palestinian leadership has been obstinate, unreasonable and flat out anti-Semitic since the beginning, and Hamas, which can only be described as a terrorist group, now controls Gaza. Further, as many Palestinians have never accepted Israel's fundamental right to exist, Israel has been subject to brutal and unrelenting attack. Indeed, much Israeli aggression has been necessary to protect its people. However, as the interposers, the primary responsibility has always lain with the Zionists. Zionism needed to figure out how to avoid pure colonialism, and it failed. And so, Israel will soon fail, too.

Netanyahu knows this, and by allying himself with the Republican Party, he has bought himself some time—the strange alliance of American evangelicals and Israeli neo-Zionists is now one of the primary forces propping the state up. However, this move has set the stage for a break in the bipartisan American support of Israel, and it's only a matter of time before the Democrats abandon Israel. And without American moral and military aid, Israel will finally become a pariah state and begin down the road of South African-style decline.

I love Israel—the two weeks I spent there at the end of my gap year were a wonderful mixture of meeting family, reveling in historical riches and floating in the turquoise blue waters of the Asi River—but at the same time, I'm convinced that the Israel we know today must come to an end. Even as I am reminded daily of the need for a Jewish state, I am simultaneously forced to conclude that a truly Jewish state can no longer exist. For while the Jews undeniably deserve their own state, the Palestinians' need for basic rights and recognition is even greater. With the death of the two-state solution, the only way to meet that Palestinian need is to integrate the Palestinian people into the Jewish state—the Israeli state. In America and Israel, the right have already recognized the reality of a one-state future. The left must finally do the same. The only legitimate fight that remains is over the character of this impending, singular, Israeli-Palestinian state.

It's beyond the scope of this column to lay out a coherent left-wing one-state solution, but morally, it is the only way forward. For the good of all, occupation must end and reunification must begin. Both peoples' claim to the land must be recognized, and new institutions in which they can both participate and thrive must be created. It will be a long and arduous process, but it can be done.

UN report says Israel a 'racist state' and 'apartheid regime'

Report 'first of its type' to conclude 'apartheid system persecutes Palestinian people'
from the Irish Times March 2017

An Israeli wall separating the Palestinian refugee camp of Shuafat from an East Jerusalem neighbourhood. Israel and the US strongly rejected the UN report. Photograph: Atef Safadi/EPA

A UN agency published a report on Wednesday accusing Israel of imposing an "apartheid regime" of racial discrimination on the Palestinian people, and said it was the first time a UN body had clearly made the charge.

Israel's foreign ministry spokesman likened the report, published by the UN Economic and Social Commission for Western Asia (ESCWA), to *Der Stürmer* – a Nazi propaganda publication that was strongly anti-Semitic.

The report concluded that "Israel has established an apartheid regime that dominates the Palestinian people as a whole". The accusation – often directed at Israel by its critics – is fiercely rejected by Israel.

UN under-secretary general and ESCWA Executive Secretary Rima Khalaf said the report was the "first of its type" from a UN body that "clearly and frankly concludes that Israel is a racist state that has established an apartheid system that persecutes the Palestinian people".

ESCWA comprises 18 Arab states in Western Asia and aims to support economic and social development in member states, according to its website. The report was prepared at the request of member states, Khalaf said.

UN spokesman Stephane Dujarric told reporters in New York the report was published without any prior consultation with the UN secretariat.

"The report as it stands does not reflect the views of the secretary-general [Antonio Guterres]," said Dujarric, adding that the report itself notes that it reflects the views of the authors.

US outrage
The United States, an ally of Israel, said it was outraged by the report.

"The United Nations secretariat was right to distance itself from this report, but it must go further and withdraw the report altogether," the US ambassador to the United Nations, Nikki Haley, said in a statement.

The Israeli ministry spokesman, Emmanuel Nahshon, commenting on Twitter, also noted the report had not been endorsed by the UN secretary general.

"The attempt to smear and falsely label the only true democracy in the Middle East by creating a false analogy is despicable and constitutes a blatant lie," Israel's UN ambassador Danny Danon said in a statement.

The report said it had established on the "basis of scholarly inquiry and overwhelming evidence, that Israel is guilty of the crime of apartheid".

"However, only a ruling by an international tribunal in that sense would make such an assessment truly authoritative," it added.

The report said the "strategic fragmentation of the Palestinian people" was the main method through which Israel imposes apartheid, with Palestinians divided into four groups oppressed through "distinct laws, policies and practices".

Refugees
It identified the four sets of Palestinians as: Palestinian citizens of Israel; Palestinians in East Jerusalem; Palestinians in the West Bank and Gaza Strip; and Palestinians living as refugees or in exile.

ESCWA hoped the report would inform further deliberations on the root causes of the problem in the United Nations, among member states and in society, Khalaf said at an event to launch the report at ESCWA's Beirut headquarters.

It was authored by Richard Falk, a former UN human rights investigator for the Palestinian territories, and Virginia Tilley, professor of political science at Southern Illinois University. Before leaving his post as UN special rapporteur on human rights in the Palestinian territories in 2014, Falk said Israeli policies bore unacceptable characteristics of colonialism, apartheid and ethnic cleansing.

The United States accused him of being biased against Israel. – (Reuters)

Israel's 'racist' Nation-State Law condemned in Westminster

From Middle East Monitor February 27, 2019

A seminar held in the Palace of Westminster by EuroPal Forum to discuss Israel's Jewish Nation-State Law in London, UK on 26 February 2019 [Jehan Alfarra/Middle East Monitor]

Hosted by British Labour MP Andy Slaughter, the seminar brought together individuals from the legal, diplomatic and public policy fields

Israel's Jewish Nation-State Law was condemned as "racist" at a seminar held in the Palace of Westminster yesterday by EuroPal Forum whose chairman, Zaher Birawi, described the legislation as "racist". The law was ratified by the Knesset in July last year. Hosted by British Labour MP Andy Slaughter and chaired by journalist and researcher Nasim Ahmed, the seminar brought together individuals from the legal, diplomatic and public policy fields. The intention was to elucidate a more nuanced understanding of the Nation-State Law while also communicating the various steps that could be taken by the international community to challenge Israel's violations of international law. The "Basic Law: Israel as the Nation-State of the Jewish People" has been criticised widely, described by Palestinians and members of the international community alike as both discriminatory and verging on apartheid.

"Much of the western world is taken up with other political problems such as Brexit," British-Palestinian lawyer Salma Karmi-Ayyoub told *MEMO*, "so it is really important that this issue doesn't fall off the agenda." Speaking at the event in parliament, Karmi-Ayyoub mentioned the implications of the Israeli law and the right of Palestinians to exercise self-determination within the State of Israel as well as in the occupied territories.

British-Palestinian academic and political commentator Professor Kamel Hawwash pointed out that the law in question states very clearly that only Jews have a right to self-determination in the land of Israel. "It is extremely important to discuss this openly here and to begin to talk to our government to explain that that's what Israel has done and what its nature is," he added. "We need to put pressure on the government to think about disassociating itself from a state that is, in practice, an apartheid state."

The Nation-State Law effectively codifies discrimination against Palestinians through the exclusive recognition of Jewish rights to self-determination in the land of Israel, thus forcing the issue of the legitimate right of return off the agenda of future Israeli-Palestinian negotiations. Furthermore, it entrenches an apartheid system in Israel through the selective status awarded to Hebrew and the removal of Arabic as an official language, and leads to the marked complication of the two-state solution through its classification of Jerusalem as the "complete and united capital of Israel".

According to international law, the city of Jerusalem — all of it — is occupied territory, having been declared to be subject to a "Special International Regime" in the 1947 UN Partition Plan from which Israel takes its legitimacy. Israel's annexation of Jerusalem has never been recognised by the international community.

Although Sinn Fein MPs don't take their seats in the British parliament, Órfhlaith Begley MP told *MEMO* that she attended the seminar specifically to discuss the implications of nation-state law. She reiterated her party's condemnation of the legislation. "We're calling upon the Irish government to condemn it also," she said, pointing out that Sinn Fein has made a number of calls for the recognition of the State of Palestine.

The seminar was part of a series organised by EuroPal Forum across Europe, including one at the European Parliament. "The aim," explained Birawi, "is to expose racist policies in the Israeli State and put before European politicians their responsibility to reject such racist legislation and put pressure on Israel to end its discriminatory practices and its illegal occupation of Palestine." The veteran activist stressed that the Nation-State Law needs to be challenged at the grassroots and parliamentary levels as a matter of urgency.

Elections and the demise of democracy
By Gershon Baskin, 28th Feb 2019 in The Jerusalem Post

Elections are a key element in any democracy – and in true democracies, they should be the highest level of celebration of the citizens' right to determine their future. But while elections are one of the pillars of true democracy, they not the only one. Majority rule is a principle of democracy. But would a true democracy allow the majority to prevent, let's say, a minority of 20% of the society from participating fully in the political life of that society?

That is what is happening in Israel today. A fifth of Israel's citizens are being delegitimized by the majority and their wannabe political representatives. Never before have the Palestinian citizens of Israel been so outcast by the majority of political parties in Jewish Israel. The demand is made of Jewish politicians across the public domain, in the media and at public events, to declare that they will not rely on the votes of 20% of the citizens, and that they will not sit with them in a coalition. And if they don't declare those things, their loyalty to the state is immediately questioned.

The prime minister and members of his party declare day and night that the Palestinian citizens of Israel seek to destroy the state. Where and when have the Arab political parties in Israel made such declarations or taken such actions? If they did, surely they would not be free men and women. They would be sitting behind bars and not participating in democratic elections.

The overwhelming majority of Palestinian citizens of Israel are law-abiding ones who contribute to the building of the state. They work in all parts of the country, pay their taxes, follow the laws, contribute to the economy, teach in the universities, fulfill our prescriptions in pharmacies and care for us all in our hospitals and clinics. And growing numbers of young Palestinian citizens are enlisting for non-military civil service.

Yes, the Arab political parties in Israel are fighting for equality. Yes, they would prefer Israel to be the state of all of its citizens and not the nation-state of the Jewish people. It is their democratic right to participate in political life in their state and to try to change the minds of all of the citizens of that state. They are not engaged in military action or terrorism against the state and its symbols, and they do not preach or practice violence.

ONE OF the leaders of the Arab parties, Ayman Odeh, is the head of a party that since 1947 has supported a two-state solution, recognizing the right of the Jewish people to self-determination.

Another leader, Dr. Ahmed Tibi, a medical doctor, has been one of the most diligent legislators since 1999. He served as an adviser to Palestinian leader Yasser Arafat with the aim of assisting Israel and the Palestinians to achieve peace. Tibi is well known as being one of the most eloquent orators on the horrors of the worst crime against humanity – the Holocaust.

Even at the far-left extreme, the Balad Party is seeking for Israel to be the state of all of its citizens, not a Jewish state – but through legitimate politics, and it is completely opposed to violence. Its founder is suspected of aiding Hezbollah during the Second Lebanon War, but exiled himself to Qatar in 2006, and has refused to face arrest, questioning and trial.

Another member of the party was arrested and convicted of smuggling cellphones into prison for Palestinian prisoners. He is serving a two-year prison term. But the political party that Azmi Bishara founded is not guilty of any crimes. It is a legitimate political party in the State of Israel representing Israeli citizens. The prime minister is suspect of committing crimes, and a former prime minister went to prison. That does not criminalize their political parties.

The demand being made from Jewish political parties – to state a priori that they will not cooperate with the Arab parties in forming a government after the elections, or in supporting a candidate other than Netanyahu to form a government – is a slap in the face to 20% of Israel's citizens and a clear sign of the demise of the core principles of democracy in Israel.

I HAVE always related to Israel as the nation-state of the Jewish people and all of its citizens. I became an Israeli citizen more than 40 years ago on the basis of Israel's Law of Return, which grants all Jews the right to become Israeli citizens.

I have defended that right over the years on the basis of two claims:

1) The Law of Return does not discriminate between citizens of Israel, it discriminates between who can become citizens of the State of Israel. Israel was dedicated, in principle, to equality between all of its citizens.

2) The hope and belief that when there is a Palestinian state next to Israel it would have its own Law of Return, granting automatic citizenship to Palestinians around the world who would like to be citizens of their own nation state.

That would provide a balance between the immigration laws of the two states that give preference to members of their own national groups. My right to be a citizen of the State of Israel, as someone who was not born in the state, should not grant me a higher status than 20% of the citizens of Israel who were born in Israel and whose direct family lineage dates back many generations in this land, and often in the exact same communities where they live today.

The principle of equality between all Israelis that is fundamental in Israel's Declaration of Independence, for me, has always been a badge of honor and a declaration of intentions of what the State of Israel seeks to be. It is clear that as long as the Israeli-Palestinian conflict exists and the Palestinian citizens of Israel have a natural and understandable allegiance to their own people living under Israeli occupation, that full equality would be impossible to implement. The Palestinian citizens of Israel will always in a way be suspect in the eyes of the Jewish majority.

Nonetheless, almost every Israeli government since 1948 has stated a desire to achieve equality, and to close the gaps between Jews and Arabs in Israel. With the absence of the principle of equality in the Nation-State Law, and the continuous incitement by the prime minister and other right-wing politicians in Israel against the Palestinian citizens of Israel, the full delegitimization of their participation in the electoral process has reached new and frightening heights.

In 1981, prime minister Menachem Begin (Likud) and education minister Zevulun Hammer (National Religious Party) hired me as the first civil servant in Israel responsible for improving Jewish-Arab relations in a new position that I created. The right-wing leaders of that time practiced democracy. Israel's first president, Chaim Weizmann, stated that Israel will be judged by the nations of the world on how it relates to its Arab minority.

Today, the future of Israel will be based on its ability to create a shared society. To do that we have to delegitimize the anti-democratic trends that are all too prevalent in the elections of 2019.

The writer is a political and social entrepreneur who has dedicated his life to the State of Israel and to peace between Israel and her neighbours. His latest book, In Pursuit of Peace in Israel and Palestine, was published by Vanderbilt University Press.

Without Saying a Word, Israeli Troops Beat Up a Blind Man in His Bed

Israeli soldiers invaded the home of a Palestinian family at night, and battered a man in the face in front of his wife and children. He's 47, blind and on dialysis, and his toes have been amputated because of diabetes

By Gideon Levy and Alex Levac Feb 28, 2019 in HaAretz

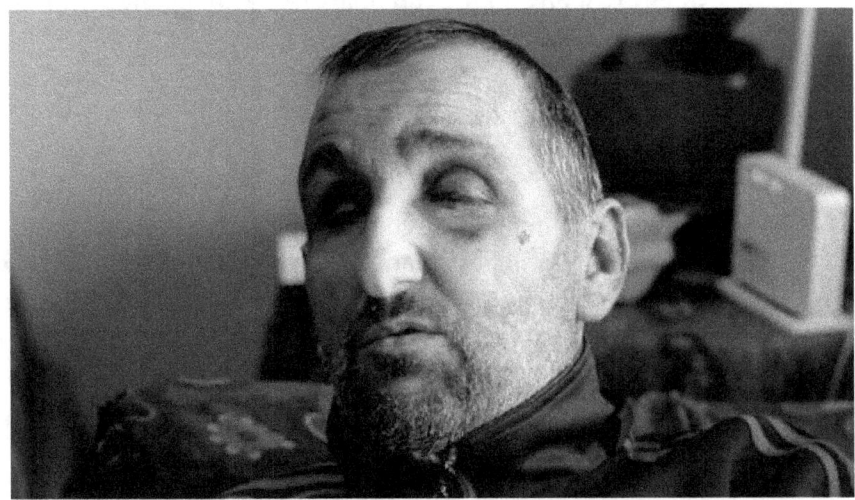

Munzer Mizhar at home in the West Bank town of Dawha, near Bethlehem. Alex Levac

He's lying on the living room sofa, next to the gas stove, trying to warm his broken body. When we visited him this week, he had just returned from the hospital and was worn out from the dialysis treatment he has been undergoing three times a week for the 11 years since his kidneys stopped functioning, as a consequence of severe diabetes.

Before that, 15 years ago, he started to lose his sight, and for the past few years he has been completely blind. Also, over the course of the last six years, he has gradually had to have toes amputated, operation after operation. His face is sallow from the dialysis.

Physically shattered, he lies there, barely able to move. He needs help getting up; he's incapable of doing anything on his own. Every few months, he travels to Jordan for the catheterization of the blood vessels in his legs, which are becoming blocked.

So yes, Munzer Mizhar, 47, is a very sick man. Still, last week, that didn't stop Israeli soldiers from pummeling him mercilessly, even after the neighbors had warned them that he was sick. Nor was his wife, an eyewitness to the attack, able to prevent the abuse of her husband despite her shouts that he was blind, too.

Nothing helped. The fists landed on his face – the blue marks are still visible, particularly below his dead eyes, now blood-red. He also has wounds on his shoulders and both hands – from his attempts to ward off the brutal assault.

It all happened while he was in his bed after 4 A.M. on February 20.

A medical technician, Mizhar was employed in a laboratory belonging to the Palestinian Authority but had to take early retirement because of his deteriorating health. He speaks good English. He and his wife Iman have four sons, the oldest 18 and triplets of 16. Iman, who is 45, has cancer, for which she's treated at Augusta Victoria Hospital in East Jerusalem, and in Jordan.

Her condition is good. She joined the conversation in their house this week but grew pale as it proceeded and had to lie down several times, eyes closed, tears welling up. The trauma of her husband's beating is still vivid, painful and hard for her to bear, perhaps even more than for him. Family members say she cowers in fright whenever the horrors of that night are recalled. They live in a well-kept home in the town of Dawha near Bethlehem.

That Wednesday, Munzer was awakened at about 4:45 A.M. by the sound of footsteps in the house. He woke his wife. He thought that maybe his sons were wandering about in the dark.

His wife opened her eyes and screamed. He didn't understand what was going on. At first they thought burglars had broken in. But Iman saw shadowy figures who had entered their room, while red laser beams sliced through the darkness toward their bed.

The specters moved without sound. Later it would emerge that the troops had silently broken down the door. After an instant, Iman realized that the intruders were soldiers. They were masked, five or six of them in the bedroom, aiming their rifles at the couple. More troops waited outside.

Iman got out of the bed, her hair exposed to the eyes of the men who had invaded her room – a very sensitive matter for them, which Munzer refers to with pain. One soldier approached the bed and without a word punched Munzer in the face. Munzer is convinced that the assailant wore brass knuckles. His face began to bleed, with a lot of blood streaming from his nose, as well as from the wounds on his hands, which ultimately failed to protect his face. He saw nothing, of course.

The West Bank town of Dawha, near Bethlehem. Alex Levac

Iman, standing next to the bed, went on shouting, but the soldiers blocked her from defending her husband. She tried to explain that he was blind and sick, but it was useless. Probably none of the soldiers understood Arabic. The soldier held Munzer's head with one hand and hit him relentlessly with the other, she says. The others just stood there. The beating went on for at least five minutes.

A light in the bathroom scattered a little light into the room. Outside it was still dark, and the soldiers didn't turn on the lights inside. Maybe that's why they didn't notice that the person being abused was helpless, blind and sick. Munzer asked the soldiers who they were. He got no reply. Iman told them she wanted to talk with the officer in charge. No one responded. Finally the blows ceased.

Iman sat Munzer up in the bed. He asked her where the children were. Then she helped him get up and led him toward a chair in the room. At first the soldiers wouldn't allow Munzer, his face streaked with blood, to sit down. They didn't ask him to identify himself and didn't say who they were looking for.

Before this his eldest son, Talal, had awoken and heard his parents shouting that there were burglars in the house. Then, from the doorway, he saw his father bleeding. His brothers also woke up. The soldiers refused to let them enter their parents' room and ordered them to raise their hands. One of the sons was overcome with dizziness and fell to the floor.

The soldiers were in the house for about 20 minutes. They didn't search for anything. None of them thought to offer the wounded Munzer medical attention. Munzer says the worst thing is that a blind person doesn't know when the next blow is coming.

Why did they hit him?

"You don't know why?" his sister Maysoun, a bitter smile on her lips, asks us. "I'm afraid to talk because you're Jews. They beat us all. The occupation beats us all. We are under occupation. This isn't the first time they beat someone for no reason, and it's not the last. What's new about it is that this time they beat a blind person."

One of the boys suggests a different explanation: Maybe they struck his father because he has a beard? True, not a full beard, but still a small beard that raises suspicion.

Maysoun is concerned that now her brother won't be allowed to travel to Jordan in June for his regular medical treatments. We tried to reassure her – after all, he didn't do anything.

Munzer Mizhar with his wife, Iman, and his sister, at home in the West Bank town of Dawha. Alex Levac

In any case, back on that Wednesday morning, the soldiers ordered the four boys to get on their knees, faces pressed to the floor, and not to move. Then they left the house.

Munzer was taken to Hussein Hospital in Beit Jala. Since the event, he has suffered from pains in his jaw and has difficulty eating solid food. To see him lying on the sofa totally helpless, trying to find a comfortable position, the remnants of his feet bandaged, occasionally closing his eyes, is to understand what the soldiers wrought.

The next day the family learned that the soldiers had been looking for Fadi Hilweh, 20, who's wanted by the army and the Shin Bet security service, though it's not clear why. He lives on the floor above. The soldiers went there first, and when they didn't find him, a Shin Bet agent known as "Capt. Nidal" ordered Hilweh's mother to contact him and have him come home.

In the meantime, the soldiers went downstairs to the Mizhars. The neighbours say that they too warned the soldiers that Munzer was blind and sick, but no one was interested. Munzer wants to know why they didn't knock on the door instead of invading the house. He would have opened the door and they could have seen for themselves that Hilweh wasn't there.

Hilweh eventually came home and was arrested. Did the soldiers think that Munzer was the wanted person, so they beat him? Even in the dark, no one could mistake a sick, blind man of 47 for a 20-year-old. "Maybe they thought [the wanted man] was Munzer, and maybe they're just violent criminals," Maysoun says. Musa Abu Hashhash, a field researcher for the B'Tselem human rights group, says quietly, "This is the most shocking case I've ever documented."

The IDF Spokesman's Office made the following statement to Haaretz: "During an operation to apprehend a wanted individual in Bethlehem, information was received that the wanted person was inside a particular building, and a search was undertaken there. During the search, a Palestinian woman tried to prevent one of the fighters from reaching a Palestinian man in the room that the fighter wanted to inspect. The fighter tried to check the Palestinian man, who reacted by grabbing at his body and his weapon, and shouted and acted disruptively. The fighter pushed the Palestinian aggressively, trying to get him under control, and as a result the man was injured. At this stage the fighter realized that the man was blind, and was not the wanted person, and tried to calm him down while allowing the man's wife to attend to him immediately. The incident was investigated and appropriate conclusions were drawn."

Iman has been in a state of depression and constant fear since that night. The boys ask whether the soldiers will come back. The family has added an extra lock to the front door. Munzer can only focus on his illness and his pain. He wakes up each every night imagining that he hears footsteps in the dark. He's certain that the soldiers are returning to give him another thrashing.

When we celebrate Israeli democracy, we celebrate the violence of occupation

In democratic countries, elections are conventionally described as 'a celebration.' But in an undemocratic reality of endless military occupation, they become an overt celebration of the violence of the powerful.

By Hagai El-Ad, from +972 25th Feb 2019

Palestinians cross the Bethlehem checkpoint, as they head to Al-Aqsa Mosque Compound in Jerusalem's Old City during Ramadan, May 18, 2018. Wisam Hashlamoun/Flash90)

"So long as I do not firmly and irrevocably possess the right to vote I do not possess myself. I cannot make up my mind — it is made up for me. I cannot live as a democratic citizen, observing the laws I have helped to enact — I can only submit to the edict of others."

Dr. Martin Luther King Jr. delivered these words in his 1957 "Give Us the Ballot" speech, part of his attempt to challenge the reality in America's Deep South, where Black people were citizens yet still denied the right to vote by various ruses. For Palestinians who have lived under Israel's rule since 1967, the mere right to vote is not even an option.

In a few months the public will go to the polls for another round of elections in which we, Israeli citizens, will vote and make decisions not only about our own fate, but also about the fate of millions of subjects who are perpetually denied political rights. The regulations and orders we dictate will continue to advance *our* interests while managing *their* lives. All they can do is submit to the edict of others.

In democratic countries, elections are conventionally described as "a celebration of democracy." But in an undemocratic reality, elections sadly become an overt celebration of violence.

Election campaigns in Israel thoughtlessly celebrate the privileges of those eligible to vote, while showing almost complete apathy to the exclusion of millions of subjects. Palestinians, of course, have no need to be reminded of their condition — they are well aware of the reality in which they live. But even so, a situation in which every few years Israelis spend months wondering exactly how they should continue to control the lives of others marks a nadir in the violence we have internalized.

Whether public discourse during the elections includes a debate on these issues, or whether politicians and the public do everything they can to avoid mentioning the occupation, the political choices Israelis make determine how to entrench the occupation regime. We determine how we will manage the enormous prison that is the Gaza Strip from the outside; how many homes we will demolish and how many communities we will displace in the West Bank; and how many Palestinian families will be deprived of their homes in East Jerusalem.

In the meantime, day by day and week by week, we are witnessing an election campaign in which the lords of the land constantly drive home their message: no one counts the subjects of military rule. As we continue to possess their lives, opinions, and feelings, we have no problem continuing to engage in our political debates over their heads. We do so openly, while taking pride in our "vibrant debate" and our "celebration of democracy." And we do so while casually and utterly negating the humanity of millions of people whose fate will also be determined for the next few years.

Immediately after the election campaign, and in the intervening years before the next one, we will rely on these "democratic elections" to both justify what we do to our subjects as well as to market this reality as an acceptable one. In this way, the election actually forms a vital component in legitimizing our ongoing control of the subjects' lives. After all, every Israeli decision, no matter how arbitrary, is seen as the product of these elections. This is an inherently violent situation, since it is impossible to justify the ongoing violence without being part of the violence itself.

The violence is manifested not only when a soldier shoots or beats a Palestinian. It is there every time a lawyer in the State Attorney's Office closes a file of a killing, or when a Supreme Court justice approves another home demolition, or when an Israeli official prevents another Palestinian student from traveling abroad to continue their studies. Their lives are in our hands, and we apply this violence through a slow, protracted, and arbitrary bureaucracy. Moreover, the presence of "democratic elections" is of great importance not only in terms of image and propaganda, but also as a crucial valve that hinders assertive action by the international community that would, at last, express its rejection of this reality.

For all these reasons, even a renowned paragon of democracy such as Knesset Deputy Speaker MK Bezalel Smotrich makes sure to join the celebration and sing the praises of democracy, while at the same time presenting his program for perpetuating the existing reality: "Even in the absence of the right to vote for a fully sovereign parliament, this is not an apartheid regime, at most it lacks a component in the basket of liberties, or rather — a deficit in democracy."

This is what millions of Israelis will do over the coming months. Another election campaign, another opportunity to determine who will "firmly and irrevocably possess the right to vote" — and who will be exposed to our violence.

Hagai El-Ad is the executive director of B'Tselem, the Israeli Information Center for Human Rights in the Occupied Territories. This article was first published in Hebrew on Local Call.

Israel's fascist sideshow takes center stage

For the first time in over 30 years, a proper Kahanist party could be entering the Knesset. But is the rise of a party that advocates for Jewish supremacy, theocracy, and 'total war' as unprecedented as the outcry has suggested?
By Natasha Roth\Published February 24, 2019 from +972

Members of the Kahanist Otzma Yehudit party Benzi Gopstein (left) Michael Ben Ari (center) and Attorney Itamar Ben Gvir (right) seen in Israeli Supreme Court in Jerusalem, March 12, 2018. (Hadas Parush/Flash90)

The last week has been an eventful one in the annals of Prime Minister Benjamin Netanyahu's dalliances with the racist ultra-right. Fresh from upsetting his authoritarian, antisemitic allies in Europe by failing to adequately maintain his recent efforts at Holocaust revisionism, Netanyahu has now paved the way for homegrown Israeli fascists to take their place — once again — in the Knesset.

The prime minister's overtures to the Jewish Power (Otzma Yehudit) party are not, in the context of his political character, surprising. His readiness to rely on white supremacists and ultranationalists abroad to prop him up provides ample evidence of the types of characters he'll make common cause with. It has also long been clear that there are very few depths Netanyahu will not plumb when his perch at the top of Israeli politics is under threat.

And that threat does, with the national elections in April looming, feel real. Faced with some of his current coalition partners failing to pass the electoral threshold, Netanyahu successfully lobbied the Jewish Home party to team up with Jewish Power, which brings the real prospect of an explicitly Kahanist party entering the Knesset for the first time in over 30 years.

Rabbi Meir Kahane, who founded the Jewish Defense League and for whom the Kahanists are named, was a fascist. He wanted to remake Israeli society by expelling Palestinians and making Jewish law the law of the land. He believed in Jewish supremacy, was fixated on ethnic purity, and declared antisemitism in the diaspora necessary in order to prevent assimilation. Violence and militarism were, for Kahane, instruments through which to ensure national rebirth.

The JDL manifestos Kahane wrote in the 1960s and '70s in New York contained seeds of this fascist ideology. The policy platform his party, Kach, ran on in the 1984 Israeli elections, and which got him elected, was explicitly fascist. It's important to state this unequivocally. Referring to 'Kahanism' without naming its ideological pedigree makes it impossible to have an honest discussion about this latest evolution in Israeli politics.

From fringe to mainstream

Kahane undoubtedly shifted the parameters of Israeli discourse during his turbulent parliamentary career. Among Kach's principles and policies were those calling for mass expulsions of Palestinians; the annexation of the West Bank, Gaza, the Golan Heights, and the Sinai; and a ban on marriage, and all sexual contact, between Jews and non-Jews — punishable by prison sentences ranging from five to 50 years. This last point was a particular obsession for Kahane: his political rallies in Israel regularly featured histrionic, concocted tales of scores of Jewish girls kidnapped and taken to Palestinian villages; and during a Kach election broadcast in the 1980s (delivered, curiously enough, in English), he warned of "the destruction of Israel not through bullets but through Arab babies."

Rabbi Meir Kahane. (Yossi Zamir/Flash90)

His party's security principles, meanwhile, continued the theme of righteous Jewish violence that informed his writings for the JDL — violence that he invested with both a biblical lineage (Bar Kokhba, Judah Maccabee) and a redemptive potential (an end to Jewish oppression). His Second Amendment-style JDL slogan, "Every Jew a .22," made aliyah in the form of a call to give the Israel Defense Forces a "free hand" when dealing with Arabs — in other words, a shoot-to-kill policy with no questions asked.

Among Kahane's other visions were an ethnically-segregated education system, which would be focused on teaching love for Israel and the Jewish people; a small government with minimal bureaucracy that would allow the flourishing of a "Jewish economy"; and the outlawing of the Israeli Communist party.

The list goes on. Above all, Kahane sought the dismantling of what passed for Israeli democracy, calling for a state based on Jewish religious law. Indeed, he believed that Judaism and "Western" democracy were fundamentally incompatible, although he was not against the temporary use of democratic institutions in order to further his other political goals.

As much as almost the entire spectrum of Israel's political establishment pronounced their shock at Kahane's rhetoric and actions, even going so far as to boycott his speeches in the Knesset, his popularity in Israel only rose after his election. Having failed to make the electoral threshold in 1973, 1977 and 1981, and after winning a single seat in the 1984 elections, Kach was projected to win four seats or more in the 1988 elections. The Israeli Election Commission barred Kach from running on the grounds that the party's platform incited racism, but by then Kahane's talk of mass expulsions was already being aired by mainstream parties in the Knesset.

Waging 'total war' against Israel's enemies

Kahane was assassinated in New York in 1990, and Israel outlawed Kach as a terror organization in 1994 (the U.S. followed a year later). But his movement lived on in Israel: the core members of Jewish Power — Baruch Marzel, Itamar Ben-Gvir, Michael Ben-Ari, and Benzi Gopstein — are all disciples of Kahane and former Kach activists. Between them, they have variously persecuted Palestinians, leftists, African asylum seekers, and the LGBTQ community.

Jewish Power's 2019 election manifesto bears a resounding resemblance to Kach's platform. The party proposes implementing Jewish law as the law of the land, and having an education system that teaches love of Israel and the Jewish people. It promises "total war" against "Israel's enemies," and seeks the annexation of the West Bank and Gaza. It calls to expel "Israel's enemies" (which should be read as Palestinians) "back to their countries of origin." At the same time, the party wants to encourage diaspora Jews to emigrate to Israel, in order to try and prevent assimilation.

Jewish Power party Michael Ben Ari speaks during a ceremony honoring Jewish extremist leader Rabbi Meir Kahane in Jerusalem, October 26 2010. (Yossi Zamir/Flash 90)

As far as security policy, the party wants "deterrence" to be restored to the Israeli army, and for the military to move from "a policy of 'containing the enemy' to one of elimination and annihilation." They want to encourage procreation and fight abortion. They envision a "Jewish democracy" that "rejects universal values." And they name their economic policy

"Jewish capitalism" — part of which proposes that once "Israel's enemies" have been expelled from the country, the security budget will be reduced by billions of shekels that can be partially reinvested in industry, small businesses and the periphery.

Total war, expulsions, annihilation, mandatory Orthodox religious law, pro-natalism, ethnic supremacism — those were Kahane's calling cards, and they are Jewish Power's, too. Thirty years ago, those policy proposals saw Kach outlawed. Today, they have led to an invitation from the prime minister, delivered via Jewish Home, to join his coalition. So what happened?

It didn't start with Kahane

It would be easy — and for many, a cold comfort — to point to men like Kahane, Netanyahu, and the Jewish Power crowd as aberrations in Israel's politics. Yet to take this stance is to suggest that Kahane's ideas, and Netanyahu's policies, are without precedent in Israel's history. And when we take an honest look at the last 70 years, can we really say they are?

Expulsion was on the lips of Israel's first prime minister, and was instrumental to the founding of the state. Intermarriage has never been possible in Israel, albeit without the threat of incarceration (a Conservative rabbi was briefly detained last year for officiating non-Orthodox weddings). Campaigns for a Greater Israel, backed by public figures from across the political spectrum, have been around since the occupation commenced, and even before. Legal status aside, Israel has been in the process of de facto annexing the West Bank for years, through a combination of demolitions, evictions, land expropriations, settlement-building, and "transfer" plans. Every discussion of the "demographic threat" that accompanies supposedly progressive two-state proposals invokes the spectre of ethnic segregation.

For the past 20 years Israeli society has been shifting inexorably to the right, with the process accelerating since Netanyahu was elected in 2009. But neither Kahane nor Netanyahu is solely responsible for brutalizing Israeli society. The roots of what we are witnessing go back much further, and to something much more fundamental about the state. The fact is that Israel has not, for a single day since its founding, been a state for all its citizens. And in this lies the raw material for the havoc that we see today.

Far-rights activists attend a ceremony honoring Meir Kahane in Jerusalem on November 17, 2016. (Yonatan Sindel/Flash90)

Indeed, the real impact of this latest political development is that it has once again blown apart the "bad apples" defense that is applied to everything from settler violence to the occupation itself. Indeed, progressive defenders of the "Jewish and democratic" balance tend to exceptionalize acts of state and social oppression against Palestinians, arguing they are signs of a political system wheezing under the strain of a 50-year military occupation and malfunctioning dangerously, perhaps beyond repair. But such protestations have long rung hollow, in much the same way that the cries of "this is not us!" did following Trump's election in the U.S. — as if white supremacy had never darkened the country's door. And as if racist state and interpersonal violence was a novelty in Israel's history.

These arguments long predate the current political moment and will, it seems, long outlive it. In the immediate term, however, Netanyahu's decision to extend the hand of power to unabashed purveyors of Israeli fascism offers us both a particular and a universal lesson: firstly, that in trying to square the circle of a "Jewish and democratic state," the latter always has, and always will, play second fiddle to the former; and secondly, that a purported democratic system which offers the trappings of true democracy to the hegemonic group alone can, even when it is functioning as intended, bring fascism into power. Israel is by no means alone in that regard.

It is, then, somewhat ironic that Rafi Peretz, the new head of the Jewish Home party, on Wednesday defended the Jewish Power merger by stating: "When the house is burning…I don't look too closely at whoever will help me put out the fire." He is right about the state of emergency — but wrong about who's holding the matches.

Information on Meir Kahane's policies and proposals, for both the Jewish Defense League and Kach, are taken from the following books: "The False Prophet: Rabbi Meir Kahane," by Robert I. Friedman (1990); "Heil Kahane," by Yair Kotler (1986); "The Story of the Jewish Defense League," by Meir Kahane (1975); and "Never Again! A Program for Survival," by Meir Kahane (1972).

Palestinians have won a moral victory, but what will happen next?

Dr Mohammad Makram Balawi March 3, 2019 from MEMO

Foreign Affairs in Berlin, Germany on 23 July, 2018 [Abdülhamid Hoşbaş/Anadolu Agency]

British Foreign Secretary Jeremy Hunt has revealed in an article published by *the Jewish Chronicle* that the UK government will vote against all Agenda Item 7 resolutions at the United Nations Human Rights Council, in response to complaints by Israel and pro-Israel advocacy groups.

Agenda Item 7, a long-standing source of frustration for the Israeli government, is focused on the rights of Palestinians under occupation, and the violation of these rights by Israel.

Writing in the paper, Hunt claimed that by singling out Palestinians for protection, Item 7 resolutions "undermine the credibility of the world's leading human rights forum".

Britain will, the foreign secretary said, vote against all such resolutions in Geneva tomorrow.

"Two years ago, the United Kingdom said that unless the situation changed, we would vote against all texts proposed under Item 7," Hunt wrote.

"Sadly, our concerns have not been heeded. So I have decided that we will do exactly what we said: Britain will now oppose every Item 7 resolution. On Friday we will vote against all four texts proposed in this way."

Hunt claimed that the decision to reject these resolutions did not mean that the government would "hold back from voicing concerns about Israel's actions", citing illegal settlements, home demolitions, and the use of lethal violence against Palestinian protesters.

He added: "We will continue to press for the abolition of Item 7, which only undermines the credibility of the world's leading human rights forum."

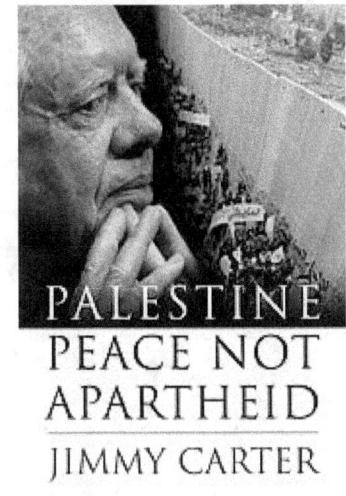

What would a non-colonial State of Israel look like?

As the Israeli elections on 9 April approach, MEMO interviews Arab MKs, current and former, as to their experiences of working within the Israeli political system, and their hopes for the future.

By Nasim Ahmed, March 3, 2019 in Middle East Monitor

Israeli Arab Knesset member, Haneen Zoabi [Middle East Monitor]

The tension between democracy and ethnocracy goes to the heart of the Israeli narrative. The founders of the state believed that they were laying the foundations of a democratic state, one that would devote itself to the benefit of "all its people". Its Declaration of Independence was clear that it was a state founded on "principles of freedom, justice and peace, guided by the visions of the prophets of Israel; it will grant full equal, social and political rights to all its citizens regardless of differences of religious faith, race or sex; it will ensure freedom of religion, conscience, language, education and culture."

Lofty ideals, indeed, although the official narrative served not only to conceal the racism inherent within Zionism but also the irreconcilable challenges arising from imposing an ethnocracy in a land already populated by people from a different ethnic group. Those who understood what Zionism entailed, such as the late writer Christopher Hitchens, opposed it in principal: "I am an anti-Zionist. I'm one of those people of Jewish descent who believes that Zionism would be a mistake even if there were no Palestinians." Hitchens, who many consider to have been one of the most powerful proponents of western liberal values and an equally powerful opponent of dogma, went on to say that he could never accept the premise of a Jewish homeland, because it was a "stupid, messianic, superstitious idea."

The tension between that idea and the ideals of Israel's founding fathers has been a recurring theme for proponents of the state and its opponents alike. Typically, supporters of Israel display the signs of being possessed by dogma. Britain's Home Secretary, Sajid Javed, for example, echoed Israel's founding narrative when he proclaimed, "If I had to go and live in the Middle East there is only one place I could possibly go. Israel!" Explaining why he would not go to any of the Muslim majority countries he added that Israel is "the only nation in the Middle East that shares the same democratic values as Britain and the only nation in the Middle East where my family would feel the warm embrace of freedom and liberty."

Javed is emblematic of those who are pro-Israel and spring to its defence armed with nothing more than clichés to face the reality of eleven million Palestinians who have never felt any "warm embrace of liberty and freedom" from Israel. They attest to the irreconcilable tension between democracy and ethnocracy woven into the Zionist paradox that has unfolded so calamitously that even former Prime Ministers of the Zionist state have voiced their concern over its drift towards becoming an apartheid state.
Few have encountered this tension in Israel more than Haneen Zoabi. The member of the Israeli parliament, the Knesset, is stepping down at the General Election next month. Nevertheless, she told me that she hopes one day to resolve the situation and transform Israel from a colonial regime to full democracy; one that does not discriminate on the basis of who is and is not a Jew. The politician from the Israeli-Arab Balad Party has been in the Knesset since 2009 and at the epicentre of the tension at the heart of Israel, the supporters of which never cease to remind us that the "only democracy in the Middle East" has Zoabi and a dozen or so other Arab members in the Knesset to prove their point.

How does she reconcile between being a member of the Knesset with her claim that Israel is not a genuine democracy? "When the US allowed African Americans to enter the bus but insisted that they sit only at the back of the bus, was that equality?" she thundered back. "You are in the Knesset but not in the seat where you can make any change, to make any real difference."

In this rhetorical bus, she added, there are 85 racist laws that prevent you from making real difference. "We always sit in the lower position. You enter the bus but you have to sit at the back. The bus you enter grants special privileges to Jews. You can shout but you don't have anything like the first amendment of the US Constitution to protect you. There is racism, there are racist articles, but there is no constitution to protect your rights."

Israeli Prime Minister Benjamin Netanyahu [ODED BALILTY/AFP/Getty Images]

The racist laws she mentioned have been the focus of campaigns by legal advocacy groups such as Adalah, the Legal Centre for Arab Minority Rights in Israel. The Haifa-based human rights group has documented every discriminatory law within the country. More than half are said to have been adopted since the 2009 election which brought to power the most right-wing government coalition in the history of the state, led by Prime Minister Benjamin

Netanyahu. The latest discriminatory law is the Jewish Nation-State Law which has been denounced for its codification of apartheid in Israel.

For Zoabi, Israeli-style apartheid has been concealed by a powerful narrative that presents the state as a liberal democracy to the rest of the world with a discourse of colonial justification. "There is a strong sense of justification that allows Israel to discriminate against its own Palestinian citizens," she explained. "There is an ethical discourse to make you feel that you must appreciate the country even if you are only given 10 per cent of your rights."

Using the classic coloniser versus the colonised dynamic, the Nazareth-born politician added that Israel also has an ethical discourse to say why it can deny Palestinians' their national rights. "There is an ethical reason why they should deny your history and identity as Palestinians, even if they give 20 per cent of our civil rights and none of our national rights. And there is a discourse to say why we should accept our inferiority and position as an oppressed people." The tragic impact of this powerful narrative, Zoabi explained, is why Israelis don't take Palestinian suffering and the discrimination faced as real suffering and real discrimination.

"The function of the state of Israel is not to be neutral to all of its citizens but to give a stronger position to the Jews at the expense of the indigenous people," she insisted. "Israel cannot guarantee individual rights to all of its citizens, because the state describes itself as a Jewish state."

Despite stepping down as an MK at April's General Election, Zoabi said that she is determined to stay involved in politics; it is, she told me, time to help to develop the Balad Party's political programme and vision. "That vision is to campaign for a state for all its citizens and to challenge the idea of a Jewish and democratic state. There is no democratic way of being a Jewish state." Her goal, she stressed, is to turn Israel into a non-colonial state. "Zionism is a colonial ideology and the only way to have democracy is to disconnect the state from Zionism."

What would a non-colonial, non-Zionist Israel look like? "We envisage a democracy. We don't say you came as colonists now you must leave; we say you came as colonists but now you have a chance to live with us."

Israel, insisted Zoabi, must not continue trying to displace and replace the Palestinians — the indigenous people — but to co-exist with them. "The only way to co-exist with us is to remove colonial objectives from the agenda and develop a state for all of Israeli citizens. It will not be at the expense of our identity and our connection with Palestinians everywhere.

Balad, meanwhile, has a democratic vision to accept all Israelis as normal human beings in a normal state. Its message to Israeli-Jews, said Haneen Zoabi, is simple: "We to would like to recognise you as a collective but within a state which doesn't identity exclusively with you, but which identifies with me and you in the same degree." Such a state will be a different state with different symbolism, and it will be a democracy. "By this, I don't just defend my rights, I also defend the Jews' right as a people because they also have the right to live in a normal state. Maybe they didn't choose to live in a racist, apartheid state but nobody has given them an alternative. Balad is offering a real alternative."

The campaign to equate anti-Zionism with anti-Semitism

By Yossi Beilin March 4, 2019 from Israeli Pulse on All- Monitor

An Israeli holds a flag in Jerusalem during a protest in support of Israel's offensive in the Gaza Strip, July 14, 2014. REUTERS/Ronen Zvulun

The Israeli government's campaign equating anti-Zionism with anti-Semitism has achieved considerable success. In May 2016, the International Alliance for Holocaust Remembrance (IHRA) decided to add "targeting of the state of Israel, conceived as a Jewish collectivity" to its definition of anti-Semitism.

French President Emmanuel Macron made similar comments in 2017 and again on Feb. 21 of this year during a meeting with the leadership of CRIF (Conseil Représentatif des Institutions Juives de France), the umbrella organization of the French Jewish community, as reported in Al-Monitor by Rina Bassist. Macron reiterated the identification of anti-Zionism with modern-day anti-Semitism and pledged that his government would define anti-Zionism as a form of anti-Semitism. Meanwhile, Jeremy Corbin, leader of the Labor Party in the United Kingdom, came in for sharp criticism when his party initially refused to adopt the IHRA's definition, criticism that eventually led to a change in Labor's position and adoption of the definition in September 2018.

Israel wants anyone seeking its friendship to identify anti-Zionism with anti-Semitism. I am not sure, however, that this is the right battle for Israel to wage, and I have a hard time understanding how this formula benefits the country. The Zionist idea envisioned all the Jews of the world gathering in Israel, but not everyone who rejects this idea is an anti-Semite.

In historical terms, the determination equating anti-Zionism and anti-Semitism is wrong. Anti-Semitism was the driving force for the creation of the Zionist movement in the second half of the 19th century by European Jews who felt they were being stifled, driven out of various professions or relegated to quotas in other fields, put on trial for crimes they did not commit and subjected to vitriol by the political right and left. The anti-Semites of the 19th century were not (necessarily) enemies of Zionism, and to some extent, they even found a common denominator with the new movement: They wanted Europe cleansed of Jews, while Zionism urged Jews to leave Europe. Thus, the haters and the hated cooperated on occasion.

The most prominent example of this kind of cooperation in modern times is the strange alliance between Israel's political right and Christian evangelists around the world who seek to ensure that at the end of time, all the Jews will convert to Christianity or be annihilated. For the evangelists, the Jews serve as harbingers of the Messiah's coming on a donkey. According to evangelical doctrine, to ensure the Second Coming of Christ, all the Jews must live in an undivided Land of Israel. For now, they are supporters of Israel and are viewed as bigger "Israel lovers" than many Diaspora Jews, keeping their vision of the end of time in the vault.

Manifestations of open anti-Semitism declined after the Holocaust and the creation of the State of Israel in 1948, as did blatant opposition to the establishment of a Jewish state, with one exception. The Islamic states, especially the Arab ones, took up the banner of hostility toward Israel and turned the notorious anti-Semitic "Protocols of the Elders of Zion" into a sort of second Quran. Their hatred of Israel was accompanied by hatred of Jews, but one cannot say that the Arabs' anti-Israel sentiment was a new cover for anti-Semitism. On the contrary, opposition to the Jewish state gave birth to manifestations of anti-Semitism in the Arab Semitic world.

There is ongoing tension between the struggle against anti-Semitism and the yearning for an ingathering of Jews under one roof as clearly manifested in comments by Prime Minister Benjamin Netanyahu in Paris after the January 2015 terror attack on a Jewish supermarket. Netanyahu, in almost spontaneous fashion, trotted out the classic Zionist response and urged French Jews to immigrate to Israel in light of the attacks against them. The French government saw this as a slap in the face. Prime Minister Manuel Valls responded that without its Jews, France would not be France. Valls saw anti-Semitism as a racist phenomenon that should be erased from French soil and believed that its mitigation lay in educating the French, not in mass Jewish migration to Israel.

Millions of Israelis hold views locating them on the spectrum between non-Zionists and anti-Zionists. Most Palestinians living in Israel, or almost all of them, regard Zionism as a movement that drove their relatives from their homes and demanded Jews' priority over them. Most if not all accept the existence of the state and fulfill their civic duties, and the majority are even proud of their country and admit its advantages over neighboring states. They also, however, regard the very idea of Zionism as the cause of their deprivation and have a hard time understanding how Jews dare declare, "The Bible is our mandate to the Land," as David Ben-Gurion famously told the Peel Commission in January 1937, and why we had to choose Palestine of all places when fleeing European anti-Semitism.

Many ultra-Orthodox Jews also oppose Zionism. They view it as a challenge to the religious concept that calls for waiting for the Messiah rather than taking the liberty of jumping the gun and establishing a Jewish state. Some among them live in Israel and boycott everything to do with the state — from the time zone on their clocks to government-issued identification cards to tax payments. Some simply express their displeasure by refusing to stand at attention during the annual sounding of sirens throughout Israel to commemorate the victims of the Holocaust and the fallen of Israel's wars. Others refuse to serve as government ministers, even though their political parties are members of the ruling coalition, so as not to bear responsibility for the sins of the secular state.

There are radical anti-Zionists among this group as well as others who repress their anti-Zionism and when asked whether they are anti-Zionists always respond, "We pray 'Next year in Jerusalem," invoking the other name of Zion. They are convinced that this response is the most crushing answer to the troublesome question.

Then there is a minority of secular Israeli Jews who are not Zionists and proud of it. They range from the "Canaanites," who in 1939 called for the integration of Jews into the region and handed out flyers opposing Zionism, to the Hebrew communists and others. All these groups are far from being anti-Semites, each opposing Zionism for reasons of its own.

One cannot ignore the link between anti-Semitism and anti-Zionism. Sometimes, anti-Zionism is, indeed, a guise for anti-Semitism, but we are not doing anyone any favors by insisting on equating the two terms. They are partially congruent, but not identical. It would be a mistake to enshrine this in law and a mistake to consider it some sort of Israeli achievement.

Yossi Beilin has served in various positions in the Knesset and in Israeli government posts, the last of which was justice and religious affairs minister. After resigning from the Labor Party, Beilin headed Meretz. He was involved in initiating the Oslo process, the Beilin-Abu Mazen agreement, the Geneva Initiative and Birthright.

A comment from a reader of this article writes|:

The efforts of the racist, apartheid state of Israel and its supporters to deflect criticism of the brutalisation of Palestinians by conflating anti-Zionism with anti -Semitism is totally perverted and immoral.

These phrases are two distinct entites : Anti-Semitism refers to ideas and behaviour which discriminates between Jews and others just because they are Jews eg. Jews are obsessed with money, Jews rule the world they dominate and run the banks etc...

In sharp contrast anti-Zionism is a political ideology which opposes Zionism.

Zionists argued that the only way to avoid persecution was to establish their own state. They achieved this in Palestine at the expense of the Palestinian people. They expelled approximately three quarters of a million indigenous Palestinians and obliterated over 400 Palestinian villages and committed numerous atrocites and crimes against humanity.

Since then the murder of Palestinians ,the continued expansion of illegal Jewish settlements, the more than 50 laws that blatently discriminate against the indigenous population, all of which are carried out in the name of Zionism led to anti Zionism.
The anti-Zionists then demand that equal rights should exist between Jews, Christinians and Muslims, a concept of equality which Jews and Israelis refuse to implement.

Israelis and Jews that support the racist state of Israel today conflate these issues in their attempt to deny their racist and evil intent against the Palestinain people hoping to avoid criticism.

Israeli army, settlers 'routinely harass' Nablus students

West Bank school's staff documented 65 Israeli violations during first semester, at least three more since January 24.
By Jaclynn Ashly, 5th March 2019, from Al Jazeera

School principal Mohammad Jaser presses a button to open the intercom system and makes a routine announcement.

"The Israeli army has been spotted near the premises," Jaser says, his voice blaring from speakers and into the classrooms of the al-Sawiyeh al-Lebban school near Nablus in the northern West Bank last month.

"Stay inside your classrooms, away from the windows, and lock the doors," he instructs the students. "Prepare for an evacuation."

The students and teachers at the mixed school, located between the villages of al-Sawiyeh and al-Lebban, have been trained to respond to incidents like this.

The school is often the target of Israeli army activity in the area and has faced numerous incidents of armed settlers entering the premises and threatening students.

The al-Sawiyeh al-Lebban school serves about 500 students, including 20 girls, from sixth to 12th grade [Jaclynn Ashly/Al Jazeera]

Due to the high frequency of violence at the school, emergency drills and training have been implemented to teach students how to respond to the incursions.

"Now, when we spot Israeli soldiers or settlers around the school, students know exactly what to do," Jaser said.

Students, for instance, receive training on how to lessen the effects of tear gas and some are trained to provide first aid to their injured peers during confrontations, he says.'They like to point their weapons at the students'

The al-Sawiyeh al-Lebban school serves about 500 students, including 20 girls, from the sixth grade until the 12th.

The school is located in Area C - which comprises about 60 percent of the West Bank under full Israeli military control - situated alongside Road 60, a shared Israeli-Palestinian road that cuts through the West Bank.

Israel's illegal Eli settlement, located on nearby hilltops, almost completely surrounds the school.

Jaser, who has been principal of the school for three years, sifts through dozens of videos and pictures of security incidents on his computer.

"This is when they came to arrest one of the students," Jaser said, as he played a video showing Israeli soldiers handcuffing a student outside the school and leading him to an Israeli army jeep.

Emergency drills and training have been implemented to teach students how to respond to Israeli incursions [Jaclynn Ashly/Al Jazeera]

During the last semester, which commenced at the end of August, the school's staff documented 65 Israeli violations at the school, and there have already been at least three documented violations since the current semester began on January 24, according to Jaser.

Abed, a teacher at the school who preferred that Al Jazeera not use his last name, says the first semester of this school year was the worst he experienced since the start of his tenure at al-Sawiyeh al-Lebban 12 years ago.

While most of the violations at the school were committed by the Israeli army, he says several times during the first semester armed Israeli settlers had also entered the school grounds, escorted by soldiers, and harassed and threatened students.

"The settlers and soldiers like to point their weapons at the students in order to frighten them," Abed told Al Jazeera.

He recounts numerous instances of Israeli aggression on the school, including troops firing tear gas at the school playground where children play football, patrolling the area and preventing students and teachers from entering school grounds, and detaining teachers and students for interrogation.

The Israeli army ordered the closure of the school but staff, students, parents, and Palestinian officials resisted [Jaclynn Ashly/Al Jazeera]

In October, the Israeli army ordered the closure of the school entirely, stating that students were throwing stones from the premises.

But the staff, students, parents, and Palestinian officials resisted and decided to open the school in defiance of the order.

Israeli forces responded by firing tear gas and rubber-coated steel bullets at the crowd gathered outside the school, injuring Palestinian Education Minister Sabri Saidam, Nablus Governor Akram Rajoub, and dozens of students and teachers.

Although the school administration succeeded in keeping the school doors open, the staff continues to feel on edge, anticipating another army closure at any moment.

As a result of these routine disruptions, "there are serious weaknesses in the teaching process", Abed told Al Jazeera. The school is often forced to evacuate the students owing to Israeli army and settler activities in the area, causing students to miss out on their classes.

"It's rare that the students are actually able to stay at the school until the last period," Abed said.

"They are being evacuated and sent home almost every day, so it affects their ability to learn."

On top of this, many parents are now afraid to send their children to the school, Abed explains, opting instead to transfer them to public schools in the nearby Salfit district or register them in private schools.

About 40 students have dropped out since the start of the school year, according to Abdulrahim Suleiman, the school's vice principal.

'Constant state of panic'

In November, Mohammad, a student at al-Sawiyeh al-Lebban who asked to use a pseudonym to protect his identity, was temporarily detained by Israeli forces on his walk back home from school.

The 17-year-old was stopped and interrogated by the soldiers for about two hours.

"They asked me about my family and had me name all of my siblings," Mohammad explained to Al Jazeera, nervously fidgeting with his hands.

"They asked me who was throwing stones at the school and what I want to be when I grow up while making jokes with each other."

The soldiers then tied plastic cuffs around the teen's wrists, blindfolded him and ordered him to lie on his back on the floor of an army jeep.

They proceeded to drive him to Israel's Huwwara checkpoint in Nablus where they handed him over to Palestinian police.

During the hours he was detained, "I was scared they would keep me and I would miss my exams and not be able to graduate", he said.

Rights groups have noted that children facing occupation-related violence often experience "nightmares, bedwetting, higher levels of absenteeism from school, higher dropout and/or transfer rates, and lower levels of educational attainment".

Furthermore, students attending schools targeted by the Israeli army and settlers have reported being in a "constant state of panic", feeling "always tired", experiencing "great difficulty" focusing on lessons, less motivation to attend school, and an increase in violent behaviour.

Zikra Daraghma, a 17-year-old student at al-Sawiyeh al-Lebban, tells Al Jazeera that she is often harassed by soldiers on her way to school. "They [soldiers] stand in our way while we are going to school and don't let us pass or make it difficult for us to get to school on time," she said.

"They always threaten and insult us. I don't even want to repeat the bad things they say to us."

Israeli violations at Palestinian schools in the West Bank have seen a marked increase over the past several months.

The United Nations has documented 111 Israeli interferences to education in the West Bank from January to December 2018, affecting 19,196 Palestinian children.

More than half of these incidents involved "live ammunition, tear gas, and stun grenades fired into or near schools by Israeli forces, impacting the delivery of education or injuring students", according to a UNICEF statement.

'We are never safe'

Al-Sawiyeh al-Lebban, along with several other schools vulnerable to Israeli-related violence in the West Bank, began implementing emergency protocol training to prepare students and staff to adequately respond to Israeli army or settler confrontations.

As part of an initiative called Schools as Zones of Peace (SZoP), led by the international NGO Save the Children, "crisis cells" - or school disaster-management committees - have been formed at vulnerable schools in the West Bank.

The cells consist of students, teachers, and the principal and are responsible for acting in an emergency, and providing leadership and training in school disaster management.

The cells lead frequent school-wide emergency drills and training to help prepare students for potential incidents.

This includes training students and teachers on how to organise an evacuation of the school, how to adequately respond to weapons commonly fired by Israeli forces, such as tear gas, and how to provide first aid.

"The most important thing is keeping the children calm," Suleiman tells Al Jazeera, noting that the organised and practised emergency response makes students and teachers feel more in control of their situation.

In addition, the Palestinian Authority (PA) received permission from Israel to station several Palestinian security guards at al-Sawiyeh al-Lebban to provide more protection for students.

The unarmed Palestinian guards are stationed around the entrances of the school and attempt to prevent the Israeli army or settlers from approaching the area. The guards also escort vulnerable children to and from school.

The school's staff told Al Jazeera that the presence of the PA security guards has significantly curbed Israeli activities in and around the school since their arrival at the start of the year.

For Daraghma, however, the presence of the Israeli army and settlers has continued to affect her and her peers.

"It affects us more psychologically," she said, "because when we see violence all around us, we can't focus on learning."

"Instead of paying attention to the lesson, we are constantly thinking about what's going to happen to us when we leave school. Will I be hurt, detained, or maybe even killed?"

"We are never safe," she added.

127 Israel aggressions on Al-Aqsa, Ibrahimi mosques in February

March 5, 2019 in Middle East Monitor

Racist graffiti sprayed next to Al-Rahma Gate by a Jewish settler in Jerusalem on 26 February 2019 [Faiz Abu Rmeleh/Anadolu Agency]

Palestinian Endowment Minister Yousef Edees said yesterday that the Israeli occupation raided Al-Aqsa Mosque more than 30 times during February.

The minister said that the Israeli occupation also prevented the call to prayer from being raised from the Ibrahimi Mosque 44 times during the same month, noting that the total number of Israeli attacks on the two holy sites reached 127 during February.

Edees noted that the Israeli occupation continues to besiege Al-Aqsa Mosque in order to partition it.

He also said that the Israeli occupation authorities deported scores of Palestinians who work at Al-Aqsa Mosque, including officials such as the Head of Jerusalem Endowment Council Sheikh Abdul-Azim Salhab and his deputy Sheikh Najeh Bkeerat.

According to the report, three Israeli gliders flew above Al-Aqsa Mosque and the military and political Israeli officials increased their raids under heavy protection from the Israeli military police. During the same month, anti-Arab and Muslim graffiti was sprayed onto the outer walls of Bab Al-Rahma in occupied Jerusalem's Old City after the area was reopened by Muslims days earlier.

FREE PALESTINE

The global solidarity movement for Palestine has reached a tipping point

by Nada Elia 1 March 2019 in Middle East Eye

An Israeli soldier aims towards Palestinian protesters in the occupied West Bank on 29 June (AFP)

"I saw the most adorable shoes yesterday, but didn't buy them," an acquaintance told me recently, explaining that since they were an Israeli brand she had refrained because of the boycott she had heard me advocate on several occasions.

"We're having a small get-together - just wine, cider, chips and dips. I promise there will be no Sabra," another friend told me, referring to the popular brand of hummus owned by a company, which has provided food and personal care packages to Israel's Golani Brigade, notorious for its human rights abuses.

These simple statements and acts of boycott, coming from individuals who until recently were "Zionist by default", reveal the distance average Americans are putting between themselves and the country they once uncritically believed was "the only democracy in the Middle East" - an oasis of civilisation in an otherwise benighted region.

Human rights abuses

Today, Israel's veneer - its once-impervious nonstick coating - is cracked beyond repair. Most people are seeing the ugliness behind the mask, the spewing lava of human rights abuses that can no longer be crusted over.

As Israeli-born actor Natalie Portman - long described as a Zionist, albeit of the liberal persuasion - recently said, Israel's new nation-state law is "racist". Portman also declined to travel to Israel last year for the Genesis Prize honouring her, leading to the cancellation of that ceremony.

Indeed, there is a growing awareness of Israel's reality in the US, the country that has long been its biggest champion, shielding it diplomatically and financing its war crimes. But this is also a global phenomenon: 2018 saw many forms of solidarity with the Palestinian struggle around the globe, from New Zealand, to India, to Nigeria, to Argentina - in sports, music, the arts, faith communities and governmental politics.

To cite but a few significant examples, an international campaign by a coalition of organisations affiliated with the boycott, divestment and sanctions (BDS) movement recently convinced Airbnb to stop listing properties in illegal Israeli settlements in the West Bank. The global community also mobilised earlier last year to convince Argentina's national football team to cancel its "friendly" match with the Israeli team in Jerusalem.

As the BDS movement explained in its Argentina campaign, "there is nothing friendly about Israel shooting Palestinian footballers". Heeding the appeal of more than 130 Palestinian clubs, Adidas also stopped sponsoring the Israel Football Association, which includes teams based in illegal settlements built on stolen Palestinian land.

Peaceful protests

Meanwhile, the Quakers became the first UK Christian church to completely divest from all companies that benefit from Israel's occupation of Palestinian land. And 39 international Jewish organisations expressed their understanding that the Palestinian people have grievances that are not rooted in anti-semitism, writing in a joint letter: "We all affirm the current call for BDS as a set of tools and tactics that should not be defined as antisemitic."

A man attends a BDS protest rally in southern France on 28 June (AFP)

In cultural news, tens of thousands of fans and activists convinced singer Lana Del Rey and other artists to withdraw from Israel's Meteor festival in a kibbutz in northern Israel, which would have been inaccessible to most Palestinians. Del Rey tweeted that she would postpone performing in Israel until she could sing for both Palestinians and Israelis.

In addition, a variety of DJs have pledged to boycott Israel, with the New-York-based collective Discwoman and others stating: "As long as the Israeli government continues its brutal and sustained oppression of the Palestinian people we respect their call for a boycott of Israel as a means of peaceful protest against the occupation."

Concern for Palestinian rights and dignity was also behind the Indian women's movement, representing more than 10 million women, endorsing BDS and demanding the release of all Palestinian child prisoners.

At the same time, Amnesty International has called for an arms embargo on Israel, while the Movement for Black Lives released an inspiring statement of solidarity with Palestinians and urged the US to end billions in annual military aid to Israel.

Academic solidarity

Even as campuses in the Global North remain hostile towards activism for justice in Palestine, students and faculty are determined to exercise their freedom of speech, and to enact solidarity in meaningful ways. The Canadian Federation of Students, representing more than 500,000 students, voted to back the BDS movement at their annual general meeting in Ottawa.

New York University is the latest US university to vote for divestment from companies that benefit from Israel's violations of Palestinian human rights, and faculty at Pitzer College in California voted to suspend its study abroad in Israel programme.

Faculty are also declining to write letters of recommendation for students seeking to study at Israeli colleges, and speaking out against Israeli abuses and for Palestinian rights, from the river to the sea.

No list can be exhaustive, but it is noteworthy that in 2018, BDS blossomed way beyond a boycott of consumer products, into direct criticism of Israel's policies and effective actions to hold the country accountable. Coalitions have emerged through an understanding of the shared struggles around immigrant rights, refugee rights, indigenous sovereignty, law enforcement violence, gender violence and more.

As the Movement for Black Lives statement explains: "We know that police officers in the United States learn the tactics of war from Israeli police forces, who come annually to train US officers in methods of oppression, surveillance and murder." Incidentally, officials in Massachusetts and Vermont both pulled out late last year from a planned training junket in Israel.

Fighting back

Social change doesn't happen because of a political proclamation. There is no trickle-down activism; it can only rise up, from the grassroots to the halls of Congress and parliament. When it reaches the point of becoming law, this is because of grassroots organising, mobilising, and persistent appeals and demands.

Even the US Congress, one of the largest bastions of Zionism outside of Israel, is changing. Two new members of Congress, Michigan's Rashida Tlaib and Minnesota's Ilhan Omar, have endorsed BDS. Tlaib said she would turn down the trip to Israel that AIPAC offers all first-year members of Congress, and lead her own delegation to Palestine instead.

Indeed, support for Israel is increasingly being viewed as a liability for progressive politicians. Minnesota's Betty McCollum has actually called out Israel's practices for what they are: apartheid.

Clearly, what we are witnessing is more than a discursive change. The disenchantment with Israel, and the growing rejection of its apartheid policies, has blown wind into the sails of BDS, with activists organising globally - and winning.

Despite attempts to criminalise boycotts, the coalitions are getting stronger, and the movement is fighting back. It's been a long struggle, and it is not over, but Palestinians have taught the world about resistance to injustice, no matter the might of the oppressor.

We have taught the world about *sumoud*, persistence. We have not given up, and we shall overcome.

Palestinians have taught the world about resistance to injustice, no matter the might of the oppressor

Keep It Up, Ilhan Omar
Neither Hamas nor a black day, but a glimmer of hope on Capitol Hill
By Gideon Levy in Haaretz March 7th 2019

Democratic Rep. Ilhan Omar in Washington, D.C., March 6, 2019.AF

Maybe Mogadishu will turn out to be the source of hope. This war-torn city was the birthplace of the most promising U.S. congresswoman today.

Ilhan Omar is not only one of the first two female Muslim members of the House of Representatives, she may herald a dramatic change in that body. "Hamas has entered the House," Roseanne Barr was quick to cry out; "A black day for Israel," tweeted Donald Trump. Neither Hamas nor a black day, but a glimmer of hope on Capitol Hill.

Maybe, for the first time in history, someone will dare tell the truth to the American people, absorbing scathing accusations of anti-Semitism, without bowing her head. The chances of this happening aren't great; the savage engine of the Jewish lobby and of Israel's "friends" is already doing everything it can to trample her.

The president mentioned removing her from the Senate Foreign Relations Committee, and Congress was set to pass a resolution, the second in one month, against uttering "anti-Semitic expressions," specifically aimed at Omar's statements.

When will Americans and Europeans stop running scared every time someone screams "anti-Semitism"? Until when will Israel and the Jewish establishment succeed in exploiting (the existing) anti-Semitism as a shield against criticism? When will the world dare to distinguish between legitimate criticism of an illegitimate reality and anti-Semitism?

The gap between these two is great. There is anti-Semitism one must fight, and there is criticism of Israel and the Jewish establishment it is imperative to support. Manipulations exercised by the Israeli propaganda machine and the Jewish establishment have managed to make the two issues identical.

This is the greatest success of the Israeli government's hasbara: Say one critical word about Israel and you're labeled an anti-Semite. And labeled an anti-Semite, your fate is obvious. Omar has to break this cursed cycle. Is the young representative from Minnesota up for it? Can she withstand the power centers that have already mobilized against her in full force?

Maybe it's important that she knows there are people in Israel crossing fingers for her?

Her success and that of her congressional colleagues, Rashida Tlaib from Michigan and Alexandria Ocasio-Cortez from New York, could be the first swallows that herald the coming of spring. This is the spring of freely expressing opinions about Israel in America. Cortez already asked this week why isn't bigotry aimed at other groups condemned just like statements against Israel are.

What, after all, has Omar said? That pro-Israel activists demand "allegiance to a foreign country"; that U.S. politicians support Israel because of money they receive from the pro-Israel lobby group AIPAC, and that "Israel hypnotized the world." What is incorrect in these statements? Why is describing reality considered anti-Semitic?

Jews have immense power in the U.S., far beyond the relative size of their community, and the blind support given by their establishment to Israel raises legitimate questions regarding dual loyalty. Their power derives from their economic success, their organizational skills and the political pressure they exert. Omar dared to speak about this.

Just imagine what Israelis and Jews would feel if Muslim Americans had the same political, economic and cultural power Jews have. Such power, above all the intoxication with power that has seized hold of the Jewish establishment, comes with a price. Omar and her colleagues are trying to collect on it.

Due to the Israel lobby, the U.S. does not know the truth about what is happening here. Congress members, senators and shapers of public opinion who are flown here ad nauseam see only Israeli victimhood and Palestinian terror, which apparently emerged out of nowhere. Islamists, Qassam rockets and incendiary balloons – not a word about occupation, expropriation, refugees and military tyranny. Questions such as where the money goes and whether it serves American interests are considered heresy. When talking about Israel one must not ask questions or raise doubts.

This cycle has to be broken as well. It's not right and it's not good for the Jews. Omar is now trying to introduce a new discourse to Congress and to public opinion. Thanks to her and her colleagues there is a chance for a change in America. From Israel we send her our wishes for success.

When will the world dare to distinguish between legitimate criticism of an illegitimate Israeli reality and anti-Semitism?

Benjamin Netanyahu says Israel is 'not a state of all its citizens'

PM has been accused of demonising Israeli Arabs in lead-up to April election

From The Guardian, 10th March 2019

Benjamin Netanyahu told a cabinet meeting Israel was the 'nation state only of the Jewish people'. Photograph: Gali Tibbon/AP

Benjamin Netanyahu has said Israel is "not a state of all its citizens", in a reference to the country's Arab population.

In comments on Instagram, the prime minister went on to say all citizens, including Arabs, had equal rights, but he referred to a deeply controversial law passed last year declaring Israel the nation state of the Jewish people.

"Israel is not a state of all its citizens," he wrote in response to criticism from an Israeli actor, Rotem Sela. "According to the basic nationality law we passed, Israel is the nation state of the Jewish people – and only it.

"As you wrote, there is no problem with the Arab citizens of Israel. They have equal rights like all of us and the Likud government has invested more in the Arab sector than any other government," he said of his right-wing party.

As the comments caused waves in Israel, Netanyahu again spoke of the issue at the start of a cabinet meeting. He called Israel a "Jewish, democratic state" with equal rights, but "the nation state not of all its citizens but only of the Jewish people".

Netanyahu has been accused of demonising Israeli Arabs, who make up about 17% of the population, in an attempt to boost right-wing turnout in elections due on 9 April.

He has continually warned that his opponents will receive the support of Arab parties and that they will make significant concessions to the Palestinians.

Netanyahu, under threat of indictment for corruption, is facing a tough challenge from a centrist political alliance led by Benny Gantz, a former military chief of staff, and Yair Lapid, an ex finance minister.

The alliance's centrist positions and its security credentials – it includes three former military chiefs of staff – have helped it beat back Netanyahu's claims that its leaders are "weak" leftists.

Arab parties would be extremely unlikely to be part of any coalition government after elections.

Arab Israelis are Palestinians who remained on their land after the 1948 creation of Israel and are largely supportive of the Palestinian cause.

Netanyahu leads what is seen as the most right-wing government in Israel's history and says he wants a similar coalition after the upcoming polls.

Only by moving beyond Zionism will Christian-Jewish dialogue progress

by RobertA H Cohen, 10th March from www.patheos.com

Christian-Jewish interfaith dialogue is looking ever more morally compromised when it comes to Israel/Palestine. When you look at the context, it's hardly surprising.

On the Christian side, there's the fear of damaging the trust and friendship built up between Jews and Christians over the last 70 years of historic post Holocaust encounter. While on my Jewish side of the conversation, we're faced with an even greater dilemma: the narrow politicisation of Judaism itself which has skewed our moral compass.

Christian guilt for the sins of antisemitic Europe across two millennia has combined with a Jewish consensus that Zionism is our best hope of longterm security. It's a joint narrative that too often creates an awkward silence from Christian leaders when confronted with the historic and on-going injustices experienced by the Palestinian people. Meanwhile, mainstream Jewish leaders encourage the silence by insisting that Zionism is central, not only to modern Jewish identity, but to Judaism itself.

Managing the interfaith debate

In recent years the rising tension in interfaith dialogue, caused by Christian communities around the world choosing to show support for Palestinian Christians, has forced the need to proactively manage the inter-communal debate on Israel.

The most recent example of this in the U.K. has been a series of events around the country organised by the Board of Deputies of British Jews and Churches Together in Britain and Ireland. The tour entitled *'Investing in Peace'* brought together Jewish Israeli and Palestinian peace activists with a message not to "take sides" but to "build bridges" through grassroots relationships. It's good as far as it goes. But it's designed not to go too far. *Investing in Peace* sets up the discussion within a paradigm of "nuance " and "balance" that ignores the real power dynamics of oppressed and oppressor. But if that true relationship is not acknowledged and confronted, neither justice nor peace are unlikely to emerge.

So, how do we get the Christian-Jewish interfaith encounter on Israel/Palestine to progress? How can we have conversations that are more honest and challenging while remaining respectful?

While I'm keen for Christian leaders to stop feeling that history places them in a moral straitjacket on Israel/Palestine, I'm going to address the rest of my observations to my own Jewish community's leadership.

A Zionist bind

Most Rabbis and Jewish community leaders in Britain, and around the world, are trapped in a Zionist bind of their own creation. They feel they cannot speak out against the behaviour of the Jewish State without risking the safety and security of the Jewish people. That's assuming they recognise (if only privately) that there is a problem to address.

For Christian-Jewish dialogue to climb to a higher level, our Jewish leadership must acknowledge the unjust reality of life for millions of Palestinians. The questions they should be asking of themselves are: *How should we speak about this truthfully? What responsibility do we have for enabling injustice to continue? What responsibility do we have for ending it?* While it would be antisemitic to accuse all Jews of being collectively and equally responsible for the condition of the Palestinians, there is an obligation to speak out when the State of Israel claims to act in the interest of Jews worldwide in defending its actions.

Neither virtuous nor victimless

Zionism was always more than just a project of European settler colonialism. The Jewish connections to the land through our liturgy, our annual cycle of festivals, and the belief in the land covenant made to Abraham and his descendants, figure large in our history and culture.

I don't doubt that most Jews still think of Zionism as a worthy and noble endeavour. Not only that, most of my fellow Jews also see it as the paramount necessity for our long-term safety and security. Against this, all other political and ethical considerations become secondary.

Zionism, once a marginal and highly contested political ideology, has succeeded like no other stream of Jewish thinking in our history. So much so, it has undergone a successful merger with Judaism itself. One can no longer see the join.
But if we continue to think of Zionism as a virtuous and victimless undertaking, it will eventually undo us, both from without and from within. In the end, there is no escaping the role of Zionism in dispossessing and marginalising a people as numerous as ourselves. The sooner we face up to the ethical implications of this, the better. Untangling Judaism from the consequences of Jewish nationalism ought to be both a theological and political priority.

I have no doubt about how difficult this will be. But nor do I doubt how essential it has become.

Post-Zionist theology

Just as mainstream Judaism reached a theological accommodation with Zionism after the Holocaust, it's now time to start thinking about a theological accommodation with post-Zionism.

Thankfully, Judaism has always been capable of adapting and responding to changing circumstances. The Babylonian exile, the destruction of the Second Temple, life in the ghettos of Christian Europe, the Holocaust, and the political triumph of Zionism – Judaism responded and adapted to all of these challenges.

And now we have a new challenge: an ethical and spiritual crisis caused by the growing understanding, by both Jews and non-Jews, that our project of national salvation has led to an on-going tragedy for another people. And in creating this tragedy, we have failed to provide ourselves with the safety and security that first motivated Zionism.

The crisis is heightened and complicated because it involves us, the Jewish people – a people with a long history of being persecuted by others. The resistance to acknowledging that we ourselves have now become 'Pharaoh' is the greatest obstacle to theological progress within Judaism. And it undermines our ability to deepen our dialogue with Christianity.

To move forward from Zionism does not entail an abandonment of Israeli Jews. Nor does it mean forgoing our belief in a Jewish homeland, or God's promises to our biblical ancestors. It does involve a reimagining of those ideas based on the fundamental understanding that God initiated the spark of life with the intent to create a humanity guided by love and justice, not inequality and oppression.

The time has come to think big, be bold and to question received wisdom. Including the wisdom that says only a 'Sparta' state in the Middle East, dependent on the good-will of global empires, will ever be able to guarantee Jewish security around the world.

Towards a new Jewish perspective

From a Jewish perspective, it's time to recognise that a denial of the injustices inflicted on the Palestinian people is undermining our ability to engage with integrity on issues of racism, discrimination and the plight of refugees around the world. These are the very issues to which Judaism and Jewish experience ought to bring considerable learning and authority. As things stand, we look hypocritical.

My advice to Jewish leaders is that national chauvinism of any kind will always be a threat to our ability to repair a fractured world or build a just society.

I'm aware that solidarity with the oppressed nearly always comes with a political cost. That's because defeating oppression, as Moses discovered, means challenging the most powerful. On this occasion, and in this situation, it is our own people who hold the power. But challenging that power is a cost that's worth paying. Otherwise, what kind of God are we being faithful to?

Note: This article first appeared in the Winter 2018/19 edition of Cornerstone magazine, a publication by the Sabeel Ecumenical Liberation Theology Center in Jerusalem.

Netanyahu says Israel will keep all land between the river and the sea

Prime minister boasts about his opposition to a Palestinian state, while victims of Iraqi pogroms lose compensation case
12th March 2019 in Middle East Eye

Israeli Prime Minister Benjamin Netanyahu stands on the west bank of the Jordan River (AFP)

Netanyahu: We'll rule all land west of the Jordan

Prime Minister Benjamin Netanyahu told lawmakers from his Likud party that Israel will continue to rule over all the land west of the Jordan River, meaning all of present-day Israel, as well as all of the occupied Palestinian territories, Mako news site reports.

"We will rule over all the territory west of the Jordan, we will be everywhere," Netanyahu said. "We won't uproot even one person. No one will be uprooted."

The Israeli premier made the comments Monday in a closed-door meeting of Likud legislators at a Jerusalem heritage centre named after Menachem Begin, the first Likud leader to rule the country.

Netanyahu recalled that former US Vice President Joe Biden confronted him over his unwillingness to permit Palestinians any territorial sovereignty, even in the future. "Joe Biden told me back then: 'You're against a Palestinian state!' I told him, 'You said it.'"

The prime minister also stated that if he forms the next government, it will be similar in composition to the current one, with one significant difference: the education minister will be from Netanyahu's own Likud party, not from a coalition partner.

In recent weeks, Bezalel Smotrich of the Union of Right-Wing Parties has expressed interest in receiving the education portfolio.

Iraq pogrom victims ineligible for full compensation
Israel's Supreme Court has decreed that Iraqi Jews who fled their country in the wake of anti-Semitic pogroms in 1941 are not eligible to receive the same financial compensation as Jews whose wartime suffering occurred on the European continent, Israeli daily Haaretz reports.

After an eight-year legal battle, the highest court in the country ruled that the Baghdad pogroms, known as the Farhud, were inspired by anti-Jewish animus that predated Nazi influence on Iraq.

As such, survivors of the pogrom will not receive an annual sum of $7,300 for their past suffering, as those of Nazi Germany, but rather of $1,000, a figure chosen by Israel's finance ministry in 2015.

"Anti-Semitism in its various forms existed before the Nazi regime rose to power, and didn't disappear after Nazi Germany was defeated," the court ruled. "There are many facets to anti-Semitism."

Though the court denied appellants the cash award they sought, the judges suggested that the state increase their compensation in any case, noting that the letter of the law is out of sync with the will of the people, who they say broadly support a larger reparations package for the Farhud victims.

Israeli Jews of Moroccan descent are also demanding that the compensation they receive for their persecution at the hands of the Vichy regime also be brought in line with the funds paid out to those who suffered directly under the Nazis.

Levi-Abekasis seeks healthy ministry, promises looser grass laws
Orli Levi-Abekasis, who is chair of the centre-right Gesher party, unveiled her faction's platform on Sunday, revealing her aspirations to head the health ministry in Israel's next government.

"Get used to this: Orli Levi-Abekasis, Israel's health minister," the lawmaker wrote in a Facebook post on Monday.

"The Israeli health system is collapsing, thousands of people are dying every year, dying needlessly," she wrote. "We cannot continue like this!"

Levi-Abekasis vowed to find a billion dollars to cover the ministry's deficit, and to invest in the country's health system an additional $3.6bn to $4.2bn over the next five years – "until we reach the OECD average".

The centre-right legislator, who left the Yisrael Beiteinu party to form her own Knesset faction in 2017, also committed to eliminating the hurdles that block Israeli citizens from purchasing marijuana legally.

"How can it be that people are denied medicine because its name is cannabis?" she asked. "Apathy, close-mindedness and disdain."

In recent days, another boutique political party that has long championed the decriminalisation of marijuana – Zehut (Identity) – polled above the electoral threshold, currently set at 3.25 percent.

If the party maintains or improves on that level of support, it will earn itself a place in the next parliament.

TV anchor to be grilled for calling abusive troops 'animals'
A television reporter who elicited widespread rage in Israel for criticising soldiers accused of badly beating a Palestinian man in front of his son will soon face a professional tribunal over her remarks, the Jerusalem Post reports.

The Btsalmo organisation, a Jewish advocacy group, is calling for Channel 13 news anchor Oshrat Kotler to be levelled with punitive sanctions for calling the Israeli soldiers featured in a news segment about the beating "human animals".

"When you send your children to the army, they are kids," Kotler said. "You send them to the territories, and they come back as human animals. This is the result of the occupation."

Three of the soldiers were recently sentenced to six months in jail, and a fourth was sentenced to three months in jail, as part of a plea deal with military prosecutors.

Israel is the only democracy in the Middle East? Netanyahu's comments have shattered that illusion

His comments that the country belongs to 'Jewish people alone' strike to the heart of the nature of Israel.

by Ben White, 11th March 2019 from The Independent

Netanyahu is desperate, in the face of an electoral challenge from former military chiefs of staff as well as the looming indictments for corruption allegations (EPA)

Israeli prime minister Benjamin Netanyahu was back in the headlines on Sunday, after declaring on social media that "Israel is not a state of all its citizens". The Likud leader later doubled down, telling his cabinet that Israel is "the nation state not of all its citizens, but only of the Jewish people".

Netanyahu's comments are the latest grim episode in an election season that will see Israelis going to the polls on 9 April. Just last month, the prime minister helped engineer an election merger that could see far-right party Otzma Yehudit (Jewish Power) enter the Knesset.

That latter piece of realpolitik in particular prompted outrage from a number of Israeli politicians, analysts and even US-based groups better known for their Israel advocacy. According to the critics, Netanyahu's boosting of the far-right and indulging of racist rhetoric endangers Israeli democracy.

Netanyahu is desperate, in the face of an electoral challenge from former military chiefs of staff as well as the looming indictments for corruption allegations. But recent developments are not just about motivating a right-wing base – the problem goes much deeper than an embattled demagogue.

Netanyahu's election manoeuvres offer an opportunity to shine a spotlight on an uncomfortable truth: namely that only under the most superficial definition can Israel be considered a democracy.

Consider the following. Millions of Palestinians are subjected to a military regime which, for 52 years, has facilitated the establishment of illegal settlements. Settlers are Israeli citizens, and vote. The Palestinians they live among – whose land the settlers inhabit and colonise – are not.

The April elections will lead to the formation of Israel's 35th government. Israel's military occupation of the West Bank, East Jerusalem and Gaza Strip began during Israel's 13th government.

Those Palestinians who do have Israeli citizenship, meanwhile, are very much second-class citizens – as Netanyahu has been at pains to emphasise.

Yes, the Jewish Nation-State law passed last year is significant in that regard, defining Israel as "the national home of the Jewish people", and asserting that "the right to exercise national self-determination in the state of Israel is unique to the Jewish people".

But the legislation was consistent with de jure and de facto discrimination going back to the very foundation of the state of Israel.

As conflict studies scholar Nadim Rouhana wrote in 2010, "there are few honest observers in Israel who dispute that a Jewish state, by definition, privileges one group of citizens over another".

This is an inequality "expressed in various ways, including in Israel's Basic Laws and its laws of land control, immigration and resource distribution" – as documented by Palestinian citizens themselves, as well as international NGOs and human rights experts.

Finally – and this is regrettably rarely taken into account – there are millions of Palestinians who, expelled from their homes in the 1948 Nakba and prevented from returning ever since, are denied their rightful citizenship and thus suffrage.

A few weeks ago, Michael J Koplow, policy director of the Israel Policy Forum, wrote an unintentionally instructive piece for Israeli newspaper *Haaretz* on Netanyahu's "embrace" of the Jewish Power party.

Koplow argued that Netanyahu's actions have "damaged one of Israel's most valuable national security assets", by which he meant that "one of Israel's most potent claims on the world stage is that it is the only democracy in the Middle East".

Yet as the facts make clear, Israel's democratic credentials are seriously lacking as soon as you go deeper than – are the people to whom we've granted citizenship able to vote?

Just last year a draft law by legislators representing Palestinian citizens was disqualified from even being debated in the Knesset plenum. Why? In calling for Israel to be a state of all its citizens, as opposed to "the state of the Jewish people", the bill violated parliamentary regulations.

Thus, the significance of the Jewish Power party and Netanyahu's racist rhetoric is in the way it makes the *claim* that Israel is a liberal democracy that much tougher to make. Netanyahu did not say anything ground-breaking on Sunday: but he is making it harder to maintain an illusion.

Racist Knesset Candidates Borrow Ideology From Labor's Occupation Pioneers

When Israeli governments in the 1960s and 1970s worked hard to steal Palestinian land while quoting God's promises to atheists, they paved the way for parties promoting Jewish supremacy

BY Amira Hass, in HaAretz, 11th March 2019

Ayelet Shaked and Bezalel Smotrich speak during a Habayit Hayehudi meeting, Jerusalem, October 15, 2019. Emil Salman

A twisted but single line stretches between Israel Galili and Bezalel Smotrich, between Yigal Allon and Levi Eshkol and Moshe Feiglin, and between Golda Meir and Yitzhak Rabin and Ayelet Shaked.

We, the Arabs and the leftists, were right when we warned during the 1960s and 1970s that the settlement enterprise was a disaster. We erred in believing that the world would intervene in time and preempt the Lebensraum impulses, the urge to create "living space." We thought that in the end, the heads of the Labor movement would learn from the expansionist impulses of other nations. After all, they were the sons and brothers of the victims of Lebensraum. But we were wrong. So now we'll have Feiglin, the latest hot name in the gallery of those preaching to expel the Palestinians, sitting in the next Knesset.

Racism is an ideology that evolves in order to justify and protect the excessive material and social rights that a certain group of people has acquired, due to years of historical circumstances. Like men, conquering nations find it hard to give up their accumulated spoils and profits and will do anything to hold onto them.

Immediately after June 1967, the Labor Alignment government cynically manipulated international law, ravaged the occupied Palestinian lands to Judaize them, and developed bureaucratic methods to reduce the number of Palestinians living in the country. One can trace the cynicism and the line that stretches from Galili to settler-leader-turned-minister Uri Ariel in a new study by the Kerem Navot organization, titled "Seize the Moral High Ground," which researches the history of orders to seize land for "temporary military purposes." Seizing Palestinian land for military purposes and then transferring it to the settlements was not invented by Likud, but by the Alignment. The Alignment holds the copyright on steadily gnawing at Palestinian land while abusing its owners to give an established settlement another road, another water pipe, another security buffer zone.

When the Labor governments worked hard to steal land on the grounds of security while quoting God's promises to atheists, they paved the way for the hundreds of thousands of Jews who are now going to vote for parties promoting the ideology of a superior Jewish race – and these are many and varied, praise God. Eshkol allowed the destruction of the Mughrabi Quarter and dispersed its Palestinian residents to the winds to make way for the Western Wall Plaza, and Allon was the first minister to move to Jerusalem's Old City.

The occupation bureaucracy they developed prevented the return home of tens of thousands of Palestinians who found themselves outside the West Bank in the summer of 1967, and restricted

Palestinian construction in Jerusalem with the help of planning laws. These governments laid the attitudinal foundations for the Third Temple, whose construction is being planned by some people with the utmost seriousness. The spirit of the mass expulsions of 1948, the desire to empty the land of Arabs, infused them.

The racist-messianic justifications have persuaded an increasing number of Jewish Israelis, because the spoils acquired have grown tremendously over the years. It's hard to give them up, and they want more. That's why Benjamin Netanyahu hastened to explain that the State of Israel is not a state of all its citizens. He fears that votes might go from him to Feiglin and Kahanist candidate Itamar Ben-Gvir.

When the world proved it could not block either the Alignment or Likud governments, the land gluttons proceeded to gorge themselves with redoubled enthusiasm. The armed, aggressive, murderous racism of the settlement messiahs and their servants is intensifying, because the inferior nation is not inferior. It is resisting. It is educated, eloquent and refuses to disappear. It is rooted in its land.

Emboldened, the Feiglins and the Smotriches will try to expel masses of Palestinians. They will fail only if all the descendents of the Alignment – not just Ta'ayush activists and a handful of anarchists – prevent it with their bodies.

Why is it hard for me to imagine the leaders of Kahol Lavan halting the trucks?

Opinion: The Fight Over Ilhan Omar Is About Something Much Bigger

I've fought for Palestinian rights for my whole career. Today I see a new generation of American Jews viewing the conflict through a new lens: equality.

by Yousef Munayyer, March 11th 2019, from BuzzFeed News

Demonstrators are arrested in front of Sen. Chuck Schumer's office in New York, 2018. Don Emmert / AFP / Getty Images

Last week began with yet another round of attacks and smears against Rep. Ilhan Omar and ended with a congressional resolution that condemned anti-Muslim discrimination for the first time. The resolution also included condemnations of many other forms of racism and bigotry, including anti-Semitism, anti-black racism, xenophobia, and anti-LGBT bigotry.

How did this happen? A diverse set of progressive actors came together and demanded that we must not exceptionalize any form of racism, but instead take exception to all of them. This intersectional approach appeared to win over key figures in both the Progressive Caucus and the Congressional Black Caucus, which seemed to make the difference in significantly shifting the language of the resolution from its initial version, promoted by the Anti-Defamation League, that focused exclusively on anti-Semitism as an indirect rebuke to Rep. Omar.

Intersectionality poses a problem for many fighting against Palestinian rights activism. That was one of the key takeaways in a report co-authored by ADL and the Reut Institute, an Israeli think tank.

This study aimed to inform what it called the "pro-Israel network" on how it can refine its strategy. It listed intersectionality as an emerging challenge that could have a "significant potential impact on Israel's legitimacy," giving oppressed groups "an important shared language with which to fight for greater recognition and inclusion."

We're seeing this play out in today's progressive politics. I've been fighting for Palestinian rights for my whole career, and while having Jewish American allies is nothing new, today I see far greater support from a new generation of American Jews, who view the conflict through a new lens: equality.

What this really reflects is a clash between two fundamentally different views of the world. The Jewish communities in the United States and Israel have roughly equal-sized populations, and in many ways embody two different responses to the very real and lengthy history of anti-Semitism and persecution: Zionism vs. equality.

Zionism's answer is that the only way to ensure the security of the Jewish people is through a Jewish state — a largely homogenous ethnoreligious nationalism where Jews dominate a nation, its laws, and its security apparatus. This answer comes at the expense of Palestinians, for whom Zionism meant the destruction of their society and their continued subjugation.

Equality provides a different answer. It sees the security of Jews as wound up in the security of other minority groups, and responds by trying to build an inclusive society where people can safely be who they are. The answer is civil rights, not majoritarian nationalism — and this means the civil rights of all. This is one reason why the Jewish community in the US has historically been at the forefront of the fight for civil rights and against racism and exclusion.

Broadly speaking, equal rights is seen as a path to security for American Jews, who are one of many minorities. In the Israeli context, where majoritarianism is politically empowering, equal rights can be viewed as a path to insecurity. These different predicaments, and the effort to achieve safety in each, come with a very different set of values.

This values divide was reflected in a Pew poll on Israeli and American Jews, published in the first month of the Trump administration. When asked what is an essential part of what it means to be Jewish, one of the largest gaps between Israeli and American Jewish respondents was to the idea of "working for justice and equality." American Jews were significantly more likely to identify this as central to their Jewish identity. Interestingly, "living in/caring about Israel" is where there was similar overlap between the groups of respondents, but in neither group was there majority support for this answer.

This tension has always existed, but over time it has been elevated or diminished. Today it is very much elevated, with factors in the US and in Israel/Palestine widening the gap.

Increasingly, American Jews view what Israel is doing to Palestinians as fundamentally contrary to Jewish values. At the same time, the Israeli government has doubled down on its entrenchment of occupation and apartheid, and its open alliance with authoritarians and enthonationalists around the world. Just this week, Israeli Prime Minister Benjamin Netanyahu reminded us that not only do millions of Palestinians living under military occupation have no right to vote, but even those who are Israeli citizens are not equal to Jews.

There's also the partisan polarization of the US–Israel relationship, driven by Netanyahu and Israel through an alliance with the Evangelical Christians that undergird the GOP. Most American Jews vote Democrat and voted for Obama, twice. They remain broadly supportive of Israel, but they don't support all Israeli policies, and Israel is not among their top voting issues. Rather, like most Americans, they prioritize issues like the economy, health care, national security, and the environment.

This broke into the open with Netanyahu's blatant political attacks on Barack Obama, the first black president, who himself embodied what a multicultural America could lead to. Many of the attacks on President Obama's Iran diplomacy came with racially coded and sometimes overt suggestions that Obama was betraying America and Israel.

This was a slightly more sophisticated form of birtherism, a higher pitched dog whistle. That might be why members of the Congressional Black Caucus skipped Netanyahu's speech before Congress in 2015, and why they spoke up behind the scenes to change language that was previously seen as clearly targeting their colleague Rep. Omar.

The partisan divide was exacerbated with the arrival of Trump, who secured the White House while displaying almost every form of bigotry and prejudice you could imagine. His words and actions emboldened white nationalists and brought a rise in hate crimes. The prime minister of Israel responded by saying there "was no greater supporter of the Jewish people" than the white supremacist in chief.

Then came Charlottesville, and then the Tree of Life synagogue shooting, where a murderous anti-Semite massacred Jews because he believed they were helping flood America with foreigners. His hatred of immigrants and Muslims reinforced his anti-Semitism and vice versa. This should remind us that these evils can not be fought in isolation, as Zionism would suggest, but rather must be opposed together as an intersectional approach would demand.

As if to demonstrate this very point, Jeanine Pirro, a talk show host on the preeminent media platform of the right, Fox News, offered a hate-filled 10-minute diatribe against Rep. Omar this weekend that was entirely built around actual dual loyalty smears. She made clear she believes Omar, a hijab-wearing African refugee, was a subversive threat to America. Her words were ugly enough that even Fox News condemned them.

The belief that injustice anywhere is a threat to justice everywhere, as famously introduced by Rev. Martin Luther King Jr., is why minorities should band together and defend one another. And a commitment to justice must also mean opposing Israel's horrific treatment of Palestinians. It all adds up to a perfect storm of growing Jewish American alienation from Israel, and increasing criticism of Zionism as a whole.

So how can you blunt that alienation, and limit the rise of Palestinian rights in mainstream politics? One way is to send a message to American Jews that even if they're appalled by the right, the left is no better. This is done by elevating a false equivalence between anti-Semitism on the left and the right.

It is a classic Zionist response to American Jews: You are not safe in a society premised on equal rights, because you are Jews, a minority with a history of persecution, and the only answer is Zionism. The right and the left have failed you and will keep failing you equally.

I doubt this will be particularly persuasive, in the short or long term. The ethnic nationalism of the right will always elevate one community at the expense of others, just as Zionism has done to Palestinians. We must work toward a vision of the world that rejects seeing the humanity and equality of people as zero sum, but rather sees them as inherently interconnected.

Yousef Munayyer is executive director of the US Campaign for Palestinian Rights.

One-state solution gains ground as Palestinians battle for equal rights
Belief in two-state solution crumbles as up to 600,000 Israeli settlers remain on occupied land
by Oliver Homes in The Guardian, 13th March 2019

Palestinians protest against a road closure by Israeli settlers opposite the Kfar Adumim settlement in the occupied West Bank. Photograph: Jaafar Ashtiyeh/AFP/Getty Images

Maybe it wasn't the wisest choice for a Palestinian activist living under the close watch of Israeli security. But Fadi Quran was obsessed and determined: he would study nuclear physics at Stanford University.

"I got stopped at the border a lot," he joked years later of the times he passed through Israeli passport control after graduating. "To be honest, when I first started I just wanted to win a Nobel prize in physics. I was 18 years old. I loved the stuff."

He wanted to use his physics degree to provide wind and solar energy to Palestinians. But the plan stalled. Israel delayed the import of the technology needed, he said, and Palestinian officials became interested and demanded a share of his company. "I was squashed."

Now 30, he sits at a plush cafe in downtown Ramallah in the West Bank, with fast internet and mochas filled with chunks of chocolate. Smartly dressed 20-somethings sit smoking and typing away on laptops. A restaurant next door sells sushi. Further up the street, there is an electric car charging station next to a tourist information centre.

It's a pleasant scene, but it's a lie, Quran says. "If you go two miles in any direction outside the centre of Ramallah, you'll find [an Israeli] settlement, or a wall, or a checkpoint or so forth." Israeli military control is not immediately visible here, he acknowledges, but that's the ingenuity of it.

Palestinians in the West Bank live under a system that was supposed to last just five years – an agreement made 25 years ago as the first step towards a self-governing country alongside Israel. Under the Oslo accords, an interim government called the Palestinian Authority (PA) was given limited control over small pockets of land, almost exclusively towns and cities, while Israel maintained control of the remainder.

But after the peace process collapsed, Israel dug in by building an extensive network of roads, military bases, settlements and quarries. Meanwhile, the PA clung to power, surviving by coordinating closely with Israeli security forces.

The PA has become a "subcontractor for the occupation", says Quran. "The other way you could frame it is postmodern Uncle Toms – people whose personal interests have become so enmeshed with the interests of the 'slave masters' that they will serve them and betray their own people's interests."

Peace has never seemed so distant. Almost two-thirds of Palestinians want the PA's 84-year-old ailing leader, Mahmoud Abbas, to resign, according to polls, and half believe the Authority "has become a burden".

Palestinians live in constant bemusement as they hear world leaders and diplomats talk as if the past quarter-century never happened. Last month, the European Union's top diplomat Federica Mogherini wrote a 3,000-word article which read like a desperate plea for Palestinians and Israelis to keep working for a two-state solution.

Foreign governments have held tight to the two-state ideal despite drastic changes on the ground. Even as they privately acknowledge it as a fading prospect, diplomats still talk of "working towards" two states.

When polled, a majority of Palestinians do not see that as a possibility. Roughly 600,000 Israeli settlers now live on occupied land with no intention of leaving. Meanwhile, Israeli politicians in cabinet talk about annexing vast swathes of the West Bank. "Almost nobody believes in the two-state solution anymore," Quran says.

A construction site in the Israeli settlement of Givat Ze'ev, in the occupied West Bank. Photograph: Baz Ratner/Reuters

Bassem Tamimi, from the village of Nabi Saleh, has a lifetime of resistance behind him. The 52-year-old points to a scar on his head from what he said was surgery after he was shaken into a coma by interrogators. His sister died after he says she was pushed down the stairs in an Israeli courthouse. His cousin was killed by a direct hit with a gas grenade. Now, his teenage daughter, Ahed, has risen to global prominence after she slapped a soldier and spent eight months in jail.

Tamimi sees the Palestinian struggle as one of fighting for ever-tinier chunks of land. When Israel was established in 1948, Palestinians were left with 22% of the land they had lived on. Under Oslo, they agreed to work towards sovereignty over that area. Now they have limited autonomy over an even smaller fraction of that.

"I fought for the two-state solution," he sighs. "I lost my friends, I lost my sister, I lost a lot of cousins, I lost my time in jail."

He has since given up on the idea of a Palestinian state alongside Israel. "Our society feels like it has lost. And this is the first time that has happened," he says. The village halted demonstrations in 2015 as too many people were being shot. "Why should Ahed fight for the life I had?" he asks.

Tamimi now advocates for one secular state in all the land shared by Israelis and Palestinians.

The idea gaining momentum, even among Palestinian officials who helped negotiate Oslo. When Donald Trump recognised the contested city of Jerusalem as Israel's capital, the senior Palestinian politician Saeb Erekat said the message was clear: "The two-state solution is over. Now is the time to transform the struggle for one state with equal rights for everyone living in historic Palestine."

Palestinians already live inside Israel with citizenship. They are families who remained in their towns and villages while others fled or were expelled in wars surrounding Israel's creation. But their life is not what other Palestinians aspire towards. The Israeli prime minister, Benjamin Netanyahu, said on Sunday: "Israel is the nation state of the Jewish people – and only it."

Neither does he back two independent states, leaving Palestinians in limbo.

Quran, the activist, is wary of calling himself a "one-stater". He knows that for many Israelis, it's a scary phrase, as it would lead to the end of Zionism in its current form. Under one state, Palestinians might make up approximately half or more of the population. That would mean Israel could cease to be a majority-Jewish country.

But his hopes appear to echo that of Tamimi. "I want everyone in this area to live under the same constitution and same social contract that provides them with freedom, justice and dignity for all."

The idea gaining momentum, even among Palestinian officials who helped negotiate Oslo. When Donald Trump recognised the contested city of Jerusalem as Israel's capital, the senior Palestinian politician Saeb Erekat said the message was clear: "The two-state solution is over. Now is the time to transform the struggle for one state with equal rights for everyone living in historic Palestine."

Palestinians already live inside Israel with citizenship. They are families who remained in their towns and villages while others fled or were expelled in wars surrounding Israel's creation. But their life is not what other Palestinians aspire towards. The Israeli prime minister, Benjamin Netanyahu, said on Sunday: "Israel is the nation state of the Jewish people – and only it."

Neither does he back two independent states, leaving Palestinians in limbo.

Quran, the activist, is wary of calling himself a "one-stater". He knows that for many Israelis, it's a scary phrase, as it would lead to the end of Zionism in its current form. Under one state, Palestinians might make up approximately half or more of the population. That would mean Israel could cease to be a majority-Jewish country.

But his hopes appear to echo that of Tamimi. "I want everyone in this area to live under the same constitution and same social contract that provides them with freedom, justice and dignity for all."

Netanyahu is right: Israel is a nation with no interest in equality
As a Palestinian citizen of Israel, I am subject to insidious discrimination that is enshrined by law – and no major party sees it as an issue
By Amjad Iraqi in The Guardian, 13th March 2019

'Most Jewish-Israelis agree that anyone who questions Jewish superiority, or Israel's rule over all people between the river and the sea, are not welcome in the public discourse.' Photograph: Gali Tibbon/EPA

As a Palestinian citizen of Israel, it is a strange experience to watch your humanity become a subject of national debate between a prime minister and a model. Responding to criticism by the well-known Israeli actor Rotem Sela this week, Benjamin Netanyahu took it upon himself to declare, via Instagram: "Israel is not a state of all its citizens. According to the nation-state law we passed [in July 2018], Israel is the nation-state of the Jewish people – and not anyone else." His assertion quickly dominated international headlines. Israeli Hollywood actor Gal Gadot (who played Wonder Woman in the 2017 blockbuster), President Reuven Rivlin, and other public figures joined the fray to defend Sela, who had posted the question: "When the hell will someone in this government convey to the public that Israel is a state of all its citizens and that all people were created equal?"

Sela's remarks are commendable. But Netanyahu is right: Israel is not a country built for all its people, a fifth of whom (more than 1.5 million) are Palestinian Arab citizens of the state. This was the case long before the "Jewish nation-state law" was enacted last year, and long before Netanyahu returned as prime minister a decade ago. Since the state's establishment in 1948, more than 65 laws have been used to restrict the rights of Palestinian citizens in all fields of life, with more being passed every year. While many of these laws may not appear discriminatory at face value, their racist impact is evident to the people they target.

For example, as a non-Jew in Israel, I cannot buy property in the vast majority of the country, and I can be barred by an admissions committee from living in a small, community town if I am not deemed "socially or culturally suitable". I am unable to study Palestinian history at a state school because it is not taught, and I could put a theatre at risk of losing state funding if I promote a play describing Israel's independence as a Nakba, or catastrophe, for the Palestinian people. If I wished to marry a Palestinian from the occupied territories, I could not bestow residency or citizenship on her so she could live with me and raise a family inside Israel; any Jew in the world, however, can fly into Ben Gurion airport and become a citizen.

In many ways, the nation-state law changes little for Palestinian citizens of the state, as the legal infrastructure for their inferior status has always been in place. And yet, by anchoring Jewish supremacy as a constitutional rule, the law also changes everything: now, Israeli courts and state bodies are obligated to carry out racial discrimination. This includes demoting Arabic from its former status as an official language, and, most dangerously, pursuing exclusive Jewish settlement as a "national value". With this law, the avenues for Palestinian citizens to combat inequality – an already Sisyphean undertaking – are narrowed even further.

This year's Israeli elections – and the spat between Sela and Netanyahu – must be understood in the shadow of this law. Until now, the political coverage has largely focused on the possibility of former army chief Benny Gantz replacing Netanyahu, or on Netanyahu's facilitation of the fascist Jewish Power party to enter the Knesset. The real issue that should be examined – and that should matter in every Israeli election – is why none of the main parties are discussing true equality, or the end of the occupation, as a central issue. The answer is simple: most Jewish-Israelis agree that anyone who questions Jewish superiority, or Israel's rule over all people between the river and the sea, are not welcome in the public discourse.

The distaste for such discussion is systemic. Last year, the Knesset Presidium refused to allow a bill entitled Basic Law: State for All Its Citizens, proposed by Balad, a secular Arab nationalist party, to be brought to the floor. Another bill entitled Democratic, Multicultural and Egalitarian State, proposed by Yousef Jabareen of an Arab-Jewish party, was dismissed in the early stages of parliamentary debates. Just last week, the Knesset's central elections committee disqualified Balad-Ra'am (a joint slate of Balad and the Islamic Movement) as well as Ofer Cassif, a Jewish member of Hadash, from running in this year's elections. (Adalah, the legal centre where I work, is representing both Balad-Ra'am and Cassif before the Israeli supreme court this week in an attempt to cancel the committee's decisions).

Although the supreme court is expected to allow their participation, this marks the sixth consecutive election in which Arab-led parties and their candidates have had to fight disqualifications. These decisions have been endorsed by rightwing and centre Jewish parties alike, accusing the Arab parties of supporting terrorism because they criticise the occupation, or denying Israel's character as a "Jewish and democratic" state because they demand a racially just society, a "state for all its citizens". What this shows again is that, as far as the Israeli political spectrum is concerned, Palestinian citizens are not to be regarded as equals, and their demands for human rights are a national threat. It should not have taken an Instagram post by a Jewish-Israeli actor to expose that reality.

• Amjad Iraqi is an advocacy coordinator at the legal centre Adalah. He is also a contributing editor at +972 magazine

Encountering Peace: A nation like all other nations?

By Gershon Baskin, March 14, 2019 in the Jerusalem Post

ARE FRANCE and Israel similar? French President Emmanuel Macron and Prime Minister Benjamin Netanyahu attend the opening ceremony of the France-Israel season event in Paris last June. (photo credit: REUTERS)

In a recent Facebook post I wrote: *"Prime Minister Netanyahu and all of the non-democratic Right and center – pay attention: In order for the State of Israel to be the democratic nation-state of the Jewish people, Israel must be the nation-state of the Jewish people and all of its citizens. Without that Israel is not Jewish and is not democratic."*

My friend and colleague Aryeh Green responded: *"Here's the thing. France is the nation-state of the French people, with full political civil and individual rights for all its citizens."*

The same can be said for every other Western nation in the world, save the United States, which by definition is a melting pot of many ethnic identities, most based on previous national identities – think of Irish Americans, Polish Americans and Italian Americans. So what's wrong with the nation-state of the Jewish people being just that: the nation-state of the Jewish people, with full civil and political and individual rights for all its citizens, whether they are Arab or Jew, whatever their religion or color of their skin or national or ethnic identity?

Your mantra of "and a state for all its citizens" is extraneous. Just as it is for France (and for the record, descendants of Poles and Italians, Irish and Spanish and other nations, can indeed gain citizenship in the land of their ancestors. Check it out. Jews aren't unique among democracies in that either.)

I post this because this is exactly the same argument that I have used many times with Palestinian friends and colleagues, and even wrote this argument in several columns I published in Palestinian newspapers. But today it is no longer true.

There are problems making that argument today after the Nation-State Law came into being; after Netanyahu's response to Rotem Sela ("Israel is not a country of all its citizens. According to the Nation-State Law that we passed, Israel is the nation-state of the Jewish nation – and its alone"); after a majority a members of the ruling Likud faction oppose the two-states solution, as well as the prime minister himself apparently; after the push by Netanyahu to empower the radical Right that supports annexation of the West Bank; and after the total delegitimization of the Arab electorate and their representatives by the majority of the Right and centre-right in Israel. There is no equality in Israel for non-Jewish citizens.

In this election campaign, there isn't even the appearance of equality for the Arab citizens. There has never been equality for the Arab citizens of Israel. Some gaps in disparities have narrowed. None have been closed. Arabs remain the poorest sector of Israel. They suffer from discrimination in every field of life possible. There used to be an appearance or a claim of equality under the law, but we all know that is not true.

There is no equality in the allocation of budgets by the state. There is no equality in labour opportunities, in transportation planning, in education, in social welfare, in public building, in public land-use planning, in policing, in the courts and in the prisons. Some justify the discrimination by declaring that the state has the right to provide benefits to those citizens who serve in the army – which are not Arabs.

But this falls short on two elements. Haredim (ultra-Orthodox) who don't serve in the army have more benefits from the state than do the Arabs; and Arabs are not relieved from military service like the Haredim, who don't serve but are simply not drafted. Not being drafted, they are not eligible for certain benefits for those who served in the army.

We are all familiar with shops and companies looking for employees that emphasize "after army service" – a code for Arabs need not apply. We all know how difficult it is for Arab students to find a place to live in Jewish cities. Discrimination is not only legal and by the government, it is deeply rooted in Israeli society as well. We all know how underdeveloped the Arab neighbourhoods are in the mixed Jewish-Arab cities, as compared to the Jewish neighbourhoods within the same jurisdiction.

How can we continue to lie to ourselves about equality in the State of Israel? Israel is not a new-born state with a weak economy. Israel is strong and developed and rich. After more than 70 years, it should not be acceptable to any of us that this discrimination continues.

Israel as the nation-state of the Jewish people is not like France – the nation-state of the French people. Anyone can potentially become part of the French nation-state. This is not the case with the Jewish nation-state. A non-Jew cannot become a member of the Jewish nation-state without changing their religion. Being Jewish is not only being a member of a nation – it is also being a member of a religion. If we talk about the nation-state of Israel, perhaps we can talk about real equality, or the possibility of real equality between all of its citizens. But if Israel is not the state of all of its citizens, there cannot be equality for all of its citizens.

If Israel would end its occupation of the Palestinian people, and the Palestinian people could assert their national identity within a given territory and achieve self-determination, perhaps we could speak about the possibility for the Palestinian citizens of Israel to express their national identity within the Palestinian state. Perhaps even holding dual citizenship with their Israeli citizenship – and then we could revisit the possibility of achieving equality for all Israeli citizens.

Israel can be the nation-state of the Jewish people, but it must also be the state of all of its citizens. Our Declaration of Independence – our vision and mission statement as a nation – emphasized the principle of equality, the principle that Netanyahu and his government have killed.

For now, I suggest we stop lying to ourselves about equality in our so-called democratic country. I hope that after the elections, we will begin to count the Arab citizens of Israel as full citizens, that the new government will once again strive for genuine equality in all fields, and that we will return to the peace process to end our occupation over the Palestinian people. Until then, let's try to be honest – at least with ourselves.

Denying Jews The Right To A State Is Anti-Semitic. So Why Is It Ok To Deny Palestinians?
By Dean Obeidallah, March 14, 2019 from the Jewish "Forward" news page

It's as if the concept of double standards was created for the Middle East conflict. One of the most glaring is the discussion surrounding self-determination for Palestinians and Israelis.

If you declare that Israel has no right to exist, you're rightfully labeled an anti-Semite. True, there are some who oppose that view, even within the Jewish community. Progressive Jewish writer Peter Beinart recently wrote an article in which he wrote that "Anti-Zionism is not inherently anti-Semitic."

But in general, if an American politician or a media figure proclaimed that they don't believe Israel has a right to exist, they would be subject to a firestorm of criticism for being anti-Semitic. They might even lose their job; just ask Marc Lamont Hill, who was let go by CNN in November for advocating a "free Palestine from the river to the sea."

When it comes to saying there should be no Palestinian state, however, there's zero backlash. No one labels you a bigot for saying that the approximately five million Palestinian Christians and Muslims living in the West Bank, Gaza and East Jerusalem are somehow not worthy of self-determination.

Did the GOP face any backlash for its 2016 platform that effectively ended its support for the creation of a Palestinian state, adding that "We reject the false notion that Israel is an occupier"? (My cousins living in the West Bank must be overjoyed to know that the occupation is finally over!)

Has there been any backlash to political pundits who have not just rejected a Palestinian state but even denied the humanity of the Palestinian people? Former Senator Rick Santorum stated point blank when he was running for President in 2012 that "all the people that live in the West Bank are Israelis. They are not Palestinians. There is no Palestinian."

Do you think CNN would have hired him if he said the same about Israelis?

The same goes for GOP icon and Fox News regular Newt Gingrich, who declared that Palestinians are an "invented" people when he came out against a Palestinian state. Clearly, if he said the same about Jewish Israelis, he would be slammed as a bigot.

Perhaps ending this double standard can play a role in ushering in a just peace for Palestinians and Israelis.

That's why we need to agree that if a person denies that either Israel or Palestine has a right to exist, they should face the same criticism.

And this rule must also apply to Israeli Prime minister Benjamin Netanyahu who continues to double and even triple down on his opposition to a Palestinian state.

We saw this again just a few weeks ago when Netanyahu made it clear he supports the never ending occupation of Palestinians as he declared, "A Palestinian state would endanger our existence." Netanyahu even slammed his more moderate opponents in the upcoming April 9th Israeli election, Benny Gantz and Yair Lapid, saying that if they win, "Sooner or later, probably sooner, they will establish a Palestinian state." That's not surprising because the last time Netanyahu ran for re-election in 2015 he made it clear to all who would listen that there will be no Palestinian state on his watch.

And just recently we learned Netanyahu was doing far more than just publicly denouncing the creation of Palestine. He was actively working to undermine any prospects of a Palestinian state by, of all things, agreeing to allow millions of dollars to flow to Hamas. Yes, that Hamas.

Why would the prime minister of Israel regularly allow large sums of money to go directly to Hamas from the Qatari government? Is it because all of a sudden Netanyahu cares about the nearly two million Palestinians living in Gaza where there's a 54 percent unemployment rate and per the World Bank, "A recent liquidity squeeze in Gaza has led to a rapid collapse in humanitarian conditions, including access to medical treatment, electricity, and clean water"?

Of course not. Netanyahu's rationale is that by propping up Hamas, it will keep the Palestinians of the West Bank and Gaza separated so that they can't unify to advocate for their own nation.

In fact, Netanyahu is not even hiding that sentiment, stating that, "whoever is against a Palestinian state should be for" allowing this transfer of millions of dollars to Hamas.

Netanyahu is the Donald Trump of the Middle East. Both have employed hate for political gain. In 2015, when Netanyahu feared losing reelection, he cried out on election day to his right wing supporters that "Arab voters are heading to the polling stations in droves." This would be akin to Trump on election day firing up his white base by warning them that blacks, immigrants and Latinos are voting in big numbers.

And earlier this week, Netanyahu again gave us his best Trump impression as he used anti-Arab bigotry to appeal to conservative voters. This time it was in response to Israeli actress Rotem Sela's plea on Instagram that Israel is, "a country of all its citizens, and all people are born equal," adding, " The Arabs are also human beings."

Well, that was too much for Bibi, who responded on Facebook that, "Israel is not a country of all its citizens." Rather, "Israel is the state of the Jewish people — and belongs to them alone."

What do you call a person who says one group of its citizens is inherently superior to the others?

It's time to have one standard across the board, for Israelis and Palestinians. Especially when we discuss this issue here in the U.S., we must be careful to apply the standard of bigotry equally to those who deny Jews and Palestinians the right to self-determination.

Dean Obeidallah hosts the daily national SiriusXM radio program, "The Dean Obeidallah Show" on the network's progressive political channel. He is also a columnist for The Daily Beast and contributor to CNN.com.

'Endless Trip to Hell': Israel Jails Hundreds of Palestinian Boys a Year. These Are Their Testimonies

They're seized in the dead of night, blindfolded and cuffed, abused and manipulated to confess to crimes they didn't commit. Every year Israel arrests almost 1,000 Palestinian youngsters, some of them not yet 13
By Netta Ahituv Mar 14, 2019 from HaAretz

Israeli forces detain Palestinian Fevzi El-Junidi, 14, following clashes in the West Bank city Hebron, December 2017. Wisam Hashlamoun / Anadolu Agency

It was a gloomy, typically chilly late-February afternoon in the West Bank village of Beit Ummar, between Bethlehem and Hebron. The weather didn't deter the children of the Abu-Ayyash family from playing and frolicking outside. One of them, in a Spiderman costume, acted the part by jumping lithely from place to place. Suddenly they noticed a group of Israeli soldiers trudging along the dirt trail across the way. Instantly their expressions turned from joy to dread, and they rushed into the house. It's not the first time they reacted like that, says their father. In fact, it's become a pattern ever since 10-year-old Omar was arrested by troops this past December.

The 10-year-old is one of many hundreds of Palestinian children whom Israel arrests every year: The estimates range between 800 and 1,000. Some are under the age of 15; some are even preteens. A mapping of the locales where these detentions take place reveals a certain pattern: The closer a Palestinian village is to a settlement, the more likely it is that the minors residing there will find themselves in Israeli custody. For example, in the town of Azzun, west of the Karnei Shomron settlement, there's hardly a household that hasn't experienced an arrest. Residents say that in the past five years, more than 150 pupils from the town's only high school have been arrested.

Omar Rabua Abu Ayyash. Meged Gozani

At any given moment, there are about 270 Palestinian teens in Israeli prisons. The most widespread reason for their arrest – throwing stones – does not tell the full story. Conversations with many of the youths, as well as with lawyers and human rights activists, including those from the B'Tselem human-rights organization, reveal a certain pattern, even as they leave many questions open: For example, why does the occupation require that arrests be violent and why is it necessary to threaten young people.

A number of Israelis, whose sensibilities are offended by the arrests of Palestinian children, have decided to mobilize and fight the phenomenon. Within the framework of an organization called Parents Against Child Detention, its approximately 100 members are active in the social networks and hold public events "in order to heighten awareness about the scale of the phenomenon and the violation of the rights of Palestinian minors, and in order to create a pressure group that will work for its cessation," as they explain. Their target audience is other parents, whom they hope will respond with empathy to the stories of these children.

In general, there seems to be no lack of criticism of the phenomenon. In addition to B'Tselem, which monitors the subject on a regular basis, there's been a protest from overseas, too. In 2013, UNICEF, the United Nations agency for children, assailed "the ill treatment of children who come in contact with the military detention system, [which] appears to be widespread, systematic and institutionalized." A report a year earlier from British legal experts concluded that the conditions the Palestinian children are subjected to amount to torture, and just five months ago the Parliamentary

Assembly of the Council of Europe deplored Israel's policy of arresting underage children, declaring, "An end must be put to all forms of physical or psychological abuse of children during arrest, transit and waiting periods, and during interrogations."

Arrest

About half of the arrests of Palestinian adolescents are made in their homes. According to the testimonies, Israel Defense Forces soldiers typically burst into the house in the middle of the night, seize the wanted youth and whisk him away (very few girls are detained), leaving the family with a document stating where he's being taken and on what charge. The printed document is in Arabic and Hebrew, but the commander of the force typically fills out the details in Hebrew only, then hands it to parents who may not be able to read it and don't know why their son was taken.

Attorney Farah Bayadsi asks why it's necessary to arrest children in this manner, instead of summoning them for questioning in an orderly way. (The data show that only 12 percent of the youths receive a summons to be interrogated.)

"I know from experience that whenever someone is asked to come in for questioning, he goes," Bayadsi notes. She's active in the Israeli branch of Defense for Children International, a global NGO that deals with the detention of minors and promotion of their rights.

"The answer we generally get," she says, "is that, 'It's done this way for security reasons.' That means it's a deliberate method, which isn't intended to meet the underage youth halfway, but to cause him a lifelong trauma."

Indeed, as the IDF Spokesman's Unit stated to Haaretz, in response, "The majority of the arrests, of both adults and minors, are carried out at night for operational reasons and due to the desire to preserve an orderly fabric of life and execute point-specific actions wherever possible."

About 40 percent of the minors are detained in the public sphere – usually in the area of incidents involving throwing stones at soldiers. That was the case with Adham Ahsoun, from Azzun. At the time, he was 15 and on his way home from a local grocery store. Not far away, a group of children had started throwing stones at soldiers, before running off. Ahsoun, who didn't flee, was detained and taken to a military vehicle; once inside, he was hit by a soldier. A few children who saw what happened ran to his house to tell his mother. Grabbing her son's birth certificate, she rushed to the entrance to the town to prove to the soldiers that he was only a child. But it was too late; the vehicle had already departed, headed to an army base nearby, where he would wait to be interrogated.

By law, soldiers are supposed to handcuff children with their hands in front, but in many cases it's done with their hands behind them. Additionally, sometimes the minor's hands are too small for handcuffing, as a soldier from the Nahal infantry brigade told the NGO Breaking the Silence. On one occasion, he related, his unit arrested a boy "of about 11," but the handcuffs were too big to bind his small hands.

The next stage is the journey: The youths are taken to an army base or a police station in a nearby settlement, their eyes covered with flannelette. "When your eyes are covered, your imagination takes you to the most frightening places," says a lawyer who represents young Palestinians. Many of those arrested don't understand Hebrew, so that once pushed into the army vehicle they are completely cut off from what's going on around them.

In most cases, the handcuffed, blindfolded youth will be moved from place to place before actually being interrogated. Sometimes he's left outside, in the open, for a time. In addition to the discomfort and the bewilderment, the frequent moving around presents another problem: In the meantime many acts of violence, in which soldiers beat the detainees, take place and go undocumented.

Once at the army base or police station, the minor is placed, still handcuffed and blindfolded, on a chair or on the floor for a few hours, generally without being given anything to eat. The "endless trip to hell" is how Bayadsi describes this process. Memory of the incident, she adds, "is still there even years after the boy's release. It implants in him an ongoing feeling of a lack of security, which will stay with him for his whole life."

Young Palestinian detainees under guard. Soldiers typically burst into the house in the middle of the night, seize the wanted youth and leave the family with a document stating where he's being taken. Breaking the Silence

Testimony provided to Breaking the Silence by an IDF staff sergeant about one incident in the West Bank illustrates the situation from the other side: "It was the first night of Hanukkah in 2017. Two children were throwing stones on Highway 60, on the road. So we grabbed them and took them to the base. Their eyes were covered with flannelette, and they were handcuffed in front with plastic cuffs. They looked young, between 12 and 16 years old."

When the soldiers gathered to light the first candle of the Hanukkah holiday, the detainees remained outside. "We're shouting and making noise and using drums, which is a kind of company thing," the soldier recalled, noting that he assumed the kids didn't know Hebrew, although maybe they did understand the curses they heard. "Let's say sharmuta [slut] and other words they might know from Arabic. How could they know we aren't talking about them? They'll probably thought that in another minute we were going to cook them."

Interrogation

The nightmare can be of differing duration, the former detainees relate. Three to eight hours after the arrest, by which time the youth is tired and hungry – and sometimes in pain after being hit, frightened by threats and not even knowing why he's there – he's taken in for interrogation. This may be the first time the blindfold is removed and his hands freed. The process usually starts with a general question, such as, "Why do you throw stones at soldiers?" The rest is more intense – a barrage of questions and threats, aimed at getting the teen to sign a confession. In some cases, he's promised that if he signs he'll be given something to eat.

According to the testimonies, the interrogators' threats are directed squarely at the boy ("You'll spend your whole life in jail"), or at his family ("I'll bring your mother here and kill her before your eyes"), or at the family's livelihood ("If you don't confess, we'll take away your father's permit to work in Israel – because of you, he'll be out of work and the whole family will go hungry").

"The system shows that the intention here is more to demonstrate control than to engage in enforcement," suggests Bayadsi. "If the boy confesses, there's a file; if he doesn't confess, he enters the criminal circle anyway and is seriously intimidated."

Imprisonment

Whether the young detainee has signed a confession or not, the next stop is prison. Either Megiddo, in Lower Galilee, or Ofer, north of Jerusalem. Khaled Mahmoud Selvi was 15 when he was brought to prison in October 2017 and was told to disrobe for a body search (as in 55 percent of the cases). For 10 minutes he was made to stand naked, along with another boy, and in winter.

The months in detention, waiting for trial, and later, if they are sentenced, are spent in the youth wing of the facilities for security prisoners. "They don't speak with their families for months and are allowed one visit a month, through glass," Bayadsi relates.

Far fewer Palestinian girls are arrested than boys. But there is no facility specially for them, so they are held in the Sharon prison for women, together with the adults.

The trial

The courtroom is usually the place where parents have their first sight of their child, sometimes several weeks after the arrest. Tears are the most common reaction to the sight of the young detainee, who will be wearing a prison uniform and handcuffs, and with a cloud of uncertainty hovering over everything. Israel Prisons Service guards don't allow the parents to approach the youth, and direct them to sit on the visitors' bench. Defense counsel is paid for either by the family or by the Palestinian Authority.

Attorney Farah Bayadsi. It's clear, she says, that the goal of the arrests "is more to demonstrate control than to engage in law enforcement."

At a recent remand hearing for several detainees, one boy didn't stop smiling at the sight of his mother, while another lowered his eyes, perhaps to conceal tears. Another detainee whispered to his grandmother, who had come to visit him, "Don't worry, tell everyone I'm fine." The next boy remained silent and watched as his mother mouthed to him, "Omari, I love you."

While the children and their family try to exchange a few words and looks, the proceedings move along. As though in a parallel universe.

The deal
The vast majority of trials for juveniles ends in a plea bargain – safka in Arabic, a word Palestinian children know well. Even if there is no hard evidence to implicate the boy in stone-throwing, a plea is often the preferred option. If the detainee doesn't agree to it, the trial could last a long time and he will be held in custody until the proceedings end.

Conviction depends almost entirely on evidence from a confession, says lawyer Gerard Horton, from the British-Palestinian Military Court Watch, whose brief, according to its website, involves "monitoring the treatment of children in Israeli military detention." According to Horton, who is based in Jerusalem, the minors will be more prone to confess if they don't know their rights, are frightened and get no support or relief until they confess. Sometimes a detainee who does not confess will be told that he can expect to face a series of court appearances. At some stage, even the toughest youth will despair, the lawyer explains.

The IDF Spokesman's Unit stated in response: "The minors are entitled to be represented by an attorney, like any other accused, and they have the right to conduct their defense in any way they choose. Sometimes they choose to admit to guilt within the framework of a plea bargain but if they plead not guilty, a procedure involving hearing evidence is conducted, like the proceedings conducted in [civilian courts in] Israel, at the conclusion of which a legal decision will be handed down on the basis of the evidence presented to the court. The deliberations are set within a short time and are conducted efficiently and with the rights of the accused upheld."

Managing the community
According to data of collected by the British-Palestinian NGO, 97 percent of the youths arrested by the IDF live in relatively small locales that are no more than two kilometers away from a settlement. There are a number of reasons for this. One involves the constant friction – physical and geographical – between Palestinians, on the one hand, and soldiers and settlers. However, according to Horton, there is another, no less interesting way to interpret this figure: namely, from the perspective of an IDF commander, whose mission is to protect the settlers.

In the case of reported stone-throwing incidents, he says, the commander's assumption is that the Palestinians involved are young, between the ages of 12 and 30, and that they come from the nearest village. Often the officer will turn to the resident collaborator in the village, who provides him with the names of a few boys.

The next move is "to enter the village at night and arrest them," Horton continues. "And whether these youths are the ones who threw the stones or not, you have already put a scare into the whole village" – which he says is an "effective tool" for managing a community.

"When so many minors are being arrested like this, it's clear that some of them will be innocent," he observes. "The point is that this has to be happening all the time, because the boys grow up and new children appear on the scene. Each generation must feel the strong arm of the IDF."

According to the IDF Spokesperson's Unit: "In recent years, many minors, some of them very young, have been involved in violent incidents, incitement and even terrorism. In these cases, there is no alternative but to institute measures, including interrogation, detention and trial, within the limits of and according to what is stipulated by law. As part of these procedures, the IDF operates to uphold and preserve the rights of the minors. In enforcing the law against them, their age is taken into account.

"Thus, since 2014, among other measures, in certain instances, the minors are invited to the police station and are not arrested at home. In addition, proceedings relating to minors take place in the military court for juveniles, which examines the seriousness of the offense that's attributed to the minor and the danger it poses, while taking into consideration his young age and his particular circumstances. Every allegation of violence on the part of IDF soldiers is examined, and cases in which the soldiers' actions are found to be flawed are treated sternly."

The Shin Bet security service stated in response: "The Shin Bet, together with the IDF and the Israel Police, operates against every element that threatens to harm Israel's security and the country's citizenry. The terrorist organizations make extensive use of minors and recruit them to carry out terrorist activity, and there is a general tendency to involve minors in terrorist activity as part of local initiatives.

"Interrogations of suspected terrorists are conducted by the Shin Bet under the law, and are subject to supervision and to internal and external review, including by all levels of the court system.

The interrogations of minors are carried out with extra sensitivity and with consideration of their young age."

Khaled Mahmoud Selvi. Meged Gozani

Khaled Mahmoud Selvi, arrested at 14 (October 2017)

"I was arrested when I was 14, all the boys in the family were arrested that night. A year later, I was arrested again, with my cousin. They said I burned tires. It happened when I was sleeping. My mother woke me up. I thought it was time for school, but when I opened my eyes I saw soldiers above me. They told me to get dressed, handcuffed me and took me outside. I was wearing a short-sleeved shirt and it was cold that night. My mother begged them to let me put on a jacket, but they didn't agree. Finally, she threw the jacket on me, but they didn't let me put my arms in the sleeves.

"They took me to the Karmei Tzur settlement with my eyes covered, and I had the feeling that they were just driving in circles. When I walked, there was a pit in the road and they pushed me into it, and I fell. From there they took me to Etzion [police station]. There they put me in a room, and soldiers kept coming in all the time and kicking me. Someone passed by and said that if I didn't confess, they would leave me in jail for the rest of my life.

"At 7 A.M., they told me the interrogation was starting. I asked to go to the toilet before. My eyes were covered and a soldier put a chair in front of me. I tripped. The interrogation went on for an hour. They told me that they saw me burning tires and that it interfered with air traffic. I told them it wasn't me. I didn't see a lawyer until the afternoon, and he asked the soldiers to bring us food. It was the first time I had eaten since being arrested the night before.

"At 7 P.M., I was sent to Ofer Prison, and I remained there for six months. In that period, I was in court more than 10 times. And there was also another interrogation, because a friend of mine was told while being questioned that if he didn't confess and inform on me, they would bring his mother and shoot her before his eyes. So he confessed and informed. I'm not angry at him. It was his first arrest, he was scared."

Khaled Shtaiwi, arrested at 13 (November 2018)

Khaled's story is told by his father, Murad Shatawi: "On the night he was arrested, a phone call from my nephew woke me up. He said the house was surrounded by soldiers. I got up and got dressed, because I expected them to arrest me, on account of the nonviolent demonstrations I organize on Fridays. I never imagined they'd take Khaled. They asked me for the names of my sons. I told them Mumen and Khaled. When I said Khaled, they said, 'Yes, him. We're here to take him.' I was in shock, so many soldiers showed up to arrest a boy of 13.

"They handcuffed and blindfolded him and led him east on foot, toward the settlement of Kedumim, all the while cursing and hitting him a little. I saw it all from the window. They gave me a document showing that it was a legal arrest and I could come to the police station. When I got there, I saw him through a small hole in the door. He was handcuffed and blindfolded.

Khaled Shtaiwi. Meged Gozani

"He stayed like that from the moment they arrested him until 3 P.M. the next day. That's a picture that doesn't leave me; I don't know how I'll go on living with that picture in my head. He was accused of throwing stones, but after four days they released him, because he didn't confess and there was no other evidence against him. During the trial, when the judge wanted to speak to Khaled, he had to lean forward in order to see him, because Khaled was so small.

"What was it like to see him like that? I am the father. That says it all. He hasn't talked about it since getting out, three months ago. That's a problem. I'm now organizing a 'psychology day' in the village, to help all the children here who have been arrested. Out of 4,500 people in the village, 11 children under the age of 18 have been arrested; five were under the age of 15."

Omar Rabua Abu Ayyash. Meged Gozani

Omar Rabua Abu Ayyash, arrested at age 10 (December 2018)

Omar looks small for his age. He's shy and quiet, and it's hard to talk to him about the arrest, so members of his family recount the events in his place.

Omar's mother: "It happened at 10 A.M. on Friday, when there is no school. Omar was playing in the area in front of the house, he threw pebbles at birds that were chirping in the tree. The soldiers, who were in the watchtower across the way here, picked up on what he was doing and ran toward him. He ran, but they caught him and knocked him down. He started to cry, and he wet his pants. They kicked him a few times.

"His grandmother, who lives here below, immediately went out and tried to take him from the soldiers, which caused a struggle and shouts. In the end, they left him alone and he went home and changed into dry pants. A quarter of an hour later, the soldiers came back, this time with their commander, who said he had to arrest the boy for throwing stones. When the other children in the family saw the soldiers in the house, they also wet their pants."

Omar's father takes up the story: "I told the commander that he was under 12 and that I had to accompany him, so I rode with him in the jeep to the Karmei Tzur settlement. There the soldiers told him not to throw stones anymore, and that if he saw other children doing it, he should tell them. From there they took him the offices of the Palestinian Authority in Hebron. The whole story took about 12 hours. They gave him a few bananas to eat during those hours. Now, whenever the children see a military jeep or soldiers, they go inside. They've stopped playing outside since then. Before the incident, soldiers used to come here to play soccer with the children. Now they've stopped coming, too."

Tareq Shtaiwi. Meged Gozani

Tareq Shtaiwi, arrested at 14 (January 2019)

"It was around 2 P.M. I had a fever that day, so Dad sent me to my cousin next door, because that's almost the only place in the village with a heating unit. Suddenly soldiers showed up. They saw me watching them from the window, so they fired shots at the door of the building, knocked it down and started to come upstairs. I got scared, so I ran from the second floor to the third, but they stopped me on the way and took me outside. The soldiers wouldn't let me take my coat, even though it was cold and I was sick. They took me on foot to Kedumim, handcuffed and blindfolded. They sat me on a chair. I heard doors and windows being slammed hard, I think they were trying to scare me.

"After a while, they took me from Kedumim to Ariel, and I was there for five-six hours. They accused me of throwing stones a few days earlier with my friend. I told them I hadn't thrown any stones. In the evening they moved me to the Hawara detention building; one of the soldiers told me I would never leave there. In the morning I was moved to Megiddo Prison. They didn't have prisoners uniforms in my size, so they gave me clothes of Palestinian children who had been there before and left them for the next in line. I was the youngest person in the prison.

"I had three court hearings, and after 12 days, at the last hearing, they told me that it was enough, that my father would pay a fine of 2,000 shekels [$525] and I was getting a three-year suspended sentence. The judge asked me what I intended to do after getting out, I told him I would go back to school and I wouldn't go up to the third floor again. Since my arrest, my younger brother, who's 7, has been afraid to sleep in the kids' room and goes to sleep with our parents."

Adham Ahsoun. Meged Gozani

Adham Ahsoun, arrested in October 2018, on his 15th birthday

"On my 15th birthday, I went to the store in the village center to buy a few things. Around 7:30 in the evening, soldiers entered the village and children started to throw stones at them. On the way home with my bag, they caught me. They took me to the entrance of the village and put me in a jeep. One of the soldiers started to hit me. Then they put plastic handcuffs on me and covered my eyes and took me like that to the military base in Karnei Shomron. I was there for about an hour. I couldn't see a thing, but I had the feeling that a dog was sniffing me. I was afraid. From there they took me to another military base and left me there for the night. They didn't give me anything to eat or drink.

"In the morning, they moved me to the interrogation facility in Ariel. The interrogator told me that the soldiers caught me throwing stones. I told him that I hadn't thrown stones, that I was on my way home from the store. So he called the soldiers into the interrogation room. They said, 'He's lying, we saw him, he was throwing stones.' I told him that I really hadn't thrown stones, but he threatened to arrest my mother and father. I panicked. I asked him, 'What do you want from me?' He said he wanted me to sign that I threw stones at soldiers, so I signed. The whole time I didn't see or talk to a lawyer.

"My plea bargain was that I would confess and get a five-month jail sentence. Afterward, they gave me one-third off for good behavior. I got out after three months and a fine of 2,000 shekels. In jail I tried to catch up with the material I missed in school. The teachers told me they would only take into account the grades of the second semester, so it wouldn't hurt my chances of being accepted for engineering studies in university."

Muhmen Teet, arrested at 13 (November 2017)

"At 3 A.M., I heard knocking on the door. Dad came into the room and said there were soldiers in the living room and wanted us to show ID cards. The commanding officer told my father that they were taking me to Etzion for questioning. Outside, they handcuffed and blindfolded me and put me in a military vehicle. We went to my cousin's house; they also arrested him. From there we went to Karmei Tzur and waited, handcuffed and blindfolded, until the morning.

Muhmen Teet. Meged Gozani

"In the morning, they only took my cousin for interrogation, not me. After his interrogation, they took us to Ofer Prison. After a day there, they took us back to Etzion and said they were going to interrogate me. Before the interrogation, they took me into a room, where there was a soldier who slapped me. After he hit me in one room, he took me to the interrogation room. The interrogator said I was responsible for burning tires, and because of that the grove near the house caught fire. I said it wasn't me, and I signed a document that the interrogator gave me. The document was also printed in Arabic, but the interrogator filled it out in Hebrew. I was taken back to Ofer Prison.

"I had seven hearings in court, because at the first hearing I said I hadn't intended to confess, I just didn't understand what I signed and it wasn't true. So they sent me back for another interrogation. Again I didn't confess. Then they sent me to interrogation another time and again I didn't confess. That's what it was like in three interrogations. In the end, my lawyer did a deal with the prosecutor that if I confessed in court – which I did – and my family would pay 4,000 shekels, they would release me.

"I'm a good student, I like soccer, both playing and watching it. Since the arrest I hardly wander around outside."

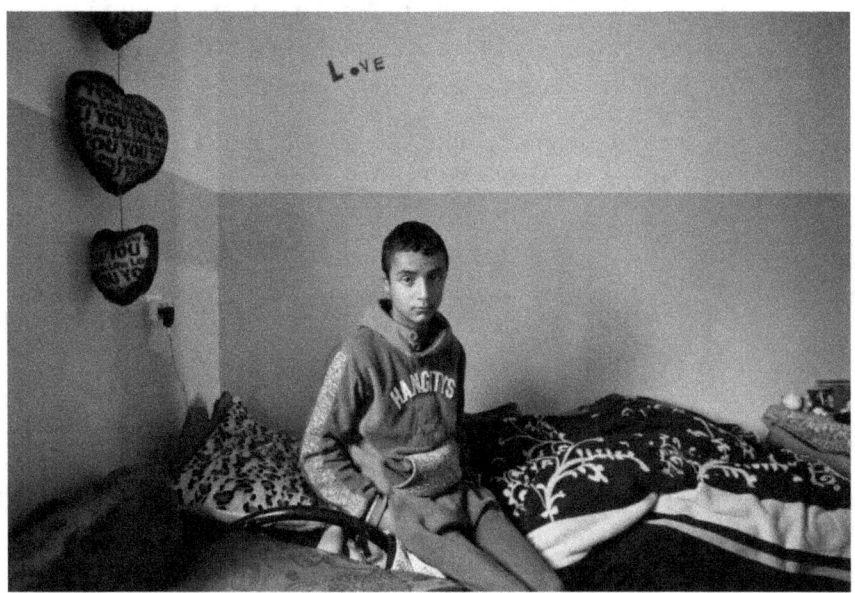

Khalil Zaakiq. Meged Gozani

Khalil Zaakiq, arrested at age 13 (January 2019)

"Around 2 A.M. someone knocked on the door. I woke up and saw a lot of soldiers in the house. They said we should all sit in the living room sofa and not move. The commander called Uday, my big brother, told him to get dressed and informed him that he was under arrest. It was the third time they arrested him. My father was also once under arrest. Suddenly they told me to put my shoes on too and go with them.

"They took us out of the house and tied our hands and covered our eyes. We went like that on foot to the base in Karmei Tzur. There they sat me on the floor with hands tied and eyes covered for around three hours. At about 5 A.M., they moved us to Etzion. On the way there in the jeep they hit us, they slapped me. In Etzion, I was sent to be checked by a doctor. He asked if I had been beaten and I said yes. He didn't do anything, only checked my blood pressure and said I could stand up to an interrogation.

"My interrogation started at 8 A.M.. They asked me to tell them which children throw stones. I said I didn't know, so the interrogator gave me a slap. The interrogation went on for four hours. Afterward, they put me into a dark room for 10 minutes and then took me back to the interrogation room, but now they only fingerprinted me and put me into a detention cell for an hour. After an hour, Uday and I were moved to Ofer Prison. I didn't sign a confession, neither about myself nor about others.

"I got out after nine days, because I wasn't guilty of anything. My parents had to pay 1,000 shekels for bail. My little brother, who is 10, has been really afraid ever since. Whenever someone knocks at the door, he wets his pants."

A Palestinian Farmer Finds Dead Lambs in His Well. He Knows Who's to Blame

The carcasses of some 10 sheep and lambs were dumped into Ibrahim Salah's well. The poisoning of its water is only one instance of what the people of his village endure at the hands of settlers from nearby Havat Gilad
Gideon Levy and Alex Levac, Mar 14, 2019 from HaAretz

Salah at his well, this week. "Why am I submitting a complaint?" he asks rhetorically. "So they won't come back again. At least I tried. What else can I do?" Alex Levac

The carcass of the large sheep lies in the shade of the olive tree, already partially eaten by the animals of the field and the birds of the sky. A swarm of flies buzzes busily in its innards. The sheep was probably pregnant, its belly was swollen; death may well have come while it was giving birth. Floating in the well are the bodies of lambs. Close to 10 dead lambs – possibly stillborn or victims of some sort of epidemic – have already been found, wrapped in tied-up garbage bags. A few pairs of disposable latex gloves are also floating in the water of the well, undoubtedly belonging to those who disposed of the dead animals.

Using a long metal rod, Ibrahim Salah, the farmer who owns the well and the nearby olive grove, is trying to fish the rest of the carcasses out of it. It's not easy because the putrid bodies – of animals that Salah says did not belong to him or his fellow villagers – are floating well beneath the top of the well.

The body of a lamb falls out of a bag onto the concrete floor next to the well. Its head is black, its bloated body, saturated with water, white. The stench is overpowering, intolerable, repellent, even after Salah has poured gallons of bleach into his 80 cubic-meter well (80,000 liters) to disinfect it. Now he'll have to bring in a generator and a pump, to extract all the water that has been contaminated by the remnants of the livestock still hidden inside. Then he'll have to bring a water tank in and rinse the well repeatedly, until it's cleansed and disinfected and the water is pure again, so he can use it to water his olive grove and for drinking.

Two days after the incident, Salah is still distraught over what he found in the well. It's not only the smell – the memory of what he saw there is equally unbearable. The well is located at the bottom of a hill on which olive trees grow, which we descended on foot this week across a boulder-strewn trail that's impassable for a standard car. We had come to view the horrific spectacle.

Salah thought he'd removed all the bodies from the well last Saturday, but on Monday when we arrived he was taken aback to see additional lambs floating in the water. He has no doubt about who did it: the settler with the all-terrain vehicle, whose name he doesn't know. He's a resident of Havat Gilad – the wild outpost that lurks behind the summit of the hill above his grove, a few hundred meters away, and the scourge of local Palestinian farmers.

In fact, the policemen and Israel Defense Forces soldiers who arrived on Sunday to look into his complaint were accompanied by the very same settler, on his all-terrain vehicle. Salah has a photograph of him on his phone, surrounded by the soldiers: a big skullcap, tzitzit, a thick beard, half a smile. Salah heard him say to the police officers, "I wanted to throw away the sheep. There was no place to throw them. I saw a well, so I threw them in." The good-heartedness of a settler from Havat Gilad.

Farata is a small, poor village in the Qalqilyah district. Salah had asked us to wait for him next to the cell-phone antenna, near his home. He was delayed for two hours at the District Coordination Office in Qalqilyah, in connection with the complaint he filed. He's 66, has seven children and speaks fluent Hebrew after years of doing renovation work in Israel, where two of his sons also work, with official permits. Until three months ago, he himself was doing renovation work at Hadera Paper, but he had decided to devote himself to tending his land.

Salah has three plots of land, with olive groves on all of them. One 18-dunam plot is adjacent to Havat Gilad. Salah is allowed access to it only twice a year, once for plowing and once for harvesting, two or three days each time and only after coordination with the IDF. This year, for example, his request to plow was turned down three times, before being scheduled for the end of the month. It's his land, while Havat Gilad is still in the process of becoming "regularized," but he's the one who's denied free access to his land.

This grove was planted by his father in 1952, around the time Salah was born. Almost every year since 2006, he's discovered that the olives have been stolen even before he arrives to harvest them. Again, he has no doubt about who's behind that. Last year, 24 of the trees were uprooted with a steam shovel. The settlers also erected a tent and a building on his land; he submitted a complaint, but to no avail.

Salah at his well.. Alex Levac

Until 2006, he worked the land together with volunteers from Rabbis for Human Rights, but since then no one dares approach the area. What will happen if we go there now? "I'll be killed on the spot, or they call in the army and take me to jail."

A second plot lies close to the village – 30 dunams of olives belonging to Salah and his sisters, which he can work without the need for "coordination." The third tract, 50 dunams of olive trees, which he planted with his own hands, is situated about two kilometers from his home. It was the well there that was contaminated.

Two weeks ago, on Friday, shepherds from Havat Gilad approached the village. They pastured their sheep on its land, in fields of wheat and barley that are now sprouting. The villagers tried to drive off the intruders. The settlers filmed the event, during which stones were apparently thrown at them, and sent the images to the police.

The law enforcement authorities went into action immediately. They suspected Salah's nephew, Baraa Salman, of throwing the stones. On that same day his car, a Peugeot 205, was impounded, and that evening, an IDF force arrested Salman at home. He's been in detention since them, awaiting trial. So much for a person who tries to defend his property.

When his nephew's car was impounded, Salah went out to the police and soldiers to try to explain to them that his nephew had not committed any crime. The soldiers, he recalls, ordered him to stand next to a wall for two hours, hands behind his back, and remain silent. "I am older than your father," he told the soldiers. "Why don't you take the settlers?" The soldiers ordered him to shut up. Then they took the car and left, before arresting his nephew that night.

Last Friday, Salah went to the nearby plot to spray the trees with insecticide. In the afternoon, after the spraying was completed, he planned to visit the second plot, where the well is located. Shepherds from the neighboring village who saw him warned him to keep away from his grove. "The settler with the all-terrain vehicle is standing next to your well," they told him. "We didn't approach, and we don't know what exactly he's doing there. But don't go – he'll kill you."

Salah heeded their advice and kept his distance. At the end of the day, he passed by and saw that the well's iron cover was missing. He went home and told himself that he would install a new cover the next day.

He went to the well on Saturday with his two sons. The water was gushing out and to his astonishment, he saw a large, dead sheep floating in the water, a dead lamb by its side. Appalled, he rushed away; he was unable to breathe, he says. He went back in the afternoon with his sons, poured bleach into the water and called both the District Coordination Office in Nablus and the head of the local village council. He was beside himself. He called the DCO in Qalqilyah, but by then it was Saturday night and there was no answer.

On Sunday, he called the organization Yesh Din: Volunteers for Human Rights. They sent their field research coordinator, Yudit Avidor, with volunteers from the NGO. They arrived later that day, saw him pulling animal corpses from the water, and stayed with him the whole day to help him file his application to the authorities. The police also arrived on the scene. Salah is now he's waiting to be summoned to lodge an official complaint, as they instructed.

"Why am I submitting a complaint?" he asks rhetorically. "So they won't come back again. At least I tried. What else can I do? More than that I can't do. If say hello to a settler, they'll take me to jail. If he hits me, they won't do a thing to him."

In 2006, settlers attacked his son Basel, who is today 40 years old, with an iron pipe. They broke his shoulder and he was taken to Meir Hospital in Kfar Sava. Salah had to pay 50,000 shekels (about $12,500) for Basel's hospitalization. No one was brought to trial.

"These are sheep that only the settlers have, intended for meat and not for milking," he explains, dispelling any doubts about the origin of the animals. Some of the lambs were also marked with red blotches on their back, a custom not practiced by the Palestinians.

"I don't know why he did it," says Salah, only partly with feigned innocence. "It's as though they just don't want the Palestinians to remain on their land."

There's a fine view from the porch of Salah's house. Havat Gilad is hidden behind the hill. We go down to the well, but hurry away, while we're still able to breathe. The stench is intolerable.

"*Israel is not apartheid state*"™   Israeli and Zionist hasbara

APARTHEID IS REAL

"Two justice systems on an ethnic basis. In other languages it's called apartheid. There's no other name for it."

Gideon Levy Sep 07, 2017

The Palestine Project

UK companies warned over involvement in Israeli war crimes - new report

From Amnesty International 16th March 2019

Travel companies have recently been criticised for their trade in the settlements © HAZEM BADER/AFP/Getty Images

Amnesty has written to all companies in the FTSE 100 spelling out dangers

Letter to Liam Fox seeks assurances that Brexit will not see the UK signing Israel trade deal that includes Israel's illegal settlements

'If you're a company operating in the settlements, then you are involved in systematic injustice' - Peter Frankental

Companies have been warned that they will be involved in human rights violations - including war crimes - if they do business in or with the illegal Israeli settlements in the West Bank, including East Jerusalem.

Amnesty has written to all companies in the FTSE 100 and FTSE 250 Index, spelling out the human rights and reputational issues of the trade in goods and services in the settlements.

All FTSE 100 and 250 CEOs - along with leading corporate law firms, the Confederation of British Industry, the Institute of Directors and the Association of British Insurers - have been sent a copy of Amnesty's new 50-page report - *Think Twice: Can companies do business with the Israeli settlements in the Occupied Palestinian Territories while respecting human rights?* - which says that while a "thriving settlement economy" might appear to provide an attractive location for international businesses, no company can involve itself in this economy without contributing to - or being linked to - human rights abuses.

The issue of business involvement in Israel's settlements recently made headlines when the US online travel company Airbnb announced it would withdraw some 200 listings for holiday properties and attractions located in settlements in the West Bank. Airbnb said the move recognised that the settlements "are at the core of the dispute between Israelis and Palestinians".

Amnesty welcomed the Airbnb announcement but the company has so far failed to implement the move. Instead, as Amnesty noted in a recent report on the online travel sector, along with TripAdvisor, Expedia and Booking.com, Airbnb is still profiting from the occupation and theft of Palestinian land and resources.

Apart from tourism, numerous other business sectors - including banking, law firms, construction companies, and food and manufacturing companies - are also heavily implicated in the perpetuation and expansion of the settlements.

Yet, under the UN Guiding Principles on Business and Human Rights, all companies have a responsibility to respect international humanitarian and human rights law wherever they operate in the world. Israel's settlements breach the Geneva Conventions and amount to war crimes, and Amnesty is warning that no company - however it may seek to justify its involvement - can do business in or with the settlements in a way that is consistent with international humanitarian and human rights law.

The Think Twice report comes ahead of the long-awaited publication of a UN database listing companies known to be operating in the settlements.

Peter Frankental, Amnesty International UK's Economic Affairs Programme Director, said:

"Whether they're a funky digital-era outfit or a decades-old FTSE 100 giant, all companies need to understand there's no way to do business in or with Israel's settlements without contributing to human rights violations against the Palestinian people.

"It's very simple - if you're a company operating in or doing business with the settlements, then you're involved in systematic injustice, discrimination and other human rights violations perpetrated by the state of Israel against Palestinians.

"We would advise all business CEOs, pension fund managers and corporate lawyers to take a good look at our report and do what it says on the cover - think twice about doing business in or with Israel's illegal settlements.

"Any involvement in the deeply exploitative settlement enterprise is bad for the Palestinian people and bad for your company, whose reputation may be tarnished for years to come.

"There's a very clear bottom line here - any profits made by a company via the settlements come at the cost of systematically violating the rights of thousands of Palestinian people."

Letter to Liam Fox

Meanwhile, in January, Amnesty wrote to International Trade Secretary Liam Fox seeking clarification on whether, post-Brexit, the UK will continue to exempt Israel's settlements from any trade agreement it reaches with Israel. Under current EU arrangements, the Occupied Palestinian Territories and products created in the illegal settlements within those territories are not covered by the EU-Israel Association Agreement, which means that settlement goods do not benefit from tariff reductions and cannot be labelled "Made in Israel".

Call on governments to legislate

As well as calling on individual companies to stop doing business in and with the settlements, Amnesty is calling on governments to make this mandatory through regulation, and to introduce laws prohibiting the import of settlement goods. Each year, hundreds of millions of pounds' worth of goods produced in the settlements are exported internationally, despite the fact that most countries around the world have officially condemned the settlements as illegal under international law. In the UK, imported settlement goods include oranges, dates, spring water and halva desserts.

The Irish Parliament is currently in the process of approving a landmark bill which would prohibit trade in goods and services with settlements, and Amnesty is calling on other countries to do likewise.

52-year occupation

During the course of nearly 52 years of occupation, more than 50,000 Palestinian homes and structures have been demolished, and tens of thousands of Palestinians have been forcibly removed. In their place, more than 600,000 Israeli settlers have been allowed to move into often purpose-built settlements, approximately 250 in number, with many of the settlements serviced by settler-only roads and guarded by a network of Israeli military checkpoints and other security infrastructure. The settlements are illegal under international law and are a war crime. In total, approximately 2,000 square kilometres of Palestinian land has been illegally appropriated for Israeli settlers in the past half-century.

You can download the full report from here: https://www.amnesty.org.uk/files/2019-03/Think%20Twice%20report.pdf?BrN9N0VX3RkzTJROuKYC46LE43hCPtTu=

6 years after Rachel Corrie was killed in Gaza, little has changed
by SINEM CENGIZ, 16*th* March 2019 from Arab News

A woman gives balloons to an Israeli soldier near the border between Israel and Gaza on its Israeli side on March 15, 2019. (REUTERS/Amir Cohen)

"No amount of reading, attendance at conferences, documentary viewing and word-of-mouth could have prepared me for the reality of the situation here," wrote Rachel Corrie. "You just can't imagine it unless you see it."

These words, describing the suffering of Palestinians she had witnessed, were in the last letter she sent to her family, shortly before her murder. Sixteen years ago today, the 23-year-old American peace activist was killed in Gaza by a bulldozer driven by an Israeli soldier.

Corrie arrived in Gaza in January 2003 at a time when the second intifada was at its peak, fueled by the demolition of Palestinian homes. On March 16, she stood in front of an Israeli bulldozer in an attempt to prevent it from demolishing the home of a Palestinian family. She thought that because she was a foreigner, the bulldozer driver would not risk harming her. She was wrong, and was crushed to death as the vehicle ran over her without stopping, according to witnesses, who said that the driver must have seen her.

The Israeli authorities deny that the driver deliberately drove over her, claiming that his view was restricted and he did not see her. Corrie dedicated her life to defending the rights of Palestinians and has become an icon of global solidarity with them. Her name is now synonymous with the Palestinian cause, and was chosen as the name for an Irish aid ship that sailed for Gaza in 2010. Her story has been told in several documentaries about Palestinian suffering, and continues to inspire activism and compassion.

The issue of settlements is one of the most contentious in the efforts to resume Israeli-Palestinian peace talks, which have been stagnant since 2014. According to a Palestine Liberation Organization report published in January, Israeli authorities approved the construction of 10,298 settlement units in the occupied territories last year, a decision that further weakens the chances for a two-state solution to the Israeli-Palestinian conflict.

Corrie dedicated her life to defending the rights of Palestinians and has become an icon of global solidarity with them.

Sinem Cengiz

The international community considers Israeli settlements to be illegal and a major obstacle to the Middle East peace process. However, Israeli Prime Minister Benjamin Netanyahu continues to use the issue of settlements as a propaganda tool for the elections in Israel next month.

On this, the 16th anniversary of Corrie's death, renewed violence in the Palestinian territories is a reminder of how little has changed since she died. Tensions have risen again due to the recent raids on the Al-Aqsa Mosque complex in East Jerusalem. The Arab League has urged the international community to put pressure on Israel to halt its "grave violations" against the mosque, while the Jordanian minister of religious affairs said "the closure of the Al-Aqsa Mosque by Israeli police constitutes blatant aggression. It is a violation of all religious and human values, understandings and agreements with Israel." Turkey also reacted harshly to the Israeli raids, saying it will not tolerate brazen attacks on holy places and the world must react.

The diplomatic status of Jerusalem, known as Al-Quds in Arabic, is a hugely complex and sensitive issue. The city is considered a holy place in Judaism, Christianity and Islam, and any change in its status risks serious repercussions across the Middle East. Its status is therefore a key issue in the Israeli-Palestinian conflict, with each side claiming the city as its capital. According to the 1993 Israel-Palestinian peace accord, the city's final status is supposed to be discussed in future peace talks.

The leaders of Turkey and Israel exchanged harsh words after Netanyahu's recent comment that "Israel is the nation-state of the Jewish people, and not anyone else." Relations between Turkey and Israel have experienced a number of ups and downs politically over the years. However, the status of Jerusalem has always been a sensitive issue. Ankara believes that East Jerusalem should be the capital of Palestine as part of a two-state solution along the lines of so-called "1967 borders." It is opposed to Israel acting as though Jerusalem is its own property, and to the "judaization" of the contested city.

Recent Israeli rhetoric and aggression seems very much related to the April 9 elections in Israel. However, such racist discourse simply stokes the fires of conflict that will claim the lives of more young people such as Corrie. It is very sad that 16 years after her death, we continue to witness such rhetoric fueling the tensions between Palestinians and Israelis.

• Sinem Cengiz is a Turkish political analyst who specializes in Turkey's relations with the Middle East.
Twitter: @SinemCngz

If Palestinians Have 22 States, Israeli Jews Have 200

The notion that the Palestinians have 22 states to go to is a blend of malice and ignorance: The Palestinians are the stepchildren of the Arab world, no country wants them and no Arab country hasn't betrayed them
By <u>Gideon Levy</u>, Mar 16, 2019 from HaAretz

Here we go again: The Palestinians have 22 states and, poor us, we have only one. Benjamin Netanyahu isn't the first to use this warped argument; it has been a cornerstone of Zionist propaganda that we've imbibed with our mothers' milk. But he returned to it last week. "The Arab citizens have 22 states. They don't need another one," he said on Likud TV.

If the Arab citizens of Israel have 22 countries, the state's Jewish citizens have almost 200. If the prime minister meant that Arab citizens could move to Arab countries, it's obvious that Jews are invited to return to their country of origin: Palestinians to Saudi Arabia and Jews to Germany.

Netanyahu belongs in the United States much more than Ayman Odeh belongs in Yemen. Naftali Bennett will also find his feet in San Francisco much more easily than Ahmad Tibi in Mogadishu. Avigdor Lieberman belongs in Russia much more than Jamal Zahalka belongs in Libya. Aida Touma-Sliman is no more connected to Iraq than Ayelet Shaked, whose father was born there. David Bitan belongs to Morocco, his birthplace, much more than Mohammad Barakeh does.

The notion that the Palestinians have 22 states to go to is a blend of malice and ignorance. Underlying it are the right wing's claims that there is no Palestinian people, that the Palestinians aren't attached to their land and that all Arabs are alike. There are no greater lies than these. The simple truth is that the Jews have a state and the Palestinians don't.

The Palestinians are the stepchildren of the Arab world. No country wants them and no Arab country hasn't betrayed them. Try being a Palestinian in Egypt or Lebanon. An Israeli settler from Itamar is more welcome in Morocco than a Palestinian from Nablus.

There are Arab states where Israeli Arabs, the Palestinians of 1948, are considered bigger traitors than their own Jews. A common language, religion and a few cultural commonalities don't constitute a common national identity. When a Palestinian meets a Berber they switch to English, and even then they have very little in common.

The suggestion that Israel's Arab citizens move to those 22 states is despicable and mean, well beyond its reference to a common language. It portrays them as temporary guests here, casting doubt on the depth of their attachment to their land, "inviting" them to get out. The amazing thing is that the ones making such proposals are immigrants and sons of immigrants whose roots in this country still need to withstand the test of time.

Palestinians are attached to this country no less than Jews are, possibly more so. It's doubtful whether the hysterical clamoring for foreign passports would seize the Arab community as it did the Jewish one; everybody was suddenly of Portuguese descent. We can assume that there are more people in Tel Aviv dreaming of foreign lands than there are in Jenin. Los Angeles certainly has more Israelis than Palestinians.

Hundreds of years of living here have consolidated a Palestinian love of the land, with traditions and a heritage – no settler can match this. Palestinians have *za'atar* (hyssop) and we have schnitzel. In any case, you don't have to downplay the intensity of the Jewish connection to this country to recognize the depth of the Palestinian attachment to it.

They have nowhere to go to and they don't want to leave, which is more than can be said for some of the Jews living here. If, despite all their woes, defeats and humiliations they haven't left, they never will. Too bad you can't say the same thing about the country's Jews. The Palestinians won't leave unless they're forcibly removed. Is this what the prime minister was alluding to?

When American journalist Helen Thomas suggested that Jews return to Poland she was forced to resign. When Israel's prime minister proposes the same thing for Arabs, he's reflecting the opinion of the majority.

From its inception, the Zionist movement dreamed of expelling the Palestinians from this country. At times it fought to achieve this. The people who survived the ethnic cleansing of 1948, the expulsions of 1967, the occupation and the devil's work in general have remained here and won't go anywhere. Not to the 22 states and not to any one of them. Only a Nakba II will get them out of here.

'The entire world knows the settlers have declared war on us'

In the occupied West Bank, Palestinians living near extremist settlements have been seeing a drastic increase in violence. Israeli authorities refuse to take responsibility, while the villagers are left to fend for themselves.

By Rami Younis and Oren Ziv 17th March 2019 in 972.mag.com

Palestinian women walk by a wall that had been hit by price tag graffiti. The graffiti reads: 'Evacuating Yitzhar = price tag.' (Oren Ziv/Activestills.org)

This past year was, by all accounts, a difficult one for Palestinians living near settlements in the West Bank. According to data provided by the Palestinian Authority's Wall and Settlement Resistance Committee, 2018 saw 614 settler attacks against Palestinians, ranging from property damage to stone throwing and lethal assault.

This constitutes an increase of 217 percent compared to the previous year; 2017 saw 284 incidents of assault, while the PA recorded 255 such incidents in 2016. As of early March, the committee documented 125 assaults — an average of more than two incidents per day.

The attacks, once referred to as "price tag attacks," are committed by extremist Jewish youth from settlements and outposts across the West Bank. Their goal is to exact a price from Palestinians for actions Israeli authorities take against the settlers, usually building enforcement in illegally built settlements. The attacks are sporadic and difficult to combat in real time.

Settler violence has steadily increased since the middle of last December, when Asam Barghouti stepped out of his car and opened fire at a group of soldiers and civilians waiting along Road 60 at the entrance to the settlement outpost of Givat Assaf. Two soldiers were killed in the attack, and another soldier and a civilian were wounded. Following the incident, far-right MK Bezalel Smotrich tweeted: "If there are terror attacks, we won't have Arabs on the roads."

Meanwhile, settlers from across the West Bank set off on a campaign of revenge. In the 24 hours following the Givat Assaf shooting, Israeli anti-occupation organization Yesh Din recorded attacks in 28 locations across the West Bank, from the Nablus area in the north to Hebron in the south. Ever since, Palestinians have been reporting an increase in settler violence. The main victims are those living next to Route 60, and particularly in villages near the settlement of Yitzhar — known for its extremism — and the settlement outposts around Shiloh, northeast of Ramallah.

It is difficult to obtain data from the Israeli side. Most incidents are not reported or are designated by the army as "confrontations" (in many cases the army arrives at the site after the settlers leave, and clashes take place between the army and Palestinian youth). B'Tselem, another Israeli anti-occupation group, investigated 129 of the violent incidents in 2018, in which four people were killed and sixteen were wounded. We tried, to no avail, to obtain information from the army and the police regarding the number of settler attacks. The Shin Bet referred us to the police, the police referred us to the army, which then sent us back to the police. No one knows — no one takes responsibility.

Layers of protection

A Palestinian woman seen outside her home in the West Bank village of Urif. She has installed two layers of metal bars to protect her home from settler attacks. (Oren Ziv/Activestills.org)

"It was completely random — that's what was so scary," says Rumel Sweiti, the editor in chief of the *Al Hayat* daily, which is published in Nablus. Sweiti, who routinely reports on the attacks, was himself the target of assault in early February. "It happened around 10 p.m. near my house in Huwara," just few miles from Yitzhar. "My house is in the northern part of the village, where the settlers have attacked many times," Sweiti adds. "They entered my yard and smashed three parked cars. I complained to the Palestinian police, now we are going to the Israeli police."

Sweiti has been attacked twice before, as have the houses of his brothers who live nearby — but this time, he says, it feels different. "Ever since the Aisha al-Rabi incident (a Palestinian woman killed by settler who threw a stone at her car, R.Y., O.Z.) [the settlers] no longer have any fear or respect for the sanctity of the Sabbath. Now they are entering people's backyards, which they did not do before, even on the Sabbath."

Not far away in Urif, a village of some 4,000 people located in the shadow of Yitzhar, the inhabitants say settlers have been trespassing on their land almost every single day since the shooting at Givat Assaf. They also say that while in the past settlers would throw stones from a distance, today they are entering people's yards.

One of these houses belongs to Munir Suleiman, a father of 10 who makes a living collective scrap metal. The back yard of his modest home — where the windows are now protected by metal bars, thanks to the help of the villagers and the local council — is full of old motorcycles and automotive parts, some of which have been smashed by settlers. "They will do anything to prevent me from earning a shekel, anything!" he says. Suleiman walks with a limp, a souvenir from a previous settler attack.

He shows us the dilapidated house, located at the edge of the village near the high school, where his children live. He long ago decided to block the house's window with stones and concrete. The local council built a fence around the house, which does little to prevent attacks.

Munir Suleiman, fro the Palestinian village of Urif, points the a bullet hole in his home, which was targeted by settlers. (Oren Ziv/Activestills.org)

Every house in the area has bars that were installed when the house was initially built, as well as an extra layer of protective black bars that give the homes a prison-like appearance. On top of the bars is metal mesh, meant to prevent stones from breaking through. Suffice it to say that none of this has helped. "They often use metal rods that cut through the mesh and break the windows despite the bars" says Munir Qadasi, a field worker from Yesh Din who comes here several times a week to document attacks.

On our tour of Urif we are joined by Muntasar Safadi, who works for the local council. He lifts his pant-leg over his ankle, revealing a wound he sustained after being shot by live fire during a demonstration three months ago. Qadasi and the other inhabitants point to the walls of the village houses, which are now pocked with bullet holes. "Sometimes they come down with the army, sometimes the army joins later, after the entire village comes out to defend itself. Then the live fire begins," says Safadi. Suleiman sits down in his yard next to a small decrepit chicken coop, telling us about one incident in which a bullet just nearly missed his head while sitting in the very same spot.

The villagers say they have tried to install security cameras, but the army immediately arrives to confiscate the film following attacks. The army does not do this in order to stop the settlers, they say, but rather to identify the young Palestinians who come out to defend their land and confront the attackers.

Several months ago, the PA held discussions about the possibility of establishing people's defense councils in every village. But operating the councils would be dangerous and problematic: even if activists are not immediately detained by Israel, the councils would require the PA to both pay salaries and provide for other resources. "All this talk about the councils is irresponsible," says Qadasi. "They want the young people to risk their lives and protect us from the settlers with their bare hands — without weapons and without salaries? It's not going to happen."

In the meantime, the inhabitants of Urif protect themselves with WhatsApp groups. "Even at 5 a.m. when someone sends an alert, you will see all the villagers coming to fight off the settlers within a few minutes," Safadi says.

"I am afraid to complain and attract attention to my house," tells us Samir Sawalma, a retired teacher who lives near Suleiman. "I am originally from Jaffa, after the Nakba we moved to Balata refugee camp. In 2000 I moved here to escape the mess there…" Suleiman does not finish the sentence, instead gesturing with resignation as he points to the reinforced windows of his house. Often, he says, he misses a doctor's appointment so as not to leave his house empty. He shows us a note he has for a doctor's appointment for the exact time we are sitting together in his yard. "I am a refugee and therefore get my health care in the camp, but the doctors are very busy. There are not enough appointments and it is important to take any available slot. But how can I leave my wife and children alone?" While we are sitting at the yard, a commercial truck stops outside the gate and the driver honks the horn repeatedly. Sawalma goes out and hugs his son who has just returned from school in the truck.

Muntasar Safadi seen in the West Bank village of Urif. 'Even at 5 a.m. when someone sends an alert, you will see all the villagers coming to fight off the settlers within a few minutes.' (Oren Ziv/Activestills.org)

"Did you notice what is going on here?" asks Safadi as he lights another cigarette. "The drivers are afraid to let the children out of the car alone without a parent to let them into the house. They fear a settler could be lurking, lying in wait for the children. As far as the driver is concerned, he could be honking the horn for another hour and not let the child exit the vehicle alone."

The distance between the high school and Yitzhar is only a few hundred feet, as the crow flies. The settlers from Yitzhar often attack the school, and when the students come out to stop them, the army arrives and disperses them with tear gas, rubber bullets, and sometimes with live fire. Dozens of tear gas canisters can be seen strewn on the ground, a testament to the frequent confrontations here.

Buy during the day, attack during the night

Huwara, a town of 9,000 inhabitants located on Road 60 between Za'atra (Tapuah Junction) and Nablus, has also been a frequent target of demonstrations and attacks by the settlers. From the yard of city hall, we can see the military post situated between Yitzhar and Huwara overlooking the area. On top of the military post flies a yellow flag with the word "Messiah" on it, most likely hoisted by settlers. The Palestinian farmers who come to work their land are required to coordinate their arrival with the Israeli army ahead of time. Access to some plots is denied throughout the year.

"Now begins what we call 'the coordination season,'" says Hawara Mayor Nasser Hawari. "We help local farmers receive confirmation from the army so they can access their land between Huwara and the settlement. Spring is approaching, and people need to plow their land, but we know that the settlers will arrive and make trouble."

Hawari, a man with a ready smile, grows serious when I ask him about what happened during last year's plowing. "The settlers know to wait for us when we come down to our land — it's like an annual ceremony. Last year, 35 settlers from Yitzhar attacked the farmers with stone and rods as the army looked on. They ruined my car, elderly people where hit on the head with stones, and a young man working on a tractor suffered panic attack and stopped breathing. It was a miracle he survived."

Hawara Mayor Nasser Hawari. 'The settlers know to wait for us when we come down to our land — it's like an annual ceremony.' (Oren Ziv/Activestills.org)

Not far from city hall is a girl's elementary school, which was the target of a settler attack in November 2018. On the wall, settlers sprayed painted the words "Yitzhar's Evacuation — Price Tag." The residents tell us that the night the school was attacked, settlers slashed the tires of several tractors belonging Bilal Hajj Jaber, who sells construction materials. When we visit him, a settler from the area is finalizing his purchase, while a teenage Palestinian loads the merchandise onto the settler's jeep. "They buy during the day and attack at night," says Qadasi. Hajj Jaber says that some of his Jewish customers condemned the attack, calling the perpetrators "dogs." He says his insurance company is unwilling to reimburse him for the damage caused by the settlers. "The insurance company told me this is a 'state of war'. For now, I can take it, but what about the others? The entire world knows that the settlers have declared war on us."

Neither the Shin Bet, the army, nor the police spokesmen responded to our questions regarding the increase of violent attacks by the settlers against the Palestinians, and did not accede to our request for additional data on the topic. In their response, the army spokesperson referred only to the claims by the inhabitants of Urif regarding the use of live fire by the army when they came under attack by the settlers, saying "The Israel Defense Forces acts to protect the security and fabric of life of all inhabitants of the region. Lately, a number of incidents occurred in the vicinity of Urif. IDF forces acted to maintain order using crowd-dispersal means. As far as we know, no live fire was used by the IDF in recent months against demonstrators in the area of the village."

This article was first published in Hebrew on Local Call.

Understanding Israel's deception regarding citizenship vs. Jewish nationality
Jonathan Ofir on March 14, 2019 from Mondoweiss

People are often confused by the difference between citizenship and nationality when it comes to Israel. This issue most recently came up in the spat between Israeli celebrity Rotem Sela who asked, "when will anyone in this government tell the public that this is a state of all its citizens," to which Prime Minister Netanyahu replied it wasn't, and said that it was a nation state of Jews alone.

This was then further confused when Netanyahu also claimed that all Israeli citizens have equal rights. What's going on here? Is Israel a state of all of its citizens, and do citizens have equal rights?

In short, I would say that Netanyahu was right about the state not being a state of all its citizens, and wrong about all citizens having equal rights.

But it's more complex than that. Israel uses this dual construct of citizenship and nationality to confuse and even downright deceive the international community – indeed even its own citizens. It is my impression that many Israelis don't even understand this fully.

The main confusion lies in the fact that Israel applies the notion of 'nationality' and 'nation' in a *radically different* manner to that which is commonly understood in most of the world today. Normally, 'citizenship' and 'nationality' are basically understood as a one thing. If you're, say, a French citizen, you're considered a French national. No French authority will consider you a 'Jewish' national – that would be racist! You're French? Be a Jew, be a Muslim, whatever – you're still a French national. On your passport it will say 'Nationality – French' – that will be your national identity.

Israel does not, repeat, does not, recognize an Israeli nationality. But we Israelis do have a notation in our passports that says: 'Nationality – Israeli'. How can this be? It is so, because Israel is lying. Israel defines 'Jewish' as a Nationality, along with over 130 other 'Nationalities' including 'Arab'. The purpose of this is to reserve exclusive national rights to Jews only, in the Nation State of the Jewish People. The 'national', institutionalized tie of Jews all over the world, by the Jewish state of Israel, is thus sweeping and extra-territorial.

This is the major, overarching paradigm that is above and beyond citizenship. It stands as a kind of ghost, a shadow, instructing all that the Jewish State does. When this is the case, 'citizenship' becomes a token, an alibi.

It would be folly to think, that when the Jewish Nation aspect is so overwhelmingly central in Zionism and in the Jewish State, that it would not have an effect on that supposedly neutral, democratic realm of citizenship. Of course it does. Yes, non-Jewish citizens can vote, but the Israeli institutions, including its parliament and its land administration apparatus is heavily biased against them. Thus, almost all of the lands in Israel are owned and administered by a state and state-affiliated institutions which have a stated priority to be biased towards 'Jewish settlement'. There is a myriad of laws which more and less directly discriminate against Palestinian citizens (see Adalah database with over 65 discriminatory laws).

And this discrimination goes beyond the citizenship *per se* – this is extremely important to understand. One of the first and most blatant examples of this discrimination is the Law of Return (1950). With its subsequent amendments, the law allows any Jew, their spouse, or even a non-Jew who is a 3rd generation descendant of a Jew, to 'return' to Israel, even if they never set foot there before, and receive automatic citizenship. 'Return' how? 'Return' in the sense that they are supposedly an affiliated part of the Jewish 'nation', arcing across the millennia and times immemorial.

All this could in theory be fine, even if it is a novel mythological application – if it were not for the fact that it has a directly related discriminatory opposite side:

While those who have never set foot in the land are allowed and welcomed to 'return', those who have been expelled from it – the majority of the Palestinian people – are not allowed to return, and not afforded the citizenship that is automatically bestowed upon Jews.

Thus, the issue of 'citizenship' here presents itself in 'absence' – millions of Palestinians should have been allowed to be equal and free citizens – but they are denied that right. How are they denied it? By ethnic cleansing and by denial of their right to return. This is called 'demographic engineering' (see UN ESCWA report on Israeli Apartheid by R. Falk and V. Tilley, 2017). Having applied the engineering (Nakba, ethnic cleansing, etc.), the state can then maintain trappings of democracy (elections, etc.), without endangering the Jewish racial supremacy rule.

Thus, the citizenship afforded by Israel to its Palestinian subjects should be seen as an aberration – an alibi for the grave crime involving the denial of citizen rights to most Palestinians.

Most all Zionists consider this aspect an absolutely clear, legitimate and mainstream position. They frown upon the fact that international law demands the Palestinian return – at the same time taking very seriously that Jewish 'right of return'. This is really Zionism 101.

But this example is only one of many, where the 'national' imperative, that is the *Jewish* nation, overshadows the role of citizenship, and in fact nullifies it – in actual fact, and in terms of its overall significance.

Simply put – Israel's 'Jewish nation state' notion is a means of colonialist dispossession of the native Palestinians. By defining them as mere "Arabs" and defining "Arab" as a nationality, Israel also eases the conscience regarding their dispossession. Thus, Netanyahu, in further clarifying his position in the recent controversy, said:

The Arab citizens [in Israel] have 22 nation states around them and they do not need another.

You see, those other states are just part of a one big Arab "nation". This Zionist concept thus robs Palestinians of their territorial belonging (and Netanyahu is certainly not the first Israeli leader to make such suggestions, they have also come from the Zionist left, see for example Golda Meir). At the same time, when it comes to the 'Jewish nation', the territorial aspect becomes overwhelmingly significant and local – Eretz Israel, the one Jewish State of all Jews everywhere – applying to a macro, global, extra-territorial Jewish 'nation'.

This is, essentially, how I think the nationality and citizenship aspects pertaining to Israel need to be viewed. The 'nation', the 'Jewish nation', is the real lifeblood of Zionism and Israel, the Jewish State. The citizenship aspect is largely cosmetic upon that, hence often used as a masking alibi for the crime against humanity which Zionism and its birthchild, Israel, represent.

About Jonathan Ofir
Israeli musician, conductor and blogger / writer based in Denmark.

Courtroom drama exposes the paradox of Israel's claim to be Jewish and democratic

Arab representatives are forced to jump through legal hoops each time they wish to campaign for Knesset seats

By <u>Orly Noy</u>, 17 March 2019 from Middle East Eye

Ofer Cassif attends a court hearing on 13 March after he was disqualified from running for the Knesset (AFP)

This has become the routine prior to elections in Israel: the Central Elections Committee, comprising legislators from various Knesset factions, disqualifies registered Arab lists or candidates, decisions that are then typically overturned by the Supreme Court on appeal.

These disqualifications are predicated on Israeli law, which specifies that a candidate or list that negates the existence of Israel as a democratic and Jewish state, or incites people to racism, cannot run. The bitter irony is that this clause, originally drafted to keep American-Israeli Orthodox rabbi Meir Kahane out, is now being wielded by his successors in an attempt to prevent Kahane's victims, Arab parties, from running. (Kahane's party, of which he was the sole representative in the Knesset in the mid-1980s, was eventually banned for being "racist" and "anti-democratic".)

This time around it was political scientist Ofer Cassif, on the Hadash-Taal list, who was disqualified by the Central Elections Committee, along with the Raam-Balad list. The Supreme Court session that heard Cassif's appeal inadvertently became a lesson on the paradox underlying the definition of Israel as Jewish and democratic.

Law of Return

The petition against Cassif was brought by Yisrael Beiteinu over statements in which Cassif compared Israel to the Nazi regime. Yisrael Beiteinu leader Avigdor Lieberman's attorney, Yoav Mani, justified the disqualification with a metaphor, noting that if no one guards the door, anyone can enter the room, rendering the inside and outside the same.

"Evil never enters with loud clanging," Mani said, "but rather quietly. The discourse of 'a state of all its citizens' is permeating the public discussion because … you have enabled it." This, from the counsel for a politician who seeks the expulsion of Arab citizens of Israel and has said that disloyal Arabs should be beheaded.

Lawyer Hassan Jabareen, the director of the Adalah legal centre who is aiding Cassif's appeal, noted that world-renowned experts on the study of fascism have also drawn comparisons between the Israeli reality and dynamics in Nazi Germany.

The discussion rapidly got to the inherent contradiction between Jewish and democratic. Justice Noam Sohlberg, a settler from Alon Shvut, persisted in wanting to hear from Cassif as to what "minimal kernel" of the definition of Israel as a Jewish state he supports. The Law of Return, which allows Jews to come to Israel and become citizens, became the litmus test.

Jabareen clarified that Cassif does not support the Law of Return, and inquired whether the Supreme Court is supposed to forbid anyone who does not support it from running for the Knesset. "You want to turn him into the Zionist left," he said sarcastically, noting by that logic, non-Zionist Haredis would also have to be denied the right to run.

Demographic war

The discussion on the Law of Return was fascinating. It was the first time I heard an establishment voice - the court - admit openly that the law was designed to ensure a Jewish majority in Israel, as opposed to the law's traditional rationale that Israel was created as a "sanctuary state" for the Jewish people.

A Jewish majority, evidently, is a moral goal in itself. According to Mani, anyone challenging this perspective should remain outside the Knesset - for if Israel wants to be both democratic and Jewish it must ensure a Jewish majority, by any means necessary. In other words, the demographic war against Arab citizens becomes part of the state's raison d'etre, and anyone who challenges it is marked as an enemy of the state.

Israeli settlers place their flag atop a Palestinian home in Jerusalem on 17 February (AFP)

According to Justice Menachem Mazuz, however, for the threat to become real there must be a programme with real prospects for success, which is not the case for Arab members of the Knesset.

If you stop and think about that, it is a truly astonishing argument. The real meaning is this: to preserve our democratic facade, we will allow the Arabs to play the parliamentary game with a non-Zionist agenda - but only so long as they have no real chance of actualising that agenda.

This is precisely the rationale that allows Balad to run its slate for the Knesset with a platform of a "state of all its citizens," denying exclusive recognition for Jewish nationalism in Israel, because the Knesset presidium will forbid the party from even submitting for deliberation any bill calling for a state of all its citizens.

Recurring humiliation

There is something very frustrating about these discussions. The Supreme Court's convoluted reasoning on the arguments of the far-right - which are more coherent than the court's own position, thanks to the simple fact that they don't even try to appear democratic - is highly disturbing from a civil standpoint. It is very troubling that Arab representatives are made to undergo this sort of humiliation each time they wish to campaign for seats in the Knesset.

Yet, there is still value in these deliberations, inasmuch as they expose another little bit of this inherent paradox. Time after time, we see that it is sufficient to scratch the surface just a little, in order to see the notion of "Zionist and democratic" completely implode.

To further highlight the absurdity, the court next addressed a demand by far-right Kahanists, Itamar Ben-Gvir and Michael Ben-Ari, that the Hadash-Taal list be disqualified from running. Ben-Gvir began: "If it looks like support for a terrorist organisation and sounds like support for a terrorist organisation, it's support for a terrorist organisation!" That was the point at which my strength gave out and I left the courtroom.

Why the media fails to cover Palestine with accuracy and empathy

A powerful Israeli lobby, reporting fatigue and the fear of being accused of anti-Semitism harms coverage, say experts.

By Alasdair Soussi 17th March 2019 from Al Jazaeera

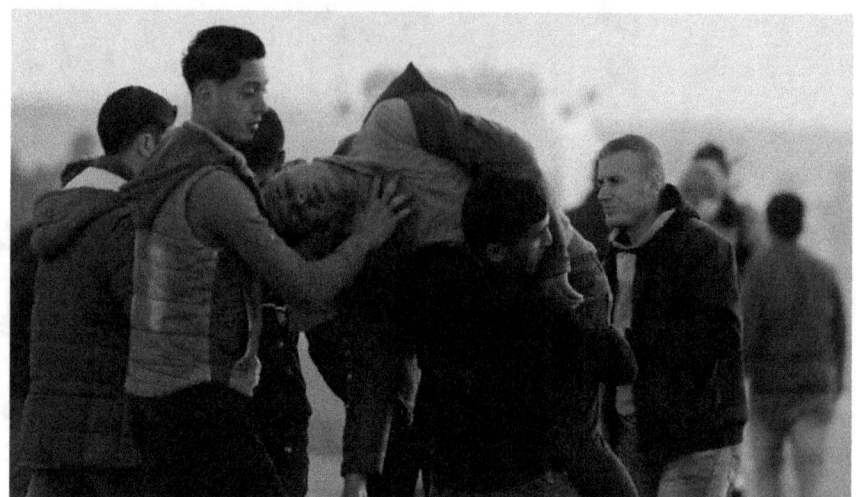

A wounded Palestinian is evacuated during a protest at the Israel-Gaza border fence, east of Gaza City on February 22, 2019 [Mohammed Salem/Reuters]

Often dubbed an open-air prison on account of Israel's and Egypt's ongoing air, land and sea blockade of the coastal enclave, Gaza is, according to Amnesty International and several other rights groups, on the brink of a humanitarian disaster.

In February, Antonio Guterres, the United Nations secretary-general, highlighted the crisis, saying that the near two million Palestinians of the besieged strip "remain mired in increasing poverty and unemployment, with limited access to adequate health, education, water and electricity".

But the mainstream media does not always succeed in telling Palestine's contemporary story with accuracy and empathy.
On Thursday, in the Scottish city of Glasgow, experts discussed the media's role in covering one of the most pressing and divisive issues in international politics.

Al Jazeera interviewed three of the panellists before the event, which was hosted by The Balfour Project, a campaign group created by British citizens to raise awareness over Britain's record in Palestine before and during its Mandate.

"You always come under particular pressure with [reporting on events in Israel and Palestine] because there is an intense and concerted Israeli media lobby - and there always was," said Sarah Helm, a former foreign correspondent for the UK's Independent newspaper. "And that includes a very intense Israeli political lobby working at every single level, which there always was too - and that was no secret and nor would they make a secret of it."
She was based in Jerusalem in the 1990s.

Helm said that her editors would often come "under pressure from the Israeli lobby in London on what correspondents out in the field were doing in a way that was not really true… [for] other foreign stories".

"Because newspapers have been got at and persuaded and pressurised by the pro-Israel lobby, the upshot over time is that the reader hasn't got a clue what this place [Palestine] is."
Today, similar concerns remain.

David Cronin, for example, who had freelanced for The Guardian, wrote in 2015 about his frustrations with the newspaper in Electronic Intifada, where he acts as an associate editor.
Having reported about atrocities against Palestinians committed by Israel, the paper was later "not keen to have me writing from Gaza", he said, adding that one editor advised him to steer clear of covering the conflict altogether.

Time and space constraints also mean that UK media reports neglect the contextual history of the conflict.

This includes the fact that seven out of 10 Gazans are registered as refugees, with many originating from families who were forced to flee their homes after Israel's foundation in 1948.
"It seems to me that certain absolutely fundamental facts have to be high up in any story," Helm said.

The Western media narrative has been dominated by Israel during the entire 70-year conflict, according to Ilan Baruch, the former Israeli ambassador to South Africa.

"Israel was brilliantly successful in offering a narrative to the western hemisphere that was embraced with little or no objective judgement," said Baruch, who resigned from the foreign service in 2011 because he felt he could no longer represent the Israeli government's policies.

Palestinian paramedics carry a wounded protester on a stretcher during clashes with Israeli forces following a demonstration near the fence along the border with Israel, east of Gaza, on March 8, 2019 [File: Mahmud Hams/AFP]

Reporting fatigue also contributes to poor media coverage. Sir Vincent Fean, a former British consul-general in Jerusalem, said that Gaza's "complex and deep-rooted" struggle has diminished the "appetite of Western media".

"In addition to the fatigue, there is also the fact that other crises in the Middle East are bloodier, like Syria and Yemen," said Fean, who was the UK's top-ranking consular officer in Jerusalem from 2010 to 2014. "They take some of the oxygen away from the issue."

In 2017, Mariam Barghouti, a Palestinian-American writer based in Ramallah, wrote in a column for Al Jazeera: "The mainstream media focus is always on Palestinian reaction and not on Israeli action and it insinuates that Palestinians are on the offence when in fact they are on the defence."

In suggesting a way forward, Helm said: "Editors must have the courage of their convictions" to insist historical context enables the reader, listener or viewer to understand the conflict.

"History has been allowed - and even recent history has been allowed - to disappear into a swamp," she said. "And everyone is terrified of putting a foot wrong and being accused of being anti-Semitic that they daren't even ask the [necessary] questions."
As several critics of Israeli government policy find themselves accused of anti-Jewish racism, Baruch, the former Israeli ambassador to South Africa, said the debate needed to move past conflating these two notions.

"Even criticising Zionism as the inspirational movement that created Israel is not anti-Semitism," he said. "[The anti-Semitism charge] is just a ploy to pull down criticism of Israel."

'I don't care about your ID': US student assaulted by Israel soldiers at Al-Aqsa
Tensions have been rising in Jerusalem in recent weeks, after Palestinians re-entered the Al-Rahma Gate area of Al-Aqsa Mosque and performed prayers there for the first time in over 15 years.
By Hanaa Hasan March 14, 2019 in Middle East Monitor,

Three American women were violently assaulted by Israeli occupation forces as they attempted to help a disabled woman at Al-Aqsa Mosque on Tuesday, despite showing soldiers their passports.

Virginia nursing student Nour Hawash, who is in Jerusalem on vacation, was taking photos with her mother and sister after midday prayers when Israeli occupation soldiers stormed the compound and started to evacuate the Dome of the Rock.

"Suddenly we heard these shots being fired and people just started running all over the place. We saw the IDF [Israeli soldiers], guns pointed, running, trying to chase people. So we just ran with everyone else to the side," Nour told *MEMO*.

The number of Israeli troops in the courtyard quickly grew, from a dozen to between 50 to 100 soldiers; Nour also saw several Palestinian men being arrested.

"They were not letting anyone near the Dome of the Rock, they had surrounded it from all its doors," the 21 year-old student says. "And there was an old lady being wheeled out as she was leaving the prayer area and she fell out of her wheelchair and she was unable to get back in. And I saw that a couple of women were trying to help her, but they were being shoved so I tried to go in as well."

However as Nour moved towards the elderly woman, she found herself shoved to the floor by an Israeli soldier, who cuffed one of her wrists and proceeded to sit on her to stop her from moving.

"That's when like ten to 15 soldiers were holding me down with their feet, trying to get my other wrist in handcuffs. And I had pulled out my passport and I told her [the soldier] that I was an American citizen and she said 'I don't care about your ID' and threw my passport to the side."

Other soldiers then dragged Nour's mother, Germeen Abdelkarim, away from her daughter and pushed her against the wall, handcuffing her, as younger sister Safa watched on frantically.

My sister was going back and forth trying to get to us, but she was being physically pushed down to the ground, and punched and shoved, they pulled her scarf off and tried to choke with it so she couldn't come near me

Nour recalls.

After being held down for more than half an hour, an Israeli guard picked up Nour's American passport from the ground and instructed the other soldiers to release her. Both her and her mother were violently shoved away, and pushed back from the Dome of the Rock close to the compound gates.

However all the doors had been barred and the family were trapped near the entrance for an hour, neither able to access the mosque nor the rest of the Old City. Even after the gates were opened, the Old City was held under lockdown for a further three hours, before the women could return to their hotel.

Nour has contacted the US embassy in Jerusalem to inform them of the family's treatment; whilst officials have said they would file a report of the incident, it is unlikely that any further steps will be taken to hold the soldiers responsible for the assault. Other than cuts and bruises, the women suffered no serious injuries.

Tensions have been rising in Jerusalem in recent weeks, after Palestinians re-entered the Al-Rahma Gate area of Al-Aqsa Mosque and performed prayers there for the first time in over 15 years. However Israeli Prime Minister Benjamin Netanyahu has affirmed that his government intends to close the gate once again, despite condemnation from Palestinian officials.
Last week, Israeli forces entered the Al-Rahma prayer area with their shoes on, in what was seen as a deliberate attempt to provoke Palestinian worshippers.
For Nour, whose mother is originally from Gaza, her experience is reflective of the reality Palestinian worshippers regularly face.

"We've always seen these things on TV and on Facebook, you've become numb to it. But actually experiencing it and witnessing the reality of the Palestinians is something completely different. It changed my perspective and honestly we are just scratching the surface of what they go through every day," she concludes.

Under the status quo agreement on Jerusalem, Israeli forces are not permitted to enter Al-Aqsa Mosque, which is under the management of the Jordanian Waqf (religious endowment), or physically attack worshippers.
However Israeli settlers regularly storm the compound in coordination with Israeli forces, performing rituals and pledging to destroy the mosque, whilst Muslim worshippers are harassed or barred from entering. Extreme settler groups have repeatedly called for increasing raids of the holy site, especially on significant Jewish holidays.

The Year of the People: The Untold Story of Gaza's 'March of Return'

By Ramzy Baroud March 14, 2019, Middle East Monitor

A Palestinian woman uses slingshot to throw stone to Israeli forces during a"Great March of Return" demonstration near Al Bureij Refugee Camp

What is the 'Great March of Return' but a people attempting to reclaim their role, and be recognised and heard in the struggle for the liberation of Palestine?

Much has been said about what the popular mobilisation in Gaza, which began on March 30, 2018, represents. Sympathetic views rightly understood the daily protests at the fence separating Israel from the besieged Gaza Strip, as a people frustrated with a protracted and inhumane blockade. Others also emphasised the fact that the protesters are mostly refugees from historic Palestine (today's Israel), who are demanding their right to return home.

Unsympathetic, dubious media reports kept poking holes in the above facts, with Israeli and pro-Israeli media falsely claiming that the popular initiative is a Hamas-driven ploy to embarrass Israel by placing people in harm's way for cheap media attention.

Nearly 250 unarmed Palestinians were killed and thousands more maimed and wounded by Israeli snipers since the protests began.

What is largely missing from the discussion, however, is the collective psychology behind this kind of mobilisation, and why it is so essential for hundreds of thousands of besieged people to rediscover their power and understand their true positions, not as hapless victims, but as agents of change in their society.

The narrow reading or the misrepresentation of the 'March of Return' speaks volumes about the overall underestimation of the role of the Palestinian people in their struggle for freedom, justice and national liberation, extending throughout a century.

Indeed, the story of Palestine is the story of the Palestinian people, for they are the victims of oppression and the main channel of resistance, starting with the Nakba – the creation of Israel on the ruins of Palestinian towns and villages in 1948. Had Palestinians not resisted, their story would have concluded then, and they too would have disappeared.

Those who admonish Palestinian resistance, including armed resistance, have little understanding of the psychological ramifications of strength – for example, the sense of collective empowerment and hope amongst the people. In his introduction to Frantz Fanon's 'Wretched of the Earth", Jean-Paul Sartre describes resistance, as it was passionately vindicated by Fanon, as a process through which "a man is re-creating himself."

And indeed, for 70 years Palestinians embarked on that journey of the recreation of the self. They resisted, and their resistance in all of its forms, moulded a sense of collective unity, despite the numerous divides that were erected amongst the people.

The 'Great March of Return' is indeed the latest manifestation of the ongoing Palestinian resistance.

It is obvious that elitist interpretations of Palestine have failed – Oslo proved a worthless, tired exercise in empty clichés aimed at sustaining American political dominance in Palestine as well as in the rest of the Middle East.

It is only when the Palestinian intellectual, guided by the resistance of her/his people, can repossess that collective narrative, that the confines placed on the Palestinian voice can finally be broken.

The crisis of the Palestinian narrative, however, is relatively recent, thus, through decided and concentrated efforts can be remedied. The signing of the Oslo Accord in 1993 shattered the relative cohesiveness of the Palestinian discourse, thus weakening and dividing the Palestinian people.

Until the Palestinian leadership is itself reclaimed by the Palestinian people as a platform for true democratic expression, it is the responsibility of the intellectual to safeguard and present the Palestinian story to the world in the most authentic, egalitarian way possible. Only then can Palestinians truly confront the Israeli Hasbara and US-Western corporate media propaganda, and finally speak unhindered.

Late Professor Edward Said wrote in 'Covering Islam,' that "facts get their importance from what is made of them in interpretation… for interpretations depend very much on who the interpreter is, who he or she is addressing, what his or her purpose is (and) at what historical moment the interpretation takes place."

Neither the Palestinian historian nor the Palestinian people are at the heart of the stories of the many interpreters of facts about Palestinian history. This predisposition is not only pertinent in the case of Palestine, but an ailment that has afflicted Middle East history, politics and journalism for decades.

Middle East historiography is "a stepchild of orientalism," wrote Dr Soha Abdel Kader, where "Middle East history bears the imprint of its birth up to the present in its use of sources, its methodology, and its isolation."

Palestinian history too faced similar obstacles, thus, for decades, persisted in forced inertia. Most notably, since the commencing of the 'peace process', Palestinian historiography largely neglected ordinary people, and remained hostage to narrating the history of the elites, their political institutions, diplomatic events, and self-indulgent understanding of conflict, whether on a socio-economic level or that of violence and war.

In the Israeli Zionist narrative, Palestinians, if relevant at all are depicted as drifting nomads, an inconvenience that hinders the path of progress – a duplicate description to the one that regularly defined the relationship between every western colonial power and the resisting natives.

Within some Israeli political and academic circles, Palestinians merely 'existed' to be 'cleansed', to make space for a different From the Zionist perspective, the 'existence' of the natives is only meant to be temporary. "We must expel Arabs and take their places," wrote Israel's founding father, David Ben Gurion. The assigning of the Palestinian people the role of dislocated, disinherited and nomadic people without worrying much about the ethical and political implications of such a decision has erroneously presented Palestinians as a docile and submissive collective. Again, they merely existed to be denied that very existence by a powerful, 'chosen', emboldened and ruthless Zionist.

This is why it is imperative that we develop a clearer understanding of the layered meanings behind the 'Great March of Return.' Hundreds of thousands of Palestinians in Gaza did not risk their lives over the last year simply because they required urgent medicine and food supplies.

Palestinians did so because they understand their centrality in their struggle. Their protests are a collective statement, a cry for justice, an ultimate reclamation of their narrative as a people – still standing, still powerful and still hopeful after 70 years of Nakba, 50 years of military occupation and 12 years of unrelenting siege.

Israel orders closure of Al-Aqsa's Rahma gate
March 17, 2019 in Middle East Monitor

Palestinians perform prayer in front of Al-Rahma Gate (Gate of Mercy) of Al-Aqsa Mosque Compound, as Israeli security forces stand guard behind them after Al-Rahma Gate was chained by Israeli police in Jerusalem on 22 February 2019 [Faiz Abu Rmeleh/Anadolu Agency

An Israeli court on Sunday ordered the closure of Al-Aqsa Mosque compound's Rahma Gate in East Jerusalem, according to local media.

The Jerusalem Magistrate's Court accepted a request by the Israeli attorney-general to renew the closure of the mosque, one of several mosques located in Jerusalem's Al-Aqsa Mosque complex.

The Bab al-Rahma Mosque was first closed by the Israeli authorities in 2003. In 2017, an Israeli court renewed the closure order.

In mid-February, Jerusalem's Religious Endowments Authority (a Jordan-run agency mandated with overseeing the city's Islamic and Christian holy sites) reopened the mosque following Palestinian protests.

The Israeli court's decision quickly drew fire from Jordan, which is responsible for Jerusalem's Islamic and Christian holy sites, saying it rejects any "prejudice to its historical situation".

"East Jerusalem, including Al-Aqsa Mosque, is part of the Palestinian land occupied in 1967 and it does not fall within the jurisdiction of the Israeli judiciary under international law," the Jordanian Foreign Ministry said in a statement.

Jordan demanded Israel revoke the decision and held it totally responsible for any serious consequences of the verdict.

Sunday's ruling came amid tension in Jerusalem since last month, when Israeli police briefly sealed the gate, sparking angry Palestinian demonstrations.

In the weeks since, the Israeli authorities have banned scores of Palestinians – including religious officials – from entering the Al-Aqsa, which for Muslims represents the world's third holiest site. Israel occupied East Jerusalem, in which the Al-Aqsa is located, during the 1967 Arab-Israeli War. It annexed the entire city in 1980 in a move never recognized by the international community.

Nightmare neighbours: What if a religious settler project took over Britain?
by *Kamel Hawwash 18 March 2019 from Middle East Eye*

To understand Israel's land grab in Palestine, imagine the backlash if similar circumstances unfolded in the UK

Palestinians demonstrate by the Israeli settlement of Modiin Illit in 2015 (AFP)

The UN Human Rights Council this month delayed publication of a promised database of companies complicit in Israel's illegal settlement enterprise.

Indulge me while I develop this scenario for you.

Imagine a situation in which an extremist British government introduces a law which determines that only British Christians have a right to self-determination in the country, and that settlements built only for Christians should be encouraged.

At a stroke, non-Christian Brits are explicitly turned into second-class citizens. Communities with majority Christian populations set up "admissions committees", to which those wishing to move need to apply for admission, which can be refused. Sound bizarre? Read on.

'The land is theirs'

One morning, you wake up and look out your window, only to find that a group of strangers have forced their way into your back garden, cordoned part of it off and started digging. You challenge them, and they tell you that this is Christian Britain, and as Christian Brits, they can build anywhere because "the land is theirs".

You politely ask them to leave, but they refuse. Instead, they begin to lay foundations, and a truck brings a caravan, into which they move. You try to rip out the fence they have set up, but a couple of burly, armed security guards appear, threaten you, and move the fence further towards your home so they can set up their caravan and toilet. They will likely be there for some time.

In despair, you call the police, hoping they will rush to your aid - but instead, they side with the squatters. You remind them that this is your land and your home, but to no avail.

They tell you to challenge the squatters in the courts. You call your neighbour to tell her what happened, only to find that she has suffered the same fate. You quickly realise that your whole neighbourhood has been taken over by people to whom it does not belong.

Your children return from school, only to find that the squatters have set up a checkpoint to control movement in the neighbourhood, and hired a security company to man it. Your children are in tears after discovering that the squatters took over the part of the garden that was their playground.

Slow wheels of justice

One of your neighbours is particularly upset, because not only did the squatters take part of his land to build a home - they took another part to build a road linking to the main road, and told your neighbour that only they can use it. To make identification of the squatter vehicles easier, they replace the traditional white number plates with yellow ones.

The wheels of justice turn very slowly, as the date for your court hearing is continuously postponed.

On your TV screen, you see politicians celebrate the growth of the squatter colonies; some even move into them, proclaiming that this is what Britishism is about: "liberating the land for Christian Brits".

Israeli activists hold a pro-settlement demonstration in 2007 (AFP)

A court hearing is scheduled in six months. The squatters turn more violent as they harass the residents, and their numbers grow. They are clearly trying to make your life so miserable that you will leave.

The court rules in favour of the squatters, but orders the fence in your garden to be moved a few yards away from your home. You wake up every morning and go to sleep every night humiliated and angry. Exacerbating matters, the squatters build a playground and a pond for their children on your land.

You try explaining to your upset and terrorised children, who now need to be accompanied to and from school, why this has happened and that it is wrong. You tell them that you are confident the squatters will all leave one day, as what they did was illegal, and you promise that you will build them an even better playground.

Turning a blind eye

But when police find out from the school that your children have been telling their friends the squatters have no right to be there, they arrest you, accusing you of inciting your children to hate the squatters. As punishment, they turn a blind eye when the squatters move their fence to take over more of your land. Now, they are within yards of your house.

The caravan has now been exchanged for a house, and your water is used to maintain the freshness of their manicured lawn, while your home receives water once a week, forcing you to buy a water storage tank.

Fearing eviction and losing hope that the courts will uphold their rights, the community calls on those who support justice to help. You ask the international community to step in, but no one seems eager to upset Christian Britain, regarding this as an "internal British matter".

Your community decides to build a database of complicit entities to shame the banks that supplied the funds, not only for the squatter homes, but now for their businesses; and the companies that supplied the construction materials, electricity and internet access that have allowed the squatter colonies to thrive.

An international human rights committee takes up the cause and promises to publish this database. The community is elated: finally, a peaceful way to pressure these companies into cutting ties with the colonies.

International complicity

But the squatters object, and their supporters pressure the committee to delay the database's publication. They accuse it of bias against Christian Britain and claim there are other "disputes" it should focus on first.

Fearing a backlash, the committee delays publication for "technical reasons". The squatters and the complicit entities breathe a sigh of relief and return to business as usual. In fact, the squatters take more land and even offer jobs to the residents - a source of cheap labour. Some take them up on it, as the economy has been damaged by the squatter enterprise.

This scenario might sound bizarre and far-fetched, but it brings home to a British audience what is happening to the Palestinian people. What I describe is their dispossession and continued humiliation.

Israel's land grab continues to this day, making it impossible for Palestinians to attain justice, freedom and equality, seven decades after Israel's creation and the expulsion of 750,000 Palestinians to make way for a Jewish majority.

The injustice should be blindingly obvious. Yet it continues unabated, as the UN's delay in publishing the settlement blacklist came amid pressure from Israel, the US and other apologists for Israeli apartheid, dispossession and oppression.

Israeli occupation demolishes residential home in Wadi Ara

Mar 18 2019 on "Days of Palestine"

Israeli occupation bulldozers demolished on Monday morning a five-storey Palestinian residential structure in Wadi Ara area in the pre-1948 occupied territories on the pretext that it was built without license.

Local sources reported that the bulldozers of the Israeli occupation destroyed a building consisting of five floors in the village of Khor Saqr in Wadi Ara.

The Israeli authorities keep demolishing Palestinian homes in the pre-1948 occupied territories on the pretext of being built without license, which Israel itself puts obstacles against it.

هذا هو الفصل العنصري !
THIS IS APARTHEID !

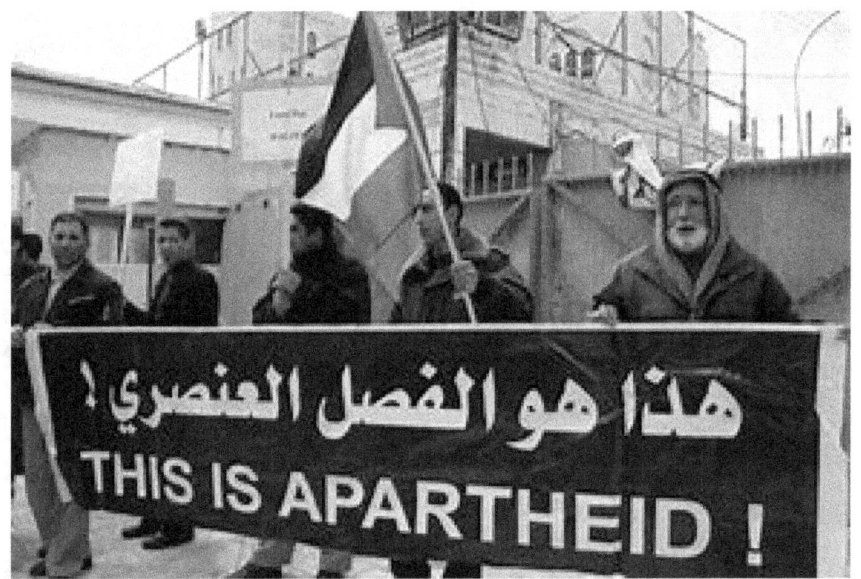

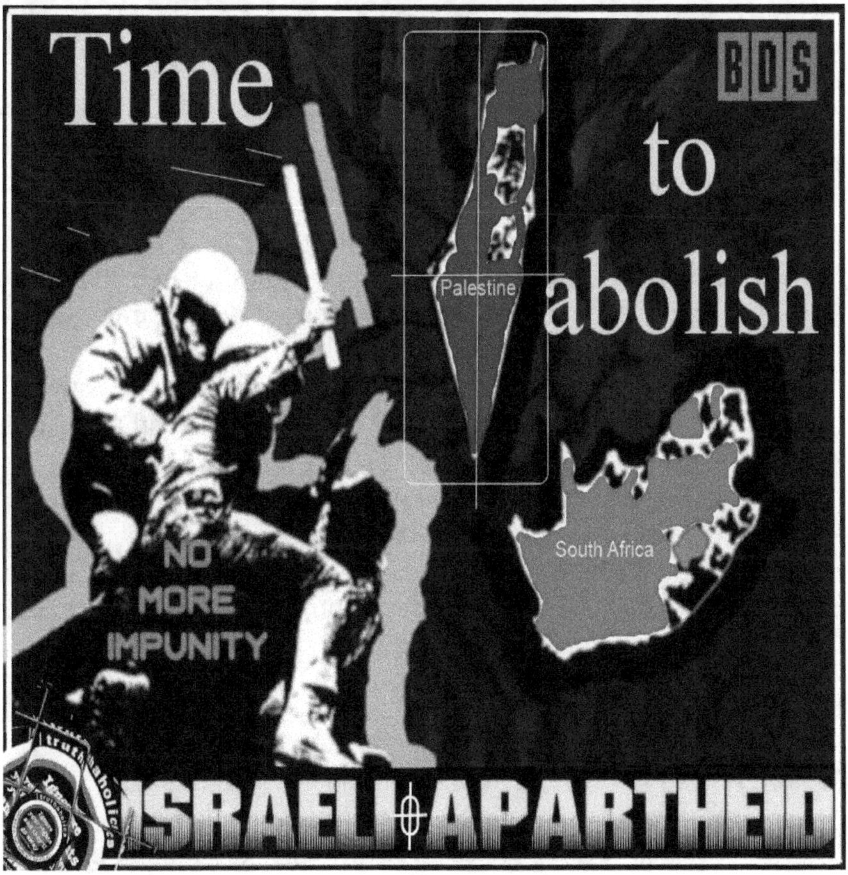

Time
BDS
to
abolish
Palestine
South Africa
NO MORE IMPUNITY
ISRAELI APARTHEID

UN experts urge Israel to stop targeting Gaza protesters
From Middle East Monitor March 19, 2019

Activists laid out 4.500 pairs of shoes in front of the Council of the EU in Belgium on 28 May 2018 to represent every person killed in the Israel-Palestine conflict in the past decade

UN war crimes investigators yesterday called on Israel to stop its snipers using lethal force against protesters in the Gaza Strip, as the anniversary approached of the start of demonstrations there, *Reuters* reported.

The Commission of Inquiry said Israel should investigate the shooting of more than 6,000 people, far beyond the criminal inquiries it has announced into 11 killings.

"The most important thing for the government of Israel is to review the rules of engagement immediately and to ensure that the rules of engagement are according to accepted international law standards," the commission's chairman Santiago Canton told the Human Rights Council.

Israel says the UN council is biased, and it boycotted the day-long debate.

Canton said Israel's Supreme Court should review the confidential rules governing lethal force after the panel found it had been "in the majority of cases authorised unlawfully".

"In a situation of crowd control, which is the way we see these demonstrations, rubber bullets could have been used," Canton told reporters, rather than "high-velocity bullets and long-range sniper rifles equipped with sophisticated optical aiming devices".

Large crowds are expected to mark the anniversary of the start of the Gaza demonstrations on 30 March, he said.
The protesters were demanding that Israel ease its blockade of Gaza and recognise their right to return to lands their families were forced out of to make way for the creation of the state of Israel in 1948.
The commission's preliminary report said last month that Israeli security forces may have committed war crimes and crimes against humanity in its response.
Canton said the independent experts were sending their confidential list of suspected perpetrators to UN human rights chief Michelle Bachelet, for forwarding to the International Criminal Court, which opened a preliminary examination of alleged Israeli abuses in 2015.

Earlier, a UN human rights investigator said Israel was depriving millions of Palestinians of access to regular clean water supplies and stripping the land of minerals "in an apparent act of pillage".

UN special rapporteur Michael Lynk said Israel "continues full-steam with settlement expansion" in the West Bank, which the United Nations and many countries deem illegal. There were 20,000-25,000 new settlers a year, he said.

Report: 449,805 Jewish settlers live in occupied West Bank
March 19, 2019 in Middle East Monitor

The number of illegal Jewish settlers who live in the occupied West Bank reached 449,805 in January this year, Israeli TV *Channel 7* reported yesterday.
According to the station, these Jewish settlers are distributed among 11 illegal settlement blocks across the occupied West Bank.

Settlements are illegal under international law, however, Israel continues with the policy with US backing.

Last year, the number of settlers was 453,159, while in 2014 it was 372,681 in the occupied West Bank, the Israeli TV said.

Israeli forces intervene in a brawl between Palestinians and Jewish settlers within in Ras Karkar village west of Ramallah, West Bank on 28 August, 2018 [Issam Rimawi/Anadolu Agency

The reported that the number of illegal Jewish settlers is expected to rise to 464,000 this year and to more than a million in 2041.

Forty-three per cent of the settlers live in the largest three settlements of Modi'in Illit, Maale Adumim, and Ariel.

The figure does not take into account settlers living in occupied East Jerusalem which Israel annex in 1967 and which the US unilaterally declared Israel's undivided capital in December 2017 in contravention to international laws and treaties signed.
Israeli Prime Minister Benjamin Netanyahu announced yesterday that construction would begin today on 840 new settlement units in the illegal settlement of Ariel in the Salfit District of the occupied West Bank.

Israel cuts water supply to 2,600 Palestinians in Jordan Valley

March 7, 2019 in MEMO

Israeli forces can be seen confiscating water pipes in the Jordan Valley [Ma'an News Agency]

Israeli forces and the Israeli Civil Administration cut the water supply to 2,600 of Palestinians living in communities in Bardala village in the Jordan Valley, northern occupied West Bank, yesterday.

Mutaz Bisharat, an official who monitors settlement activity in Tubas/Jordan Valley, told *Ma'an* that Israeli forces cut off water supply for 60 per cent of residents of the Bardala village; amounting to 2,600 people.

Israeli forces also cut off water supplies for 1,800-2,000 dunams (445-494 acres) of Palestinian agricultural lands that must be continuously irrigated.

Bisharat added that Israel claims that water sources in the area are illegal, adding that this cannot be true because the water comes from wells in the village and inside Palestinian lands.

He pointed out that as Israeli forces cut off water supplies for Palestinians, they construct wells for Israeli settlers.

Bisharat called upon international and humanitarian institutions to immediately intervene to stop Israeli violations of human rights.

The Jordan Valley forms a third of the occupied West Bank, with 88 per cent of its land classified as "Area C" which falls under full Israeli military control.

Jordan Valley residents mostly live in enclaves closed off by Israeli military zones, checkpoints, and more than 30 illegal Israeli settlements.

Brazen Settlement Expansion Underscores Urgency to Publish Database

Item 7 General Debate, 18th March 2019 from Human Rights Watch

As Israeli authorities expand settlements at an "unprecedented high level," in the words of a recent European Union report, it is more urgent than ever that the High Commissioner for Human Rights release the long-awaited report on the database of businesses facilitating illegal Israeli settlements. Settlements are at the root of serious, systematic violations of Palestinian rights, undermining their livelihoods and economy.

The disappointing further delay in publishing the database further entrenches corporate involvement in the abuses stemming from illegal settlements, in violation of their own responsibilities to avoid such complicity. The High Commissioner has a responsibility to fulfil the mandate entrusted to her by the Human Rights Council and commit to a clear date for publishing this vital report. We note that the High Commissioner has confirmed that the report will be published "in coming months," and we encourage her to take all steps necessary to ensure it is available for consideration by the Council at its June session. States should support publication as a measure of transparency in line with UN Security Council Resolution 2334 and to reaffirm the international consensus on the illegality of settlements.

In addition, the Human Rights Council should ensure appropriate follow-up to the conclusion of the UN Commission of Inquiry on the 2018 Gaza Protests that members of the Israeli security forces and their commanders may have committed war crimes and crimes against humanity. We encourage the High Commissioner to give the International Criminal Court prosecutor access to information about alleged perpetrators shared with her office by the Commission of Inquiry. This includes material about any officials who issued unlawful open-fire orders sanctioning the firing on protesters who posed no imminent mortal danger, who bear direct criminal liability, so they can face possible criminal prosecution.

The High Commissioner should also share this information with credible national judicial authorities, so they can pursue appropriate crimes under the principle of universal jurisdiction.

States should also suspend assistance to the agencies within the Palestinian Authority and Hamas security forces that are systematically arresting and torturing critics and opponents, as Human Rights Watch recently reported. Not a single security officer was convicted for these abuses in 2016 and 2017, the latest years for which we have data. These abuses will continue so long as impunity remains the norm.

Finally, we note that for the first time, the lead sponsors have tabled the accountability resolution under item 2 (relating to the work of the High Commissioner) rather than item 7 (relating to the human rights situation in the OPT).

The onus is now on those states that have used item 7 as a shield for refusing to support the resolution, most notably certain members of the European Union, to demonstrate they were acting in good faith by now supporting the resolution on its merits.

A British Palestinian MP seeks recognition for Palestine in the home of the Balfour Declaration

By Yvonne Ridley March 18, 2019 in MEMO

Layla Moran, British Member of Parliament of Palestinian descent

Britain's first Member of Parliament of Palestinian descent is preparing for a historic debate on Friday to have the government give official recognition to the state of Palestine in what she says is probably the "most personal and poignant" piece of legislation she has submitted since arriving in Westminster.

Rising political star Layla Moran, a Liberal Democrat, sent shock waves through the ranks of the Conservative Party when she overturned a 10,000 majority at the 2017 General Election to take Oxford West and Abingdon which was previously regarded as a safe Tory seat. Now she's making more waves with the second reading of her Private Members Bill this week to have Palestine recognised by Britain as a state.

Since Moran's arrival in Westminster, occupied Palestine, especially the Gaza Strip, has endured some of the worst violence inflicted by the brutal Israeli occupation. In an article on Monday for *The House*, parliament's in-house magazine, she wrote: "Just a few months ago, following the anniversary of the Nakba [the

Catastrophe of the creation of Israel in 1948], horrific images of the dead or injured Palestinian men, women and children were everywhere. The violence was unjustifiable and unacceptable. My heart broke for Palestine and Palestinians. I have family there; it's part of who I am."

She went on to point out that US President Donald Trump's "inflammatory" decision to move the US embassy to Jerusalem in the same period added to the acute feelings of injustice. "His decision and rhetoric served as a catalyst for the violence and to demonstrate his disregard for the peace process, the two-state solution, and Palestine."

Moran, who is being tipped as a possible leader of the Lib Dem Party, explained that, "Watching from my still new position on the green benches I felt, and still feel, a responsibility to do all I can to help restore hope to Palestinians. I now walk through the halls of the place that implemented the Balfour declaration [sic] all those years ago and I believe that Britain has an obligation under that declaration. We have a historic responsibility to speak up. Peace can only be attained through a two-state solution but for as long as those two states are not equal it is unreasonable to put the responsibility of peace talks solely on their shoulders."

Trump's move of the US Embassy to Jerusalem was another stark reminder of the inequality between Israel and Palestine, she added. "It was also a reminder that the UK can and must use its voice, through the [UN] Security Council and all other platforms, to contribute towards a resumption of peace negotiations based on a two-state solution with Jerusalem as a shared capital. Not only do we have a responsibility to do so through our role in the Balfour declaration, but it is also the right thing to do."

The article is extremely critical of the peace process which, she says, is "nowhere to be found" and she accuses members of the international community of ignorance if they don't understand that the process is now "a fallacy". Accusing extremists on both sides of hijacking the agenda she is critical of Hamas, claiming that the movement's "presence is setting the dialogue back considerably."

Last November Moran made more headlines with a scathing attack on Donald Trump when he plunged the UN Relief and Works Agency for Palestine Refugees (UNRWA) into a financial crisis by cutting Washington's annual donation to the agency. As UNRWA's largest donor state, this had a huge effect on the essential services provided to millions of Palestinian refugees, including education, healthcare and social services.

With America edging closer to imposing a "deal of the century" on the Palestinians, Moran insists that it is more important than ever for Britain to step up and use its influence and voice. "The UK can help restore a sense of hope for Palestinians, we can help bring the parties back to the negotiating table, and we can help level the playing field. But we can only do that if we recognise the state of Palestine. Saying that we believe in a two-state solution without recognising one of those states ourselves would be laughably hypocritical if it weren't so damaging."

In 2012, the UN General Assembly granted Palestine the status of a non-member observer state. To date, it has been recognised by 137 of the 193 countries in the world which are UN members.

According to Moran, her bill will pave the way for Palestine's long "overdue recognition" as a state by the British government. "I am Palestinian," she concludes. "There is a Palestinian state, and it is time for the UK to recognise that."

Moran's mother, Randa, is a Palestinian Christian from Jerusalem and the MP still has family living in the West Bank city of Ramallah. Her British father's diplomatic career took the family all over the world. She speaks four languages as well as English — French, Arabic, Spanish and Greek — and is not the only one in her family to enjoy a high profile. Her great-grandfather, Wasif Jawhariyyeh, was a celebrated writer who wrote extensive memoirs about Palestinian life under Ottoman and British rule, before fleeing Palestine after the State of Israel was created.

The 36-year-old's performance on Friday will be scrutinised closely by the Palestinian Ambassador in London, Dr Husam Zumlot. He told *MEMO* last year that the forthcoming debate on statehood will create the right atmosphere for a "just peace" in the Middle East as an entry point to discussion and an incentive to peacemaking. Before moving back to London where he studied for his PhD, Zumlot was the Palestine Liberation Organisation's main diplomat in the United States until, last September, the Trump administration closed the PLO's office in Washington as part of an effort to block moves against Israel at the International Criminal Court.

Should her Private Member's Bill succeed it will be extremely poignant that Palestine's statehood is recognised thanks to a British Palestinian legislator in Westminster, where the controversial declaration was penned by Lord Arthur James Balfour in 1917. Is it an omen that Layla Moran entered parliament in the centenary year of Balfour's letter to Lord Walter Rothschild promising British support for a "national home for the Jewish people" in Palestine? We will know if it is on Friday.

How local resistance challenges power structures in Palestine

By Timothy Seidel, Alaa Tartir 16 March 2019 in Middle East Eye
Despite Israel's flagrant violations of international law, the transformative potential of a mobilised and resilient people should not be overlooked

Palestinians protest in the Gaza Strip on 20 April 2018 (AFP)

On 23 January, Israeli bulldozers razed some 15 dunams (3.7 acres) of Palestinian agricultural lands in the Wadi al-Samn area of southern Hebron in the occupied West Bank.

Days earlier, in the village of Battir, Israeli bulldozers razed and leveled another 15 dunams of Palestinian agricultural lands, uprooting about 60 olive trees. Battir is on the UNESCO world heritage list for its terrace farming and irrigation channels.

Also in January, Israeli settlers chopped down 40 Palestinian-owned olive trees in al-Mughayyir village in Ramallah. The village has come under increasing attacks by Israeli settlers, according to the Ma'an News Agency, including the running-over of flocks of sheep, uprooting of trees, seizure of land, and burning of local mosques.

Escalating violence
The escalation of settler violence was evident again this past week, when Israeli settlers attacked Mughayyir. The UN human rights office said it was "deeply concerned about the protracted and extremely violent attack" that led to the killing of Hamdi Naasan, a 38-year-old father of four.

Since Israel's occupation of the West Bank, including East Jerusalem, in 1967, more than half a million Israelis have moved into Israeli settlements in occupied Palestinian territory, in violation of international law.

Settler violence has social and economic effects, with the UN noting: "Olive-based livelihoods in many areas of the West Bank are undermined by Israeli settlers who uproot and vandalize olive trees, and by intimidation and the physical assaults on farmers during the harvest itself." The number of violent incidents has been on the rise.

According to the Israeli human rights group B'Tselem, "settler violence and vandalism takes place with full backing by the Israeli authorities. Sometimes soldiers take part in the assault; at other times, they stand idly by. The police [make] no substantial effort to investigate the incidents, nor ... to prevent them or stop them in real time."

Settler-colonial violence in the West Bank benefits Israel because it has "gradually dispossessed Palestinians of more and more areas in the West Bank, paving the way for a state takeover of land and resources".

In our new book, *Palestine and Rule of Power: Local Dissent vs. International Governance*, we explore the structures and processes that explain these expressions of violence and Palestinian resistance. In particular, we examine the impacts of settler-colonialism and neoliberalism in Palestine today, along with forms of everyday resistance to both.

Legacy of settler-colonialism
As the opening stories illustrate, the role of land is central in settler-colonial struggles. Our book takes a close look at the legacy of settler-colonialism in Palestine - how it has destroyed in order to replace, and renamed in order to erase.

'Apartheid Road' has a wall along its length, dividing Palestinian and Israeli drivers (AFP)

The second expression of power our book considers is the neoliberal political and economic order defining appropriate behaviour in late modernity, seen most clearly in Palestine in the state-building project. Over the last quarter-century, since the Oslo Accords and the establishment of the Palestinian Authority, the rule of power has been displayed through institution-building agendas and commitments, and expressed in terms of humanitarianism, foreign aid and dependency.

Richard Falk, the former UN special rapporteur for human rights in Palestine, says this neoliberal approach to "peace" has set the stage for what US President Donald Trump calls "the deal of the century" - the essence of which is an economic agenda that, when applied to the structural realities of Palestine, ends up hardening security and softening resistance without changing the victimisation of Palestinians.

Our book explores how neoliberalism and settler-colonialism interact to express a specific kind of power that rules in Palestine today, while also looking at resistance and local dissent.

Such resistance was recently evidenced when Palestinian, Israeli and international activists shut down the recently opened "Apartheid Road" near Jerusalem, which has a wall along its entire length, dividing Palestinian and Israeli drivers.

It has also been observed each Friday as thousands of Palestinian civilians in Gaza have participated in the Great March of Return, calling for an end to the Israeli siege and demanding their right of return.

Mobilising aid
Various elements aim to silence this local resistance; international aid is a key instrument mobilised for this purpose. While international aid had failed to bring a lasting peace to Palestine-Israel, it has successfully set the rules for a securitised version of peace and securitised processes of state-building and political reforms, which criminalise Palestinian resistance.

Falk notes that the achievements and potential of ongoing resistance efforts, as well as their critique of the effects of relying on a neoliberal reconstruction of a people living under oppression, offer important insights into what is happening in Palestine and what needs to be done if a just peace is ever to be realised.

Despite Israel's flagrant violations of international law and the stark failure of the formal Palestinian leadership to address the aspirations of the Palestinian people, the transformative potential of a mobilised, resourceful and resilient people should not be overlooked.

- *Timothy Seidel* *is an assistant professor at Eastern Mennonite University, and* *Alaa Tartir* *is a programme adviser to Al-Shabaka: The Palestinian Policy Network. Tartir and Seidel are the co-editors of Palestine and Rule of Power: Local Dissent vs. International Governance, Palgrave Macmillan, 2019.*

When it comes to condemning Hamas, Israel should look in the mirror
by Muhammad Shehada, 19th March 2019 from The New Arab.

Over the last few days, thousands of Gazans have taken to the streets as part of the "We Want to Live" campaign, in protest of the worsening living conditions in the besieged enclave.

The politically neutral and decentralised movement has emphasised that it doesn't stand against any Palestinian party, but mainly aims to end all policies that make Gaza unlivable; including Hamas' increased taxation over consumer goods, the Palestinian Authority's economic sanctions on Gaza, the intra-Palestinian division and most importantly, Israel's blockade.

Unfortunately, and to the dismay of most Palestinians, the protests were violently suppressed by Hamas' security forces, fearing they would distract from the pressure that Gaza's Great Return March protests have been putting on Israel to ease its blockade.

Hamas leaders even went so far as to state that they believe Israeli and PA intelligence were trying to infiltrate and mislead the crowds to cause unrest in the Strip.

Confirming Hamas' concerns, Israeli propagandists were delighted by the scenes of Palestinians beating one another.

They hastened to engage in an unprecedented show of disingenuous sympathy with Gazans; such events are an opportunity for Israel to further demonise Hamas and blame the brutalities of the status quo solely on the Palestinian leadership.

Suddenly, Netanyahu's spokesperson, Ofir Gendelman, shamelessly acknowledged the misery of Gaza's slow death, blaming none of it on decades of Israeli occupation, or the blockade and regular military assaults that have rendered Gaza almost unlivable. Hamas, and Hamas alone - Gendelman claimed - was the reason for all of Gaza's pain.

Even more outrageous, was Gendelman's admission that all Gazans really want is a "better life, freedom and social justice," and that "they deserve it". Suddenly, there was no more crying out that Gazans are "beasts" - solely dedicated to "destroying Israel".

Other infamous Netanyahu mouthpieces stated that Israel "supports" Gaza's freedom of expression and quest for emancipation. Freedom from what, if not from the blockade and occupation that squeezed the last breaths of life out of Gaza and caused its people to explode?

More ironically, Israel's ambassador to the UK, Mark Regev, posted a video in which he juxtaposed the latest Gaza protests with the ongoing Great Return March at Gaza's separation fence. For Regev, the protests dispersed by Hamas were "real," while the anti-blockade protests were Hamas orchestrated "riots," as if Gazans have suffered nothing from the 12-year-long Israeli siege.

Indeed, Regev deliberately ignored that many of those "real" protesters were the same activists who marched at the front lines in Gaza's Return March, where Israel killed 259 unarmed protesters and wounded more than 30,000.

Similar to the Great Return March, the "We Want to Live" protests also repeatedly, and desperately picked on Israel's aim to demonise the unarmed Palestinian masses

The narrative flipped from Palestinians burning tyres and hurling stones in "anti-Hamas protests," to it being a battle for freedom.

If all this is to prove one thing, it's that for Israel's delusional denialists, there's no looking into the mirror.

Instead, there is essentially a conditional qualifier to acknowledge Gaza's slow death, and its people's call for freedom. Put simply: If

Gazans protest Israel then it's terrorism, otherwise it's a struggle for freedom.

The audacity of this hypocritical selectivity and politicised sympathy with Gaza's suffering - which has been mainly caused by the miseries that Israel has visited upon Gaza's civilian population for decades - was compounded by the disgusting crocodile tears shed by every single Israeli propagandist that condemned Hamas' use of violence to disperse the protests.

However, Netanyahu's mouthpieces purposefully ignore that when it comes to extreme brutality, crimes against humanity, silencing critics and repressing freedoms, Israel instantly sticks out as one of the world's most glaring examples of state-sanctioned terrorism against a largely defenseless population.

It may well be true that in one instance this week, Hamas security forces opened fire in the air to disperse the crowds; but in comparison with Israel's long-standing use of live-fire carefully-calibrated to inflict the severest of casualties on Palestinian protesters; there were no reports of injuries caused by Hamas' few shots in the air.

In response to the activists who were severely beaten by Hamas' security forces, almost all Palestinian political factions - including several Hamas leaders - have denounced the use of violence against Gazan protesters, and are calling for an investigation and an official apology.

Of course people have every right to criticize Hamas' shameful repression of the Gaza protests.

But Israel holds no moral ground to ever criticise any inter-Palestinian affairs when it has consistently chosen to bully, intimidate and abuse Gazans for more than a decade in order to turn them against each other.

The same Israeli government that is now capitalising on the Gazan opposition to Hamas' economic policies, is the very same government that's been sending cash to Hamas, in order to keep

Palestinians divided and prevent the realisation of Palestinian statehood.

Finally, if Israel was really concerned with Gaza's wellbeing, at the very least, its government would not have paved the way to power of a widely-denounced supremacist terrorist group; Otzma Yehudit, which is solely dedicated to the ethnic cleansing of Palestinians.

Muhammad Shehada is a writer and civil society activist from the Gaza Strip and a student of Development Studies at Lund University, Sweden. He was the PR officer for the Gaza office of the Euro-Med Monitor for Human Rights.

UN expert: 'Israel's policy of usurping Palestinian natural resources has robbed the Palestinians of vital assets'

By Yumna Patel on March 19, 2019 on Mondoweiss

In a new report issued Monday by the UN Human Rights Council, officials condemned a number of Israel's ongoing policies in the occupied Palestinian territories, including Israel's exploitation of Palestinian natural resources and its impacts on the environment, and the catastrophic effects the 12-year siege has had on the Gaza Strip.

The report states that as an occupying power, Israel has a responsibility to ensure that Palestinians enjoy "the full panoply of human rights enshrined in international law, in order to protect their sovereignty over their natural wealth."

In what could amount to several human rights violations, Israel has overseen the degradation of the Palestinian water supply, the exploitation of Palestinian natural resources, and the defacing of their environment.

Michael Lynk, UN Special Rapporteur on human rights in the Palestinian territories, said in the report that "Israel's policy of usurping Palestinian natural resources and disregarding the environment has robbed the Palestinians of vital assets, and means they simply cannot enjoy their right to development."

The report reads:

For the almost five million Palestinians living under occupation, the degradation and alienation of their water supply, the exploitation of their natural resources and the defacing of their environment is symptomatic of the lack of any meaningful control they have over their daily lives as Israel, the occupying power, exercises its military administrative powers in a sovereign-like fashion, with vastly discriminatory consequences.

Lynk highlighted three key impacts of Israel's policies on the Palestinian environment and natural resources, including the inability of West Bank Palestinians to control their water supplies, the lack of clean drinking water in Gaza, and Israel's practice of disposing of hazardous waste in so-called "sacrifice zones" in the West Bank.

"As of 2017, more than 96% of Gaza's coastal aquifer – the main source of water for residents of Gaza – has become unfit for human consumption," Lynk said.

He attributed the lack of clean drinking water in Gaza to over-extraction because of the territory's extremely dense population, contamination with sewage and seawater, Israel's blockade, "and asymmetrical wars which has left Gaza's infrastructure severely crippled and with a near-constant electricity shortage."

He went on to condemn Israel's policy of extracting natural and mineral wealth from the Dead Sea, located partially in the occupied West Bank, "for its own benefit, while the Palestinians were denied any access to those resources."

"States are obligated to ensure that the enjoyment of human rights is not affected by environmental harm, and to adopt legal and institutional frameworks that protect against any environmental damage that interferes with the enjoyment of human rights," Lynk said.

The report itself ends in dramatic and condemnatory fashion:

An occupying power that took its responsibilities under international law seriously would rule in the best interests of the population under occupation, and aim to end its alien rule as soon as reasonably possible. It would recognize that the territory's natural wealth, environment and resources belongs to the protected people. As such, it would encourage them to assume increasing authority and management over this wealth as a necessary precondition for a short and successful occupation, and a peaceful and cooperative future. An occupying power governed by these principles would not pillage. It would respect both public and private property. Any development or use of the natural resources would be conducted strictly within the limits of usufruct. It would seek to conserve and to preserve. Above all, it would not appropriate the occupied territory's natural resources for its own gain or exploitation.

Israel has strayed extremely far from these legal responsibilities. Indeed, its temporary-permanent occupation of the Palestinian territory has been the photo negative of what is required of a faithful occupying power. During its five decades as occupant, it has appropriated private and public property without lawful authority. It has regarded the Palestinian territory as its own for acquisitive purposes and someone else's territory with respect to the protection of the people under occupation. Its expropriation of Palestinian hydro resources breaches both international humanitarian and human rights law, and scorns the principles that underlie the right to water. Its usurpation of the territory's natural resources and its disregard for its environment robs the Palestinians of vital assets that it requires should it ever achieve its freedom. The right to development in Palestine has become a dead letter. Can we not do the math to understand that these realities belie any visible path to Palestinian self-determination, and instead lead to a darker future that portends dangers to both peoples?

Yumna Patel is a multimedia journalist based in Bethlehem, Palestine. Follow her on Twitter at @yumna_patel

ENCOUNTERING PEACE: ISRAEL 2019 AND THE ABSENCE OF PEACE
by Gershon Baskin, Jerusalem Post, 20th March 2019

Israeli peace activist on the Gaza border.. (photo credit: REUTERS)

On Tuesday, I lectured to a group of 50 teenagers at the Nahshon pre-army academy in Sderot. I always enjoy meeting these mechanistim who take an extra year before being drafted into the IDF to focus on leadership development, volunteerism and making a commitment to the improvement of our society. They share the same activist attitude that reminds me of my own youth movement days in Young Judaea some 44 years ago. They were very engaging and interested in what I had to say. As always, a group of them followed me out of the room at the end of my talk, and their questions kept coming, even at the expense of their lunch break.

When I entered their classroom, I noticed a poster board they had produced from an earlier activity, on which was listed 20 issues to consider prior to voting on April 9 in what will be their first election. The list included issues such as a party's platform and ideology, its economic plans, the integrity of its leaders, the consistency of the party's policies and actions, the track record of the candidates, the homogeneous nature of the party, security and whether the party will pass the 3.5% threshold. The one missing element that was obvious to me, but is completely missing in this election campaign, is the issue of peace, and our relations with our Palestinian and Arab neighbors. Peace is not only missing in reality, it has disappeared from the political campaign – whose outcome will shape the future of this country for years to come.

I can't blame these 18-year-old Israelis, or their teachers and guides. Peace is absent from the Israeli debate and absent from the agenda of the governments that have led this country in recent years. For most of the last 70 years, the aspiration of peace was part of the stated agenda of most political parties in Israel and part of the agenda (at least in declaration) of past governments. But "peace" has become a dirty word in the Israeli lexicon, equivalent to "Left," post-Zionist and anti-Zionist, and almost likened to treason.

We just marked the 40th anniversary of the Israeli-Egyptian peace treaty. Officially, we also have peace with Jordan. Netanyahu has boasted about Israel's close relations with a number of other moderate Sunni states in the region which share the common enemy and threat from Iran.

The Israeli public is sophisticated enough to understand that the relations with Egypt, Jordan and other Arab countries are not what was once dreamed about when we envisioned genuine peace. Were we just naïve dreamers in the past? Was the aspiration for peace just the empty words of politicians? Can we as a Jewish state in the Arab and Muslim Middle East allow ourselves to remove this from our agenda and our goals? I, obviously, believe that we cannot and we should not.

Oslo was a failed peace process. Olso was not peace. We never reached peace with the Palestinians. We never reached an agreement with them on all of the core issues that we agreed to negotiate when we signed the Declaration of Principles between the Government of Israel and the Palestine Liberation Organization in September 1993. All of those innocent Israelis and Palestinians who were killed after the beginning of the peace process were not the victims of peace, nor the victims of Oslo. They were the victims of the continuation of the conflict and the failure to make peace.

Oslo failed after years of negotiations, and both sides are responsible for its failure. Both sides breached each one of the six agreements that were signed in the framework of Oslo. Both sides are responsible for the failure to reach a permanent status agreement. Both sides rejected the offers made by the other side as being insufficient in their eyes to end the conflict. On both sides of the conflict, there is a firm assertion that there is no partner for peace on the other side. This is not the sole observation of Israelis. Palestinians do not see a partner in Israel. Both sides have very legitimate reasons to believe that the other side is not a partner, and it seems with each passing day that there are more reasons for that belief.

The absence of peace from the agenda of Israel's elections is a reflection not only of the difficulties in reaching peace but also, and perhaps even more so, a statement that the status quo of not having a partner is all right. It seems to the public, and apparently also to the politicians, that the status quo for Israel is acceptable, or better than the option of actually working to develop a partnership with the other side. Negotiations with the enemy are hard. Concessions have to be made. Physical assets – land – has to be turned over. Jerusalem has to be on the table. Developing cooperation, working together, confronting extremists from within – taking controversial positions – these are all elements that have to be met with directly by responsible governments and statesmen and women.

The acceptance of the non-existence of a partner allows our current and future leaders to escape from dealing concretely with the primary existential issue facing Israel – the question of our borders, and the human makeup of the people living under the control of our country and their basic political and human rights.

Throughout this crucial election season, we continue to lie to ourselves that with 50% of the people living between the Jordan River and the Mediterranean Sea being Palestinian, Israel can remain the democratic nation-state of the Jewish people. We can pass laws in the Knesset defining ourselves as the nation-state of the Jewish people only, and we can tell ourselves that we are a nation living under the laws that we create – but that does not change the reality that part of Eretz Yisrael is also Palestine, and that there is another people living under our control who do not live under democracy and will never be part of the Jewish State of Israel.

The political pundits can call this old politics or naïve or whatever names they wish to use – but this is our reality and it will not change until we go back to the basics: that we must return to negotiations with our neighbors and this must be done by governments. This is their responsibility and duty, and it is our duty as citizens to force them to do their jobs.

CHURCH LEADERS REPRESENTING OVER 50 MILLION CHRISTIANS URGE "ECONOMIC PRESSURE" AGAINST ISRAEL

Taken from the BDS South Africa web site 20th March 2019

American and African Christian leaders, representing churches with over 50 million members, have issued a joint statement comparing the situation of Palestinians under Israeli occupation to that of black South Africans under Apartheid. The statement follows a "Pilgrimage Group Visit" to Israel-Palestine by a delegation of American and African church leaders. Part of the joint statement reads:

"WE VISITED PALESTINIAN COMMUNITIES AND HOMES WHERE PEOPLE ARE NOT ALLOWED TO HAVE FREEDOM OF MOVEMENT OR SELF-DETERMINATION [...]

WE VISITED A REFUGEE CAMP OF DISPLACED PERSONS WHO STILL HOLD THE KEYS TO THEIR HOMES CONFISCATED OVER 70 YEARS AGO.
WE MET AND HEARD STORIES OF MEN, WOMEN AND CHILDREN WHO HAVE THEMSELVES OR FAMILY MEMBERS BEEN VICTIMS OF STATE SANCTIONED VIOLENCE IN THE FORM OF DETENTION, INTERROGATION, TEARGASSED, BEATINGS, FORCED CONFESSIONS AND DEATH…

WE MET WITH FAMILIES WHO ARE FIGHTING TO KEEP THEIR HOMES FROM BEING TAKEN FOR JEWISH SETTLEMENTS AND DEVELOPMENTS [...]

WE SAW THE PATTERNS THAT SEEM TO HAVE BEEN BORROWED AND PERFECTED FROM OTHER PREVIOUS OPPRESSIVE REGIMES [INCLUDING] THE EVER-PRESENT PHYSICAL WALLS THAT WALL IN PALESTINIANS IN A POLITICAL WALL REMINISCENT OF THE BERLIN WALL [...] ROADS BUILT THROUGH OCCUPIED PALESTINIAN VILLAGES, ON WHICH PALESTINIANS ARE NOT PERMITTED TO DRIVE; AND HOMES AND FAMILIES DIVIDED BY WALLS AND BARRIERS [...]

THE HEAVY MILITARIZATION OF THE [PALESTINIAN] WEST BANK WAS REMINISCENT OF THE MILITARY OCCUPATION OF NAMIBIA BY APARTHEID SOUTH AFRICA [AND] THE LAWS OF SEGREGATION THAT ALLOW ONE THING FOR THE JEWISH PEOPLE AND ANOTHER FOR THE PALESTINIANS; WE SAW EVIDENCE OF FORCED REMOVALS [...]."

In their statement the church leaders conclude with urging for the option of "economic pressure" and commit to "work alongside the oppressed Palestinian people, to advocating in our own countries among our governments for actions and policies that will help lead to a resolution of the conflict". Click here for the full Church statement.

.The human rights and Palestine solidarity organization, BDS South Africa, welcomes this latest move by Christian leaders. We call on all Christians worldwide to play the role in Israel-Palestine once played by Churches in the isolation of and struggle against Apartheid – to celebrate the God of love and justice, through action! Let's jointly walk with Palestinian Christians, Muslims, our Jewish Israeli allies and all other progressive people around the world in opposing Israeli apartheid, and follow in the footsteps of all our Prophets who insisted on speaking truth to power. It was, after all, Jesus Christ himself who instructed us to "open your mouth for the speechless […] and plead the cause of the poor and needy" (Proverbs 31:8,9) to "defend the poor and orphans; do justice to the afflicted and needy" (Psalm 82:3) and "Dispense true justice and practice kindness and compassion" (Zechariah 7:9).

Story of Ahmad Manasra: Killed while trying to save a family from Israeli soldiers

Manasra rushed a wounded father to hospital. When he went back to save the wife and daughters, he was shot to death.
From PNN Bethlehem, 21st March 2019

On Wednesday night, a Palestinian Youth named Ahmad Jamal Manasra (26) was shot dead by Israeli soldiers at Al-Nashash military checkpoint south of Bethlehem while trying to save a Palestinian family from IOF.

According to local sources, Alaa Ghayada, with his wife and two daughters, was driving back from a family visit from Nahhalin to Irtas town in Bethlehem, passing through Al-Nashash checkpoint. While on the traffic lights, their car was hit from the back by another car. As soon as Ghayada went down to check what happened, an Israeli soldier opened fire at him from her military watchtower. He sustained critical injuries from an exploding bullet (dumdum).

At the time, Ahmad Manasra was driving in the street and rushed to help the injured. He took Ghayada to the closest hospital, and promised him to go back for his family as well. As soon as he went back to save the wife and two daughters, soldiers opened fire at him. He was shot by eight bullets, six of them in his upper body.

Today, Alaa Ghayada remains in critical conditions, while his wife was also injured in the shooting, while Manasra was killed immediately.

Following the killing, hundreds of people went out to the streets chanting for him, while Bethlehem city went on a general strike for his soul, preparing for his funeral today.

Manasra is the fourth Palestinian to be killed by IOF within three days.

Ashrawi: Failure to hold Israel accountable is boosting its extremist racist politics
PNN, Ramalla, 20th March 2019

PLO Executive Committee Member Dr. Hanan Ashrawi in a statement on Tuesday condemned Israeli demolition of a school in the Shu'fat refugee camp, saying this assault on the rights of Palestinian children to an education is part and parcel of the relentless Israeli plans to uproot Palestinians from the occupied city of Jerusalem.

"Israel's policy of home and property demolition is designed to make life conditions impossible for Palestinians in order to displace them from their homes, businesses, and schools and bring them with Israeli settlers in the ever-expanding illegal settlement regime," Ashrawi said. "This policy of displacement and replacement is at the heart of Israel's ongoing colonial occupation, which Israel is working hard to make permanent and irreversible," she added.

Ashrawi noted that the demolition coincides with the ongoing discussions of Israel's egregious and widespread violations of human rights in the Occupied Palestinian Territory, including East Jerusalem, exposing Israel's abject disregard to international law.

"This also coincides with unprecedented expansion of illegal Israeli settlements and the grave escalation of violence against the Palestinian population, especially in Jerusalem," she said.

"As revealed in the discussions at the UN Human Rights Council, it is evident that the international community has a serious human rights and impunity crisis at hand. Israel is committing serious and pervasive human rights violations with impunity because the international community is abdicating its responsibility to hold Israel accountable for its actions," Ashrawi added.

Ashrawi concluded by saying this international failure also feeds into and encourages the right wing and fascism frenzy in Israeli politics, as evident in the objectionable campaign video by Israel's so-called justice minister promoting fascism as an element of democracy. This shameful display of unabashed supremacist ideology must push all responsible international actors committed to human rights and the prospects of the two-state solution to action. Rather than shying away from their responsibilities, states must take swift action to stop this downward spiral of violence, racism, and impunity."

Israel Votes 2019 - The need for political partnership

By Ron Gerlitz from "fathom, journal.org" March 2019
Ron Gerlitz, the Co-Executive Director of Sikkuy, The Association for Civic Equality in Israel, argues that only a political alliance between the Jewish left, the Jewish centre, and Arab citizens has a chance of preventing the Israeli right from continuing in power and that such an alliance is feasible.

Then Defence Minister, Moshe Ya'alon speaks with Leader of the of the Joint Arab list, Ayman Odeh in the assembly hall of the Israeli Parliament on March 28 2016. Photo by Yonatan Sindel. Flash90.

Three large segments of the Israeli public – the Jewish left, Jewish Centre and the country's Arab citizens – face tremendous political challenges in modern day Israel. Substantial differences in ideology and identity separate them, yet the same ultra-right-wing government is battering them all, and all three are seeking an end to that. The best way to oust the present right-wing government is to create a political alliance among the three, and such an alliance, even if not the close to being forged at present, is entirely possible. As things stand now, there *is* no other way. The right wing is consolidating its rule by all possible means, and the prospect of leftist and centrist parties collectively obtaining 61 seats is negligible. If the 10 to 13 seats projected for the current configuration of parties representing Arab citizens (Balad-Raam and Hadash-Taal) are not counted toward the base of support for the next government, there will be no reasonable chance to form a non-right-wing government.

Prime Minister Netanyahu understands this very well and that's why his election campaign has gone on the offensive against Benny Gantz and Yair Lapid, who head the new centrist Blue and White party. Netanyahu accuses them of harbouring extremely dangerous plans, including the intent to form a government reliant on the support of Arab citizens. "It's Bibi or Tibi" he repeats at every opportunity. This theme continues a well-worn and constant effort by the right wing to delegitimize Arab participation in the governing coalition. In light of this, the failure to somehow create a working partnership of the Jewish left, the Jewish centre, and Arab representatives will actually be furthering the chief project of Israel's right wing.

There are two common misperceptions about such a partnership. Among the Jewish mainstream, the misperception that the Arab political leadership is not a valid partner in this respect is attributable primarily to decades of increasingly intense right-wing incitement against both Arab leaders and Arab voters. Meanwhile, the Arab public believes it has no partner in the Jewish left and centre, a conviction undoubtedly reinforced by **Avi Gabbay's drastic pronouncement in October 2017** that he would not join a government which includes the Joint Arab List. The same lesson was hammered home again in early March 2019, when the new centrist party, Blue and White, **supported a disgraceful decision by the Knesset to disqualify the Balad-Raam Arab list from competing in the April election**, a decision **subsequently overturned** by the High Court of Justice who decided to allow the list to take part in the election.

Here, I argue that the typical conclusions drawn in this regard were made in error, and that a reasonable political partnership enabling regime change is politically feasible. Under certain conditions, moreover, it would enjoy broad support from the Arab public and most of the Arab political leadership. Certainly, the Jewish left and centre would consider supporting such a move in order to return to power.

BLUEPRINT FOR PARTNERSHIP: THE RABIN PRECEDENT OF A CIVIL MAJORITY

The second Rabin administration (1992-1995) was the first and so far the only government to rely on the Arab members of the Knesset. In the 1992 elections, Labor won 44 seats, Meretz 12, Hadash 3, and the Arab Democratic Party 2. Shas, which won 6 seats, initially joined the government before leaving in 1993 when the Oslo Accords were signed in September 1993. Rabin's government subsequently became a minority government (with 56 seats) and was supported from the outside by the parties representing the Arab public; Hadash and the Arab Democratic Party. These two Arab parties, it should be noted, voted with the government from the outset in July 1992, with such support becoming critical in enabling the Rabin administration to remain in power once it became a minority government.

The Rabin government shattered the undemocratic notion that the government's base of support must be a Jewish majority, by relying instead on a civil majority. **The agreement between Rabin and the representatives of the Arab voting public** was that so long as the government strove for peace with the Palestinians and advanced equality for Arab citizens of Israel, Hadash and the Arab Democratic Party would prevent the right from ousting the government. Both sides kept their end of the bargain. The Arabs supported the government through every no-confidence motion that threatened to topple it, and for two years had unprecedented influence on government policy. While they were not formally part of the coalition, their support enabled the government not merely to survive but to also carry out the most dramatic moves since the establishment of the state – recognition of the PLO in exchange for the recognition of Israel's right to exist in peace and security, the signing of the Oslo Accords, and Israel's military withdrawal from Gaza and Jericho. The government also took preliminary but important steps to redress longstanding discrimination toward Arab citizens – ending the embarrassing discrimination in child support allowances, recognition for several unrecognised Arab communities, and adding momentum to budget allocations for Arab local authorities. The change in policy and rhetoric was palpable, and there are many in Arab society who both recognise that time as the golden era of their relations with the state and support the re-establishment of such a government. Indeed, an early March op-ed in the New York Times by MK Ayman Odeh argued just this.

The partnership enabled the left to return to power 15 years after the electoral upset of 1977 and to promote unprecedented steps toward reconciliation with the Palestinians, as well as enabling the Arab political leadership to initiate new progress toward reducing socioeconomic gaps and changing policies in a way consonant with the national aspirations of the Palestinian people.

This fragile political understanding between the Zionist left and the Arabs endured many hardships. But the agreement was honored by both sides until a lone right-wing extremist ended it by assassinating the prime minister.

While the Oslo process did not ultimately lead to peace, we cannot know what might have been without Rabin's murder and the subsequent election of Netanyahu, who set his sights on destroying the Oslo Accords. In any case, the shared political objective of the Jewish left and centre, as well as today's Arab leadership, is for the Government of Israel to once again try again to reach peace with the Palestinians – something a right-wing government will not do.

TOWARDS A NEW BLOCKING MAJORITY

I will describe here, a blueprint for a less-than-close partnership in which the Arab MKs are not members of a centre-left coalition but instead support it externally as a so-called blocking majority, as was the case during the second Rabin government. I will also describe what could make this possible in the current or future elections and what actions need to be taken in order to build such a partnership and replace the current government.

In recent years, supporters of the Jewish centre and left in Israel, have witnessed a drastic deterioration of the values they hold dear. The government and the man who leads it do damage to the rule of law and to the independence of the nation's highest court, while augmenting the settlements and reinforcing the occupation. The prime minister and members of his cabinet, regularly incite against the left and against Arabs. Many people believe that the current administration, corrupt and frightened, is leading the country over the edge and into the abyss.

Meanwhile, **Arab citizens are subject to unprecedented and incessant political assault.** Notwithstanding the economic interests behind recent government movement toward more equitable budgeting policies for Arab towns, on nearly all other fronts, the government continues to systematically, frontally and uninhibitedly undermine the rights of Arab citizens. The wave of legislation eroding their civil rights and legal status was epitomized by the now-notorious Nation-State Law in July of 2018 and has been compounded by slanderous ministerial mudslinging that depicts Arab leaders as traitors who collaborate with the enemy, repeated attempts to undermine Arab political representation, and plenty more villainy of that nature.

The majority of Arab citizens, along with the Jewish centre and left understand that the only way to alter this vicious reality is to displace the rightist government. However, none of these three groups can achieve that alone. It can only be done by a government led by the centre or the left and supported in one way or another by the MKs who represent the Arab public, as in the second Rabin administration, which owed its existence to the support of the Arab MKs. Such a government would represent the majority of the citizenry, who despite their significant disagreements and disparities, can still agree on the practical directions that the government of Israel must foster. This majority can, and must, be translated into a functional partnership that will replace the current government.

In a normal democratic system, the parties that represent most Arab citizens would be an integral part of a future governing coalition, but the prospects for that in the current climate seem dim. The external support from Arab MKs for a centre-left government, however (in exchange for fulfilment of a list of demands, naturally), without their being an actual part of the government but while functioning as part of its base of support – *is* an achievable goal and should be a key action objective for anyone interested in a change of government in this next or any future election.

WHY CONVENTIONAL WISDOM IS WRONG

Conventional wisdom says that this is political fantasy and unachievable. In fact, that view is the outcome of three factors: a systematic proactive approach by the right, targeting just such a potential partnership; irresponsible declarations by politicians on all sides of that potential partnership; and barriers that may seem intractable but are not. Here is a list:

To begin with, the Jewish centre and left and the Arab mainstream straddle the two sides of the Zionist-Palestinian conflict. In this potential political partnership, each would accord political legitimacy to the other. Given our reality in which most Arab citizens see Zionism as a racist movement, the Jewish centre and left will find it hard to politically connect with them. Arab citizens likewise find it difficult to connect with a government that adheres to the Zionist ideology that brought them the Nakba and the loss of their homeland. The clear recognition that the alternative to this partnership must be disastrous for both sides, however, is what can make such an arrangement possible.

Secondly, and this is a central impediment, the Jewish public, and the influential figures who shape Jewish opinion on the left and in the centre, believe that Arab political leaders are not prepared to accept such a development. This inaccurate view is based on inadequate familiarity with the Arab political leadership in Israel. The vast majority of that leadership understands that the only route to curbing the government's political attacks against Arab citizens and perhaps also moving us closer to an end to the occupation is via the replacement of this rightist government with a government of the centre-left. If they have an opportunity to choose, in exchange (of course) for clear demands, Arab political leaders will support such a government from the outside in order to block another right-wing government.

THE POSITION OF THE ARAB PARTIES

It is worth examining the position taken on this issue by each of the four parties that represent Arab citizens and are running in April 2019 on two lists, each of which comprises two parties. Members of Knesset from Hadash (an Arab-Jewish party, the full name of which is The Democratic Front for Peace and Equality) speak out consistently on the matter, declaring publicly that they will not be the ones to prevent putting an end to the rightist government. Their message is very clear: If the election results make it possible, **they will join a blocking majority** to enable and support a non-right-wing government.

According to MK Yousef Jabareen of Hadash, their constituency will support this move under certain circumstances. Of significance to this discussion is the fact that the participation by Hadash in a blocking majority during the second Rabin government was led at the time by Tawfiq Zayyad, a distinguished and respected national figure among Arab citizens. This creates support in principle for the process and will make it easier for Arab politicians to tread the same ground again, given suitable circumstances. Jabareen's view is that the realities of an extreme right-wing government under Netanyahu oblige the Arab public to pursue responsible decision making. These are the conditions he believes must be the basis for negotiations about joining a blocking majority: A government that accords full equality for Arab citizens, including reparative affirmative action; that will work to end the occupation based on the 1967 borders, under a clear timetable; and that will guarantee the Arab parties a real ability to exert their influence on decision making, especially in relation to the status of the Arab public and to the question of peace.

MK Ahmad Tibi, who heads the Taal party, was interviewed at length by the Calcalist in February 2019, and declared himself ready to join a blocking majority to prevent another government headed by Netanyahu. The key conditions he sets are: Extensive budgetary allocations for Arab towns, including for housing; an effective struggle against violence in Arab communities; recognition of the unrecognised Bedouin villages in the Negev; annulment of the Nation-State Law; and the appointment of an MK from one of the Arab parties to the chairmanship of the Knesset Finance Committee.

MK Abd Al Hakeem Haj Yahya of Raam (the Islamic Movement's southern branch) said in September 2017 that he supported a political partnership with the left to achieve a change of government and these positions align with the position traditionally taken by the party. The Balad party takes the opposite position, but they are in the minority among the Arab public. A recent survey from November 2018 suggested that 64% of the Arab public support the idea of the Arab parties' joining the government; 80% think that the Arab parties should support the government from the outside in exchange for fairer budgets.

The idea that Arab MKs can't be partners in a process like this was reinforced by the Joint List's decision not to sign a surplus-votes agreement with Meretz in the 2015 elections. The conclusion however, is unwarranted, because it fails to take into account the peculiar circumstances then prevailing, just a short time after the formation of the Joint List. The opposition expressed by part of the list, the absence of an orderly decision making mechanism, and other special circumstances gave rise to a situation whereby signing the agreement could have led to the dismantling of the Joint List when it had only just been created. The crucial individuals in favour of signing the agreement understandably felt that doing so was not worthwhile if it were to precipitate the dismantling of the partnership only just established. But that's not a sign of things to come. In an October 2017 radio interview, MK Ahmad Tibi said that not signing the surplus-votes agreement with Meretz had been a mistake. And Joint List chairman MK Ayman Odeh has already said unequivocally, more than once, that not signing the agreement was a mistake that would not be repeated.

Bottom line, at least three of the four parties representing Arab citizens are expected to support joining such a blocking majority under certain conditions. A thorough understanding of Arab politics leads to the conclusion that, should the votes of Arab members of Knesset be required to form a government of the centre and left that would unseat the right wing government, most of those votes would be forthcoming.

THE POSITION OF THE JEWISH LEFT AND CENTRE

Within the Jewish left and centre, there is strong disagreement on this subject. Meretz unequivocally supports such a step, and Labor tends to support it. There are, however, many opponents within the new centre party, Blue and White. Some among the Labor leadership and even more among the leaders of the centrist parties are still deluding themselves that they will be able to form a government with 61 Knesset seats without the Arabs. Yet this posture is hard to fathom, at least considering the balance of power in the current Knesset, where the leftist and centrist parties (including Kulanu which may or may not join such a government) have a total of 50 seats. Even after the announcement of the Attorney General's decision to indict the prime minister, and following the meteoric rise of Gantz and Lapid's new party in the polls, the polls as of early March give the centre and left parties (including Kulanu but excluding the ultra-Orthodox parties) only 51 seats.

Worth bearing in mind is that in the last forty years, the left has held power only twice, and both times Arab citizens played a significant role in the victory: It was their representatives who supported the second Rabin government. In 1999 too, when there was a direct election for Prime Minister as well as for the Knesset, Arab votes provided the numbers that put Ehud Barak ahead of

Netanyahu. Hence many from the left and some of the leadership of the centre understand very well that the present government cannot be replaced unless Arab citizens are part of the new government's base of support.

RABIN WANTED TO REMAIN PRIME MINISTER; HE HAD NO OPTION EXCEPT ARAB SUPPORT

A few years ago, in an interview I conducted with former Labor MK Moshe Shahal, we discussed a series of meetings he had attended in the 1990s with Hadash chairman Tawfiq Zayyad, during which they forged the understandings which in July 1992 became the basis of Hadash support for the Rabin government. When I asked him how super-security-oriented Rabin had agreed to a minority government reliant on the Arabs, he replied: "Rabin wanted to remain Prime Minister, and he had no other option except Arab support."

The possibility thus exists that after the April 2019 or future elections, circumstances could push the head of the largest party in the centre-left bloc into such a partnership.

Thus far, however, playing the hand dealt by Prime Minister Netanyahu with his accusations about their intention to rely on Arab MKs as their base of support for forming a government, the Blue and White party has refrained from any reference whatever to a possible obstructive bloc with the Arabs.

If the only way though, that Gantz or another future leader in the centre-left bloc can be prime minister turns out to be adding the Arabs to his government's base of support – whether because Likud declines to join their government, because they are politically pressured not to form a national unity government with Likud, or they decide to do something substantive vis-à-vis the Palestinians – the chances are that he will follow Rabin's path and invite the Arabs to join a blocking majority in support of the government.

The outlines of the partnership between the Zionist left and the Arabs during the second Rabin administration, over twenty years ago, must now become the minimum objective for a political partnership allowing the formation of a new centre-left government and perhaps laying the foundations to enable the Arab leadership to join the coalition. Bear in mind that such a partnership, which need not be conditioned on first bridging the deep ideological gaps between the Zionist left and centre and the Arab leadership, can still determine the objectives which the government should be pursuing and what it must refrain from doing. That sort of functional agreement is certainly possible.

CALL TO ACTION

In order to push ahead with this, the relevant stakeholders should not wait for the elections or the day after. The notion that removing the current government is impossible has generated a sense of despair among all three of the potential partners and could well lower the turnout on election day, especially among Arabs. Lower turnout could mean the loss of some seats for the Jewish-centre-left-Arab bloc, a failure to prevent a new rightist government, and a missed opportunity for the kind of positive process that could have followed the election. To seize the opportunity for real change, concrete steps must be taken immediately to encourage the idea on both sides that an alternate scenario is both possible and desirable.

Here, then, is a call to action: Political activists, thinkers and doers, those in civil society, academia and from the political world, must begin work on creating a public atmosphere supportive of this option. They should demand that the leadership on both sides promote it, and should begin writing about it without delay, describing how this political partnership would look: What are the conditions for supporting a government from the outside? Different versions of a potential agreement should be drafted to address different scenarios, including an agreement to outline the dimensions of support from the outside for a centre-left government as well as the conditions for joining the coalition (even though the latter is a very low-probability scenario).

The field of relations between Jewish and Arab citizens is full of ideas, including in writing, about the existing situation and potential final agreements addressing the relationships and the regional situation. The existing documents, however, do not address the crucial matter of political partnerships that could enable the establishment of a government in Israel that would eventually secure an end to the occupation and stabilize these relationships in a positive way.

Thus far, various figures among the Arab leadership have proposed different requirements: the revocation of recently passed discriminatory legislation like the Nation-State Law; real steps to advance equality for Arab citizens, including an end to home demolitions in the Negev; expansion of the jurisdictional areas of Arab towns; significant steps to reduce discriminatory budgeting; and the appointment of Arabs to head Knesset committees. This is about taking steps that are real and substantial from both a practical and a symbolic standpoint, and they are partially implementable immediately. Moreover, the Arab leadership will naturally also demand that serious negotiations be started with the Palestinians, en route to ending the occupation.

Demands such as these, although challenging for the Jewish left and centre, do not contradict the centre-left worldview, so it is reasonable to anticipate a positive response that will assure the support of most of the Arab Knesset members for the new government. And as long as the conditions are met, most of the Arab public will also support this – exactly as they did for the Rabin government.

The political leadership of the Jewish centre-left and of the Arabs must do their part to promote the atmosphere required to breathe life into this partnership after the elections. They will need to speak out strongly to counter voices in both the Jewish and Arab public that try to portray supporters of this idea as politically weak and insufficiently nationalistic.

But even now, especially now, while Prime Minister Netanyahu is leading a no-holds-barred campaign trumpeting the "danger" of such a partnership, the level-headed and responsible leadership on both sides can and should pave the way for a successful working partnership. The leadership of the centrist parties, and of Labor and Meretz and the Arab parties, must move to establish a mechanism to press ahead with thinking and discussion about this, and the party memberships must start pressuring their leaders to act. It is important to create quiet agreements about non-participation in the delegitimisation of the other side, and about refraining from attacking the other side in a way that delegitimises a future partnership. As a trust-building measure, the leadership of the centre and left must avoid supporting any step designed to disqualify any Arab Knesset member or faction and must actively and consistently oppose the attack that the present government is leading against Arab citizens. Regrettably, the new centrist party, Blue and White, decided in March 2019 to support the disqualification of the Arab list Balad-Raam from competing in the upcoming elections for the Knesset (a decision that was later overturned by the High Court of Justice). Undoubtedly this unworthy manoeuvre reduces the chances of creating such a partnership, and serious confidence-building steps will be required on the part of Blue and White if they eventually decide to form such partnership after the election.

THERE IS NO ALTERNATIVE

Given all of the foregoing, a functional political alliance along the lines proposed here will necessarily be a complicated and difficult process on both sides: For the Arabs, it won't be easy to go from being constantly in the opposition to supporting the government, and there are forces in Arab society that will attack such an alliance. On the other side, having become much stronger in recent years, the right will unleash a firestorm against a government that allies with the Arabs, since the delegitimization of Arabs by the regime in power is one of the big political achievements of the right. The streets will be full of demonstrators and the Shin Bet will need to protect the prime minister very well this time.

Perhaps the prospects for such an alliance to come about are not bright. But for those who hesitate I would ask – what's the alternative? In practical terms, what do you propose to do in order to prevent the continuation of right-wing rule, which is corrupting the country, severely damaging the foundations of democracy, leading to ever more violent confrontations with the Palestinians under occupation, destroying the relations between citizens, and liable finally to drown us in blood? There is only one way to prevent this nightmare: To establish a reasonable, rational political partnership between the Jewish left and centre and Arab citizens, one that will enable the government of Israel to try, again, to end the Israeli-Palestinian conflict and give all our children hope and a future in this land.

The article, translated from the Hebrew by Deb Reich, appeared originally in Hebrew and Arabic in September 2018 in "Achievable Alliances" edited by Amir Fakhoury and published by the Research Center of the School for Peace at Neve Shalom~Wahat al-Salam. It has been updated to cover the recent developments of the April 2019 election campaign. Ron Gerlitz is the Co-Executive Director of Sikkuy, The Association for Civic Equality in Israel; the opinions expressed here are his own.

ISRAELI APARTHEID vs S. AFRICAN APARTHEID

	Israel	South Africa
Jewish or White-only cities, housing, buses & restaurants	✓	✓
Violent gov't removal from cities based on religion or race*	✓	✓
Forced Segregation in school by race or religion	✓	✓
Less funding for schools based on race or religion	✓	✓
Mandatory IDs indentifying persons by race or religion*	✓	✓
Gov't Restrictions on where non-Jews & Whites can travel*	✓	✓

END ISRAELI APARTHEID | Apartheid is government policy of racial discrimination & segregation

AdsAgainstApartheid.com

*Defined by the U.S. State Dept as pillars of South African Apartheid

Israel again turning Temple Mount into a time bomb

By Akiva Eldar March 21, 2019, Israel Pulse, Al Monitor

Al-Aqsa Mosque reflects on the floor next to a gate to the compound known to Jews as Temple Mount and to Muslims as the Noble Sanctuary, in Jerusalem's Old City, March 14, 2019.

The government of Israel scored another victory in its struggle against Palestinian Muslims on March 17 when the Jerusalem Magistrate's court issued a temporary closure order against the contested site known as) on the Temple Mount compound. It is now up to Public Security Minister Gilad Erdan to instruct police to reseal the site the court shut down in 2003.

Given the sensitive nature of the area, revered by both Muslims and Jews, this hot potato will likely end up on the desk of Prime Minister Benjamin Netanyahu. A decision to enforce the court order could ignite flames in Jerusalem and the West Bank and spark a crisis in relations with Jordan. However, a stay of the order and acceptance of the Muslim decision last month to reopen the site and use it as a mosque would play into the hands of the political right vying with Netanyahu's Likud for every vote in the April 9 elections. Chair of the Muslim Waqf in Jerusalem Sheikh Abdelazeem Salhab on Feb. 18 warned, "The mosque is a red line." He added, "No Muslim would give up a single grain of its sand." Salhab also said the Waqf, the custodian of the site, planned to renovate the structure and reopen it as a mosque and as offices.

Following the latest court order, the Jordanian Foreign Ministry announced that it does not recognize the authority of an Israeli court over East Jerusalem, including Al-Aqsa Mosque compound, which it views as territory unlawfully occupied by Israel since 1967.

On the other side, the New Right party announced March 6, "Allowing the Waqf to revamp the Gate of Mercy site is a capitulation to terrorist thuggery." The party urged Netanyahu "not to surrender to terrorism." "Laws are enforced with an iron fist not by giving in to a gang of hooligans that identifies weakness and abuses it," said the party.

The last time Netanyahu decided to flex his muscles on the Temple Mount, giving in to similar political pressure in July 2017 and going along with police recommendations to place metal detectors at the gates of the compound, violent protests erupted in East Jerusalem and the West Bank.

In a March 7 article on the Ynet website, lead researcher of the left-wing Ir Amim nonprofit Aviv Tatarsky recalled that at the time, police assured those opposed to the metal detectors that "the Palestinians will simply have to get used to them." No sentence refutes more clearly the accepted assumption that as an alternative to ending its occupation and conflict with the Palestinians, Israel had opted to manage the conflict. In fact, the precise definition of Israel's policy is "fanning the conflict," and nowhere does this policy fuel the flames higher than on the Temple Mount.

The Jerusalem syndrome is not confined to the walled Old City. The right-wing government aims to bury the 1993 Oslo Accord with the Palestinians and use it as a tool to dig the grave of the two-state solution — a solution not feasible in any way absent a change in the current legal status of East Jerusalem.

At the end of January, by virtue of the 1995 interim agreement with the Palestinians (known as Oslo II), Erdan signed a periodic injunction banning the Palestinian Authority (PA) from "opening, operating a representative office, holding a meeting or any activity within Israel's territory."

The order limits the activity of the Orient House, which served as the headquarters of the PLO in East Jerusalem, and of other institutions, including the East Jerusalem Chamber of Commerce, the Supreme Council for the Arab Tourism Industry, the Palestinian Prisoners Club, the Center for Palestinian Studies, and the Office for Social and Statistical Studies. In signing the order, Erdan said, "Extending the closure of the Palestinian institutions is a message to the PA and the residents of East Jerusalem that the State of Israel does not intend to relinquish its sovereignty in East Jerusalem and will not allow any [other] foothold there."

Erdan based his statement on the 1967 decision by the Israeli government to apply Israeli law on east Jerusalem — a decision later anchored in Israeli law. This decision contradicts international law and the stances of UN member states, including the United States. Those states do not recognize the ''unification'' of the city.

It seems that Erdan had forgotten (or maybe he relies on people's short memory) the April 2003 Road Map for Peace in the Middle East, approved by the Sharon-Netanyahu government and unanimously adopted by the UN Security Council. The document, as it appears on the Knesset and Foreign Ministry websites, stipulates that as a first stage and by the end of that year, Israel would reopen the East Jerusalem Chamber of Commerce and other closed Palestinian institutions in the east of the city. The reopening was to be conditioned on these institutions operating only in accordance with previous agreements between the sides.

Israel has not implemented a single line of that clause. Rather, the government has been trying to push out the Palestinian presence from the eastern part of the city, especially from the Old City Basin. The Gate of Mercy/Bab al-Rahma conflict is a typical example of the use Israel makes of the Jewish narrative about Jerusalem while denying the Muslim narrative. Indeed, Muslim worshipers were the ones to break into the Bab al-Rahma building last month, but it was Israel that locked it 16 years ago.

Ran Bar-Yaakov, a Jerusalem researcher of Bab al-Rahma, refuted this week prevailing Israeli-right claims that the site was never used as a Muslim prayer house. Writing in Haaretz, he noted that Bab al-Rahma served as a separate mosque in both the early Arab and Mamluk periods. In his 2014 book, "Eretz Israel in Medieval

Arabic Sources (634-1517)," researcher Uri Tal cites the impressions of an 11th-century traveler to Jerusalem who described "a handsome mosque decorated with all types of carpets, with an allocation of servants, into which many people come to pray."

The first episode of a documentary series by filmmaker Roni Koban titled "The Exceptions," which aired on March 17 on the Kan public broadcasting channel, provides a peek at individuals and groups plotting to demolish Al-Aqsa and other mosques on the Temple Mount to make way for a third Jewish temple. These religious zealots operate unhindered and even enjoy the support of prominent public figures, chief among them the popular ultra-right candidate running for the Knesset, former Knesset member Moshe Feiglin, and Likud Knesset member Yehuda Glick. As far as they are concerned, the Muslims are foreign invaders who should have no part of Jerusalem.

Such victories in the war over competing narratives, closure orders of worship sites in Jerusalem and bans on the activity of civil society bring to mind the saying, "Any more victories of this kind and we are doomed." Throughout history, Jews, Muslims and Christians lived peacefully in the Old City as good neighbors. Jerusalem is far too dear to be abandoned in the hands of politicians and far too volatile to be left in the hands of religious zealots, who would set it on fire.

Why the US decision about Golan Heights, West Bank and Gaza is dangerous
Mohsen Abu Ramadan 22 March 2019 in Middle East Eye

Druze Arabs on the Israeli-occupied Golan Heights hold an anti-election protest outside a municipal polling station in Majdal Shams (Reuters)

The US government's decision to drop the word "occupied" in referring to the Golan Heights, West Bank and Gaza Strip comes as an extension of US policy under President Donald Trump, who has adopted the positions of Israeli Prime Minister Benjamin Netanyahu's rightwing government entirely.

Last year, Trump moved the US embassy to Jerusalem and recognised the city as the capital of Israel. He froze US aid to the Palestinian refugee agency, UNRWA, and demanded a redefinition of Palestinian refugee status by excluding new generations, which would reduce the number of refugees from more than five million to around 40,000.

Expanding settlements

The Trump administration also decided that the continuous expansion of Israeli settlements was not an obstacle to the peace process, knowing that the US ambassador to Israel, David Friedman, is a major supporter of the settlement enterprise.

In addition, the US closed the Palestine Liberation Organisation office in Washington and froze US aid to Palestinians, estimated, according to OECD data, at nearly $7.3bn from 1993 to 2017.

It did not end there. The US government enacted laws to prohibit providing funds to the families of Palestinian political prisoners and individuals killed by Israel, under the pretext of "fighting terrorism".

It also considers any form of criticism of Israel to be anti-semitic, including the boycott, divestment and sanctions (BDS) movement, which is a legal and peaceful form of protest.

These developments are part and parcel of how the US assumes it will deal with the Palestinian issue: through the removal of political solutions based on the Palestinian people's right to self-determination, in accordance with international law and resolutions.

The US aims to replace such plans with Netanyahu's vision for the conflict - that is, to find humanitarian solutions based on economic peace for Palestinian residents. In this vision, the Gaza Strip is separated from the West Bank, and Palestinian communities are turned into scattered enclaves. The goal is to eliminate the foundations of Palestinian national identity.

'Deal of the century'

As the Trump administration's plans become apparent in accordance with the yet-to-be-announced "deal of the century", and as the Palestinian people's right to self-determination is undermined, Arab-Israeli relations are undergoing a process of normalisation to bypass the 2002 Arab Peace Initiative announced in Beirut.

The initiative offered normalised relations with Israel, provided that it withdrew from the Palestinian territories occupied in 1967, and enabled the establishment of a Palestinian state on those lands. At the recent Warsaw summit, the path for Arab-Israeli relations was forged through the creation of a common "enemy", Iran - part of misleading Zionist propaganda that sees a joint Arab-Israeli interest in confronting the "Iranian threat".

The goal, however, is really to create a smokescreen and provide Israel with an opportunity to enter and dominate Arab markets and resources.

A Palestinian boy waves a national flag in Jerusalem on 15 March (AFP)

While Iranian-Arab differences and disagreements cannot be ignored, they can be solved through negotiation and dialogue. This can be achieved in a manner that safeguards the interests of all the parties within an orderly framework - on the basis of not interfering in the internal affairs of the countries involved - and that maintains respect for their sovereignty, interests and wealth.

If this is achieved, the main threat remains the Israeli occupation, which aims to become a major military and economic force that can control the region.

Flouting international law

The US decision to remove the word "occupied", in violation of international law and UN resolutions, gives the Israeli government ample scope to widen its settlement project. This will allow for the confiscation of more land, the transfer of residents and the elimination of any chance for a Palestinian state, paving the way for the official annexation of the Palestinian territories by Israel.

The recent US decisions on Palestine, not to mention other global issues, are not surprising. Trump does not believe in the rules of international law, codified after the Second World War.

Instead, he believes, as colonisers did, that military and economic tools alone are effective in international and domestic political equations, without regard for mutual interests or the principles of international law and human rights, including the right to self-determination.

In this context, the US decision to drop the word "occupied" not only undermines the foundations of international law regarding the occupied territories, but it adopts the Zionist narrative, which describes these lands as a "historic and religious right" for the Jews.

It also cements the denial of Palestinian and Syrian rights, aiming to tear apart the historical ties of the original residents with their land. This decision gives legitimacy to the occupation by allowing it to do as it pleases with these lands, without accountability.

It gives the reins to the settlement frenzy, imposing new facts on the ground in violation of UN Security Council Resolution 2334, which condemns settlements - and it paves the way for possible annexation of these lands by stating that they fall under "Israeli control".

How will Palestinians respond?

This decision strikes at the basis of all initiatives calling for a two-state solution, including the Arab Peace Initiative. It works to prepare public opinion for Israel's solution to the occupied territories, which is based on the administration of the people without the land, dispossessing Palestinians and disregarding refugees' right of return.

Finally, the decision works to "legislate" the transfer of the US embassy to Jerusalem - and the recognition of the city as the capital of the occupation's state - by excluding Jerusalem from being considered part of the occupied territories.

In the face of this reality, and amid the inherent dangers of the US decision, Palestinians must formulate a plan to confront this based on the Palestinian narrative, which must become relevant again on an Arab and international scale.

It is also necessary that the nature of the conflict is highlighted: that it requires national liberation based on international resolutions to fight settler-colonial, Zionist, discriminatory policies - policies that are supported by the US government.

You have the power to stop apartheid: An open letter to AIPAC

American Jews, who play such a central role in what happens in Israel, can put an end to the oppression of Palestinians on both sides of the Green Line. But only if they tell Israelis that enough is enough.

By Marzuq al-Halabi, 22nd March 2019 from +972

Prime Minister Benjamin Netanyahu speaks at the AIPAC Conference in Washington DC, on March 6, 2018. (Haim Zach/GPO)

Dear AIPAC leaders,

In one of his most famous poems, "Think of Others," Palestinian national poet Mahmoud Darwish asks the reader to keep the *other* in mind at all times. This, he writes, should apply whether we are preparing breakfast, paying our water bill, or declaring war. I wonder, then, whether you, as you take part in your annual conference next week think about *us* over here? Do you think about me or my 19-year-old daughter Shaden, who these days is head over heels in love?

Jewish people across the world have much influence over what is happening in Israel, a fact that to a large degree also affects my fate. Thus, as the third wheel in your relationship with the state in which I live, allow me to ask a few simple, banal questions. Ordinary questions, like those in Darwish's poem.

Before you invite Prime Minister Benjamin Netanyahu to address the conference goers, ask him about the daily, unbridled incitement against Israel's Palestinian citizens, people yearn for a decent life, as do all the people of the world — as do you, Jewish-American citizens of the United States. Ask him and his friends about who gave them the right, the power, and the justification to pass the Jewish Nation-State Law, which creates a hierarchy between communities and nationalists, and which is a gateway to a racist state?

When they come to Washington D.C. to speak about the right of the Jewish people in its homeland, ask them about the rights of people such as myself, non-Jews, in their homeland. Do you know of Jewish values that undermine values of universalism, human rights, and democracy? Would you accept a situation in which American Jews are prevented from having the same rights as other citizens?

My questions, of course, pertain to citizens of Israel inside the Green Line. These are residents of the State of Israel whose land was expropriated and never returned, even if it was never put to use. These are citizens, a third of whom are internal refugees, uprooted from their villages and towns in 1948 and forbidden to return, even if they live just a stones throw away. This is the lived reality of 100,000 residents of the unrecognized villages in the Negev, living on borrowed time.

Bedouin women collect their belongings from the ruins of their demolished homes in the village of Umm al-Hiran, Negev desert, January 18, 2017. (Hadas Parush/Flash90)

These people are the indigenous minority from before the 1948 war and the Nakba, making up 20 percent of the general population that lives on 3.2 percent of this country's land. A relatively quiet national minority compared to others living under similar circumstances. A population that gave its blessing to the peace process and the Oslo Accords, one which has always taken its citizenship seriously. This goes for the Druze community as well, which forged a blood pact with the Israeli state, at least until the passing of the Jewish Nation-State Law.

And what about the occupied territories, the Gaza ghetto, and the daily injustices that long ago have been transformed into an apartheid regime? My apologies, but there is no other term that accurately describes what happens every day, every hour, in the West Bank. Jewish-only roads, fences, walls, checkpoints, closure, collective punishment, military operations against a civilian population, and nationalistic settlers, who make the lives of the Palestinians miserable.

Recently, as I made my way to a meeting of the Global Forum of the National Library of Israel, I passed through the city of Modi'in, which was partially established on land conquered in June 1967. There I saw fenced-off Palestinian villages with only one or two entries, under the control of Israeli soldiers. I saw a terrifying wall, which dismembers not only the land but also the lives of those who are forbidden from traveling freely — an elementary right of all people. Speaking to one of the discussion groups, I told them exactly what I had witnessed.

The separation wall in Shuafat refugee camp, in the background is Israeli settlement of Pisgat Ze'ev, East Jerusalem, January 24, 2017. (Anne Paq/Activestills.org)

From a bird's eye view, Israel has never had it better: Military, economic, political, and strategic superiority over the Palestinians and the neighboring Arab countries. It appears that the feeling of being drunk on power has far surpassed the euphoria that took hold of the Jewish community following Israel's victory in June 1967. This new feeling has left Jews in a stupor, effectively legitimizing Kahanism, hyper-nationalism, racism, and belligerence. The Jewish Nation-State Law was born out of this very feeling.

We are on the verge of witnessing Israel turn from an ethnic democracy into a full-fledged apartheid state, and there is no one left to put the genie back in the lamp. Right-wing leaders are exploiting the situation they created in order to frighten Jews in

Israel and across the world of even the slightest possible change in the status quo. Meanwhile, they have succeeded in delegitimizing not only Palestinians on both sides of the Green Line, but any Jewish citizen who believes in human rights. They have not succeeded in establishing a so-called Start-Up Nation, but rather a terrified citizenry subject to constant fear-mongering. The government takes advantage of this fear to justify the occupation's crimes.

The feeling of total victory pushes Israelis to believe that the time has come to defeat the Palestinians once and for all. Yet life has its own set of rules. The fading relevance of the Green Line is creating a demographic balance between Jews and Palestinians between the river and the sea. To deal with this fact, the government will try to deepen its control over six million Palestinians. Oppression will lead to a cycle of resistance, subsequent greater oppression, followed by a popular uprising. More power will lead to expulsions, ethnic cleansing, and crimes against humanity. American Jews could end up paying the price for Israel's actions, and the world may no longer be able to look you in the eyes.

Palestinian protesters seen at the Gaza border fence, during a 'Great Return March' protest, Gaza Strip, September 28, 2018. (Mohammed Zaanoun/Activestills.org)

We can move toward a process of historic reconciliation only after the sense of Jewish supremacy is replaced by generosity, out of the understanding that the Jewish question is intertwined with that of the Palestinian question — that both will be solved between the river and the sea in historic Palestine. And while reconciliation is naturally a long and arduous process, it is preferable to apartheid.

AIPAC leaders, you who live thousands of miles from here, must listen to the voices of those who are not invited to deliver speeches at your annual conference — those whose voices were silenced or purposefully distorted. Please, do not believe those who tell you how good we have it in the Land of Zion. At the very least, cast doubt on what they say.

You, who play such a central role in what happens in Israel, can prevent the worst from happening. Tell them "no more." Perhaps then we can bring an end to the injustices.

Yours,
Marzuq al-Halabi
Jerusalem
Marzuq Al-Halabi is a jurist, journalist, author. He writes regularly for Al-Hayat. This article was first published in Hebrew on Local Call.

Israeli soldiers break into Palestinian school, arrest 10-year-old

Fully armed soldiers enter the school in occupied Hebron, threaten teachers, and take away a child they likely exceeded their authority to arrest because of his age.

By Meron Rapoport 21st March 2019, from +972

Fully armed Israeli soldiers forced their way into a Palestinian school in the occupied West Bank city of Hebron and took away a 10-year-old boy this week The age of criminal culpability is 12 years old under both Israeli civilian and military law.

While the soldiers likely exceeded their authority in this case, it would hardly be the first time that has happened. Israeli soldiers have been documented arresting and detaining far-younger Palestinian children over the years, particularly in Hebron.

The incident this week took place at the Haj Ziad Jaber School in of Hebron, a city in the West Bank where hundreds of Israeli soldiers are permanently stationed alongside hundreds of Jewish settlers and tens of thousands of Palestinians.

While the Jewish settlers living in the same city are subject to Israeli civilian law, Palestinians, even those living on the same street, are subject to military law and can be arrested by Israeli troops — a foreign army — at any time.

According to a report in Ma'an News, which published a video of the incident, the soldiers forced their way into the school and snatched the child from his classroom. On its Facebook page, the school wrote that the boy is a fourth grader.

In the video, an Israeli army officer can be seen grabbing the boy, who appears very young. A few Palestinian adults, including the school's vice principal, try and stop the soldiers from taking the child.

Another Israeli soldier can be seen pushing an older Palestinian man, who Ma'an identified as the vice principal. When yet another Palestinian educator tries explaining to the soldiers that these were small children, the Israeli officer responds in Hebrew, "they threw stones, I don't care how old they are," adding that he would take them to an Israeli police station.

When the vice principal asks the Israeli soldiers to explain what is happening in Arabic, the army officer responds, again in Hebrew: "I don't give a crap about your Arabic."

Most Palestinians do not speak Hebrew and the vast majority of Israeli soldiers, even those in roles that require them to interact with the occupied Palestinian population on a daily basis, do not speak Arabic.

At a certain point in the video, the Israeli officer is seen speaking into his radio, ordering more soldiers to enter the school, saying "there are teachers jumping all over me." Another soldier then threatens to break the arm of another of the Palestinian educators.

When one of the Palestinian educators asks to speak with a higher-ranking Israeli officer, the officer who originally forced his way into the school to detain the small child responds, "talk to whoever you want, I don't give a crap."

Eventually, after the Israeli army reinforcements filled the elementary school's hallways, each clutching an assault rifle, the soldiers take away the 10-year-old Palestinian child and at least one of the adults.

According to Ma'an, "local sources" said that Palestinian authorities attempted to intervene at that point and that the boy was released some time later.

Gaby Lasky, an Israeli attorney who specializes in human rights in the occupied Palestinian territories, said that because the age of criminal culpability is 12, "the soldiers did not have the authority to arrest the boy."

"Every soldier, and definitely every officer, should know that there is no legal authority to arrest or put on trial a child of that age," Lasky explained. Even entering school grounds during school hours with weapons, without a warrant, and without coordinating with the school's administration, is something that should be forbidden. Usually, she said, even the army avoids doing so.

Lasky said she planned to file a complaint against the soldiers for entering the school grounds and arresting the young child

An Israeli army spokesperson responded by claiming that a group of students had thrown stones toward Israeli cars in the Jewish settlement in Hebron, and that following that incident, a "[military] force conducted a warning chat with the pupils, but they were not arrested."

Nevertheless, the spokesperson added, "the incident will be investigated and regulations will be clarified accordingly."

Meron Rapoport is an editor at Local Call, where a version of this article first appeared in Hebrew.
Full videos of this "arrest" are available on YouTube at https://youtu.be/hobWLm6OB7Y?t=4

And whilst you're at it go watch https://youtu.be/kYIaTLL6_d0?t=27 …. Which illustrates the dual legal systems which apply in the West Bank, abusive oppressive military laws for the Palestinians, lax and lenient laws – often not upheld - civil law for the land grabbing Zionist settlers. Aparteid in action laid bare for all to see. Sheer evil.

Israel deprives Palestinians of clean water, UN says

March 20, 2019 from Middle East Monitor

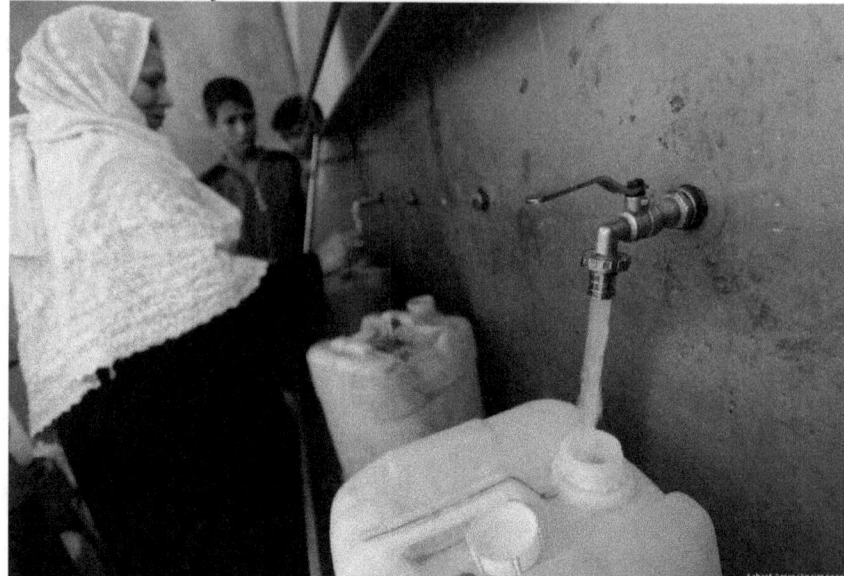

Palestinians fill their bottles at a water purification station due to the lack of clean water in Gaza on 5 November 2013 [Ashraf Amra/Apaimages]

Israel deprives Palestinians of benefiting from natural resources of water which constitutes a "violation of legal responsibilities as an occupying power," Special UN Rapporteur on the Situation of Human Rights in Occupied Palestinian Territory Michael Lynk said.

"For nearly five million Palestinians living under occupation, the degradation of their water supply, the exploitation of their natural resources and the defacing of their environment, are symptomatic of the lack of any meaningful control they have over their daily lives," Lynk said.

He gave these remarks as he presented a report on the impact of the occupation on the environment and natural resources to the Human Rights Council in Geneva.

"Israel's policy of usurping Palestinian natural resources and disregarding the environment has robbed the Palestinians of vital assets, and means they simply cannot enjoy their right to development.

Its approach to the natural resources of the Occupied Palestinian Territory has been to use them as a sovereign country would use its own assets, with vastly discriminatory consequences.

The report said people living under occupation should be able to enjoy their full rights as enshrined in international law, in order to protect their sovereignty over their natural wealth.

"However, Israeli practices in relation to water, extraction of other resources and environmental protection, raise serious concerns."

"With the collapse of natural sources of drinking water in Gaza and the inability of Palestinians to access most of their water sources in the West Bank, water has become a potent symbol of the systematic violation of human rights in the Occupied Palestinian Territory," the Special Rapporteur said.

"As of 2017, more than 96% of Gaza's coastal aquifer – the main source of water for residents of Gaza – has become unfit for human consumption. The reasons include over-extraction because of Gaza's extremely dense population, contamination with sewage and seawater, Israel's 12-year-old blockade, and asymmetrical wars which has left Gaza's infrastructure severely crippled and with a near-constant electricity shortage.".

The Rapporteur said natural and mineral wealth from the Dead Sea, which is partly within the occupied West Bank, were being extracted by Israel for its own benefit, while Palestinians were denied access to them.

"States are obligated to ensure that the enjoyment of human rights is not affected by environmental harm, and to adopt legal and institutional frameworks that protect against any environmental damage that interferes with the enjoyment of human rights," Lynk said.

There are serious concerns about Israel's practice of disposing of hazardous waste in so-called "sacrifice zones" in the West Bank. The impact of Israel's practices may be felt not only by Palestinians, but also by Israelis and others in the region, the Rapporteur said.

The report also questioned the ongoing use of excessive force by Israeli security forces against demonstrators in Gaza, and the near humanitarian catastrophe in the territory caused by the blockade.

Lynk also expressed fears about the fate of Palestinian families in East Jerusalem – nearly 200 of whom are at risk of forced eviction – and concern for human rights defenders facing increasing attacks on their credibility and pressure on funding.

"We must understand that these issues and violations block any visible path to Palestinian self-determination, and are instead leading to a darker future that heralds danger to both peoples," he said.

Israel again turning Temple Mount into a time bomb

By *Akiva Eldar* March 21, 2019 , Israel Pulse, Al Monitor

Al-Aqsa Mosque reflects on the floor next to a gate to the compound known to Jews as Temple Mount and to Muslims as the Noble Sanctuary, in Jerusalem's Old City, March 14, 2019. REUTERS/Ammar Awad

The government of Israel scored another victory in its struggle against Palestinian Muslims on March 17 when the Jerusalem Magistrate's court issued a temporary closure order against the contested site known as Bab al-Rahma (Gate of Mercy) on the Temple Mount compound. It is now up to Public Security Minister Gilad Erdan to instruct police to reseal the site the court shut down in 2003. Given the sensitive nature of the area, revered by both Muslims and Jews, this hot potato will likely end up on the desk of Prime Minister Benjamin Netanyahu.

A decision to enforce the court order could ignite flames in Jerusalem and the West Bank and spark a crisis in relations with Jordan. However, a stay of the order and acceptance of the Muslim decision last month to reopen the site and use it as a mosque would play into the hands of the political right vying with Netanyahu's Likud for every vote in the April 9 elections. Chair of the Muslim Waqf in Jerusalem Sheikh Abdelazeem Salhab on Feb. 18 warned, "The mosque is a red line." He added, "No Muslim would give up a single grain of its sand." Salhab also said the Waqf, the custodian of the site, planned to renovate the structure and reopen it as a mosque and as offices. Following the latest court order, the Jordanian Foreign Ministry announced that it does not recognize the authority of an Israeli court over East Jerusalem, including Al-Aqsa Mosque compound, which it views as territory unlawfully occupied by Israel since 1967.

On the other side, the New Right party announced March 6, "Allowing the Waqf to revamp the Gate of Mercy site is a capitulation to terrorist thuggery." The party urged Netanyahu "not to surrender to terrorism." "Laws are enforced with an iron fist not by giving in to a gang of hooligans that identifies weakness and abuses it," said the party. The last time Netanyahu decided to flex his muscles on the Temple Mount, giving in to similar political pressure in July 2017 and going along with police recommendations to place metal detectors at the gates of the compound, violent protests erupted in East Jerusalem and the West Bank.

In a March 7 article on the Ynet website, lead researcher of the left-wing Ir Amim nonprofit Aviv Tatarsky recalled that at the time, police assured those opposed to the metal detectors that "the Palestinians will simply have to get used to them." No sentence refutes more clearly the accepted assumption that as an alternative to ending its occupation and conflict with the Palestinians, Israel had opted to manage the conflict. In fact, the precise definition of Israel's policy is "fanning the conflict," and nowhere does this policy fuel the flames higher than on the Temple Mount.

The Jerusalem syndrome is not confined to the walled Old City. The right-wing government aims to bury the 1993 Oslo Accord with the Palestinians and use it as a tool to dig the grave of the two-state solution — a solution not feasible in any way absent a change in the current legal status of East Jerusalem.

At the end of January, by virtue of the 1995 interim agreement with the Palestinians (known as Oslo II), Erdan signed a periodic injunction banning the Palestinian Authority (PA) from "opening, operating a representative office, holding a meeting or any activity within Israel's territory." The order limits the activity of the Orient House, which served as the headquarters of the PLO in East Jerusalem, and of other institutions, including the East Jerusalem Chamber of Commerce, the Supreme Council for the Arab Tourism

Industry, the Palestinian Prisoners Club, the Center for Palestinian Studies, and the Office for Social and Statistical Studies. In signing the order, Erdan said, "Extending the closure of the Palestinian institutions is a message to the PA and the residents of East Jerusalem that the State of Israel does not intend to relinquish its sovereignty in East Jerusalem and will not allow any [other] foothold there."

Erdan based his statement on the 1967 decision by the Israeli government to apply Israeli law on east Jerusalem — a decision later anchored in Israeli law. This decision contradicts international law and the stances of UN member states, including the United States. Those states do not recognize the "unification" of the city. It seems that Erdan had forgotten (or maybe he relies on people's short memory) the April 2003 Road Map for Peace in the Middle East, approved by the Sharon-Netanyahu government and unanimously adopted by the UN Security Council. The document, as it appears on the Knesset and Foreign Ministry websites, stipulates that as a first stage and by the end of that year, Israel would reopen the East Jerusalem Chamber of Commerce and other closed Palestinian institutions in the east of the city. The reopening was to be conditioned on these institutions operating only in accordance with previous agreements between the sides.

Israel has not implemented a single line of that clause. Rather, the government has been trying to push out the Palestinian presence from the eastern part of the city, especially from the Old City Basin. The Gate of Mercy/Bab al-Rahma conflict is a typical example of the use Israel makes of the Jewish narrative about Jerusalem while denying the Muslim narrative. Indeed, Muslim worshipers were the ones to break into the Bab al-Rahma building last month, but it was Israel that locked it 16 years ago.

Ran Bar-Yaakov, a Jerusalem researcher of Bab al-Rahma, refuted this week prevailing Israeli-right claims that the site was never used as a Muslim prayer house. Writing in Haaretz, he noted that Bab al-Rahma served as a separate mosque in both the early Arab and Mamluk periods. In his 2014 book, "Eretz Israel in Medieval Arabic Sources (634-1517)," researcher Uri Tal cites the impressions of an 11th-century traveler to Jerusalem who described "a handsome mosque decorated with all types of carpets, with an allocation of servants, into which many people come to pray."

The first episode of a documentary series by filmmaker Roni Koban titled "The Exceptions," which aired on March 17 on the Kan public broadcasting channel, provides a peek at individuals and groups plotting to demolish Al-Aqsa and other mosques on the Temple Mount to make way for a third Jewish temple. These religious zealots operate unhindered and even enjoy the support of prominent public figures, chief among them the popular ultra-right candidate running for the Knesset, former Knesset member Moshe Feiglin, and Likud Knesset member Yehuda Glick. As far as they are concerned, the Muslims are foreign invaders who should have no part of Jerusalem.

Such victories in the war over competing narratives, closure orders of worship sites in Jerusalem and bans on the activity of civil society bring to mind the saying, "Any more victories of this kind and we are doomed." Throughout history, Jews, Muslims and Christians lived peacefully in the Old City as good neighbors. Jerusalem is far too dear to be abandoned in the hands of politicians and far too volatile to be left in the hands of religious zealots, who would set it on fire.

What is 'apartheid'?

Apartheid is a crime against humanity in accordance with the 2002 Rome Statute of the International Criminal Court. Three conditions must be fulfilled for a practice to be labelled as "apartheid":

South Africa	Israel/ Palestine	
✓	✓	Two or more racial groups must exist;
✓	✓	The ruling racial group must carry out inhumane practices against the other racial group or groups;
✓	✓	These inhumane practices must be carried out in a methodological and institutional manner by the ruling race, whose objective is to perpetuate this situation;
✗	✓	Currently practiced through laws and other official regulations?

"Apartheid" is a legal term, not an insult.

It's the most suitable label to describe Israel's treatment of millions of Palestinians over the last seven decades.

The Palestine Project

Talk of Golan annexation leaves out those expelled from it

President Trump's recognition of Israel's annexation of the Golan Heights has been widely celebrated by Israelis. But do those same Israelis know of the hundreds of thousands of people expelled from the territory during the 1967 war?

By Tom Pessah March 24, 2019 in +972 Magazine

Members of the Druze community in the Golan Heights protest the decision of President Donald Trump to recognize Israeli sovereignty in the territory, Majdal Shams, March 23, 2019. (Basel Awidat/Flash90)

The vast majority of Israelis are still unaware that over 130,000 residents of the Golan Heights were expelled during from their villages, towns, and cities during the 1967 war. In fact, over the past decades, the territory has become a "consensus" issue among most Israelis, with many seeing no reason to return it. So while President Trump stunned the world last week by recognizing Israel's annexation of the Golan, in Israel almost everyone celebrated the move.

Like in the case of Palestinian refugees, for decades the official Israeli line was that the Golan's inhabitants simply fled of their own accord. according to Syrian estimates, however, only approximately 50,000 of them escaped Israeli bombardments and left alongside the surrendering Syrian army. Israeli soldiers admitted in interviews that many residents stayed behind and waited to return to their villages, while others attempted to re-cross the armistice lines.

The IDF would turn to the same methods used against Palestinians in 1948 to prevent the return of the new refugees to their homes — razing entire villages to the ground, driving out the residents, and shooting "infiltrators." Whether through direct expulsion or prevention of return, Israel was effectively ethnically cleansing the Golan.

Israeli soldiers drive a captured Syrian army vehicle on the outskirts of the city of Quneitra in the Golan Heights, June 11, 1967, a day after the war ended. (Moshe Milner/GPO)

Many of the refugees remain on the Syrian side of the border, in the Damascus and Dara areas, leaving them vulnerable to the deadly impact of the civil war in the country. According to Al-Marsad Arab Human Rights Centre in the Golan Heights, the current number of refugees and their descendants is estimated at 500,000.

Only one group was permitted to remain: some Between 6,000-7,000 Syrian Druze, who mostly live in four villages in the northern Golan, many of whom have relatives in Syria who are not permitted to return to their villages. The Israeli authorities assumed that following the 1967 war, the Golan Druze would become loyal Israeli citizens, echoing the decision made by the Druze leadership inside Israel in 1948. In practice, the Golan Druze have been resisting Israeli control for over 50 years. Today there are 22,000 Druze in the Golan, but only 1,700 have accepted Israeli citizenship, and the residents there continue to protest the occupation of their land, with many imprisoned for their political activities.

Israel would eventually annex the Golan in 1981, a decision that, until Trump's recent announcement, was universally condemned. Following annexation, the Israeli authorities attempted to force the local residents to carry an Israeli I.D. card. The Golan Druze responded with a six-month general strike, which included protests and public burnings of the government-issued cards. Druze working in various industries in northern Israel preferred to lose their jobs than violate the strike. According to one source, Israeli soldiers were ordered to shoot at protesters — a command they refused. Despite imposing a curfew, cutting the residents' telephone access, and preventing the entry of journalists and doctors, the Israeli government was forced to reach an agreement with the residents and to issue cards with an "unspecified citizenship," rather than an Israeli one.

In the meantime, the Israeli government was hard at work in building settlements across the newly-occupied territory. Today, the Golan's Jewish population consists of some 22,000 settlers living in 32 settlements (unlike those in the West Bank, Israelis do not typically refer to the Jewish localities in the Golan Heights as settlements). Each of those settlements was built on the land of former Syrian towns and villages, of which there are still visible ruins.

Israel has reportedly offered several times to return some of the Golan to Syria during previous rounds of peace negotiations, yet no agreement has ever been reached (Netanyahu reportedly discussed a withdrawal to 1967 lines in 2010).

Today, Israel still maintains restrictive residency rules, while continuing to demolish homes and confiscate land from the Golan Druze. The Israeli authorities have also revoked the residency of around 100 Druze, have refused to clear the area of landmines — relics of the 1967 war, which repeatedly claim lives
— while ensuring the separation of families on both sides of the border. Rather than maintaining internal "consensus" on the Golan Heights, both Israel's leaders and citizens should be paying more attention to the voices of those most affected by Trump's announcement.

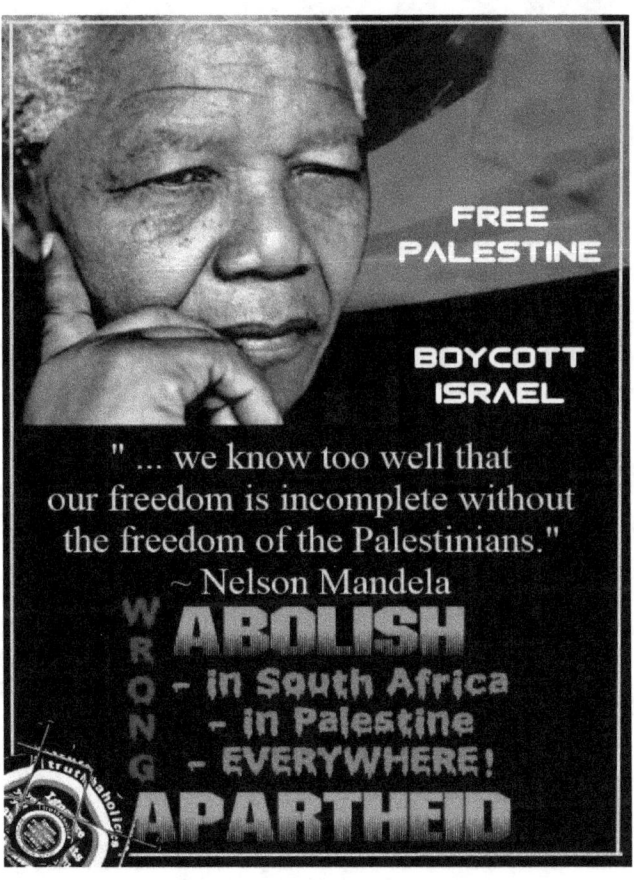

On a Clear Day in the West Bank, You Can See the Israel You Lost Forever

A visit to a settlement leader whose vision of Israel's future borders includes parts of Syria, Iraq, and Lebanon and even Iran

by Bradley Burston, 24th May 2019 from HaAretz

Daniella Weiss in her house in the settlement of Kedumim Meged Gozani

HAVAT GILAD, West Bank — It took me a long time, many visits to the West Bank, before I realized that this is the place where dreams come to die.

Dreams of a democratic Israel, one which respects and values minorities. Dreams of a free and independent Palestine. Dreams of peace.

Many of my friends had dreams like that when we moved from North America to Israel as young people in the 1970s. But we watched those dreams get crushed, one after another, cut down and trampled and intentionally rendered impossible by the settlement movement, its allies, and the extremists on both sides who play into their hands.

At the same time, in this, the eternal capital of the zero-sum, there are settlers aplenty who will tell you, without the merest ounce of cynicism, that they are living the dream.

A few weeks ago I paid a visit to one of them, Daniella Weiss: prophetess, politician, fanatic, great-grandmother.

I came to her home in the settlement of Kedumim to ask her, a person whose long-ago predictions for the future have already largely come to pass, what she believes lies in store for Israel in the long term.

More than forty years ago, when my friends and I were struggling to found a kibbutz in central Israel, Weiss saw something which we did not. It was something in the occupied territories, a settlement project, then non-existent, which would in time effectively come to run the state of Israel as a whole.

"I came to Shomron with the idea of it becoming an inseparable part of the state of Israel," Weiss says, using the Hebrew term for the northern West Bank, the biblical Samaria.

Weiss, her husband and their two small children were part of the group of 10 families who in 1975 became the first settlers in the region.

It was clear to her from the very beginning – even before the beginning – the goal, the way things were going to take place, the way they would eventually look here: "Just as I saw the small state of Israel with millions of people, I was going up the hills [of the West Bank] to see the state of Israel getting broader and bigger, with millions of Jews settling the hills. That was the picture."

Bradley Burston and his wife Varda Spiegel during solidarity action with Palestinians in the West BankCourtesy of Bradley Burston

'My philosophy blocked the two-state solution'

From the very beginning, Weiss had a sense that this was an undertaking which would utterly transform Israel. From the very beginning, Weiss's creed never changed.

She wanted then, and wants today, to bring the country to a standstill, to set it on its ear, to convert it to her way of thinking, "because my revolution affects not my life, but the life of every single person there, even if he doesn't know it."

At that very time, in the mid-70s, as Weiss and her group were squatting on land which had in part been confiscated from neighboring Palestinian villages, my friends and I were establishing a lost colony of Woodstock near the ancient site of Gezer - young people whose dreams were shaped by what they sensed had gone wrong in America, and what might just go right in Israel.

We dreamed that Israel could progress on a path toward a true social democracy, expanding existing government safety nets for the disadvantaged, building on pioneering models of health care, education, collective ownership, affordable housing, agriculture and industry.

To prepare me for this new reality, the kibbutz movement trained me to be a shepherd.

What we failed to recognize, what we did not want to acknowledge, was something that Weiss already sensed: The revolution of the labor movement, which had founded Israel and run it for decades, was dying of old age. In time, the revolution of the settlers would take its place.

Just as members of kibbutz and moshav collectives had wielded disproportionate influence across many spheres of life in Israel, particularly in government and the military, they would be supplanted by true believers of settlement, among them settlers themselves – like Weiss's neighbor, the often openly bigoted firebrand politician Bezalel Smotrich.

In her suburban-style home in Kedumim – whose population has now grown from those 10 tent-squatter families to nearly 10,000 residents – Weiss cordially welcomes us, a film crew from Haaretz, widely viewed by settlers as an institution so left-wing as to constitute an enemy.

She and I realize that we have often been at the same place at the same time: She as a settler, me as an occupying soldier; she as a settler, me as an anti-settlement protester; she as a settler, me as a journalist from a hated media outlet.

Daniella Weiss in the settlement of Havat Gilad ahead of a planned evacuation, 2003 Milner Moshe/GPO

She expresses sympathy for my political distress, my obsolete dreams, and concedes that the settlement movement has been instrumental in shaping the reality I so abhor. And yet, she continues, for her, the overriding feeling is one of satisfaction, "that my philosophy has had the upper hand, and indeed, it blocked the two-state solution."

How do you react, I ask her, when someone says those words, two-state solution?

"First of all, I know that it will not happen. Practically, we see here hundreds of thousands of Jews. We see even in the eastern neighborhoods of Jerusalem 300,000 Jews in the areas which were liberated in the Six Day war, so where will there be a [Palestinian] state? Even Netanyahu understands that [the most] he can afford to do here for the Arabs is no more than autonomy."

A state just for Jews

Weiss takes us on a tour of the unauthorized settlement outpost of Havat Gilad, "Gilad's Farm," long a flashpoint of violence. She was instrumental in founding the outpost, built as a memorial to the murder of a settler, a murder which led to acts of vengeance against Palestinians, then spirals of bloodshed, concentric vicious circles which have yet to be broken.

There is a stretch of soil here, rocky, pale as death, which, when you add water, sticks to your shoes like nothing else.

Weiss, who knows these things, tells me to avoid stepping in a certain unremarkable, shallow-looking puddle.

"It's like quicksand," she says. I look down, thinking of the Hebrew homonym – botz tova'ni – in a play on words, "mud that makes demands."

The ridges surrounding us are dotted with settlements. One of them, Har Bracha, boasts high-rise apartments. We were both there when she helped found it, on Independence Day 1983. I was on leave from reserve duty in Lebanon, my pregnant wife and I among a group of Peace Now protesters hoping to stop the settlers. I ask Weiss to look again into the future.

"Would you like Israel to expand further, beyond Gaza, beyond Judea and Samaria? Would you like Israel to extend beyond the Jordan River?"

"Yes, I want to have for the Jewish nation the promised land from the bible, the land that was promised to Abraham, Isaac and Jacob, from the Euphrates to the Nile. And I'm sure it will be. Of course, I cannot know how many years it will take, because it wasn't specified by our prophets."

A line of marchers walking along a road during a two day hike in the West Bank, organized by the settler organization "Gush Emunim". 1975. Moshe Milner/GPO

Settlement of Kedumim, 1982. Zaslavski Avraham/GPO

"What about southern Lebanon?"

"It is part of it. All of it. Even parts of Syria. Part of Iraq. Part of Iran. It's huge! This is the promised land. The only question I have is, 'Why does it take so much time?' But I also learn from the prophets that the plan of God is not a human plan."

"Do you think you have any way of convincing people that that would be a good idea?"

"I've convinced many. All the people that are connected with a movement that I run, and many, many, many religious people are sure that this will be the future. Many people believe in it."

"When the Likud party was Herut," she says, referring to the staunchly right-wing party founded by Menachem Begin in 1948, "when it was [Ze'ev] Jabotinsky, the right-wing parties and movements believed in the promised land in biblical terms. So I don't see anything extreme in my approach. This is the basic Jewish approach. The clearer we make this point, the better it will be for all of us – for Jews and Arabs alike. That this is going to be a state just for Jews."

What will life be like in that future Israel?

"I believe that the future of the state of Israel is a religious country run by religious laws. Yes. So I believe," she says.

Moreover, "Only when you take the bible completely, all of it, on the personal and national and human, universal level, only then do you feel free."

I change the subject. Or so I think.

"Let's say that under a certain administration in Washington and a certain coalition in Israel, the government decides its time to move some settlers elsewhere. How do you feel about that idea?"

Young settlers at the unauthorized Havat Gilad outpost, northern West Bank, 2003. Moshe Milner / GPO

"We will not let it happen. I know it happened there – I know it happened in Gaza. I'm fully aware of these things. But thank God, we have passed here the line where things like that can happen again. Because in the communities around here there are 500,000 Jews – half a million Jews. And this is power. To evacuate here means five times the evacuation of Jews from [Inquisition-era] Spain."

"Do you oppose the evacuation of even one?"

"Even one settler."

"From anywhere, even from settlements which Israel considers completely illegal?"

"No doubt," she says, adding, "The settlement movement is very strong, and affects all fields of Israeli society, atmosphere and politics."

She notes that there are now 250 settlements in the West Bank, nearly the total number of kibbutzim that existed when we founded Gezer.

In the end, our small kibbutz, a moribund labor movement and the weaknesses and inconsistencies of Israeli democracy were no match for the single-minded crusade of the settlers, with their Old Testament vision, scope and antipathy to compromise.

The funeral procession of slain Rabbi Raziel Shevach at the Havat Gilad outpost, January, 2018. Olivier Fitoussi

"I could spend my life as a great-grandmother. No, but I'm dedicated to the covenant between God and the Jewish nation, in Sinai, where we got orders," she says. "What I see is the direct blessing of God. Now we are in a time of redemption. And in a time of redemption, the blessing of God is immediate."

I'd come to the West Bank to see how they did it. How they won. How they ruined any chance that the extraordinary Israel we moved here hoping for could become reality.

What I learned was that the settlers are nowhere near done yet.

'You have to brainwash all the time'

When I talk to young North American Jews, by far the strongest element in their alienation from Israel is the settlement movement, the strength of the occupation and what the occupation represents in terms of the denial of rights to millions of Palestinian people.

"It is very clear to me why the young Jewish generation in the United States in North America are very much aggravated by what people like me do here," says Weiss. "It's very clear."

"People say to me, why don't you explain to the Jews of the United States what it is exactly behind your thinking? I explain," she laughs, "'You have to brainwash all the time. You have to say it, to explain it, to live it, to cope with it.'"

"You know, we have a family confrontation," she continues. "My husband says to me every week, 'Why do you speak to your children all the time about Zionism, pioneers in Judea and Samaria, settling and settling?' And all my family are settlers here. Because this is the only way to continue Zionism. If there is no enthusiasm, there is no sex. If there is no sex, there is no pregnancy. If there is no pregnancy, there are no babies. This is the problem in the United States today.

"Also, [regarding] the young Jewish generation, when they come here, if they come here, and they live [here] a few months, and they encounter difficulties, and they cope with the things we cope [with], not just in the settlements but in the state of Israel, they gradually change their mind."

"Now, you may ask," she says to me, "but you live here, and you know the things that I've said, and you do not change your mind. 'Okay. Why didn't the brainwashing work on me?' Because I didn't do it on you. Two hours of a meeting is not brainwashing. I do it to my children a few hours every day. My husband says to me, 'What do you do all the time?' I brainwash."

Let me suggest why the brainwashing didn't work on me. In an Israeli army uniform I got plenty of brainwashing from many people in several languages. In the context of that uniform I occupied northern Sinai, southern Lebanon, this area, Gaza, East Jerusalem, I occupied everything that it was possible to occupy. And all that I have come away with was: It's occupied. That's all I've managed to come away with.

"This brings me to the very primitive analysis of mine. About the left-wing mind."

Earlier in our conversation, when I'd told Weiss that I would not buy wine made in her settlement, nor in any West Bank settlement, she'd told me that this did not upset her at all. She said, "There is a right-wing mind and a left-wing mind. These are two different creations. You have a left-wing mind."

"Let's say your victory is final. The West Bank stays in Israeli hands. Why shouldn't the Palestinians here have full rights, in particular the right to vote?"

"The reason that the Arabs of Judea and Samaria cannot have the right to vote for the Knesset is because if the Arabs should have a right to vote, it's dangerous to the future of the Jewish nation in the land of Israel."

In the future, she continues, "It will all become a Jewish state. The Arabs can be here [in the West Bank], not as citizens with full rights, but just human rights. But not the right to vote for the Knesset."

There is no point in changing what [Israel's first prime minister] David Ben-Gurion did in granting citizenship to Arabs within the pre-1967 borders, she continues, "but by no means [can we] enlarge the right of Arabs to vote for the Knesset, God forbid, to Arabs who live here."

Why should the Palestinians agree to this?

"If we utter these words clearly, and we are self-confident that this is the truth - and it's not anti-democratic, and it's not against human pride – then the Arabs will be affected by it. They will know that the Jews have come here to stay. For good. Forever."

I mention that President Reuven Rivlin of the former Herut party and the founding generation of Likud has suggested that the Palestinians of the West Bank be granted the right to vote in Israeli elections.

"Rivlin," she laughs, "has become a leftist since he became a president."

"Some on the far right think the solution is expelling the Palestinians from here: transfer."

"I am very much not for the idea of transfer. I believe that the right thing for us to do – us, the Jews – is to establish more and more [West Bank] communities and encourage more and more Jews to come to Israel. Immigration from the United States from England, from France."

This, after all these years, is what I know, and Daniella Weiss does not:

They won't come. Those millions of Jews from America. They're not coming now. They won't come specifically because of what the settlement movement has done to Israel. And this is how I leave her: "I am worried. I am worried that this is the place that will result in the end of Israel."

"Oh no," she says, with the broadest of smiles. But not at all in a cruel way. She is absolutely sincere. And matter of fact.

"This is the future of Israel."

Palestine: 'Israeli war crimes should go to international court'

March 24, 2019 in Middle East Monitor

Ibrahim Khraishi, Permanent Observer Representative of the State of Palestine to the UN speaks at the UNHCR special session on "the deteriorating human rights situation in the occupied Palestinian territory, including East Jerusalem", at the United Nations Office in Geneva, on 18 May 2018 [Elma Okic / UN Geneva / Flickr]

Israeli crimes against peaceful Palestinian protesters in Gaza should go to the International Criminal Court (ICC), said the Palestinian ambassador to UN in Geneva on Sunday.

Ibrahim Khraishi's call came after the UN Human Rights Council on Friday passed a resolution on strengthening the UN presence in the Israeli-occupied Palestinian territory.

The council said it was "gravely concerned" by the findings of the UN-appointed independent international commission of inquiry, which said Israeli forces may have committed war crimes and crimes against humanity during the peaceful Great March of Return protests.

"That report should be transmitted to the ICC by the commissioner," Khraishi told *Anadolu Agency*, referring to Michelle Bachelet, who heads the council.
Khraishi said that Israeli forces target all people, not sparing children, the disabled, the media, or healthcare providers.

Expressing his hope that the report will go to the ICC, Khraishi said court prosecutors should start investigating Israeli war crimes. Earlier this month, US Secretary of State Mike Pompeo said **restrictions of entry to the US will be placed on investigators examining alleged war crimes** involving Israel

Mentioning British Foreign Secretary Jeremy Hunt saying his country would oppose all anti-Israeli resolutions at the council, Khraishi said: "Our cause was started by Britain's Balfour Declaration more than 100 years ago. After their mandate, they encouraged Israeli gangs to kill our people and evict them from their houses."

He went on to say that under the British mandate in Palestine, Israeli forces had damaged more than 500 villages and cities.

Khraishi criticised British "double standards" towards Palestinians, saying:

[the UK] is always asking for accountability everywhere but when it comes to Israel, they are the protectors and they encourage a culture of impunity.

Since March of last year, more than 250 Palestinians have been killed and thousands more injured by Israeli army fire during protests demanding the right of Palestinian refugees to return to their homes in historical Palestine from which they were driven in 1948 to make way for the new state of Israel.

They also demand an end to Israel's 12-year blockade of the Gaza Strip, which has gutted the coastal enclave's economy and deprived its roughly two million inhabitants of many basic commodities.

Israeli forces have recently been targeting Gaza with airstrikes, alleging that burning kites and balloons were sent from Gaza to the Israeli side.

Last week, on March 15th, the Israeli airforce carried out a staggering 100 air strikes in the Gaza Strip. Following the air strikes, Israel warned it would continue to use "uncompromising force" against the Palestinian people in the Gaza Strip should the UN Security Council not condemn the alleged launching of two rockets towards Tel Aviv. For it's part, Hamas said that Israel is causing new crises in the Gaza Strip through its military escalation and targeting of Palestinian resistance sites and civilian facilities.

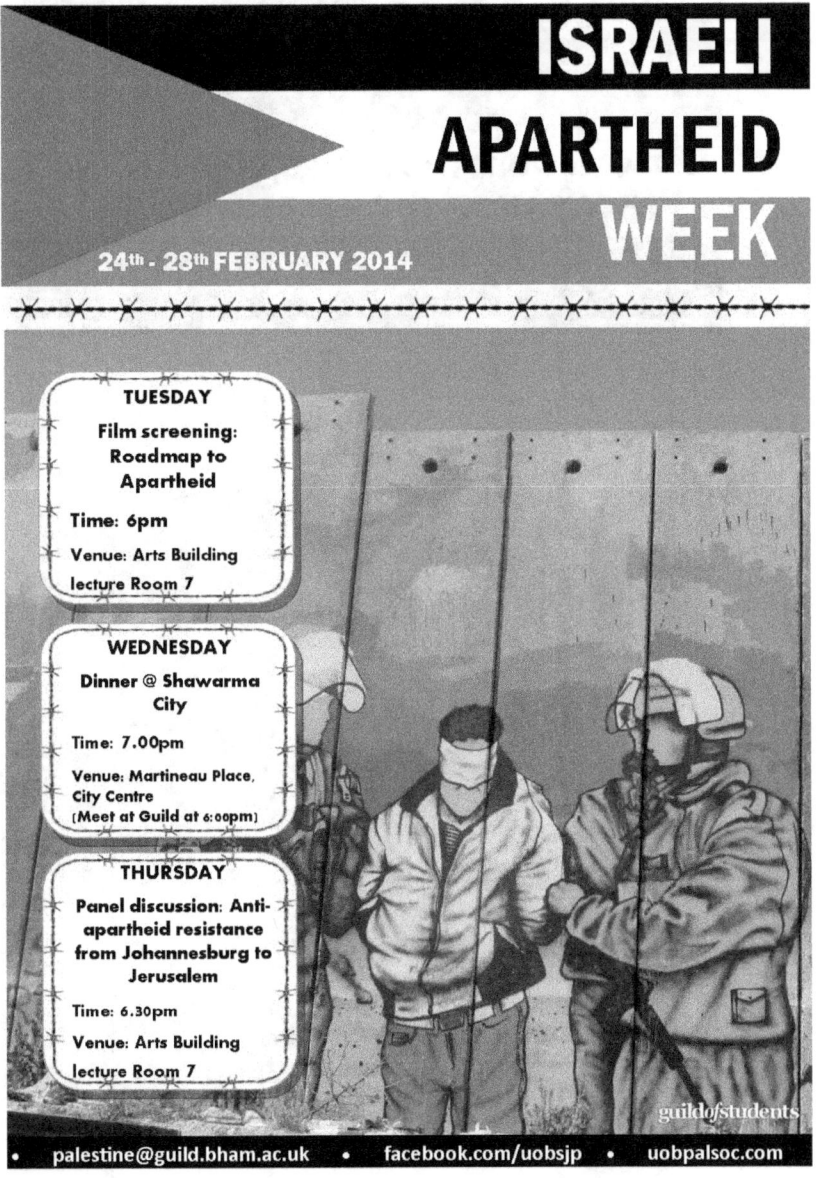

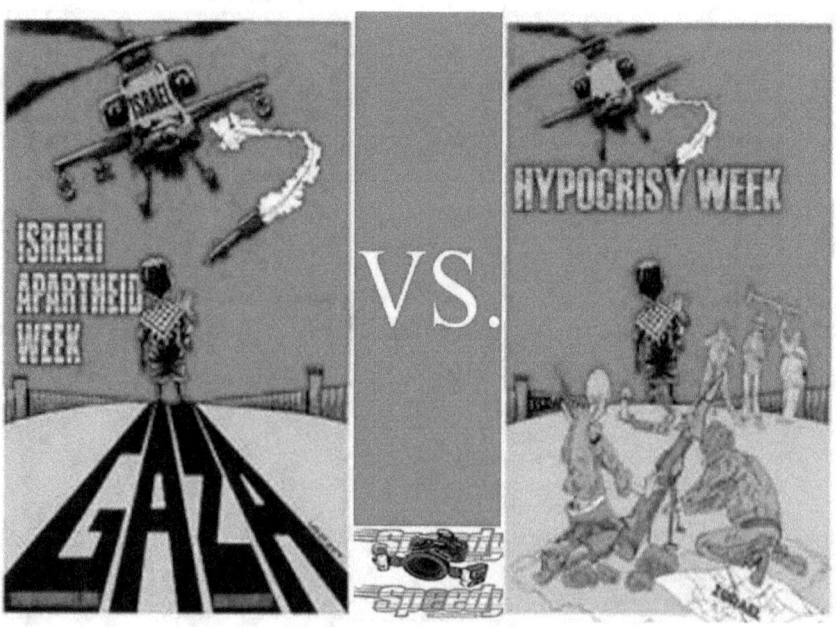

Israeli Troops Got Off Easy After Abusing a Palestinian Family. Here's What Actually Happened

A family of shepherds living in miserable tents, a father and son brutalized at the hands of Israeli soldiers: The painful and ongoing saga of the Shalada family of Kobar

By Gideon Levy and Alex Levac Mar 22, 2019 in HaAretz

Houlod Shalada with her siblings Anjoud and Yassin at the family's tent this week. Alex Levac

No one talked about the victims. For a moment it seemed as though the three soldiers from Netzah Yehuda, the ultra-Orthodox battalion of the Israel Defense Forces, who were convicted this month of abusing two Palestinians – and given ridiculously low sentences, after an outrageous plea bargain – were the victims. For a moment it seemed as though their beating of a bound father and his son in an army jeep was limited to what was seen in the video clip released for public viewing: a few blows to the head, some verbal humiliation. For a moment it seemed as though the father, Ziad Shalada, 44, and his son, Mahmoud, 22, who have been charged with abetting terrorism, are members of a dangerous, sophisticated terrorist squad. For a moment it was possible to think all that – until we visited the family's tent this week in the village of Kobar, near Ramallah.

The Shaladas' tents are pitched on the edge of the village, past the last of its houses. We've never seen anything more pitiful. There's a large tent containing an old, rickety television in the center, and next to it two small tents, even more wretched. Together, these house the sheep and the family – parents and their 11 children. Originally from the town of Sa'ir, near Hebron, the family moved here in the mid-1980s with their flock. Ziad works as a garbage collector in Kobar with his old tractor, and the 40 sheep supplement their income.

This past Monday, a large sheep was dying at the entrance to the sleeping tent. Its head lurched backward, its body heaved, its breathing grew heavier; the sight was altogether unbearable. Another sheep huddled around the tractor, licking it, apparently having despaired of looking for food. The shepherd and father of the family and his eldest son are still in jail – victims of the abuse meted out by soldiers from the Netzah Yehuda battalion of the Kfir infantry brigade, which is deployed solely in the West Bank. The two Shalada men are suspected of having aided the terrorist Assam Barghouti, who was convicted of murdering two soldiers and a newborn, who was removed from his mother's womb after she was wounded, in shooting attacks last December in the West Bank settlement of Ofra and in the Givat Assaf settler outpost. Father and son have been in custody since then, leaving the family without a source of income.

Seventeen-year-old Anjoud Shalada, barefoot and dressed in rags, rolls about on the ground. She suffers from cerebral palsy, spends her days on the tent floor, moving about with the aid of her hands. Her clothes and her body are covered in filth. She, her sisters and her little brothers were eyewitnesses to the beating her father took at the hands of the soldiers on the night of January 8. No one has recovered from the trauma of the event. They haven't returned to the tent where the soldiers detained them, because it still scares them.

Their uncle, Iyad Shalada, 46, who lives in another tent, located on the slopes of the nearby town of Bir Zeit, brought us here, together with Iyad Hadad, a field researcher for the Israeli human rights organization B'Tselem. Only the eldest daughter, Houlod, 19, her 5-year-old brother Yassin, and the paralyzed Anjoud, hidden behind a tarpaulin, were in the family's tent when we arrived. The other siblings were at school or somewhere else.

The mother of the family, Hadija, 39, and her son Mohammed, 18, were in court at the Ofer base, in the hope of seeing their loved ones during the proceedings that day. But they arrived too late, or perhaps the hearing took place earlier than scheduled; either way, they didn't succeed in seeing them for even a fraction of a second. The next hearing in their case is set for June 15. The family will not see the two men until then, nor are they likely to hear anything about their condition. Sheep and cats wandered in and out of the tent. The television was broadcasting "Palestine Today" with a raspy sound.

At 3 A.M. on January 8, the Shaladas woke up in a panic to the sight of a ferocious dog and then dozens of masked men invading their tent. Later, it turned out that the men were members of the Border Police's special anti-terror force (Yamam, in Hebrew). The family thought thieves were raiding them. They had been sleeping, as usual, on mattresses that were laid out every evening on the floor of the big tent. The dog pounced on 6-year-old Hussein, putting its paws on the chest of the petrified little boy, who was barely awake; the combatants didn't restrain it. The boy's parents, brothers and sisters shrank in horror.

The policemen, accompanied by a civilian and an officer who were not in masks, spread out in the tent. Houlod recounts the chaos and fear. An articulate young woman who attended school until the ninth grade, she describes in great detail the unforgettable horrors of that night, when the children screamed and cried with dread and their parents tried to protect them.

The Shalada family's tent in Kobar, this week. Alex Levac

The policemen first seized Ziad, and wouldn't permit him to dress, Houlod says; he remained in his undergarments and galabiya. They pushed him into a corner and ordered everyone else into an adjacent tent. It was bone-chillingly cold – there's no coal stove in the smaller tent – and the floor was muddy from the rain. Anjoud had to be carried out; the Border Policemen refused to allow her to remain in bed. Ziad's hands were bound behind him and his interrogation began. Houlod heard shouts. She says she saw troops punching and kicking his face and his body. She wasn't able to hear what he was being asked.

"We pleaded for our father," Houlod says. "We were shaking with cold and fear." The invaders went on beating and questioning Ziad. Houlod tried to go to him, but a policeman punched her in the face; another struck her from behind on the shoulder and she fell to the ground. She was in pain for three days, she tell us now. She recalls hearing the Israelis calling her father "Sheikh Hamas." He had never before been arrested, with the exception of 11 days when he was a boy.

Houlod will never forget the moment when the policemen distributed food among themselves and started to eat. "It was very hard. The children are shouting, Father is yelling, everyone is cold, and they're eating in our tent as though it's their home. That made us really furious."

After more than half an hour of questions and blows, the Border Police took Ziad to an empty dwelling nearby. He later told his lawyer that they beat him at length there. They made him lie on the floor, jumped on him, kicked him and hit him with a belt. According to Houlod, that went on for an hour. Finally, Ziad was taken to a jeep and the soldiers drove off. By now, morning had come.

A short time later, about 20 soldiers returned to the tent where the stunned family was huddled. The soldiers asked where Mahmoud was, claiming that his father had asked that he join him. Mahmoud was handcuffed and blindfolded and taken outside.

Then the jeep journey to the Beit El base began, during which father and son were brutalized, only a small segment of which was made public in the video clip.

The commander of the Netzah Yehuda battalion, Lt. Col. Nitai Okashi, would later say: "There was no doubt in my mind that the auxiliary company had to execute the activity in order to settle accounts with the terrorist who killed two of the unit's fighters, in order to generate a feeling of success among the fighters." No one considered removing this battalion commander from his post for his remarks: The soldiers were maliciously sicced on the helpless victims in order "to generate a feeling of success."

Sacks of flour and mattresses are heaped in a corner of the tent. The sheep outside is taking its last gasps. During the 20 days that followed, the family didn't hear a word about the fate of their loved ones. Only then did a lawyer from the Palestinian Prisoners Club meet with Mahmoud – Ziad was still being denied access to a lawyer – and he called the family to say that the young man was in a very bad way: He was incapable of answering questions from the lawyer, his face was swollen from beatings, bruises were visible on his body and he was unable to stand on his feet.

Houlod and Yassin Shalada. Alex Levac

A few days later, Mahmoud told the lawyer that in the jeep the soldiers removed his blindfold and said: Watch what we are doing to your father. They beat Ziad relentlessly on the head, in the presence of his handcuffed son. Details of the abuse appear in the more than 300 pages of the indictment against the soldiers who administered it.

Houlod's phone rings. It's her mother, Hadija, from the court. She didn't get to see her husband and her son. Now she is trying to pay for their canteen purchases. The lawyer,

Mamoun al Hashim, had told her that Ziad has internal bleeding in his stomach as a result of the blows he took. He already was suffering from kidney disease, and he also suffers from backaches.

Houlod herself saw her father and her brother for the first time in a court hearing on February 15. She was not allowed to exchange a word with them, nor even to gesture in their direction, for fear of being expelled.

"I don't know how to put it," she says of the hearing. "It was so sad. My father suddenly had become so old, and so worn out, and my brother, too." A week earlier, her mother saw them for the first time in the courtroom; she had warned her daughter that their condition was very bad. Ziad's face was still swollen and streaked with bruises from the pummeling, and Mahmoud looked very thin. Ziad could not even stand up in the courtroom. The next time Hadija saw him was two weeks later, and his condition had improved. Their interrogation by the Shin Bet security service in the police station in the Russian Compound in the center of Jerusalem had concluded, and they were transferred to Ofer Prison for the duration of their trial.

The Israel Police provided Haaretz with the following statement: The individuals suspected of providing assistance to the terrorist who carried out the attack at Givat Assaf were arrested by a force from the Police Anti-Terror Unit [Yamam], without resistance and without the need for force.

The claims that the suspects were beaten [by police] before being turned over to the IDF are not substantiated, and a check undertaken by the appropriate authorities determined that the conduct of the fighters of the anti-terror unit was impeccable.

According to Houlod, her brother is accused of having encountering Assam Barghouti, who was on the run in the wake of the murders, in the pasture, and who asked to be taken to the tent, where Ziad hid him. She maintains that they hadn't known Barghouti before and that she didn't see him in their tent compound. She had heard about the trial of the soldiers who abused her father and her brother, and about the verdict, but she wasn't interested. She asks only why the commanding officers weren't tried.

Houlod believes that the fact that the soldiers turned her father and her brother into cripples, physically and mentally, is more than enough punishment for anything they did, and the army should release them immediately. She and the other children have seen the clip of the beating.

"It was awful," she says. "I wish I hadn't seen it. To see your father being beaten cruelly while he is helpless; to see soldiers with heavy rifles beating my father and my brother on the head, while they can't defend themselves. It was awful."

This doesn't need to happen: Another pre-election war on Gaza

We need leaders who can talk about ending the siege, about ending the occupation, about equality, freedom, and security as the only solution for both Israelis and Palestinians.

By Haggai Matar and Oren Ziv, 25th March 2019 in +972

Israeli security forces assess the damage to a home in central Israel that was destroyed by a rocket fired overnight from Gaza, Mishmarot, March 25, 2019. (Oren Ziv/Activestills.org)

The rocket fired from Gaza that destroyed a home and wounded seven people in central Israel Monday morning, took Israelis by surprise. On the one hand, that's totally understandable; we aren't used to rocket fire in the Tel Aviv area, and certainly not rockets that exact such a devastating price. An attack on civilians, on a sleeping family, is a terrifying thing.

On the other hand, the attack is surprising only if we disconnect it from all the stories that don't get any airtime: unarmed protesters shot on the Israel-Gaza fence almost every week (only recently, a 14-year-old was shot dead by Israeli snipers), several deadly incidents West Bank in recent weeks, along with attacks and other steps being taken against Palestinian prisoners held in Israeli jails.

When we talk about Palestinian aggression, hardly anyone mentions the fact that since the beginning of the year, Israeli security forces have killed 30 Palestinians in Gaza and the West Bank.

The rocket attack is a surprise only if we allow ourselves to forget the wider context of the daily reality of occupation — from arrests of Palestinian children in their classrooms to settler attacks on Palestinian farmers — or the siege on Gaza, which has left the Gazans impoverished and hopeless.

None of this justifies attacks on Israeli civilians, of course, but it should remind us that Israel is the one attacking Palestinian civilians on a daily basis. We cannot lose sight of that context when we talk about what may come next.

In response to the rocket attack Monday morning, Prime Minister Netanyahu said Israel would "respond with force." (At the time of publication, those attacks had begun.) Deputy Defense Minister Eli Ben Dahan, who visited the destroyed house in the moshav of Mishmarot, described the Israeli government's three options: continue shooting on "empty depots" in Gaza, re-occupy the strip, or re-institute Israeli's targeted killing program.

Education Minister Naftali Bennett said that Hamas must be "subdued," while Netanyahu rival Benny Gantz, whose campaign ads bragged of sending Gaza back to the Stone Age, blamed Netanyahu for the rocket attack for not striking Hamas and Gaza harder. Far-right politicians demanded Gaza be "flattened."

Some residents of Mishmarot, however, took a different tone. Yoni Wolf, whose family lives in the house that was destroyed by the rocket, told reporters Monday morning that Israel must "regain not only its deterrence but also its sanity." Another resident of the town said one of his former employees, a Palestinian man from Gaza, called to ask how he was doing. "Not everybody hates us," he said.

The danger is that now, following the attack on Mishmarot, in light of the upcoming elections, and in an attempt to maintain his image as "Mr. Security," Netanyahu could be dragged into the deadliest and most devastating round of violence we have seen since the last Gaza war in 2014

Palestinian protesters take part in the weekly Great Return March demonstration near the Israel-Gaza fence, east of Rafah, in the southern Gaza Strip, March 22, 2019. (Abed Rahim Khatib/Flash90)

But there is another way. We can stop the bloodshed. We do not have to wage another pre-election war. We can stop speaking in empty slogans about destroying the Hamas regime. These are lies, they have always been lies. What we need is leader who can talk about negotiations, ending the siege and the occupation, about equality, freedom, and security as the only solution for both Israelis and Palestinians.

This article was first published in Hebrew on Local Call.

Gaza hit by Israel after Hamas denies rocket attack on Tel Aviv

25th March 2019 from Palestinian News network

There are reports in Gaza that the offices of Hamas politburo chief Ismail Haniyeh have been hit. The Israeli occupation army confirmed the attack.

Only a few hours after the Palestinian resistance movement Hamas denied it had launched a rocket attack toward Tel Aviv, the Israeli military says it has begun striking the besieged Palestinian territory.

The Israeli military said on Monday it had started hitting Hamas targets throughout the Gaza Strip.

Palestinian security officials and Hamas media outlets said a naval position of the resistance movement was targeted by at least two strikes west of Gaza City.

In northern Gaza, another target was a large training camp run by Hamas.

The new Israeli aggression against the coastal enclave came after Tel Aviv authorities said earlier on Monday that a long-range rocket launched from the Gaza Strip had struck an area near Tel Aviv in central Israel, wounding seven people.

The early morning attack on Mishmeret, an agricultural town north of Tel Aviv, came a day after Israeli warplanes bombed the besieged enclave ahead of the anniversary of Gaza fence protests at the weekend.

It forced Israeli Prime Minister Benjamin Netanyahu to cut short his trip to Washington immediately after meeting US President Donald Trump later on Monday, his office said.

A Hamas official, who asked not to be named, told AFP on Monday, "No one from the resistance movements, including Hamas, has an interest in firing rockets from the Gaza Strip towards the enemy."

He added that the same message had been conveyed to Egypt, which intervened to broker a ceasefire and prevent Israel from launching another war on Gaza after tensions escalated last year.

Earlier Monday, the Israel Occupation Forces said that the rocket, which struck a home in the community of Mishmeret in the early hours of the morning, was fired from a Hamas position near Rafah in the southern Strip, some 120 kilometers away. The military said the rocket was manufactured by the group.

The military sent two infantry brigades and armored forces to southern Israel and is preparing to call up thousands of reservists, including some from the Air Defense Command, the Intelligence Corps and the Home Front Command.

'No country can rewrite history': Trump's Golan decision widely condemned
Several countries have slammed Washington's recognition of Israeli 'sovereignty' over Syria's Golan Heights
From Middle East Eye 25th March 2019

Several countries have slammed Donald Trump's decision to recognise Israel's "sovereignty" over the Syrian Golan Heights, calling the move a brazen attempt to set aside international law.

The Syrian government was amongst the first to condemn the US president's announcement on Monday, with a foreign ministry official calling it a "blatant assault on Syria's unity and sovereignty".

Syrian official calls US decision a 'blatant assault' on country's sovereignty (Reuters/File photo)

"Trump neither has the right nor the legal authority to legitimise the occupation and theft of others' land by force," the Syrian official told state-run SANA news agency.

Earlier on Monday, Trump signed an executive order stating that the United States officially recognises "that the Golan Heights are part of the State of Israel". He justified the move on the basis that the territory, which Israel occupied after the 1967 war, is critical for Israel's security."Today I'm taking historic action to promote Israel's ability to defend itself," Trump told reporters.

Israel annexed the Golan Heights in 1981 in a move that was never accepted by the international community.

Today, tens of thousands of Israeli settlers live in communities across the occupied area.

'No country can rewrite history'

The US president's move, which was first announced late last week, is the latest in a series of major policy announcements pursued by the Trump administration in the face of widespread criticism and backlash.

The Lebanese foreign ministry rejected Trump's decision on Monday, saying that it breaks the basic rules of international law. Beirut also warned Israel that only a just peace will help it maintain its security, not military power and expansionism. "The Golan Heights is Arab, Syrian land, and no proclamation will change that reality. No country can rewrite history by transferring the ownership of land to another country," the ministry said in a statement.

For his part, Sheikh Naim Hassan, a Lebanese Druze spiritual leader, denounced the US decision, saying that the people of the Golan Heights have historically stuck to their Arab roots, rejecting Israeli attempts to erase the Arab heritage of the local population.

Most Syrians in the Golan Heights are Druze, a mystical monotheistic sect that branched off from mainstream Islam. "The Arab allegiance of the Druze in Golan alongside their brethren in the nation will not be bent by the [US] decisions, decrees and even assaults," Hassan said, as reported by Lebanon's news agency NNA.

Turkish Foreign Minister Mevlut Cavusoglu also said the US "once again ignored international laws" by recognising Israel's hold on the Syrian territory. "However, this decision will never legitimise Israel's annexation" of the Golan Heights, Cavusoglu said, as reported by Anadolu news agency.

The spokesman for Turkish President Recep Tayyip Erdogan also condemned the move, saying it was especially cynical as it took place just "as Israel bombards Gaza".

The Israeli military carried out several air strikes on the Gaza Strip late on Monday, hours after a rocket was fired from the coastal Palestinian enclave into a community north of Tel Aviv, injuring seven people. The decision to recognise Israel's "sovereignty" over the Golan Heights "as Israel bombards Gaza is manifestation of [an] anti-peace mentality", said Ibrahim Kalin, the presidential spokesman, as reported by Anadolu.

Netanyahu hails decision

The American-Arab Anti-Discrimination Committee, a Washington-based advocacy group, called Trump's decision an "outrageous violation of international law".

It cited five United Nations resolutions that explicitly call on Israel to withdraw from territories it occupied after the 1967 war, including the Golan Heights. "It is the obligation of the US Congress and the Trump administration, as well as the United Nations and the international community, to uphold its own international agreements and fundamental principles of human rights that it claims to promote in its foreign policies," the group said in a statement.

Trump's decision had one major supporter: Israeli Prime Minister Benjamin Netanyahu. Speaking at the White House on Monday, Netanyahu said that by recognising Israeli "sovereignty" over the Golan Heights, Trump had proven to be the greatest US president in history.

"Over the years, Israel has been blessed to have many friends who sat in the Oval Office, but Israel has never had a better friend than you," Netanyahu told Trump.

Analysts have said that Washington's decision to recognise Israel's hold on the Golan aims to boost Netanyahu's chances at re-election in the 9 April elections.

The Israeli premier is facing a stiff challenge from ex-Israeli army boss Benny Gantz, who was also in Washington this week to shore up support during an address at pro-Israel lobby group AIPAC's annual conference.

Netanyahu cuts short US trip as Israel begins attack on Gaza

March 25, 2019, from Middle East Eye

Flame and smoke blow up after Israeli fighter jets carried out airstrikes towards points of Izz ad-Din al-Qassam Brigades, the armed wing of Hamas, in Rafah, Gaza on 15 March, 2019 [Abed Rahim Khatib/Anadolu Agency]

Israeli Prime Minister Benjamin Netanyahu has cut short his trip to the US, after Israel called up reservists in preparation for a new attack on the Gaza Strip.

Netanyahu had been due to spend two days in the US, today visiting US President Donald Trump at the White House and tomorrow addressing the American Israel Public Affairs Committee (AIPAC) conference in Washington DC.
He announced this morning however that he would now only briefly visit President Trump, before returning to Israel "to manage our operations up close". Before leaving, Netanyahu – who is also

Israel's defence minister – reportedly held a remote meeting with the Israeli army's chief of staff, the chief of Israel's intelligence agency Shin Bet, and the head of Israel's National Security Council, *Haaretz* reported.

Palestinians inspect wreckage after Israeli fighter jets carried out airstrike towards a building belonging to Hamas, in Gaza City, Gaza on 15 March 2019. [Ashraf Amra – Anadolu Agency]

This comes after Israel today deployed two army brigades to the Gaza fence and called up reservists for aerial units in preparation for a potential assault on the besieged Strip. Chief of Staff of the Israeli army, Aviv Kohavi, ordered two brigades be sent to Israel's Gaza Division which, according to the *Times of Israel*, "represent[s] over 1,000 additional soldiers deployed to the area, a significant troop increase".

Israel has also locked down the Gaza Strip, closing the Kerem Shalom (Karm Abu Salem) and Erez (Beit Hanoun) crossings which allow goods and medical supplies into the enclave. Israel has also reduced the fishing zone it imposes off Gaza's coast, further blockading the territory. At the time of writing, Israel had just begun its attack on the Strip, with Palestinians living there bracing for further attacks overnight.

The Israeli army has claimed these measures are a response to rocket fire from the Gaza Strip. The alleged rocket hit a house north of Tel Aviv, leaving seven wounded. Israeli army spokesperson, Ronen Manelis, claimed the rocket was fired by Hamas – which governs the Gaza Strip – a claim that Hamas denies.

Damaged building is seen after Israeli fighter jets carried out airstrikes towards points of Izz ad-Din al-Qassam Brigades, the armed wing of Hamas, in Rafah, Gaza on March 15, 2019. (Abed Rahim Khatib – Anadolu Agency)

A Hamas official told *Agence France Press (AFP)*: "No one from the resistance movements, including Hamas, has an interest in firing rockets from the Gaza Strip towards [Israel]."
That this has occurred just two weeks before Israel's upcoming general election on 9 April is significant for a number of reasons. Firstly, Netanyahu's visit to the US was widely expected to act as a pre-election PR exercise, demonstrating the strong relations between him and the Trump administration. Netanyahu has been keen to stress this relationship throughout his campaign, using billboards of the pair shaking hands and pointing to President Trump's decision to move the US embassy to Jerusalem in May as evidence that Netanyahu has "got things done".

This tactic appeared to be holding true once again last week, as President Trump tweeted that "it is time for the United States to fully recognise Israel's sovereignty over the Golan Heights". The decision – which reversed decades of US foreign policy under which the Golan Heights was declared "Israeli occupied" in line with international law – was seen as an election gift for Netanyahu, and a potentially much-needed boost to his struggling poll numbers. President Trump was slated to sign a decree recognising Israeli sovereignty over the Golan Heights while Netanyahu was in the US, though it is now unclear when this will go ahead.

In addition, by cutting the trip short Netanyahu has not only deprived himself of this PR opportunity but also left the AIPAC conference open to his biggest electoral rival, Benny Gantz. In what was interpreted as a blow to Netanyahu, earlier this month it was announced that Gantz would give the keynote speech at AIPAC, an opportunity that would represent his first major address to the US.

In a statement about the keynote, Gantz's Blue and White (Kahol Lavan) alliance said: "Gantz will use his speech to emphasise that, after the election, he will work to rebuild the relationship with American Jewry and ensure that Israel will once again enjoy the support of its friends across the spectrum in the United States".

Giving his AIPAC address today, Gantz said: "Our thoughts and prayers go out to the families whose homes were attacked by a rocket this morning in Israel. The strong resilient people of our nation were attacked yet again, forced to live with constant reminders of our enemies' hate and unwillingness for change." The former chief of staff of the Israeli army also praised Netanyahu for the decision to cut his trip short, saying: "I will return to Israel today as well to stand, and if needed, to fight in defence of our people […] I am a soldier. That is who I am. That is what I do."

Gantz was less supportive of Netanyahu on Twitter, however, writing: "Those who do not respond with force and instead [pay] Hamas […] now get rockets in the Hasharon region [north of Tel Aviv]. Will [Netanyahu …] finally focus on the security of the citizens of the state and not on his legal issues," referring to the myriad corruption investigations levied against the prime minister.

Israeli Prime Minister Benjamin Netanyahu has cut short his trip to the US, after Israel called up reservists in preparation for a new attack on the Gaza Strip.

Netanyahu had been due to spend two days in the US, today visiting US President Donald Trump at the White House and tomorrow addressing the American Israel Public Affairs Committee (AIPAC) conference in Washington DC.

He announced this morning however that he would now only briefly visit President Trump, before returning to Israel "to manage our operations up close". Before leaving, Netanyahu – who is also Israel's defence minister – reportedly held a remote meeting with the Israeli army's chief of staff, the chief of Israel's intelligence agency Shin Bet, and the head of Israel's National Security Council, *Haaretz* reported.

This comes after Israel today deployed two army brigades to the Gaza fence and called up reservists for aerial units in preparation for a potential assault on the besieged Strip. Chief of Staff of the Israeli army, Aviv Kohavi, ordered two brigades be sent to Israel's Gaza Division which, according to the *Times of Israel*, "represent[s] over 1,000 additional soldiers deployed to the area, a significant troop increase".

Israel has also locked down the Gaza Strip, closing the Kerem Shalom (Karm Abu Salem) and Erez (Beit Hanoun) crossings which allow goods and medical supplies into the enclave. Israel has also reduced the fishing zone it imposes off Gaza's coast, further blockading the territory. At the time of writing, Israel had just begun its attack on the Strip, with Palestinians living there bracing for further attacks overnight.

The Israeli army has claimed these measures are a response to rocket fire from the Gaza Strip. The alleged rocket hit a house north of Tel Aviv, leaving seven wounded. Israeli army spokesperson, Ronen Manelis, claimed the rocket was fired by Hamas – which governs the Gaza Strip – a claim that Hamas denies. A Hamas official told *Agence France Press (AFP)*: "No one from the resistance movements, including Hamas, has an interest in firing rockets from the Gaza Strip towards [Israel]."

That this has occurred just two weeks before Israel's upcoming general election on 9 April is significant for a number of reasons. Firstly, Netanyahu's visit to the US was widely expected to act as a pre-election PR exercise, demonstrating the strong relations between him and the Trump administration. Netanyahu has been keen to stress this relationship throughout his campaign, using billboards of the pair shaking hands and pointing to President Trump's decision to move the US embassy to Jerusalem in May as evidence that Netanyahu has "got things done".

This tactic appeared to be holding true once again last week, as President Trump tweeted that "it is time for the United States to fully recognise Israel's sovereignty over the Golan Heights". The decision – which reversed decades of US foreign policy under which the Golan Heights was declared "Israeli occupied" in line with international law – was seen as an election gift for Netanyahu, and a potentially much-needed boost to his struggling poll numbers. President Trump was slated to sign a decree recognising Israeli sovereignty over the Golan Heights while Netanyahu was in the US, though it is now unclear when this will go ahead.

In addition, by cutting the trip short Netanyahu has not only deprived himself of this PR opportunity but also left the AIPAC conference open to his biggest electoral rival, Benny Gantz. In what was interpreted as a blow to Netanyahu, earlier this month it was announced that Gantz would give the keynote speech at AIPAC, an opportunity that would represent his first major address to the US.

In a statement about the keynote, Gantz's Blue and White (Kahol Lavan) alliance said: "Gantz will use his speech to emphasise that, after the election, he will work to rebuild the relationship with American Jewry and ensure that Israel will once again enjoy the support of its friends across the spectrum in the United States".

Giving his AIPAC address today, Gantz said: "Our thoughts and prayers go out to the families whose homes were attacked by a rocket this morning in Israel. The strong resilient people of our nation were attacked yet again, forced to live with constant reminders of our enemies' hate and unwillingness for change."

The former chief of staff of the Israeli army also praised Netanyahu for the decision to cut his trip short, saying: "I will return to Israel today as well to stand, and if needed, to fight in defence of our people […] I am a soldier. That is who I am. That is what I do."

Gantz was less supportive of Netanyahu on Twitter, however, writing: "Those who do not respond with force and instead [pay] Hamas […] now get rockets in the Hasharon region [north of Tel Aviv]. Will [Netanyahu …] finally focus on the security of the citizens of the state and not on his legal issues," referring to the myriad corruption investigations levied against the prime minister.

However, commentators have speculated that the threat of another war on the Gaza Strip could actually be of benefit to Netanyahu's re-election bid. Netanyahu has been criticised as weak on Gaza, with the right-wing claiming he has failed to "deal effectively with Hamas". One such critic is co-founder of the New Right (Hayemin Hehadash) party and current Education Minister, Naftali Bennett, who has long advocated for a heavy-handed approach to Gaza.
In a statement today, the New Right party said: "Israel's deterrence has collapsed, and we have to say honestly, Netanyahu failed against Hamas. The release of the terrorists, the fear of destroying their homes, the restraint in the face of the rockets to the south – all of these led Hamas to stop being afraid of Israel."

If Netanyahu now responds forcefully against the Gaza Strip, he could win the support of those portions of the electorate who support Bennett's interpretation. The *Times of Israel* points out that, weeks before Israel's 2009 and 2013 elections, Israel launched its 2008 and 2012 wars on the Strip after being spurred on by "appeals for a strong retaliation" to alleged rocket fire. If the same happens again, with just 15 days to go until the election, Israel could face a "khaki election" in which the country goes to the ballots during wartime.

This prospect has not been lost on the Palestinian factions, with the Palestinian Liberation Organisation (PLO)'s Executive Committee saying in a statement that "Netanyahu's government is seeking to use these developments [for] the Israeli elections early next month, as well as for the benefit of Netanyahu personally [and] his allies in the far right."

Trump's stance on the Golan Heights will allow Israel to operate with impunity elsewhere

Washington is ignoring international law and consensus, bolstering Benjamin Netanyahu's position ahead of the forthcoming elections

By Jonathan Cook in The National 24th March 2019

An Israeli soldier stands next to signs pointing out distances to different cities, on Mount Bental, an observation post in the Israeli-occupied Golan Heights. Reuters/Ronen Zvulun

When President Donald Trump moved the US embassy to occupied Jerusalem last year, effectively sabotaging any hope of establishing a viable Palestinian state, he tore up the international rulebook.

Last week, he trampled all over its remaining tattered pages.

He did so, of course, via Twitter.

Referring to a large piece of territory Israel seized from Syria in 1967, Mr Trump wrote: "After 52 years it is time for the United States to fully recognize Israel's Sovereignty over the Golan Heights, which is of critical strategic and security importance to the State of Israel and Regional Stability."

Israel expelled 130,000 Syrians from the Golan Heights in 1967, under cover of the Six Day War, and then annexed the territory 14 years later – in violation of international law. A small population of

Syrian Druze are the only survivors of that ethnic cleansing operation.

Replicating its illegal acts in the occupied Palestinian territories, Israel immediately moved Jewish settlers and businesses into the Golan.

Until now, no country had recognised Israel's act of plunder. In 1981, UN member states, including the US, declared Israeli efforts to change the Golan's status "null and void".

But in recent months, Israeli prime minister Benjamin Netanyahu began stepping up efforts to smash that long-standing consensus and win over the world's only superpower to his side.

He was spurred into action when the Bashar Al Assad – aided by Russia – began to decisively reverse the territorial losses the Syrian regime had suffered during the nation's eight-year war.

Israel itself used the Golan as a base from which to launch covert operations to help Mr Assad's opponents in southern Syria, including Islamic State fighters. Iran and the Lebanese militia Hezbollah, meanwhile, tried to limit Israel's room for manoeuvre on the Syrian leader's behalf.

Iran's presence close by was how Mr Netanyahu publicly justified the need for Israel to take permanent possession of the Golan, calling it a vital buffer against Iranian efforts to "use Syria as a platform to destroy Israel".

Before that, when Mr Assad was losing ground to his enemies, the Israeli leader made a different case. Then, he argued that Syria was breaking apart and its president would never be in a position to reclaim the Golan.

Mr Netanyahu's current rationalisation is no more persuasive than the earlier one. Russia and the United Nations are already well advanced on re-establishing a demilitarised zone on the Syrian side of the separation-of-forces line. That would ensure Iran could not deploy close to the Golan Heights.

Mr Netanyahu is set to meet Mr Trump in Washington tomorrow, when the president's tweet will reportedly be converted into an executive order.

The timing is significant. This is another crude attempt by Mr Trump to meddle in Israel's election, due on April 9. It will provide Mr Netanyahu with a massive fillip as he struggles against corruption indictments and a credible threat from a rival party, Blue and White, headed by former army generals.

Mr Netanyahu could barely contain his glee, reportedly calling Mr Trump to tell him: "You made history!"

But, in truth, this was no caprice. Israel and Washington have been heading in this direction for a while.

In Israel, there is cross-party support for keeping the Golan.

Michael Oren, a former Israeli ambassador to the US and a confidant of Mr Netanyahu's, formally launched a plan last year to quadruple the size of the Golan's settler population to 100,000 within a decade.

The US State Department offered its apparent seal of approval last month when it included the Golan Heights for the first time in the "Israel" section of its annual human rights report.

This month, senior Republican senator Lindsey Graham made a very public tour of the Golan in an Israeli military helicopter, alongside Mr Netanyahu and David Friedman, Mr Trump's ambassador to Israel. Mr Graham said he and fellow senator Ted Cruz would lobby the US president to change the territory's status.

Mr Trump, meanwhile, has made no secret of his disdain for international law. This month, his officials barred entry to the US to staff from the International Criminal Court, based in The Hague, who are investigating US war crimes in Afghanistan.

The ICC has made enemies of both Washington and Israel in its initial, and meagre, attempts to hold the two to account.

Whatever Mr Netanyahu's spin about the need to avert an Iranian threat, Israel has other, more concrete reasons for holding on to the Golan.

The territory is rich in water sources and provides Israel with decisive control over the Sea of Galilee, a large freshwater lake that is crucially important in a region facing ever greater water shortages.

The 1,200 square kilometres of stolen land is being aggressively exploited, from burgeoning vineyards and apple orchards to a tourism industry that, in winter, includes the snow-covered slopes of Mount Hermon.

As noted by Who Profits, an Israeli human rights organisation, in a report this month, Israeli and US companies are also setting up commercial wind farms to sell electricity.

And Israel has been quietly co-operating with US energy giant Genie to explore potentially large oil reserves under the Golan. Mr Trump's adviser and son-in-law, Jared Kushner, has family investments in Genie. But extracting the oil will be difficult, unless Israel can plausibly argue that it has sovereignty over the territory.

For decades the US had regularly arm-twisted Israel to enter a mix of public and back-channel peace talks with Syria. Just three years ago, Barack Obama supported a UN Security Council rebuke to Mr Netanyahu for stating that Israel would never relinquish the Golan.

Now Mr Trump has given a green light for Israel to hold on to it permanently.

But, whatever he says, the decision will not bring security for Israel, or regional stability. In fact, it makes a nonsense of Mr Trump's "deal of the century" – a regional peace plan to end the Israeli-Palestinian conflict that, according to rumour, may be unveiled soon after the Israeli election.

Instead, US recognition will prove a boon for the Israeli right, which has been clamouring to annex vast areas of the West Bank and thereby drive a final nail into the coffin of the two-state solution.

Israel's right can now plausibly argue: "If Mr Trump has consented to our illegal seizure of the Golan, why not also our theft of the West Bank?"

AIPAC Is Playing The Victim, But It's Palestinians Who Are Being Silenced

by [Peter Beinart](#) March 25, 2019 in Forward News

So far, the theme of AIPAC's 2019 Policy Conference has been peril, not just to Israel, but to AIPAC itself. AIPAC's CEO accused unnamed critics of "trying to silence each of us."

AIPAC President Mort Fridman declared that, "none of us are willing to be silenced."

House Majority Leader Steny Hoyer warned of forces that seek "to silence others through exclusion, disenfranchisement, or fear."

AIPAC
✔ *@AIPAC*
Mar 24, 2019

Replying to @AIPAC @LeaderHoyer

"Together, we cherish dissent and value criticism of leaders and policies. That's a good thing. It's what makes our democracies stronger."

AIPAC
✔ @AIPAC

"...However, what weakens us is when, instead of engaging in legitimate debate about policies, someone questions the motives of his or her fellow citizens or tries to silence others through exclusion, disenfranchisement, or fear." #AIPAC2019
10:43 PM - Mar 24, 2019

On its face, this is odd. No American politician has suggested that AIPAC be prevented from holding conferences or advocating positions or that it face any restrictions that wouldn't apply to other lobbies. At the same conference where AIPAC's leaders claim that their rights to freely speak and assemble are in danger, those leaders will in the coming days host the Vice President and the leaders of both parties in both houses of Congress.

Yes, one freshman member of congress, Ilhan Omar, has suggested, flippantly, that AIPAC wields power because its supporters give politicians money, which is true but incomplete: AIPAC also wields power because of a strong cultural, ideological and religious affinity for Israel, particularly on the right.

Yes, Omar later suggested that groups like AIPAC "push for allegiance to a foreign country," which is simplistic and misleading: AIPAC members are both proudly loyal to the government of the United States and uncritically supportive of the government of Israel. They reconcile these two impulses by denying that American and Israeli interests ever conflict.

Yes, the liberal activist group MoveOn urged Democratic presidential candidates not to attend this year's AIPAC conference, and most complied.

But none of this means, even remotely, that AIPAC is being silenced. To the contrary, when it comes to free speech, AIPAC is not victim but victimizer.

It is a major force behind the Combatting BDS Act, which in the words of the American Civil Liberties Union, would encourage states to "require state contractors — including teachers, lawyers, newspapers and journalists, and even students who want to judge high school debate tournaments — to certify that they are not participating in politically motivated boycotts against Israel."

Thus, according to the ACLU, the bill "would encourage states to adopt unconstitutional measures intended to suppress protected political expression."

AIPAC is also pushing the Anti-Semitism Awareness Act, which directs the US government to define "denying the Jewish people their right to self-determination" as anti-Semitism.

AIPAC
✔ *@AIPAC*

AIPAC supports the bipartisan, bicameral Anti-Semitism Awareness Act that directs the @usedgov to use a widely-accepted definition of anti-Semitism. Thank you @PeterRoskam @RepTedDeutch @RepDougCollins @RepJerryNadler @SenatorTimScott @SenBobCasey. Read→ https://bit.ly/2sg1UkX

Rep. Ted Deutch
✔ *@RepTedDeutch*
Anti-Semitism is on the rise in schools & on college campuses, and we must do more to stop this troubling trend.

I introduced the Anti-Semitism Awareness Act to help the Education Dept. protect students from the most insidious and modern forms of anti-Semitism.

Anti-Semitism Awareness Act

"I've heard far too many stories from Jewish students of the anti-Semitism they face in schools and on college campuses every day. Jewish students, like students of any religion, should not live in fear of attacks because of their religion. They shouldn't have to fear wearing Judaic symbols or expressing their support for Israel. As we work to combat all forms of discrimination and hate, Congress must act to protect Jewish students on campus, and this legislation would help the Education Department stem this troubling trend."

Thus, a student who called for transforming Israel from a Jewish state into a secular state with equal rights for all would be guilty of bigotry. Which is one reason the ACLU has warned that the law would "chill the speech of students, faculty, and other members [of] campus communities around the country."

Why does AIPAC exaggerate the threats to its rights while ignoring its role in threatening the rights of others? Because permanent victimhood creates moral license.

Decades ago, the late Rabbi David Hartman warned of the "moral narcissism" that leads some Jews, because of our traumatic history, to "judge others, but refuse to be judged."

That's how AIPAC and other establishment American Jewish groups function today. They describe Israel as perennially facing existential threat. Listen to AIPAC and you'll likely never know that the Palestine Liberation Organization recognized Israel's existence in 1993, that the entire Arab League offered to do the same in 2002 if Israel permitted a Palestinian state in the West Bank and Gaza Strip and found a "just" and "agreed upon" solution for Palestinian refugees, and that Israel is the sole Middle Eastern nation with nuclear weapons.

Of course, Israel does face genuine threats, as evidenced by Hamas' recent, despicable, missile attacks. But by ignoring Israel's massive power advantage, and describing the Jewish state as forever at risk of another Holocaust, AIPAC frees Israel of moral responsibility.

If Israel's adversaries — even the mostly unarmed protesters who last year marched towards the fence that encloses Gaza — constitute an existential threat, then anything Israel does to defend itself is legitimate. Countries on the brink of extinction have only one moral responsibility: to survive.

By now describing itself as under assault from forces that threaten its basic rights, AIPAC is applying the victimhood narrative it has long applied to Israel to itself.

And in so doing, it is giving itself the same moral license. If Omar and those activists who support BDS and a secular, binational state between the Jordan River and the Mediterranean Sea really threaten to "silence" AIPAC — if American Jews' right to participate politically is now in jeopardy — then why shouldn't AIPAC use any means necessary to protect itself.

If anti-Zionism really menaces the safety of American Jewish students on campus, then banning it is simply self-defense.

It's a grand exercise in v'nahafoch hu, the turning upside down that Jews celebrated last week during Purim. In truth, it is pro-Palestinian, not pro-Israel, activists who face legislation in congress that could criminalize their speech. And it is Palestinians in Gaza—not Israelis—who face the existential threat of living in a territory that, according to the United Nations, will be unfit for human habitation by next year

Facing these realities would require that AIPAC's leaders — rather than taking refuge in Jewish victimhood — confront the moral responsibilities of Jewish power, which is something, sadly, the organization still refuses to do.

Peter Beinart is a Senior Columnist at The Forward and Professor of Journalism and Political Science at the City University of New York. He is also a Contributor to The Atlantic and a CNN Political Commentator.

U.S. Golan Recognition Proves Israel Can Retain Occupied Territories, Senior Israeli Official Says

The statement draws a comparison between the Golan Heights and the West Bank, both occupied in 1967

By Noa Landau, 26th March 2019 in HaAretz

A general view shows the town of Majdal Shams near the ceasefire line between Israel and Syria in the Israeli-occupied Golan Heights, March 25, 2019. \ AMMAR AWAD/ REUTERS

The U.S. recognition of Israeli's sovereignty over the Golan Heights proves Israel can retain occupied territories captured in a defensive war, a senior Israeli diplomatic source said Tuesday.

According to the source, who was present aboard Israeli Prime Minister Benjamin Netanyahu's flight from Washington to Israel, "Everyone says you can't hold an occupied territory, but this proves you can. If occupied in a defensive war, then it's ours."

The statement draws a comparison between the Golan Heights and the West Bank, both occupied in 1967. Right-wing Israeli parties estimate that recognition of Israeli sovereignty in the Golan Heights will serve as the basis for a future annexation of Area C in the West Bank.

The source praised the "historically and diplomatically important" move by the Trump administration, citing the "total" support of a superpower such as the U.S.

On Monday, U.S. President Donald Trump met Prime Minister Benjamin Netanyahu to sign a presidential proclamation officially recognizing the Golan Heights as Israeli territory on Monday, thus formalizing a move announced with a tweet earlier on Thursday.

In a joint press conference, Trump said: "We do not want to see another attack like the one suffered this morning north of Tel Aviv," adding: "Our relationship is powerful." Trump then said: "We will confront the poison of anti-Semitism."

The international community does not recognize Israeli sovereignty over the area, the European Union issued a statement Friday that it will not change its position regarding the Golan Heights: "The position of the EU has not changed. The European Union, in line with international law, does not recognize Israel's sovereignty over the territories occupied by Israel since June 1967, including the Golan Heights, and does not consider them to be part of Israel's territory."

United Nations Secretary-General Antonio Guterres said on Monday that it is "clear that the status of Golan has not changed," according to UN spokesman Stephane Dujarric.

The international community does not recognize Israeli sovereignty over the area, the European Union issued a statement Friday that it will not change its position regarding the Golan Heights: "The position of the EU has not changed. The European Union, in line with international law, does not recognize Israel's sovereignty over the territories occupied by Israel since June 1967, including the Golan Heights, and does not consider them to be part of Israel's territory."

United Nations Secretary-General Antonio Guterres said on Monday that it is "clear that the status of Golan has not changed," according to UN spokesman Stephane Dujarric.

File photo U.S. President Donald Trump and Israel's Prime Minister Benjamin Netanyahu hold up a Golan Heights proclamation after a meeting in the White House, March 25, 2019. Brendan Smialowski/AFP

"The UN's policy on Golan is reflected in the relevant resolutions of the Security Council and that policy has not changed," Dujarric said. A UN Security Council resolution adopted by the 15-member body in 1981 declared that Israel's "decision to impose its laws, jurisdiction and administration in the occupied Syrian Golan Heights is null and void and without international legal effect." It also demanded Israel rescind its decision.

Only around 12 per cent of the Golan's Druze hold Israeli citizenship, as most still reject it on nationalist grounds citing an allegiance to Syria.

The event is overshadowed by an escalation between Israel and Gaza that forced Netanyahu to cut his U.S. trip short.

Trump's Golan Heights decision: Endorsing illegal annexation
By David Morrison 25th March 2019 from Middle East Eye

Israeli Prime Minister Benjamin Netanyahu (R) and US President Donald Trump speak upon the latter's arrival at Ben Gurion International Airport in Tel Aviv on 22 May 2017 (AFP)

"After 52 years it is time for the United States to fully recognize Israel's sovereignty over the Golan Heights, which is of critical strategic and security importance to the State of Israel and Regional Stability!"

Those were the words of US President Donald Trump in a tweet on 21 March 2019. Most likely, they will become official US policy when Trump meets Israeli Prime Minister on his visit to Washington to address the annual policy conference of AIPAC, the American Israel lobby on 26 March.

A gift to Netanyahu

A fortnight later on 9 April, there is a general election in Israel. Netanyahu is in the fight of his life to retain his premiership. He is being challenged by a new entrant into Israeli politics, the former head of the Israeli military Benny Gantz.

The timing of Trump's announcement is a political gift to Netanyahu. On the same day the prime minister received a political gift from US Secretary of State Mike Pompeo, who visited the Western Wall in Israeli-occupied East Jerusalem with him.

By so doing, Pompeo tacitly recognised Israeli sovereignty over East Jerusalem (see below).

The US could be reasonably accused of interference in the Israeli general election.

US recognition of Israeli sovereignty over the Golan Heights was foreshadowed during the Trump presidential campaign by his advisory team on Israel - a team consisting of Jason Greenblatt, who is now Trump's chief negotiator on Israel-Palestine (along with his son-in-law, Jared Kushner), and David Friedman, who is now US ambassador to Israel.

A joint statement by Greenblatt and Friedman on 2 November 2016 contained the following short but very significant sentence: "The false notion that Israel is an occupier should be rejected."

If that principle is implemented in full, the Trump administration will recognise all of the West Bank as Israeli sovereign territory, as well as the Golan Heights. It is not inconceivable.

Israel's record of violations

Israel took over the Syrian Golan Heights by force in June 1967 and around 100,000 Syrians were driven out or fled in the process. This Syrian territory has been under Israeli military occupation ever since.

Residents of the Golan Heights raise Syrian banners during a protest against the backing of Israel's capture of the Golan Heights by the US president, on 23 March (AFP)

In 1981, Israel annexed the territory. On 17 December 1981, the Security Council passed resolution 497 demanding that Israel reverse its annexation. The resolution declared that:

"The Israeli decision to impose its laws, jurisdiction and administration in the occupied Syrian Golan Heights is null and void and without international legal effect" and demanded that "Israel, the occupying power, should rescind forthwith its decision".

Israel refused to do so and it remains in violation of resolution 497 to this day.

The US voted for resolution 497, which was passed unanimously. In other words, it was US policy in December 1981 and until recently that the Golan Heights were Syrian territory, that Israel didn't have sovereignty over them. Trump is now proposing to reverse that. To do so is in clear breach of Security Council resolution 497.

It is also in breach of Security Council resolution 2254 on Syria passed on 18 December 2015, in which the Security Council "reaffirm[ed] its strong commitment to the sovereignty, independence, unity and territorial integrity of the Syrian Arab Republic, and to the purposes and principles of the Charter of the United Nations".

In December 1981, the Security Council declared that the Golan Heights were Syrian territory, and it hadn't altered that opinion by December 2015, so when resolution 2254 speaks of the "territorial integrity of the Syrian Arab Republic" that includes the Golan Heights.

An act of aggression

The Rome Statute of the International Criminal Court now defines the crime of aggression and specifies the following as an "act of aggression":

"The invasion or attack by the armed forces of a State of the territory of another State, or any military occupation, however temporary, resulting from such invasion or attack, or any annexation by the use of force of the territory of another State or part thereof."

There is no doubt that Israel's military occupation of the Golan Heights for the past 52 years constitutes an act of aggression against the Syrian state.

Instead of the US taking steps to persuade Israel to cease this aggression and return the Golan Heights to Syria – which it could easily do by threatening to curtail military aid to Israel – the US is now proposing that Israel be rewarded for its aggression by keeping the territory it has seized permanently.

Israel has established more than 30 Jewish-only settlements in the Golan Heights with an estimated 20,000 settlers. This colonisation of occupied territory has involved the commission of war crimes by Israel on a grand scale.

Article 8.2(b)(viii) of the Rome Statute defines "the transfer, directly or indirectly, by the Occupying Power of parts of its own civilian population into the territory it occupies" to be a war crime.

In other words, when a state, which is occupying territory not its own, transfers some of its own civilians into that territory that process constitutes a war crime under international law.

There is little doubt that Israel's colonisation programme in the Golan Heights (and in the West Bank, including East Jerusalem) has involved the commission by Israel of a tsunami of war crimes as defined in the Rome Statute.

Israel 'not an occupier'

It is clear that the principle set out by Greenblatt and Friedman in November 2016 that "the false notion that Israel is an occupier should be rejected" is being steadily implemented by the Trump administration.

For example, it has now been reflected in US State Department documents, which no longer refer to the West Bank (including East Jerusalem), Gaza and the Golan Heights as "occupied".

Earlier country reports on human rights practices for Israel/Palestine were titled Israel and the Occupied Territories (see, for instance, the 2016 report), the 2017 report, published on 20 April 2018, is titled "Israel, Golan Heights, West Bank and Gaza", though the Golan Heights are still described as "Israeli-occupied" in the text. The latter has been amended to "Israeli-controlled" in the 2018 report published on 13 March 2019.

On 16 November last year, there was an indication that the Trump administration was about to cease regarding the Golan Heights as "occupied" by Israel - at a UN General Assembly committee, the US opposed a resolution condemning Israel's occupation of the Golan Heights for the first time, having abstained in previous years.

Despite the US opposition, the committee went on to approve a draft resolution by 151 votes to 2 with 14 abstentions. Only Israel joined the US in voting no. It wasn't a complete surprise, therefore, when on 21 March 2019 Trump rejected the notion that Israel is an occupier in the Golan Heights.

On the same day, as I mentioned above, accompanied by the Israeli prime minister and the US Ambassador to Israel David Friedman, the US Secretary of State Mike Pompeo visited the Western Wall in Israeli-occupied East Jerusalem.

According to Israeli press reports: "His is the first-ever visit of a top US diplomat to the Western Wall with an accompaniment of an Israeli official". By entering East Jerusalem with the Israeli prime minister at his side, the US secretary of state tacitly recognised Israeli sovereignty over East Jerusalem.

By contrast, when Trump became the first sitting US president to visit the Western Wall on 22 May 2017, the visit was described as "private" and he wasn't accompanied by the Israeli prime minister or any other high-ranking Israeli official.

The president hasn't formally rejected the notion that Israel is an occupier in East Jerusalem, but it's a fair bet that he will. Can it be long before he follows suit with regard to the West Bank as a whole and rejects completely the notion that Israel is an occupier, as prescribed by Greenblatt and Friedman in November 2016?

ENCOUNTERING PEACE: GAZA – NOW AND FOREVER

Despite its name, the protests and violence have nothing to do the right of return of Palestinian refugees and their descendants to their original homes now in the State of Israel.

BY GERSHON BASKIN MARCH 27, 2019 FROM JERUSALEM POST

TANKS DEPLOYED near the Gaza border. (photo credit: REUTERS)

March 30 will mark the 43rd Land Day (since the first Land Day in 1976) and will be one full year since the outburst of the weekly "March of Return" on the Gaza-Israel border. According to Israeli Internal Security Minister Gilad Erdan (and despite Diaspora Affairs and Education Minister Naftali Bennett's statement that soldiers are afraid to shoot), Israel has killed some 250 Palestinians along the border this past year, and injured some 25,000.

Despite its name, the protests and violence have nothing to do the right of return of Palestinian refugees and their descendants to their original homes now in the State of Israel. The violence and protests launched by Gaza civil society activists, and quickly taken over by Hamas, are meant to be a constant reminder that Palestinians are not going anywhere, and that the situation in which they live is totally unacceptable.

Israel does not hold sole responsibility for the horrible situation of Gaza. Hamas is perhaps the main party responsible for the demise of Gaza and the unlivable conditions there. But Israel, and later Egypt, have enforced a siege and closure on Gaza since 2005, when Israel disengaged from the coastal enclave. In 2007, when Hamas took control of Gaza by force from the Palestinian Authority, Israel's isolation policy – later supported by Egypt, and in the past year by the Palestinian Authority as well – has squeezed Gaza dry and made life there intolerable.

Three wars have taken place in the recent years, as well uncountable numbers of "cycles" of hit-and-retaliation between Hamas and the "Palestinian factions" in Gaza and Israel. The last cycle took place this week. Normally, Egypt comes to the rescue and enables the sides to pull back from the brink of another war. Hamas declares a ceasefire and Israel declares that quiet will be answered by quiet. Israel never agrees to announce that a ceasefire understanding has been reached. But the quiet does not last for long.

Along with the ceasefire non-agreements, understandings have been put on the table that include easing the siege, planning for an internationally secured seaport, allowing Palestinian goods from Gaza to leave Gaza, allowing students from Gaza to get to universities outside of Gaza, enabling Palestinian workers in Gaza to work in Israel, enabling normal Gazans to travel to the West Bank and beyond, enabling peace activists from Gaza (yes they do exist) to attend peace activities in Israel, increasing Gaza's ability to produce electricity, increasing supplies of healthy fresh water, and allowing Gaza to be a normal territory which is allowed to trade with the world.

Generally what happens is that Israel increases the size of the area for Palestinian fishermen to bring in their daily catch (fish is one of the main sources of protein in Gaza), which usually lasts only for a few days or a few weeks at best. Israel also recently allowed Qatar to send money to Gaza and to allow fuel to get in to power up the only electricity plant there. Basically, the payments were seen by Israel as buying additional quiet time.

THIS WEEK'S round was actually not started because of something new or changed in Gaza. It seems that the current round actually began from pressure created by a change of policy in the Hamas wing of the Rimonim Prison, where the Israel Prison Service (IPS) applied a technology which blocks the ability of the prisoners to use cellphones that are smuggled into the prisons. The IPS claims that Palestinian prisoners use their cellphones to direct terrorist operations from their prison cells to their activists in the West Bank. Prisoners and prisoner advocacy organizations claim that while some calls might be used for that purpose, the illegal phones are mainly used by prisoners to be in contact with their families. The "security" wings of Israeli prisons where Palestinian prisoners are held – as opposed to the criminal wings where both Israeli and Palestinian normal thieves, rapists and non-political murderers are held – have no public pay phones available for the prisoners. They and their support groups claim that if there were such phones available, the IPS could easily monitor all of the calls made, and the need for prisoners to have illegal cellphones would be reduced by a huge percentage.

The adaption of the blocking system against cellphones was too much for the prisoners to accept, and protests began in the prison accompanied by unprecedented violence. In a society where there have been more than one million people in Israeli prisons since 1967, every family in Palestine – in the West Bank and Gaza – has personal experience with prisons.

In addition to the prison situation, the unilateral deductions made by Israel in tax transfers to the Palestinian Authority because of its payments to the families of Palestinian prisoners, including terrorists, have led the PA to refuse to accept any transfers at all from Israel in protest. This has created an enormous burden on the Palestinian budget which cannot be met, and on PA employees, including security service personnel, who are not receiving even half of their salaries.

Add to that the PA decision not to transfer any money to Gaza, and we have the outburst of protests in Gaza against Hamas that were then crushed by Hamas with a heavy hand, all of which plays in the background to what we are witnessing this week. And we don't know how the March 30 events will pass – how much violence and how many additional casualties there will be.

On top of all of this, we have Israeli elections on April 9. I can't help but think that the current round, whatever happens, has already served the electoral interests of our prime minister. When under attack, the Israeli people rally in solidarity with each other, with the army, around the flag and around their leader.

The flare-up in Gaza serves Prime Minister Benjamin Netanyahu's interests. It has already turned attention away from submarines, shares and profits in his cousin's companies, and three indictments waiting to be issued for corruption. Netanyahu is once again Mr. Security – weighing decisions carefully, consulting with his advisers and the military commanders, and making careful, cautious decisions. Yet the situation over the past 10 years has not changed. The people of the south of Israel continue to be hit with rockets, incendiary balloons and kites – with red alerts sending them to shelters, as poverty and despair continue to fester in Gaza.

When will we all finally learn that there is no military solution for Gaza? None. Even reconquering Gaza and killing all of the current leaders of Hamas will only produce, more quickly, the next generation of young Palestinian leaders with hatred in their hearts and a willingness to fight and die for Palestine with their actions.

Palestinians are not going anywhere. Gaza will not disappear. Gaza will not sink into the sea. And the notion that deterrence can be created – which will make the two million people in Gaza accept their lot – is a lot of hot air produced by a lot of Mr. Securities and retired generals.

Drunk with power: How Trump is destroying the Middle East

by David Hearst 27 March 2019 from Middle East Eye

If you want to know who will pay the price of a re-energised Trump, the answer is the Palestinians

US President Donald Trump during a meeting with Israeli Prime Minister Benjamin Netanyahu in the Oval Office at the White House in Washington, DC, 25 March 2019 (AFP)

Special Counsel Robert Mueller's investigation has ended in the worst possible way for a large coalition of forces that hoped to see the back, or at least the beginning of the end, of US President Donald Trump.

While low-hanging fruit has fallen, Trump and his family have wriggled out of some of the most searching questions asked of a sitting president.

Questions about obstruction of justice are not over, but the Mueller firecracker has fizzled, Trump has rebounded and his pursuers are once again back on the defensive.

The prospect of a second Trump term now seems more likely.

Seismic shifts
Washington will almost certainly not be the only place to feel the seismic shifts in power that have taken place this week. If you want to know who will pay the price of a re-energised Trump, the answer is already before you: the Palestinians.

While the final act of the Mueller drama has played out, another one has unfolded almost below the radar.

This is as consequential to the Middle East as this president - who can fire an FBI director investigating him, or dangle pardons before potential witnesses - is at home.

Trump gifted Benjamin Netanyahu, the Israeli premier, the Golan Heights - a prize all other US presidents, Republican and Democrat, have rightly backed away from, and one which the EU has emphatically today rejected.

The Golan Heights on the Syrian border was captured at the same time as the West Bank was. If you allow Israel to keep this piece of occupied territory, there is nothing stopping Israel from now annexing part or all of the West Bank.

Which is exactly the point a senior official on Netanyahu's plane back from Washington made to a Haaretz reporter. He said: "Everyone says you can't hold an occupied territory, but this proves you can. If it's occupied in a defensive war, then it's ours."

Trump's logic in handing the Golan to Israel was simple, and one which he clearly explained on Fox News.

It was very much like his decision to move the US embassy to Jerusalem. "I was inundated with calls from all over the world, the leaders, mostly the leaders saying 'please don't do it, don't do it'. I did it and it's been done and it's fine."

In other words, "I got away with Jerusalem, so I can get away with the Golan."

In God's name
Piece by piece, dunam by dunam, Trump and Netanyahu have dismantled a Palestinian state and any negotiated means to obtain one. Trump has ended all US contributions to UNWRA, the UN agency which has become chief employer, educator and sustainer of the Palestinian refugee camps.

Donald Trump (L) and Benjamin Netanyahu hold up a Golan Heights proclamation on 25 March 2019 in Washington (AFP)

He will deny visas to lawyers for the International Criminal Court investigating Israeli war crimes. He has declared anti-Zionism anti-Semitic. He has taken Jerusalem and Golan Heights off the table and now declared occupiers can keep the land they conquered. And he has done all this in God's name.

Could it be, Secretary of State Mike Pompeo was asked, that President Trump is destined to help save the Jewish people from the Iranian menace?"As a Christian, I certainly believe that's possible," Pompeo, who was visiting Israel, replied.

"It was remarkable - so we were down in the tunnels where we could see 3,000 years ago, and 2,000 years ago - if I have the history just right - to see the remarkable history of the faith in this place and the work that our administration's done to make sure that this democracy in the Middle East, that this Jewish state remains," he said.

"I am confident that the Lord is at work here," Pompeo concluded.

A new mandate
This is what Trump, fettered by an ongoing Mueller inquiry, has already achieved. What will Trump, unchained from these constraints, now do in the Middle East? What would a new mandate for Trump and a re-elected Netanyahu look like for the Palestinians?

The first target in this salami slice war will be the annexation of Area C which contains most of the settlers and constitutes 61 per cent of the territory of the West Bank. The second will be the imposition of a pliant successor to a moribund Mahmoud Abbas. The third would be a military offensive in Gaza to finish Hamas off once and for all.

Trump is right. To their undying shame, the Western-backed leaders of the Arab states are all cheering him on.

The next generation of Arab leaders, Mohammed bin Salman of Saudi Arabia, Mohammed bin Zayed of Abu Dhabi, Abdel Fattah el-Sisi of Egypt, have clearly placed their own trading and security relationship with Israel over their fathers' historic pledges to protect and fight for the Palestinians.

They have stopped even pretending to maintain the boycott of the state they have yet to recognise, pending an agreed Palestinian settlement.

All are silent about the destruction of the Palestinian claim in this conflict.

Drunk with power

The Palestinians are well and truly alone. Trump and Netanyahu, two of the most destructive leaders for the Middle East, are drunk with power.

A drunk is about the last person to sense the dangers that rational and sober people see.

From 1948 to 1965, the Palestinians stayed dormant against Israel with no leaders to represent them, but they emerged to form a resistance movement in Fatah and other groups, whose cause united the Arab world and dominated it for three decades.

Inaction does not equal acquiescence. The absence today of a Palestinian leadership that can win rights and land for an occupied people does not amount to surrender. It's not game over.

Soberly, the only other flag to be seen in the seas of pro-democracy campaigners in Algiers is the Palestinian one. Rationally, the state of Israel is as hated and feared on the Arab street as it has ever been. Arab leaders whose legitimacy is paper thin depend on Israel as never before.

Any new wave of the Arab Spring, which we might well be seeing in Algeria, would change that.

A Palestinian protester waves his national flag as smoke billows from burning tyres during a demonstration along the border between the Gaza strip and Israel on 8 June 2018 (AFP)

The great mass of Arab public opinion, abandoned and suppressed by its leaders, will not stay still or inert. It will start to move in other directions. Europe is out of touch and consumed with its own disunity. Russia is out of the game.

The next war
That leaves two regional powers left to keep the Palestinian torch aflame - Turkey and Iran. The Turkish President Recep Tayyip Erdogan now plans to convert Istanbul's Hagia Sophia into a mosque in direct response to Trump's recognition of Israel's claims over East Jerusalem and Golan Heights.

Originally built as a cathedral by the Byzantine Emperor Justinian, it was converted into a mosque after the Ottoman conquest of Istanbul and then converted into a museum by Kemal Ataturk, the founder of modern Turkey.

The move is a clear signal that two can play the game of moving religious furniture around in a sensitive region.

"Now, Trump tries to declare Jerusalem as [Israel's] capital. He is giving Golan Heights to occupier Israel. Of course you will get a response from Turkey," he said.

Trump, as George W. Bush before him, terminally misunderstands how the Middle East works. Iran expands as a regional power in the vacuum created by Western overreach, miscalculation and eventually withdrawal. All it has to do is wait for the prize to drop in its lap.

Right now, Iran's most effective pro-consul, Qassem Soleimani, is meeting every single Sunni Arab group and politician that he can - Iraqi, Egyptian, Syrian, Palestinian. All those who fought Iran and Hezbollah bitterly in Syria are now finding a new ear and a new interlocutor in this man.

Trump and Netanyahu are not conquering the Middle East, but they could well be re-aligning it for the next war to come. Israel, unleashed and unbound, is the last power on earth to see clearly the damage it is doing and the generations of conflict it is engendering.

The winner takes all. It will indeed but not in the way it iDavid Hearst is the Editor in Chief of the Middle East Eye. He left The Guardian as its chief foreign leader writer. In a career spanning 29 years, he covered the Brighton bomb, the miner's strike, the loyalist backlash in the wake of the Anglo-Irish Agreement in Northern Ireland, the first conflicts in the breakup of the former Yugoslavia in Slovenia and Croatia, the end of the Soviet Union , Chechnya, and the bushfire wars that accompanied it. He charted Boris Yeltsin's moral and physical decline and the conditions which created the rise of Putin. After Ireland, he was appointed Europe correspondent for Guardian Europe, then joined the Moscow bureau in 1992, before becoming bureau chief in 1994. He left Russia in 1997 to join the foreign desk, became European editor and then Associate Foreign Editor. He joined The Guardian from The Scotsman, where he worked as education correspondent.magines now.

The Sadists Who Destroyed a Decades-old Palestinian Olive Grove Can Rest Easy

Another Palestinian village joins the popular protest, its inhabitants no longer able to bear attacks by settlers. Vandals have butchered a grove of 35-year-old olive trees in the village. The tracks led to a nearby settler outpost

Gideon Levy and Alex Levac Jan 24, 2019 in HaAretz

Vandalism in an olive grove in the West Bank village of Al-Mughayyir. Alex Levac

Who are the human scum who last Friday drove all-terrain vehicles down to the magnificent olive grove owned by Abed al Hai Na'asan, in the West Bank village of Al-Mughayyir, chose the oldest and biggest row, and with electric saws felled 25 trees, one after another? Who are the human scum who are capable of fomenting such an outrage on the soil, the earth, the trees and of course on the farmer, who's been working his land for decades? Who are the human scum who fled like cowards, knowing that no one would bring them to justice for the evil they had wrought?

We're unlikely ever to get the answers. The police are investigating, but at the wild outposts of the Shiloh Valley, and Mevo Shiloh in particular, where the perpetrators' tracks led, they can go on sleeping in peace. No one will be arrested, no one will be interrogated, no one will be punished. That's the lesson of past experience in this violent, lawless, <u>settlers'</u> country.

The story itself makes one's blood boil, but only the sight of the violated grove brings home the scale of the atrocity, the pathological sadism of the perpetrators, the depth of the farmer's pain upon seeing that his own God's little acre was assaulted by the Jewish, Israeli, settlers, believers, destroyers – just three days before Tu B'Shvat, the Jewish Arbor Day, the holiday of the trees celebrated by the same people who destroyed his grove. This is how they express their love for the land, this is a reflection of the encroacher's fondness for the earth and for nature.

And on a boulder at the far end of the grove they left their calling card, smeared on a rock: a Star of David smeared in red, shamefaced, shameful, a Mark of Cain that stigmatizes everything it stands for, and next to it, the word "Revenge." Revenge for what?

The 25 felled trees lie like corpses after a massacre on the fertile brown, plowed earth. Twenty-five thick trunks stand bare and decapitated, their roots still deep in the earth, their tops gone, the work of a malicious hand – now mere dead lumber after years of having been tended, cultivated and irrigated. It was the most impressive row of trees in the grove; the destroyers moved along it with satanic deliberateness, sawing mercilessly. When, walking amid the stumps in the grove, the distraught owner Na'asan said that for him the act was tantamount to murder, his words made perfect sense. When we were just arriving there, his wife had phoned and begged him not to visit the grove, for fear he would not be able to abide the sight. Na'asan has cancer.

In the briefcase of documents he always carries with him is a copy of the official complaint he submitted to the Binyamin district station of the Israel Police, despite the fact that he knows nothing will ever come of it, that it will be buried like every such complaint. Anyone who wanted to apprehend the rampagers could have done it that same day: Mevo Shiloh, where the tracks of the all-terrain vehicles led, is a small settler outpost – violent and brazen.

The way to Al-Mughayyir, located south of Jenin, passes through the affluent town of Turmus Ayya, many of whose residents live most of the year in the United States, only visiting their splendid homes in the summer. The village, with a population of 3,500, is separated from the town by pasture land where sheep are now grazing. Everything is lushly green.

Abed al Hai Na'asan, with a butchered olive tree. The people of Al-Mughayyir say their problems have never been with the army, only with the settlers. Alex Levac

In the center of Al-Mughayyir, a few men are standing next to an official vehicle of the Palestinian Authority. Personnel from the Palestinian Ministry of Agriculture have arrived to assess the damage suffered by the farmers; at best the ministry gives them a symbolic amount of compensation. Such is the deceptive semblance of a government that supposedly protects helpless farmers.

Everyone in the village knows that the PA can do nothing. So, about two months ago, the residents launched a popular protest, just as citizens of other villages before them have done – from Kaddoum, Nabi Saleh, Bil'in, Na'alin and others. Every Friday, they gather on their land, which lies on the eastern side of the Allon Road, and are confronted by a large number of army and Border Police forces, who disperse them with great quantities of tear gas that hangs like a pall over Al-Mughayyir, and with rubber bullets, rounds of "tutu" bullets (live 0.22-caliber bullets). Then come the nighttime arrests. Overnight this past Sunday, the troops arrested another seven villagers who took part in the demonstrations; 35 locals are currently in detention. This is the method Israel uses to suppress every popular protest in the territories.

According to the villagers, their sole demand is removal of the Mevo Shiloh outpost, which was established without a permit on a half-abandoned Israel Defense Forces base that overlooks their fields. The settlers burn the Palestininans' fields, allow their sheep to graze on their land without permission, chase away the villagers' flocks and perpetrate various "price tag" operations – hate crimes – against them.

In the previous such assault, on November 25, eight cars were damaged. The graffiti, documented by Iyad Hadad, a field researcher for the Israeli human rights organization B'Tselem, leave little to the imagination: "Death to the Arabs," "Enough administrative orders," "Revenge," "Price Tag" – and also the unfathomable "Regards to Nachman Rodan."

The people of Al-Mughayyir say their problems have never been with the army, only with the settlers. Here the war is for control of the land. It is a primeval, despairing war in which law, property rights and ownership play no part – what counts is the violence that can be perpetrated, under the aegis of the occupation authorities. When, one day, these people are forced to give up their land in the wake of the violence, the settlers will chalk up yet another impressive achievement in their effort to chop up the West Bank into separate and disconnected slices of territory. This week, when we drove across village land toward Mevo Shiloh, the villagers who rode with us begged us to turn around at once. So great is their fear of the settlers, that even when they crossed their fields in a car with Israeli plates, accompanied by Israelis, they were seized by dread.

The home of Amin Abu Aaliya, head of the village council, is perched atop a high hill, overlooking all the houses in his village and the fertile valley where his lands lie. In the winter sun that shines on the holiday of the trees, he serves a local pastry stuffed with leaves of green za'atar (wild hyssop), baked by his wife, who doesn't join us. When we ask him to "Tell her it was delicious," he replies, "She mustn't get a swelled head."

The view from the roof of his elegant home is indeed stunning. Scratchy music that blares from an old Citroen Berlingo down below heralds the arrival in the village of a vendor selling the sweet cotton candy known here as "girls' hair." In the middle of the village, young people are decorating one of the houses with flags of Fatah and Palestine: A resident of the village is due to return home today after serving two years in an Israeli prison, and a festive welcome is being prepared for him.

The West Bank village of Al-Mughayyir. Alex Levac

The Allon Road, which was paved in the 1970s and runs north to south in the eastern part of the West Bank, with the aim of severing its territories from the Kingdom of Jordan, also separated Al-Mughayyir from most of its land, about 30,000 dunams (7,500 acres), located east of the road. The villagers grew used to that over the years. They also forgave the expropriation of land for the road and afterward for its widening. There is no safe place for them to cross the Allon Road with their herds, to access their land but they grew used to that, too. Sometimes the army blocks the dirt road that leads from the village to their land and they are cut off from it, unless they decide to take a long bypass route there. A matter of routine.

The people of Al-Mughayyir also learned how to live with the former existence of the military base of Mevo Shiloh, which dominated their land. They even came to terms with the Adei Ad outpost, whose members also assaulted them. But then the IDF evacuated the base and the settlers seized it. An internet search reveals that the settlers were ostensibly removed from this outpost a few years ago. But mobile homes sprout from the high hill that overlooks the village's fields, and alongside them, large structures used for farming. Mevo Shiloh is alive and kicking.

The villagers say that the Civil Administration, a branch of the military government, promised them in the past that the outpost would be evacuated, but that didn't happen. Lacking the funds to wage a legal battle, and not believing it would produce results anyway, they embarked on their Friday demonstrations.

I asked whether they had first consulted with other locales that have waged similar struggles. "There was no need to," the council head said. "You don't need consultation when you are in the right. We feel unsafe on our own land. How are we to protect ourselves and our lands? It's a natural reaction: Either to turn to violence or to popular protest. We chose the path of popular protest."

The dirt path that leads east from the village toward the Allon Road reflects the events here in the past two months. Empty canisters of the tear gas fired at the demonstrators hang from electrical cables, the ground is strewn with the remnants of scorched tires and with stone barriers. During the Friday protest two weeks ago, 30 villagers were wounded by rubber-coated metal bullets. The troops film the demonstrators and raid the village at night to arrest them – standard procedure in the villages of the struggle. Close to 100 residents have been detained during the past two months.

A dense cloud of tear gas hangs over Al-Mughayyir during the demonstrations and, according to council head Aaliya, even wafts upward to his house high on the hill. In some cases the settlers join the security forces to disperse the demonstrations, throwing stones at the protesters.

Na'asan, whose trees were ravaged, arrives at Aaliya's house and shows him a copy of the complaint he filed with the Binyamin police: "Confirmation of submission of complaint." The space for the details of the incident is empty. The space for the place of the event contains the following, word for word: "Magir RM in the forest, nursery, grove, field." The charge: "Damage to property maliciously." Hebrew only, of course. "File No. 31237."

The police arrived at the grove last Friday, two hours after Na'asan discovered what had happened and reported it to the Palestinian Coordination and Liaison office. They said the ATV tracks seemed to lead to Mevo Shiloh. According to Na'asan, while the police were in the grove, a few settlers stood on the hill opposite and watched. The police are now investigating.

About 20 members of Na'asan's extended family subsist thanks to this grove, which before the attack boasted a total of 80 trees of different ages, all meticulously cultivated. Standing here now, he says he'll have to clear away those that were felled and bandage the stumps against the cold.

That's the only way they will perhaps sprout new branches, which he will have to tend. It will take another 35 years for the grove to return to its former state. Na'asan is 62. This grove grew together with his children, he says. He knows there's little chance he'll be around to see it recover.

Is Trump's Golan move another Balfour Declaration?

March 28, 2019 in Middle East Monitor

Trump proclaims Syrian Golan Heights as the territory of Israel - Cartoon [Carlos Latuff/MintPressNews]

The Balfour Declaration was issued in 1917 by the then British Foreign Secretary, Arthur Balfour, who viewed "with favour the establishment in Palestine of a national home for the Jewish people". Although Balfour's statement in a letter to a leading Zionist was only 67 words long, its impact has lasted for more than a century.

On Monday, at a time when the Middle East is in turmoil, Donald Trump signed an official proclamation recognising Israel's sovereignty over the occupied Syrian Golan Heights. Given that both the former British Foreign Secretary and current US President have given away land that was never theirs to dispose of, is Trump's decision another Balfour Declaration?

Trump's Golan decision was taken at the wrong time, not least because he is hoping to pass his peace plan for the Middle East and this decision is likely to be an obstacle. The Arab and Islamic countries already lack enthusiasm for his "deal of the century", and his Golan move is only going to irritate them more; at the very least, it is unlikely to win them over. This, in turn, will certainly encourage Iran and Hezbollah to take a stronger approach towards both the US and Israel.

Recognising Israeli sovereignty over the Golan Heights will not, in any way, contribute to regional stability, as Trump may believe. What's more, it further reduces the chances of Syrian-Israeli negotiations any time soon. Thus, although Trump may think that he is a man of peace, he is becoming increasingly unstable in the way that he takes unilateral decisions, whether deliberately or not.

Speaking to John Quigley, Professor of Law at the Moritz College of Law at the Ohio State University, he reminded me that the Golan Heights are Syrian territory which Israel seized and occupied by military means in 1967. "Seizure and occupation create no sovereignty," he explained. "President Trump's statement that he considers the Golan to belong to Israel has no bearing on the [official, legal] status of the territory. Regardless of whether a territory is occupied by aggression or in defence, though, occupation does not bring sovereignty. Israel is in violation of international law with its occupation."

Perhaps Trump took this step now as a favour to his ally Benjamin Netanyahu during a key General Election campaign in Israel; it will undoubtedly win the Prime Minister some votes. It may also help to divert public attention from the corruption allegations that Netanyahu is facing. This highlights the fact that Trump does not seem to understand how international relations work; to him, it's all about personal relations.

Moreover, the US has been respecting for over five decades UN Security Council Resolutions 242 and 338, but Trump has managed to make it look as if Washington not only breaks resolutions and agreements but also has no respect for what previous administrations have agreed to. This will not help the search for peace because it serves to confirm that the US can no longer be an honest broker in the Arab-Israeli conflict.

What makes Trump's latest move in the region even more provocative is that he gives the clear impression that he thinks that the Golan is his land to give away to whomsoever and whenever he wishes. What will his next move be? To give Israel the Egyptian Sinai Peninsula as well? In acting without any care for the consequences of his decisions, he is only creating more chaos in the Middle East.

The Golan announcement also has an impact on neighbouring countries such as Jordan and Lebanon, who share borders with the territory and now face an additional security threat as, indeed, does the rest of the region. Trump has given legitimacy to Netanyahu's government to claim more territory in the name of "Israel's security" at the cost of everyone else's and with Washington's obvious approval.

While the Arabs never particularly liked US policy in the Middle East, they generally had some respect for the country. That has now gone, and America's reputation has been damaged. Trump invites hatred not only of his policies but also of the US establishment itself. Furthermore, with half an eye on his own re-election campaign, he may have thought that this decision will encourage Jewish Americans to support him. He is mistaken, though, to assume that all Jews favour Netanyahu's government. Yet again, we may well see that he has miscalculated and this, like other moves in the Middle East, may backfire on the US President.

US to recognise Israel sovereignty over Golan – Cartoon [Sabaaneh/MiddleEastMonitor]

Israel is targeting the Great March of Return anniversary with vile propaganda

March 28, 2019 in Middle East Monitor

Palestinian protestor seen during a weekly "Great March of Return" demonstration near the Israel-Gaza border, on March 22, 2019 [Mohammad Asad / Middle East Monitor]

At first, it was a rocket, Israel claimed, which prompted another round of bombing of the civilians in the Gaza Strip. After damaging 500 Palestinian homes, and with talk of the Zionist state increasing its military presence on the nominal Gaza borders, the first anniversary commemorating the Great March of Return protests on 30 March is being cited as the next stage for the colonial entity's premeditated bloodshed.

Former Israel Defence Forces (IDF) Chief Benny Gantz is still pushing for more violence and has, once again, mentioned a return to targeted assassinations of Palestinians if he is elected next month. According to Gantz, current Israeli Prime Minister Benjamin Netanyahu's strategy is failing to deter Hamas in Gaza.

However, since Israel's 2014 military offensive codenamed Operation Protective Edge, Netanyahu has focused more on normalising the many forms of violence which Israel implements against Palestinians. During the years of "calm", as described by Gantz, Israel was engaged constantly in human rights violations which attracted much less scrutiny than the massacres it committed during the summer of 2014.

When Israeli media claims that "Israel and Hamas prepare to square off" and uses the Great March of Return protests as the premise for yet more IDF violence, it is clear that deterrence, which was Israel's excuse for previous atrocities, no longer forms part of Netanyahu's strategy.

The aim is to portray Palestinian resistance as violent while using an array of deadly violence which the international community, in its complicity, will have no qualms about passing off as legitimate "self-defence", even if war crimes and crimes against humanity are committed.

Unlike what happened at the start of the Great March of Return protests on 30 March last year, when even mainstream media reported widely on the atrocities committed by Israel, the planned attacks on demonstrators will this time likely garner support for its "self-defence and security" narrative because, lest anyone forgets, one rocket fired from Gaza landed north of Tel Aviv.

Israel alone is manipulating the context of the demonstrations to promote a "square off". It is erasing the history of a whole year of peaceful demonstrations in pursuit of legitimate demands and, as a result, is also preventing Palestinians from owning their own narrative by depicting the protests as irrational gatherings which require deadly force to disperse them.

It is worth remembering that throughout last year, the UN insisted on depicting the protests as the Palestinians' reaction to the Israeli-led blockade, rather than the collective and very legitimate demand to return to their land.

Now that the UN has dutifully condemned one single rocket and aligned itself unequivocally with Israel, it stands to reason that the institution will attempt to suggest that there is some equivalence between a vast, military presence on the Israeli side of the border and Palestinians gathering peacefully to demand their rights, unarmed and no match for tanks, missiles, and snipers.

Prolonging violence is Israel's latest tactic. Having opponents to this strategy within Israeli society is strengthening the objective of normalising aggression.

Continuing its assault on Gaza is not just an appendage to Netanyahu's election campaign; if Palestinians are constantly deprived of political opportunities to articulate their demands, Israel can also continue to impose its own narrative and the international community will follow suit. Most likely, this time, the UN will distance itself further from the Palestinian right of return and fully endorse, albeit with the same hypocritical expressions of "concern", the Israeli spin that any Palestinian civilians killed by IDF snipers and bombs were legitimate targets posing a threat to the soldiers hundreds of metres away. We must reject such vile propaganda.

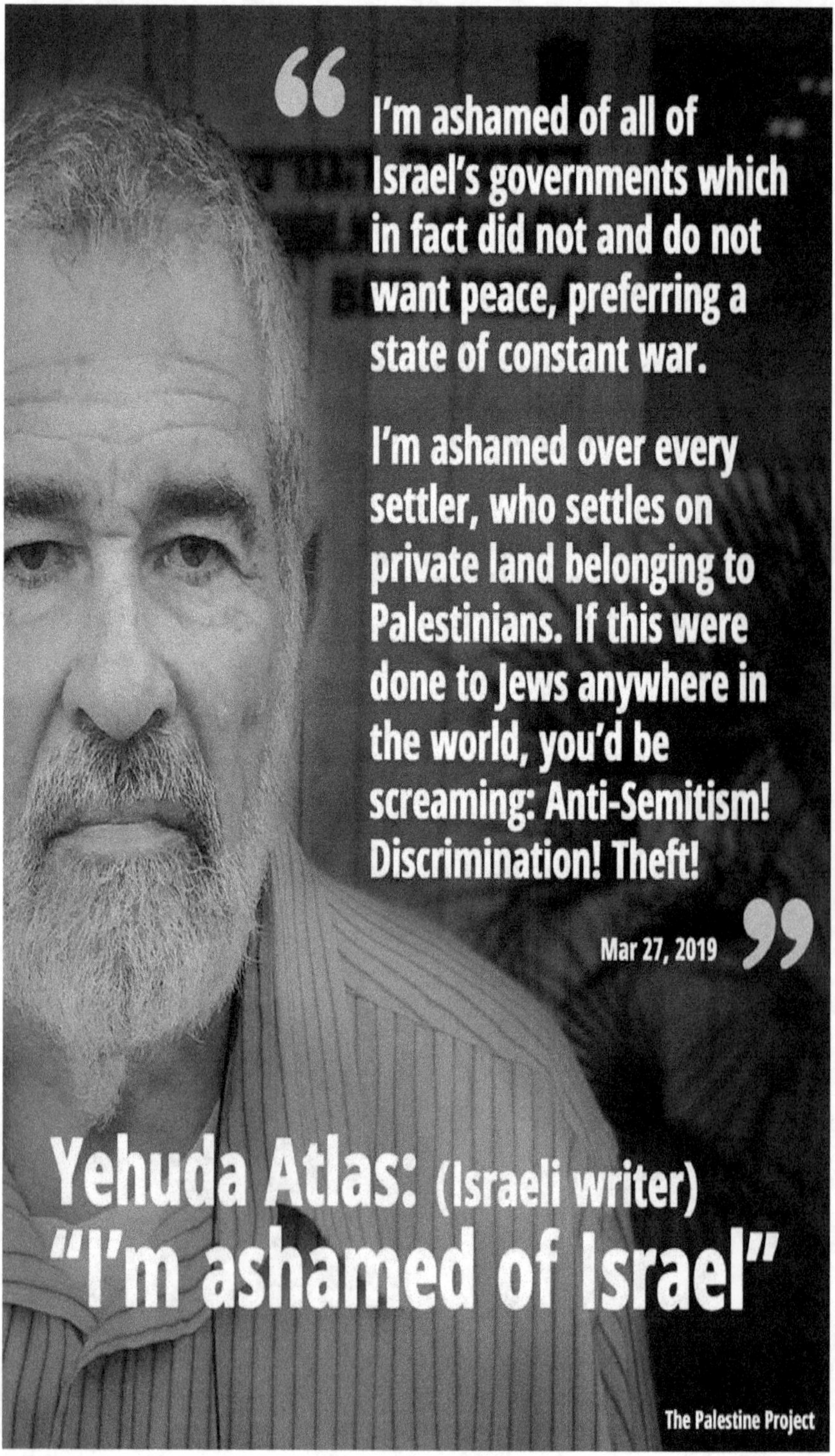

> I'm ashamed of all of Israel's governments which in fact did not and do not want peace, preferring a state of constant war.
>
> I'm ashamed over every settler, who settles on private land belonging to Palestinians. If this were done to Jews anywhere in the world, you'd be screaming: Anti-Semitism! Discrimination! Theft!

Mar 27, 2019

Yehuda Atlas: (Israeli writer)
"I'm ashamed of Israel"

The Palestine Project

Israel should see Abbas as a partner for peace

Israeli right-wing politicians actually hope for an outburst of violence in the West Bank, even if all politicians know that there is a path to peace with Palestinian President Mahmoud Abbas.

Ephraim Sneh March 28, 2019, Israel Pulse in Al-Monitor

REUTERS/Mohamad Torokman. *Palestinian President Mahmoud Abbas gestures during a meeting with the Palestinian leadership in Ramallah, West Bank, Dec. 22, 2018.*

The idea that the Gaza Strip will eventually erupt is entirely predictable.

It should be obvious to everyone that 2 million people living in such dire humanitarian circumstances and controlled by a terrorist organization is the kind of explosive material that will inevitably blow up sooner or later.

On the other hand, the explosion that is unpredictable is the one in the West Bank. There are two main reasons for the sense of relative stability that permeates that region. The first is the constant, stubborn effort by the Shin Bet, with military backing from the Israel Defense Forces (IDF), to thwart terrorism. The second is security cooperation with the Palestinian Authority (PA) and its security forces.

They are under orders from President Mahmoud Abbas, first and foremost, to prevent terrorist attacks, even though he is subjected to profound and widespread public criticism because of this. The contribution of the Palestinian security cooperation to preventing terrorism is enormous.

But the current state of stability is threatened by a series of recent developments. Should these coincide, they could cause everything to blow up and result in a major conflagration. These developments are:

- Incessant efforts by Hamas to instigate terrorist attacks in the West Bank. In 2018 alone, the Shin Bet prevented 480 attempts to launch attacks in the West Bank, 219 Hamas terrorist cells were arrested and, most tellingly, 560 attempts by individual assailants were stopped.
- An increasing sense that there is no diplomatic way out of the situation. The Arab world is busy with its own troubles, and the hills of the West Bank are being covered by settler homes. Meanwhile, the establishment of a Palestinian state — the national aspiration of the Palestinian people — seems more remote than ever, if not completely impossible. Twice in the past, this sense of isolation and hopelessness resulted in an intifada: in December 1987 and in September 2000. I was head of the Civil Administration in the West Bank in 1987 and deputy defense minister in 2000, so when I look at the current situation, I can't help but say to myself, "How similar they are!"
- The absence of any positive diplomatic developments on the horizon and the lack of achievements resulting from the Abbas policy — of rejecting terror and insisting on continued security cooperation with Israel — weaken the authority of the West Bank political leadership. At the same time, Hamas and other extremist factors have grown stronger.
- The economic situation in the West Bank, which is significantly better than that of Gaza, has nevertheless been getting worse. This can be attributed to two significant cuts to the budget of the Palestinian Authority. The first is the confiscation of half a billion shekels from tax money ($138 million) that the Israeli government collected on behalf of the PA. The second is the result of US budget cuts

to various Palestinian institutions, including the security forces that operate alongside us. The financial duress facing the PA could lead to its paralysis and even its collapse, which would certainly expedite any volatile development.
- The US administration has changed its historic role. For the past five decades, every American administration, regardless of whether it was Republican or Democrat, attempted to serve as a calming, moderating influence, intent on bringing the two sides in the conflict closer together. The Trump administration abandoned the traditional, moderating attitude of his predecessors and became a provocateur instead, fanning the flames of the conflict, even if indirectly, rather than extinguishing them. The damage the Trump administration caused to the United Nations Relief and Works Agency for Palestine Refugees in the Near East, the weakening of the PA through financial cuts and its hindering of security collaboration between Israel and the Palestinians were not intended to better the security situation in Israel. They were designed to appease Israeli Prime Minister Benjamin Netanyahu and his inner circle politically. If US President Donald Trump's "deal of the century" would blatantly reflect this stance, the deal on its own could trigger the next explosion.
- The Palestinian West Bank population is keeping close watch on Israel's actions in the Gaza Strip. Qatari money given to Hamas in a kind of protection racket supports the predominant assumption among Palestinians that Israel only understands force, and that the only way to get anything from Israel is by firing a rocket at it, not by extending a hand.
- The last development is potentially the most dangerous. It involves the sharp rise in violence among the radical settlers known as the Hilltop Youth. According to Palestinian figures, while there were 284 cases of attacks on Palestinians in 2017, the number ballooned to 614 in 2018. In the first quarter of 2019, which is not yet over, there have been at least 125 incidents. One such incident alone is enough to ignite a major conflagration.

When I say a major conflagration in the West Bank, I mean that the Palestinian-Israeli conflict will once again become violent and encompass a geographic area that includes all the cities, villages and refugee camps throughout the entire West Bank. In military terms, this is an "intercommunal conflict," or rather a civil war between those who are citizens and those who are not. There is no set mechanism to end such a conflict. It lasts a long time, has numerous casualties and leaves hundreds of thousands of people uprooted. One terrifying example of this is Syria.

Intercommunal conflict in the West Bank will impact all areas of life in Israel. The economy, exports and tourism will all suffer. Israel's diplomatic isolation will intensify. The IDF will return to policing duties, impacting its readiness for war, as happened on the eve of the Second Lebanon War in 2006.

Decision-makers are well aware of the scenario I presented and its serious consequences. Just last year, the heads of the Shin Bet and the IDF presented it to the Cabinet, as well as to the Knesset's Foreign Affairs and Defense Committee. But no one jumped up to prevent it or at the very least, to prepare for it.

The reason is that some of the more extreme leaders of the right want precisely this scenario to happen. As far as they are concerned, it is the only way to obtain 100% control over the Greater Land of Israel — the land between the Mediterranean and the Jordan River — without bearing the burden of controlling a population over half of which is Palestinian. They hope that the steps taken to impose collective punishment, which will become necessary due to the scope of the violence, will result in the mass emigration of Palestinians eastward, across the Jordan River. They will legitimize maintaining the occupation of the West Bank by force and keeping it under military rule. Supporters of this scenario believe that it is the best and only way to ensure that Arabs do not become the majority population in the land between the Jordan River and the Mediterranean. The more centrist group of right-wing leaders is aware of the risks inherent in an ethnic war in the West Bank but is not willing to come into conflict with a significant part of their voter base in order to give up control of about one-fifth of Israel's total territory, just to establish a Palestinian state.

Unfortunately, even most of Israel's center-left leadership has accepted the false premise that "there is no partner for peace." And yet, the Palestinian leader who always wanted negotiations with Israel is none other than Abbas. He has the receipts to prove it too, just as he does for his active opposition to violence and terrorism and his insistence on continuing security collaboration with Israel. All members of the Cabinet, and all those who served in a senior official position and are now political leaders, know this to be true. They were exposed to it in the briefings they heard and in the intelligence reports they read. They know that the statement, "Abbas is not a partner for peace," is a lie.

It is true that Abbas is not a partner for continuing the status quo, nor is he a partner for expanding the settlements. He is, however, a partner for serious, in-depth negotiations and has already proved as much. Toward the end of Ehud Olmert's time as prime minister, the two men engaged in many extensive discussions, which resulted in a series of understandings, not bridging all the differences. All that was left were a few minor differences, which any fair and authoritative mediator can resolve.

When they engaged in these negotiations, Abbas was president of Palestine (he still is) and Olmert was the elected prime minister of Israel. If a new Israeli government does not want to see the current situation deteriorate into intercommunal conflict in the West Bank between the settlers and the Palestinians, it will have to revisit the Olmert-Abbas understandings and simply use them as the basis for negotiations.

IDF Prepares for Large Scale Campaign
March 29, 2019 from Jerusalem on Line

Israeli Prime Minister Benjamin Netanyahu has said that he has ordered the army to prepare for a full-scale campaign in the Gaza Strip ahead of the planned clashes over the weekend.

"I ordered to deploy forces in preparation for a large-scale offensive.

All citizens of Israel must know that if we have to enter Gaza, we will do it with force and confidence, after having exhausted all possibilities, "said Netanyahu, who is also Minister of Defense.

The comments come as the army prepares for major riots along the security fence this Saturday, during the first anniversary of the "March of Return" protests and after the last escalation earlier in the week.

"We are operating on several fronts simultaneously. Not far from here are the Golan Heights, where President [Donald] Trump recognized our sovereignty three days ago. This is a great achievement for Israel. Beyond the Golan Heights is Syria and also Iran.

Iran is constantly trying to bring far-range precision missiles to Syria, very advanced and very lethal. We will not allow it, and our actions against Iran's attempts to militarily entrench itself in Syria continue all the time, "the prime minister said.

Earlier, the Israeli army announced that it attacked a group of Palestinians who threw explosives tied to balloons from the northern Gaza Strip towards southern Israel. Gaza sources reported t hat three people were injured.

Israeli artists join Palestinians in urging Eurovision contestants not to play Tel Aviv

Open Letter on March 29, 2019 in Mondoweiss

Dear Eurovision contestants,

We are Israeli artists, musicians, filmmakers, and authors. Many of us signed a letter supporting Palestinian calls to relocate the Eurovision Song Contest from Tel Aviv. Here's why.

We, as Jewish Israelis who yearn to live in a peaceful, democratic society, recognize that there is no way to achieve that without ending our government's oppression of millions of Palestinians. A society can't be considered democratic if it keeps a military rule over millions, denying them basic rights, including the right to vote. What does democracy mean when one fifth of Israeli citizens, Palestinian Arabs, are denied equal rights by law?

Our young men and women are obliged to serve in the Israeli occupation army, participating in perpetrating all sorts of crimes against Palestinians, including maintaining an illegal siege of Gaza.

"We will forever live by the sword," promised our fanatic prime minister Benjamin Netanyahu. Well, we do not wish to live by the sword! We want to live normal, peaceful lives, without oppressing or subjugating anyone. We don't want our children to join an army that most of the world accuses of committing war crimes and crimes against humanity.

In Tel Aviv itself Israel displaces the indigenous Palestinians of Jaffa using economic and legalistic means, evicting families, demolishing homes, and neglecting and defunding whole neighborhoods.

You are due to perform at the Tel Aviv Expo center, on the ruins of the Palestinian village of al-Shaykh Muwannis, whose residents were forcibly displaced and never allowed to return.

We have thought deeply about your scheduled performances. On one hand, it would so wonderful to hear your music and your messages of inclusivity. On the other, this message will be delivered in Tel Aviv, which Israel uses as means of public relations, to distract from its military occupation, apartheid policies, and ethnic cleansing against the indigenous Palestinian people. It would be the perfect diversion.

We, as artists, can't sit silent as our Palestinian counterparts suffer silencing, dehumanization and violence, and we ask you to join us in speaking out. Palestinian artists have urged you to pull out of Eurovision, and we join their call, for their sake and for our own futures.

Sincerely,

Anat Even, filmmaker
Ohal Grietzer, musician
Avi Hershkovitz, film director
Liad Hussein Kantorowicz, performance artist
Noki Katan, Techno DJ
Hagar Ophir, installation and performance artist
Michal Sapir, musician, writer
Yonatan Shapira, musician
Eyal Sivan, documentary filmmaker
Danielle Ravitzki, musician, visual artist
Eyal Vexler

Why is Britain providing cover for Israel's human rights abuses?

by Kamel Hawash, 28th March 2019 from Middle East Eye

As the US recognised Israeli sovereignty over the Golan Heights, Britain opted to oppose all UN Human Rights Council resolutions on Israeli violations of Palestinian rights

Palestinian protesters march at the Gaza fence on 22 March (AFP)

It was a bad day for Palestinians, but even worse for the long-term status of international law. I would go so far as to label 21 March "Black Thursday".

First, US President Donald Trump recognised Israel's sovereignty over the Syrian Golan Heights, illegally occupied since its capture in 1967. Then, British Foreign Secretary Jeremy Hunt announced that Britain would oppose "every Item 7 resolution" at the UN Human Rights Council (HRC) on Israeli violations of Palestinian rights.

Rabidly pro-Israel

Trump's Golan announcement came via Twitter: "After 52 years it is time for the United States to fully recognize Israel's Sovereignty over the Golan Heights, which is of critical strategic and security importance to the State of Israel and Regional Stability!"

Emboldened by an anti-Palestinian and rabidly pro-Israel US administration, the extremist Israeli government is out to get what it can while that administration is in office.

Last year, Trump recognised Jerusalem as Israel's capital and moved the US embassy to the holy city. Then, he cut US funding for the Palestinian refugee agency, UNRWA, and his team began to search for ways to end Palestinian refugees' claims to the right to return to their homes. More recently, the occupied Palestinian territories lost their "occupied" designation.

All of these actions are in breach of international law, and counterproductive to any efforts to bring peace to the troubled holy land.

The UNHRC, established in 2006, is "an inter-governmental body within the United Nations system responsible for strengthening the promotion and protection of human rights around the globe and for addressing situations of human rights violations."

Refusal to obey international law

In 2007, the council voted to make Israel's actions a permanent agenda item. Under Item 7, human rights abuses by Israel and its continued illegal occupation of Arab lands would be reported on. It is interesting to note that out of the 47 members, only Canada voted against this decision.

As expected, Israel and its supporters in the US were outraged. They accused the council of bias and of singling Israel out. Yet, Israel's human rights abuses - both before and since that decision - and its refusal to obey international humanitarian law confirm the need for that designation.

US President Donald Trump speaks in Washington on 27 March (AFP)

The UK continues to consider Israel an ally, despite its blatant disregard for international law, its human rights abuses and its refusal to implement 705 UN General Assembly resolutions. According to a 2002 study by Professor Steven Zunes of San Francisco University, Israel held the record for ignoring UN Security Council resolutions.

While the UK has condemned some of Israel's policies, including settlements, home demolitions and evictions, it has taken no concrete actions to hold it to account. Where it matters, including when Israel is accused of committing war crimes or crimes against humanity, the UK has sided with Israel's "right to self-defence".

This has been particularly evident at the HRC. In 2009, Britain chose not to vote when the Goldstone report into Israel's assault on Gaza earlier that year accused it of war crimes. This was despite the UN's High Commissioner for Human Rights insisting that it was time to end the "culture of impunity" prevailing in Israel and the Palestinian territories.

True colours

Taking its lead from the US, which left the council last year, former UK foreign secretary Boris Johnson announced that the UK would "move next year to vote against all resolutions introduced under Item 7".

On the eve of the UNHRC's 40th meeting in Geneva this month, Hunt chose the Jewish Chronicle to confirm that Britain would "oppose every Item 7 resolution. On Friday we will vote against all four texts proposed in this way."

Surely, Britain's decision to provide cover for a foreign state's human rights abuses should have been announced in the mass media, rather than a UK pro-Israel publication catering to some parts of the Jewish community. In so doing, he might also have contributed to the conflation of the UK's Jewish community with Israel, which is dangerous.

The UK ultimately voted against all resolutions under Item 7, including the Palestinians' right to self-determination. In a statement explaining its decision, the Foreign Office tried to justify this as an act not against the individual resolutions, but against the council's decision to keep Item 7.

Bizarrely, it claimed some satisfaction that the accountability resolution, which had been moved to Item 2, resulted in a UK abstention.

The UK's true colours in defending Israel came to the fore again when it abstained on the motion to adopt the report of the independent international commission of inquiry on the protests in the occupied Palestinian territories, which found "reasonable grounds" to believe that during Gaza's Great March of Return, Israeli soldiers committed violations of international human rights and humanitarian law.

Who is getting special treatment?

The UK's explanation was that it could not support a resolution that failed to investigate the role of non-state actors, particularly Hamas. The decision was roundly condemned by a coalition of charities, which called it a "dereliction of its responsibility". Shadow Foreign Secretary Emily Thornberry pressed the government further, noting that its actions effectively told Israeli authorities: "We refuse to find fault with your actions."

Both Britain and the US are not only shielding Israel from accountability for its crimes; they are damaging the standing of international law and international humanitarian law. They are also emboldening Israel to continue to feel that it can operate above the law.

If evidence was needed to confirm this, a tweet by Israeli MK Bezalel Smotrich should do. In the wake of Trump's decision to recognise Israel's sovereignty over the Golan, he called on the US president to also "recognise our sovereignty over the West Bank. God willing, we will work to achieve this soon. We hope to see your support, too."

Trump and his administration have used a combination of "facts on the ground" and "biblical" arguments to justify their decisions in support of Israel, which breach international law. Turning a blind eye to illegal facts on the ground sends a dangerous message to aggressors that their aggression can be accepted with time, and that no accountability will follow.

As for biblical justifications, surely today's "universal bible" is international law, painstakingly developed to replace the law of the jungle for the benefit of mankind.

If the status of international law is further eroded, simply for Israel's sake, then who is being singled out for special treatment?

Hundreds killed, thousands wounded: A year of Gaza rallies

Palestinians to mark a year of Great March of Return protests after UN found Israel may have committed war crimes.

by Ben White 28 Mar 2019, from Al Jazeera

The UN published a damning indictment of Israeli forces' conduct in suppressing the protests [Majdi Mohammed/AP Photo]

Palestinians in the Gaza Strip are set to mark the one-year anniversary of the Great March of Return protests, anticipating more of the same lethal violence that has characterised Israel's approach since the demonstrations began.

Last month, the United Nations Commission of Inquiry (COI) published a damning indictment of Israeli forces' conduct in suppressing the protests.

According to the COI, Israeli soldiers have been deliberately shooting civilians, killing and maiming protesters - including children, as well as journalists and medics.

The COI's findings were welcomed by human rights groups who last year unsuccessfully challenged the army's rules of engagement and its shooting policy in Israel's Supreme Court.

Those rules permit soldiers to target so-called "main inciters" - civilians deemed to be encouraging protesters to approach the fence.

"Israel has simply invented the concept of 'main inciters,'" Professor Kevin Jon Heller, associate professor of public international law at the University of Amsterdam, told Al Jazeera.

"No such status exists under international humanitarian law (IHL) or international human rights law (IHRL). Under IHL, you are either a combatant or a civilian. Under IHRL, force of any kind requires the target to pose some kind of actual threat," Heller continued.

"You can't simply shoot someone in the leg because you think they are leading a demonstration. And lethal force requires the target to post an imminent threat to life."

Legal rights centre Adalah was one of the groups which challenged Israel's response to the protests in the courts. "Israel - including the army, the government, and the Supreme Court - is recreating international law to fit its practices", said Suhad Bishara, a lawyer at Adalah who petitioned against the use of sniper fire.

"In a combat situation, IHL applies and civilians should be protected. In a law enforcement paradigm under IHRL, civilians are protected. So, what Israel has done is create new concepts that do not exist under international law to justify the killing of civilian protesters," Bishara told Al Jazeera.

As two Israeli legal experts wrote in an assessment of the Supreme Court's ruling, the government's position "conflates and obfuscates the international legal frameworks at play, creating an extremely pliable set of rules that can be manipulated depending on the exigencies of the moment".

A key part of Israel's approach to the protests is the designation of Gaza as an "enemy entity", which dates back to a September 2007 security cabinet decision.

It is this definition which "gives the green light to many illegal practices", said Bishara, whose colleagues at Adalah are currently challenging in the courts a decision to prevent any Palestinian in Gaza from seeking compensation on the basis they live in an "enemy entity".

"For the sniper, everyone on the other side of the fence is seen de facto as a threat; either you are officially affiliated to Hamas, or you are protecting them somehow. The Israeli Supreme Court categorised the demonstrators as participating in hostilities and determined that, as such, 'they lose their protection'. This is how you criminalise everyone as a potential threat - according to these broad, arbitrary, and inaccurate definitions, Israel is saying there is almost no civilian society in Gaza."

Hundreds killed, thousands wounded

According to Palestinian health officials, more than 250 Palestinians have been killed since the protests began and thousands more have been injured.
In its report, the UN found that 189 Palestinians were killed between March 30 and December 31 last year.

Israel's response to the Great March of Return protests is only the latest in a series of actions in Gaza that have drawn international condemnation.

During the 50-day offensive in 2014, for example, Israeli officials were slammed for a policy that saw Palestinian family homes repeatedly targeted over supposed links to armed faction members.

Haydee Dijkstal, an international criminal and human rights lawyer from 33 Bedford Row, told Al Jazeera that the steps taken by Israel with respect to Gaza since the 2005 withdrawal of settlers signify "a trend away from the concept of proportionality, and a retreat from protections that civilians are guaranteed under international humanitarian law".

"To categorise a whole family, groups of protesters or an entire residential area in such a way that innocent civilians could be targeted or designated as acceptable collateral damage suggests an attempt to create a justification for indiscriminate attacks and collective punishment which does not exist under international law", she added.

Israel has responded to the COI and other criticism from local and international human rights groups with the same basic message: the Great Return March protests are organised by terrorists, and the overwhelming majority of those shot have been terrorists.

A key part of Israel's public relations campaign has been figures disseminated by the Meir Amit Intelligence and Terrorism Information Centre, once described by an Israeli security journalist as a "pipeline" for "assessments that the Military Intelligence research division does not want directly associated with it".

Meir Amit's "analyses" of Great Return March casualties is - by its own admission - reliant on "circumstantial evidence", with a mere "affiliation" or "link" to any Palestinian political faction enough to classify a protester as a "terrorist". Meir Amit has categorised children as young as 13 as "terrorists", as well as slain journalist Yaser Murtaja.

The centre's "statistics" are cited by Israeli diplomats, as well as pro-Israel publications with headlines like: "Firm Proof That Most Palestinians Killed in Gaza Protests Had Terrorist Ties".

By contrast, Israeli human rights group B'Tselem has concluded that, out of 190 identified fatalities among demonstrators, only 53 - or 28 percent - were confirmed as "participating in hostilities", a designation the NGO assigns based solely on an individual's active membership in an armed faction.

The UN COI, meanwhile, stated that "at least 29 of those killed at the demonstration sites were members of Palestinian organized armed groups".

For international law experts like Dijkstal, Israel's ongoing approach to Gaza "risks providing an example whereby creating overly broad policies and categorisations could be used to suppress opposition or protest, and individuals exercising their fundamental human rights to free expression and peaceful assembly are unlawfully targeted under the guise of being a threat".

"Israel constantly stretches the limits of IHL and IHRL to justify its use of force against Palestinians," said Heller.

"Instead of using international law as a minimal standard designed to protect civilians, Israel uses it as a 'war manual' ... looking for loopholes and basing its actions on unreasonable and legally flawed interpretation, founded on a morally repugnant world view," a B'Tselem spokesperson told Al Jazeera.
"This is not a legalistic or theoretical issue: this guise of legality legitimizes Israel's immoral, lethal policies in the eyes of both the Israeli public and the international community, which allows Israel to persist in its action with their fatal outcomes."

Palestinian Great March of Return:
Counting the human cost

At least 60 Palestinian demonstrators in Gaza were killed as the Israeli army fired live ammunition, tear gas and firebombs at protesters assembled along several points near the fence with Israel. More than 2,700 others were wounded.

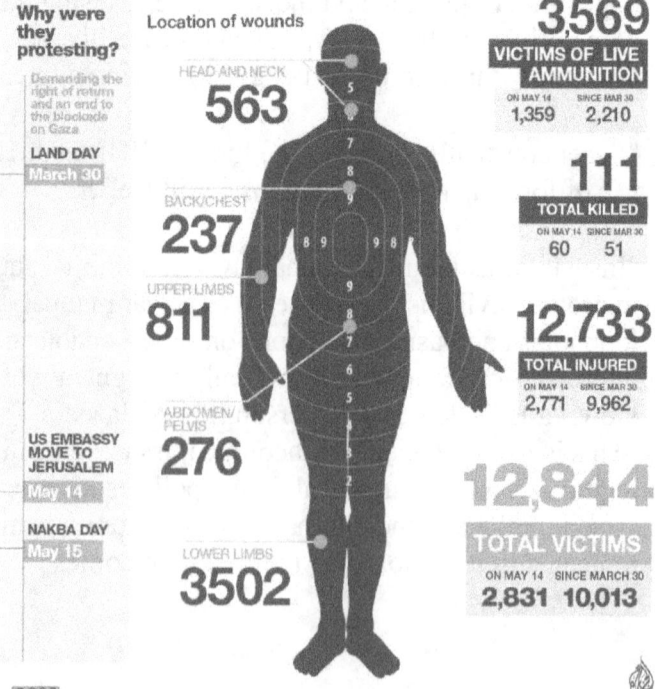

Why were they protesting?
Demanding the right of return and an end to the blockade on Gaza

LAND DAY
March 30

US EMBASSY MOVE TO JERUSALEM
May 14

NAKBA DAY
May 15

Location of wounds

HEAD AND NECK: 563
BACK/CHEST: 237
UPPER LIMBS: 811
ABDOMEN/PELVIS: 276
LOWER LIMBS: 3502

3,569
VICTIMS OF LIVE AMMUNITION
ON MAY 14: 1,359
SINCE MAR 30: 2,210

111
TOTAL KILLED
ON MAY 14: 60
SINCE MAR 30: 51

12,733
TOTAL INJURED
ON MAY 14: 2,771
SINCE MAR 30: 9,962

12,844
TOTAL VICTIMS
ON MAY 14: 2,831
SINCE MARCH 30: 10,013

SOURCE: PALESTINIAN MINISTRY OF HEALTH IN GAZA | AS OF 3pm (12:00 GMT) MAY 16, 2018
@AJLabs ALJAZEERA

What have the Palestinians gained from a year of protests along the eastern Gaza fence?

March 29, 2019, by Motasem A Dalloul in Middle East Monitor

Palestinian protestors seen during a weekly "Great March of Return" demonstration near the Israel-Gaza border, on 22 March, 2019 [Mohammad Asad/Middle East Monitor]

On 30 March last year, the Palestinians in the Gaza Strip took part in the Great March of Return, an example of popular resistance initiated by activist Ahmad Abu Rtema and then adopted by the factions. They then established the National Committee for the Great March of Return and Breaking the Siege in order to run the protests. Protests have been held weekly ever since.

The Committee adopted the goals laid down by Abu Rtema, which remain an end to the 12-year-old Israeli-led siege imposed on the territory, and highlighting the right of Palestinian refugees to return to their homes and land inside what is now called Israel, from where their families were forced out by Zionist terrorists prior to the creation of the state in 1948.

Over the past year, Israeli occupation forces have killed 273 protesters and wounded more than 25,000 others. The so-called Israel Defence Forces also carried out several military operations while trying to suppress the protests, prompting the Palestinian resistance groups to respond by targeting Israeli cities and towns with homemade rockets. This, in turn, prompted urgent international mediation, with Egypt and the UN getting involved in an effort to calm the situation.

Putting the bloodshed to one side, the Palestinian factions and many observers argue that the protests have achieved a lot on the political, national and humanitarian levels. They have, for example, put the Palestinian issue back to the top of the regional and international agendas. The protesters have also undermined the implementation of the US "deal of the century", which has not yet found the quiet and stable environment necessary for it to be unveiled.

Perhaps more than anything else, the protests have exposed the brutal reality of the Israeli occupation state, which claims to be a beacon of democratic values. Israel used lethal force against peaceful, unarmed protesters who, according to the UN and other international bodies, posed no danger whatsoever to its soldiers. The shocking death toll illustrated the fact that Israel has no respect for the right of the Palestinians to demonstrate in support of their legitimate right of return to their land.

In addition, the protests led to qualitative progress in the fractured relationship between the Palestinian resistance factions and a number of countries in the region, especially Egypt, which has been mediating a truce between the Palestinian resistance groups in Gaza and the Israeli government.

Palestinian resistance activists in the occupied West Bank have been inspired by what they have seen in Gaza, as have the millions of Palestinians in the refugee camps in neighbouring states and in the wider diaspora. They have seen their right of return being discussed at the highest levels.

Regarding the national gains, the Great March of Return protests are the largest ever popular resistance action. The fact that they are now coordinated by the unified National Committee is significant. This body, which includes rival factions, has had an impact on all national activities organised by any of the Palestinian factions in the Gaza Strip. This unity was reflected in the formation of the

Joint Control Room for the military wings of the factions, which has been taking decisions regarding resistance efforts.

On the humanitarian side, the protests have pushed Israel to ease its siege imposed on Gaza, even before any comprehensive understanding or truce has been agreed. In an effort to reduce or end the protests, Israel has allowed more electricity, paid for by Qatar, into the Gaza Strip; allowed Qatar to fund a job creation programme for 13,000 unemployed graduates and workers in the enclave; increased the fishing zone; allowed more exports and imports; afforded monthly cash payments to over 10,000 poor families; and opened the Rafah Crossing for people and trade. This has had a very positive impact on the devastated Gaza economy.

The Great March of Return protests have, therefore, achieved much for the Palestinians in the still besieged territory. Moreover, they have also shown that when they are united, the people are capable of great things, making everyone much more optimistic about achieving their national goals.

Suffering in Gaza isn't a humanitarian issue, it's an Israeli political decision

Recent rockets fired into central Israel by armed groups in Gaza were not 'mistakes,' as both Hamas and Israel claim. The counter-intuitive context, Tareq Baconi explains, is a Hamas attempt to get Israel back onboard with a cease-fire agreement. Excerpts from The +972 Podcast.

Hamas and Israel reached a cease-fire agreement last November following months of Egyptian-mediated negotiations. Under that agreement, Israel was supposed to ease restrictions on the movement of people and goods in and out of Gaza. Hamas was supposed to curtail protests along the fence.

Tareq Baconi, Ramallah-based analyst for the International Crisis Group and author of "Hamas Contained: The Rise and Pacification of Palestinian Resistance," believes that two rockets fired into central Israel by militants in Gaza in recent weeks were attempts by Hamas and other Palestinian factions "to pressure Israel into meeting its obligations under that cease-fire agreement" and adopt a more sustainable policy toward Gaza.

The Gaza Strip is facing an unprecedented crisis, Baconi explained on The +972 Podcast. In addition to the humanitarian and economic crises created by Israel's 12-year blockade, the Palestinian Authority has stopped paying tens of thousands of Gazans their salaries and pensions.

Furthermore, the staggering number of Palestinians killed and maimed during a year of the Great March of Return protests has had its own impact on the health system and economy. Many in Gaza, Baconi said, "would tell you they have nothing to lose."

Indeed, the Great Return March and the recent flare up are connected, according to Baconi.

Below are excerpts of the interview, which can be heard in full on The +972 Podcast. Look for us on iTunes or wherever you get your podcasts.

"From day one, before the protests had even been initiated, [Israel] adopted an open fire and live fire policy against these civilians at staggering cost in terms of the loss of human life. But what that means as well is that popular mobilization on its own failed to compel Israel to revisit its blockade or its policies of isolation and failed to compel the international community to bring pressure on Israel to deal with the Gaza Strip differently."

"In other words, the lesson that came out of the Gaza Strip was that only force works. Only when Hamas got involved was there an opening to start talking in terms of cease-fire negotiations and to bring more pressure on Israel. Only when the protests appeared to be more destructive and more intense to the peripheral communities within Israel did Israel respond."

It's interesting that once civil society took matters into its own hands, the way to ease the blockade again was to put the Great March of Return protests under Hamas' wing. It sort of keeps control with Hamas.

"This is the biggest tragedy of the Great March of Return. It was very much a movement that was inspiring when it started and I think Palestinians — not just in the Gaza Strip, but everywhere — are talking about shifting to a rights-based struggle. They're talking about shifting their struggle to an anti-apartheid struggle, to one that demands equality and freedom across the land, from the river to the sea."

"The Gaza Strip, and what's been happening over the course of the past year, shows how treacherous that path is. It shows how worrying it is for Palestinians to mobilize on the grassroots level because they face unprecedented challenges. They face challenges from Israel […] that has no qualms killing and firing at civilians who are engaged in popular protests, but you also see internal challenges where Palestinian factions co-opt and mobilize for their own factional interests."

"There's a real question here for Palestinians — for Palestinians who believe in civil disobedience and popular protests but who also do not believe in armed struggle, and do not believe in firing rockets at civilian populations in Israel. There's a real question as to how to disrupt life in Israel in a way that allows for their demands to be heard without allowing their protests to be quashed."

We're also seeing internal divisions, both with Hamas and the Palestinian Authority, but also between Hamas and Islamic Jihad. Is the recent flare-up, the rocket that was fired last Monday, connected to Hamas' ability to control other factions as well?

"I do not think this rocket fire […] was a result of those complications. I do think that there were many reasons that this specific rocket was fired. The broader reason is the cease-fire discussions, and this is Hamas' way of trying to compel Israel to meet its cease-fire obligations before the election."

"[Hamas] believes that the [Netanyahu government] isn't going to escalate before the elections. So it believes that this is its best shot to force some kind of concession before the elections. But there are more immediate factors," Baconi added, mentioning disturbances and Israeli measures against Palestinian prisoners inside Israel, tensions on the Temple Mount/Haram al-Sharif, as well as the Israeli army's expanded incursions in the West Bank.

It has been said that these rockets were accidentally fired. Can you shed light on some of what's happening there?
"In terms of the two rockets that were fired on March 14, the narrative that came out of that incident was that the rockets were fired by mistake. That was the story that Hamas leaders gave the Egyptian delegation that happened to be in the Gaza Strip on the day of the rocket fire. And that was also the story that was put forward by Israel's own security establishment."

"But I don't believe the story that the rockets were fired by mistake. This narrative allows Hamas to claim that it still is abiding by its policy of not firing rockets and [it gives] Israel leeway to not respond in force or through a major escalation. But at the same time, it is a demonstration of Hamas' willingness and capacity to fire rockets if Israel doesn't meet its obligations under the cease-fire."

"So it's basically a fig leaf that allows both parties to pretend that they're still interested in averting an escalation, but also reminding the other that they could go toward an escalation if the cease-fire doesn't hold."

The Trump administration this week recognized the Golan Heights as Israeli territory. It also recently committed to more humanitarian aid for Gaza. How does this affect everything that's going on?
"The way the Trump Administration is dealing with the question of Palestine is somehow paradoxical because on the one hand you hear about the administration wanting to alleviate humanitarian suffering in the Gaza Strip, and on the other hand you see them defunding UNRWA, which in many instances is a matter of life and death for Palestinians in Gaza."

"So what's clear in the Trump policies is that there is an effort to de-politicize the Palestinian question. Money is taken away from UNRWA in order to redefine who and what a Palestinian refugee is, and money is injected into the Gaza Strip, or planned to be injected into the Gaza Strip, to fund infrastructure projects or to fund economic development."

"The Gaza Strip is suffering because it's under blockade; it's under blockade because of a political decision by Israeli governments to maintain the segregation of two million Palestinians, away from Israeli control. That decision is a political decision. The Gaza Strip is not an economic challenge to be resolved. The situation of the Gaza Strip, as in the West Bank and East Jerusalem, won't be alleviated until Palestinian political rights are addressed."

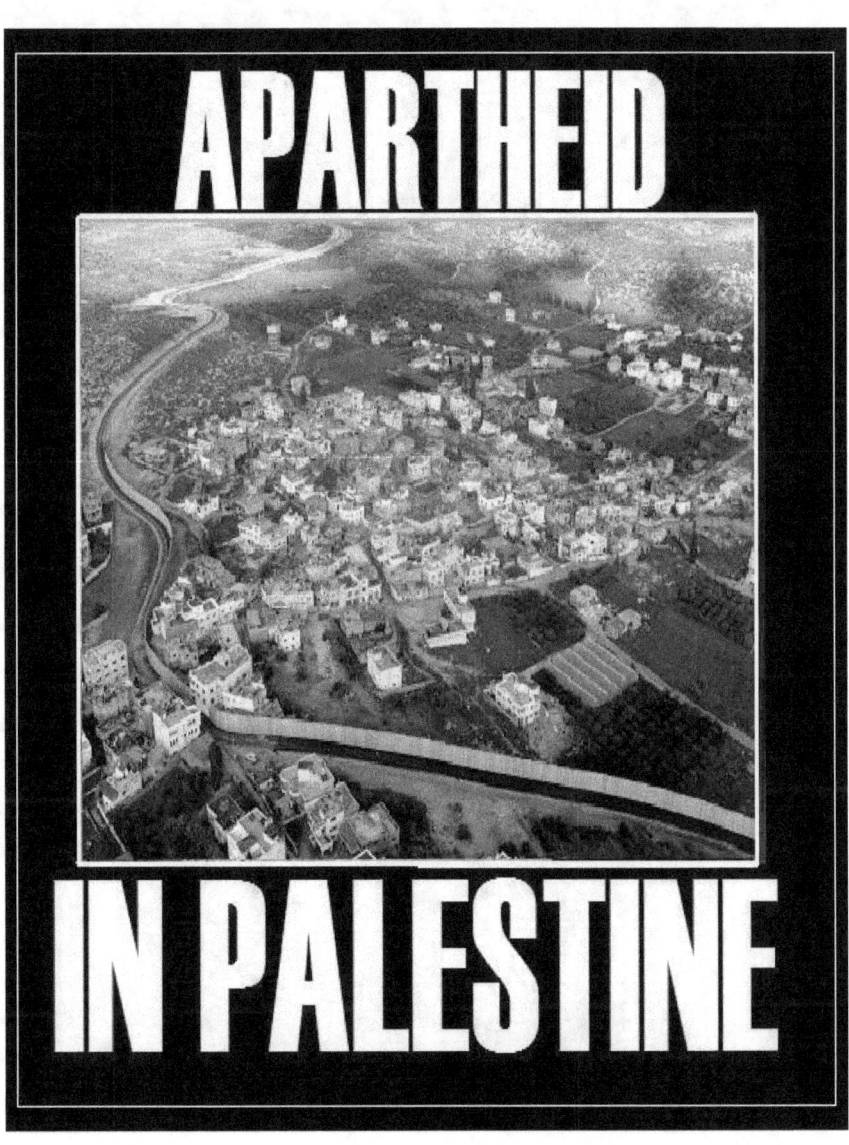

Israel kills four during March of Return anniversary protest

Tens of thousands gather in Gaza in largely restrained demonstrations, as Palestinians elsewhere mark Land Day

30th March 2019 from the Middle East Eye

Tens of thousands of Palestinians demonstrated in the Gaza Strip on Saturday, marking the one-year anniversary of the Great March of Return protest movement that has rocked the besieged enclave.

Gaza's Health Ministry reported four deaths from gunfire: a 21-year-old man and three 17-year-old boys. However a repetition of previous protests, where as many as 60 people have been killed in one day, was averted.

Adham Amara was shot in the face, Tamer Abu al-Kheir was shot in the chest and Bilal Mahmoud al-Najjar was also shot. They were all 17. Their deaths mean 52 children have been killed by Israeli forces in Gaza since the Great March of Return began, according to Save the Children.

Now some 200 Palestinians have been killed overall as Israel has cracked down on protests that have become a weekly occurrence.

A Palestinian man checks the damage following an Israeli air strike in the southern Gaza Strip city of Khan Yunis, March 10, 2019. (Abed Rahim Khatib/Flash90)

Ahead of Saturday's protest, Palestinian factions called for calm, and around 8,000 members of security were deployed along Gaza's 65km frontier with Israel to stop protesters from reaching the boundary fence.

The efforts appeared to be largely successful, with the assistance of an Egyptian delegation that has been brokering negotiations with Israel and the Strip's rulers Hamas. Both the Egyptians and Hamas' leader in Gaza, Yahya Sinwar, appeared near the frontier to urge restraint.

Hamas hopes an agreement with Israel can help ease the blockade that is crippling the deprived coastal enclave. Khalil al-Hayya, a senior member of Hamas' politburo, told MEE that the protests can help implement such an agreement.

"Today I salute the people who participated in their thousands in this protest, despite the hunger," he said on Saturday.

"Tomorrow, the Egyptian delegation is to receive a timeframe for the implementation of the truce understandings. These crowds are the kind of pressure on the Israeli occupation that will make it to commit to its pledges."

Israeli crackdown

Palestinians protest in Gaza (Reuters)

Despite the protesters' restraint, Israeli forces met the demonstrations with live fire, rubber bullets and teargas.

Nizar Abu Amro, a paramedic with the Medical Relief Association NGO, told MEE that Israeli forces were using a new type of gas on the protesters.

"They used nerve gas and another strange kind of teargas, which is yellow. We do not know anything about its contents, but it causes strange disorders," he said. The gas was first seen two days ago in Jabalia in Gaza's south, and Abu Amro said it is now being tested to determine what it is.

Several Palestinians described Israeli forces firing on protesters despite being some distance from the frontier. An MEE correspondent east of Gaza's al-Burij refugee camp witnessed the military heavily firing teargas at Palestinians despite them being 300 metres away from the boundary fence.

According to the Gaza health ministry, 244 Palestinians were wounded across the Strip, five of which were in critical condition. A paramedic was among those injured.

'We do not fear their fire'

A year ago the Great March of Return kicked off calling for Gaza's 11-year siege to be lifted and for the right of return for Palestinians locked out of their ancestral homes now in Israel.

Speaking to MEE as he toyed with empty teargas canisters, Hussein Swedan, 15, said he had every intention of returning to the central Israeli city of Ramla, where his family was expelled from in 1948.

"I came here to tell the world and the Israeli occupation that I will never forget the land of my fathers and grandfathers. We have a home in Ramla and we will one day return to it," he told MEE."I tell the Israeli occupation that we do not fear their fire."

In Malaka, east of Gaza City, Iktimaal Hamad told MEE that Palestinian women's place at the forefront of the protests was crucial.

"The Palestinian woman has brought forth something so precious and valuable for the sake of the Palestinian cause, and will always be on the frontlines confronting the challenges, confronting the plots that she is exposed to," she told MEE.

Nearby was Attallah al-Feeyomi, 19, who was shot in the leg in the same spot during an earlier protest, leading to amputation.

He is one of at least 136 Palestinians to have had a limb amputated after being shot while protesting this year, according to Gaza health ministry statistics

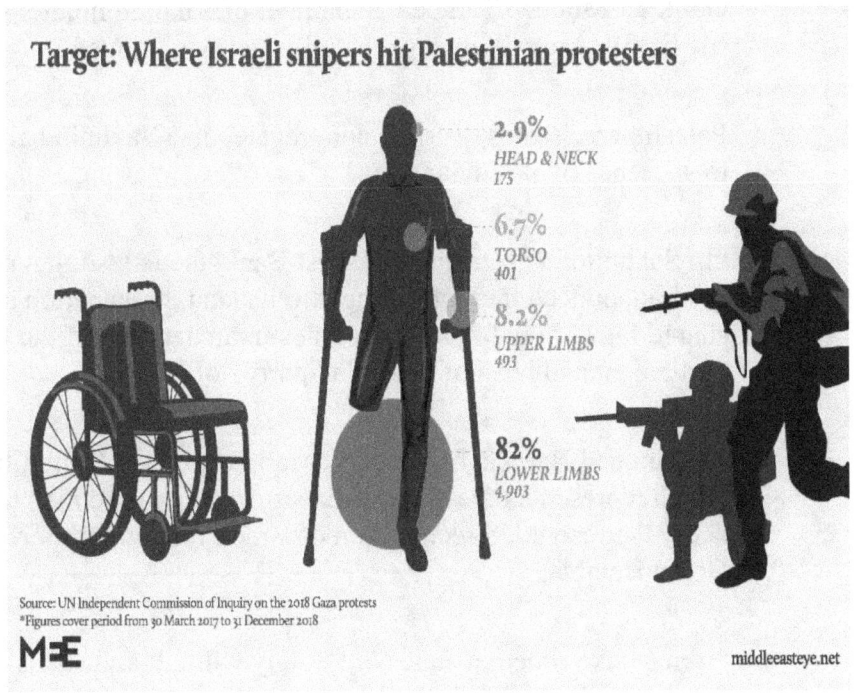

"We are here to break the siege on the Gaza Strip and call on the occupation to leave our lands," he said.

"They have weapons, tanks, planes and guns that are internationally prohibited. We have our rocks."

Land Day honoured

Saturday also saw the anniversary of Land Day, when in 1976 Israeli attempts to expropriate Arab land were met with widescale protests. Land Day has subsequently become a cause celebre for all Palestinians, hence the March of Return's start date. Outside the illegal Israeli settlement of Beit El in the occupied West Bank, a demonstration turned violent, as Palestinians resisted the Israeli military presence by burning tyres and throwing rocks.

Meanwhile, in Sakhnin, a town in Israel's Galilee, 2,000 Palestinian citizens of Israel braved poor weather to march and protest. "We feel united in all parts of Palestine, from Gaza to the Galilee," Muneeb Tarabeh, a member of Sakhnin municipality, told MEE. "We are rallying against all Israeli violations."

Palestinian citizens of Israel congregated in a Sakhnin hall to listen to speeches by politicians.

"In Sakhnin, in Gaza and the West Bank, the Palestinian people have announced their attachment to its land, to its nation and its shared fate," Jamal Zahalka, a Palestinian member of the Israeli parliament and head of the Balad party, told MEE.

Mohammed Baraka, head of the Arab Follow-Up Committee, which represents Palestinian citizens of Israel, used his platform to decry the recent US recognition of Israeli rule over the Syrian Golan Heights.

"It may take time but states of tyranny will fall and states of freedom will rise," he told the crowd. "Trump's declaration granting the Golan to Israel, this declaration will fall because there is no right over our right."

How Israel is working to remove Palestinians from Jerusalem

Residents and analysts say Israel is stepping up its bid to displace Arabs in the disputed city

By [Jonathan Cook](#), 31st March 2019, in "The National"

An Israeli flag flutters at Mount of Olives with the Old City of Jerusalem and its Dome of the Rock mosque in the centre, March 27, 2019. AFP

The 350,000 Palestinian inhabitants of occupied East Jerusalem are caught between a rock and hard place, as Israel works ever harder to remove them from the holy city in which they were born, analysts and residents warn.

That process, they say, has only accelerated in the wake of US President Donald Trump's decision a year ago to relocate the American embassy to Jerusalem, effectively endorsing the city as Israel's exclusive capital.

"Israel wants Palestinians in Jerusalem to understand that they are trapped, that they are being strangled, in the hope they will conclude that life is better outside the city," said Amneh Badran, a politics professor at Jerusalem's Al Quds university.

Since Israel seized the eastern part of Jerusalem in 1967 and then illegally annexed it in 1981, it has intentionally left the status of its Palestinian population unresolved.

Israeli officials have made Palestinians there "permanent residents," though, in practice, their residency is easily revoked. According to Israel's own figures, more than 14,500 Palestinians have been expelled from the city of their birth since 1967, often compelling their families to join them in exile.

Further, Israel finished its concrete wall slicing through East Jerusalem three years ago, cutting some 140,000 Palestinian residents off from the rest of the city.

A raft of well-documented policies – including house demolitions, a chronic shortage of classrooms, lack of public services, municipal underfunding, land seizures, home evictions by Jewish settlers, denial of family unification, and police and settler violence – have intensified over the years.

At the same time, Israel has denied the Palestinian Authority, a supposed government-in-waiting in the West Bank, any role in East Jerusalem, leaving the city's Palestinians even more isolated and weak.

All of these factors are designed to pressure Palestinians to leave, usually to areas outside the wall or to nearby West Bank cities like Ramallah or Bethlehem.

"In Jerusalem, Israel's overriding aim is at its most transparent: to take control of the land but without its Palestinian inhabitants," said Daoud Alg'ol, a researcher on Jerusalem.

Like others, Mr Alg'ol noted that Israel had stepped up its 'Judaisation' policies in Jerusalem since the US relocated its embassy. "Israel is working more quickly, more confidently and more intensively because it believes Trump has given his blessing," he said.

Demographic concerns dominated Israel's thinking from the moment it occupied East Jerusalem in 1967, and subordinated it to the control of Jewish officials in West Jerusalem – in what Israel termed its newly "united capital".

City boundaries were expanded eastwards to attach additional Palestinian lands to Jerusalem and then fill in the empty spaces with a ring of large Jewish settlements, said Aviv Tatarsky, a researcher with Ir Amim, an organisation that campaigns for equal rights in Jerusalem.

The goal, he added, was to shore up a permanent three-quarters Jewish majority – to ensure Palestinians could not stake a claim to the city and to allay Israeli fears that one day the Palestinians might gain control of the municipality through elections.

Israel has nonetheless faced a shrinking Jewish majority because of higher Palestinian birth rates. Today, Palestinians comprise about 40 per cent of the total population of this artificially enlarged Jerusalem.

Israel has therefore been aggressively pursuing a twin-pronged approach, according to analysts.

On one side, wide-ranging discriminatory policies – that harm Palestinians and favour Jewish settlers – have been designed to erode Palestinians' connection to Jerusalem, encouraging them to leave. And, on the other, revocation of residency rights and the gradual redrawing of municipal boundaries have forcibly placed Palestinians outside the city – in what some experts term a "silent transfer" or administrative ethnic cleansing.

Israel's efforts to disconnect Palestinians from Jerusalem are most visibly expressed in the change of Arabic script on road signs. The city's Arabic name, Al Quds (the Holy), has been gradually replaced by the Israeli name, Urshalim, transliterated into Arabic.

The lack of services and municipal funding and high unemployment mean that three-quarters of Palestinians in East Jerusalem live below the poverty line. That compares to only 15 per cent for Israeli Jews nationally.

Despite these abysmal figures, the municipality has provided four social services offices in the city for Palestinians, compared to 19 for Israeli Jews.

Only half of Palestinian residents are provided with access to the water grid. There are similar deficiencies in postal services, road infrastructure, pavements and cultural centres.

Meanwhile, human rights groups have noted that East Jerusalem lacks at least 2,000 classrooms for Palestinian children, and that the condition of 43 per cent of existing rooms is inadequate. A third of pupils fail to complete basic schooling.

But the biggest pressure on Palestinian residents has been inflicted through grossly discriminatory planning rules, said Mr Tatarsky.

In the areas outside the wall, Palestinians have been abandoned by the municipality – and receive no services or policing at all.

Israel's long-term aim, said Mr Tatarsky, had been exposed in a leak of private comments made by Israeli Prime Minister Benjamin Netanyahu in 2015. He had proposed revoking the residency of the 140,000 Palestinians outside the wall.

"At the moment, the government is discussing putting these residents under the responsibility of the army," Mr Tatarsky said.

That would make them equivalent to Palestinians living in Israeli-controlled areas of the West Bank and sever their last connections to Jerusalem.

Meanwhile, on the inner side of the wall, Palestinian neighbourhoods have been tightly constrained, with much of the land declared either "scenic areas" or national parks, in which construction is illegal, or reserved for Jewish settlements. The inevitable result has been extreme overcrowding.

In addition, Israel has denied most Palestinian neighbourhoods' masterplans, making it all but impossible to get building permits.

"The advantage for Israel is that planning regulations don't look brutal – in fact, they can be presented as simple law enforcement," said Mr Tatarsky. "But if you have no place to live in Jerusalem, in the end you'll have to move out of the city."

An estimated 20,000 houses – about 40 per cent of the city's Palestinian housing stock – are illegal and under threat of demolition. More than 800 homes, some housing several families, have been razed since 2004.

As well as the large purpose-built Jewish settlements located on Palestinian land in East Jerusalem, several thousand extremist settlers have taken over properties inside Palestinian neighbourhoods, often with the backing of the Israeli courts.

Mr Tatarsky noted that Israel has been accelerating legal efforts to evict Palestinians from their homes over the past year, with close to 200 families in and around the Old City currently facing court battles.

When settlers move in following such evictions, Ms Badran said, the character of the Palestinian neighbourhoods rapidly changes.

"The settlers arrive, and then so do the police, the army, private security guards and municipal inspectors. The settlers have a machine behind them whose role is to make life as uncomfortable as possible for Palestinians. The message is: 'You either accept your subjugation or leave'."

In Silwan, where settler groups have established a touristic archaeological park in the midst of a densely populated Palestinian community just outside the Old City walls, life has been especially tough.

Mr Alg'ol, who lives in Silwan, noted that fortified settler compounds had been established throughout the area, many dozens more Palestinian families were facing evictions, excavations were taking place under Palestinian homes, closed-circuit TV watched residents 24 hours a day, and the security services were a constant presence. Many hundreds of children had been arrested in recent years, usually accused of stone throwing.

Israel's newest move is the announcement of a cable car to bring tourists from West Jerusalem through Palestinian neighbourhoods like Silwan to the holy sites of the Old City.

Mr Tatarsky said touristic initiatives had become another planning weapon against Palestinians. "These projects, from the cable car to a series of promenades, are ways to connect one settlement to the next, bisecting Palestinian space. They strengthen the settlements and break apart Palestinian neighbourhoods."

Mr Alg'ol's family was one of many in Silwan that had been told their lands were being confiscated for the cable car and a new police station.

"They want to turn our community into an archaeological Disneyland," he said. "And we are in the way. They plan to keep going until we are all removed."

A German Affair, Not Just a Love Story in Palestine

Why does Israel discriminate against foreign citizens who marry Palestinian residents of the West Bank?
Amira Hass Mar 31, 2019 from HaAretz

Josefin Herbach and Abdelrahman Salaymeh in Hebron Tomer Appelbaum

Diplomatic representatives of Germany, France, Spain and the United States attended an Israeli Supreme Court hearing last Thursday, even though the petition being heard related to a German citizen and her right to live with her Palestinian spouse in their own home in Hebron. The couple, whose request for family unification was rejected by Israel, are Josefin Herbach and Abdelrahman Salaymeh. "I was very tense during the hearing," said Salaymeh. "For the judges this was just another file, for us it's our entire life."

The diplomats did right to attend the hearing, since this individual case is tied to a general matter of principle: Why on earth does Israel forbid citizens of these countries to live peacefully and securely with their Palestinian spouses in Bethlehem, Ramallah or Jenin? Why does Israel discriminate against U.S., South American and European citizens, in comparison to other citizens of those same countries, only because they married Palestinians who are residents of the West Bank (and Jerusalem), and not Jews?

This question is addressed to all countries that have diplomatic, military, economic and cultural ties with Israel: Why the hell do you consent to Israel turning some of your citizens, who are equal before your law, into citizens who are inferior to your other citizens, devoid of the right to determine their family life? Why do you accept such discrimination, which is based on ethnicity, if not on racist considerations?

Spoiler: The hearing was short. Justices Uzi Fogelman, Anat Baron and Yosef Elron decided not to discuss the petition, since this is what the state asked for. The state is still in the process of formulating a new policy, the judges and petitioners were told for the hundredth time. Thus, there was no discussion of the individual case of Herbach and Salaymeh or of the principle raised by the petition, namely the blatant state intervention in the family lives of Palestinians. It was agreed that Herbach's visa would be extended by another six months, with the state updating the court on September 1 with regard to any new policy.

A reminder: Herbach and Salaymeh met and fell in love in 2015, while she was studying Arabic in Hebron, where he was her teacher. They got married in November 2015. Israel controls all borders, determining which foreigners get entry or residence visas for the West Bank and the Gaza Strip. In January 2016, Israel extended Herbach's visa by only six days, demanding that she leave when it expired.

Since then she has been living in her house under a temporary injunction issued by the High Court of Justice in response to a petition filed by attorneys Yotam Ben-Hillel and Leora Bechor, requesting a stay of her deportation. Her residence visa is extended every few months, but she's restricted to the West Bank only, forbidden to enter Israel. On the eve of the latest hearing she was given a one-day entry pass into Jerusalem.

In June 2017 the state refused the couple's request for family unification, namely, the granting of permanent resident status in the West Bank to Herbach. Israel controls the Palestinian population registry in the West Bank and Gaza. It alone determines to whom the Palestinian Authority can issue a resident identity card, meaning a resident status. The reason given for denying Salaymeh's request for family unification: "This is a political issue. According to current policies and in accordance with the standpoint of political echelons, requests for family unification in this area [the West Bank] are approved only in exceptional cases or in special humanitarian circumstances."

A couple who fall in love and want to live together is not a humanitarian case, and definitely not an exceptional one. If Herbach were to marry, for example, a settler in Kiryat Arba, which is built on Hebron land, the attitude towards her would be quite different. She would obtain permanent resident status, possibly citizenship, and until that happened, her visas would get extended without her heart rate jumping beforehand and without her needing to run to the High Court. When the request was denied, attorneys Ben-Hillel and Bechor composed a new petition.

As mentioned, the debate on the individual case and the principle involved was deferred. "There is no point in arguing the merit of the case since the state has no position," explained Justice Fogelman on Thursday. "The issue requires an extension due to the period we're in [election] – this issue has wider aspects."

Ben-Hillel explained that West Bank families in which one spouse is a foreigner live in legal limbo; on one hand, the state makes it difficult for that spouse to obtain a residence visa, or it shortens its duration. "Once you could get a visa for a year, now, if you're lucky, you get one for three months," he said. On the other hand, family unification is only approved in rare and exceptional humanitarian circumstances, with no details given as to what these are.

Sharon Hoash-Eiger, attorney for the state, asked that the petition be struck from the record and that should a new policy, if formulated, leads to another denial of the request for unification, the couple could submit a new petition. Ben-Hillel rejected this. The judges decided not to strike the current petition.

"It makes it a bit easier to know that we're not the only ones," said Salaymeh, referring to at least 30,000 other families whose requests for unification are gathering dust after Israel froze any processing of these cases. Because according to Israel, the family life of Palestinians is a political issue, not a legal one, and definitely not a fundamental human one.

Win or lose, Netanyahu has already cemented his legacy

In his 10 years in power, Netanyahu has engaged in race-baiting against his own citizens, declared the occupation a permanent feature of Israeli reality, and shifted both the national and international conversation on Palestine. It is time to acknowledge that these are no mere trends — but his very legacy.

By Edo Konrad, April 2, 2019 in +972

Israeli Prime Minister Benjamin Netanyahu attends a memorial ceremony for Golda Meir at Mount Herzl cemetery, Jerusalem, November 18, 2018. (Noam Revkin Fentonl/Flash90)

Ten years after he was elected prime minister, it is nearly impossible to imagine an Israel without Benjamin Netanyahu at its helm. An entire generation of Israelis has come of age in the Netanyahu era, and much of what young Israelis have internalized about politics, about their identity, and about Israel is the result of the legacy he has already left behind — regardless of whether he is re-elected.

In 10 years of Netanyahu's rule, the prime minister has emboldened and been emboldened by some of the most extremist elements in Israeli society, engaged in race-baiting against his own citizens, cozied up to authoritarian and anti-Semitic leaders around the world, meddled in the internal politics of Israel's greatest ally, and declared the occupation a permanent, integral feature of the Israeli reality.

What he's done differently, whether deliberately or unwittingly, is lay out in the open what previous prime ministers thought best to not openly acknowledge or declare. Israeli leaders have always been lenient toward Jewish radicals, implemented undisguised discriminatory policies against Palestinian citizens, struck deals with despotic regimes around the world, and entrenched the settlement enterprise in the occupied territories.

One of the most defining features of Netanyahu's legacy, however, is the way in which Israeli civil and political discourse has changed on his watch. To understand the way he has changed Israel, one must first understand the ways in which Netanyahu himself was transformed by the office. While he was always viewed as an outsider in Israeli politics, even within his own party, for years the prime minister retained a certain outward respect for Israel's minorities, the rule of law, and democratic norms.

Brazilian President Jair Bolsonaro and Israeli Prime Minister Benjamin Netanyahu seen during a visit to the Western Wall, Jerusalem's Old City, April 1, 2019. (Yonatan Sindel/Flash90)

That all changed around the last elections, says Amir Fuchs, who heads the Israeli Democracy Institute's Defending Democratic Values Program. "Some believe Netanyahu was always against the Israeli judicial system and the rule of law — but that's simply not true," Fuchs explains. "Before 2015, the prime minister spoke out against attacks on the courts by politicians to his right, while surrounding himself with Likud moderates such as Benny Begin and Dan Meridor or rivals from the political center such as Tzipi Livni and Yair Lapid. He did not, for example, initially openly support the Jewish Nation-State Law. That eventually ended up changing."

The day of the 2015 elections, in a last-ditch effort to save his campaign, Netanyahu warned that left-wing organizations were busing Arabs to the polls "in droves."

Palestinian citizens take part in a protest against the Jewish Nation-State Law, central Tel Aviv, August 12, 2018. (Oren Ziv/Activestills.org)

"That was racism pure and simple, and it marked a shift from the way Netanyahu had previously expressed himself," adds Fuchs. "After the elections, he became swept up in the incitement against Israel's Arab population led by those further to his right."

The disdain for both Israel's judicial system and its minorities would, over the next few years, be translated into actions, as Netanyahu began capitulating and even championing radical right-wing legislative initiatives such as the "override bill" (which would defang the High Court's ability to overturn unconstitutional laws) and the Jewish Nation-State Law, which constitutionalizes Jewish supremacy in Israel. Whereas in previous governments Netanyahu relied on moderates like Ehud Barak and Livni to form his coalition, this time around he surrounded himself with right-wing hardliners who pushed the prime minister to support a slate of far-right and nationalist laws, both vis-à-vis the Palestinians and democratic values and institutions.

Each of Netanyahu's governments have been more nationalist than the one that came before. As the right grew in power, playing to the most extremist elements of its base, its ideology "steadily moved from the drawing board to the law books to the real world," Michael Schaeffer Omer-Man recently wrote. Those governments passed laws to muzzle free speech, legalize the theft of Palestinian land in the West Bank, harass human rights activists and organizations, delegitimize nonviolent resistance to the occupation, ensure dissenters are banned from entering the country, and stripping Arabic of its status as an official language, among others.

But it is the attacks on Palestinian citizens that have come to define the changes we have seen in Netanyahu's Israel. The kind of unabashedly racist rhetoric that was once the bread and butter of fringe political groups like the followers of Meir Kahane or strongmen like Avigdor Liberman has become a legitimate part of the public discourse.

"Over the past 10 years, we have seen a tsunami of incitement by the successive Netanyahu governments toward the Arab public," says Basha'er Fahoum-Jayoussi, a Palestinian legal scholar based in Haifa.

"The Israeli ear has become trained to equate of Arabs with terror, and no one bats an eye," Fahoum-Jayoussi told +972 just days after the prime minister gave an interview to Channel 12 News, in which he claimed, on primetime television, that Israel's Arab parties support terrorism.

Successive Netanyahu governments have legitimized rhetoric about Palestinian citizens that Israelis, even in the mainstream, may have thought to themselves but never dared say out loud. The last few years have seen a number of watershed moments in that process. Perhaps the most blatant was when in 2016 over 1,700 wildfires erupted across Israel-Palestine, top members of Netanyahu's government blamed Palestinians for starting an "arson intifada." The claims turned out to be almost entirely baseless.

An Israeli Tax Authority worker checks the damage inspects the damage caused to a restaurant following a wildfire near Jerusalem, November 28, 2016. (Yonatan Sindel/Flash90)

But it was the passing of the Jewish Nation-State Law that was, for many Arab citizens, a sign that no matter how seriously they took their citizenship, Israel would always view them as inferior. Although Netanyahu had several times blocked the law — the equivalent of a constitutional amendment in the Israeli system — in 2018 he pushed it through and now claims it as the crown jewel of his legislative victories.

"By attacking Palestinians, Netanyahu goes for the lowest common denominator in order to unify Israelis," says Fahoum-Jayoussi, while noting that his government also earmarked NIS 10-15 billion to help close economic gaps plaguing Israel's Arab community. The dissonance, she says, creates a "kind of schizophrenia, which ultimately ensures we remain dependent on the government's good graces."

In the occupied territories, Netanyahu's legacy has been simpler. Although when he took office in 2009 he famously declared his support for a two-state solution in his "Bar Ilan speech," he has now built around him a coalition of annexationists, opponents of the two-state solution, and openly declares that Israel will never give up control of the entire territory between the Jordan River and the sea.

"It's hard to know whether Netanyahu believed in the two-solution when he delivered the speech at Bar Ilan," says Assaf David, the co-founder and academic director of the Forum for Regional Thinking. "But as time went on, he began to understand that Israel needs to go to war against Palestinian nationalism."

A group of protesters wave a Palestinian flag while trying to take cover during the demonstration, east of Gaza City, March 30, 2019. (Mohammed Zaanoun/Activestills.org)

To carry out that war, Netanyahu has held fast to three ideological pillars: declaring Israel's military rule over the West Bank, including the settlement enterprise, permanent; turning the West

Bank and Gaza into two separate, distinct entities; and quashing any and all semblance of Palestinian nationalism or resistance to Israeli rule, while treating the conflict as a zero-sum game.

"At the heart of Netanyahu's policy over the past 10 years has been the attempt to 'de-nationalize' the Palestinian cause," says David. "Once he buried the possibility for a Palestinian state, his next step was to destroy Palestinian national consciousness. This kind of thinking has long existed on the right, but this prime minister is the first to actually implement and lead it. Now we see the political center and parts of the center-left going along with this mentality."

An election campaign poster showing Prime Minister Benjamin Netanyahu in Jerusalem, April 2, 2019. (Yonatan Sindel/Flash90)

That hasn't been an easy task. Netanyahu has led two wars in Gaza, leading to a bloody stalemate with no end on the horizon, and saw a wave of knife attacks, shootings and car-rammings take place on his watch. Anti-occupation Israelis who insist on a national conversation about the effects of Israel's policies on Palestinians have been labeled traitors, and the push to annex the West Bank has not only become mainstream, it is now a central goal of many governing parties.

In the eyes of many Israelis, all of that translates into a sustainable situation with relatively low casualties on the Israeli side. Rather than moving toward a solution, Israelis remain content with a reality in which they were not forced to choose between making any drastic political decisions.

"Netanyahu has always been easily pressured by those around him, which means he can easily be dragged to the right," says Anat Saragusti, a veteran Israeli journalist and peace activist. "He prefers to manage the conflict without taking on too many military excursions. Aside from the devastation of the 2014 Gaza war, he has remained mostly restrained."

As long as violence directed at Israelis remains relatively low and international powers aren't willing to place real pressure on Israel to come to an agreement with the Palestinians, the Israeli public would not have to decide between either a two-state or a one-state solution, both of which would exact enormous political and material costs. Under Netanyahu, Israelis have gotten used in the comforts of the status quo: relative quiet coupled with eternal occupation.

"The occupation is viewed by Israelis as a relic of the 90s," Saragusti continues. "Who talks about the occupation today? We don't physically see it, it hardly appears in the media, except for on the fringes, and politically it is a non-story."

Of course, removing the Palestinian question from the Israeli political agenda — and that of the world — was not entirely Netanyahu's doing, and it was only possible with broader regional changes that led to shifting priorities in the Arab world.

The Arab Spring, says David, heightened the Sunni world's sense of danger from growing Iranian power, allowing Netanyahu to begin forming quiet alliances with Arab states that had previously considered the Jewish state their sworn enemy.

The proxy war between the Arab states and Iran, and the widespread effects of the Syria's refugee crisis, meant that the Sunni world had shifted its focus away from Palestine, David says.

"Arab states care about their stability and the Syrian refugee crisis — they don't have time to worry about Palestinian refugees or the Israeli-Palestinian conflict."

Prime Minister Benjamin Netanyahu meets with Sultan of Oman Qaboos bin Said. (Photo courtesy of the Israeli Prime Minister's Office)

"Now, the Palestinian national movement is facing a major crisis vis-à-vis the Arab world, and the lack of pressure on Israel, coupled with the growing pressure on the Palestinians from every direction, could eventually lead to an implosion that could force Israel to take back full military control of the West Bank or Gaza," David added.

It is time to acknowledge that the influence and changes Benjamin Netanyahu has had on Israel and its society, the region, and the international discourse on Palestine, are not mere trends but his very legacy. Whether he is reelected to build on that legacy or leaves it for others to cope with is almost beside the point.

"Rhetoric has the power to create reality, and the kind of rhetoric that has sprouted here is increasingly dangerous," Saragusti concluded. "People are afraid of identifying as left-wing, while Palestinian citizens are increasingly being pushed out of the democratic game — once you push minorities out of this game, what does this say about our democracy? This should have the political leadership extremely worried. Netanyahu has led this move and created a recipe for disaster."

The Year of the People: The Untold Story of Gaza's 'March of Return'

By Ramzy Baroud, March 14, 2019 from Middle East Monitor

A Palestinian woman uses slingshot to throw stone to Israeli forces during a"Great March of Return" demonstration near Al Bureij Refugee Camp in Gaza City, Gaza on 8 March, 2019 [Hassan Jedi/Anadolu Agency]

What is the 'Great March of Return' but a people attempting to reclaim their role, and be recognised and heard in the struggle for the liberation of Palestine?

Much has been said about what the popular mobilisation in Gaza, which began on March 30, 2018, represents. Sympathetic views rightly understood the daily protests at the fence separating Israel from the besieged Gaza Strip, as a people frustrated with a protracted and inhumane blockade. Others also emphasised the fact that the protesters are mostly refugees from historic Palestine (today's Israel), who are demanding their right to return home.

Unsympathetic, dubious media reports kept poking holes in the above facts, with Israeli and pro-Israeli media falsely claiming that the popular initiative is a Hamas-driven ploy to embarrass Israel by placing people in harm's way for cheap media attention.

Nearly 250 unarmed Palestinians were killed and thousands more maimed and wounded by Israeli snipers since the protests began.

What is largely missing from the discussion, however, is the collective psychology behind this kind of mobilisation, and why it is so essential for hundreds of thousands of besieged people to rediscover their power and understand their true positions, not as hapless victims, but as agents of change in their society.

The narrow reading or the misrepresentation of the 'March of Return' speaks volumes about the overall underestimation of the role of the Palestinian people in their struggle for freedom, justice and national liberation, extending throughout a century.

Indeed, the story of Palestine is the story of the Palestinian people, for they are the victims of oppression and the main channel of resistance, starting with the Nakba – the creation of Israel on the ruins of Palestinian towns and villages in 1948. Had Palestinians not resisted, their story would have concluded then, and they too would have disappeared.

Those who admonish Palestinian resistance, including armed resistance, have little understanding of the psychological ramifications of strength – for example, the sense of collective empowerment and hope amongst the people. In his introduction to Frantz Fanon's 'Wretched of the Earth", Jean-Paul Sartre describes resistance, as it was passionately vindicated by Fanon, as a process through which "a man is re-creating himself."

And indeed, for 70 years Palestinians embarked on that journey of the recreation of the self. They resisted, and their resistance in all of its forms, moulded a sense of collective unity, despite the numerous divides that were erected amongst the people.

The 'Great March of Return' is indeed the latest manifestation of the ongoing Palestinian resistance.

It is obvious that elitist interpretations of Palestine have failed – Oslo proved a worthless, tired exercise in empty clichés aimed at sustaining American political dominance in Palestine as well as in the rest of the Middle East.

It is only when the Palestinian intellectual, guided by the resistance of her/his people, can repossess that collective narrative, that the confines placed on the Palestinian voice can finally be broken.

The crisis of the Palestinian narrative, however, is relatively recent, thus, through decided and concentrated efforts can be remedied. The signing of the Oslo Accord in 1993 shattered the relative cohesiveness of the Palestinian discourse, thus weakening and dividing the Palestinian people.

Until the Palestinian leadership is itself reclaimed by the Palestinian people as a platform for true democratic expression, it is the responsibility of the intellectual to safeguard and present the Palestinian story to the world in the most authentic, egalitarian way possible. Only then can Palestinians truly confront the Israeli Hasbara and US-Western corporate media propaganda, and finally speak unhindered.

Late Professor Edward Said wrote in 'Covering Islam,' that "facts get their importance from what is made of them in interpretation… for interpretations depend very much on who the interpreter is, who he or she is addressing, what his or her purpose is (and) at what historical moment the interpretation takes place."

Neither the Palestinian historian nor the Palestinian people are at the heart of the stories of the many interpreters of facts about Palestinian history. This predisposition is not only pertinent in the case of Palestine, but an ailment that has afflicted Middle East history, politics and journalism for decades.

Middle East historiography is "a stepchild of orientalism," wrote Dr Soha Abdel Kader, where "Middle East history bears the imprint of its birth up to the present in its use of sources, its methodology, and its isolation."

Palestinian history too faced similar obstacles, thus, for decades, persisted in forced inertia. Most notably, since the commencing of the 'peace process', Palestinian historiography largely neglected ordinary people, and remained hostage to narrating the history of the elites, their political institutions, diplomatic events, and self-indulgent understanding of conflict, whether on a socio-economic level or that of violence and war.

In the Israeli Zionist narrative, Palestinians, if relevant at all are depicted as drifting nomads, an inconvenience that hinders the path of progress – a duplicate description to the one that regularly defined the relationship between every western colonial power and the resisting natives.

Within some Israeli political and academic circles, Palestinians merely 'existed' to be 'cleansed', to make space for a different From the Zionist perspective, the 'existence' of the natives is only meant to be temporary. "We must expel Arabs and take their places," wrote Israel's founding father, David Ben Gurion.

The assigning of the Palestinian people the role of dislocated, disinherited and nomadic people without worrying much about the ethical and political implications of such a decision has erroneously presented Palestinians as a docile and submissive collective. Again, they merely existed to be denied that very existence by a powerful, 'chosen', emboldened and ruthless Zionist.

This is why it is imperative that we develop a clearer understanding of the layered meanings behind the 'Great March of Return.' Hundreds of thousands of Palestinians in Gaza did not risk their lives over the last year simply because they required urgent medicine and food supplies.

Palestinians did so because they understand their centrality in their struggle. Their protests are a collective statement, a cry for justice, an ultimate reclamation of their narrative as a people – still standing, still powerful and still hopeful after 70 years of Nakba, 50 years of military occupation and 12 years of unrelenting siege.

Palestinians protesting during the Great March of Return in the Gaza Strip in 2018. (Photo by Mati Milstein)

One year has passed since Palestinians in the blockaded Gaza Strip launched the **Great March of Return protests**, which continue to be held every Friday along the fence with Israel.

Most discussions around the protests focus on the Israeli military's brutal response to the demonstrations, and the impunity with which Israeli snipers use live fire to **intentionally kill or wound** Palestinian protestors, without fear of consequences. Adalah warned Israeli authorities again this week not to continue its policies at this weekend's anniversary of the march.

As Adalah, Al Mezan and our partners have found – and as the 2018 UN Commission of Inquiry confirmed – these actions violate international law, and yet Israeli authorities have proven to be **unwilling to properly investigate or punish** the perpetrators for their crimes.

However, it is also crucial to remember why Palestinians in Gaza launched the march in the first place: to reclaim their **right to return** to their homeland.

This is why the demonstrations began on 30 March – **Land Day** – which marks Palestinians' resistance to the state's expropriation of mass tracts of their land in Galilee in 1976. During these protests, six unarmed Palestinian citizens of Israel were killed by police.

The Palestinian struggle to defend their land and homes remains as vital today as it was 43 years ago.

Just this year, for example, Israeli authorities announced plans to **forcibly transfer 36,000 Bedouin citizens** from their homes in the Naqab, in order to make way for a military industrial zone, a phosphate mine, and expanded highways - plans that Adalah is challenging before Israeli courts and planning committees.

A Bedouin woman in the Naqab village of Umm al-Hiran surveys the remains of her home after its demolition by Israeli authorities in 2017. (Photo by Mati Milstein)

These plans are being given legal backing by **discriminatory legislation** such as the Jewish Nation-State Law (JNSL), which enshrines Jewish supremacy as a constitutional rule and bears the distinct characteristics of apartheid.

[Article 7](#) of this law, which calls on the state to promote Jewish settlement as a national and constitutional value, will intensify Israel's racist land policy on both sides of the Green Line and put thousands more Palestinians at risk of displacement and dispossession.

The Israeli elections next month foreshadow a continuation of these policies in Israel and in the 1967 Occupied Territories. As a result, Palestinians' rights to their lands, their livelihoods and their lives are under greater threat than ever.

These plans are being given legal backing by **discriminatory legislation** such as the Jewish Nation-State Law (JNSL), which enshrines Jewish supremacy as a constitutional rule and bears the distinct characteristics of apartheid.

Article 7 of this law, which calls on the state to promote Jewish settlement as a national and constitutional value, will intensify Israel's racist land policy on both sides of the Green Line and put thousands more Palestinians at risk of displacement and dispossession.

The Israeli elections next month foreshadow a continuation of these policies in Israel and in the 1967 Occupied Territories. As a result, Palestinians' rights to their lands, their livelihoods and their lives are under greater threat than ever.

Encountering Peace: The birth of the state of Palestine in Gaza

Gershon Baskin, April 4, 2019, in Jerusalem Post

On October 12, 2003, a group of former Israeli and Palestinian negotiators, including former chief of staff Amnon Lipkin-Shahak, completed a 50-page comprehensive draft permanent-status agreement for peace and the establishment of an independent Palestinian state in the West Bank and Gaza with East Jerusalem as its capital. That December 1, the Swiss government hosted the formal launching of the "Geneva Initiative" in the Swiss city, with hundreds of Israeli and Palestinian public officials and citizens in attendance, including this author.

These were the darkest, bleakest days of the Second Intifada, and operation "Defensive Shield" aimed at crushing the Palestinian uprising and the Palestinian Authority. This was a period that had witnessed the very bloody end of the Oslo peace process and the hope that one day peace could be a reality.

Ariel Sharon was prime minister, and the bellicose words and actions of Israel's best-known general were felt with great pain by the Palestinians throughout the territories. Israelis were living in fear during this period of the most horrific acts of terrorism, led by suicide murderers who were blowing themselves up and killing hundreds in buses, cafes and shopping malls across the country. Every Saturday evening during this period, a very small group gathered in Paris Square near the prime minister's house, calling to keep the hope of peace alive. I was one of those at the square. It was a very depressive time.

In the months prior to October 2003, I heard from my friend, the late Ron Pundak – who led the Geneva Initiative – that great progress had been made and that soon, a full agreement would be reached. As non-officials who no longer held positions of responsibility, these brave people, who were all previously official negotiators, wanted to demonstrate that a partner for peace existed on both sides of the conflict and that there were solutions to every single issue in conflict – including borders, security, Jerusalem and refugees.

As the details of the draft agreement became known around the world and in Israel and Palestine, statements of support came pouring in. In November 2003, US secretary of state Colin Powell responded to the Geneva Initiative: "The US remains committed to the President's two-state vision and to the road map, but we also believe that projects such as yours are important in helping to sustain an atmosphere of hope, in which Israelis and Palestinians can discuss mutually acceptable resolutions to the difficult issues that confront them."

In December, president Bush said: "[The Geneva Accord] is productive, so long as they adhere to the principles [to] fight off terror; that there must be security; and there must be the emergence of a Palestinian state that is democratic and free." While international and local support for the Geneva Initiative was increasing, prime minister Sharon's opposition to the accord became more resolved, understanding that an Israeli-Palestinian agreement based on Geneva would mean a Palestinian state in the West Bank. Sharon had to stop the support behind the initiative.

On December 18, Sharon dropped the bombshell at the annual Herzliya Conference. Completely unexpected and out of character, Sharon – who just a year before had compared Netzarim, a small Israeli settlement in Gaza, to Tel Aviv – suddenly announced that Israel would unilaterally withdraw from all of the Gaza Strip, removing every Israeli citizen from there, including some 9,000 settlers and IDF personnel. Suddenly, the entire world was caught up in the new Israeli initiative to disengage from Gaza. Geneva was now forgotten.

The international community, led by US president Bush, took the disengagement very seriously. Together with the other three Quartet partners (the UN, EU and Russia), the US created a Disengagement Authority and brought in former World Bank president James Wolfensohn to head it. The primary basis for the international community's engagement in the disengagement was that through coordination and cooperation between Israel and the PA, the successful transference of Gaza from Israel to the Palestinians would lead to similar developments in the West Bank. But this is not at all what Sharon had in mind.

Sharon refused to coordinate and cooperate with the Palestinian disengagement coordinating mechanism headed by Mohammed Dahlan, with more than 12 committees formed for that purpose. Sharon made it very clear that he was not going to cooperate with Palestinian Authority President Mahmoud Abbas or Dahlan, and stated that Abbas is not a partner. In fact, he said, "He is a chick with no feathers." Sharon's plan was coherent and fully developed, even if it remained outside of public knowledge – locally or internationally.

When Israel withdrew from Gaza in 2005, Israel demolished all of the settlements, not leaving anything that could have been used, for example, to resettle Palestinian refugees. Israel shut the gate out of Gaza and sealed it hermetically. Prior to the disengagement, Israel shut down the Erez Industrial Zone on the Israeli side of the border and also essentially stopped the work that was being developing in the Karni industrial zone – on the Gaza side of the border.

With the closure of Gaza, the coastal enclave's economy came to a standstill. Gush Katif's recently-transferred 4,000 square meters of hothouses went bankrupt quickly as their produce aimed for the Israeli market was left to rot on the border. Israel froze the transfer of taxes collected on behalf of the Palestinian Authority. The PA's ability to govern Gaza was severely compromised.

Sharon suffered from a stroke on January 4, 2006. Then 24 days later, Hamas won the PA parliamentary elections. Sharon would not have been surprised, as was most of the world. Hamas was credited with ousting Israel, and Abbas was punished for negotiating with Israel without achievements. The following year, Hamas kicked the PA out of Gaza in a bloody coup d'état. The Gaza disengagement would now become the first step toward Israeli withdrawal from the West Bank. The Gaza disengagement was perceived as a dramatic failure from the point of view of Israel.

Now we are witnessing the final stages of the implementation of the plan devised by Sharon, and likely to be completed if Netanyahu wins the elections on April 9. Gaza will be recognized as a Palestinian state and Hamas will be transformed from a terror organization into a state with a no-war, no-peace relationship with Israel. Hamas will gain international recognition, and any possible international pressure on Israel to withdraw from the West Bank or east Jerusalem will be removed.

Netanyahu and his right-wing government will begin their plan for the annexation of the West Bank. Sooner, not later, Israeli control and annexation over the West Bank will become officially a new form of apartheid – a state with two separate legal structures: one for citizens and one for several million non-citizens. These steps will mark the beginning of the next stage of the Israeli-Palestinian conflict. It will not end, and the Palestinian demand for full equality will be formally launched as the two-state solution is abandoned – either seen as already implemented with Gaza being the Palestinian state, or seen as irrelevant with the occupation and Israeli control continuing over the West Bank and east Jerusalem – and Gaza still under almost full Israeli control and domination.

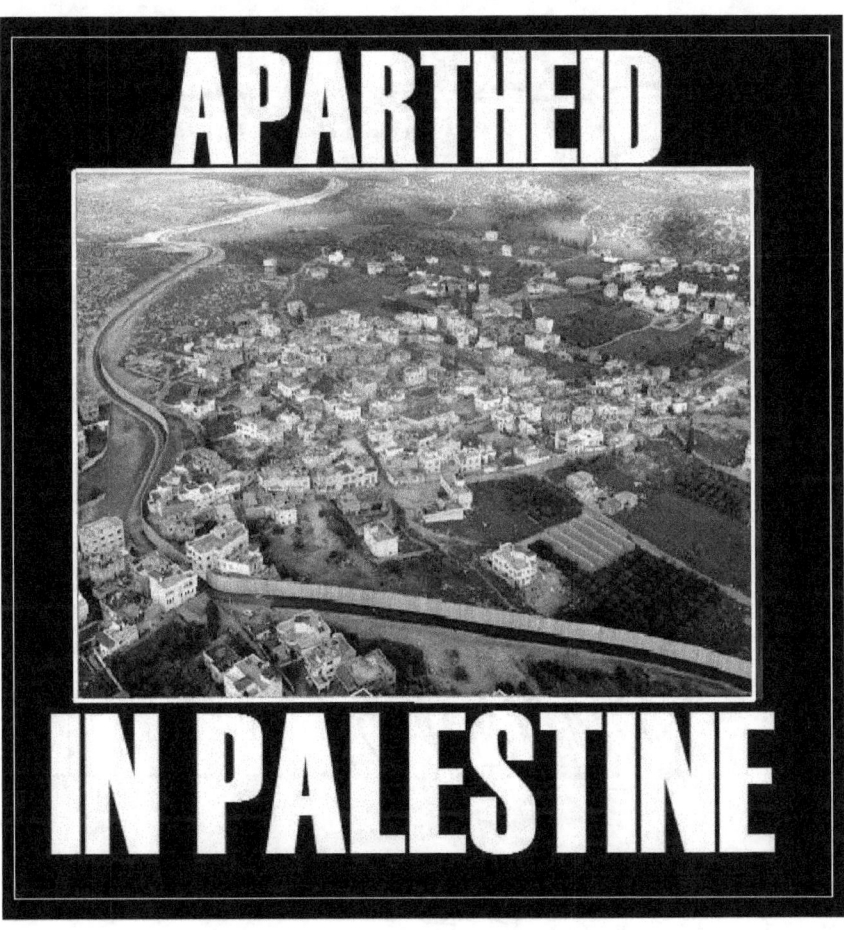

Israel demolishes Al-Araqeeb Bedouin village for 142nd time
April 4, 2019, from Middle East Monitor

A woman from al-Araqib Bedouin village can be seen gesturing towards Israeli bulldozers on 4 April 2019 [Ma'an News]

Israeli bulldozers demolished the unrecognised Bedouin village of Al-Araqeeb in the Negev desert in southern Israel for the 142nd time, on Thursday, *Ma'an News* has reported.
Locals reported that Israeli bulldozers, escorted by Israeli police forces, demolished residential structures and tents of Al-Araqeeb villagers, leaving women, children and the elderly without a shelter.

Villagers said that they insist on remaining in their village, adding that they will keep re-building their village.

The Israeli demolitions of Al-Araqeeb are carried out in attempts to force the Bedouin population to relocate to government-zoned townships.

Like the 34 other Bedouin villages "unrecognized" by Israel, Al-Araqeeb does not receive any services from the Israeli government and is constantly subjected to the threats of expulsion and home demolition.

These "unrecognised" villages were established in the Negev soon after the 1948 Arab-Israeli war following the creation of the state of Israel, when an estimated 750,000 Palestinians were forcibly expelled from their homes and made refugees.

Many of the Bedouins were forcibly transferred to the village sites during the 17-year period when Palestinians inside Israel were governed under Israeli military law, which ended shortly before Israel's military takeover of Gaza and the West Bank, including East Jerusalem, in 1967.

Now more than 60 years later, the Bedouin villages have yet to be legally recognised by Israel and live under constant threats of demolition and forcible removal.

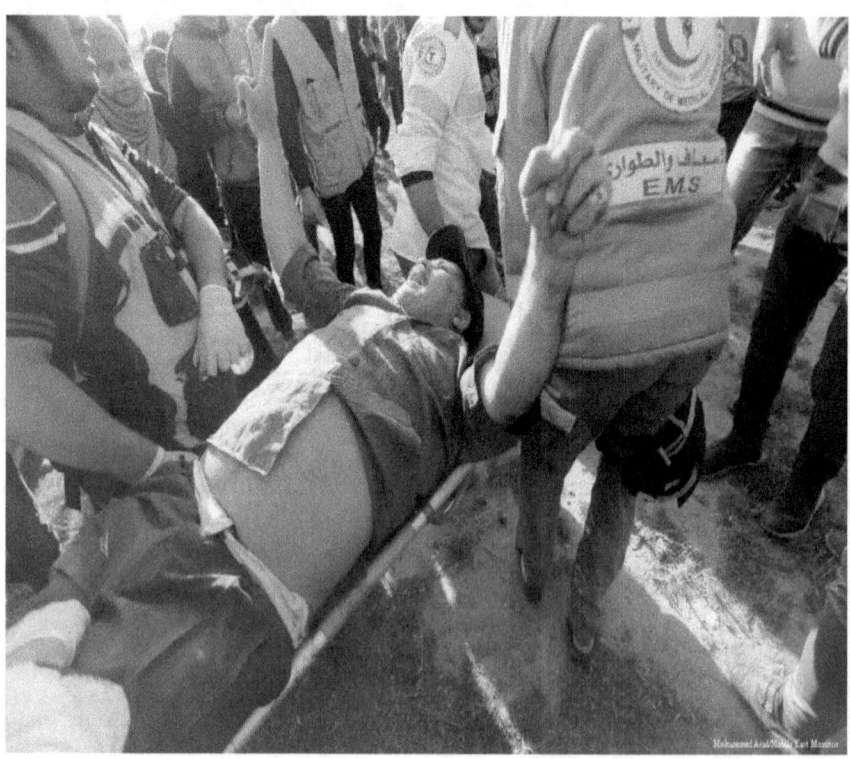

Liberty leads the people: fighting for a decent life in Gaza

Amjad Ayman Yaghi *The Electronic Intifada* 5 April 2019

The photograph by Mustafa Hassouna that made Aed Abu Amro an instant icon..Anadolu Agency

When Aed Abu Amro held a Palestinian flag aloft during one of the Great March of Return protests last year on the boundary between Gaza and Israel, the last thought on his mind was that he would become an internet sensation.

But a picture of the shirtless Aed, slingshot and flag in hand and enveloped by the smoke from tear gas, went viral almost instantly.

It sparked comparisons with a painting from the European Romantic period and made him an instant icon of the Palestinian resistance.

The photo was taken on 22 October by Mustafa Hassouna of the Turkish Anadolu press agency. And it so happened that in composition, lighting and motif, the picture closely resembles

"Liberty Leading the People," a painting by the French painter Eugène Delacroix.

That the subject of the 1830 painting was the struggle for liberty during the revolution in France the same year – with liberty represented by a woman, bare-chested, carrying a French flag – only added to the poignancy of Hassouna's photo.

For Aed, the global reaction to the photo was an eye-opener.

"I was amazed by how quickly the photo spread," Aed told The Electronic Intifada in a recent interview.

The comparisons to Delacroix's painting made him proud, he said, and have encouraged him to carry on, even if inadvertently becoming an icon has also come with a responsibility.

"People consider the photo a symbol of the resistance. This has made me determined to remain steadfast and stay among those rejecting the Israeli blockade. It's great to become a symbol, but the occupation is still imposing its siege."

The cost of protest
Aed, 20, had been a regular at the Great March of Return protests, spurred originally, he said, by the December 2017 announcement by Donald Trump, the US president, that he would move the US embassy to Jerusalem.

He remembers watching Al Jazeera with his father, Jamal Sadi Abu Amro, that day. After the announcement was made, his father had turned to him and said: "Nothing has been left to us anymore… The Palestinian cause is lost."

So when the Great March of Return protests started a year ago, Aed was there.

"I felt," Aed said, "that if nothing else, our revolution of the youth could express our rejection of Trump's announcement."

He made new friends at the protests, friendships forged in tear gas and under a hail of bullets.

But his activism also came at a cost. He has been hit several times by tear gas grenades, friends have been wounded and one, Ahmad Yaghi, 25, was killed last August.

On 5 November 2018, a bullet strafed Aed's left leg at a coastal protest against the naval blockade, leaving him wounded but undeterred. He returned to the Great March of Return protests within days.

Then on 23 November back at the fence east of Gaza City, Aed was shot again, this time in his right leg, and this time more seriously.

Doctors told him he had been struck by a so-called butterfly bullet, a projectile that opens up on impact for maximum effect.

The bullet caused severe damage to his knee and other bones in his leg, leaving him unable to move his toes and in need of constant pain medication.

It forced him to stop going to the protests.

It also forced him to stop going to the gym.

The perfect body
The gym was Aed's escape and his hobby. One of six siblings, five of whom still live at home in the al-Zaytoun neighborhood of Gaza City, he has devoted many hours to building his physique and getting away from his family's crowded home.

Aed competed successfully in competitions in the 55 kg (121 lb) bodybuilding weight category in local gyms, most recently in July 2018.

"I was the best bodybuilder in the East Gaza region at 55 kg. I was preparing myself for the Gaza Strip bodybuilding championship on 26 November. But then I was wounded."

The injury has been extensive. The white stabilizers on his leg are due to come off at any time now, but he still needs surgery on tendons in his toes, as well as a knee operation.

When he is recovered, he said, he wants to return to the protests. But his father is ambivalent.

"I can't prevent Aed from going to the protests," Jamal, 48, told The Electronic Intifada. "He is badly affected by the siege and the poverty, he wants to express his anger at the repression he has suffered since birth in our occupied society."

The photo of Aed Abu Amro has been compared to this 1830 painting by Eugene Delacroix, "Liberty Leading the People."

Jamal, who is unemployed and relies on the wages his five sons occasionally bring back from jobs in factories or elsewhere, said he hoped Aed – who used to work in a cigarette stall not far from home – would return to his sport.

"I believe sport can send a message to the world, that Aed can have an impact if he is a distinguished athlete representing Palestine in foreign competitions."

For now, however, the focus is on the necessities. For months, Jamal said, he has been trying to secure painkillers, antibiotics and antibacterial soap for Aed, scarce commodities in Gaza, where all imports are under severe Israeli restrictions.

He has had to borrow money to buy medicine, he said, and has reached out to various charities to help him secure more.

A life under occupation
Aed has known only occupation, blockade and war. Born in 1999, he lived through the second intifada and three all-out Israeli military assaults on Gaza, as well as the 12-year Israeli-enforced blockade that has left Gaza on the brink of a humanitarian catastrophe.

He was 15 during the last war on Gaza in 2014. The family had to evacuate their home after a number of houses near them were bombed. When they returned, he learned that his friend and contemporary Fayez Yasin had been killed.

"I used to ask my dad when I was young: 'Why do they kill children and women? Why do their airplanes launch rockets instead of flying as normal planes?'" Aed told The Electronic Intifada. "I didn't imagine that when I grew up I would still live with occupation, blockade and the theft of Palestinian land."

He is puzzled too by what he read in Israeli papers, especially in the comment sections under articles, after his photo went viral.

"People called me a terrorist! I can't remember a day when we didn't have an electricity blackout. I've watched dozens of people killed, including friends. I've seen whole neighborhoods destroyed. And people called me a terrorist!"

These days, Aed spends most of his time with two close friends, Mahmoud Abu Marsa and Ahmad Bahlool, both 20, and like Aed unemployed. All are desperate for a better life.

"I am proud of him," Abu Marsa told The Electronic Intifada. "He represents the youth of Gaza, all of us who grew up with wars and a siege that has deprived us of any decent opportunities."

He is missed at the protests, Abu Marsa said. Bahlool said Aed was always the strongest and boldest, willing and able to retrieve and carry the wounded to safety.

Bahlool is convinced that Aed was deliberately targeted after the photo went viral.

"The occupation wanted to say: 'You aren't a hero.' But what people don't see is that behind this photo, Aed is just a 20-year-old who is fed up with waiting. We love life. We want to live a decent life."

Amjad Ayman Yaghi is a journalist based in Gaza.

Israeli elections: Why Jews should vote for a Palestinian national party
By Orly Noy 3 April 2019 from Middle East Eye
A vote for Balad would allow us to be partners for change in the deepest possible sense

Electioneering in Israel has entered the home stretch, with party propaganda – and public discourse in general – degenerating into a mixture of slogans, mudslinging and distortions, even more glaring than usual.

Amid this turmoil, Jews of conscience are trying to decide how to cast their vote. For those who do not identify as Zionist, the main possibilities are the two Arab parties into which the Joint Arab List has split: Hadash-Taal and Raam-Balad.

Superficial political discourse

The first combines the communists and Ahmad Tibi's party, and the second combines Balad and the Islamic Movement's southern branch. Apart from the question of voting for Islamic candidates, the second alternative raises one of the more challenging questions in Israeli political thought: the place of Jews in the Palestinian national movement.

An Israeli flag flutters, with Jerusalem's Old City in the background, on 27 March (AFP)

Balad is a Palestinian national party, which, in the frightfully superficial political discourse conducted in Israel, is enough to brand it as nationalist in the extreme. That's a lie, and it must be refuted.

In general, extreme nationalism is a concept that prioritises the national over the individual, and one specific nationality over others. The national approach of Balad is the obverse of both of these.

Firstly, Balad does not talk about Palestinian nationalism as exclusive, but rather as something alongside Jewish-Israeli nationalism; it demands recognition of both national entities. From a national Palestinian perspective, this is a far-reaching position, because it proposes recognition by this country's indigenous people of the Jewish nationalism imposed upon it as a legitimate nationalism, and not a colonial one.

Unchaining nationalism from Zionism

The only precondition is unchaining this Jewish nationalism from Zionism. The Zionist position, even in its most progressive version – as represented by Meretz, for instance – offers Palestinian citizens civil rights, but not national collective rights. The right of national recognition is accorded to Jewish citizens only.

Israel's <u>nation-state law</u> is just a more blatant expression of this basic Zionist stance, highlighting the fact that it is impossible to talk about equal civil rights in a reality of national oppression. It's not coincidental that since the founding of the state, not a single new Arab city has been built. The aspiration to create a "Jewish and democratic" state in Israel makes a demographic war against its non-Jewish citizens inevitable.

A Palestinian waves the national flag during a protest in Gaza on 30 March (AFP)

Secondly, the nationalism of Balad does not position itself above the individual, but rather is a means for people to actualise their individual rights, including their collective rights.

In a reality where national identity is most influential in shaping the space and place of the individual in the hierarchy of power, national liberation is a necessary step on the path to civic equality; in other words, to the establishment of a true democracy, which is the second foundation upon which Balad's ideology rests.

From here comes the answer to the question of why Jews should support a Palestinian national party. In the present reality, this is the only path towards real democratisation of the country, and its release from the bonds of exclusive Jewish nationalism and the narrowing of the civic-democratic space to which that nationalism inherently leads.

Coming to grips with privilege

True, it's much easier and more tempting to join a movement that defines itself as Jewish-Arab, such as Hadash, even if the party's percentage of Jewish members is negligible.

This self-definition is morally very appropriate, but it blurs the extreme asymmetry that exists between the positions of these two national entities, so the fact that it tends to focus more on the discourse of equality is not surprising. That, too, is an appropriate discourse, but its horizons are limited while there is still this essential inequality in the most influential component shaping the political reality: national identity.

This is something that should be significant for us, as Jews who are interested in a radical change in the status quo. It requires us to come to grips with the privilege that we cannot be released from if all we do is chant slogans along the lines of: "Jews and Arabs refuse to be enemies."

Balad invites us, as Jews, to take a step back from the euphoria of partnership and get behind the national Palestinian project – the only thing that can bring authentic meaning to that partnership.

It's not a simple challenge. We, as Jews, are not accustomed to taking a backseat. But so long as we have not set out on this journey from the most deeply rooted point of departure, the result won't rise beyond slogans that enthuse us at demonstrations but ultimately lead nowhere.

In this sense, Balad is inviting us to be partners for change in the deepest possible sense. We must simply take a deep breath and embrace a conceptual shift in the hierarchy. This appears to be the most significant thing we can do in the upcoming elections.

Annexation Will Free Israel From the Fake Commitment to Liberty and Equality
By Yossi Klein, 4th April 2019 in HaAretz

A man carrying a boy walks past the remains of a Palestinian house in Beit Jala, West Bank, April 2, 2019. Mussa Qawasma / Reuters

Two hard slaps, one on each cheek, is what we need to give ourselves in order to wake up from this dream of the only democracy in the Middle East. Two smacks in the face to understand that the election – <u>with bots or without</u> – do not make a democracy out of a country where 2.5 million out of the 10 million people who live in it have no civil rights. Two slaps to remind us that we are only extras in the show that opens Tuesday – and closes Wednesday.

The <u>election</u> on Tuesday is a "let's pretend" performance of democracy. Our participation is just a bit of one-off background scenery lacking any influence. In a true democracy, a <u>man pursued by the law</u> does not impose elections on 9 million people as a means to avoid a trial. In a normal democracy, we don't hold an election over corruption. You are tried for corruption, not elected. We hold elections over education, religion, economics and a 71-year-old war.

The fate and future of our children, not that of <u>Benjamin Netanyahu</u>, will be determined by this war. We have been sweeping this war under the carpet, even though it is what gave birth to the aggression and corruption that have brought us to where we are today. But we are not talking about this war and not dealing with it. There is nothing to talk about. No one to talk to and nothing to talk about.

When nothing is on the agenda in the election except for Netanyahu's future, it is clear that what came before Tuesday will be what comes after it. But it will be even more flawed, more extreme, crazier. This is not a "crucial" election, it is only crucial for Netanyahu. The choice between one nationalist right and a different nationalist right is critical only for the right. The destruction of the legal system is more fateful, the internal rift is more painful, but we are in denial, insisting stubbornly on business as usual, driving a car without brakes – but making sure to signal on the curves.

Two smacks in the face will wake us up, not just from the illusion that we are living in a democracy but also the illusion that it really bothers us one way or the other. It's simply not true. Is there anything that can convince us not to busy ourselves with the psychoses of the candidates and return to the reality of the checkpoints and <u>arresting children</u>?

Yes, there is such a thing. Annexation of the Palestinian territories and imposing Israeli law on 2.5 million people without rights will convince us. Only then will we be able to look in the mirror and admit sadly – though with a certain amount of relief – that we are finished with democracy. Because only annexation will force us to realize that even now we are a country without any borders, and that 20 percent of its residents lack rights.

When we sober up from the illusion of democracy, we will understand that for years we have been without it, wearing the emperor's new clothes and not understanding why we are seen as crazy. Annexation will remove the restraints of having to act like a normal country. It will be something liberating, wild, uninhibited – we will be the crazy, violent guy who fled the hospital, we will not be embarrassed about anything, we will be like Donald Trump, like Itamar Ben-Gvir, like South Africa.

Annexation will free us from the fake commitment to liberty and equality, rescue us from the lie of "the most moral army in the world," and enrich the dictionary with words like "transfer," "expulsion," "exile," and "voluntary emigration." Nothing will stop us; one who doesn't stop at red lights no longer pays any attention to stop signs.

After the annexation, we will have here – as we have now – over 11 million people. More than Sweden and similar to Belgium. But in Sweden and Belgium everyone is equal before the law, and here they aren't. When the law preventing the investigation of a sitting prime minister, whether it is called the French Law, the Portuguese Law or the Law to Save Netanyahu from Prison, we will no longer be a country with two sets of laws, but a country with three sets of laws: One set for the Arabs, another set for the Jews and a special set for selected, powerful, strong Jews who work night and day on our behalf.

They will continue to do little for us and a lot for themselves. We will be an island of Sicilian protection rackets in the middle of a shark-filled sea. Tough men in sunglasses will then pass through the neighborhood, everyone will know who they are, and they won't deny it. True, they'll say, we're not saints, but show us someone who'll protect you better than we will. After all, what are they asking for? For us to put the slip of paper in the envelope that we know we should put there. And remember, they'll tell us, they have a lot of cousins to feed.

Israel Fears Words as Palestinian Voices Grow
Pro-Palestinian accounts get suspended on social media platforms all the time
Apr 05 2019 from "Days of Palestine

Pro-Palestinian accounts get suspended on social media platforms all the time. It shouldn't happen, but it does. We sometimes object, sometimes win, often lose, sometimes the suspensions and deletions are barely noticeable, and in other cases, such as this one, a pattern emerges that muddies the ground and makes it sink-able for everyone.

Palestinian Voices is an upcoming news outlet run by young people, that gives children and other youngsters a free platform to publish their stories — factual, fictional or otherwise. It's a new venture with a thousand learning curves yet to be swerved and dunams of space to hone unchartered skills in the search for professionalism and leadership. It's exciting to see it unfold.

Recently, not one, not two, but three members of the team have had their accounts destroyed. Twitter's waste disposal unit has been busy recently. One by one, these young, ambitious journalists and reporters working to bring us the news from Palestine are being forcibly taken from us; metaphorically — erased in the night.

And the outcry — is there one?
The act of silencing signifies terror: a fear of words, a fear of third person experience, a fear of the message and of its meaning. Dangerously, it undermines the fundamental vision that free speech, discussion and debate are tools to education and empowerment. Censorship undermines democracy.

Censorship is sinister
Punishing students for their speech robs our public debate of needed voices, says Sonja West — professor in First Amendment Law at the University of Georgia; it teaches children that censorship is acceptable. It isn't.

Ironically, in the beginning, sites such as Twitter and Facebook were built to give everyone a fair crack and importantly, an equal voice. Their collusion with the Israeli government has led them into a dark alley, trying to extinguish young people's words, seize their opinions, and gag their reports — the freely written, freely read and freely shared is no longer free, unless of course, it sings for Israel.

But where does the silencing come from? Who would agreeably work at the behest of Israel to decide who can and who can't write. Other young people? Middle-aged lobbyists sitting round a glass table scratching out the tongues of their teenage enemies? Censorship is indeed sinister.

For now, these accounts are gone. But they return — of course they do. In the face of adversity, Palestine and everything Palestinian, always returns.

The Israeli Election Choices: Apartheid or Ethnic-Cleansing

"Whether Netanyahu and his coalition with the fascist Jewish Power party—that openly advocates the ethnic cleansing of Palestinians—or Gantz, who prides himself on bombing Gaza back to the 'Stone Ages,' none of the major parties support a two-state solution or equality for Palestinians in a single state."

DIANA BUTTU

Diana Buttu, Ramallah-based political analyst, former advisor to Palestine Liberation Organization Chairman Mahmoud Abbas and Palestinian negotiators, and Palestinian citizen of Israel:

"For Palestinians—whether citizens of Israel or living under undemocratic Israeli military rule in the West Bank and Gaza Strip—these elections are the equivalent of a choice between Trump and Trump. Whether Netanyahu and his coalition with the fascist Jewish Power party—that openly advocates the ethnic cleansing of Palestinians—or Gantz, who prides himself on bombing Gaza back to the 'Stone Ages,' none of the major parties support a two-state solution or equality for Palestinians in a single state.

"Rather, this election will likely result in an even more extreme, right-wing extreme government than the last—which was the most right-wing in Israel's history: an outcome that does not bode well for Palestinians, the region, or the world. This will happen irrespective of whether Netanyahu is elected or Gantz, as virtually none of the parties that will make it into the Knesset support Palestinian freedom or equality."

NOURA ERAKAT

Noura Erakat, Human rights attorney and Assistant Professor at George Mason University, former legal counsel to the U.S. House of Representatives and advocate for Palestinian refugee rights at the UN, and author of *Justice for Some: Law and the Question of Palestine* (2019):

"It is way past time for the international community to scrutinize Israel's racial system of governance and nothing helps demonstrate that more than Israel's elections. A broad swath of candidates are running on explicitly anti-Palestinian campaigns that mobilize voters by fomenting fear, declaring that Israel is a nation-state of

"That is to say nothing of the nearly 5 million Palestinians excluded from voting who have lived under Israel's military rule for over five decades. Palestinians in the West Bank and Gaza are neither citizens of Israel nor sovereigns of their own state, because Israel covets Palestinian land and resources. Continuing to tout Israel as a democracy today is as laughable and dishonest as saying that Donald Trump is a centrist reformer aimed at achieving racial justice. It is high time we be honest about these basic facts."

REBECCA VILKOMERSON

Rebecca Vilkomerson, Executive Director of Jewish Voice for Peace, a national organization inspired by Jewish tradition to work for the freedom, equality, and dignity of all the people of Israel and Palestine:

"The divide between Jewish American and Jewish Israeli values, as expressed through votes, has never been greater. Regardless of the outcome in the Israeli elections, the viable candidates and parties who could form a governing coalition range from right-wing to outright fascist. None support Palestinian statehood, rights, or equality.

"This election reinforces the need for pressure from outside Israel—including Boycott, Divestment and Sanctions (BDS)—for any hope of significant changes in Israeli policies towards the Palestinian people or progress towards peace."

Israelis have some serious decisions to make
By Rev. Dr Mae Elise Cannon, April 3, 2019 in Middle East Monitor

Most Israelis see themselves as having a major decision to make on 9 April. Looking at Israel as an American Christian, I think the decision has two aspects: who will govern Israel following the General Election, and how will this determine Israel's future direction vis-a-vis the Palestinians. Americans in general, and America's Christians interested in Israel in particular, will be more influenced by the future direction of Israeli politics and policies than by the outcome of the election.

The Middle East is seeing many decisions for change: the Pope has made a historic visit to the Arabian Peninsula and said mass in the United Arab Emirates; Israeli Prime Minister Benjamin Netanyahu made an official visit to Oman, without the previously anticipated backlash; and the US President is pulling ground troops out of Syria. Some choose to continue down the same roads as in the past, but that too is a decision.

The organisation I lead, Churches for Middle East Peace (CMEP), has long been a friend to Israelis. We are also a friend to Palestinians, and others seeking peace in the Middle East. As such, we have been very critical of Israel's occupation policies. We have also been critical of Hamas terrorism and the Palestinian

Authority's withholding of resources from its own people. And we have long criticised anti-Semitism here in the US. There is a significant power imbalance between Israelis and Palestinians. While there are legitimate grievances on both sides, the abuse of power in the ongoing occupation of the Palestinian people must be acknowledged and brought to an end.

A protest in support for Palestine at Times Square in New York, US on 20th May 2018 [Mohammed Elshamy/Anadolu Agency]

Americans, like Israelis, are coming to a crossroads. Most Americans have long supported Israel, while at the same time opposing some Israeli policies. Also like Israelis, for several decades Americans have thought their policy arguments with each other needed to stop at the water's edge. The US had a consistent (if occasionally horrendous) foreign affairs outlook and policy. However, this standpoint is ending. Israel's policies are becoming a bone of contention among Americans, as evidenced on Capitol Hill in response to the controversial statements made by Representative Ilhan Omar.

There are many reasons for this contentiousness, among them Netanyahu's efforts to take sides in US partisan politics. A more important reason is that Americans are taking a fresh look at where things are going. Not only are some up and coming American politicians openly hostile to Israel's occupation policies, but far more are also beginning to ask whether the US should make sacrifices to its own principles in order to support that occupation. Whole Christian denominations, historically friendly to Israel, are looking at whether to disinvest in the occupation. Some already have.

Minnesota Democratic Congressional-elect Ilhan Omar speaks at an election night results party on 6 November 2018 in Minnesota, US [Stephen Maturen/Getty Images]

The big decision for Israelis after 9 April is that second one that they will consider; whether to continue down the present road or change direction. The occupation is 51 years old. Do Israelis want their grandchildren to keep doing occupation military service in the West Bank? Do they think it is healthy for them and produces the society that Israelis want for their future? Will keeping up the blockade on Gaza, which Israel started well before Hamas came to power there, make security better for Israelis in the future? Or would it be better to change course, to build instead of destroy, to strengthen instead of oppress?

Of course, the second decision Israelis will make after the election has consequences for Israel, but it also has consequences for its future with Americans. Do Israelis prefer a future where they subjugate Palestinians and divide Americans into pro- and anti-Israel camps? The US is a democracy, imperfect often, but power in the US does reliably swing from one side eventually to the other. Does it help Israel to get more Americans to take sides for and against? Does it help to make Israel a partisan issue in the US?

Opposition to the occupation among Americans, in general, is growing, paradoxically as opposition to Boycott, Divestment and Sanctions (BDS) and other ways of expressing anti-occupation views are also increasing. The anti-occupation view is not opposition to the existence of the State of Israel. Indeed most Americans — whether Christian, Jewish or of other faiths — support two viable and secure states, Israel and Palestine, but see this as a diminishing possibility because of current settlement expansion and one-sided US policies. The opposition to BDS has many strands, too.

Choosing which way to go to the future will be hard for Israelis. They have most of the power and a strong aversion to being seen as the ones who give without gaining. The only way for Israelis to truly achieve and secure a stable future for their state is to protect and ensure the same rights for their Palestinian neighbours. Israel will not benefit by dividing Americans.

Israeli elections: Creating a front against apartheid

By Oren Yiftachel 3 April 2019 from MiddleEast Eye

A new discourse that reflects the reality on the ground is urgently needed to energise democratic forces, both in Israel/Palestine and overseas

Settlements in the occupied West Bank have created new facts on the ground (AFP)

The Israeli election campaign, in full force less than two weeks before the vote, has oscillated between discussions of corruption and terrorism.

Critically, however, the election campaign appears to be shunning, at all costs, the central topic that will determine Israel's future: the apartheid system gradually shaping Jewish-Palestinian relations.

Those who made peace their agenda – such as former foreign minister Tzipi Livni – have fallen by the wayside. Even US President Donald Trump's recent intervention, recognising Israel's claim to sovereignty in the Golan Heights, has ignited debate mainly over the future of the northern front, rather than over the likely future annexation of Palestinian lands.

The silencing on this topic only makes its long-term impact more severe, like an untreated disease. The democratic camp must create a local and international front against apartheid to save the country from this bleak future, led by Prime Minister Benjamin Netanyahu and his allies.

Geographic blindness

Long years of incitement against the very idea of peace and Palestinian statehood - against human rights organisations and "the left" in general - are having an effect. Many progressive Israelis having been raising new (and important) flags, such as women's rights and gay rights, environmental protection and social justice. Resistance to Israel's oppression of Palestinians can, it seems, wait for another day. But this is a dangerous illusion.

This overlooking produces geographic blindness, unmatched in any other election campaign globally. On the one hand, millions of Palestinians controlled by Israel are not counted as voters and have no say in determining the government that will shape their lives. On the other, hundreds of thousands of Jewish settlers - who reside in the same areas - are considered fully fledged citizens, and are likely to determine who forms the next government.

It is important to remember that the Palestinian territories and their five million Palestinian inhabitants are going nowhere. Israel settles these territories in a continuing colonial project, ruling Palestinians with a violent iron fist. Despite the charade of Palestinian "self-rule" in small enclaves, known as Areas A and B, recent Israeli interventions have exposed the real masters of Palestine.

These have included the stopping of tax transfers to the Palestinian Authority, constant invasions of the Israeli army into Palestinian "self-ruled" areas and frequent killings, the Israeli transfer and distribution of Qatari cash to Gaza, and the bombing at will of dozens of Palestinian targets after rocket attacks.

Creeping apartheid

Israel controls the area between Jordan and the Mediterranean Sea in a near-total manner. But the geographic blindness through which Israeli electoral politics "see" Jews but not Palestinians points to a deeper transformation, best described as creeping apartheid.

Under this decades-long system, several broad types of citizenships have been created and institutionalised as "separate and unequal". Jews possess full citizenship anywhere on the land, while Palestinians are fragmented into inferior legal categories: second-class Israeli citizens, "residents" of East Jerusalem, "subjects" of the West Bank and Gaza, or refugees in the camps.

Israel's separation wall is considered illegal under international law (AFP)

The parallels to apartheid South Africa are clear: Jews are akin to "the whites", Palestinians in Israel are the "coloureds", and their brethren in the West Bank and Gaza are "the blacks".

Geographically, the hundreds of settlements in the West Bank have been connected to the rest of Israel, while Palestinians are locked into their enclaves, which resemble Bantustans, on both sides of the Green Line.

This has transformed the military - and putatively "external" and "temporary" - occupation into an internal, civil and permanent rule. This was recently codified through the nation-state law, which declares Israel to be the homeland of the Jews, where only they enjoy the right to self-determination, and which promotes Jewish settlement of the entire area.

Israel's economic policies - which channel the vast majority of resources to Jews, while Judaising land and stifling Palestinian development - are another plank in the "separate and unequal" structure. Palestinians have contributed to the deadlock through years of terrorism, but the power to change direction remains firmly in their hands.

Distorted definitions

This requires the redrawing of political definitions and struggles. The language of "right versus left" is distorted, painting Israel as a normal state with a conservative nationalist camp, competing against a more progressive liberal camp. In such "normal" states, the right-left struggle is contained within clear demographic and political boundaries. No camp demands to rupture those boundaries, annex new territories or subject millions to colonial rule against their will.

Yet in Israel's forthcoming election, this is precisely the agenda of all parties associated with Likud circles and beyond, including all the Jewish religious parties, amounting to more than half the parliament (but representing perhaps a quarter of the people under Israeli rule).

These politicians object to the establishment of a Palestinian state and support continuing Israeli control over the entire land, against international law and the will of the Palestinians.

This was made even more blatant by the inclusion of the racist Otzma Yehudit (Jewish Power) party in the "legitimate" conservative camp, after decades in which all Jewish parties rejected such a partnership.

The masks have thus been taken off – this is a colonial project against Palestinian rights and those supporting the Palestinian struggle, and the main tool is the emerging apartheid state.

The struggle against this agenda begins by naming it correctly. This is not a "right-wing agenda", but an emerging apartheid bloc. This is not a mere struggle between two national movements; it is colonialism. It is likely that after the election, the apartheid reality will deepen, creating greater geographic, legal and economic barriers to equality and democracy.

The new political map of the Palestinian territories will likely look increasingly like the black Bantustans in pre-1994 South Africa, with the expected support of the US regime and the silent compliance of Russia, India and even Europe.

International coalitions

What should the democratic and progressive forces do? First, in the short time before the elections, the obvious apartheid reality should be flagged everywhere. All who believe in democracy must create a joint front against apartheid.

This is a common denominator that can unite forces, from the moderate right to Arab parties, despite large differences on other topics. Calling for a front against apartheid will put the topic in the public spotlight, cracking the current geographic and political blindness.

The old tropes of "democracy here and occupation there" or "left versus right" are dead. The Bar-Ilan speech in which Netanyahu discussed a two-state solution a decade ago, is dead. A new discourse that reflects the true political agenda and the reality on the ground is urgently needed to energise democratic forces, both in Israel/Palestine and overseas.

This is particularly relevant to Jewish communities around the world that are often at the forefront of the fight for democracy and human rights, but that usually remain silent on Israeli crimes. It is equally important for supporters of the Palestinian struggle for justice to face the new reality.

Public discourses do not change overnight. The front against apartheid will have to work after the elections and gather every possible ounce of support to combat the dangers ahead. It will have to create Jewish-Palestinian and international coalitions, mobilise international law, command media attention and occupy the streets.

The solutions to the current apartheid scenario may vary. Similar protracted conflicts in Northern Ireland, Bosnia, Macedonia, Colombia and South Africa have displayed a range of solutions: partition, confederation, federation, or a united binational or liberal democratic state.

All are possible in Israel-Palestine, although confederation appears most likely. But first, the front against apartheid must be established to halt the deterioration – the sooner the better.

IDF puts Palestinians under closure as Israelis go to the polls

While Jewish Israelis will be able to move freely in and out of the occupied West Bank, millions of Palestinians — even those with entry permits issued by the Israeli army — will be on lock-down.

By Edo Konrad, April 8, 2019 from +972

Illustrative photo of Israeli soldiers voting at a portable ballot box, near Bethlehem in the West Bank. (Nati Shohat/Flash90)

As millions of Israeli citizens head to the polls to vote on Tuesday, the Israeli army will put Palestinians in the West Bank under complete closure and will seal the Gaza Strip entirely. Movement within the West Bank should not be affected.

This means that as Israeli citizens living in settlements across the occupied territories may move freely back and forth across the Green Line separating Israel and the West Bank, millions of Palestinians are barred from doing so.

Even those tens of thousands of Palestinians who have permits to work inside Israel every day — primarily in construction and maintenance jobs — will not be allowed to go to work that day.

Unlike Israelis, for whom Election Day is a paid holiday, they will not be compensated for the one-day leave imposed on them by the Israeli military.

Palestinians in the Gaza Strip, for whom leaving requires months-long processes of applying and waiting for an Israeli military permit, which is often denied, will be entirely stuck.

The closure is scheduled to begin at midnight Monday, April 8, and end at midnight on April 9. The army says it will make humanitarian and medical exceptions on a case-by-case basis out of humanitarian basis.

Palestinians living in the West Bank and most in East Jerusalem — 2,953,000 in total — are not eligible to participate in Israel's democratic system. That same system, which others get to vote in, rules nearly every aspect of their lives, decides where they can or cannot travel, where they can live, whether they can hold political protests, where they may or may not build, and in some cases even what they can and cannot say. The nearly half a million Israeli settlers who live in the West Bank are not only subject to a different set of laws, they have the right to vote in elections that can change those policies if they have grievances.

In the Gaza Strip, the Israeli army decides what goods may be imported and exported, where fishermen can fish, how much electricity is available on a daily basis, who can enter and exit the territory, and who can travel between different areas of the occupied Palestinian territories. None of the 1,961,000 people living there have a say in those policies.

Closures during elections, as well as Jewish and Israeli holidays, are a routine procedure that Israeli authorities say is intended to prevent terror attacks. As Israeli sociologist Yael Berda told +972 earlier this year, the closures were first introduced as a punitive policy with the beginning of the First Intifada. The suicide bombings of the 90s increased those closures as preventative measures during holidays or visits by major world leaders, and there were times when closures on all of the occupied territories could last between 70 to 80 days.

Trucks at the Kerem Shalom crossing, the main passage point for goods entering Gaza from Israel, in the southern Gaza Strip town of Rafah, July 24, 2018. (Abed Rahim Khatib/ Flash90)

Curiously, the more-than 36,000 Palestinians who work inside Israeli settlements in the West Bank — where they have direct contact with Israeli citizens — will not be affected by the closure.

While Palestinians in the West Bank are barred the right to vote and the ability to travel freely, the soldiers tasked with carrying out the day to day of military occupation were given the privilege of kicking off the 2019 elections.

In the run-up to the elections, the IDF established 130 makeshift polling stations for soldiers on duty. At Ofer Military Base, which houses an infamous military court and prison, Israeli soldiers took part in the early voting process, allowing them to enjoy the fruits of the democratic process.

Lawyers Worldwide Urge International Court: Investigate Israeli Crimes

Apr 08 2019, from Days of Palestine

On the eve of the first anniversary of the "Great March of Return" at the Gaza border, lawyers and jurists around the world are calling on the prosecutor of the International Criminal Court (ICC) to investigate and prosecute Israeli crimes against the Palestinians.

Today, the International Association of Democratic Lawyers presented a petition from the International Lawyers Campaign for the Investigation and Prosecution of Crimes Committed Against the Palestinian People to Fatou Bensouda, chief prosecutor of the ICC. The petition urges Bensouda to initiate a full investigation and prosecute violations of international humanitarian law and international human rights law committed by Israeli officials in the Occupied Palestinian Territories. The petition has garnered the support of tens of thousands of lawyers worldwide.
The petition condemns "the unimaginable atrocities that have been committed and continue to be committed by Israel against Palestinian civilians which deeply shock the conscience of humanity."

It cites the well-established legal principle that victims of gross violations of international human rights law and serious violations of international humanitarian law "have a right to a remedy and reparation."

The petition denounces "the failure and refusal" of Israel to hold accountable "those suspected of committing crimes against Palestinian civilians," which has resulted in "abandoning the rule of law and replacing it with widespread impunity for Israeli officials who have sanctioned and for Israeli individuals who have perpetrated such crimes."

Israel Bombs Gaza Ahead of Great March of Return Anniversary

On March 25 and 26, in anticipation of the forthcoming election and the anniversary of the Great March of Return,
Israel pummeled Gaza with dozens of airstrikes, instilling terror in 2 million Palestinians.
On Saturday, March 30, tens of thousands of Palestinians are planning to walk toward the Gaza border to commemorate the March 30, 2018, launch of the Great March of Return. For the past year, during the weekly protests, tens of thousands of Palestinians have demanded an end to the Israeli blockade of Gaza and the right to return to their homeland. In response, Israeli forces have engaged in violent and illegal repression against demonstrators.

UN Commission Documents Crimes by Israeli Leaders

On March 18, the United Nations Commission of Inquiry on the 2018 Protests in the Occupied Palestinian Territory, convened by the UN Human Rights Council, issued a 252-page report of its findings on the Great March of Return demonstrations.
"We present this comprehensive report with an urgent plea to Israel to immediately ensure that the rules of engagement of their security forces are revised to comply with international legal standards…. The excessive force that took place on 30 March, 14 May and 12 October 2018 must not be repeated," Commission Chair Santiago Canton told the Human Rights Council.
The Commission found "reasonable grounds to believe that during these weekly demonstrations, the Israeli Security Forces killed and gravely injured civilians who were neither participating directly in

hostilities nor posing an imminent threat to life. Among those shot were children, paramedics, journalists, and persons with disabilities. 183 people were shot dead, another 6,106 were wounded with live ammunition."

Unless acting in lawful self-defense, the Commission noted, "intentionally killing a civilian not directly participating in hostilities is a war crime. Serious human rights violations were committed which may amount to crimes against humanity."

The Commission concluded that the Israeli Security Forces' "conduct also violated international humanitarian law, which permits civilians to be targeted only when they 'directly participate in hostilities.' This purposefully high threshold was not met by demonstrators' conduct, in the view of the Commission, with one possible exception."

Furthermore, the Commission stated, "Targeting unarmed demonstrators purely on the basis of their current or former political views, or their current or former membership of an armed group — and not on their conduct at the time — is impermissible in the view of the Commission."

The Commission recommended that the government of Israel:

- Prohibit the use of lethal force against civilians who pose no imminent threat to life;
- Make sure the rules of engagement don't sanction lethal force against "main inciters" as a status. Ensure the rules only allow lethal force as a last resort, where the target poses an imminent threat to life or is participating directly in hostilities;
- Do not allow targeting based solely on actual or alleged affiliation with a group rather than conduct;
- Investigate all protest-related killings to determine whether war crimes or crimes against humanity have been committed with a view toward accountability;
- Ensure prompt and effective remedies for those unlawfully killed or wounded; and
- Immediately lift the blockade on Gaza.
The Commission's report will be forwarded to the ICC.

Petition Seeks Accountability in International Court for Israeli Leaders

In the summer of 2014, Israeli forces killed 2,200 Palestinians, nearly one-quarter of them children and over 80 percent of them civilians, in an operation dubbed "Operation Protective Edge." The following January, Bensouda opened a *preliminary examination* into the situation in Palestine. In a preliminary examination, the Office of the Prosecutor determines whether there is sufficient evidence of crimes of sufficient gravity falling within the ICC's jurisdiction, whether there are genuine national proceedings, and whether opening an investigation would serve the interests of justice and of the victims.

The petition from the International Association of Democratic Lawyers urges Bensouda to take the next step — from a *preliminary examination* to a full *investigation* into Israeli crimes against the Palestinian people. In an investigation, the Office of the Prosecutor gathers evidence, identifies suspects, and asks ICC judges to issue an arrest warrant or a summons to appear.

On April 8, 2018, in light of Israeli actions during the Great March of Return, Bensouda stated that "any new alleged crime committed in the context of the situation in Palestine may be subjected to my Office's scrutiny. This applies to the events of the past weeks and to any future incident." She added, "I am aware that the demonstrations in the Gaza Strip are planned to continue further. My Office will continue to closely watch the situation and will record any instance of incitement or resort to unlawful force." She added, "Violence against civilians – in a situation such as the one prevailing in Gaza – could constitute crimes under the [ICC's] Rome Statute."

Bensouda noted, "Any person who incites or engages in acts of violence including by ordering, requesting, encouraging or contributing in any other manner to the commission of crimes within ICC's jurisdiction is liable to prosecution before the Court, with full respect for the principle of complementarity."

"Complementarity" means the court will take jurisdiction only over people whose home country is unwilling or unable to genuinely investigate and prosecute.

Israel has demonstrated its unwillingness to mount an impartial investigation into Operation Protective Edge. In August 2018, the Israeli military absolved itself of any wrongdoing in that operation. The lawyers' petition was inspired by the International Association of Democratic Lawyers' previous international call for lawyers to support the campaign to free Nelson Mandela in the 1980s. Just as that campaign "proved to be for those living under Apartheid in South Africa," the current petition "is an essential first step in securing equal justice under law" for the Palestinian people.

Netanyahu doubles down: 'Palestinian sovereignty…is dead'

April 8, 2019, in Middle East Monitor

US Secretary of State Mike Pompeo (L) meets Israeli Prime Minister Benjamin Netanyahu at Prime Ministry Office in Jerusalem on 20 March 2019 [Kobi Gideon/Anadolu Agency]

Israeli Prime Minister Benjamin Netanyahu told Israeli media in an interview yesterday that he intends to annex West Bank settlements, "if possible with American support".

According to *the Jerusalem Post*, Netanyahu told *Arutz 7* that he intended to "apply Israeli law to the communities in Judea and Samaria [the West Bank]" during "the next term".
Asked whether the Trump administration was aware of these plans, Netanyahu replied: "Sure", adding: "They [the US] will react as they will react. We will see. These are my principles."

The Likud leader also doubled down on his vow not to remove illegal settlements.

"If we do not tear out the settlers, then who are they going to live under? They are going to be under Palestinian sovereignty? That is dead," he declared.

Those who live in the settlements, "will be under Israeli sovereignty," he added.

Netanyahu further elaborated to *Arutz 7*:

The Palestinians can have all the powers to govern themselves, but none to threaten us, which means we maintain security control. We don't uproot anyone. We don't divide Jerusalem.

"My friend [former US vice president] Joe Biden, who may be running for the presidency of the US [in 2020], said, 'Bibi, that is not a state. That is not sovereignty.' I said, 'Joe, you call it what you will. This is what it is. These are my positions. I am not changing these positions.'"

Meanwhile, in an interview with *Army Radio*, "the prime minister clarified that he does not intend to annex all of the West Bank, just the places in Area C where the settlements are located", the paper added.
"A Palestinian state will not be created, not like the one people are talking about. It won't happen."

Israeli army to raze eight Palestinian homes in Masafer Yatta

Apr 08 2019 on Days of Palestine

The Israeli occupation army on Sunday notified Palestinian citizens of its intent to demolish eight homes in Masafer Yatta, south of al-Khalil in the West Bank.

Local official Rateb al-Jabour reported that Israeli forces stormed the villages of ar-Rakeez and al-Mafqara in eastern Yatta and handed citizens home demolition notices.

Four of these homes belong to three brothers and their sister from the family of al-Hamameda in ar-Rakeez village. They were also handed a notice ordering them to remove a mobile toilet.

In al-Mafqara village, the Israeli army also notified two brothers from the family of Hamameda and a widow of its intent to remove four homes belongings to them. Two of these homes are a mobile house and a tent.

Israel arrests 21 Palestinians in West Bank raids

Apr 08 2019 from Days of Palestine

The Israeli occupation forces (IOF) arrested 21 Palestinians during overnight raids carried out across the occupied West Bank, on Monday.

In a statement, the IOF claimed that the individuals had been detained for "suspected involvement in popular hostile activities".

It, however, did not elaborate on the nature of these alleged "activities".

The Israeli army carries out frequent arrest campaigns across the West Bank -- including occupied East Jerusalem -- on the pretext of searching for "wanted" Palestinians.

According to Palestinian figures, roughly 5,700 Palestinians -- including a number of women and children -- are currently languishing in Israeli detention facilities.

Just a normal day in Palestine I guess (Editor)

There are no fig leaves left to cover the uncomfortable and illegal facts about Israel

By Professor Kamel Hawwash April 8, 2019 in Middle East Monitor

Israeli forces intervene in Palestinians during a protest against construction of Jewish settlement within 43rd anniversary of Palestinian Land Day in Ramallah, West Bank on March 29, 2019. [Issam Rimawi - Anadolu Agency]

There is nothing left of the rotten fig leaves which have been used to cover Israeli Apartheid. On 19 July last year, Israel's parliament and main democratic institution, the Knesset, passed the racist Nation-State Law, which gave the right to self-determination in Israel only to Jews. In the run up to tomorrow's General Election, Prime Minister Benjamin Netanyahu pointed Israel's Arab citizens to the 22 Arab countries to which they could move.

Emboldened by US President Donald Trump's recognition of Israeli sovereignty over the illegally occupied Syrian Golan Heights, Netanyahu's appetite for more land theft has turned to the West Bank. He declared that Israel must exercise security control west of the River Jordan and insisted that he will not move a single

Jewish settler out of the illegal settlements, whether in the blocs or isolated areas.

Given that the current incumbent of the White House will give his blessing to Israel's illegal actions once they are sold to him by his Zionist advisers as facts on the ground, Netanyahu has thus laid the ground for Trump's recognition of Israeli sovereignty over the West Bank, possibly in his second term. I am prepared to predict that once the Israeli election is over, the US Ambassador to Israel, David Freidman, will be encouraging Netanyahu to speed up his annexation of the West Bank, to enable him to ask the US President to recognise the annexation as a fact on the ground in this term.

Israel has passed the Nation-State Law becoming officially an Apartheid State – Cartoon [Sabaaneh/MiddleEastMonitor]

Trump is currently the milch cow that keeps giving to Israel so why not milk him for what it is worth, while he is still around? Why risk delaying US recognition of Israeli sovereignty over the whole of historic Palestine from the River Jordan to the Mediterranean Sea to a second Trump term, when the American electorate might elect someone else, who may balk at recognising illegal acts? In other words, they may say "sell, sell, sell" in the financial markets, but here it is "take, take, take".

It has become abundantly clear since Trump's election and his choice of advisers on the Israel-Palestine peace process, that what Netanyahu wants, he gets. The Israeli premier must be pinching himself as he sits back in Jerusalem wondering if this is for real. The situation is such that if Netanyahu wanted to be America's Godfather, Trump might just oblige once his son in law Jared Kushner tells him that it is appropriate and long overdue. Bizarre? Of course it is. However, note that Trump recently referred to Netanyahu as the Prime Minister of Jewish American citizens when addressing the Republican Jewish Coalition in Las Vegas: "I stood with *your* prime minister at the White House to recognise Israel's sovereignty over the Golan Heights." (Emphasis added.)
Instead of being troubled by Israel's naked racism, Trump legitimises law breaking to the detriment of the international order and the status of international law. It is worth remembering that his National Security Advisor, John Bolton, has warned the International Criminal Court and its judges against investigating atrocities committed by only two countries, the US and Israel. Netanyahu and Trump are drunk on power and are prepared to treat international law as subservient to their wishes, excusing Israeli breaches but not those of other countries.

This also applies to Israel crying wolf and accusing the Boycott, Divestment and Sanctions (BDS) campaign of anti-Semitism when it is the target due to its illegal actions and oppression of the Palestinians; it is quick to call for sanctions against Iran, Iraq and Syria, though. Another example of its self-declared exceptionalism relates to its calling the fence with Gaza an internationally recognised border — alone amongst all UN member states, Israel has never declared its borders — but refusing to withdraw to the internationally recognised Armistice ("Green") Line with either Palestine or Syria. It is one law for Israel and another, as it sees fit, for others.

What further emboldens Netanyahu is the weak response to his illegal actions by other members of the international community. Take, for example, Israel's recent announcement that it was advancing plans for more around 5,000 settlement units, all illegal under international law. Just as Britain's acting Foreign Minister for the MENA region, Mark Fields, published a statement condemning Israeli settlements, Netanyahu was announcing his intention to annex the West Bank, in which these illegal units were to be constructed. Condemnation alone has proven to be not only inadequate in its self but also coupled with growing trade links with Israel, which is at best illogical and at worst hypocritical.

housands of demonstrators from the Druze community stage a protest against the "Jewish Nation-State" law that was approved last month by the Israel's parliament, at Rabin Square in Tel Aviv, Israel on August 04, 2018 [Daniel Bar On / Anadolu Agency]

As Israelis head to the polls tomorrow, they should realise that the label of racism and Apartheid is not only an accurate description of the Netanyahu government's policies, but also reflects badly on those who elect them. I do not throw accusations of racism around lightly. However, a state which claims to be a democracy but is institutionally racist against its own non-Jewish citizens, as evidenced by over 60 discriminatory laws, and which is selective when it comes the application of international law, must face the consequences that come with this.

Israelis cannot claim that it is not them at fault, but this or that government, given that the majority have elected successive governments that have moved towards far-right extremism and whose Justice Minister recently sprayed herself with "fascism" in an election ad. If their governments do not reflect their views, will they elect a Knesset which reverses the Nation-State Law, gives all

Israeli citizens equal rights, pledges an end to the occupation and welcomes Palestinian refugees home? They can do this on 9 April, but will they? Sadly, even if they wished to do so, they will not find a party to vote for which is genuine about wanting peace. Their choice of candidates is limited to those who advocate "hard Apartheid" or "soft Apartheid".

Apartheid, though, is Apartheid, and it is a crime against humanity. That is what Israel is all about in 2019. It has no fig leaves left to cover this fact.

Israeli press review: Annexation and immunity on the menu for Netanyahu
Israeli media takes stock of what to expect in the wake of a heated election
In Middle East Eye, 10th April 2019

Israeli Prime Minister Benjamin Netanyahu, leader of the Likud party, walks through the Mahane Yehuda market in Jerusalem (AFP)

With victory secured, Bibi seeks immunity
Writing in Haaretz, the paper's editor-in-chief Aluf Benn predicts Benjamin Netanyahu will pursue immunity from prosecution and annexation of parts of the West Bank.

Facing a raft of indictments over corruption allegations, Netanyahu will likely make a deal with his future right-wing coalition partners ensuring they pass legislation that will give him immunity, Benn writes.

In return, those nationalist-religious parties will seek a vow from Netanyahu that he will lobby US President Donald Trump to include Israeli annexation of the West Bank's Area C - which represents 60 percent of the occupied Palestinian territory - in his "Deal of the Century" peace plan.

To help achieve his goals, Netanyahu will continue to erode the power of the Supreme Court, which has proved problematic for him and his coalition partners in the past.

Already, a showdown between the Israeli right and the judiciary over the controversial nation-state law is brewing.

"The first test is approaching: The present High Court will decide whether or not to hear petitions to throw out the nation-state law, in contrast to the united position of the right-wing parties that deny the court's power to invalidate basic laws," Benn writes.

Fewer women, more ultra-Orthodox
The new Knesset is notable for having fewer female members and more religious ones, Ynet reports.

Twenty-nine women were elected on Tuesday, down from 36 in the outgoing parliament.

Out of the 120 Knesset seats, 42 go to Mizrahi Jews - the term used to refer to those of Middle Eastern origin - Ynet reports. All eight of ultra-Orthodox party Shas's seats will be held by Mizrahis.

A full quarter of the new Knesset will be held by religious or ultra-Orthodox members. Seventeen seats will go to ultra-Orthodox candidates, up from 13, while another 14 are to be handed out to nationalist-religious politicians.

Representation of Palestinian citizens of Israel– including Druze – is dropping from a high of 16 to just 12 seats.

Meanwhile, the new Knesset will see a record number of openly LGBTQ members, who will hold five seats.

A period of reflection for Palestinian parties
The Jewish nation-state law was a game changer for parties representing Palestinian citizens of Israel, Jack Khoury writes in Haaretz.

Following a poor turnout and calls for a Palestinian boycott, he writes, the Hadash, Raam, Taal and Balad parties need a moment of introspection to reassess their political message.

"The Arab Knesset members could justifiably argue that most of the time, they do act for the good of their constituents. But in the shadow of the extreme-right government and its campaign to delegitimize them, led by Netanyahu, they had little influence," Khoury writes.

"The enactment of laws like the so-called 'nation-state law' contributed enormously to the loss of faith in the Israeli establishment and in the Knesset."

The failure of the four parties to stay together in the Joint List, which won 13 seats in 2015, also contributed to the sense of apathy in the community.

"Despite their attempts at displaying unity, they didn't connect on the ground, leading to internal fighting over their conflicting narrow interests. This exacerbated the disgust among voters who don't particularly identify with any one of the parties," Khoury writes.

"Those people may have voted in 2015, but this time, they just stayed home."

Naftali Bennett pins hopes on soldiers
The New Right party of Naftali Bennett and Ayalet Shaked faces the embarrassment of not making the Knesset's 3.25 percent threshold, news site Ynet reports, but they are hoping soldiers save the day.

"They hoped to secure the defence and justice portfolios - but according to the polls they won't even make the threshold".

In his speech on election night following the exit polls, Bennett sounded optimistic, according to Ynet.

"We have patience, faith and nerves of steel. The New Right will pass," Bennett said.

The former education minister has spent much of his career touting the military, and predicted that the votes of soldiers, which are counted last, could see his party through.

"The soldiers will take care of us," he said.

Encountering Peace: The view from the Left
By Gershon Baskin April 10, 2019 In The Jerusalem Post

BENJAMIN NETANYAHU – the elections were all about him. (photo credit: REUTERS)

The view from the Left

Netanyahu did it again. Despite three indictments for corruption hanging over his future, despite the gaps between rich and poor and increasing costs of living, despite the collapsing health system, despite spending hours in traffic jams every week, despite the periodic barrage of rockets from Gaza, despite the perception of giving into Hamas and paying protection money, Benjamin Netanyahu will remain Israel's prime minister.

Israel is a very divided society. Yet it is difficult to determine that the division is over ideology and visions for the future of Israel. Israel divided its votes equally between Netanyahu and Benny Gantz. But the Arab citizens of Israel failed to bring out the vote. One of the two Arab parties did not make it over the threshold – and they will surely pay the price for it. Moshe Feiglin's Zehut Party, surprisingly, failed to cross the threshold, and that is good news.

The best news is that the Bennett-Shaked union of the New Right will also be out of our lives for the coming months, perhaps years. However, the agenda that Shaked set in place with the aim of eliminating the ability of the Supreme Court to deal with constitutional issues will likely advance.

Along with the bad news is the shrinking of the Labor Party and its more ideological sister, Meretz. Both Labor and Meretz need to rethink their futures.

Israel continues to move to the Right. Gantz and his party of generals will bring new life to the opposition, where they will primarily focus on bringing down Netanyahu after his hearing regarding his criminal indictments. The assumption this morning is that the cases against Netanyahu are so solid that within a year, he will be forced to resign, and then Israel will most likely head to the polls once again, this time without the unbeatable Netanyahu heading the Likud.

For now, it seems that what there was is what there will be. Avigdor Liberman may be heading back to the Defense Ministry.

Kahlon will be heading back to the Finance Ministry. The right-wing religious union will probably demand the education portfolio and maybe the Justice Ministry.

None of the real issues on Israel's agenda were even discussed during the election campaign. The critical issues – of determining Israel's borders, the future of the occupied territories, the Palestinian issue, and the issue of peace – have never been further from the public political debate than in this election campaign. Issues concerning Israel's economic policies and direction, what was called just a few years ago "social justice," were also not on the agenda. The issues of the environment and climate change, which is on the agenda of young people all around the world, was also not on the agenda in these elections.

The Israeli elections were about one main issue: Benjamin Netanyahu, and here is where the public seems most divided. Those of us who see Netanyahu as corrupt, divisive against Arabs and leftists, an annexationist without any hope in the world of ending Israel's occupation over the Palestinian people, are extremely sad this morning.

The other side is celebrating its victory, and will now hold Netanyahu to his words: that the criminal files against him are nothing and will quickly disappear; that he will annex at least the Jewish settlement blocs accounting for 20-40% of the West Bank; that he will eliminate the Hamas threat in Gaza; and that he will continue to march into the arms of waiting Arab leaders in the region, without giving in to the Palestinians.

What I see from the Left side of the political map is the continuing weakening of the rule of law; increasing threats to Israel's Supreme Court; continued provocation with the Palestinian Authority that will lead to a sharp increase in violence; little chance of changing the situation vis-à-vis Gaza; and no changes regarding the regional threats. It seems hard to believe that after his hearing on the cases of corruption, the indictments will not be issued and then Netanyahu will have his "day in court." Except that his day in court will be many, many days and months, and it is hard to understand how he will be able to run the country that needs most of his time to be prime minister. For this reason, it is likely his coalition partners will advance a law or a mechanism to enable him to delay his legal battles until he is no longer prime minister, and that could be years from now.

The most important unknown is President Donald Trump's "deal of the century," which is supposed to be presented, finally, in the near future. If it is, as I expect, a pre-cooked deal between Trump and Netanyahu, it will be a total non-starter for the Palestinians, who will immediately reject it. Then Netanyahu will be able to freely embrace it, even if there are elements in the plan that he rejects. Netanyahu will blame the Palestinians, once again for rejecting peace, and say that Israel has no partner.

Netanyahu will be able to state that Israel accepts the plan as a basis for negotiations and we are, once again, waiting for there to be a Palestinian partner. Following this, he is likely to move forward with his plans for annexing large chunks of the West Bank. The action that will put a final blow to the option of two states, except, as I wrote last week, he will begin the process of convincing the world that the two-states solution already exists, with Gaza being a Palestinian state.

He will also bring new life into what was called the "Jordanian option," telling West Bank Palestinians that they already have Jordanian citizenship, and if they want they are welcome to remain in areas A and B of the West Bank under the corrupt Palestinian Authority, or to leave to Jordan or elsewhere.

President Abbas's days are numbered for sure – as a result of age, too many years in office, or his inability to offer any hope to his people. The Palestinian people will also have their day at the polls in the not too distant future. Without any positive political horizon for them, it is likely that they too will end up with a government which is not interested in peace with Israel.

For reasons that completely escape me, most Israelis who I meet seem content and even happy with their situation. This is an aspect of Israeli society that we will have to revisit. For me personally, I am very worried about our future.

Israeli airstrike targets agricultural land east of Gaza
Two Gazans arrested near border fence
Apr 09 2019 in Days of Palestine

An Israeli warplane on Monday evening bombed an agricultural tract of land in the east of al-Bureij refugee camp in central Gaza, with no known reason.

According to eyewitnesses, an Israeli drone fired at least one missile at an empty agricultural piece of land near the border fence in the east of al-Bureij camp.

The airstrike only caused material damage to the place.

In a separate incident, the Israeli occupation forces rounded up on the same day two Palestinian young men near the border fence in southern Gaza.

According to the Hebrew website 0404, the young men were unarmed and tried to infiltrate into Israel.

Israeli army bulldozes lands, opens fire at workers in Gaza
Apr 10 2019 from Days of Palestine

On Wednesday morning, the Israeli occupation bulldozers infiltrated into a border area in the Gaza Strip, while soldiers opened fire at Palestinian workmen in Rafah south of the Gaza Strip.

Local sources reported that four armored bulldozers left a military post in the east of Rafah and entered a border area to level lands. They added that Israeli soldiers also opened fire at a group of Palestinian workers as they were collecting aggregate in a border area to the northeast of Rafah, with no reported casualties.

FAQ: Deir Yassin Massacre
from the Institute for Middle East Understanding April 2010

71 Years Today: April 9, 1948, three Zionist militias - the Haganah, Irgun and Stern Gang -- attacked the Palestinian village of Deir Yassin, located west of Jerusalem. More than 100 men, women, and children were massacred. Some were mutilated and raped before being murdered. Twenty-five men from the village were paraded through Jerusalem and then

executed in a nearby quarry. Those able to escape fled to East Jerusalem.

PHOTO: Ruins of homes left empty from the Deir Yassin Massacre, 1986. (Source: deiryassinremembered.org)

The massacre at Deir Yassin is one of some two dozen documented massacres of Palestinian civilians by Zionist forces seeking to transform Palestine into a Jewish state. If the import of catastrophes were gauged only in numbers of people slaughtered, Deir Yassin may not have taken on its central role in the Palestinian national consciousness. However, the terror at Deir Yassin triggered a mass flight of Palestinians who feared for their own lives. When Israel was established, more than 700,000 Palestinians lost their homes and belongings, their farms and businesses, their towns and cities. Jewish militias, and later, the Israeli army, drove them out. Israel rapidly moved Jews into the newly-emptied Palestinian homes. This tragic event and its consequences lie at the core of the Palestinian/Israeli problem.

What happened in the Palestinian village of Deir Yassin and why does it matter today?

In the early morning of April 9, 1948, three Zionist militias - the Haganah, Irgun and Stern Gang -- attacked the Palestinian village of Deir Yassin, located west of Jerusalem. More than 100 men, women, and children were massacred. Some were mutilated and raped before being murdered. Twenty-five men from the village were paraded through Jerusalem and then executed in a nearby quarry. Those able to escape fled to East Jerusalem.

Word of the terror attacks spread rapidly, causing many Palestinians to flee, fearing for their lives. Within a year of the massacre, Deir Yassin, which had been emptied of Palestinians, was re-populated with Jewish immigrants and its name was removed from the map.

For Palestinians, Deir Yassin became the symbol of the sudden loss of their homes and homeland and the near destruction of their society, a situation which endures until today. When Israel was established sixty years ago, more than 700,000 Palestinians were exiled and 78 percent of the land of historic Palestine was lost.

Today, Palestinian refugees are still deprived of their internationally-recognized right to return to their homeland. In the West Bank, Israel continues to seize land for Israeli-only settlements and Israeli-only roads.

Who carried out the massacre?

The Haganah, which became the Israeli army, fired mortars at the village while the Irgun and Stern Gang attacked from close range. At the time of the massacre, David Ben-Gurion, Israel's 1st prime minister, directed Haganah policy; Menachem Begin, Israel's 6th prime minister, led the Irgun; and Yitzhak Shamir, Israel's 7th prime minister, was a leader of the Stern Gang.

What resulted from the Deir Yassin massacre?

As news of the massacre spread, the ensuing terror triggered the mass flight of Palestinians. A few days after the attacks, in fact, the Irgun asserted that the incident advanced "terror and dread among the Arabs in all the villages around, in Al Maliha, Qaluniya and Beit Iksa a panic flight began..." The flight of Palestinian refugees fit into the plans of Zionist military and political leaders at the time. During the first week of April, a concerted campaign — known as Plan Dalet — to systematically expel Palestinians from areas sought for the soon-to-be-founded state of Israel went into effect. Zionist forces conducted eight major military operations against Palestinian cities and villages between April 1st and May 15th when Israel declared independence and Arab states intervened in response to the growing refugee crisis. Some 250,000 Palestinians had been expelled by then.

Was Deir Yassin an isolated incident?

No. While Deir Yassin may be the most infamous, Israeli historian Benny Morris documents 24 massacres of Palestinians conducted by Zionist, and then Israeli, forces in 1948. According to Morris:

In some cases four or five people were executed, in others the numbers were 70, 80, 100. There was also a great deal of arbitrary killing. Two old men are spotted walking in a field - they are shot. A woman is found in an abandoned village - she is shot. There are cases such as the village of Dawayima [in the Hebron region], in which a column entered the village with all guns blazing and killed anything that moved. The worst cases were Saliha (70-80 killed), Deir Yassin (100-110), Lod (250), Dawayima (hundreds) and perhaps Abu Shusha (70).... The fact is that no one was punished for these acts of murder. Ben-Gurion silenced the matter. He covered up for the officers who did the massacres.

The Irgun and Stern Gang also attacked British and United Nations institutions and officers who they believed stood in the way of the Zionist enterprise in Palestine. The Irgun was responsible for the bombing of the King David Hotel, which was used as British military headquarters, in Jerusalem in 1946. Ninety-one people were killed. The Stern Gang assassinated Lord Moyne, the British minister of state for the Middle East, in 1944, attempted to assassinate Harold MacMichael, the High Commissioner of Palestine, in 1944 and assassinated Count Folke Bernadotte, the United Nations representative in the Middle East, in 1948.

What was the total destruction and how it is still relevant today?

In total, at least 450 Palestinian towns and villages were depopulated due to Zionist military attacks or fear of such attacks. Most of these were demolished. By the end of 1948, more than 700,000 Palestinians - two-thirds of the Palestinian population - were exiled and their society was destroyed. Even today, a Jew from anywhere in the world is welcome to settle in Israel, while Palestinians with the keys and deeds to their seized homes do not enjoy the right to return.

Remembering Deir Yassin

Benjamin Netanyahu's reelection underlines Israel's apartheid reality

By SAREE MAKDISI, APR 10, 2019, The Los Angeles Times

Israeli Prime Minister Benjamin Netanyahu, accompanied by his wife Sara, greets supporters at the Likud Party headquarters in Tel Aviv on election night early on April 10. (Thomas Coex / AFP / Getty Images)

The results of Israel's elections reveal a stark reality: Not only will Benjamin Netanyahu almost inevitably form a coalition government even further to the right than the one he already heads, but the country's Jewish electorate has given its resounding endorsement to the policies for which he stands.

Netanyahu ran a manifestly racist electoral campaign, reaching out to embrace politicians who openly espouse the desire to expel Palestinians from the state and promising to annex parts of the West Bank, dealing probably a final blow to the moribund two-state solution.

What Israeli voters want, clearly, is precisely what is on offer: more dispossession of Palestinians, more home demolitions, more indiscriminate bombing campaigns, more shooting of protesters, more settlements, more restrictions on Gaza and on Palestinian life in general, and deeper and deeper inequality between Jews and non-Jews in Israel and in the territories over which it rules.

The bloc led by Benny Gantz hardly offered much of a difference. Gantz's own electoral campaign prominently featured a series of videos called "Only the Strong Survive," which gloated over how many Palestinians the former army chief of staff had killed and how proud he was to have bombed parts of Gaza "back to the Stone Age."

One video limply offered, "It's not shameful to be striving for peace."

In the end, Gantz's tough-guy claims were clearly not enough to convince Israeli voters to depart from a wily politician they knew for a fact — because he's been doing it for so long — would continue to subjugate the Palestinians.

The voters reaffirmed the de facto or de jure realities Palestinians have long faced. Last year, Israel legally enshrined a Jewish nation-state law that formalized the superior status of Jews over non-Jews, officially relegating Arabic — the language spoken by the 20% of the state's citizens who are Palestinian — to a secondary status, elided Palestinians' ongoing presence in and claim to their ancestral land, directed the government to "encourage and promote" Jewish settlement and thereby further segregation, and declared that the right to self-determination in the state is reserved for Jews alone.

Netanyahu himself announced on Instagram in March that Israel is "the nation state not of all its citizens but only of the Jewish people."

International law has a word to describe a state that discriminates along racial lines like this: apartheid.

Two sets of numbers indicate how institutionalized this apartheid is. First, although Israel exerts control over territory (including the occupied West Bank, East Jerusalem and Gaza) inhabited by around 13 million people, only 5.8 million — 80% of them Jews, according to Israel's Central Election Committee — are eligible voters.

When you add to these shameful figures the millions of registered Palestinian refugees living outside Israel and the occupied territories, in enforced exile solely because Israel refuses to allow them to return home, the reality becomes even more stark: Israel's elections, far from being legitimately democratic, are in fact a manifestation of minority rule.

Millions of disenfranchised Palestinians have no say over the structures and patterns of their everyday lives. They are subject to whatever Jewish Israeli voters think they deserve, which is essentially further dehumanization.

But if the Palestinians had the right to vote, what would they vote for? They may not have elections, but opinion polls consistently show that when asked which Palestinian leader they trust the most, the overwhelming winner (48% in the most recent poll conducted by the reputable Jerusalem Media and Communications Centre) is "none of the above."

And when asked which party they support, the answer is consistently neither Fatah, which controls the Palestinian Authority, (28%) nor Hamas (10%), but "don't trust anyone" (41%).

A solid majority prefer negotiations to armed struggle and an increasing number want a single state, shared with Jews. (Only 0.4% want an Islamic state to replace Jewish state of Israel.)

The takeaway from Israel's election is simple: The two-state solution is dead. What remains is a single racist state whose beneficiaries are satisfied with their government and whose victims are deeply unhappy and desperate for something new: a transition from an apartheid state to a genuinely democratic one in which Palestinians are treated as equal citizens with Israeli Jews, not disenfranchised brutes.

Saree Makdisi is a professor of English at UCLA.

Trump paves way for Israel to expand settlements in Golan
by Ahmad Melhem, April 11, 2019, Palestine Pulse in Al Monitor

Israel's Ministry of Housing has confirmed government plans to develop the Golan Heights to accommodate 250,000 Israeli settlers there by 2048, when the country marks its 100th anniversary. The plan, prepared by the ministry in cooperation with the Golan Regional Council and the Council of Katzrin settlement, was revealed one week after US President Donald Trump announced March 25 that the United States would recognize Israel's sovereignty over the Golan Heights.

The plan is to build 30,000 new housing units in Katzrin, build two new settlements, create 45,000 jobs, develop transportation networks, including railways and airports, and clear land mines from 80,000 dunums (almost 20,000 acres). No further details were available regarding when the plan will be implemented and whom it might employ.

"Revealing a long-term plan to Judaize the Golan would not have been possible without the US decision," Antoine Shalhat, director of the Palestinian Forum for Israeli Studies (MADAR), an independent research center in Ramallah, told Al-Monitor. Successive US administrations had always considered the Golan Heights occupied territory.

In December 1981, the Israeli Knesset passed a law to annex the Golan Heights and impose Israeli jurisdiction over it. However, the UN Security Council passed Resolution 497, which considered the Israeli law null and void and called for canceling it.

"Launching this settlement plan in the Golan Heights is proof of the US decision's power in Israel. It allows it to set in motion settlement, tourism, economic and demographic projects," Shalhat said, adding, "The plan was already thought up and immediately introduced as soon as Trump announced his decision."

Israel seized the Golan Heights from Syria in 1967 and has refused to give it up since. The Israeli government held a Cabinet session there in April 2016, during which Prime Minister Benjamin

Netanyahu pledged to keep the Golan Heights "forever" and called on the world to recognize Israel's sovereignty there.

Israel had appointed members and heads of local councils in the Golan until Interior Minister Aryeh Deri decided in October to hold elections for local authorities in the four villages there: Majdal Shams, Baqatha, Masada and Ein Qiniya.
The mostly Druze population, however, rejected the elections and Druze candidates in Baqatha and Masada withdrew, while voter turnout in Majdal Shams and Ein Qiniya was low.

Yet Israel still completely controls the Golan villages and their residents.

According to statistics from Al-Marsad, an Arab human rights center in the Golan Heights, around 26,000 Syrians live in the Golan. Israel has established 34 settlements, with some 26,000 settlers living there, according to Human Rights Watch. Compared with settlement rates in the West Bank, which Israel also seized in 1967, the number of settlements in the Golan Heights is low.

Shalhat said the reason for the difference was that "during Israeli-Syrian negotiations, there has been an unofficial Israeli approval for returning the Golan Heights to Syria in exchange for normalization and signing a peace treaty." He added, "This position was expressed by former Israeli Prime Minister Yitzhak Rabin during the negotiations between 1993 and 1996." However, with Trump's decision, such an arrangement is no longer an option.

Meanwhile, Trump's decision was met with popular condemnation and protest in the Golan Heights. On April 2, 300 Syrian Druze demonstrated against the decision and against a project approved by the Israeli government in 2014 to build 31 wind turbines, arguing that the Golan Heights would remain Syrian territory, the Yedioth Ahronoth daily newspaper reported.

"Trump's decision is complementary to his decision to recognize Jerusalem as the capital of Israel [and proves] the lack of respect for international law that considers the Golan Heights occupied land," political activist Salman Fakhreddine, who lives in Majdal Shams, told Al-Monitor.

"We have been living under occupation for 50 years now, and Trump's decision will not change anything. In the end, this land is occupied Syrian territory and its sovereignty goes to the Syrian state, which is obliged to liberate it," he said.

"We, as residents, are doing our duty toward our land, which is limited to popular peaceful resistance. We insist on rejecting the occupation and not recognizing it," he said.

"Settlement activity in the Golan Heights has not stopped since 1967, and the [April 1] announcement of the settlement plan comes under [the rubric of] Israeli election propaganda," Fakhreddine said. "Settlement activity in the Golan Heights in recent years has not been as urgent to Israel as it is in the West Bank, [which is] close to the center of the state. But it will now focus on its expansion here, and we cannot [do anything] but hold on, because the land we stand on is all we have left."

Majd Abu Saleh, a lawyer who lives in Majdal Shams, told Al-Monitor, "Trump's decision will not change our affiliation with Syria and our refusal to be part of Israel. We have expressed this through popular demonstrations in the villages of the Golan Heights. Under occupation, we will never accept this decision."

He said, "Israel has been trying to Judaize the Golan Heights since the first day it set foot here and established its settlements. Trump's decision will only encourage it to further Judaize the area."

"We are familiar with the policy of Judaization and imposing a fait accompli that Israel has been pursuing for years to force its sovereignty and control over the Golan Heights. But we, as civilians under occupation, will always stand against it," Abu Saleh said. "The biggest effort will have to be on the Syrian state's part as well as the Arab world to restore the Golan Heights."

Residents can only take to the streets to protest against Trump's recognition of Israeli sovereignty over the Golan Heights. In light of the ongoing war in Syria, the US decision has given Israel the green light to carry out its settlement projects in the Golan Heights as it pleases.

Israel kills a child, injures 66 in the 54th Friday of the March of Return

Great March of Return will continue until achievement of its goals in full

Apr 12 2019 from Days of Palestine

The 54th Friday of the Great March Of Retrun - Days Of Palestine Photos

Israeli occupation forces (IOF) have once more opened fire on Palestinians who took part in the 54th Friday of the peaceful protests "Great March of Return" along the border between the besieged Gaza Strip and occupied territories, killing a child and injuring at least 66 others.

The Ministry of Health reported that Israeli occupation snipers shot one child and injured 66 others including two paramedic volunteers in the 54 th Friday of the peaceful Great March of Return, east of Gaza.

The child **Mysara Musa Ali Abu Shalof**, 15, was shot in the abdomen, east of Jabalia, the Ministry Of Health affirmed.

The spokesperson of the Ministry of Health added that the volunteer paramedic Kamal Al-Shahri severely suffocated during his humanitarian work, east of Khan Younis.

In another statement the Ministry of Health reported that the volunteer paramedic Bilal Abu Foul of the Palestinian Red Crescent Society (PRCS) was hit with a tear gas canister in his hand during his humanitarian work east of Jabaliya.

Meanwhile the Higher National Commission of the Great March of Return said that the march will continue until achievement of its goals in full.

Since the beginning of the Great March of Return and breaking the siege on 30 March, 2018, **at least 271 were killed** and **more than 16,656 were injured** with different injuries by the Israeli occupation forces.
The Gaza Strip has been under an "Israeli" siege since June 2007. The blockade has caused a decline in living standards as well as unprecedented unemployment and poverty.

Rethinking the nature of the Palestinian-Israeli conflict

The narrative of occupation granted Israel legal and political cover to continue with its settler colonisation unabated

by Jeremy Wildeman , Emile Badarin 11 April 2019 from Middle East Eye

A Palestinian demonstrator (L) argues with an Israeli settler during a protest against Jewish settlements in Jordan Valley near the West Bank city of Jericho November 17, 2016 (REUTERS)

The results of the recent Israeli election indicate that another far-right government coalition will be formed under the leadership of Prime Minister Benjamin Netanyahu, who campaigned on a promise to annex the West Bank.

As with all previous Israeli governments, the expected Netanyahu-led coalition will continue to suppress the Palestinians, but this time it may do so without rhetorical and policy reference to the Oslo Peace Process and "occupation".

In so doing, any distinction between the territories that Israel occupied in 1967 and was established on in 1948 will rapidly disappear.

Occupied no more

The US has already paved the way for such a future. Recently, the US administration stopped referring to the West Bank, Gaza Strip and the Syrian Golan Heights as "occupied territories" in its annual human rights report.

This was preceded by President Trump's recognition of Israeli sovereignty over Jerusalem in December 2017 and then the Golan Heights, which Saeb Erekat, a senior Palestinian official, considers a prelude to recognising Israel's annexation of the West Bank.

To be sure, previous US administrations have already conceded that parts of the West Bank, the so-called Jewish "settlement blocs", must be annexed to Israel.

Israel conquered and occupied the West Bank, Gaza, East Jerusalem and other Arab territories like the Golan Heights in June 1967. Since then, the international community has labelled those areas "occupied" under international law.

The Trump administration has though displayed a willingness to forego international law in its foreign policy, aligning itself fully behind the Israeli project to colonise the entirety of historic Palestinian.

Since conquering the Palestinian territories in 1967, Israel has violated the rules of occupation stipulated in the 1907 Hague Regulations and the Fourth Geneva Convention. It has operated as a settler-colonial state, which wants a conquered land without the original people on it.

This aim can only be achieved through the elimination of the indigenous presence from most of the land, in violation of international law.

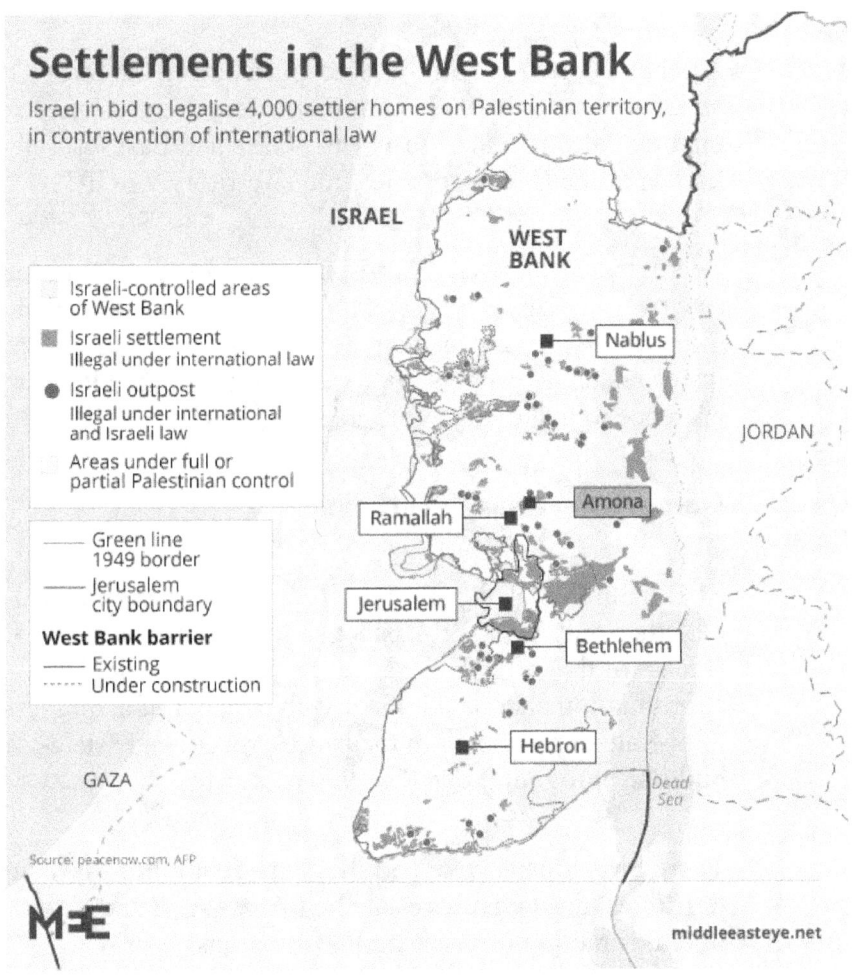

Elimination is the settler-colonial state's guiding principal, purposed as "a sustained institutional tendency to supplant the indigenous population".

Israel took this approach from the start of its own "state-building" in Palestine, when it eliminated much of the Palestinian presence on the land.

In 1948, it seized 78 percent of Palestine and forcibly expelled over half of the native population (about 800,000 people) and destroyed more than 500 of their villages. On that land the settler-colonial state of Israel emerged.

After an aborted 1956 foray into Gaza during the Suez Crisis, Israel again expanded in 1967 and took the remaining 22 percent of historic Palestine: the West Bank, Gaza and East Jerusalem – known as the Occupied Palestinian Territory, or OPT.

There, Israel followed a 1963 plan to conquer and enforce military rule over the OPT. This time though it did not succeed at immediately driving as many Palestinians off their land and has instead taken a different approach to reducing the Palestinian presence to make space for Israeli settlers.

Occupation versus colonisation

Starting in the 1970s, fervent settlement construction and a network of settler-only bypass roads began to push Palestinians into specific "areas" of the OPT. This paved the way for further land expropriation and, paradoxically, this model of dispossession came to operate in parallel with the peace process and "state-building" programme in the 1990s.

There Palestinians were corralled into ever more shrinking spatial territories, discursively re-labelled Areas A, B and C within a neo-liberal paradigm of peace and negotiations.

Encircled by ever more settlements, bypass roads and the Separation Wall, each area (i.e. Palestinian town or city) has been blockaded into a gated enclave with Israeli-controlled entrances and exits that Israeli forces close or open at will.

This has allowed Israel to complete a spatial redesign of the entire OPT into a gigantic matrix of control. There Gaza has been tragically transformed into the world's largest open-air prison, and the West Bank a "swiss cheese" of smaller and isolated open-air prisons and enclaves.

Palestinians carry placards denouncing the Israeli prime minister's recent decision not to renew the mendate of The Temporary International Presence in Hebron (TIPH) on 30 January (AFP)

So, without resorting to the blatant mass expulsion of Palestinians carried out in 1948, Israel has effectively been eliminating the Palestinian presence from the majority of the OPT by restricting their presence to specific controllable and gated "areas".

Those areas encompass just an extremely small percentage of the original Palestinian land, with Israeli settlers brought in to populate land the Palestinians are removed from.

Yet, despite clear evidence of settler colonial practices in Palestine, and the use by most of the international community of settler colonial terminology like "settlements", "land expropriation", "population transfer", "separation wall", "frontier" and "settlers", most observers – particularly in the West – still tend to discount settler colonialism as a thing of the past.

Legal and political cover

In October 2009, by acceding to an "agreed on outcome" that would permit ongoing Israeli settlement expansion, the Obama Administration buried the Two-State solution that the Peace Process is built upon.

At the same time, the narrative of occupation, discursively packaged alongside the two-state settlement and political process, granted Israel legal and political cover to continue with its settler colonisation unabated.

In this way occupation has been useful as a term employed conceptually to reinforce the hollow paradigm of a negotiated settlement, while the last bits of the OPT are settled and annexed into Israel.

This narrative also allows the international community to avoid taking the hard but necessary steps of enforcing international law, supporting democracy and defending human rights, while providing them with a faux framework to craft policy for an alternative reality that does not exist.

Further, this framework has fragmented the Palestinians, altered their political priorities and put their resistance against dispossession into disarray. Meanwhile, it has provided some Arab and Western states with an alibi to continue normalising and strengthening their relationship with Israel, so long as there are 'negotiations' to end the occupation.

While one Israeli political leader after the other declares they will not give up control over the OPT, the Trump administration aims to end the Palestinian struggle for self-determination, and the right of return for Palestinian refugees, by discontinuing use of the term occupation as part of the "deal of the century".

Yet, this also exposes how deeply false the narrative of occupation, a two-state solution and a negotiated settlement have become.

Colonial elimination

For generations now, Israel has been engaged in colonial elimination. Whereas occupation is characterised by temporariness, the process of settler-colonisation and elimination are permanent.

So, a deepened cooperation between the Trump administration and Netanyahu governments over the annexation of Palestinian lands is inadvertently offering a chance to reframe the OPT as colonised, not occupied, further doing away with the artificial distinction created between Palestinian territories conquered in 1967 with those from 1948.

This offers an opportunity to rethink the nature of the Israeli-Palestinian struggle as one of decolonisation for all of the peoples in the entirety of historic Palestine.

Such decolonisation would be the first step towards building a shared future based on humanity, justice, equality and democracy for all.

With the Israeli Election, the Plight of Palestinians Has Gotten Even Worse
The election should dispel any doubts that Israel will grant Palestinians freedom and rights without outside pressure.
By [Yousef Jabareen](#) 12th April 2019 from The Nation

Now that the results of Israel's national election is in, it's becoming increasingly clear that Prime Minister Benjamin Netanyahu has won his fifth term in office (his fourth consecutive term) and will lead the next government, after running a campaign that was once again based on exploiting racism and xenophobia against Palestinian citizens of Israel and other non-Jews. It's also increasingly clear that Israeli society's descent into right-wing extremism and fascism continues, with President Donald Trump cheering from the sidelines.

During the campaign, Netanyahu once again made unmistakably clear that he believes Palestinian citizens of the state, like myself, who make up about 20 percent of Israel's population, are second- or third-class citizens, unwelcome outsiders in our own land. In response to a recent social-media post by an Israeli actress about Palestinian citizens of Israel, Netanyahu wrote that "Israel is not a state of all its citizens," but rather it "is the nation-state of the Jewish People—and them alone"; this was a reference to the "nation-state" law passed last summer. A few days later, echoing the calls of right-wing extremists who want to ethnically cleanse Palestinians from Israel and the occupied territories, he declared that Palestinian citizens of Israel "have 22 other Arab countries" where they can go live.

A man walks by a campaign billboard for Benjamin Netanyahu days before the 2019 Israeli elections. (AP Photo / Oded Balilty)

Even more alarming, Netanyahu engineered a deal that will end up bringing the overtly racist and fascist Jewish Power party—whose members advocate the expulsion of Palestinians—into the next government if he forms it. Jewish Power leaders are disciples of the notorious right-wing extremist Meir Kahane, whose Kach party is considered a terrorist organization by the US government. After surviving mass ethnic cleansing during Israel's establishment in 1948, Palestinian citizens of Israel must now face the likelihood that advocates of what Israelis euphemistically call "transfer" will hold senior positions in the next government.

For years, as Israel has tried to avoid being labeled an "apartheid" state internationally, Israel's government under Netanyahu has implemented measures to cement a regime that systematically discriminates against non-Jews, in both the occupied territories and inside Israel's pre-1967 borders. Last summer, Israel's parliament (of which I am a member) passed the "Jewish Nation-State law," which might be more accurately called the Jewish Supremacy law. It enshrines in Israel's quasi-constitutional laws the supremacy of Jewish citizens and openly declares that the right to self-determination in Israel is "unique to the Jewish people." This is akin to Congress officially declaring that the United States belongs to white Christians only, with inferior status afforded to nonwhite, non-Christian citizens—including indigenous Americans.
The passage of the nation-state law, which is now being used to justify racism toward Palestinian citizens of Israel, comes in addition to some 60 other laws that already discriminated against us in practically every aspect of life, from housing and employment, to education, health care, and family reunification rights, many of which date to the founding of the state. With Netanyahu's next government promising to be even more hard-line and extreme than the last, our plight will surely worsen even further.

While Netanyahu and other Israeli leaders continue to drift to the far right, Palestinians in Israel are working towards a future where Jews and Arabs can live together in freedom and equality, regardless of their race or religion. Last summer, shortly before the nation-state law passed, I introduced a bill calling for full equality for all Israeli citizens, and one of my fellow Palestinian Knesset members introduced a separate bill calling for Israel to be a state for all of its citizens. In our inclusive, multicultural vision, racial, ethnic, and religious differences would be appreciated, so that all children grow up feeling valued by society. The state's wealth would be invested equitably for the benefit of all. Arabs and Jews would enjoy the same opportunity to have a good job, a home, and a dignified life. Arabic and Hebrew would be on the same footing as official languages, and state symbols would be inclusive and not reflect the identity of one group to the exclusion of others.

Under my (party's) political platform, Palestinians in the occupied territories would enjoy self-determination in a state alongside Israel, and Palestinian citizens of Israel would enjoy full equality. In the end, my bill was voted down, and my colleague's was banned even from being debated. Yet we persist, because we have no other choice. We cannot abandon our children to a future of permanent second-class status and subjugation.

After more than 70 years of systematic dispossession and discrimination, and more than 50 years of brutal military rule over millions of disenfranchised Palestinians, it is finally time for the world to acknowledge that Israel has established a full-blown apartheid regime in the occupied territories that is creeping into Israel itself. The results of this election should dispel any lingering doubts that Israelis will ever grant Palestinians our freedom and rights without significant outside pressure.

The reactionary ideology that dominates Israel—of racism and religious superiority—must be rejected. Israeli leaders must be sent the unequivocal message that apartheid was wrong in South Africa and it is wrong in Israel/Palestine, too. It is time for the international community to stand in support of Palestinians who are working for an inclusive, progressive future, where all the peoples of the Holy Land can live in freedom, with justice and equality.

How the left also dehumanises Palestinians in Gaza

By imbuing Gazans with mythical bravery, the left is failing the task of recognising Palestinian humanity.

by Susan Abulhawa, 12th April 2019 from Al Jazeera

Palestinian demonstrators take cover while Israeli soldiers are seen on their military vehicle during a protest in the southern Gaza Strip on December 21, 2018 [File: Ibraheem Abu Mustafa/Reuters]

Along the political spectrum, from the far left to extreme right, and spanning racial and ethnic lines, nearly everyone who has something to say about protesters in Gaza seems to fail the task of recognising Palestinian humanity. If it's coming from the right, the narrative is of terrorists, rockets and Hamas, a legitimate Palestinian resistance fully cemented as the Boogieman in the western imagination.

From the left, the stories are the stuff of legends, portraying unfathomable Palestinian heroism, courage and "sumud", an Arabic word romanticised in English to convey epic Palestinian steadfastness.

At both ends of the spectrum, defenceless Palestinians are larger than life, unlike other humans, either superhumanly posing a threat to highly armed soldiers several football fields away, or displaying supernatural courage and fearlessness before near-certain death.

The latter narrative, which manages to sentimentalise unspeakable misery is so enticing that even Palestinians have taken up this framing.

Nothing to lose

Just days ago, I watched a video of a young man who was shot in the legs. He limps along, falls and gets up, only to be shot again. The scene repeats over five or six bullets before the man cannot get up again and others come to evacuate him. The headline and comments extolled the "brave young man" who continued to stand up to his oppressor despite being hit multiple times in his legs.

As a Palestinian mother, I saw something else in that man, young enough to be my son. Maybe he was utterly divested of hope and robbed of the will to live a life encased in the barbaric, malicious, and creative savagery of Israel's siege on Gaza. A young man who has probably known little more than fear, despair, want, and impotence to do anything. Maybe a young man with nothing to lose, someone already bled of his rightful life, attempting a single moment of dignity in defiance, knowing, and maybe hoping, it would be his last. And maybe this is what the soldier saw, and chose instead to add the trauma of amputated limbs to a tortured man feebly raising a small rock with no will or energy to even throw it.

Maybe his motivation was nationalism. Maybe it was the hope of securing money for his family following his martyrdom or injury. Maybe he thought his death would give his people an inch towards liberty. Maybe it was the only thing left for him to do. We cannot know what is in the hearts of those who put their bodies between bullets and despair. But we can be sure that their motivations are painfully human. There is nothing godlike to see or fetishise.

Reductive analyses

There is no doubting the courage required to stand up to hateful, murderous Israelis, but narratives that imbue Palestinians with mythical bravery are harmful. They propose an otherworldly ability to withstand what no human should be forced to withstand, and they obscure the very human and very dark reality of life in Gaza, which has led to rates of suicide never before seen in Palestinian society.

Individuals in Gaza have different reasons for joining the Great March of Return, but the prevailing analyses are reductive, often coupling epic Palestinian bravery with non-violent resistance, because western imaginary cannot abide armed resistance, no matter how enduring or merciless the violence inflicted on them. The kind of heroism that is connected with guns is the exclusive purview of western soldiers. The only moral resistance available for the oppressed in the western psyche is exclusively non-violent. This means that the case for Palestinian liberty and dignity collapses the minute we fly an incendiary kite or fire a rocket towards a state that has been eviscerating Palestinian society and Palestinian bodies for decades. We see the same phenomenon around reactions in the United States when Black Americans rise up and do not perfectly conform "peaceful" and "nonviolent" protest, despite the centuries of denigration and marginalisation they have endured.

It does not help that even some Palestinians reinforce this notion by dismissing Hamas or downplaying any form of armed resistance as outliers in an otherwise ideal and tidy protest of a preternaturally strong and valiant oppressed people.

Gaza is a death camp

But the truth must be said, and the truth is abysmally ugly and bleak. There is nothing for the world to romanticise in Gaza. Nothing to idealise. Gaza is a death camp. Death and suppression technology is "the Jewish Nation's" single greatest export and Gaza is the human laboratory where Israeli arms manufacturers fine-tune their wares on the bodies, psyches and spirits of Palestinians. It is a wretched existence that spares none of the two million prisoners in that concentration camp.

Israel has turned Gaza, once a great city at the intersection of trade across three continents, into a black hole of dreams. Gaza is hope's coffin, an incinerator of human potential, and extinguisher of promise. People can barely breathe in Gaza. They cannot work, cannot leave, cannot study, cannot build, cannot heal. By all accounts, the tiny strip is unlivable, literally unfit to sustain life. Nearly 100 percent of the water is undrinkable. Youth unemployment is so high that it makes more sense to measure employment, which stands at a pathetic 30 percent. Approximately 80 percent of the population lives below the poverty line. Most residents get just a few hours of electricity every day. The sewage system has collapsed. The healthcare system has been stretched to its breaking point and hospitals are closing for lack of vital supplies and fuel, which Israel often prevents Palestinians from buying or even receiving from donors. This ineffable misery is intentional. Israel designed and made it. And the world allows it to persist.

Discourse of 'Sumud'

When our lives, resistance and struggle are framed in mythical terms, not only does it obscure our humanity, but it diminishes the depravity of Israel's control over millions of Palestinian lives. The discourse of sumud set us up for failure at every turn. On one hand, it supposes that Palestinians can endure anything. On the other hand, it suffuses the unuttered assumption that Palestinians deserve to be free because we are good, brave, nonviolent and steadfast.

But the truth is that we are nothing more, or less, than human. We are collectively neither monsters nor heroes, and even the worst of us are entitled to live free of foreign occupation. It must be said again and again that our struggle against our tormentors is legitimate in every form, whether nonviolent or violent. It must be said again and again that however we fight, our resistance is always self-defence. It must be said again and again that our right to life and dignity is not predicated on measures of our collective goodness, bravery or steadfastness. Ultimately, the left must stop fabulizing Palestinians and instead look squarely into the gruesomeness of the despair and anguish of Gaza, which I suspect most of us cannot even imagine.

Susan Abulhawa is a Palestinian writer and the author of the international bestselling novel, Mornings in Jenin (Bloomsbury

2010). She is also the founder of Playgrounds for Palestine, an NGO for children.

Gaza: Israel targeted Marches of Return with 'lethal' gas bombs
Apr 09 2019, from Days of Palestine

Palestinian Ministry of Health in Gaza said that the levels of injuries of people who arrived at the hospitals during the March of Return and breaking the siege reveal the occupation's deliberate intentions in killing and mutilation. Ashraf Al-Qudra, the ministry's spokesperson, added: "The Israeli occupation forces' use of lethal force against civilians in the east of Gaza Strip has resulted in the martyrdom of 271 citizens and the injury of 16,500 others."

Al-Qudra revealed that the occupation had used different types of live bullets, in addition to unidentified and non-coded gas bombs that cause health repercussions for the injured people.

Al-Qudra stressed that the occupation has developed its repressive methods using metal and tear gas bombs as a tool for killing and maiming, which resulted in the death of 6 citizens, including four children, as well as the injury of dozens by various distortions.

The Ministry of Health called on the concerned authorities to monitor the Israeli occupation's violations and use of lethal tools out of their standard characteristics.

Since 30 March 2018, Palestinians have been participating in peaceful marches near the fence separating the Gaza Strip and the occupied Palestinian territories in 1948 to demand the return of the refugees to their towns and villages from which they were displaced in 1948, and the breaking of the imposed siege on Gaza.

As an Israeli, I Oppose the Occupation
By <u>Oren Rimon Or</u>, 9th April 2019 in The Harvard Crimson

The Undergraduate Council's vote to fund Israeli Apartheid Week generated more conversation than anyone had expected. When prominent newspapers framed the UC decision as controversial, and when members of Harvard Hillel claimed that IAW risks the safety of Jewish students on campus, there is a need to remind ourselves of some definitions that were lost during this week.

I am an Israeli Jewish student and I am against the appeals made by some Hillel members to the UC. I am against the occupation, but my religion has nothing to do with it and neither does anyone else's religion. The situation in Israel-Palestine is political and is a matter of human rights and justice, not one of ideology or religion as we so often hear.

The fact that certain Jewish students feel attacked by IAW has no connection to their religious affiliation. These students feel attacked because of their political views. They feel attacked because they support a country that was politically criticized and condemned during the events held last week. As a Jewish Israeli student, IAW did not deal with my religion. It did, however, challenge the political actions of the country I come from. As long as we wish to adhere to democratic values, IAW, as any other political activity, should not be silenced.

The blur between anti-Semitism and criticism of Israel is a phenomenon that we should all resist. A religion and a government's policy are fundamentally different things. Anti-

Semitism and anti-Zionism are not the same, and we should refrain from putting them under the same umbrella.

The fact that we even need to emphasize this raises concerns. Claiming that by criticizing Israel one makes a claim about Jewish people in general is in fact an anti-Semitic statement. There are many Jewish people around the world that have no connection to Israel. Jewish people, like anyone else, have the right to adopt their own political views. Attributing Zionism to any Jewish student on this campus violates their right to freedom of thought and as a Jewish student, I am glad that the UC decided to differentiate between the two.

Many people make this exact mistake by starting with a political argument that slowly slips into a religious one, until the two seemed unseparated. This silences voices that should be heard and we should resist that. Today, students know that by criticizing Israel they take the risk of being falsely accused of anti-Semitism. I am an Israeli Jewish student and I criticize my government; would you call me anti-Semitic? I have spent 22 years there, all my beloved ones are there, together with my past and probably my future. But those years have brought me, like other editorial contributors, to be "silent no longer." Unlike them, however, I say silence no more to the occupation.

When you spend years in Israel you have two choices: seeing the occupation or closing your eyes in front of it. Twenty-two years were absolutely enough for me to see that we live under a system that discriminates between people based on their national identity. Twenty-two years were enough to see houses in the West Bank and East Jerusalem being demolished by Israel in front of their Palestinians owners' eyes. It was enough to see the Israeli settlers' freedom of movement in stark contrast to the harsh restrictions on Palestinians' movement, it was enough to see the deprivation of water, the arrests of children and the bombings on Gaza. Twenty-two years on this land were enough, and are definitely too long, to say silence no more to the occupation.

We should all remain silent no more in the face of those who wish to prevent freedom of speech on our campus as well. Falsely accusing students who take political stands of anti-Semitism hurts our fundamental right to speak. I chose to participate in a student panel held at the beginning of the week, because of my political beliefs, because as an Israeli and as a human being I resist the occupation and support human rights. In the panel, I was asked whether I am afraid to voice my political opinions in this campus. More than anything else, the silence of voices is what we should all be afraid of, if not terrified of.

We should all say: silence no more. During the last week, Harvard students said it loudly.

Oren Rimon Or '22 lives in Weld Hall.

Israel's new government will offer Palestinians a few crumbs, nothing more
April 12, 2019 in Middle East Monitor.

Prime Minster of Israel, Benjamin Netanyahu greets supporters on 10 April, 2019 in Tel Aviv, Israel [Amir Levy/Getty Images]

After securing 36 seats in the Knesset, and with other right-wing parties winning at least 30, it is obvious that the leader of Israel's Likud party, Benjamin Netanyahu, is going to form the next — his fifth — government. Although he is not as pragmatic a leader as others, mainly those on the Left, he played his election cards very openly, and his agenda includes destroying every Palestinian dream.

The Palestinian Authority, Palestine Liberation Organisation and Fatah leader Mahmoud Abbas said on Tuesday that he is ready to work with any Israeli government which is ready for peace. That was before the result of the Israeli General Election was known; it is doubtful if the new Israeli government will be looking for peaceful solutions to the decades-old conflict in historic Palestine. "We will not abandon our rights and will not accept the [American] deal of the century," insisted Abbas. "We are open if Israel accepts the UN resolutions for peace." He has not commented on the election result, but his senior aide Saeb Erekat has: "The Israelis voted for the party which does not want to end the occupation and is opposed to the two-state solution."

Israeli columnist Boaz Bismuth wrote in *Israel Hayom* that Netanyahu's agenda is based upon fulfilling Jewish aspirations at the expense of Palestinian rights. Bismuth referred to the adoption of the Jewish Nation-State Law as an example. "And here's the problem: when the 20th Knesset passed the important nation-state law, which had the support of the vast majority of the people, the Left objected to it, arguing that it was racist because it did not include a clause spelling out equality for all citizens. It was obvious to most of the public that equality had no place in the law because this is not a country for all its citizens, but rather the Jewish state." Where does this leave the Palestinians inside Israel and in the occupied territories? The Democratic Front for the Liberation of Palestine (DFLP) expects Likud to adopt more extreme policies on Palestinian rights. "Likud will form the government," explained Talal Abu Zarifa, a senior official of the DFLP in Gaza. "Hence, it needs to adopt more extreme policies in order to attract the extreme right wingers to join its coalition. The result will surely be a government which disrespects Palestinian rights."

Bismuth may have given us a hint about what Netanyahu's Likud is thinking, but one senior member of the party has made it very clear what it is going to do on the ground. Speaking to *Channel 12 TV*, Yisrael Katz stressed that the new Israeli government would not be a national unity administration, but a right-wing government that will impose Israeli sovereignty over the occupied Palestinian West Bank.

With elections weeks away, Israel pounds Gaza – Cartoon [Sabaaneh/MiddleEastMonitor]

Palestinian Professor of Political Science Hanna Isa is based in the occupied West Bank. He confirmed that this is exactly what the Likud-led coalition will do. "Jerusalem has already gone," Isa told me, "and Israel is going to annex area C, which is home to 350,000 Palestinians and 400,000 Israeli Jewish settlers. The settlers will be granted Israeli identity cards which will make them Israeli citizens. The crumbs will be left for the Palestinians."

Prof. Isa believes that the new Israeli government will not wait too long to carry out this step, which he expects to be part of Donald Trump's "deal of the century". He thinks that the US President will announce the details of his deal on 15 May, Nakba Day; the 71st anniversary of the creation of the state of Israel. "The date is symbolic and significant," Isa added. "On 15 May, Israel was established, and on 15 May, Palestine will vanish."

The Israeli opposition parties have said that they will make things "miserable" for the government. "The Knesset will be a battleground," they claim, but they will not be fighting to give the Palestinians anything. Why should they? There is no pressure on Israel internationally to compromise on any issue of importance; what Israel wants, it gets, even if that means a racist state in which only Jews are equal citizens while the non-Jews are treated as second class and worse.

The crumbs that any Israeli government, right or left, will give the Palestinians will be no more than small fragmented pieces of their homeland "in which they could have municipal services, such as garbage collection; raise a Palestinian flag; and, most importantly, continue security coordination with Israel." That is the reality which should force Mahmoud Abbas and his PA to end what he has called "sacred" security collaboration without delay.
Only unity will succeed in getting the Palestinians anything at all; the PA's current policies are completely discredited and ineffective. We can always sit, cap in hand, and wait for Israel to toss us some crumbs, of course, but the people of Palestine have more dignity and self-respect than that. The sooner that Abbas realises this and acts accordingly, the better for us all.

This was an election Nakba of their own making for Israel's frustrated Arab citizens
April 12, 2019 from Middle East Monitor

Efforts to bring an end to the right wing, anti-peace policies of Israeli Prime Minister Benjamin Netanyahu have clearly fallen short of their goals. One thing is certain, though; the blame for his survival falls squarely on the shoulders of Israel's Arab community.

One must always take a cautious approach to anything that Israel does, including its complex election process, but the results of Tuesday's General Election show clearly that Netanyahu's survival is in a large part due to Israeli Arabs who somehow believed that it's better to bury their heads in the sand and pretend that the 70-year nightmare doesn't exist than to go out and vote. Although the choice of government boiled down to two slates led on the one hand by extremist Apartheid advocate Benjamin Netanyahu, and on the other by former Israel Defence Forces Chief of Staff General Benny Gantz, whose politics are very similar to Netanyahu's, Israel's Arab citizens could have had a say in the outcome. They fluffed it.

The Arab voters in Israel missed the obvious third alternative, to vote for their own interests in an increasingly hostile environment. In the fight to defend the civil rights of Israel's 1.8 million Arab citizens and reverse the state's quarter century of frustrating the peace process, Tuesday's result is an election Nakba for the Palestinians. Netanyahu has the advantage over his rival Gantz, and his new government will be more repressive than before.

Israeli Likud Party campaign material and posters of Prime Minister Benjamin Netanyahu strown on the floor following election night on April 10, 2019 in Tel Aviv, Israel [Jack GUEZ/AFP/Getty]

So much was at stake and yet 50 per cent of Arab Israelis eligible to vote allowed racist provocation to push them into a self-destructive protest abstention. Not only has the number of Arab parties with seats in the Knesset fallen, but voter apathy has also sent a signal to everyone that their concerns are insignificant on the road ahead. The Arab Israelis helped to strengthen Netanyahu's grip on power. Even worse is the fact that in the face of one of the most racist, anti-Arab campaigns in Israel's history – which is replete with anti-Arab racism in any case — the country's Arab citizens buried their heads in the sand rather than fight for change.

Netanyahu called for the annexation of all of Israel's settlements in the West Bank and much of the available land, isolating the Palestinian population in disconnected Bantustans. Election rhetoric was filled with scaremongering about the so-called Arab voter threat changing Israel and forcing it to accept Palestinian statehood. On election day, around 1,200 Netanyahu activists were given cameras to take to polling stations in Arab areas, a disgraceful form of intimidation and bullying in a country which claims to be a democracy; indeed, "the only democracy in the Middle East".

After almost losing, Benjamin Netanyahu comes 1st in 2019 Israeli election – Cartoon [Sabaaneh/MiddleEastMonitor]

Netanyahu's victory spells doom for many of the Palestinian national objectives and increases the challenges in the fight against institutional racism and the struggle for Palestinian independence.

Although Netanyahu's Likud Party slate was thought to have tied with Gantz's Kahol Lavan Party on 35 seats each, the final results show that Likud actually won 36 seats, one more than Kahol Lavan. In order to get the minimum 61 seats needed to form the government in the 120-seat Knesset, Netanyahu will depend on forging a coalition with other right-wing parties.

The relative failure of Gantz in his first election campaign not only spells doom for Israel's fast-disappearing political Left, but also means an even more gloomy future for Israel's Arab population. This will be Netanyahu's fifth term in office as Prime Minister. The man who helped destroy the Oslo Peace accords of the 1990s is now well placed to destroy Palestinian civil rights and bury the hope of statehood permanently.

If he succeeds in forging a coalition, Netanyahu will use it as a mandate to advancehis anti-Arab platform which includes a call to annex occupied West Bank land, while enclosing Palestinians in Bantustans which might function like mini-Gaza Strips. Although Israel withdrew its military presence and illegal settlements from Gaza in 2005, it has since maintained a smothering blockade that has turned Gaza into an open-air prison subject to Israel's political and military whims. Both legally and practically, Israel is still the occupying state.

A similar fate lies in wait for major Palestinian population centres in the West Bank, such as Ramallah, Nablus, Hebron and Jenin. Annexation, which Netanyahu's party has advocated for years although he himself has publicly opposed it, would mean a tougher occupation with more restrictions that will push the two state solution into oblivion. It would also bury any hopes of a single, democratic state for all people living between the River Jordan and the Mediterranean Sea.

Moreover, the new political reality will put pressure on US President Donald Trump to favour Israel's political needs even more than he does at the moment. In the past year, Trump has promised to unveil a peace plan for Israelis and Palestinians described as the "deal of the century", while simultaneously agreeing to nearly everything that Israel has demanded: Washington has recognised Jerusalem as Israel's "undivided" capital; moved the US Embassy from Tel Aviv to Jerusalem; and recognised Israel's sovereignty over the Syrian Golan Heights, which it has occupied since the 1967 Six Day War.

No one really knows what the Trump deal actually offers and Netanyahu's victory gives America the opportunity to change the final details. Trump has said that he will unveil it only after the Israeli election, and now he can change the plan from one that gives Palestinians a foundation for independence to one that pushes statehood off the agenda altogether. It is possible that he will propose that Jordan and Egypt can provide land for a "Palestinian state" to be controlled by the two Arab countries. That would fall in line with Israel's political charge to encage major Palestinian populations in the West Bank.

Death to the Arabs' sprayed on the election posters of Arab members of the Israeli Knesset during the 2019 election campaign on 8 April 2019 [Furat Nasser/Facebook]

Regardless of what Trump unveils, his "deal of the century" is irrelevant, as it is rejected by Israel, rejected by the Palestinians and rejected by most of the Arab world. What is really relevant, though, is how the Arab countries will deal with Israel's increased control over the Palestinians. Most of them are embedded deeply into Israel's reality, albeit behind closed doors.

On the ground, of course, Israel has already enclosed its own Arab citizens in "virtual Bantustans" by approving almost 70 laws which discriminate against non-Jews, including the "Jewish Nation-State Law" which opened the door to a more aggressive and troubling future wherein Arab interests are undermined. Such legislation meant that ballot papers this week were printed in Hebrew only, even in Arab areas; Arabic is no longer an "official" language of the self-declared "Jewish State". Over the past decade or so, Israel has been gradually eliminating Arabic from road signs and other aspects of public life.

Apathy on the part of Arab voters and divisions within the once powerful coalition called "The Joint List" means that Arab parties fell well short of their potential to hold 24 seats in the Knesset. Instead of the Joint List's 13 seats, the predominantly Arab Ra'am Balad slate took just four, with Hadash-Ta'al doing marginally better with six. This weakened parliamentary representation also weakens the ability of Arab leaders to speak out against rising discrimination against non-Jewish citizens of Israel.

Is the idea of having more control over their own destiny so very frightening for Israel's Arabs? Or is it that the Palestinian leadership within Israel and across the diaspora is so uninspiring that doing nothing is better than fighting for one's dignity?

The Arab Israeli response to the unprecedentedly racist election campaign was crippled by self-imposed hurdles. The Palestinians in Israel trivialised the value of their votes more than they have ever been marginalised in the 71 years of their "non-existent" existence in the State of Israel. At a time when they could easily have united to increase voter turnout, they fractured themselves and stayed at home.

It was different in 2015. When Netanyahu's right-wing government raised the minimum threshold for party slates to qualify for a seat in the Knesset to 3.5 per cent of the vote, the Arab Israelis rose above their selfish rivalries and went to the polls "in droves", as the racist Prime Minister described it. Despite the obvious intention to try to exclude the many small Arab parties whose representatives have been demonised, threatened with lawsuits and in some cases jailed for their criticism of Israel's racist, Apartheid policies, the now defunct Joint List took 13 seats. Now the Arab parties have just 10.

Like all things Arab, apparently, reality outlives reason. Israel's Arab political parties can blame the election results on Arab despair, paranoia, intimidation, oppression and racist rhetoric by the right-wing Jewish parties, but the truth is that the Arabs have no one to blame but themselves. More marginalised than ever before, the Palestinians are now reeling from an election Nakba which leaves them with no meaningful role in forging their own destiny. That's what happens when you choose not to vote. Israel's Arab citizens have scored an own goal of epic proportions.

The Israeli escalation in Jerusalem requires urgent international intervention
April 14, 2019: Dr. Hanan Ashrawi from PLO Dept of public diplomacy and policy

The PLO Executive Committee strongly condemns the recent Israeli escalation against Jerusalem, including demolition of Palestinian homes, repeated arrests of senior officials like the Governor of Jerusalem Adnan Ghaith, as well as provocative raids on Muslim and Christian holy sites by Israeli Ministers.

The Israeli establishment is clearly emboldened to escalate its campaign of forced expulsion, murder, and theft of Palestinian land and resources. This is evident in the recent aggressive actions by the Israeli occupation authorities in occupied Jerusalem, which are part of a comprehensive plan against the Palestinian people, which reflects the racist, extremist, and colonial nature of Israel's policies against the Palestinian people.

These incendiary, illegal, and hostile Israeli actions coincide with the election of the most extreme rightwing Knesset in Israeli history and the US administration's irresponsible endorsement of their agenda.

This includes recent statements by US Secretary of State, Mike Pompeo that signaled the administration's tacit endorsement of Benjamin Netanyahu's pledge to annex large parts of the occupied West Bank, which is a flagrant violation of international law, including the UN Charter. This political endorsement of illegality and hostility threats to destroy any prospect of political resolution to the conflict and undermines the standing and integrity of international law as the universal framework and standard to conflict resolution.

States that willfully violate international law, like Israel, must be held accountable for their actions, including through international accountability mechanisms like the international criminal court. This is an international responsibility incumbent upon all states. Furthermore, we call on responsible states that opposed the Trump administration's unilateral and unlawful decision to recognize Jerusalem as the capital of Israel to assume their responsibilities and act to deter Israel's dangerous actions.

Israel delivers demolition notices to 13 Issawiya homes
April 10th 2019 Ma'an News Agency

The Israeli municipality of Jerusalem delivered demolition notices to residential structures in the Issawiya neighborhood, on Wednesday.

Muhammad Abu al-Hummus, member of a local follow-up committee, said that joint teams from the Israeli municipality and police raided the neighborhood and delivered demolition notices, summons for 13 residential structures, under the pretext that they were built without the Israeli-issued building permits.
Abu al-Hummus pointed out that some of the notified buildings were built more than 15 years ago.

Some of the buildings were identified as belonging to the Mahmoud, Darwish, Hamdan and al-Zaatari families.
Abu al-Hummus added that the Israeli municipality inspector took footage of dozens of buildings and homes in the neighborhood. Tensions increased in the neighborhood following the delivery of notices.

Israel uses the pretext of building without a permit to carry out demolitions of Palestinian-owned homes on a regular basis. Israel rarely grants Palestinians permits to build in East Jerusalem, though the Jerusalem municipality has claimed that compared to the Jewish population, they receive a disproportionately low number of permit applications from Palestinian communities, which also see high approval ratings.

For Jewish Israelis in occupied East Jerusalem's illegal settlements, the planning, marketing, development, and infrastructure are funded and executed by the Israeli government. By contrast, in Palestinian neighbourhoods, all the burden falls on individual families to contend with a lengthy permit application that can last several years and cost tens of thousands of dollars.

Israel to demolish Palestinian homes in Jerusalem "peace forest", but Israel settlement will remain

14th April from The New Arab

Israel regularly demolishes Palestinian homes built without permits [Anadolu]

Hundreds of Palestinian located in a "peace forest" in occupied East Jerusalem will lose their homes after an Israeli court rejected an appeal against their demolition.

The Jerusalem municipality has attempted to change the zoning of the "peace forest" so that the demolition ruling does not apply to structures built by Jewish Israelis in the area.

Many houses in occupied East Jerusalem are built without licenses, allowing Israel to order their demolition.

Palestinians say it is near impossible to obtain building permits from the Israeli state.

The Jerusalem District Court upheld a decision to demolish 60 buildings in the neighbourhood because the houses are located in a national Israeli "peace forest".

The "peace forest" is a green space intended to connect East and West Jerusalem and promote coexistence between Israeli and Palestinian communities.

The area is zoned as a public space or forest, hence the building of residential homes is not allowed.

Residents have previously attempted to seek authorisation for existing building and permission for new builds with the assistance of architects and lawyers.

Their plan was rejected in 2008 for "contradicting" a new zoning plan for the city.

"It's not that we didn't want to obtain a building permit, they wouldn't allow us to," said Walid Shweiki, a resident of the area, told *Haaretz*.

"Your family grows, you have a wife and children. Where can you go and live? On the street? You need some place."

The city filed indictments against the home owners in a local court and obtained demolition orders, but the process was delayed when three families appealed to the district court.

Their appeals were rejected two weeks ago, setting the stage for 500 people to lose their homes.

"There are clear planning and construction laws and the High Court has ruled that whoever decides to build without appropriate permits can complain only to themselves for deciding to take the law into their own hands," ruled the judge.

Despite order the demolition of unlicensed Palestinian homes citing zoning regulations, the city has advanced a plant to cancel the zoning of the "peace forest" upon the request of a pro-settlement NGO.

NGO Elad works to move Jewish residents into Palestinian neighbourhoods in occupied East Jerusalem, as well as promoting tourism and archeological initiatives in the area.

Elad has built camping and tourism structures in the "peace forest" without building permits.

Demolition orders were initially issued against those structures, but the city retroactively granted a request by Elad for building permits, *Haaretz* reported.

The NGO's plans did not involve construction, only the development of land for leisure and sport activity, the Jerusalem Municipality claimed

The Israel Land Authority has also granted Elad use of the land for 15 years in return for a fee of 400,000 shekels ($110,300).

There was no competitive bidding process or public announcement of the deal, which was revealed under a freedom of information request.

A hotel with 1,100 rooms is also currently being built in the area with the support and funding of the Israeli tourism ministry.

"The site is a strategic tourist destination," said the ministry.

Azzun village sealed off by Israeli forces for 19th day

April 14, 2019, in Middle East Monitor

Azzun village sealed off by Israeli forces for 19th day on 14 April 2019 [Maan News]

The main entrance of the Azzun village, in the northern occupied West Bank district of Qalqiliya, has remained sealed off by Israeli forces for 19 consecutive days, according to local sources on Sunday, *Ma'an News* has reported.

Israeli forces sealed off the village's main entrance with large cement blocks 19 days ago, preventing passage in both directions and forcing Palestinian residents to take a different route to reach other districts.

The Israeli army claimed that the seal off was in response to Palestinian youths cutting a piece of the Israeli-erected electric fence.

However, locals confirmed that the main goal is illegal Israeli settlement expansion in the area.

Azzun is surrounded on all sides by areas under Israeli military control and an Israeli settlement bloc sits directly to the south. It has one of the highest rates of detainees per capita of all villages in the occupied West Bank, including many children.

Eurovision: Material girl Madonna shuns Palestine solidarity
by Ruby Hamad, 10th April 2019 in The New Arab

Madonna is set to perform two songs at the interval of Tel Aviv Eurovision [Getty]

Like much of the world, Australia has been obsessed with Eurovision long before it first took part in the annual singing and songwriting talent competition in 2015.

SBS, a publicly-funded television station has been broadcasting the spectacle every year since 1983.

And although Eurovision has never been my deal, I also see no value in trashing it without a good reason. Why criticise something that brings others joy? We could certainly all use some, especially if that joy is more or less harmless.

But this year is a different story: This year it isn't harmless.

The contest takes place in the home country of the previous year's winner, and with last year's competition won by Israeli performer Netta, Eurovision 2019 is set to begin in Tel Aviv on May 14.

Since this is I guess, a cultural event, this means Eurovision 2019 conflicts with the BDS (Boycott, Divestment, and Sanctions) movement, and Palestinian organisers have explicitly asked performers to refrain from taking part in this year's competition.

Regardless of anyone's feelings on BDS in general, it's not asking a great deal to abstain from participating - whether as contestants or viewers - in a celebration of this magnitude.

Eurovision showcases a multitude of nationalities and countries coming together in one big glitzy global party. It's also a celebration that will be taking place mere kilometres from where the rights of Palestinians are being violated on a daily basis.

Given the history of the misnamed Israel-Palestine conflict (can it truthfully be deemed a "conflict" when it consists largely of one powerful side exercising its brute power over the other?) an escalation of the violation of the human rights of Palestinians may have seemed impossible, but somehow it isn't.

In the last two–three weeks alone:

Israel announced plans to formally annex the West Bank, surprising literally no-one who has more than a passing knowledge of the conflict and has long given up on the possibility of Israel permitting a two-state solution.

This annexation will make the illegal Israeli settlements on land illegally confiscated from Palestinians formally part of Israel proper but will not extend to those Palestinians living in the West Bank. They will remain stateless and under occupation on their own ever-dwindling land.

Israel closed the crossings into the West Bank and Gaza for a 24-hour period during the national elections, once again cutting off Palestinians from the outside world altogether, and demonstrating its complete and utter control over their lives in the process.

Israel has continued to greet Palestinian protestors at the Gaza border with gas bombs, snipers and all-out assault. Children, journalists and medics have not been spared the carnage.

Amid this backdrop, the saccharine sweetness that is Eurovision with its pretensions of acceptance and tolerance is rather on the nose.

Perhaps anticipating a lukewarm global reception, Israel is pulling out the big guns - no pun intended - this week, announcing that Madonna will perform two songs at an interval during competition during the festivities.

Material Girl or no, it's really not a lot to ask that people abstain this once.

We're always told now is not the time to talk about Palestine and other assaults by the West on the Middle East.

It wasn't the time when Hillary Rodham Clinton was running for president and we objected to her ultra-hawkish views on the region. Her 2016 election campaign policies included a promise to take the US-Israel alliance "to the next level," as well as promising yet more money, more weapons and tougher sanctions on Israel's "enemies."

In a campaign speech, she also scolded Palestinian leaders "to stop inciting violence, stop celebrating terrorists as martyrs and stop paying rewards to their families," before going on to condemn the "alarming" BDS movement as "anti-Semitic."

It also wasn't the time to talk about Palestine and the Middle East when some Facebook posts emerged from Wonder Woman herself, aka Israeli actress Gal Gadot, that expressed enthusiastic supported for the 2014 assault on Gaza. Gadot praised the IDF for "protecting" Israeli citizens from terrorists, and, like Clinton, also laid the blame for the conflict firmly on the shoulders of Palestinians.

And now, apparently, it's not the time because people seem to think having a party is just so much more important than the human rights of Palestinians.

Australian entry Kate Miller-Heidke brushed off the criticism, rejecting appeals to cancel her appearance by claiming she wants to go to Israel to learn more about the conflict and meet with

Palestinians. We all know this is a copout. Apart from the privileged ignorance of being able to blithely admit to not knowing about what is happening there, this betrays a deliberate decision to ignore the Palestinians speaking out to her right now, requesting she and others not to attend the event.

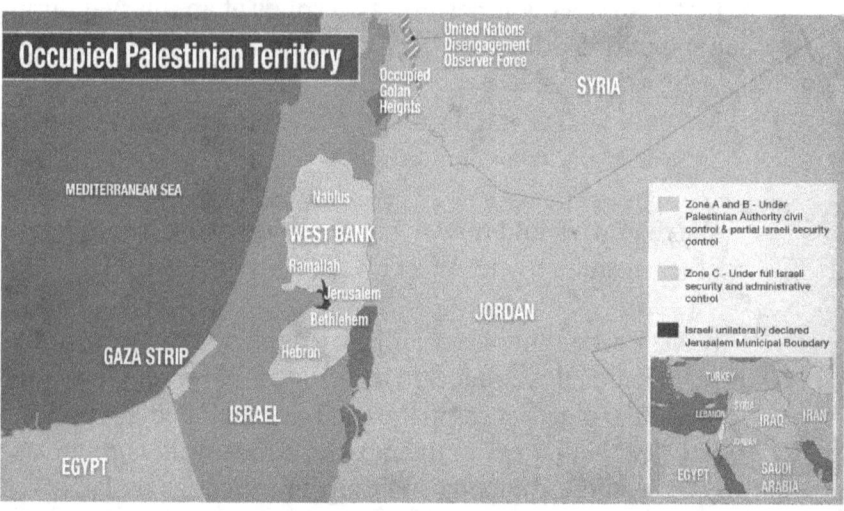

Yes, we all have a right to make our decisions on our political beliefs and actions. We also have a right to critique and respond to the actions of others.

After so many years of Palestinians and their allies racking our brains wondering what exactly it is going to take to make the world care enough to do something about their ongoing persecution and occupation, that the world's response is to literally sing and dance on their graves and on their ongoing struggle, is a pill that is not so much bitter to swallow as it is outright impossible.

Now is the time we stop making excuses for the inexcusable.

There are many struggles and oppressions in this world, but there are few we can actually do something about.

Those of us who reside in and are citizens of the West can do something about Palestine because it is our governments, our diplomatic support, and our dollars that help to make their oppression possible.

This is why we seem to be missing such a golden opportunity; the boycotting of Eurovision 2019 has the potential to be powerful enough to extend beyond the realm of symbolism and into the realm of meaningful action.

Now is the time. Even if you don't agree with BDS in general, a kitschy talent quest is not more important than the struggle of a people for life, dignity and self-determination.

Given this urgent context, it's sadly easy to see that anyone who publicly supports this year's Eurovision is clearly more interested in pursuing their personal pleasure, than in alleviating the pain of others.

To go on ignoring this ongoing calamity of our own making just so we can feel good about participating in something for our own fleeting pleasure is a screaming siren announcing we have decided that our entertainment is more paramount than the lives and suffering of other people.

Actions can sometimes change the course of history for the better. If only we were brave enough and cared enough to say together: Enough is enough. Set Palestine free.

Ruby Hamad is a writer and Phd candidate in media and postcolonial studies at the University of New South Wales. Born in Lebanon and raised in Australia, she splits her time between Sydney and New York.

Europe must stand by the two-state solution for Israel and Palestine

High-ranking former European politicians urge the EU to reject any US Middle East peace plan unless it is fair to Palestinians

15th April 2019 from The Guardian

Palestinians attend the Great March of Return at the Israel-Gaza border on 12 April 2019. Photograph: Anadolu Agency/Getty Images

We are reaching out at a critical point in time in the Middle East, as well as in Europe. The EU is heavily invested in the multilateral, rules-based international order. International law has brought us the longest period of peace, prosperity and stability our continent has ever enjoyed. For decades, we have worked to see our Israeli and Palestinian neighbours enjoy the peace dividends that we Europeans have through our commitment to that order.

In partnership with previous US administrations, Europe has promoted a just resolution to the Israeli-Palestinian conflict in the context of a two-state solution. To this date, despite subsequent setbacks, the Oslo agreement is still a milestone of transatlantic foreign policy cooperation.

Unfortunately, the current US administration has departed from longstanding US policy and distanced itself from established international legal norms. It has so far recognised only one side's claims to Jerusalem and demonstrated a disturbing indifference to Israeli settlement expansion. The US has suspended funding for the UN agency for Palestinian refugees (UNRWA) and for other programmes benefitting Palestinians – gambling with the security and stability of various countries located at Europe's doorstep.

Against this unfortunate absence of a clear-cut commitment to the vision of two states, the Trump administration has declared itself close to finalising and presenting a new plan for Israeli-Palestinian peace. Despite uncertainty as to if and when the plan will be released, it is crucial for Europe to be vigilant and act strategically.

We believe that Europe should embrace and promote a plan that respects the basic principles of international law as reflected in the agreed EU parameters for a resolution to the Israeli-Palestinian conflict. These parameters, which the EU has systematically reaffirmed during past US-sponsored talks, reflect our shared understanding that a viable peace requires the creation of a Palestinian state alongside Israel on borders based on the pre-1967 lines with mutually agreed, minimal and equal land swaps; with Jerusalem as the capital for both states; with security arrangements that address legitimate concerns and respect the sovereignty of each side and with an agreed, fair solution to the question of Palestine refugees.

Europe, by contrast, should reject any plan that does not meet this standard. While sharing Washington's frustrations about the unsuccessful peace efforts of the past, we are convinced that a plan that reduces Palestinian statehood to an entity devoid of sovereignty, territorial contiguity and economic viability would severely compound the failure of previous peace-making efforts, accelerate the demise of the two-state option and fatally damage the cause of a durable peace for Palestinians and Israelis alike.

It is, of course, preferable for Europe to be working in tandem with the US to solve the Israeli-Palestinian conflict, as well as to address other global issues in a strong, transatlantic alliance. However, in situations in which our vital interests and fundamental values are at stake, Europe must pursue its own course of action.

In anticipation of this US plan, we believe Europe should formally reaffirm the internationally agreed parameters for a two-state solution. Doing this in advance of the US plan establishes the EU's criteria for supporting American efforts and facilitates a coherent and unified European response once the plan is published.

European governments should further commit to scale up efforts to protect the viability of a future two-state outcome. It is of the utmost importance that the EU and all member states actively ensure the implementation of relevant UN security council resolutions – including consistent differentiation in accordance with UN security council resolution 2334, between Israel in its recognised and legitimate borders, and its illegal settlements in the occupied territories.

Furthermore, recent escalating efforts to restrict the unhindered work of civil society have made European support for human-rights defenders in both Israel and Palestine, and their critical role in reaching a sustainable peace, more important than ever.

Israel and the occupied Palestinian territories are sliding into a one-state reality of unequal rights. This cannot continue. For the Israelis, for the Palestinians or for us in Europe.

Right now, Europe is facing a defining opportunity to reinforce our shared principles and long-held commitments in relation to the Middle East peace process and thereby manifest Europe's unique role as a point of reference for a rules-based global order.

Failing to seize this opportunity, at a point in time when this order is unprecedentedly challenged, would have far-reaching negative consequences.

Douglas Alexander *Former minister of state for Europe, United Kingdom*
Jean-Marc Ayrault *Former foreign minister and prime minister, France*

Carl Bildt *Former foreign minister and prime minister, Sweden*
Włodzimierz Cimoszewicz *Former foreign minister and prime minister, Poland*
Dacian Cioloș *Former prime minister and European commissioner, Romania*
Willy Claes *Former foreign minister and Nato secretary general, Belgium*
Massimo d'Alema *Former foreign minister and prime minister, Italy*
Karel De Gucht *Former foreign minister and European commissioner, Belgium*
Uffe Ellemann-Jensen *Former foreign minister and president of the European Liberals, Denmark*
Benita Ferrero-Waldner *Former foreign minister and European commissioner for external relations, Austria*
Franco Frattini *Former foreign minister and European commissioner, Italy*
Sigmar Gabriel *Former foreign minister and vice-chancellor, Germany*
Lena Hjelm-Wallén *Former foreign minister and deputy prime minister, Sweden*
Eduard Kukan *Former foreign minister, Slovakia*
Martin Lidegaard *Former foreign minister, Denmark*
Mogens Lykketoft *Former foreign minister and UN general assembly president, Denmark*
Louis Michel *Former foreign minister and European commissioner, Belgium*
David Miliband *Former foreign secretary, United Kingdom*
Holger K Nielsen *Former foreign minister, Denmark*
Marc Otte *Former EU special representative to the Middle East peace process, Belgium*
Ana Palacio *Former foreign minister, Spain*
Jacques Poos *Former foreign minister, Luxembourg*
Vesna Pusić *Former foreign minister and deputy prime minister, Croatia*
Mary Robinson *Former president and United Nations high commissioner for human rights, Ireland*
Robert Serry *Former UN special coordinator for the Middle East peace process, the Netherlands*
Javier Solana *Former foreign minister, Nato secretary general and EU high representative for common foreign and security*

policy, Spain
Per Stig Møller *Former foreign minister, Denmark*
Michael Spindelegger *Former foreign minister and vice-chancellor, Austria*
Jack Straw *Former foreign secretary, United Kingdom*
Desmond Swayne *Former minister of state for international development, United Kingdom*
Erkki Tuomioja *Former foreign minister, Finland*
Ivo Vajgl *Former foreign minister, Slovenia*
Frank Vandenbroucke *Former foreign minister, Belgium*
Jozias van Aartsen *Former foreign minister, the Netherlands*
Hubert Védrine *Former foreign minister, France*
Guy Verhofstadt *Former prime minister, Belgium*
Lubomír Zaorálek *Former foreign minister, Czech Republic*

Access to clean water is a human right, so why is Palestine an exception?
Apr 15 2019 from Days of Palestine and Middle East Monitor

Free access to clean water is a basic human right. This is not just a common-sense assertion, but also a binding legal commitment enshrined in international law. In November 2002, the UN Committee on Economic, Social and Cultural Rights adopted "General Comment No. 15" regarding the right to water: "The human right to water is indispensable for leading a life in human dignity. It is a prerequisite for the realisation of other human rights." (Article I.1)

The discussion on water as a human right culminated years later in UN General Assembly resolution, 64/292 of 28 July, 2010. It explicitly "recognises the right to safe and clean drinking water and sanitation as a human right that is essential for the full enjoyment of life and all human rights."

It all makes perfect sense. There can be no life without water. However, like every other human right, it seems, the Palestinians are denied this one too.

There is a water crisis affecting the whole world, and it is most pronounced in the Middle East. Climate change-linked droughts, unpredictable rainfall, lack of centralised planning, military conflicts and more have resulted in unprecedented water insecurity.

The situation is even more complicated in Palestine, though, where the water crisis is related directly to the more general political context of Israel's occupation: apartheid, illegal Jewish settlements, siege and war. While much attention has rightly been given to the military aspect of the Israeli occupation, the state's colonial policies involving water receive far less attention, but they are a pressing and critical problem.

Ashraf Amra Indeed, total water control was one of the first policies enacted by Israel after the establishment of the military regime following the occupation of East Jerusalem, the West Bank and Gaza Strip in June 1967. Israel's discriminatory policies – its uses and abuses of Palestinian water resources – can be described as "water apartheid".

Excessive Israeli water consumption; the erratic use of dams; and the denial of Palestinians of the right to their own water or the digging of new wells, have all left vast and possibly irreversible environmental consequences. They have fundamentally altered the aquatic ecosystem altogether.

In the West Bank, Israel uses water to cement existing Palestinian dependency on the occupation. It uses a cruel form of economic dependency to keep Palestinians reliant and subordinate. This model is sustained through the control of borders, military checkpoints, collection of taxes, closures, military curfews and the denial of building permits. Water dependency is a centrepiece of this strategy.

The "Interim Agreement on the West Bank and the Gaza Strip", known as the Oslo II Agreement, signed in Taba, Egypt in September 1995, crystallised the unfairness of Oslo I, which was signed in September 1993. Over 71 per cent of *Palestinian* aquifer water was made available for Israeli use, with just 17 per cent allocated for Palestinian use.

Even more appallingly, the new agreement invited a mechanism that forced Palestinians to buy their own water from Israel, further cementing the client-owner relationship between the Palestinian Authority and the occupying state.

Israel's Mekorot water company, a wholly-owned government entity, misuses its privileges to reward and punish Palestinians as it sees fit. In the summer of 2016, for example, entire Palestinian communities in the occupied West Bank went without water because the PA failed to pay Israel massive sums of money to buy back water taken from Palestinian natural resources. Bewildering, isn't it? And yet many are still wondering why Oslo failed to deliver the much-coveted "peace".

Look at the numbers in order to appreciate this water apartheid: Palestinians in the West Bank use about 72 litres of water per person per day, compared to 240-300 litres for Israelis. The political responsibilities of such unequal distribution of available water resources can be attributed to both the cruel Israeli occupation and the short-sighted vision of the Palestinian leadership.

The situation in Gaza is even worse. The territory will be officially "unliveable" by 2020, according to a UN report. *That's next year.* The main reason for this grim prediction is Gaza's water crisis.

According to a study conducted by international charity Oxfam, "Less than four per cent of fresh water [in Gaza] is drinkable and the surrounding sea is polluted by sewage." Oxfam researchers concluded that water pollution is dangerously linked to a dramatic increase in kidney problems in the Gaza Strip. Gaza's water and sanitation crises are worsening as frequent shutdowns of the enclave's only functioning power plant are killing any hope for a remedy.

The US-based RAND Corporation found that one-fourth of all diseases in the besieged Gaza Strip are waterborne. RAND estimations are no less dramatic. It reports that, based on World Health Organisation (WHO) standards, 97 per cent of Gaza's water is not fit for human consumption. In terms of human suffering, this reality can only be described as horrific.

The hospitals in the Gaza Strip are trying to fight the massive epidemic of illness and disease caused by dirty water while underequipped, suffering electricity cuts and lacking any clean water themselves. "Water is frequently unavailable at Al-Shifa, the largest hospital in Gaza" the RAND report continues. "Even when it is available, doctors and nurses are unable to sterilise their hands to carry out surgery because of the water quality."

According to the environmental media platform Circle of Blue, out of Gaza's 2 million residents, only 10 per cent have access to clean drinking water.

"My children get sick because of the water," Madlain Al-Najjar, a mother of six living in the Gaza Strip, told Circle of Blue. "They suffer from vomiting and diarrhoea. Often, I can tell that the water is not clean, but we have no other option."

Britain's *Independent* reported on the story of Noha Sais, a 27-year-old mother of five, living in Gaza. "In the summer of 2017, every one of Noha's children suddenly fell ill, uncontrollably vomiting and were soon hospitalised. Gaza's filthy Mediterranean waters had poisoned them.

"The youngest, Mohamed, normally a healthy and boisterous five-year-old, contracted an unknown virus from the sea, which took over his body and brain. Three days after the trip, he slipped into a coma. A week after that he died."

Noha told the newspaper that, "The doctors said the source of the infection was a germ that came from the polluted seawater, but they couldn't work out exactly what it was. They just said to me even if my son recovered, he would never be the same – he would be a vegetable."

Many similar cases are reported across Gaza, and there is no end in sight. Israel's water policies are facets of a much larger war against the Palestinian people intended to reinforce its colonial control.

Judging by the evidence, Zionists didn't "make the desert bloom," as Israeli propaganda claims. Since its establishment on the ruins of more than five hundred Palestinian towns and villages destroyed between 1947 and 48, Israel has done the exact opposite.

"Palestine contains vast colonisation potential which the Arabs neither need nor are qualified to exploit," wrote one of Israel's founding fathers and first Prime Minister, David Ben Gurion, to his son Amos in 1937. Zionist Israel, though, has done more than just "exploit" that "colonisation potential"; it has also subjected historic Palestine to a relentless and cruel campaign of destruction that is yet to cease.

This is likely to continue as long as Zionism prevails in Israel and occupied Palestine; it is a racist, hegemonic and exploitative ideology. If access to clean water is indeed a human right, why is the world allowing Israel to make Palestine and its people an exception?

Internet news and comment

- Australians For Palestine - http://www.australiansforpalestine.com/
- Desert Peace - http://www.desertpeace.wordpress.com/
- Dissident Voice - http://www.dissidentvoice.org/
- Electronic Intifada - www.electronicintifada.net
- Intifada Palestine – http://www.intifada-palestine.com/
- Ma'an News Agency - http://www.maannews.net/eng/
- Middle East Monitor - http://www.middleeastmonitor.org.uk/
- Middle East Online - http://www.middle-east-online.com/english/
- Mondoweiss - http://mondoweiss.net
- My CatbirdSeat - http://www.mycatbirdseat.com/
- Palestine Chronicle - http://www.palestinechronicle.com/
- Palestine Information Centre - http://www.palestine-info.co.uk/en/
- Redress Information & Analysis – http://www.redress.cc/
- Ramallah Online - http://www.ramallahonline.com/
- Sabbah Report - http://www.sabbah.biz/
- Salem News - http://www.salem-news.com/
- The People's Voice - http://www.thepeoplesvoice.org/
- Uruknet - http://www.uruknet.info/
- Veterans Today – http://www.veteranstoday.com/
  Nimr Jamal - http://www.countdown2040.com/index.php
- The Forward Independent - http://forward.com
- Muftah - http://muftah.org
- The Nation - http://www.thenation.com
- Arab News – www.arabnews.com
  Jerusalem Post - http://www.jpost.com/
- Middle East Eye - http://www.middleeasteye.net/
- Red Pepper - https://www.redpepper.org.uk/israel-palestine/
- Days of Palestine – daysofpalestine.com
  Americans for Middle East Understanding - http://www.ameu.org/home.aspx
- Mufta - https://muftah.org/about/
- The Palestine Project - https://www.facebook.com/PalestineProjectPage/
- Palestine News Network (PNN) – english.pnn.ps
- Adalah - https://www.adalah.org

Helpful organisations

- www.btselem.org - The Israeli Information Centre for Human Rights in the Occupied Territories
- www.icahd.org - Israeli Committee Against House Demolitions
- www.ifamericansknew.org
- www.kairospalestine.ps
- www.sadaka.ie - The Ireland Palestine Alliance
- www.scottishpsc.org.uk
- www.twinningwithpalestine.net
- www.vivapalestina.org

Other books compiled by Godot Hussein.

Two months in Palestine 2017

The Stench from Israel

Israel – the Broken State